PĀLI LITERATURE AND LANGUAGE

WILHELM GEIGER

TRANSLATOR

BATAKRISHNA GHOSH

GYAN

Published by

Gyan Publishing House
5, Ansari Road
Daryaganj, New Delhi-110002
Phone: 011-47034999, 9811692060
E-mail: books@gyanbooks.com

Distribution Network
gyanbooks.com
India, USA, Canada, UK, Australia

ISBN: 978-93-6920-539-4 (PB)

First Published, 1916

2nd Impression 2025

Printed at: Gyan Press, Delhi.

PĀLI LITERATURE AND LANGUAGE
Author: WILHELM GEIGER, Translator: BATAKRISHNA GHOSH

PĀLI LITERATURE AND LANGUAGE

BY

WILHELM GEIGER

EMERITUS PROFESSOR OF INDO-IRANIAN PHILOLOGY AT THE UNIVERSITY OF MUNICH

AUTHORISED ENGLISH TRANSLATION

BY

BATAKRISHNA GHOSH, DR.PHIL. (MUNICH),
D.LITT. (PARIS)

LECTURER IN SANSKRIT AND GERMAN AND COMPARATIVE PHILOLOGY, CALCUTTA UNIVERSITY,
PROFESSOR OF GERMAN AND FRENCH, VIDYASAGAR COLLEGE; PRABODH BASU
MALLICK PROFESSOR OF INDIAN PHILOSOPHY, NATIONAL COUNCIL OF
EDUCATION, BENGAL, JOINT-EDITOR, "INDIAN CULTURE"

TABLE OF CONTENTS

	Page
Preface	xi
Abbreviations	xiii
Introduction	1

The notion of Pāli; linguistic strata inside P. (I-II)—P. as artificial language; its land of origin (III-VII).—Basis of P. a Māgadhī (VIII-X).

PART I. PĀLI LITERATURE

I. The Canonical Literature	9
1. Origin and Authenticity of the Canon (1-4)	9
2. Classification of the Pāli Canon, Editions, Translations (5-6)	13
3. Vinaya-Piṭaka (7)	15
4. Sutta-Piṭaka (8)	16

Dīgha-Nikāya and Majjhima-N. (9).—Saṃyutta and Aṅguttara N. (10).—Khuddakapāṭha, Dhammapada, Udāna, Itivuttaka (11).—Suttanipāta, Vimāna- and Petavatthu (12).—Thera- and Therī-gāthā, Jātaka (13).—Niddesa, Paṭisambhidāmagga, Apadāna, Buddhavaṃsa (14).

5. Abhidhamma-Piṭaka (15)	22
Individual works of the Abh.-P. (16)	23
Supplement: The Paritta (17)	24
II. The Non-Canonical Literature	25
I Period: From the Completion of the Canon to the 5th century A.D.	25

The Aṭṭhakathā (18).—Nettippakaraṇa, Peṭakopadesa, Suttasaṃgaha (19).—Milindapañhā (20).—Dīpavaṃsa (21).

II Period: From the 5th century to the 11th century ...	28

Works of Buddhaghosa (22).—Jātakaṭṭhavaṇṇanā (23).—Dhammapadaṭṭhakathā (24).—Buddhadatta, Ānanda, Dhammapāla (25.—Culla-Dhammapāla, Upasena, Mahānāma, Kassapa, Vajirabuddhi, Khema, Anuruddha (26).—Khudda- and Mūla-sikkhā (27).—The Mahāvaṃsa (28).—Anāgatavaṃsa and Bodhivaṃsa (29).—Kaccāyana (30).

PAGE

III Period: From the 12th century to the Modern Age ... 38

Sāriputta and the Ṭīkās (31).—Sāriputta's pupils (32).—Chapada (33).—Dāṭhāvaṃsa, Thūpavaṃsa, Jinālaṃkāra, Jinacarita (34).—Mahāvaṃsa-Ṭīkā (35).—Vedehathera (36).—Buddhappiya (37).—Continuation of the Mahāvaṃsa (38).—Sārasaṃgaha, Saddhammasaṃgaha (39).—Lokappadīpasāra, Pañcagatidīpana, Buddhagbosuppatti (40).—Saddhammopāyana, Telakaṭāhagāthā (41).—Burmese authors (42).—Authors of the 17th Century (43).—Modern works (44).—Linguistic literature (45).—Works of the school of Kaccāyana (46).—Continuation of same (47).—Moggallāna (48).—Moggallāna's pupils (49).—Saddanīti (50).—Dictionaries (51).—Root lists (52).—Miscellaneous (53).

PART II. GRAMMAR OF PĀLI

Literature 59

A. *Phonology*

1. Sound-system and Accent 61

Scripts (§ 1).—Sound-system (§ 2, 3).—Accent (§ 4).

2. The Law of Mora 63

Law of Mora (§ 5).—Character of syllables (§ 6).—Long before double-consonance (§ 7).—Shortening as result of Svarabhakti (§ 8).

3. The Vowels ā̆ ī̆ ū̆ 65

e for *a* before double-consonance (§ 9).—*i* and *u* (§ 10).—*e*, *o* from ī̆, *ū* (§ 11).

4. Representation of the Vowels ṛ, ḷ 66

a, *i*, *u* from ṛ (§ 12).—ṛ becomes consonantal (§ 13).—*u* from ḷ (§ 14).

5. Diphthongs and their Representation 68

e, *o* from *e*, *o*, *ai*, *au*; *i*, *u* from *e*, *o* (§ 15).

6. Influence of Neighbouring Vowels or Consonants on the Vowels 69

PAGE

Influence of following vowels (§ 16).—Influence of preceding vowels (§ 17).—Influence of consonants on vowels (§ 18).

7. Influence of Accent on vocalism 70

Reduction of vowel of the second syllable (§ 19).—Syncope (§ 20).—Weakening of pre-tonic syllable (§ 21).—Shortening of unstressed final syllables (§ 22).—Shortening of the second syllable (§ 20).—Effect of the expiratory accent (§ 24).

8. Saṃprasāraṇa and the loss of syllable through Contraction. 73

Saṃprasāraṇa (§ 25).—*e*, *o*, from *aya*, *ava* (§ 26).—Contraction (§ 27).—The prepositions *upa* and *apa* (§ 28).

9. Increase of syllables through Svarabhakti 76

Generalities (§ 29).—Svarabhakti *i* (§ 30).—Svarabhaktis *a*, *u* (§ 31).

10. Quantitative Changes in Composition and under stress of Metre 78

Influence of Metre (§ 32).—Protraction and Contraction of vowels in Compounds (§ 33).

11. Irregularities of vocalism (§ 34) 80

12. Consonants in Free Position 81

Intervocalic mutes (§ 35).—Drop of intervocalic mutes (§ 36).—*h* for Aspirates (§ 37).—Softening of surds (§ 38).—Hardening of sonants (§ 39).—Aspiration and loss thereof (§ 40).—Change in place of Articulation (§ 41).—Cerebrals for Dentals (§ 42).—*r*, *l*, *ḷ* for *d*, *n*, *ṇ* (§ 43).—*l* for *r* (§ 44).—*r* for *l* (§ 45).—Alternation between *y* and *v* (§ 46).

13. Dissimilation and Metathesis (§ 47) 91

14. Consonant-groups 91

Combination of two Consonants 91

Generalities (§ 48).—Consonant-groups containing *h* (§ 49).—Combination of Sibilant with Nasal (§ 50).—Laws of Assimilation (§ 51).—Progressive Assimilation (§ 52).—Regressive Assimilation: mute before nasal, liquid, semi-vowel (§ 53).—Regressive Assimilation: sibilant before liquid or semi-vowel;

PAGE

nasal or *l* before semi-vowel; the groups *vy*, *vr* (§ 54).—Dentals and *ṇ* before *y* (§ 55).—The group *ks* (§ 56).—The groups *ts*, *ps* (§ 57).

Combination of more than two Consonants 101
Generalities (§ 58).—Details (§ 59).

15. Sporadical Aberrations in Sound-groups 103
h for sonant aspirates (§ 60).—Softening of Tenues, hardening of Mediae (§ 61).—Aspiration and Loss thereof (§ 62)—Changes of Consonant-classes (§ 63).—Cerebrals for Dentals (§ 64).

16. Metathesis in sound-groups and loss of Syllable through Haplology (§ 65) 106

17. Sandhi 107
Initial and final (§ 66).—Compositional Sandhi (§ 67).—External Sandhi: Generalities (§ 68).—Similar Vowels in Sandhi (§ 69).—Dissimilar Vowels in Sandhi (§ 70).—*e*, *o* and nasal vowels before vowels (§ 71).—Filling hiatus by consonants (§ 72).—Inorganic Sandhi-consonants (§ 73).—Confrontation of vowel and consonant (§ 74).

B. *Word-formation*

I. Noun (Substantive and Adjective) 115

1. Generalities 115
Nominal stems (§ 75).—Gender (§ 76).—Number and Case (§ 77).

2. *a*-declension 118
Masculines and neuters in *a* (§ 78).—Individual forms (§ 79).—Māgadhisms (§ 80).—Feminines in *ā* (§ 81).

3. *i*- and *u*-declension 122
Masculines in *i*, *u* (§ 82).—Individual forms (§ 83).—Stem *sakhi* (§ 84).—Neuters in *i*, *u* (§ 85).—Feminines in *i* (*ī*), *u* (*ū*) (§ 86).—Stems *sirī*, *hirī*, *itthī* (§ 87).

4. Diphthong-stems (§ 88) 127

5. Radical stems (§ 89) 127

PAGE

6. *r*-declension 128

Agent nouns (§ 90).—Words of relationship (§ 91).

7. *n*-Declension 130

Masculines in *an* (§ 92).—Stems *san*, *yuvan*, *maghavan*, *puman* (§ 93).—Neuters in *an* (§ 94).—Subst. and Adj. in *in* (§ 95).

8. *nt*-declension 134

Adjectives in *ant* (§ 96).—Present Participles in *nt* (§ 97).—Stems *arahant*, *sant*, *bhavant* (§ 98).

9. *s*-declension 138

Neuters in *as* (§ 99).—Masculines and Feminines in *as* (§ 100).—Neuters and Masculines in *is*, *us* (§ 101).

10. Adverbs and Comparison 140

Adverbs (§ 102).—Comparison (§ 103).

II. Pronoun 142

Personal Pronouns of first and second person (§ 104).—Pronoun of the third person (§ 105).—Strengthening of pronouns by other pronouns (§ 106).—Pronouns *esa*, *ena*, *tya*, *tuma* (§ 107).—Pronoun *ayaṃ* (§ 108).—Pronoun *asu* (§ 109).—Relative Pronoun (§ 110).—Interrogative Pronouns (§ 111).—Other Pronouns (§ 112).—Pronominal Adjectives (§ 113).

III. Numerals 152

1. Cardinal Numbers 152

The numbers 1 and 2 (§ 114).—The numbers 3 to 10 (§ 115).—The tens, hundreds, etc. (§ 116).—Application of Numerals (§ 117).

2. Ordinals, Distributives, Fractional Numbers, Numeral Adverbs, Numeral Adjectives and Numeral Substantives.

Ordinals (§ 118).—Distributives, etc. (§ 119).

IV. Verbal System 158

1. Generalities (§ 120) 158

PAGE

2. Present-system with Indicative, Subjunctive, Imperative and Optative 159

A. Present Indicative 159

Flexion (§ 121).—Remarks thereon (§ 122)

B. Subjunctive (§ 123) 160

C. Imperative 161

Flexion (§ 124).—Remarks on Active (§ 125).—Remarks on Medium (§ 126).

D. Optative 164

Flexion (§ 127).—Remarks on Active (§ 128).—Remarks on Medium (§ 129).

E. The Verbal Classes of Sanskrit in Pali 166

1. Thematic Conjugation 166

Class I (§ 130).—Roots in *i*, *ī*; root *bhū* (§ 131).—Redupl. roots of Cl. I (§ 132).—Roots *gam*, *yam*, *ruh* (§ 133).—Class VI (§ 134, 135).—Class IV (§ 136).—Roots *jar*, *śar*, *mar* (§ 137).—Root *jan*, Roots in *ā* (§ 138).—Class X, Causatives, *e*-flexion (§ 139).

2. Athematic Conjugation 175

Class II (§ 140).—Roots *as*, *brū* (§ 141).—Class III; Root *dhā* (§ 142).—Root *dā* (§ 143).—Class VII (§ 144).—Class IX (§ 145).—Roots *grah*, *mā*, *bandh* (§ 146).—Class V (§ 147).—Roots *śak*, *āp* (§ 148).—Class VIII, with root *kar* (§ 149).

3. Future with Conditional 183

Two Types: Paradigms (§ 150).—Type Ia (§ 151).—Type Ib (§ 152).—Roots in *r* (*kar*, *har*) and root *han* (§ 153).—Type II (§ 154).—New formations from Present stems of the Thematic Conjugation (§ 155).—New formations from Present stems of the Athematic Conjugation (§ 156).—Conditional (§ 157).

4. Aorist 190

Generalities (§ 158).—Four Types: Paradigms (§ 159).—Type I (§ 160).—Type II (§ 161).—Roots *kar*, *bhū*, *vac* (§ 162).—Type III (§ 163).—Historical forms from roots in mutes and sibilants (§ 164).—New formations after Type III (§ 165).—

PAGE

Type IV (§ 166).—New formations after Type IV from Present Stems of the Thematic Conjugation Cl. I and VI (§ 167).—Cl. IV and X (§ 168).—New formations from Present Stems of the Athematic Conjugation (§ 169).—Details (§ 170).

5. Perfect (§ 171) 202

6. Periphrastic Constructions 202

Periphrastic Future (§ 172).—Periphrastic Perfect (§ 173).—Periphrastic Constructions with Present Participle and Gerund (§ 174).

7. Passive 204

Passive formation with *ya* (§ 175).—Passive formation with *iya* (§ 176).—Flexion; Passive Aorist in *i* (§ 177).

8. Causative 207

Unmodified roots and *a*-roots (§ 178).—Roots with internal *i*, *u* and with final ī̆ ū̆; details (§ 179).—Roots in *ā* (180).—New formations with *āpaya*, *āpe* (§ 181).—Double-causatives (§ 182).—Flexion (§ 183).

9. Desiderative (§ 184). 211

10. Intensive (§ 185) 211

11. Denominative 212

Formations with *āya* (§ 186).—Formations with *aya* (*e*) and *āpaya* (*āpe*) (§ 187).—Formations with *a*, *ya*, *iya* (§ 188).—Flexion (§ 189).

12. Verbal Nouns 214

1. Participles of Present and Future—Active 214

Participles in *nt*, *nta*, (§ 190).—Participles in *māna* (§ 191).—Participles in *āna* (§ 192).—Participles from Futural Stem (§ 193).

2. Participles of the Preterite 217

Participles in *ta* (§ 194).—Participles in *ita* (§ 195).—New formations in *ita* from Present Stems (§ 196).—Participles in *na* (§ 197).—Active Participles of Preterite (§ 198).

PAGE

3. Participles of Future—Passive 221

Participles in *tabba*; New formations (§ 199).—Root *bhū* and *e*-stems (§ 200).—Participles in *anīya*, *aneyya* (§ 201).—Participles in *ya* (§ 202).—Participles in *tāya*, *tayya*, *teyya* (§ 203).

4. Infinitives 224

Infinitives in *tave*, *tuye*, *tāye*, *tase*. Datives of Verbal Nouns used as Inf. (§ 204).—Infinitives in *tuṃ* (§ 205).—New formations in *tuṃ* from Present Stems (§ 206).—Inf. in compounds with *kāma* (§ 207).

5. Gerunds 226

Generalities (§ 208).—Historical forms in *tvā*, *tvāna*, *itvā*, *itvāna* (§ 209).—New formations from Present Stems (§ 210).—Gerunds in *tūna* (§ 211).—Gerunds in *ya* (§ 212).—Gerunds in *iya* and New formations (§ 213).—Gerunds in *yāna*.

INDEX 233

PREFACE

The following English version of Professor Geiger's "Pāli Literatur und Sprache" offers more than the German original, for much new material, supplied by Professor Geiger himself, has been incorporated into it. Professor Geiger also secured the permission of the German Publishers.

I distinctly remember that at the first lecture on Pāli I attended at the Munich University I was taught the Law of Mora, the corner-stone of Pāli Phonology. My astonishment, therefore, can be well imagined when I discovered that many of the Czars of Pāli in India have never even *heard* of this law! It is all the more remarkable, because Professor Geiger's work is well known in our University and is in fact one of the text-books prescribed for M.A. students in Pāli. On account of the language difficulty, however, our students have not hitherto been able to make full use of it. There was thus a clear case for translating Professor Geiger's work into English.

The translation was completed on 29th June, 1937. But the Calcutta University Press, always busy with a thousand things, could not pay undivided attention to printing it. Hence the inordinate delay in bringing out this translation, which at least some students of Pāli are anxiously waiting for.

In references to Prose texts, line too has been given throughout; thus A.I.2^3 = Aṅguttara-Nikāya, vol. I, p. 2, l. 3.

My thanks are due first of all to Professor Geiger, my honoured teacher and my teacher's teacher. I am grateful also to Professors Suniti Kumar Chatterji, Prabodh Chandra Bagchi, Sailendra Nath Mitra and Beni Madhab Barua for the interest they evinced in this translation.

31st December, 1942. BATAKRISHNA GHOSH

ABBREVIATIONS

A.	denotes	Aṅguttara-Nikāya, ed. by Morris and Hardy, 5 vols.
AbhKM.	,,	Abhandlungen für die Kunde des Morgenlandes.
AbhP.	,,	Abhidhamma-Piṭaka.
AIC.	,,	E. Müller, Ancient Inscriptions in Ceylon, London 1883.
Ak.	,,	Aṭṭhakathā.
AMāg.	,,	Ardha-Māgadhī.
Ap.	,,	Apabhraṃśa.
BB.	,,	Beiträge zur Kunde der Indogermanischen Sprachen, ed. by Bezzenberger.
Beitr.	,,	E. Kuhn, Beiträge zur Pāli-Grammatik.
Bodh.	,,	Mahābodhivaṃsa, ed. by Strong.
BR.	,,	Sanskrit-Wörterbuch von O. Böhtlingk und R. Roth, 7 vols., St. Petersburg 1855 ff.
Bu.	,,	Buddhavaṃsa, ed. by Morris.
Catal.	,,	Catalogue.
Co.	,,	Commentary.
Cp.	,,	Cariyāpiṭaka, ed. by Morris.
CV.	,,	Cullavagga.
D.	,,	Dīgha-Nikāya, ed. by Rhys Davids and Carpenter, 3 vols. Parts translated by R. O. Franke.
DCo.	,,	Sumaṅgala-Vilāsinī, Comm. on D., I, ed. by Rhys Davids and Carpenter.
Dh.	,,	Dhammapada, ed. by Fausböll.
DhCo.	,,	The Commentary on the Dhammapada (Dhammapadaṭṭhakathā), ed. by Norman, 4 vols.
Dhk.	,,	Dhātukathā, ed. by Gooneratne.
Dhs.	,,	Dhammasaṅgani, ed. by E. Müller.—Trans. by Mrs. Rhys Davids.
DhsCo.	,,	Atthasālinī, Comm. on Dhs., ed. by E. Müller.
Dial.	,,	Dialogues of the Buddha, Trans. by Mr. and Mrs. Rhys Davids, 2 vols. (SBB. II, III).

Dpvs.	denotes	Dīpavaṃsa, ed. and trans. by Oldenberg.
D. und M	,,	Geiger, Dīpavaṃsa und Mahāvaṃsa.
Gdhvs.	,,	Gandhavaṃsa, ed. by. Minayeff.
GGA.	,,	Göttingische Gelehrte Anzeigen.
GN.	,,	Nachrichten der Kgl. Gesellschaft der Wissenschaften zu Gött'ngen.
IA.	,,	Indian Antiquary.
IF.	,,	Indogermanische Forschungen, ed. by Streitberg.
Iv.	,,	Itivuttaka, ed. by Windisch.—Trans. by Moore.
Jā.	,,	Jātaka (quotations from the Canonical Gāthās).
JāCo.	,,	Jātaka Commentary (quotations from the prose parts of the Jātakaṭṭhavaṇṇanā, ed. by Fausböll, 7 vols).
JAs.	,,	Journal Asiatique.
JMāh.	,,	Jaina-Māhārāṣṭrī.
JPTS.	,,	Journal of the Pāli Text Society.
JRAS.	,,	Journal of the Royal Asiatic Society.
Kacc.	,,	Kaccāyana, ed. and trans. by Senart.
Kh.	,,	Khuddakapāṭha, ed. by Childers.—Trans. by Sei lenstücker.
Kvu.	,,	Kathāvatthuppakaraṇa, ed., by Taylor.
KZ.	,,	Kuhns Zeitschrift für vergleichende Sprachforschung.
LSprS.	,,	Geiger, Literatur und Sprache der Singhalesen, Strassburg 1900.
M.	,,	Majjhima-Nikāya, ed. by Trenckner and Chalmers, 3 vols.
Māg.	,,	Māgadhī.
Māh.	,,	Māhārāṣṭrī.
Mhvs.	,,	Mahāvaṃsa, ed. by Geiger—Trans. by Geiger.
Milp.	,,	Milindapañhā, ed. by Trenckner.—Trans. by Rhys Davids, 2 vols. (=SBE. XXXV, XXXVI).
MV.	,,	Mahāvagga.

Nām.	denotes	Subhūti, Nāmamālā.
Nett.	,,	Nettippakaraṇa, ed. by Hardy.
Notes	,,	Trenckner, Notes to the Milindapañhā (JPTS. 1908, 102 ff.).
OB.	,,	Orientalische Bibliographie.
P.	,,	Pāli.
Paiś.	,,	Paiśācī.
PD.	,,	Childers, Dictionary of the Pāli Language.
PGL.	,,	Andersen, Pāli Reader, II. Pāli Glossary.
PGr	,,	Pāli Grammar; 1. Minayeff, Pāli Grammar; 2. E. Müller, Simplified Grammar of the Pāli Language; 3. R. O. Franke, Gesch. und Krit. der einheim. Pāli-Grammatik.
Pkr.	,,	Prākrit.
PkrGr.	,,	Pischel, Gramm. der Prākrit-Sprachen, Strassburg 1900.
PLB.	,,	Bode, Pāli Literature of Burma.
PR.	,,	Andersen, Pāli Reader.
Ps.	,,	Paṭisambhidāmagga, ed. by Taylor.
PTS.	,,	Pali Text Society.
Pu.	,,	Puggalapaññatti, ed. by Morris.
Pv.	,,	Petavatthu, ed. by Minayeff.
PvCo.	,,	Paramatthadīpanī III., Co. on Pv., ed. by Hardy.
Rasav.	,,	Rasavāhinī, ed. by Saraṇatissa.
S.	,,	Saṃyutta-Nikāya, ed. by Feer, 5 vols.
Ś.	,,	Saurasenī.
Sāras.	,,	Sārasaṃgaha, ed. by Somananda.
Sāsvs.	,,	Sāsanavaṃsa, ed. by Bode.
SBB.	,,	Sacred Books of the Buddhists, ed. by Rhys Davids.
SBE.	,,	Sacred Books of the East, ed. by Max Müller.
Sdhs.	,,	Saddhammasaṃgaha, ed. by Saddhānanda.
Skr.	,,	Sanskrit.
Smp.	,,	The Historical Introduction to Buddhaghosa's Samanta Pāsādikā, ed. by Oldenberg in Vin. III, 283 ff.

Sn.	denotes	Sutta-Nipāta, ed. by Andersen and Smith.
SP.	,,	Sutta-Piṭaka.
SV.	,,	Sutta-Vibhaṅga.
Th1.	,,	Theragāthā, ed. by Oldenberg.
Th2.	,,	Therīgāthā, ed. by Pischel.
Th2Co.	,,	Paramatthadīpanī, Co. on Th2., ed. by J. E. Müller.
Ṭī.	,,	Ṭikā.
Ud.	,,	Udāna, ed. by Steinthal.—Trans. by Strong.
Vbh.	,,	Vibhaṅga, ed. by Mrs. Rhys Davids.
Vin.	,,	Vinaya-Piṭakaṃ, ed. by Oldenberg, 5 vols.
VP.	,,	Vinaya-Piṭaka.
-vs.	,,	-vaṃsa.
VT.	,,	Vinaya Texts, trans. by Rhys Davids and Oldenberg, 3 vols. (=SBE. XIII. XVII. XX.).
Vv.	,,	Vimānavatthu, ed. by Gooneratne.
VvCo.	,,	Paramatthadīpanī IV, Co. on Vv., ed. by Hardy.
WZKM.	,,	Wiener Zeitschrift für die Kunde des Morgenlandes.
ZDMG.	,,	Zeitschrift der Deutschen Morgenländischen Gesellschaft.

PĀLI LITERATURE AND LANGUAGE

INTRODUCTION

I. By Pāli is understood the language in which is composed the Tipiṭaka, the sacred scriptures of Ceylon and Hinter India, and its ancillary literature. The word *Pāli* however signifies only "text," "sacred text."[1] If we use this word to designate the language, it is merely a convenient abbreviation for *pālibhāsā*. Synonymous with *pālibhāsā* is *tantibhāsā*.

Pāli is an archaic Prākrit, a Middle-Indian idiom, which is characterised by the same peculiarities which distinguish the Middle-Indian from the Old-Indian.[2] Pāli, however, cannot be directly derived from Sanskrit; for it shows a number of characteristic features which suggest its closer relation to Vedic. Thus the ger. in *-tvāna* (beside *-tvā*), the forms *tehi*, *yehi*=Ved. *tebhis*, *yebhis* (as opposed to Skr. *tais*, *yais*), etc. This has always to be borne in mind when in the following Pāli forms are compared with Sanskrit forms. The former cannot be derived from the latter but stand beside them as later formations.

II. Pāli is not a homogeneous language. Numerous double forms reveal it to be a mixed dialect. Dialectical particularisms are found in it in large numbers. Yet, however, stages of development associated with periods following one after another can be clearly distinguished in the history of the Pāli language. Four different stages can be distinguished:

1. The language of the Gāthās, *i.e.*, the metrical pieces. It is of a very heterogeneous character. On the one hand, it contains many archaic speech-forms which are distinguished from the Old-Indian forms only phonologically; on the other hand, there are also used in it in large numbers such new formations as are wholly characteristic of Pāli, and they are often crossed by the archaic forms

1 *Cf.* the expression *iti pi pāli*, *e.g.*, Th2Co. 61[8], where *pāli*=*pāṭho*. Further, *pāli* "sacred text" as distinct from *aṭṭhakathā*, Dpvs. 20. 20; Mhvs. 33. 100; Sdhs. JPTS. 1890, p. 58[b].

2 R. O Franke, Strassburg 1902, Pāli und Sanskrit, p. 90 ff..

which may occur side by side with them, not seldom even in one and the same verse. In some cases the exigencies of metre might have determined the choice of the forms to be used. Particularly in those cases where verses out of an older language were translated into a later one, the use of archaic forms was liberal, because it afforded a closer approximation to the original.

2. The language of the canonical prose. It is more homogeneous and uniform than the language of the Gāthās. The archaic forms diminish more and more in number and partly disappear altogether. The use of new formations is no longer accidental or arbitrary as in the oldest period of the language, but is governed by more rigid rules.

3. The later prose of the post-canonical literature, as of the Milinda-book, the great commentaries, etc. It is based on the canonical prose and reflects its artificial and erudite usage. The difference between the first and the second period is therefore much greater than that between the second and the third. The latter is further characterised by a still more restricted use of the archaic forms.

4. The language of later artificial poetry, which no longer possesses a homogeneous character. The authors derived their knowledge of the language and borrowed the speech-forms indiscriminately from older and later literature, and their propensity to archaism and Sanskritism is more pronounced or less in different cases.

III. There is now on the whole a consensus of opinion that Pāli bears the clear stamp of a "Kunstsprache," *i.e.*, it is a compromise of various dialects. This has been most emphatically declared by H. Kern.[1] Minayeff's[2] opinion stands close to his. But already E. Kuhn[3] rightly pointed out that the problem is not solved merely by defining Pāli as an artificial language—its solution is only deferred by it. "Even an artificial and literary language, which on occasions draws materials from all possible dialects, must have had as its foundation a particular dialect." For Pāli now arises the question, which region of India was the home of that language which was the basis of Pāli.

[1] Over de Jaartelling der zuidelijke Buddhisten en de Gedenkstukken van Açoka den Buddhist, Amsterdam 1873, p. 18.

[2] Pāli Grammar, p. xlii.

[3] Beiträge zur Pāli-Grammatik, Berlin 1875, p. 9.

IV. According to the tradition current in Ceylon, Pāli is Māgadhī, *Māgadhānirutti*, *Māgadhikabhāsā*, that is to say, the language of the region in which Buddhism had arisen. This is very important, for strengthened by this argument the Buddhistic tradition makes the further claim that the Pāli-Tipiṭaka is composed in the language used by Buddha himself [1] and therefore in contrast to all other collections it alone represents the original canon. For this reason Māgadhī is also called *Mūlabhāsā* [2] as the basic language in which the words of Buddha were originally fixed, whereas the other versions are regarded as secondary variations.

V. Weighty arguments have however been urged against the view that Pāli is a dialectical form of Māgadhī or is based on it. Precisely the chief distinguishing features of Māgadhī, as we know them from the grammarians and from the inscriptions and the dramas, are unknown to Pāli. These features are: 1. the mutation of every *r* into *l* and every *s* into *ś*, and 2. the ending *-e* in N. Sg. Masc. and Neut. of *a*-stems and of consonantal stems inflected like them. Pāli however retains the *r* (its change into *l* is indeed frequent but not the rule), and possesses no *ś* at all, but only *s*, and the nominal forms mentioned above end in it with *-o*, or *-aṃ*. For this reason already Burnouf and Lassen [3] contested the theory that Pāli is a Magadha-dialect.

VI. Westergaard,[4] and after him E. Kuhn,[5] consider Pāli to be the dialect of Ujjayinī, because it stands closest to the language of the Asoka-inscriptions of Girnar (Guzerat), and also because the dialect of Ujjayinī is said to have been the mother-tongue of Mahinda who preached Buddhism in Ceylon. R. O. Franke reached a similar conclusion by altogether different means.[6] In his attempt to locate Pāli by eliminating all those Indian popular dialects which, on account of their peculiar linguistic features, cannot be regarded as the source of Pāli, he finally reached the conclusion that its original home was "a territory,

[1] *Cf.* Buddhaghosa: *ettha sakā nirutti nāma sammāsaṃbuddhena vuttappakāro Māgadhiko vohāro*, comm. to Culla-Vagga V. 33.1. See Samantapāsādikā, ed. Saya U Pye, IV. 416^{10}.

[2] Sdhs., JPTS. 1890, pp. 55^{23}, 56^{21}, 57^{19}.

[3] Essai sur le Pāli, Paris 1826.

[4] Über den ältesten Zeitraum der indischen Geschichte, p. 87.

[5] Beitr., p. 6 ff. *Cf.* Muir, Original Sanskrit Texts, II^2, p. 356.

[6] Pāli und Sanskrit, p. 131 ff. By Pāli I of course always understand what has been called "literary Pāli" by Franke.

which could not have been too narrow, situated about the region from the middle to the western Vindhya ranges." Thus it is not improbable that Ujjayinī was the centre of its region of expansion. Sten Konow[1] too has decided in favour of the Vindhya region as the home of Pāli. In his opinion there is a closer relationship between Pāli and Paiśācī, and differing from his predecessors in the field, particularly from Grierson,[2] he seeks the original home of Paiśācī not in North-West India but in the region of Ujjayinī.

VII. Oldenberg[3] considers Pāli to be the language of the Kaliṅga country. He considers the legend of Mahinda and his mission to be unhistorical. In his opinion Buddhism, and with it the Tipiṭaka, was introduced into Ceylon rather in course of an intercourse between the island and the neighbouring continent extending over a long period. As regards the character of the language, he compares it above all with that of the inscription of Khandagiri, which, in his opinion, agrees with Pāli on essential points. Also E. Müller[4] considers the Kaliṅga country to be the home of Pāli. He bases his conclusion on the observation that the oldest settlements in Ceylon could have been founded only from the opposite mainland and not by people from Bengal or thereabout.

VIII. A consensus of opinion regarding the home of the dialect on which Pāli is based has therefore not been achieved.[5] Windisch[6] therefore falls back on the old tradition—and I am also inclined to do the same—according to which Pāli should be regarded as a form of Māgadhī, the language in which Buddha himself had preached. This language of Buddha was however surely no purely popular dialect, but a language of the higher and cultured classes which had been brought into being already in pre-Buddhistic times through the needs of inter-

[1] The home of Paiśācī, ZDMG. 64. 95ff., particularly 103 f., 114 f., 118.

[2] The Paiśācī Languages of North-Western India, Asiatic Society Monographs, Vol. VIII, 1906; Pischel, Gramm. der Prākrit-Sprachen, § 27.

[3] The Vinaya Piṭaka I, London 1879, p. L ff.

[4] Simplified Grammar of the Pāli Language, London 1884, p. III.

[5] I refer particularly to H. Lüders, Bruchstücke buddhistischer Dramen, Berlin 1911, p. 40 ff.; A. Berriedale Keith, Pāli, the Language of the Southern Buddhists, Ind. Hist. Qu. I, 1925, p. 501 ff.; P. V. Bapat. The Relation between Pāli and Ardhamāgadhi, *Ibid.*, IV. 1928, p. 23 ff.

[6] Über den sprachlichen Charakter des Pāli, in the Actes du XIVe Congrès International des Orientalistes. Algère 1905, prem. partie, Paris 1906, p. 252 ff. Windish's opinion is similar to that of Winternitz, A History of Indian Literature, Vol. II, p. 13.

communication in India.[1] Such a *lingua franca* naturally contained elements of all the dialects, but was surely free from the most obtrusive dialectical characteristics. It was surely not altogether homogeneous. A man from the Magadha country must have spoken it in one way, and a man from the districts of Kosala and Avanti in another, just as in Germany the high German of a cultured person from Württemberg, Saxony or Hamburg shows in each case peculiar characteristic features. Now, as Buddha, although he was no Magadhan himself, displayed his activities mainly in Magadha and the neighbouring countries, the Māgadhī dialect might have imprinted on his language its own characteristic stamp. This language could have therefore been well called Māgadhī even if it avoided the grossest dialectical peculiarities of this language. As Windisch has rightly pointed out, after the death of the master, a new artificial language must have been evolved out of the language of Buddha. Attempts were made to retain the teachings of Buddha in authentic form, and to impose this form also upon those portions which, although derived from the monastic organisations of the various provinces, were gradually incorporated into the canon. In connection with the designation of the canonical language as Māgadhī, Windisch also refers to the Ārṣa, the language of the Jaina-suttas. It is called Ardha-Māgadhī, *i.e.*, "half-Māgadhi." Now it is surely significant that the Ardha-Māgadhī differs from Māgadhī proper on similar points as Pāli.[2] For Ardha-Māgadhī too does not change the *r* into *l*, and in the noun inflexion it shows the ending *-o* instead of Māgadhic *-e* at least in many metrical pieces. On the other hand, as I believe to have myself observed, there are many remarkable analogies precisely between Ārṣa and Pāli in vocabulary and morphology. Pāli therefore might be regarded as a kind of Ardha-Māgadhī. I am unable to endorse the view, which has apparently gained much currency at present, that the Pāli canon is translated from some other dialect (according to Lüders, from old Ardha-Māgadhī). The peculiarities of its language may be fully explained on the hypothesis of (*a*) a gradual development and integration of various elements from different parts of India, (*b*) a long oral tradition extending over several centuries, and (*c*) the fact that the texts were written down in a different country.

IX. I consider it wiser not to hastily reject the tradition altogether but rather to understand it to mean that Pāli was

[1] For a graphic description, see Rhys Davids, Buddhist India, p. 140 ff.

[2] Pischel, Gramm. d. Pkr. Spr., p. 15.

indeed no pure Māgadhī, but was yet a form of the popular speech which was based on Māgadhī and which was used by Buddha himself. It would appear therefore that the Pāli canon represents an effort [1] to reflect the *Buddhavacanaṃ* in its original form. This theory would have been refuted if it could be proved that the Pāli canon must have been translated from some other dialect. Sylvain Lévi[2] has tried to prove this. He points out a number of termini such as *ekodi*, *saṃghādisesa*, etc., in which a sonant appears in the place of a surd. From these data he infers the existence of a pre-canonical language in which the softening of intervocalic surds was the rule. I do not consider Lévi's arguments to be convincing. Firstly, because all these etymologies given by Lévi are uncertain. Secondly, because the softening of surds takes place not only in the "termini" but also in a large number of other words.[3] Moreover, in my opinion, no special case should be made out of this phonological phenomenon. For they merely represent one of the various dialectical peculiarities which are met with in Pāli. Thus, for instance, we find equally frequent cases of the opposite process (hardening of a sonant) as well as various other features which considered together prove the mixed character of the Pāli language.

X. If Pāli is the form of the Māgadhī used by Buddha, then the Pāli canon would have to be regarded as the most authentic form of the *Buddhavacanaṃ*, even though the teachings of the master might have been preached and learnt from the very beginning in the various provinces of India in the respective local dialects. This conclusion has been drawn—wrongly, in my opinion—from Cullavagga V.33.1=Vin. II.139. Here it is related, how two Bhikkhus complained to the master that the members of the order were of various origins, and that they distorted the words of Buddha by their own dialect (*sakāya niruttiyā*). They therefore proposed that the words of Buddha should be translated into Sanskrit verses (*chandaso*). Buddha however refused to grant the request and added: *anujānāmi*

[1] I say this intentionally; for, as the Pāli canon is the result of a long development extending over more than one century, it would naturally contain much that is unauthentic. It may have also lost much that is authentic and is preserved in other canons.

[2] Journal Asiatique, sér. 10, t. XX. p. 495 ff.

[3] Cf. below, § 38 f.

bhikkhave sakāya niruttiyā buddhavacanaṃ pariyāpuṇituṃ. Rhys Davids and Oldenberg [1] translate this passage by "I allow you,[2] oh brethren, to learn the words of the Buddhas each in his own dialect." This interpretation however is not in harmony with that of Buddhaghosa, according to whom it has to be translated by "I ordain the words of Buddha to be learnt in *his* own language (*i.e.*, in Māgadhī, the language used by Buddha himself)."[3] After repeated examinations of this passage I have come to the conclusion that we have to stick to the explanation given by Buddhaghosa. Neither the two monks nor Buddha himself could have thought of preaching in different dialects in different cases. Here the question is merely whether the words of Buddha might be translated into Sanskrit or not. This is however clearly forbidden by the Master, at first negatively and then positively by the injunction beginning with *anujānāmi*. The real meaning of this injunction is, as is also best in consonance with Indian spirit, that there can be no other form of the words of Buddha than in which the Master himself had preached. Thus even in the life-time of Buddha people were concerned about the way in which his teaching might be handed down as accurately as possible, both in form and in content. How much more must have been the anxiety of the disciples after his death! The external form was however Māgadhī, though according to tradition it is Pāli.[4]

[1] Vinaya Texts III = Sacred Books of the East, XX, p. 151.

[2] In the text there is no *vo*! But I think this word was indispensable for the interpretation given by the English translators in order to get something with which to connect *sakāya niruttiyā*. According to the actual text *saka* may be connected only with *buddhavacanaṃ*. For the meaning "ordains, decides" for *anujānāti*, cf. Vin., I. 45^{25}, 83^{31}, $85^{19,24}$, 94^{13}, etc.

[3] Cf. above, p. 3, f.n. 1.

[4] See Fr. Weller, Zeitschr. für Buddhismus, 1922, pp. 211-13 and my reply, *Ibid.*, pp. 213-14.

PART I

PĀLI LITERATURE

Preliminary notice. 1. Previous works: J. d' Alwis, A descriptive Catalogue of Sanskrit, Pāli, and Sinhalese Literary Works of Ceylon, Colombo 1870.—H. Oldenberg, Catalogue of Pāli MSS. in the India Office Library, London 1882 (App. to JPTS. 1882).—L. de Zoysa. A Catalogue of Pāli, Sinhalese and Sanskrit MSS. in the Temple Libraries of Ceylon, Colombo 1885—Catalogues of MSS.: JPTS. 1882, 50 ff.; 1883, 133 ff.; 1885, 1 ff.; 1888, 108 ff. Also Fausböll, Catal. of the Mandalay MSS. in the Ind. Off. Libr., JPTS. 1896, 1 ff.

2. Short surveys and descriptions of particular aspects: H. Kern, Manual of Indian Buddhism, Strassburg 1896, pp. 1-11.—Rhys Davids, Buddhism, London 1910, p. 18 ff.; Buddhist India, London 1903, p. 140 ff.—E. Hardy, Der Buddhismus, Münster i. W. 1890, p. 159 f.—Winternitz, Die Religionen Indiens; Der Buddhismus in Bertholet's Religionsgeschichtliches Lesebuch, 1911, p. 214 ff. Wickremasinghe, Catal. of the Sinhalese MSS. in the Brit. Mus., London 1900, Introd.—M. Bode, The Pāli Literature of Burma, London 1909.—S. Z. Aung, Abhidhamma Literature in Burma, JPTS. 1910-12, p. 112 ff.

3. Comprehensive treatment in Winternitz, A History of Indian Literature, Vol. II, pp. 1-423, Calcutta 1933.—G. P. Malalasekera. The Pāli Literature of Ceylon, London 1928.—B. C. Law, History of Pāli Literature, 2 vols., London 1933. In view of these special treatises it is permissible for me to be very brief with the contents and the historical importance of the chief works. They are therefore a necessary supplement to the present work.

An important source book is the Gandhavaṃsa, edited by Minayeff, JPTS, 1886, p. 54 ff. Index to it by M. Bode, *Ibid.* 1896, p. 53 ff.

I. THE CANONICAL LITERATURE

1. *Origin and Authenticity of the Canon*

1. The Pāli canon is known under the name Tipiṭaka (Skr. Tripiṭaka), *i.e.*, "Threefold basket," because it consists of three main parts: Vinaya-Piṭaka, Sutta-Piṭaka and Abhidhamma-Piṭaka. It is the canon of the Theravāda school which itself belongs to the Vibhajjavādins.[1] According to tradition, which on essential points is probably quite dependable,[2] its compilation began immediately after the death of Buddha about 483 B.C.,[3] at the council of Rājagaha. It was further developed a hundred years later at the council of Vesālī, the chief cause of which was the cropping up of certain wrong views which were threatening to undermine monastic discipline. At the third council under king Asoka (264 to 227 B.C.)[4] the canon in all its essential parts seems to have been brought to a formal completion.

[1] On the relation between the two designations, see Oldenberg, Vin. I, p. XLI ff.; Geiger Mahāvaṃsa transl., App. B. 14b.

[2] The history of the councils is based mainly on CV. XI. LII = Vin. II. 284. ff,; Dpvs. Chaps. 4-5.54, 7.34 ff,; Mhvs. Chaps. 3-5. Also Buddhaghosa's Samantapāsādikā, Introd. (Oldenberg, Vin. III. 283 ff.) and Sumaṅgalavilāsinī (ed. Rhys Davids and Carpenter. PTS. 1886 p. 2 ff.). Further Geiger, Mhvs. transl., p. LI ff. For the history of the Pāli canon, cf. Oldenberg, Vin. I, p. XL ff.; Buddhistische Studien, ZDMG. 52, 1898, p. 613 ff.; Buddha[6], p. 84 ff.; Oldenberg and Rhys Davids, Vin. Texts I = SBE.XIII, Introd.; Rhys Davids, Dialogues of the Buddha I = SBB II. Preface; Winternitz, A Hitory of Indian Literature, Vol. II. 1 ff. (cf. literature given under f.n. 1). More sceptical about the tradition are Minayeff, Recherches sur le Bouddhisme, trad. par Propignan. Paris 1894; L. de La Valée Poussin, Conciles Bouddhiques I. Le Muséon N.S.6, 1905, p. 213 ff.(cf. I.A. 37, 1 ff., 81ff.); Barth, Rev. de l' hist. des religions 5, 1882, p. 237 ff.; 28, 1893, p. 277 ff.; 42,1900, p. 74 ff.; Sylv. Lévi, Les saintes écritures du Bouddhisme, Paris 1909, and particularly R. O. Franke, The Buddhist Councils, JPTS. 1908, p. 1. ff; Dighanikāya transl., 1913, p. XLII ff.

[3] For the sake of brevity I only refer to Winternitz, Ibid., p. 4, as well as the data given by me in Mhvs. transl., p. XXII ff.

[4] Kashi-Prasad Jayaswal (Journ. As. Soc. Bengal, N.S. IX, Nr. 8 and 9, p. 317 ff.) has calculated the year of Asoka's accession to the throne to be 276 B.C., and his coronation at 272 B.C.

This council is specially associated with the formation of the Abhidhamma, for according to tradition, the Thera Tissa Moggaliputta is said to have recited at it the Kathāvatthuppakaraṇa. This book contains the refutation of 252 different wrong teachings and is included among the works of Abhidhamma.[1] The third council was also of importance on account of the resolution to send missions to neighbouring countries. The tradition is here supported in an interesting manner by epigraphical discoveries.[2] Mahinda (Skr. Mahendra), the son of king Asoka,[3] went to Ceylon as the messenger of the teachings of Buddha. He brought to Ceylon the canon in its Theravāda form.

2. The gradual formation of the canon may be imagined to have come about in the way, that in particular monastic orders the memories of the speeches and dialogues of the master were kept alive so far as they were known at all. Hence the introductory words *evaṃ me sutaṃ* "so have I heard." At larger gatherings, as at the councils, these particular contributions were examined and given monastic sanction in favourable cases. In this way the material grew up continually and was classified into particular collections. Such an origin of the canon renders it understandable that already at the beginning there was given the possibility of the formation of different schools.[4] On the occasion of the second council, therefore, there arose in the church the schism of the Theravādins and the Mahāsāṃghikas. The main body of the canon therefore should have been collected in the first two centuries after the death of Buddha. Titles such as *dhammakathika, peṭakin, suttantika, pañcanekāyika*[5] occurring in inscriptions of the 3rd century B.C. prove that already at that time the canon must have been divided in the same manner as in later days. Of the seven texts which were specially recommended for study by king Asoka in Bhabra edict, four or five may be traced in the

[1] Mhvs. 5.278.

[2] Cf. Rhys Davids, Buddhist India, p. 299 ff.; Geiger, Mhvs. transl, p. XIX f.

[3] According to the tradition recorded by Hiuen-thsang in the Si-yu-ki, Mahinda was Asoka's brother. Cf. St. Julien, Mém. sur les Contrées Occidentales par Hiouen-Thsang II. 140.

[4] The story of Purāṇa in CV.XI. 1. 11 (=Vin. II, 289 f.) is very important in this respect. Purāṇa comes to Rājagaha where Buddha's disciples had assembled after his death. He is asked to take part in the council but he courteously declines saying that he would prefer to adhere to what he had himself heard from the Master's lips.

[5] Cf. Hultzsch, ZDMG. 40.58; Bühler, Epigraphia Indica II. 93; Rhys Davids, Buddhist India, p. 167 f.; Winternitz, *op. cit.*, pp. 13 ff.

Pāli canon with tolerable certainty.[1] It is also very remarkable that the name of Asoka, who is so much praised in all Buddhist orders, has never been mentioned in the canon. The assumption is justified therefore that in Asoka's time the formation of the canon had been practically completed. In the first few centuries however the canon used to be handed down orally. The Tipiṭaka along with its commentary Aṭṭhakathā was fixed in writing, according to a notice in Dpvs. and Mhvs., which gives the impression of being quite trustworthy, only under king Vaṭṭagāmani, *i.e.*, a few decades before the beginning of the Christian era.[2]

3. Many peculiarities of the Pāli canon may be understood only if the way in which it came about is kept in view and it is remembered that it was handed down orally for nearly four hundred years. As the contributions to the canon came from different places at different times various contradictions could not be avoided, as has been pointed out by R. O. Franke.[3] We can thus also understand the schematic character of the canon and the numerous repetitions occurring in it. It is in the nature of an oral tradition that events and situations of common occurrence should be described in stereotyped form in the same words.[4] Much of what repeatedly occurs in the text was without doubt compulsory for the monks to learn. I consider as such the continually repeated synonymous expressions, the discussions in question and answer which almost look like formularies for the examinations which the monks had to pass,[5] the parables and similes, and the mnemonic verses. It has to be pointed out however that apparently even from the beginning the sacred texts were used for purposes of preaching.[6] Under such circumstances it was unavoidable

[1] *E.g.*, Ariyavāsā = D. III. 269 ff., Anāgatabhayāni = A. III. 105-108, Munigāthā = Sn. 207-221 (ed, D. Anderson and H. Smith), Moneyyasutta = A.I. 273, Lāghulovāda = M. I.414-420. For literature on this point, see Winternitz, *op. cit.* p. 16 ff.

[2] Dpvs. 20.20-21; Mhvs. 33.100-101.

[3] JPTS. 1908, p. 2 ff.; WZKM. 24,17 ff.; Dīghanikāya transl., p. XLIX.

[4] Thus, for instance, the greetings (M.I. 16^{16}, 40^{12}; D.I. 159^{3}, 161^{3}, etc.), the concluding words after a religious instruction (Vin. I. 16^{31}. D.I. 85^{7}, M. II. 39^{12}, S.I. 70^{6}, etc.), or the description of the various stages of the *jhāna* (Childers, P. Dict., *sub voce*), etc.

[5] Cf., for instance, the series *taṃ kiṃ maññatha, cakkhuṃ niccaṃ vā aniccaṃ vā ?* etc. M. III, 271 ff.; 277 ff. ; S. IV. 105 ff , etc.

[6] Recitation of such particular pieces is regarded as something self-evident in Dpvs. 8.6 ff., 12.84 ff., 13.7 ff., Mhvs. 12.29 ff., 14.58 and 63, 15.4 ff. (the Bālapaṇḍita-

that those texts which were familiar to every Bhikkhu should again and again thrust themselves into the sacred tradition. Of particular importance is the fact that not at all very seldom in one and the same collection two or more pieces follow each other having absolutely the same contents and wording, distinguished merely by the names of persons and places.[1] It is clear that in these cases we have to do with differences in tradition dating from the very beginning. When the collection of individual pieces began, the redactors quite naïvely arranged the variants one after another without trying to solve the problem of their authenticity. And finally, also the influence of purely literary activity might not have been quite negligible when the collections were compiled and written down. It is clear that the main tendency was to offer the material in as full a form as possible. It is not at all surprising therefore that from collections which were already existing whole pieces were taken into new collections whenever there seemed to be a sufficient reason to do so.[2] It however remains unknown which of the various forces was most potent in any particular case, and it is not at all unlikely that this question will never be solved satisfactorily.

4. It will be clear from what has been said above, in what sense we can speak of the authenticity of the canon. None will claim today that all that is contained in it is derived from Buddha himself. But without doubt it contains a mass of utterances, speeches and teachings of the Master, as they were impressed on the memory of the disciples in their more or less accurate form. It is however impossible to read, *e.g.*, the Mahāparinibbāṇasutta,[3] without getting the impression that here we are confronted with the actual reminiscences of the last days of the Master. Other texts, on the other hand, might be imitations of existing types, which were at least impregnated with the spirit of Buddha. Others again are purely monastic fiction. Such is the case, for instance, when in the Vinaya all the individual regulations about

suttanta mentioned in Mhvs. 15.4=Dpvs. 13.13=M. III. 163 ff.; wrongly Mhvs. trans. (p. 97. f.-n. 2). Cf. further, DhCo. I. 129 ff.

[1] Thus, for instance, Sutta 124, 125, 126 in S. IV. 109 f.; also Sutta 191, 192= S. IV. 162 ff. Cf. further S.I. 220-222 with 224, etc.

[2] Cf. the Sāmaññaphalasuttanta in D. I. 71 ff. with the Mahāassapura and the Mahāsakuludāyi-suttanta in M.I. 274 ff., II. 15 ff. The Selasuttanta occurs in Sn., p. 102 ff. and M. II. 146—in the latter perhaps interpolated later, for the preceding Suttanta deals with the same subject.

[3] D. II. 72 ff.

monastic discipline are attributed to the Master. Here too the formulated laws were modelled after certain types. But, on the other hand, we should not be too sceptical. The main body of the canon had at all events come into being in the first two centuries after the death of Buddha—at a time when the memory of the master might have been still fresh.[1] And we have indeed no reason to doubt the honest intention of the Bhikkhus. If we always keep in view the fundamental difference between the Greek and the Indian mode of thought, then it may perhaps yet be said that the picture of Buddha stands out of the Pāli canon in the same way as that of Socrates out of the writings of Xenophon and Plato.

2. *Classification of the Pāli Canon, Editions, Translations*

5. Beside the division of the canon into three Piṭakas "baskets"[2] the tradition of southern Buddhism knows also other divisions of the canon.[3] Thus 1. the division into five Nikāyas consisting of the first four Nikāyas of the Sutta-Piṭaka (D., M., S., A.), as well as the Khuddaka-Nikāya which in this connection comprehends also Vinaya and Abhidhamma.—2. The division into nine Aṅgas [4] is only formal. They are Sutta, Geyya, Veyyākaraṇa, Gāthā, Udāna, Itivuttaka, Jātaka, Abbhutadhamma and Vedalla.[5] By "Sutta" is meant all the dialogues of Buddha along with some pieces out of the Suttanipāta. All pieces composed in mixed prose and verse are called "Geyya." The "Veyyākaraṇa" includes the

[1] Sometimes the canonical works themselves betray the fact that they were composed long after Buddha. Thus, already in the Theragāthās, when Pārāpariya (v. 920-948) complains about the degenaration of discipline within the monastic order. In Petavatthu IV.3.1 is mentioned a King of Suraṭṭha, named Piṅgalaka. According to the commentary (PvCo.p.244) he should have lived two hundred years after the death of Buddha. This should give us however the lowest time limit, excepting of course occasional later additions.

[2] For the meaning of the word Piṭaka, see Winternitz *op. cit.*, p. 8, f.-n. 3.

[3] DCo. I. 22 ff.; DhsCo., pp. 25 ff.; Sārasaṃgaha, ed. Somananda, pp. 36 ff.; Dpvs. 4.15; Gdhvs., JPTS. 1886, pp. 55 ff. The nine Aṅgas are mentioned also in the canon itself: M.I. 133[24], A II. 7[2], 103[10], 108[1], Vin. III, 8[7], Pu. 43[29].

[4] According to the records of northern Buddhism there are twelve Aṅgas. Wassilieff, der Buddhismus 1, p. 109; Burnouf, Introd. sur le Bouddhisme, pp. 51 ff.; Kern, Manual of Ind. Buddhism, p. 7.

[5] Childers, PD. under these words.

Abhidhamma and some other texts. "Gāthās" are pieces composed solely in verse. The titles "Udāna," "Itivuttaka" and "Jātaka" will come up again for discussion below as parts of the Khuddaka-Nikāya. The Suttas which deal with supernatural conditions and powers are called "Abbhutadhamma." The meaning of the title "Vedalla"[1] is not clear.—Finally, from quite a mechanical point of view, the canon is divided into 84,000 Dhammakkhandhas,[2] *i.e.*, individual pieces or lectures.

6. Editions: 1. The edition in Siamese script printed in Bangkok at the cost of King Chulalongkorn in 39 vols. in which are still wanting the Jātakas, Avadāna, Vimāna- and Petavatthu, Thera- and Therīgāthā, Buddhavaṃsa, Cariyāpiṭaka. A monumental new edition of the whole Tipiṭaka in 45 vols. was executed by the late King of Siam (in Siamese script, printed in Bangkok).

2. The Rangoon Edition of the "Hanthawaddy Printing Works" in Burmese script (not available to me), 20 vols., containing Vinaya- and Abhidhamma-Piṭaka, as well as the Dīgha-Nikāya of the Sutta-Piṭaka.[3]

3. Editions of individual texts, printed in Sinhalese script in Ceylon: Dīgha-Nikāya published by W. A. Samarasekara, Colombo 1904 f. (see JPTS. 1912, p. 142); Majjhima-Nikāya, Colombo 1895 ff. (JPTS. 1912, p. 147); Saṃyutta-Nikāya, ed. B. Amarasiṇha, Welitara 1898 ff. (JPTS. 1912., p. 150); Aṅguttara-Nikāya, ed. Devamitta, Colombo 1893 ff. (JPTS. 1912, p. 137).

4. Individual texts published by the Pali Text Society in Roman characters comprehending most of the texts of the Sutta and Abhidhamma Piṭaka. See below. Oldenberg's edition of the Vinaya, Fausböll's edition of the Jātakas are special supplements.

Translations of individual texts by Rhys Davids, Oldenberg, Franke, K. E. Neumann, Dutoit, etc., have been mentioned below. There are moreover: T. W. Rhys Davids, Buddhist Suttas I, SBE. XI.—K. E. Neumann, Buddhistische Anthologie, Texte a. d. Pâli-

[1] In the list of Aṅgas in northern Buddhism, Vaipulya corresponds to Vedalla. But there is also a northern Buddhist work Vaidalya. Schiefner, Târanâtha's Gesch, des Buddhismus in Indien, p. 302.

[2] Childers, PD. under the word.

[3] Lanman, Pali Book Titles, Proc. Amer. Acad. of Arts and Sciences. XLIV, No. 24. 1909, p. 667.

Kanon übers, Leiden 1892.—Warren, Buddhism in Translations (also non-canonical texts), Harvard Or. Ser. III, Cambridge Mass. 1896.—Dutoit, Leben des Buddha, eine Zusammenstellung aller Ber. a. d. kanon. Schriften der südl. Buddhisten, Leipzig 1906.—Winternitz, Die Religionen der Inder: der Buddhismus (Bertholet's Religionsgeschichtl. Lesebuch, separate edition), Tübingen 1911.—H. Oldenberg, Reden des Buddha, München 1922—K. Seidenstücker, Pāli Buddhismus in Übersetzungen, München-Neubiberg 1923.

3. *Vinaya-Piṭaka*

7. The Vinaya-Piṭaka[1] contains the monastic rules of the order of Buddhist monks. It consists of the following parts:

1. Suttavibhaṅga: (*a*) Pārājika, (*b*) Pācittiya;
2. Khandhaka: (*a*) Mahāvagga, (*b*) Cullavagga.
3. Parivāra.

1. The Suttavibhaṅga is based on the Pātimokkha.[2] This is very probably one of the oldest texts, containing the formulary for the ceremony of confession, as it was performed on Uposatha-days in the monastic orders. The SV. is a commentary on this text. The individual transgressions are divided into categories in the order of their seriousness: *pārājikā dhammā* entailing excommunication from the order, *saṃghādisesā dh.*, *aniyatā dh.*, then *pācittiyā dhammā*, *pāṭidesaniyā dh.*, *sekhiyā dh.* In SV. a story is always given at first stating when the particular transgression was committed for the first time. Then follows in the words of the Pātimokkha the respective regulation for the expiation of the transgression, as well as a philological explanation of it and a casuistic discussion of individual cases and possibilities. To the Mahāvibhaṅga meant for the monks there is added at the end of the SV. also a Bhikkhunīvibhaṅga of similar

[1] The Vinaya-Piṭakaṃ, one of the principal Buddhist holy Scriptures in the Pāli Language, ed. H. Oldenberg, 5 vols., London 1879-83.—Vinaya Texts, transl. by T. W. Rhys Davids and H. Oldenberg, parts I, II, III (=SBE. XIII, XVII, XX), London 1881-85.—For the Gāthās occurring in the Vin. see R. O. Franke, WZKM. 24. 1 ff. On the whole problem, see Winternitz, *op. cit.*, p. 21 ff.

[2] Minayeff, Prātimoksha Sūtra, St. Petersburg, Akad. 1869; Dickson, The Pātimokkha, JRAS. 1875, p. 1 ff. Translation in Rhys Davids and Oldenberg, VT. I. 1 ff. Cf. Ibid., p. X ff., as well as the discussions about the relation between he Pāt. and SV. in Oldenberg, Vin. I, p. XV ff.

character.—2. The Khandhakas represent the positive counterpart to the SV. They contain the regulations which determine the course of life within the monastic order. The Mahāvagga consists of the first ten Khandhakas. Its introductory chapter gives a history of the time, from the Saṃbodhi to the founding of the first Saṅgha in Benares. The Cullavagga is but the continuation of the MV. At its end are added two supplementary Khandhakas (XI and XII) which contain the story of the first two Councils. Closely connected with the Khandhakas are the *kammavācā*, which are formularies for the various acts of the Church to be undertaken by the order. Seven such formularies are known, of which the *upasampadā-kammavācā*, the formulary for the ceremony of the initiation of a member into the order, is still much used among the southern Buddhists.[1] All the *kammavācā* known to us agree with the corresponding regulations of the Khandhakas, which are themselves only a collection of such formularies with more detailed explanation and justification.—3. The Parivāra, consisting of nineteen sections, is of later origin. In all probability it was originated only in Ceylon. This is certain of the introductory verses.[2] It is a manual of instruction about the contents of the Vinaya—a *mātikā* (table of contents) without any value of its own.

4. *Sutta-Piṭaka*

8. To the Sutta-Piṭaka belong firstly the first four Nikāyas—Dīgha-Majjhima-, Samyutta- and Aṅguttara-Nikāya. They are the "collections" of Suttas or Suttantas, *i.e.*, of speeches and dialogues of Buddha, or occasionally of his first disciples with their followers. Their form is prose sprinkled with verses. The individual Suttas vary according to the place and time of their origin. Instead of *nikāya* also the term *āgama*[3] is used: Dīghāgama, etc. This is the expression universally used in northern Buddhist literature. The Sutta-Piṭaka

[1] F. Spiegel, Kammavakya, Palice et Latine ed. Cf. further Dickson, JRAS. VII, N. Ser., p. 1 ff; Baynes, JRAS. 1892, p. 68 ff.; Bowden, JRAS. 1893, p. 159 ff. Seven Kammavācās have been printed by Frankfurter, Handbook of Pāli, p. 141 ff. and Takakusu, Pali Chrestomathy, p. 40 ff Cf. also Rhys Davids (and Clauson), JPTS. 1907, 1 ff.

[2] It is said in it of Mahinda and the other messengers that they came "hereto" (*idha i.e.*, to Ceylon), and then a number of famous Theras of the island are mentioned, including even Ariṭṭha, the nephew of king Devānaṃpiyatissa, Mhvs. 19.66.

[3] Childers, PD., *sub voce.*

is the chief source of our knowledge of the dhamma. It is therefore often directly called *dhamma* as opposed to *vinaya*.[1]

9. 1. The Dīgha-Nikāya "long collection" contains the longest Suttas.[2] As a collection it was complete already at a very early time, the Brahmajālasutta of D. is quoted in Saṃyutta-Nikāya IV. 286[12] R. O. Franke[3] wanted to prove that the D. is a "homogeneously conceived literary work" and "a homogeneous work of some literatus." This is certainly wrong.[4] Such a view militates against the fact that also inside the D. there are found contradictions just as in the canon taken as a whole. The external relations which Franke[5] has proved to exist between individual Suttas only explain why a particular Sutta came to occupy a particular place in the collection. Nothing more can be inferred from them. A peculiar importance attaches to the 16. Sutta of the D., the Mahāparinibbāṇa-sutta,[6] a running description of the events of the last weeks of the life of Buddha.—The number of Suttas in D. is 34; it is divided into three parts (Vagga): Sīlakkhandhavagga (1-13), Mahāvagga (14-23), Pāṭikavagga (24-34).

2. The Majjhima-Nikāya "middle collection" contains Suttas of middle length.[7] Their value is very unequal; some (*e.g.*, Nr. 82,

[1] On the importance of the SP., cf. Rhys Davids, Buddhism (Amer. Lect. on the Hist. of Religions), p. 59.

[2] The Dīgha-Nikāya, ed. Rhys Davids and Carpenter, 3 vols., London, PTS. 1890, 1903, 1911.—Translation : T. W. Rhys Davids and C. A. F. Rhys Davids, Dialogues of the Buddha, transl., Parts I, II London 1899, 1910. = SBB II, III (Suttas 1-23); K. E. Neumann, Reden Gotamo Buddho's aus der längeren Sammlung Dīghanikāyo des Pali-Kanons übers. Bd I, II, München 1907, 1912; R. O. Franke, Dīghanikāya, das Buch der langen Texte des Buddh. Kanons in Ausw. übers., Göttingen und Leipzig 1913.—On the Gāthās in D., cf. R. O. Franke, JPTS. 1909, pp. 311-384.

[3] D. übers., pp. XXX, XLII. Cf. also by the same author : Das einheitliche Thema des Dīganikāya, WZKM. 27. 198 ff.

[4] Franke's theory has been rejected not only by me (D. Literaturztg. 1914, No. 26 col. 1637 f.) but also by C A. F. Rhys Davids (JRAS. 1914, p, 467), as well as by H. Oldenberg (Archiv f. Religionswissensch. 17.627).

[5] ZDMG. 67. 409 ff.

[6] Translated by Rhys Davids, SBE. XI, p. 1 ff., SBB. III, p. 71 ff. ; Dutoit, Leben des Buddha, p. 221 ff,; K. E. Neumann, Die letzten Tage Gotamo Buddho's, München 1911; R. O. Franke, D. übers., p. 179 ff. On the relations between this Sutta and the Avadānaśataka of the Nepalese tradition, see Speyer, ZDMG. 53. 121 ff.

[7] The Majjhima-Nikāya, Vol. I ed. Trenckner, Vols. II, III ed. Chalmers. London, PTS. 1886, 1898, 1899.—Translation : K. E. Neumann, Reden Gotamo Buddho's aus der mittl. Samml. Majjhimanikāyo des Pali-Kanons übers., 3 vols, Leipzig 1896-1902.—On the Gāthās in M., cf. R. O. Franke, WZKM. 26 171 ff,

88. 93) belong to the most beautiful pieces in the canon.—The number of Suttas in M. is 152, divided into three groups of fifty (paṇṇāsa): Mūlapaṇṇāsa (1-50), Majjhimapaṇṇāsa (51-100), Uparipaṇṇāsa (101-152). As in the case of D., in M. too R. O. Franke would recognise no collection but an artificial literary work (schriftstellerisch verfasstes Werk), to which the Suttanipāta stands in relation of dependence.[1]

10. The third and fourth Nikāyas are more pronouncedly later and supplementary collections. In extent they considerably exceed D. and M.—3. The Saṃyutta-Nikāya[2] gets its designation from the fact that its Suttas are grouped together (saṃyutta) according to their contents. The Sakka-Saṃyutta, for instance, contains those Suttas in which the god Sakka plays a rôle, the Bojjhaṅga-Saṃyutta is composed of those pieces in which the seven "elements of the highest knowledge" are discussed,[3] etc. The most famous Sutta in S. is the Dhammacakkappavattanasutta, which contains the first sermon of Buddha with which he began his career as a world teacher.[4]—The number of Saṃyuttas is 56, and that of the Suttas 2,889; the whole is divided into 5 parts (vagga).

4. The Aṅguttara-Nikāya (literally: "by-one-limb-more-collection")[5] is divided into 11 sections (nipāta). They are called Eka-Nipāta "section of one," Duka-Nipāta "section of two," etc., up to Ekādasa-Nipāta "section of eleven." Every section contains Suttas dealing with subjects which are in some way or other connected with the number of the corresponding section. The first Sutta in the Eka-Nipāta, for instance, deals with the *one*, which more than anything else darkens the mind of man, that is, woman. The section of five begins with Suttas[6] which deal with the *pañca sekhabalāni*, etc. Various

[1] R. O. Franke, Die Zusammenhänge der Majjhimanikāya-Suttas, ZDMG. 68. 473 ff.; Majjhimanikāya und Suttanipāta, WZKM 28. 261 ff.

[2] The Saṃyutta-Nikāya of the Sutta-Piṭaka, ed L. Feer, 5 vols., London, PTS. 1884-98; Vol. VI Indexes by Mrs. Rhys Davids, 1904.—German translation by Wilhelm Geiger, München-Neubiberg, I, 1930; II, 1925.—The Book of the Kindred Sayings (Saṃyutta N.) trans. by Mrs. Rhys Davids and F. Woodward, 5 vols., London 1917-30.

[3] S. I. 216 ff.; V. 63 ff.

[4] S. V. 420 ff=Vin. I. 10 ff.

[5] The Aṅguttara-Nikāya, Vols. I, II, ed. Morris, London, PTS 1885, 1889; Vols. III-V, ed. E. Hardy, Ibid., 1896-1900; Vol VI, Indexes by M. Hunt, 1910. Cf. Leumann, GGA. 1899. Nr. 8, p. 585 ff.—Translations: B. Nyāṇatiloka, Reden des Buddha, a. d. Aṅguttara-Nikāya, übers. und erl., 5 vols., München-Neubiberg 1923 ff.

[6] A. III. 1 ff.

combinations are resorted to in the Nipātas of higher designations for which no corresponding subject could be found. Thus Sutta 28 of the "section of nine" is made of 5+4, Sutta 11 of the "section of eleven" of 3+3+3+2, etc.[1] In this scholastic method of grouping of subjects the A. resembles the Abhidhamma.—The number of Suttas is at least 2,308; the Nipātas are divided into *vaggas* containing as a rule 10 Suttas each. The largest number of Suttas contained in a *vagga* is 262; the lowest number is 7.

11. The 5th Nikāya of the Sutta-Piṭaka is the Khuddaka-Nikāya "the collection of short pieces." It contains texts of the most diverse characters, and it is significant that among the Buddhists of Ceylon, Burma and Siam there is no complete agreement as to the pieces belonging to it. In Ceylon Khuddaka-Nikāya is considered to consist of: 1. the Khuddakapāṭha[2], a collection composed of only 9 short Sutta-like pieces. It is clearly a prayer book of daily use. Three of the Suttas (Nrs. 5, 6, 9) occur also in Suttanipāta. Quite popular in character is the Tirokuḍḍasutta (Nr. 7) which deals with the Petas, the departed souls. It bears the character of a magic hymn. Particular verses out of it are still recited in Ceylon and Siam on the occasion of the cremation of dead bodies, as is reported by Seidenstücker.—2. The Dhammapada[3] is a collection of 423 memorial verses—a famous anthology of Indian Spruchweisheit. According to contents it is divided into 26 parts (vagga). Sometimes several consecutive verses form one close group—a small poem in itself. More than half the verses may be found also in other canonical texts. The compiler of the Dh. however certainly did not depend solely on these canonical texts but also made use of the great mass of pithy sayings which formed a vast floating literature in India.—3. The Udāna[4] is a collection of solemn sayings of Buddha, mostly in metrical form. Accompanying stories in prose give the occasions on which they

[1] A. IV. 407, V. 326.

[2] Khuddaka Pāṭha, by R. A. Childers, JRAS., N.S. IV, 1870, p. 309ff.; Khuddaka-Pāṭho, Kurze Texte...übers. u. erl. von Seidenstücker, Breslau 1910. Cf. 17.

[3] Dhammapadam......Palice ed., Latine vert.......V. Fausböll, 1825; new edition by same, London 1900. Of translations I mention the English one by M. Müller (SBE. X, Part I, Oxford 1881, new edition 1898) and the German ones by L. von Schroeder ("Worte der Wahrheit"), Leipzig 1892, and Dhamma-Worte, verdeutscht von R. O Franke, Jena 1923. Further literature in Winternitz, pp. 80-84.

[4] Udânam, ed. P. Steinthal, London PTS. 1885. The Udāna...transl. by Strong, London 1903. Udāna, German translation by K. Seidenstücker, Augsburg 1920.

were uttered. Altogether we have 82 stories divided into 8 parts (vagga)—4. The Itivuttaka[1] "Thus-has-been-said" closely resembles the Udāna. It contains the Master's sayings on morality. The number of the individual pieces, which are composed in a mixture of prose and verse, is 112. They are called Suttas and they either repeat the same thoughts at first in prose and then in verse, or in such a manner that the portions in prose and verse supplement each other. Like A. the Iv, is divided into Nipātas (Eka-. Duka-, Tika-, Cotukka-Nipāta), and the latter are again divided into vaggas.

12. 5. The Suttanipāta[2] of the Khuddaka-Nikāya is very archaic in character. Its first four parts (vagga) consist of 54 pieces; the 5th, called Pārāyaṇavagga, is a running poem in 18 sub-sections, and it contains the questions which the 16 disciples of Bāvarī ask Buddha, as well as their answers. Some pieces of the Sn. are like Ākhyāna-poems in character. Narrative stanzas sometimes alternate in them with dialogue-stanzas, as for instance in the Nālakasutta (III. 11), or, as in the Selasutta (III. 7), the speeches are in verse and the introductory or connecting portions in prose.—6. Vimānavatthu[3] and 7. Petavatthu[4] belong to the later and the least happy parts of the canon. Their later origin—perhaps a short time before the third council—is proved less by their contents than by their language which is not always impeccable, the mention of Piṅgalaka,[5] etc. The Vimānavatthu describes the grandeur of celestial palaces, in which the Devas live in reward of some good act performed in lifetime. It consists of 83 stories in seven parts (vagga). The Petavatthu consists of 51 stories in four vaggas, and it describes the sorrowful fate of the spirits or restless souls (peta), which have to expiate for the sins committed in lifetime.

[1] Iti-Vuttaka, ed. E. Windisch, London, PTS. 1889; Sayings of the Buddha, the Iti-Vuttaka, transl. by J. H. Moore, New-York 1908; Itivuttaka, German translation by K. Seidenstücker, Leipzig 1921. On the text, cf. Moore, JPTS, 1906-7, p. 176 ff.

[2] The Sutta-Nipāta, ed. V. Fausböll, I. Text, II. Glossary, London; The Sutta-Nipāta, new ed. by D. Andersen and H. Smith, London, PTS. 1913. Translation by V. Fausböll, The Sutta-Nipāta transl. SBE. X., Part 2, Oxford 1881. A concordance of the Gāthās of Sn. by R. O. Franke, ZDMG. 63. 1 ff., 255 ff. 64 1 ff.

[3] The Vimāna-Vatthu, ed. Gooneratne, London, PTS. 1886 (uncritical). On the commentary on Vv., see below. 25. 3.

[4] Petavatthu, ed. Minayeff, London PTS. 1888. W. Stede, Die Gespenstergeschichten des Peta Vatthu, Leipzig 1914.

[5] Cf. above, p. 13, f.-n. 1.

13. Like Vv. and Pv. also 8. the Theragāthā and 9. Therīgāthā [1] are metrical in form. These are collections of strophes which are attributed to renowned monks (Thera) and nuns (Therī). Often several strophes together form short poems. There is no doubt that these strophes contain much that belongs to the authentic Buddhistic literature of the earliest times. Many verses however might have been fabricated by the collectors or the redactors on the basis of fragmentary reminiscences. As for the authors, the ascription of verses to a particular monk or a particular nun might in most cases be quite arbitrary. It is however not impossible that in some cases the ascription of verses to these authors is based on a dependable tradition. The Thera- and the Therīgāthās can on no account be regarded as a "homogeneous work of a single intellect," even if due concession is made in this respect for the notorious utilisation of existing gāthās.[2] The number of Theragāthās is 1,279, and that of Therīgāthās 522; the former are divided into 21 and the latter into 16 Nipātas, called Eka-, Dukanipāta, etc., according as they contain one strophe or more attributed to one and the same author.—10. The Jātakas [3] are a collection of strophes which from the beginning presuppose accompanying prose narratives. Each of the latter contains the story of the Buddha in one of his earlier existences. Only the verses however were regarded as canonical; the prose narrative was left more or less to the discretion of the reciters. The strophes are very different in character. Sometimes they give the morals of the story, sometimes the questions and answers of the characters in the story form the subject of the verses, and sometimes the verses represent both the dialogue and the narrative. In the later Jātakas the narrative verses are predominant and they often combine to form ballads or epic poems. In the face of such diversity I cannot understand how "the mass of the Jātaka-Gāthās as a whole" may be regarded as "the personal product of a single author." [4] The Jātaka verses are doubtless a "collection." This is suggested also by its quite

[1] The Thera- and Therī-Gāthā, ed. H. Oldenberg and R. Pischel, London, PTS. 1883.—Translations: K. E. Neumann. Die Lieder der Mönche und Nonnen Gotamo Buddho's, Berlin 1899; Mrs. Rhys Davids, Psalms of the Early Buddhists, I, II, London PTS., 1909, 1913.

[2] R. O Franke, ZDMG. 63.16[11].

[3] Cf. below in 23 for literature.

[4] R. O. Franke, WZKM. 20. 318. For the contrary view cf. Winternitz, *op. cit.*, pp. 122-23. Moreover Franke himself modifies his statement to such an extent that it is quite doubtful whether in his own opinion too the expression "author" should not be replaced by "redactor."

artificial division into Nipātas as in the case of Thera- and Therīgāthās. The "section of ones" (Ekanipāta) consists of verses of which only one at a time belongs to a particular story; in the "section of twos" two verses belong to each story, etc.

14. The last pieces of the Kh. N. are 11, the Niddesa, a commentary to a part of the Suttanipāta, traditionally ascribed to Sāriputta. This text has not yet been edited.—12. The Paṭisaṃbhidāmagga,[1] dealing with the knowledge attained by the Arahant, belongs rather to the Abhidhamma literature both in form and contents.—13. The Apadāna,[2] most parts of which are still unedited, is a collection of legends in verse, in which are glorified the noble deeds (Apadāna) of Buddhistic saints in previous existences. This work is certainly one of the youngest in the canon, but hardly younger than the Avadānas of the Sanskrit Buddhist literature.—14. The Buddhavaṃsa[3] is also metrical in form; in 28 cantos it delineates the story of 24 former Buddhas as well as of Gotama Buddha, recited by the latter himself.—15. The Cariyāpiṭaka[3] is a selection of 25 metrical Jātakas. Buddha himself explains in them how in previous existences he had fulfilled the ten Pāramitās "perfections," which are the pre-condition of Buddhahood. In the first four Nikāyas the doctrine of the Pāramitās is still unknown. Winternitz[4] rightly characterises the Cp. as the artificial production of "an excellent monk who was anything but a poet" and who manufactured edifying stories for the elucidation of the doctrine on the basis of the existing Jātakas. There were various recensions of the Cp.[5] One of them is mentioned in the Nilānakathā of the Jātaka-book, but only two-thirds of the stories agree with ours.

5. *Abhidhamma-Piṭaka*

15. The Abhidhamma is not a systematic philosophy, but merely a supplement to the *dhamma*.[6] The work belonging to it mostly

[1] Paṭisaṃbhidāmagga, ed. A. C. Taylor I, II, London, PTS. 1905, 1907. Index by M. Hunt, JPTS. 1908, p. 152 ff.

[2] Texts out of the Apadāna in E. Müller's edition of Th2Co. See below, 25·2. Cf. further, E. Müller, Verhandlungen des X. Orientalisten-Kongr. in Genf. 1894, I. 165 ff.; L. Feer, JAs. 1883, s. 8, t. I, p. 408, 433 ff.

[3] The Buddhavaṃsa and the Cariyāpiṭaka, ed. R. Morris, London, PTS. 1882.

[4] Buddh. Lit., p. 164.

[5] Charpentier, Zur Gesch. des Cp., WZKM. 24, 1910, p. 351 ff.

[6] Rhys Davids, Buddhism (Amer. Lect.), p. 62.

contain merely detailed elucidations of various topics dealing with ethics, psychology or theory of knowledge which are mentioned in the canon. Its form is throughout scholastic. The themes are schematically classified; they are not properly defined but rather described by multiplying synonyms and they are brought into all possible combinations considered as they are from the most different points of view. The Abhidhamma is highly venerated particularly in Burma. The first suggestions of the Abhidhamma are found already in the dry and schematic enumerations in the Aṅguttara-Nikāya of the Sutta-Piṭaka, the last two Suttantas of the Dīgha-Nikāya[1] and similar pieces.

16. The following seven works belong to the Abhidhamma: 1. Dhammasaṅgaṇi[2] "enumeration of psychical phenomena,"—a psychological work.—2. Vibhaṅga[3] "differentiation," a supplement and continuation of the preceding.—3. Kathāvatthu,[4] which has been already referred to in 1. It is perhaps historically the most important book in the Abhidhamma. I consider the tradition about its origin to be quite trustworthy.—4. The Puggalapaññatti[5] "description of individuals" deals with the various personalities and characters in the form of questions and answers.—5. The Dhātukathā or the Dhātukathāpakaraṇa[6] "discussion of the elements" deals with the various psychic phenomena and their relation to the categories.—6. The Yamaka[7] "book of pairs" is a work on applied logic, and it derives its name apparently from the fact that all psychic phenomena are considered in it in the light of a particular thesis and its opposite antithesis.—7. The Paṭṭhānappakaraṇa or Mahāpaṭṭhāna[8] is a voluminous work. It deals with causality, but is very difficult to understand. The best European expert in the Abhidhamma, Mrs. Rhys Davids, says of this

[1] The Saṃgīti-and the Dasuttarasuttanta D. III. 207 ff., 272 ff.

[2] The Dhammasaṅgaṇi, ed. E. Muller, London. PTS. 1885; C. Rhys Davids. A Buddhist Manual of Psychological Ethics, being a translation of the Dhamma-Saṅgaṇi, London 1900.

[3] The Vibhaṅga, ed. Mrs. Rhys Davids, London. PTS. 1904.

[4] Kathāvatthu, ed. A. C. Taylor I, II. London. PTS. 1894, 1897.

[5] The Puggala-Paññatti, ed. R. Morris, London. PTS. 1883; Nyānatiloka. Puggala Paññatti, das Buch der Charaktere übers., Breslau 1910.

[6] The Dhātu Kathā Pakaraṇa and its commentary, ed. E. R. Gooneratne, London, PTS. 1892.

[7] The Yamaka, ed. C. Rhys Davids I, II, London, PTS. 1911, 1913.

[8] Only the first part of the Dukapaṭṭhāna has been edited by Mrs. Rhys Davids. London, PTS. 1906. Cf. JPTS, 1896. 33-34.

work[1]: "the text remains very difficult and obscure to the uninitiated Western mind, and I am far from pretending to solve any one of its problems."

Supplement : The Paritta

17. The Paritta or Mahāparitta[2] is a collection of canonical texts for popular magical use. In Ceylon such Paritta-ceremonies (Sgh. *pirit*) are still in vogue. As Seidenstücker says, such ceremonies are performed on various occasions, such as the building of a new house, death, illness, etc.[3] On these occasions the texts collected in the Paritta are recited. There are altogether 28 pieces, of which 7 are taken from the Khuddakapāṭha (cf. **11.** 1), which seems to have been a predecessor of the Paritta. Also in Burma the Paritta is held in high esteem by laity. It is not known when the present Paritta was compiled. Magical rites are, however, known in Buddhism from the earliest times. It is said of Buddha himself,[4] that he taught a "snake charm" to his disciples: it is significant that the purpose of the charm is to completely envelop the snakes with one's own spirit of benevolence (*mettena cittena pharitum*), so that it may not do any harm to anybody. It is also said in the book of Milinda that the *parittā* were taught by Buddha.[5] Of the six texts which are then cited as examples, five are found in our Paritta. The commentary of the Dhammapada relates[6] of a great exorcism, which was performed by Ānanda during the life-time of Buddha by means of the Ratanasutta of the Suttanipāta.

1 Duka Pṭh. I, Preface, p. XIV.

2 The text in Frankfurter, Handbook of Pali, pp. 81-139. Cf. Seidenstücker, Khuddaka-Pāṭho, p. 29 ff. M. Bode, Pali Lit. of Burma, p. 3 f. The word *parittā* signifies "Protection (from evil spirits)"; *parittāsutta* "magical cord (tied round the wrist as an amulet)" JāCo. I, 396[13] (here also *parittāvālikā*), Mhvs. 7.14; *parittaṃ karoti* "performs a magical ceremony." JāCo. II. 34[16].

3 Cf. also JRAS.. Ceylon Branch, VII, Nr. 28, p. 38; VIII. Nr. 29, p. 321 ff.

4 Vin II, 109-110; A. II. 72.

5 Milp. p. 150f. Cf. M. Bode, ibid.

6 DhCo, III. 441 ff.

II. THE NON-CANONICAL LITERATURE

I Period

From the Completion of the Canon to the 5th Century A D.

18. According to the Indian tradition it was Mahinda who brought to Ceylon along with the canon also an Aṭṭhakathā, a commentary on it. The authenticity of this tradition however cannot be proved. It is at all events certain that in Ceylon already at an early time there was a commentary literature of considerable magnitude and multifarious contents. On this commentary literature is based not only the later commentaries such as those of Buddhaghosa, but also the historical literature beginning with the Dīpavaṃsa. This Aṭṭhakathā of Ceylon seems to have been still existing and accessible even in the 12th century.[1] In the opening verses of his Vinaya-commentary, the Samantapāsādikā, Buddhaghosa mentions the Aṭṭhakathā as the source of his own work.[2] Buddhaghosa says that the Aṭṭhakathā was composed in the (old) Sinhalese language. In order to make it accessible to the Bhikkhus, and at the suggestion of the Thera Buddhasiri, he translated it into Pāli. The chief source was the Mahā-Aṭṭhakathā; but he turned into account also the materials of other commentaries, such as the Mahāpaccarī- and the Kurundī-Aṭṭhakathā. The two Ṭīkās on Smp., the Vajirabuddhi and the Sāratthadīpanī,[3] mention moreover the Cullapaccarī, the Andhaṭṭhakathā, the Paṇṇavāra, and the Saṃkhepaṭṭhakathā. According to the Saddhammasaṃgaha (14th century) the Mahā-Aṭṭhakathā was the commentary on the Sutta-Piṭaka, the Mahāpaccarī on the Abhidhamma, and the Kurundī on Vinaya.[4] Also the Gandhavaṃsa[5] mentions the same three Aṭṭha-

[1] This is quite evident from the data of the Mahāvaṃsa-Ṭīkā, ZDMG. 63. 549-550. R. O. Franke's objection (D. XLV[35]) may be met simply by consulting the contents of the passages of the Mhvs. Ṭī. quoted by me.

[2] Edited by Saya U Pye I.2[1] ff. Cf. also the introductions to the Sumaṅgalavilāsinī, Manorathapuraṇī, etc.

[3] In Minayeff, Prātimoksha, p. VII, note 10. Look there for the meaning of the title.

[4] Sdhs., JPTS. 1890, p. 55f. Cf. also Minayeff, Recherches sur le Bouddhisme, p. 284. It is however remarkable that Buddhaghosa does not mention the Kurundī as the chief source of his Smp.

[5] Gnvs., JPTS. 1886, pp. 59 and 68.

kathās, and in fact the Aṭṭhakathā par excellence (*i.e.*, the Mahā-A.) is ascribed to the Porāṇācariyā, and the two others are regarded as works of the Gandhācariyā—which clearly shows that they are later. Nothing has been directly preserved of all these Old Ceylonese Aṭṭhakathās.

19. There are preserved from the time before Buddhaghosa: 1. The Nettippakaraṇa "book of guidance," also called simply Netti, and 2. the Peṭakopadesa "instruction on the Piṭaka" or the Peṭaka.[1] In Burma these two works are regarded as canonical.[2] As the titles show, they serve as introduction to the teachings of Buddhism. According to tradition they were composed by Mahākaccāyana, one of the most prominent disciples of Buddha.[3] This is however certainly not true. The author was probably Kaccāyana by name and was hence identified with the renowned disciple of Buddha. The same was the case also with the grammarian Kaccāyana. The problem of the time of origin of these two works has been discussed by E. Hardy[4] in the light of both internal and external evidences. He assigns to them a date about the beginning of the Christian era. In connection with the Netti and the Peṭaka let us also mention 3. the Suttasaṃgaha[5] "collection of the Suttas." It is the only comprehensive anthology of Suttas as well as of texts such as Vimānavatthu, etc. We know nothing about the time of its origin or about its author. This work has however to be mentioned here because, along with Netti, Peṭaka and the book of Milinda, it is considered in Burma to belong to the "canonical" Khuddaka-Nikāya.[6]

20. The Milindapañhā[7] "Questions of Milinda," contains in the style of Suttas a dialogue between King Milinda and the Thera Nāgasena about the most important problems of Buddhism.[8] In contents

[1] The Netti-Pakaraṇa with extracts from Dhammapāla's commentary, ed. E. Hardy, London, P.T.S. 1902 (Cf. J. d' Alwis, Catal., p. 70 ff.); Specimen des Peṭakopadesa (Dissertation) by R. Fuchs, Berlin 1908.

[2] M. Bode, Pali Lit. of Burma, p. 4 f.

[3] Gnvs. p. 49. The authorship of Mahākaccāyana is claimed for the Netti both in the introductory verses and at the end.

[4] Netti, Introd., p. VIII ff.

[5] Oldenberg, Catal., p. 80, Nr. 44; Fausböll, JPTS. 1896, p. 31, Nr. 92.

[6] Cf. f.-n. 2.

[7] This is probably the correct title.

[8] The Milindapañho...ed. V. Trenckner, London 1880.—Translations: Rhys Davids, The Questions of King Milinda, transl., I, II. = SBE XXXV, XXXVI, London 1890, 1894. Cf. R. Garbe, ein histor. Roman aus Altindien, Rodenbergs Deutsche Rundschau,

the book represents the orthodox point of view of the Theravādins. As the quotations occurring in it show, the canon known to the author does not differ in anything from the Pāli canon.[1] Milinda is the Indian form of the name of the Graeco-Bactrian king Menander (end of the 2nd century B.C.), who was evidently well disposed towards Buddhism, but of whom it remains unknown whether he actually became a Buddhist.[2] Our Milindapañhā is very probably based on a Buddhistic Sanskrit work, composed in North-West India about the beginning of the Christian era.[3] The translation into Pāli took place in Ceylon, already before Buddhaghosa who quotes it repeatedly. The original work was much shorter as the Chinese translations show.[4] The real contents of the work ended with Chapter 2, at the end of which we find in our Pāli text the remark: *Nāgasena-Milindarāja-pañhā niṭṭhitā.* Its Introduction too was much shorter in the original than in the Pāli version. It was considerably extended in Ceylon by various additions after existing models.[5] It is not improbable that there were various versions of it in Pāli; also the fragments of a metrical version are found in the Pāli text.

21. To the works of the age before Buddhaghosa belongs also the Dīpavaṃsa "the island chronicle,"[6] a history of Ceylon up to the end of the reign of Mahāsena (325-352 A.D.). As Buddhaghosa knows the Dpvs., it must have been composed between 352 and about 450 A.D. Regarded from the literary point of view it is certainly a very weak performance. The author possessed only a very imperfect knowledge of Pāli and in language he is wholly dependent on his sources by

Vol. 112, p. 261 ff., 1902; F. O Schrader, Die Fragen des Königs Menandros I, Berlin 1907; Winternitz, Buddhist Lit., p. 174 ff. A translation of the Milp. was begun also by Nyānatiloka, fascicles 1-3. Leipzig 1914.

[1] Rhys Davids, Questions I, p. XIV ff.

[2] See Rhys Davids, Questions I. p. XIX ff.; V. Smith, Early History of India, pp. 187, 226; von Gutschmid, Gesch. Irans, p. 104 ff.

[3] Rhys Davids, Questions I. p. XLV ff.

[4] B. Nanjio. Catal. of the Buddhist Tripiṭaka, Nr. 1358; E. Specht. Deux Traductions Chinoises du Milindapañho (with Introduction by Sylv. Lévi). Transact. IXth Congress of Or. I., London 1893, p. 520; Takakusu, JRAS. 1896, p. 1 ff.; E. Specht, JAs. sér. 9, t. VII, 1896, p. 156.

[5] Thus, as Rhys Davids, *Ibid.*, I, p. 8, f.-n. 2 has noticed, the story of the dispute with Purāṇa-Kassapa and Makkhali-Gosāla is only an echo of the introduction to the Sāmaññaphalasuttanta, D.I. 47. The story of Nāgasena's relation with Rohaṇa (Milp. 8[19] ff.) corresponds, as I have to point out, exactly to the story related in Mhvs. 5. 131 ff.

[6] The Dīpavaṃsa...ed. and transl. H. Oldenberg, London 1879; W. Geiger, Dīpavaṃsa und Mahāvaṃsa, Leipzig 1905. Cf. IA. 35, 1906, p. 153 ff.

studying which he collected his materials. R. O. Franke was quite right in all this.[1] But he is quite wrong when, confusing form with contents, he refuses to recognise in Dpvs. any historical value. In contents the Chronicle is based on the historical portions of the old Aṭṭhakathā. That the informations given in it are not quite imaginary [2] is proved by its frequent agreement with the tradition current in continental India. The Dpvs. is therefore the vehicle of an old historical tradition, and it is the duty of historical criticism to examine it minutely and assess its worth.

II Period

From the 5th to the 11th Century

22. The beginning of the 2nd period is characterised by commentaries which were composed on the Tipiṭaka and which are based on the Ceylonese Aṭṭhakathā. Buddhaghosa is the greatest figure in this commentary literature. He was born in a Brahmin family of Northern India and came to Ceylon during the reign of king Mahānāma (458-480). He studied the Tipiṭaka and the Aṭṭhakathā in the Mahāvihāra of Anurādhapura and afterwards showed a very fruitful literary activity. The details about his life as handed down by tradition are probably nothing but legends.[3] The commentaries composed by him on the Tipiṭaka are the following [4]:

I. Vin. 1. Samantapāsādikā [5] = Co. on Vinaya-Piṭaka
2. Kaṅkhāvitaraṇī [6] = Co. on Pātimokkha

[1] WZKM. 21. 203 ff., 317 ff. My reply in ZDMG. 63. 540 ff., and again Franke, D., Introduction, p. XLIV f. Winternitz, Buddh. Lit., p. 210 ff. has accepted my view.

[2] When Franke, JPTS. 1908, p. 1 says "that in the absence of any sources, the last-named work—namely, precisely this same Dpvs.—must be considered as standing unsupported on its own tottering feet," he is expressing as clearly as possible that the author of the Chronicle had freely invented his data! Who can however say that seriously?

[3] Buddhaghosuppatti, ed. Gray; Mhvs. 37. 165 ff. (Colombo edition); Sdhs. 51ff.; Sāsvs. 28 ff. Cf. Minayeff, Recherches sur le Bouddhisme, p. 189 ff.; Winternitz, Buddh Lit., p. 190 ff. Cf. B. C. Law, The Life and Work of Buddhaghosa, Calcutta and Simla 1923. Of the commentaries on the Tipiṭaka, many have been published in Bangkok (Siamese script), Rangoon (Burmese script), Colombo (S. Hewavitama Request, 1917 ff., Ceylonese script). The editions of the PTS. are given in the regular reports of the Society. Edition of the Visuddhimagga by C. A. F. Rhys Davids, 2 vols., PTS. 1920-21.

[4] Gnvs., p. 59; de Zoysa, Catal., pp. 2-3.

[5] Edited in Burmese script by Saya u Pye, 4 vols., Rangoon 1902, 1903. The historical Introduction in Oldenberg, Vin. Piṭ. III. 283 ff. For a Chinese version of it, see Takakusu, JPTS. 1896, p. 415 ff.

[6] Unpublished.

II.	SP. 3. Sumaṅgalavilāsinī [1]	= Co. on	Dīgha-Nikāya
	4. Papañcasūdanī [2]	= ,, ,,	Majjhima-Nikāya
	5. Sāratthapakāsinī [3]	= ,, ,,	Saṃyutta-Nikāya
	6. Manorathapūraṇī [4]	= ,, ,,	Aṅguttara-Nikāya
	7. Paramatthajotikā	= ,, ,,	Khuddaka-Nikāya, Nr. 1, 5
III.	Abh P. 8. Atthasālinī [5]	= ,, ,,	Dhammasaṅgaṇi
	9. Saṃmohavinodanī [6]	= ,, ,,	Vibhaṅga
	10. Pañcappakaraṇaṭṭhakathā [7]	= ,, ,,	Abh P., Nr. 5, 4, 3, 6, 7

The commentaries of the Abhidhamma seem to have borne the general designation Paramatthakathā.[8] Also the commentaries on the Jātaka and the Dhammapada are ascribed to Buddhaghosa, about which further below. Also the Apadānas are said to have been commented upon by him.[9] While still in India he is said to have composed work called Ñāṇodaya, as well as an Atthasālinī [10] which was probably a first sketch of the later commentary on Dhammasaṅgaṇi.

Along with the commentaries of Buddhaghosa should be mentioned also his Visuddhimagga "Path of purification." [11] It is a kind

[1] Edited by Saya u Pye, 3 vols., Rangoon 1903. Further the Sumaṅgala-Vilāsinī, Part I, ed. Rhys Davids and Carpenter, London, PTS., 1886. Of a Singhalese edition (by Saranaṅkara) in Ceylon 3 parts only have appeared.

[2] 5 fascicles have appeared of a Sinhalese edition from Colombo (1898-1911).

[3] Colombo edition, Parts 1-7 (1900-11).

[4] Edition by Dharmārāma (Singh. script), Peliyagoda 1893-1907; second edition 1904-13.

[5] Atthasālinī, ed. E. Müller, London, PTS., 1897. Further edition by Saya u Pye, Rangoon 1902.

[6] Edition by Saya u Pye, Rangoon 1902.

[7] Edition by Saya u Pye, Rangoon 1902. The commentary on Kyu. was edited by Minayeff, JPTS. 1889, p. 1 ff.; that on Dhk. by Gooneratne as appendix to the edition of this text, London, PTS., 1892, p. 114 ff.; that on Yam. by Mrs. Rhys Davids, JPTS. 1912, p. 51 ff.

[8] Gnvs. 59^{25}.

[9] Gnvs. 59^{27-30}. Cf. de Zoysa, Catal., p. 2. Nr. 13; Fausböll, JPTS. 1896, p. 31, Nr. 91.

[10] Sāsvs. 31^{5-6}.

[11] Visuddhi-Magga with Singhalese paraphrase Colombo 1890 ff. (JPTS. 1912, p. 154). Cf. de Zoysa, Catal., p. 16. An analysis of the Vism. by Warren, JPTS. 1893 p. 76 ff. Translations by same, Buddhism in Translations, pp. 145, 150, 155. etc. Cf. also Carpenter, JPTS. 1890, p. 14 ff.

of encyclopaedia of Buddhist doctrine divided into three parts: *sila*, *samādhi*, *paññā*. The origin of this work, which is held in high esteem by the Southern Buddhists of the present day, is shrouded in legends of all kinds.[1]

23. Whether the Jātakaṭṭhavaṇṇanā,[2] the commentary on the Jātaka-verses mentioned above in **13** under Nr. 10, was also composed by Buddhaghosa, is not certain. The Jātaka-commentary[3] as it appears in Fausböll's edition, contains in all 547 stories, which are referred to former births of the Buddha and which are therefore called Jātakas "birth stories." Every story consists of four parts: 1. the canonical Gāthās; 2. the Atītavatthūni, "the stories of the past," *i.e.*, the prose narratives belonging to the Gāthās; 3. the Paccuppannavatthūni "stories of the present," in which is described the occasion on which the particular Jātaka was told, along with the appended *samodhānāni*, in which is mentioned what characters have been assumed at present by the persons in the Jātaka; 4. the Veyyākaraṇāni, the "commentaries," in which the verses are explained word by word.[4] The whole work is preceded

[1] Cf. Mhvs. 37. 184 ff. (Colombo edition). Sāsvs. 30[6], 31[18].

[2] The Jātaka together with its Commentary...ed. by V. Fausböll, 6 vols., London 1877-96 (7th vol. contains the indices by D. Andersen). Preliminary to this edition the author published the following three studies: (*a*) Five Jātakas Copenhagen 1861, (*b*) The Dasaratha-Jātaka, Copenhagen 1871, (*c*) Ten Jātakas, Copenhagen 1872.—Translations: Rhys Davids, Buddhist Birth Stories or Jātaka Tales I, London 1880; The Jātakas, transl. by various scholars under the editorship of E. B. Cowell, 7 vols., Cambridge 1895 1913; Dutoit, Jātakam, das Buch der Erzählungen aus früheren Existenzen Buddhas, übers, Leipzig 1908 ff.

[3] See L. Feer, JAs., sér 7, t. V, 357 ff. and VI, 243 ff. (1875); sér. 9, t. V. 31 ff., 189 ff. and t. IX. 288 ff. (1895, 1897). See von Oldenburg, JRAS. 1893, p. 301 ff.; L. Feer, Proceedings of the XI Oriental Congress, Paris 1899, Sect. 1, p. 151 ff; R. O. Franke, BB. 22. 289 ff. (1897), as well as WZKM 20. 317 ff. (1906); T. W. Rhys Davids, Buddhist India, p. 189ff. (1903); H. Oldenberg, Lit. des a. Ind., p. 103 ff. (1903); Charpentier, ZDMG. 66.38 ff., particularly p 41, f.-n. 2 (1912). An excellent treatment of the subject is given by Winternitz, Buddh. Lit., pp. 113-56 (1933). I am inclined to attach more importance to the Jātakas as a source of knowledge about Indian culture about Buddha's time than Winternitz is prepared to do. I agree with the judgment given by Bühler, Indian Studies III (Sitzungsber. d. Wiener A. d. W., phil.-hist. Cl., Vol. CXXXII), p. 18 ff.

[4] The various portions are not as sharply divided as may be suggested by the typographical contrivances in Fausböll's edition. The hand of the redactor may be perceived often and again in the relations between them. Thus *e.g.*, in II. 205[13], as Franke has pointed out, the phrase *tam eva udapānaṃ* of the Atītavatthu belongs to the Paccuppannavatthu.

by an introduction called the Nidānakathā, which contains the story of the Buddha in his earlier existences and in his last birth up to the dedication of the Jetabanavihāra in Sāvatthī.

In external form the Jātaka-commentary is in my opinion the work of a priest of Ceylon,[1] be he Buddhaghosa[2] or some other scholar not far from him in time. But the author has taken his material from the old Aṭṭhakathā.[3] The Aṭṭhakaṭhā again is based on oral tradition. There is no doubt that from the very beginning the Gāthās were handed down together with the stories—without the latter the former often give no sense at all. But the two portions have been handed down in different manners. The verse portion was fixed and unchangeable; but the prose portion containing the story was left more or less to the discretion of the rhapsodists. This also explains the contradictions which are sometimes found between the verses and the prose, and which was certainly present already in the Aṭṭhakathā.[4] In short, the Jātakas are of the type of Ākhyānas,[5] but it is far from the truth that all the Jātakas are of this type. Also stories without any verse were incorporated into the collection. Such are, for instance, the Jātakas with the Abhisaṃbuddhagāthās,[6] in which the Gāthās are not placed in the story itself but are fathered on Buddha at the end in the *samodhāna*. On the other hand, particularly in the Jātakas of the last books, in which the connecting prose shrinks almost into nothing in comparison with the verses, we see how the epic poetry is being gradually developed out of the older Ākhyānas. The Jātakas were utilised at a very early time for the purpose of didactic sermons. This explains their extraordinary popularity from the early days of the Buddhist Church[7] to the

[1] Cf. JāCo. IV. 490[20], V. 254[1].

[2] According to E. Müller, Gurupūjākaumudī, p. 54 ff., Buddhaghosa himself was the author.

[3] The Aṭṭhakathā is often mentioned also in the Jātaka Thesaurus, and that in contradistinction from Pāli, the canonical text consisting of the Gāthās, JāCo. II. 294[8,9]; 299[4,5]; VI. 279[29] etc.

[4] Cf. H. Lüders, NGGW. 1897, p. 40 ff.; Hertel, ZDMG. 60. 399 ff. (also 68. 64 ff); Charpentier, ZDMG. 62. 725 ff.; Winternitz, *Ibid*, p. 119, f.-n. 2.

[5] Oldenberg, JPTS. 1912, p. 19 ff. against A. B. Keith, JRAS., 1911, p. 985.

[6] Senart, JAs. sér. 9, t. XVII. 385 ff.

[7] Hence pictures of scenes out of the Jātakas already in the Indian art of the 3rd century B.C.; Rhys Davids, Buddhist India, p. 198 ff. See, von Oldenburg. JAm-Or. Soc. XVIII. 1897. p. 183 ff.; Hultzsch, JRAS. 1912, p. 406; A. Foucher, L'art gréco-bouddhique du Gandhāra, I. 1905, p. 270 ff.

present day. The contents of the Jātakas are not however specifically Buddhistic, but the common property of the Indian people as is proved, *inter alia* by the numerous points of similarity and agreement between the Jātakas and the epics.[1] But the Buddhists have adapted these folk-tales and drawn them into their own sphere. Examples are not wanting which show how such folk-tales became Jātakas.[2] The process of incorporation takes place in the Paccuppannavatthūni. They are therefore later elements than the Atītavatthūni, although I believe that they too belonged to the Aṭṭhakathā. The difference between the scenes of action is very striking.[3] The "stories of the past" are mostly referred to Western and Northern India (Gandhāraraṭṭha, etc.), but the "stories of the present" to the East (Kosalaraṭṭha, Magadharaṭṭha, etc.).

24. The Dhammapadaṭṭhakathā[4] is later than the Jātaka-Commentary. According to the introductory verses, which are however quite stereotyped, it is the Pāli translation of an original Singhalese Aṭṭhakathā. In my opinion it is quite improbable that Buddaghosa[5] himself was the author of this commentary. But it is quite probable that this later work was greatly influenced by older prototypes. The Dhammapadaṭṭhakathā gives to every Gāthā or every group of Gāthās of the Dh. a particular story supposed to be a sermon (Dhammadesanā) of Buddha himself, at the end of which he recites the respective verses. These stories are more specifically Buddhistic than the Jātakas. Buddhistic priests and saints are the main characters in them. Not infrequently even Jātakas proper, the Atītavatthūni, are introduced: legends of a previous birth of one of the characters in the main story. Several of these interpolated stories may be traced in the Jātaka-Commentary,[6] and, on the other hand,

[1] Cf. Winternitz, Buddh. Lit., p. 122, f.-n. 3.

[2] Thus, for instance, the story of the quail in S. V, 146 ff. had become the Jātaka II. 59 f., the story of Dīghāvu in Vin. I. 342 ff. has become Jāt. III. 211 ff.; Rhys Davids, Buddhist India, p. 194; Winternitz, *Ibid.* p. 115. On the other hand the Sutta in M. II. 45 ff. is a true Jātaka although it is not contained in our collection; Rhys Davids, p. 196.

[3] Fausböll, Jāt. VII, postscript, p. VI ff.

[4] The Commentary of the Dhammapada, ed. H. C. Norman, London, PTS., 4 vols. 1906-14; Dhammapadaṭṭhakathā, ed. Nāṇissara, Colombo 1891-1906.

[5] Gnvs., p. 59^{27}, 88^{27}.

[6] Cf., *e.g.*, DhCo. I. 265 ff. with JāCo. I. 199 ff.; DhCo. III. 124 ff. with JāCo. II. 165 ff.; DhCo. III. 141 ff. with JāCo. III. 333 ff.

many of its main stories correspond to the Paccuppannavatthūni of the Jātakas.[1] The literary style is largely influenced by the numerous quotations from the Jātakas, the Nikāyas, from Vimāna- and Petavatthu, and from Suttanipāta and Vinaya.[2] The numerous cases of agreement in contents between the DhCo. and other works[3] can naturally be explained also on the hypothesis of common borrowing from a third source.

25. Along with Buddhaghosa should be mentioned:—1. Buddhadatta, who was his contemporary according to tradition.[4] He is reputed to be the author of the *Madhuratthavilāsinī* (or *Madhurattha-pakāsanī*), a commentary on the Buddhavaṃsa, as well as of the *Vinayavinicchaya*, a compendium of the Vinaya in Pāli verse, the *Uttaravinicchaya* of similar contents,[5] the *Abhidhammāvatāra*,[6] a handbook of Buddhist metaphysics, as well as a *Jinālaṃkāra*, which is certainly not the work of the same name which will be described below (**34**.3). With the possible exception of the first-named work, everything is problematic about them. There might have been a scholar named Buddhadatta at the time of Buddhaghosa, but it appears to me that the tradition has ascribed to him also the work of a namesake of his who lived at a later age.—2. Ānanda, of continental India,[7] is the author of the *Mūlaṭīkā* or *Abhidhamma-Mūlaṭīkā*,[8] the oldest sub-commentary to the Aṭṭhakathās of Abhidhamma. He is said to have composed it at the instance of Buddhamitta, who moved also Buddhaghosa to write his Papañcasūdanī.[9] If that is true, then

[1] Compare, *e.g.*, DhCo. I. 239 ff. with JāCo. I. 114 ff.; DhCo. III. 178 ff. with JāCo. IV. 187 ff.

[2] Cf. the indices in Norman's edition.

[3] Thus the stories DhCo. III. 104 ff. and 290 ff. = VvCo. 75 ff. and 220 ff.; the story II. 112 ff. occurs in Buddhaghosa's Manorathapūraṇī; the motif of the story I. 129 ff. reappears in Mhvs. 32.63 ff.

[4] Sāsvs. 29[28], 73[31]; Gnvs. 66[27]. Of the works attributed to Buddhadatta there have now been edited Abhidhammāvatāra, Rūpārūpavibhāga, Vinayavinicchaya and Uttaravinicchaya by A. P. Buddhadatta, PTS. 1915 and 1927.

[5] Gnvs. 59[31], 69[5] ff.; de Zoysa, Catal., p. 2; Fausböll, JPTS. 1896, p. 18, Nr. 31. For the last two works, see below, p. 40, f.-n. 1.

[6] Sdhs. IX. 13 (JPTS. 1890, p. 62); de Zoysa. p. 5; Fausböll, p. 35; S. Z. Aung, JPTS. 1910-12, p. 123.

[7] Gnvs. 66[27].

[8] De Zoysa. p. 3; S. Z. Aung, p. 120 f.; Gnvs. 60[3]; Sāsvs. 33[16].

[9] Gnvs. 68[13], [30], 69[18]; Sāsvs. 33[16].

Ānanda and Buddhaghosa were contemporaries.—3. Dhammapāla of Padaratittha [1] composed a commentary called *Paramatthadīpanī* [2] on those parts of the Khuddaka-Nikāya, which had not been commented upon by Buddaghosa: Udāna, Itivuttaka, Vimāna- and Petavatthu, Thera- and Therīgāthā and Cariyāpiṭaka. Moreover, he is supposed to be the author of a commentary on the Visuddhimagga called *Mahāṭīkā* or *Paramatthamañjūsā* as well as a commentary on the Netti, the *Nettippakaraṇassa Atthasaṃvaṇṇanā*, a Ṭīkā to this his own work, called *Līnatthavaṇṇanā*, and also a Ṭīkā *Līnatthapakāsanī* on the Aṭṭhakathās of the first four Nikāyas, a Ṭīkā on the Jātakaṭṭhakathā as well as on Buddhadatta's Madhuratthavilāsinī, and finally an Anuṭīkā on the Ṭīkā of Abhidhammaṭṭhakathā.[3] The four last-named works seem to be lost to-day. It seems that in this case too the tradition has fathered on Dhammapāla, who might have been a younger contemporary of Buddhaghosa,[4] the works of various Theras [5] of the same name, as he had made it his life's task to supplement the commentaries of Buddhaghosa. Dhammapāla's date would be one century later if he is identical with the Dhammapāla of the Nālandā-Monastery who was Hiuen-thsang's teacher's teacher.[6] Yet however, like E. Hardy,[7] I consider this identity to be yet unproved.

26. The number of the old commentators may be completed by adding the following names: 1. Culla-Dhammapāla, a pupil of Ānanda, author of *Saccasaṃkhepa* "Elements of Truth;" [8] 2. Upasena,

[1] Sāsvs. 33[11].

[2] De Zoysa, p. 2; Fausböll, p. 29 f., Nr. 87, 88. The commentary on the Therīgāthās has been edited by E. Müller and that on Peta- and Vimānavatthu by E. Hardy, London, PTS., 1893, 1894, 1901.

[3] Gnvs. 60. On the Netti-commentary and its Ṭīkā, cf. Fausböll, p. 41 f., Nr. 132, 133.

[4] The (Singhalese) Nikāyasaṃgraha (ed. Wickremasinghe), p. 24 mentions one after another Buddhaghosa, Buddhadatta, Dhammapāla. Similarly Gnvs. 60, Sāsvs., 33.

[5] The Gnvs. knows four different Dhammapālas. See E. Hardy, Netti, Introd., p. XII.

[6] Thus according to Steinthal, Udāna, pref. p. VII; Rhys Davids and Carpenter, DCo I, pref. p. VIII. On the traditions about Dhammapāla recorded by Hiuen-thsang in Si-yu-ki, see. St. Julien, Mém. sur les Contrées Occidentales I. 287 ff., 452 ff., II, 119 f; see further Schiefner, Tāranātha, p. 160 ff.; Takakusu, I-tsing, p. LVII, 179, 181; B. Nanjio, Catal. of the Chinese Tripiṭaka, App. I, p. 347, Nr. 16.

[7] ZDMG. 51, 103 ff.

[8] Gnvs. 60[30]; Sāsvs. 34[3]; Sdhs. IX. 16. De Zoysa, Catal., p. 11; Fausböll, JPTS. 1896, p. 35, Nr. 120; S. Z. Aung, *ibid.*, 1910-12, p 123.

author of a commentary on the Niddesa [1] called the *Saddhammappajotikā* or *Saddhammaṭṭhitikā*; 3. Mahānāma, author of the *Saddhammappakāsinī*, a commentary on the Paṭisambhidāmagga [2]; 4. Kassapa, author of *Mohavicchedanī* and *Vimaticchedanī* [3]; 5. Vajirabuddhi, author of the *Vajirabuddhi*, a Ṭīkā on the Samantapāsādikā.[4] In Gnvs. a Mahā- and a Culla-Vajirabuddhi are distinguished, both from Jambudīpa, the continental India. The former is reputed to have written a work called *Vinayagaṇḍhi*; 6. Khema, author of the *Khemappakaraṇa*,[5] who is mentioned with Culla Dhammapāla, as well as with 7. Anuruddha, the author of the *Abhidhammatthasaṃgaha*, the most read handbook on Abhidhamma,[6] on which the greatest theras of the 12th century have written Ṭīkās. Anuruddha is also the author of two other works in the field of Abhidhamma, namely, *Paramatthavinicchaya* and *Nāmarūpapariccheda*. There are two Ṭīkās on each of them.[7]

27. Two other short but important texts have still to be mentioned, which belong to the Vinaya: the *Khuddasikkhā* of Dhammasiri and the *Mūlasikkhā* of Mahāsāmin.[8] They are short compendiums on monastic discipline, for the most part in verse and evidently meant to be learnt by heart. There are various commentaries on them, as well as Singhalese translations. Judging by

[1] Gnvs. 61^{11}, 70^{23}; Sāsvs. 33^{15}. De Zoysa, p. 2, Nr. 11.

[2] Gnvs. 61^{3}, 70^{16}, Sāsvs. 33^{14}. De Zoysa, p. 2, Nr. 12. Wickremasinghe (Catal. of Singh. MSS., p. XII) would identify Mahānāma with the author of the Mahāvaṃsa. In Gnvs. both are however clearly distinguished and in 61^{9} the latter is called Nava-Mahānāma.

[3] Gnvs. 60-61, Sāsvs. 33^{34}. The first work is mentioned in S. Z. Aung, JPTS. 1910-12, p. 124, and the second work is perhaps identical with the *Vimativinodanī*, a Ṭīkā on Smps., de Zoysa, p. 3; Fausböll, p. 13, Nr. 17.

[4] Gnvs. 60^{21}, ^{25}, 66^{28}, ^{29}. Fausböll, p. 19, Nr. 35.

[5] Gnvs. 61^{28}; Sāsvs. 34^{3}; Sdhs. IX. 17; Nikāyasaṃgraha 24^{17}. De Zoysa, pp. 7-8 (where Vācissara has been mentioned as author); Fausböll, p. 36, Nr. 120.

[6] Abhidhammattha-Saṅgaha (ed. Rhys Davids), JPTS. 1884, p. 1 ff. On Ceylon editions, see de Silva, JPTS. 1912, p. 136; Compendium of Philosophy, being a translation of the Abhidhammattha-Saṅgaha by S. Z. Aung, ed. by Mrs. Rhys Davids, London, PTS., 1910.

[7] Gnvs. 61^{24}; Sāsvs. 34^{1}, Sdhs. IX. 14. De Zoysa, pp. 9, 10; Fausböll, p. 36. Nr. 120; M. Bode, Pali Lit. in Burma, p. 104 with foot-notes 5, 6; S. Z. Aung, JPTS. 1910-12, p. 123.

[8] Khuddasikkhā and Mūlasikkhā, ed. E. Müller, JPTS. 1883, p. 86 ff. De Zoysa, Catal., pp. 8, 9; Sāsvs. 33^{38}, Sdhs. IX. 12. On their use in Burma, see M. Bode, PLB., p. 6.

their language, they can be hardly placed before the 11th century. A lower limit is furnished by their mention in the Galvihāra-inscription of king Parakkamabāhu I (second half of the 12th century) in Polonnaruwa.[1] These texts were held in high esteem already at that time.

28. The chronicle-literature of Ceylon owes to the second period its most important work, the *Mahāvaṃsa* of Mahānāma.[2] It covers the same period of history as the Dīpavaṃsa in almost the same order. The dry Chronicle has been here made into an artificial epic poem by drawing much new material from the Aṭṭhakathā. The kings Devānampiyatissa (247-207 B.C.) and Duṭṭhagāmaṇi (101-77 B.C.) are the central figures of the first and the second parts respectively of the Mahāvaṃsa.[3] According to Indian notions the Mahāvaṃsa is a commentary on Dīpavaṃsa. For this reason the commentary of the former is called Tīkā. I think Fleet[4] was right when he connected the passage Mhvs. 38.59 with the origin of our poem. In that case the date of its composition would fall in the beginning of the 6th century A.D. (under king Dhātusena). The original Mahāvaṃsa ends abruptly in 37.50 with the words *Mahāvaṃso niṭṭhito*. The later continuers have evidently destroyed the final portion in order to be able to impose their additions.

29. To the Buddha-legend belong—1. the *Anāgatavaṃsa* of Kassapa,[5] a prophecy on the future Buddha Metteyya in metrical form fathered on Gotama Buddha. According to tradition[6] the author is identical with Thera mentioned in **26**.4.—2. the *Boddhivaṃsa* or *Mahābodhivaṃsa* of Upatissa,[7] a story of the sacred tree in Anurādhapura with a long introduction reaching back to the Buddha Dīpaṃkara. The work is composed in prose and presents, with the

[1] E. Müller, AIC., pp. 88, 122.

[2] The Mahâwanso in Roman characters with the trans. subjoined ..Vol. I, by G. Turnour, Ceylon 1837; The Mahávaṇsa...rev. and ed. by H. Sumangala and DAdS Batuwantudawa, Colombo 1883; The Mahāvaṃsa, ed. by W. Geiger, London, PTS., 1908.—Translation : The Mahāvaṃsa, or the Great Chronicle of Ceylon, transl. by W. Geiger, assist., by M. Bode, London, PTS., 1912.

[3] For details, see Geiger, Dīpavaṃsa und Mahāvaṃsa, Cf. above, **21**.

[4] JRAS. 1909, p. 5, f.-n. 1.

[5] Anāgata-vaṃsa, ed. Minayeff., JPTS. 1886, p. 33 ff.

[6] Gnvs. 60-61.

[7] The Mahābodhivaṃsa, ed. S. A. Strong, London, PTS., 1891; Mahabódhivansa by Upatissa......rev. by Sarananda, Colombo 1891.

exception of a few independent notices, a compilation out of older sources such as Nidānakathā, Mahāvaṃsa, etc. As I have tried to prove, [1] it was composed probably in the first half of the 11th century.

30. The grammarian Kaccāyana belongs to the age posterior to Buddhaghosa. His work *Kaccāyanavyākaraṇa* or *Kaccāyanagandha* [2] is considered to be the oldest Pāli grammar. R. O. Franke [3] has, however, shown that even before Buddhaghosa and Dhammapāla there must have been a fixed grammatical system, which was different from that of Khccāyana and was perhaps based on the grammar of Bodhisatta. [4] The chief weakness of Kaccāyana's system lies in the fact that it ignores the historical relation of Pāli with Sanskrit. He gives an exposition of Pāli wholly out of itself. Moreover it does not at all give an exhaustive treatment of the linguistic material. Kaccāyana has naturally nothing to do with Mahākaccāyana, the disciple of Buddha.[5] He is also different from the Kātyāyana who in the 3rd century B.C. wrote the Vārttikas on Pāṇini's grammar. He is moreover to be distinguished from the author of the Netti and the Peṭaka. Without doubt he is later than Buddhaghosa, for otherwise the latter would have followed him in his grammatical terminology as the author of the classical Pāli grammar. A higher limit for the date of Kaccāyana may be obtained from the fact that he utilised, besides the Kātantra of Śarvavarman and Pāṇini along with his commentators, also the Kāśikā (7th century).[6] Besides this *magnum*

[1] Dīpavaṃsa und Mahāvaṃsa, p. 84 ff.; Wickremasinghe, Catal. of Sinh. MSS., p. XIV. The view of Strong, that Upatissa was a contemporary of Buddhaghosa, is of course untenable.

[2] d' Alwis, An Introduction to Kachchāyana's Grammar of the Pāli Language, Colombo 1863; d' Alwis, Catal., p. 89 ff.; Kachchāyano's Pāli Grammar...by Fr. Mason, Toungoo, 1868-70; Kaccāyanappakaraṇam......per E, Senart, JAs., sér. 6, t. XVII, 1871, p. 193-544; Kaccāyana, ed......and transl. by Vidyabhusana, Calcutta 1891; E. Kuhn, Kaccāyanappakaraṇae Specimen, Halle, 1869, and Specimen alterum, 1871. On the whole problem of Kaccāyana's grammar, see R. O. Franke, Gesch. und Krit. der einheim. Pāli-Grammatik und-Lexikcgrophie, Strassburg 1902; Subhúti, Nāmamālā, p. V ff.

[3] PGr., p. 3. Cf. d' Alwis, Catal., p. 67 ff.

[4] Franke, PGr., p. 2.

[5] It is doubted also in Ceylon. See de Zoysa, Catal, p. 28; Subhúti, Nām., p. VI.

[6] Franke, PGr., p. 18. Already Windisch, Ber. d. K. Sächs. Ges, d. W. 1893, p. 244 f. pointed out that K.'s Grammar must at all events be later than the 4th century.

opus two other grammatical works, *Mahāniruttigandha* and *Culla-niruttigandha*, are ascribed to him. [1] Out of the numerous commentaries on Kaccāyana I mention here only the *Nyāsa* of Vimalabuddhi, which is also called *Mukhamattadīpanī*. [2] He seems to belong to the period we are dealing with because already towards the end of the 12th century Chapada wrote a commentary on it called *Nyāsapradīpa*.[3]

III Period

From the 12th Century to the Modern Age

31. There was a great upward swing in the literary activity of Ceylon during the glorious reign of Parakkamabāhu I (1153-1186). Under his auspices the Thera Mahākassapa is said to have held a council[4] with the purpose of providing Ṭīkās in the Magadha-language to the Aṭṭhakathās, particularly of Buddhaghosa. The following is the list of the Tīkās:—

1.	Sāratthadīpanī	Ṭī on	Samantapāsādikā (Vin.)
2.	Paṭhama-Sāratthamañjūsā	,, ,,	Sumaṅgalavilāsinī (D.)
3.	Dutiya-Sāratthamañjūsā	,, ,,	Papañcasūdanī (M.)
4.	Tatiya-Sāratthamañjūsā	,, ,,	Sāratthappakāsinī (S.)
5.	Catuttha-Sāratthamañjūsā	,, ,,	Manorathapūraṇī (A.)
6.	Paṭhama-Paramatthappakāsini	,, ,,	Atthasālinī (Dhs.)
7.	Dutiya-Paramatthappakāsinī	,, ,,	Sammohavinodanī (Vbh.)
8.	Tatiya Paramatthappakāsinī	,, ,,	Pañcappakaraṇaṭṭhakathā (Dhk., etc.).

Of these Tīkās the *Sāratthadīpanī* by Sāriputta [5] has been preserved. The same Thera is the author of another Ṭīkā on Papañcasūdanī, named *Līnatthapakāsanā*.[6]

[1] Gnvs, 59[12]. De Zoysa, p. 22 mentions a Cullanirutti, said to be one of the oldest Pāli-grammars, Subhúti, Nâm., p. XXVIII calls their author Yamaka.

[2] Gnvs. 60[23]; Subhúti, p. IX; de Zoysa, p. 25; Franke. p. 22 f. Cf. Fausböll. JPTS. 1896, p. 47. Nr. 149. The Porāṇa-Kārikā is said to be still older. It has nothing to do with the Kārikā of Dhammasenāpati (Gnvs. 63[34], 73[21]). Cf. Fausböll, p. 47, Nr. 148. 13; de Zoysa, p. 24; Subhúti, p. LXIX.

[3] A very late commentary on the Nyāsa is the *Niruttisāramañjūsā* of the Burmese monk Dāṭhānāga (middle of the 17th century). Cf. Subhúti, p. X; de Zoysa, p 25; Franke, p. 28; M. Bode, PLB., p. 55.

[4] Sdhs. VIII (JPTS. 1890, p. 58 ff.). That the council had been actually convened is epigraphically attested, E. Müller, AIC., pp 87, 120 ff. Cf. Mhvs. 78, 34.

[5] De Zoysa, Catal., p. 3; Fausböll, JPTS. 1896, p. 12, Nr. 14, 15, 16.

[6] Fausböll. p. 28 f., Nr. 83, 84.

The account of the council of Mahākassapa closely follows the stories of older councils. It is probable that the council gave the impetus for the composition of such Ṭīkās and therewith initiated an era of remarkable literary activity, carried on mainly by Sāriputta and his pupils. As a work of Sāriputta is mentioned, beside the two already referred to above, the *Vinayasaṃgaha* "Compendium of the Vinaya."[1] According to the Gnvs. he is said to have composed also the *Sāratthamañjūsā* on the Manorathapūraṇī.[2]

32. Of Sāriputta's pupils are to be mentioned: **1.** Saṃgharakkhita as the author of a *Khuddasikkhā-Ṭīkā* (see **27**). It is called "new Ṭīkā," and was therefore probably later than the Porāṇa-Ṭīkā attributed to Mahāyasa. Both the Ṭīkās have been preserved in MSS.[3]—2. Buddhanāga, the author of a Ṭīkā on the Kaṅkhāvitaraṇī (**22**, Nr. 2) called *Vinayatthamañjūsā*[4] which likewise exists only in manuscript.—3. The Gnvs. (62, 66) mentions 18 works of Vācissara. The following commentary-works of this author still exist in manuscript: (*a*) *Mūlasikkhā-Abhinava-Ṭīkā* (see **27**), which is evidently later than the Porāṇa-Ṭīkā of Vimalasāra.[5] (*b*) *Simālaṃkārasaṃgaha*, belonging to the sphere of Vinaya, on the boundaries of sacred districts,—the monks living in them had to jointly perform the ecclesiastical duties.[6] (*c*) *Khemappakaraṇa-Ṭīkā* on the work mentioned in **26**.6.[7] (*d*) *Nāmarūpaparicchedа-Ṭīkā* on the work of Anuruddha[8] mentioned in **26**.7. (*e*) *Saccasaṃkhepa-Ṭīkā* (**26**.1), older than Sumaṅgala's Ṭīkā on the same work.[9] (*f*) *Abhidhammāvatāra-Ṭīkā*[10] on the well-known work of Buddhadatta (**25**.1). (*g*) *Rūpārūpavibhāga*,[11] like the works from *c* to *f*, belonging to the

[1] Fausböll, p. 17, Nr. 30; Subhûti, Nâm., p. 7 f. The work was also called *Pālimuttakavinayasaṃgaha* or *Mahāvinayasaṃgahappakaraṇa*. Cf. the works mentioned in de Zoysa, pp. 11 and 15. Cf. **43**.1.

[2] Gnvs. 61[30-31] 71[10-11]. A grammatical work of Sāriputta will be mentioned below.

[3] De Zoysa, Catal., p. 8; Wickremasinghe, Catal., p. XVI. Cf. also **46**.2, **53**.1.

[4] Gnvs. 61-62; Fausböll, JPTS. 1896, p. 17, Nr. 28. Cf. de Zoysa, p. 15, where however no author is mentioned.

[5] De Zoysa, p. 9.

[6] De Zoysa, p. 13. Also other works on the same subject are mentioned here.

[7] De Zoysa, p. 8.

[8] De Zoysa, p. 9.

[9] De Zoysa, p. 12; Fausböll, p. 37, Nr. 121.

[10] De Zoysa, p. 5.

[11] De Zoysa, p. 11 (without mentioning the author); Fausböll, p. 36, Nr. 120.

Abhidhamma. There are mentioned, besides, *Vinayavinicchaya-Ṭīkā* and an *Uttaravinicchaya-Ṭīkā* (25.1)[1]; a Ṭīkā called *Sumaṅgalappasādanī* on the Khuddasikkhā; a *Yogavinicchaya*, a *Paccayasaṃgaha* etc. It is quite possible that these works were composed by different Theras of the same name. There were at all events several Vācissaras[2]—4. Sumaṅgala composed a Ṭīkā on Anuruddha's Abhidhammatthasaṃgaha (**26**.7) which was titled *Abhidhammatthavibhāvanī*[3] and another Ṭīkā on the Abhidhammāvatāra (**25**.1) called the *Abhidhammatthavikāsanī*,[4] as well as a *Saccasaṃkhepa-Ṭīkā*,[5] which is also called the Abhinavaṭīkā (cf. above 3 *e*). All the three works exist in MSS.

33. Saddhammajotipāla or Chapada[6] belongs to the circle of Sāriputta's disciples. He was a native of Burma, but he received his education in Ceylon, where he stayed from 1170 to 1180 according to tradition. Of his works (cf. also **30**) the following belong to the sphere of Vinaya: (*a*) *Vinayasamuṭṭhānadīpanī*, (*b*) *Pātimokkhavisodhanī*[7], (*c*) *Vinayagūlhatthadīpanī*,[8] in which the difficult passages of the Vinaya have been discussed, as well as (*d*) *Sīmālaṃkārasaṃgaha-Ṭīkā*[9] on **32**.3*b*. To the Abhidhamma belong (*e*) *Mātikatthadīpanī*, (*f*) *Paṭṭhānagaṇanānaya*, (*g*) *Nāmacāradīpa*,[10] as well as his best-known work (*h*) *Abhidhammatthasaṃgahasaṃkhepa-Ṭīkā*,[11] a commentary on the work of Anuruddha mentioned in **26**.7. Finally

[1] The Ṭīkās mentioned by de Zoysa, p. 15, 14 probably belong hereto. As author of the first work he mentions Revata, but he does not mention the name of the author of the second. In Fausböll, p. 19, Nr. 32 and 33 an anonymous Ṭīkā on the Vinayavinicchaya, called the *Līnatthappakāsinī*, has been mentioned, which however should not be confounded with the work of the same name referred to in 25.3.

[2] Should not the Vācissara mentioned in Mhvs. 81.17 ff. have been the pupil of Sāriputta?

[3] De Zoysa, p. 5; Oldenberg, Catal., p. 84, Nr. 58; Fausböll, p. 38 f, Nr. 123; cf. also **42**.1.

[4] De Zoysa, p. 5.

[5] De Zoysa, p. 12.

[6] Gnvs. 64[19], Sāsvs 39, 40, 65, 74. Cf. M. Bode, PLB., p. 17 ff.; S. Z. Aung, JPTS. 1912, p. 124 f. Cf. also **46**.1.

[7] De Zoysa, Catal., p. 11.

[8] *Ibid.*, p. 15.

[9] *Ibid.*, p. 13.

[10] *Ibid.*, p. 9; S. Z. Aung, p. 124.

[11] De Zoysa, p. 12; Oldenberg, Catal., p. 85, Nr. 54; Fausböll, JPTS, 1896, p. 39. Nr. 123; S. Z. Aung, p. 125. According to the introductory verses the work was composed at the instance of King Vijayabāhu (1186-87). Not so in Gnvs. 74[14].

there is still to mention (*i*) the *Gandhasāra*, apparently an anthology of sacred texts.—In connection with Chapada let us also mention the Burmese monk Sāriputta or Dhammavilāsa, who died in the year 1246. He received his ordination from Ānanda, one of the four Theras who accompanied Chapada on his journey back to Burma from Ceylon. Dhammavilāsa is the author of the oldest Burmese law-book *Dhammavilāsa-Dhammasattha*, which is the basis of the later legal literature of the Burmese.[1]

34. The pupils of Sāriputta displayed their activity also in the field of Buddhistic legends and ecclesiastical history. In this connection are to be mentioned—1. The *Dāṭhāvaṃsa* of Dhammakitti,[2] who in the concluding verses declares himself to be a pupil of Sāritanuja. It is clear from the introductory verses that the poem was composed at the beginning of the 13th century.[3] It deals with the story of Buddha's tooth-relic and adds to the tradition recorded in the Mahāvaṃsa a few notices which were very probably culled from the local tradition of Ceylon.—2. The *Thūpavaṃsa* of Vācissara,[4] who was probably Sāriputta's pupil. It is written in prose and is merely a compilation of pieces from Nidānakathā, Samantapāsādikā and Mahāvaṃsa with its Ṭīkā. It was composed in the first half of the 13th century. The later Singhalese version may be ascertained to have been composed between 1250 and 1260.—3. The *Jinālaṃkāra* of Buddharakkhita,[5] a poem composed in a very ornate language and in very artificial metres, which already bears all the signs of the artificial poetry of India.[6] It describes the life of Budda till the Sāṃbodhi. In the concluding verses (271 ff.) the author gives his own

[1] M. Bode, PLB., p. 31 ff.

[2] Dāṭhāvanso...by Dhammakirti...ed. Asabha Tissa, Kelaniya 1883. The Dāṭhāvaṃsa (ed. Rhys Davids), JPTS. 1884, p. 108 ff. A Ṭīkā on Dāṭhāvs. is mentioned by Fausböll, JPTS. 1896, p. 45, Nr. 142.

[3] Geiger, Dīpavaṃsa und Mahāvaṃsa, p. 88 ff. According to Wickremasinghe, JRAS. 1896, p. 200 ff., there were five different Dhammakittis. The first of them is the author of Dāṭhāvs.

[4] Pāli Thūpavaṃśaya ed. Dhammaratana, Ceylon 1896. Cf. Geiger, *ibid.*, p. 92. The Gnvs. 70^{18} of course mentions the Thūpavs., but not among the works of Vācissara and without giving the name of the author.

[5] Jinālaṅkāra...by Buddharakkhita, ed. Gray, London 1894. The Jinālaṅkāra by Buddharakkhita, transl. into Sinh. and ed. by W. Dīpaṅkara and B. Dhammapāla, Galle 1900.

[6] The author is said to have himself composed a Ṭīkā on his work. Cf. also Gray. Introd., p. 8 f.

name and mentions the year 1700 (after Buddha = 1156 A.D.) as the time of its composition.[1] With the Jinālaṃkāra ascribed to Buddhadatta (**26**.1) our poem has therefore nothing to do, even if any real value attaches to this datum.—4. The *Jinacarita* of Medhaṃkara[2] is likewise a highly artificial poem which in conventional form deals with a subject similar to that of the Jinālaṃkāra. The Gnvs. 62^{24}, 72^{7} mentions this author immediately after Vācissara,[3] Sumaṅgala and Dhammakitti, and thus evidently takes him to be the pupil of Sāriputta. The author says in the concluding verses that he had composed his work in a Pariveṇa erected by King Vijayabāhu. This seems to be a calculated and intentional homage, which however could have a point in it only if the prince was still living. It is therefore permissible to think that Vijayabāhu III (1225-29) is here referred to by the author, and Medhaṃkara would thus be a contemporary of Vācissara.

35. The Ṭīkā on the Mahāvaṃsa[4] is of great importance for information about the Ceylonese tradition. It is called *Vaṃsatthappakāsinī.*[5] Its author is unknown. As for its date, an upper limit is furnished by the reference to Dāṭhopatissa II (about 670 A.D.), and a lower limit by the fact that the Pāli-Thūpavaṃsa (**34**.2) quotes it profusely. If the Mahābodhivaṃsakathā quoted in it is identical with our Bodhivaṃsa (**29**.2), then we get a still closer upper limit for it. The MhvsṬī. is certainly older than the first supplement to the Mahāvaṃsa by Dhammakitti (**38**), because it breaks off at the same place where the original Mahāvaṃsa (**28**) ends. It is probable therefore that the MhvsṬī. was composed in the 12th century. Its importance lies in the fact that it offers a mass of supplementary notices to the Mahāvaṃsa culled from the Aṭṭhakathā. In this way it reveals to us the richness of the contents of the Aṭṭhakathā, which was still available at the time.[6] The MhvsṬī. is therefore a fruitful

[1] See also Gnvs. 72^{9}; Sdhs. IX. 21.

[2] Jinacarita, ed. Rouse, JPTS. 1904-05. p. 1 ff. Jinacarita...ed. and transl. by Ch. Duroiselle, Rangoon 1906. On the various Medhaṃkaras, see Rouse, p. 2; Wickremasinghe, Catal., p. 21*a*, 35*b*, 119*a*.

[3] Rouse has evidently misunderstood the construction; *kārite* in 469 belongs to *pariveṇavare* in 470.

[4] Mahāwaṃsa Ṭīká or Waṃsatthappakásiní, rev. and ed. by Baṭuwantuḍáwe and Ñáṇissara Bhikshu, Colombo 1895; Vaṃsatthappakāsinī ed. by G. P. Malalasekera, 2 vols. PTS. 1935.

[5] On what follows, cf. Geiger, Dīpavaṃsa und Mahāvaṃsa, p. 34 ff.

[6] Cf. above, p. 25, f.-n. 1.

source of information about the indigenous tradition, the historicity of which however has naturally to be tested separately in each case.

36. Vedehathera belongs to the 13th century, as has been proved by the researches of d'Alwis and Sten Konow.[1] According to the notices in his works, he belonged to the Brahmin family of Vippagāma. He was a "forest-dweller" and a pupil of Thera Ānanda also called *araññāyatana*. His works are: (a) The *Samantakūṭavaṇṇanā* "description of the Adam's Peak."[2] The poem deals with the story of Buddha's life and particularly the legends of his three visits to the island of Ceylon. On the occasion of his third visit he left on the summit of the Samantakūṭa his *śrīpada*, the print of his left foot. The verses 722-46 give a description of the sacred hill, which has given the name to the whole poem consisting of 796 strophes.—(b) The *Rasavāhinī*,[3] a collection of prose stories, which, according to the introductory words, are based on a Ceylonese original. This original was translated into Pāli by Raṭṭhapāla in the Mahāvihāra, and the translation was revised by Vedehathera. Altogether the Rasav. contains 103 stories, of which 40 are derived from the Jambudīpa, the continent of India, and 63 from Laṅkādīpa, Ceylon. These are fables, legends, sagas and religious tales. The original work had very probably drawn the material from the Aṭṭhakathā. Hence the frequent quotations with *tenāhu porāṇā*. In the present Pāli version the Mahāvaṃsa has been drawn upon profusely; some of the stories are based on the Apadānas and the Jātaka-book. The *Sahassavatthuppakaraṇa* "the book of thousand stories" was probably in contents connected with the Rasav. and it is said toha ve been reintroduced into Ceylon from Burma.[4]

[1] D'Alwis, Catal., pp. 221-25; Sten Konow, Vedehathera, Skrifter udgiven of Videnskabsskelskabet i Christiania, hist.-filos. Kl. 1895, Nr. 4.

[2] Samanta Kūṭa Warṇanâ...transl. into Sinh. and ed. by W. Dhammânanda and M. Ñâṇissara, Colombo 1890.

[3] Rasavahini...by Vedeha Maha Thera, ed. Saraṇatissa, 2 parts, Colombo 1901 and 1899. Selected pieces have been edited and translated by Spiegel, Anecdota Palica, Leipzig 1845, p. 15 ff.; Sten Konow, ZDMG. 43, 1889, p. 297 ff.; D. Andersen, Studier fra Sprog- og Oldtidsforskning, Nr. 6, Kopenhagen 1891 (not available to me); Pavolini, Giornale Soc. As. Ital. VIII, 179 ff., XI, 175 ff. An analysis of the work has been given by Pavolini, La Materia e la Forma della Rasavâhinī, *ibid*, XI, 35 ff.

[4] De Zoysa, Catal., p. 20. On a *Sahassavatthaṭṭhakathā* four times mentioned in the MhvsṬī., see Geiger, Dīpavaṃsa und Mahāvaṃsa, p. 52.

37. A contemporary of Vedehathera was Buddhappiya, the author of the *Pajjamadhu*,[1] a poem which in 104 artistic stanzas glorifies the external beauty of Buddha and also his wisdom. In the last stanza but one, the author gives his own name and says that he is a pupil of Ānanda, who is doubtless the same person as Vedehathera's teacher.—The *Attanagaluvihāravaṃsa*[2] was composed probably about the same time as the Pajjamadhu,—in the second half of the 13th century. It is written in a mixture of prose and verse and gives the story of the death of Sirisaṃghabodhi (Mhvs. 36.91 ff.) and his wife as well as of the founding of the Attanagalu monastery on the spot where they died. As the anonymous author (v. 3) himself admits, he was induced to compose this poem by the priest Anomadassin, who is probably the person to whom, according to Mhvs. 86.37 f., in the reign of Parakkamabāhu II (1229-1246), was entrusted the Attanagalu monastery, furnished with new buildings by the minister Paṭirāja.

38. The Mahāvaṃsa of Mahānāma (**28**) was continued under the special title *Cūlavaṃsa* "Short Chronicle" and made into a narrative covering the whole history of Ceylon.[3] According to tradition the first author to continue the work was Thera Dhammakitti, who according to Mhvs. 84.12 ff. came to Ceylon from Burma in the reign of Parakkamabāhu II (first half of the 13th century). An evident supplement to the later Mhvs. begins with Chap. 90.104 after the close of the reign of Parakkamabāhu IV which began in the year 1284. The second part of the Mhvs. (Chaps. 37-90) which ends here describes above all the glorious age of Parakkamabāhu I (1153-1186).[4] In order to round off the concluding portion of the Mhvs., let us mention here that in the second half of the 18th century, according to Mhvs. 99.78ff., the king Kittisiri had the chronicle extended up to his own time. This third part is made up of the Chapters 90 (from verse 105) to 100. In Chapter 101 are then given notices up to the arrival of the English in Ceylon.

[1] Edited by Gooneratne, JPTS. 1887, pp. 1-16. Also the Pajja Madhu...by Buddhapria, ed. Devamitta, Colombo 1887. Cf. **56**.4.

[2] The Pali Text of the Attanagaluwansa and its ancient translation...by d'Alwis Colombo 1887. Cf. d'Alwis, Catal., p. 11 ff., particularly 32 f.; de Zoysa, Catal., p. 17.

[3] The Mahawansa, from the thirty-seventh chapter, ed. H. Sumangala and DAdS. Batuwantudawa, Colombo 1877. Translation: The Mahávaṇsa, Part II.... transl. by L. C. Wijesiṇha, Colombo 1889; Cūlavaṃsa, Text (2 vols.) and Translation (2 vols.), by Wilhelm Geiger, PTS. 1935.

[4] Chaps. 67-79, See Copleston, JRAS., Ceylon Branch, Nr. 44, 1893, p. 60 ff.

39. To the transition period from the 13th to the 14th century belongs 1. the *Sārasaṃgaha* of Siddhattha,[1] a work on Buddhism in prose mixed with verses. The author gives his own name in the concluding verses of the work and also says that he was a pupil of Buddhappiya. If thereby the author of the Pajjamadhu is meant, then we have for the Sārasaṃgaha the date suggested above. A lower limit is at all events furnished by the reference to it in the Moggallānapañcikāpadīpa composed in 1457 A.D. Some idea of the contents of the Sāras is furnished by its chapter-headings: the Chaps. 1-3, for instance, deal with *buddhānaṃ abhinīhāra, tathāgatassa acchariyāni and pañca antaradhānāni*, Chaps. 13-15 with *sīlāni, kammaṭṭhānāni, nibbāṇa*, and Chaps. 30-34 with the *Nāgā, Supaṇṇā, Petā, Asurā, Devā*[2]; the last chapter contains a *lokasaṃṭhiti* (cosmology).—2. Somewhat later is the *Saddhammasaṃgaha* of Dhammakitti Mahāsāmin.[3] This is probably the last of the Dhammakittis known to us, who was active towards the end of the 14th Century.[4] In the 9th Chapter various authors and works are enumerated, the latest of them belonging of the 13th century. The Sdhs. in 40 chapters gives a history of the Buddhist church (without furnishing much new information) from the Councils in India to the period mentioned just above, and ends with a hymn in praise of the doctrine and a blessing for its study.

40. To the 14th century belongs: 1. the *Lokappadīpasāra*. According to Sāsvs. 48 it was composed by a Burmese monk named Medhaṃkara, who had prosecuted his studies in Ceylon.[5] The work deals with various forms of existence in the *saṃkhāraloka*, in the hell, among the Petas, in the animal world, in human life, in the *sattaloka*, and in the *okāsaloka*. The different topics are further elucidated by various legends. The 5th chapter, for instance, which deals with the forms of human existence, has drawn many stories from the Mahāvaṃsa.—Allied with it in content is 2. the *Pañcagatidīpana*,[6] a poem in 114 strophes, which describes the five possible

[1] Edited by Somananda, Brendiawatta 1898. Cf. Oldenberg, Catal., p. 125, Nr. 108.

[2] For the *termini*, see Childers PD.

[3] Saddhamma Saṃgaho, ed. N. Saddhānanda, JPTS. 1890, p. 21 ff.; de Zoysa, Catal., p. 19 f. Cf. 46.5.

[4] See above, p. 41, f.-n. 3.

[5] Oldenberg, Catal., p. 126, Nr. 109; Fausböll, JPTS. 1896, p. 42, Nr. 184; M. Bode, PLB., p. 35 f.

[6] Edited by L. Feer, JPTS. 1884, p. 152 ff.

forms of rebirth in hell, as animal, as Peta, as man, or as god. Nothing is known about its author or the time of its origin.—3. The *Buddhaghosuppatti*[1] should belong to the 14th century if its author Mahāmaṅgala is the same man as the grammarian Maṅgala (**53**.2*b*). This short work is a biography of Buddhaghosa, and it is referred to also in the Sāsvs. 30[20], where this famous commentator is dealt with. The author has made use of the data left by the *pubbācariyā* "the former teachers."

41. By way of appendix I would like to mention here two poems of which the authors and the time of origin are unknown: 1. The *Saddhammopāyana*, a collection of 621 (including the concluding verses 629) strophes in 9 chapters in praise of the law of Buddha.[2] It begins with a description of the 8 *akkhaṇā*, the miseries of the *dasa akusalāni* and the sorrowful lot of the Petas, and then goes over to the conceptions of *puñña* and *phala* and describes the individual meritorious acts (*dāna*, *sīla*, etc.,) and ends with *appamāda*.—2. The *Telakaṭāhagāthā*[3] the "oil-cauldron-verses." These 98 strophes are ascribed to a Thera who was condemned to be thrown into a vessel full of boiling oil. He had been falsely accused of indirectly rendering help in an intrigue of the wife of King Tissa of Kalyāṇī. This story belongs to the cycle of sagas centering round Rohaṇa, and it is touched in the Mahāvaṃsa (22.12ff.), and is related at greater length in later sources.[4] The boiling oil cannot injure the Thera and he pronounces those strophes in which certain fundamental conceptions of the teaching of Buddha are elucidated. They deal with death and the thought of death, of transience, of suffering, and of the unreality of the soul, etc.

42. From the 15th century onwards the activity of the Burmese monks comes to the forefront. The special subject of their study is Abhidhamma. I mention here 1. Ariyavaṃsa,[5] who lived in Ava during the reign of Narapati (1442-68). He wrote (*a*) *Maṇisāramañjūsā*, a commentary to Sumaṅgala's Abhidhammatthavibhāvanī (**32**.4); (*b*) *Maṇidīpa* Ṭīkā on Buddaghosa's Atthasālinī (**23**.8)[6]; (*c*) *Jātakavi-*

[1] Buddhaghosuppatti ..ed. J. Gray, London 1892

[2] Edited by R. Morris, JPTS. 1887, p. 35 ff.

[3] Edited by E. R. Gooneratne, JPTS. 1884, p. 49 ff.

[4] Rasav. II. 57 ff.; Rājāvali 21[14].

[5] M. Bode, PLB., p. 42f.; Gnvs. 65[1], 75[5].

[6] De Zoysa, Catal., pp. 8, 9; Fausböll, JPTS. 1896, p. 40, Nr. 124.

sodhana, a work on the Jātakas.—2. Saddhammapālasiri, a contemporary of the former and author of *Nettibhāvanī*, [1] a Ṭīkā on the Netti (19).—3. Sīlavaṃsa,[2] somewhat later than the above mentioned writers, was the author of the *Buddhālaṃkāra*, a poetical version of the story of Sumedha in the Nidānakathā.—4. Raṭṭhasāra,[3] who versified various Jātakas.—The poem *Kāyaviratigāthā*,[4] also belonging to the 15th century, is anonymous; it deals with the ways of overcoming sensuality.—To the 16th century [5] belong 5. Saddhammālaṃkāra, the author of a *Paṭṭhānadīpanī* on the Abhidhamma-work mentioned in **16**.7, and 6. Mahānāma, the author of the *Madhusāratthadīpanī*, a sub-commentary on the Mūla-Ṭīkā (**25**.2).—In the same century, the Wagaru-Dhammasattha composed in the Talaing language was translated into Pāli [6] by Buddhaghosa under the title *Manusāra* (the original work was composed towards the end of the 13th century, somewhat later than the Dhammavilāsa-Dhammasattha referred to in **33**). The Manusāra is the basis of the whole legal literature of Burma, composed partly in the native language, and partly both in Burmese and Pāli, as for instance the *Manuvaṇṇanā* (18th century) and the *Mohavicchedanī* (19th century).

43. In the 17th century we have to mention 1. Tipiṭakālaṃkāra,[7] the author of (*a*) *Visativaṇṇanā*, a commentary on the 20 introductory verses of the Atthasālinī (**22**.8), and (*b*) *Yasavaḍḍhanavatthu* and (*c*) *Vinayālaṃkāra*, a commentary on Sāriputta's Vinayasaṃgaha (**31**).—2. Tilokaguru,[8] author of (*a*) *Dhātukathā-Ṭīkāvaṇṇanā* and (*b*) *Dhātukathā-Anuṭīkāvaṇṇanā*, the two commentaries on the Dhātukathā (**16**.5), and (*c*) *Yamakavaṇṇanā* and (*d*) *Paṭṭhanavaṇṇanā* on the corresponding books of the Abhidhamma (**16**.6, 7).—3. Sāradassin,[9] author of a *Dhātukathāyojanā* (on **16**.5),—4. Mahākassapa,[10] author of the *Abhidhammatthagaṇṭhipada* which deals with the difficult termini of the Abhidhamma.—To the 18th century belongs 5. Ñāṇābhivaṃsa,[11]

[1] S. Z. Aung, JPTS. 1910-12, p. 121.
[2] M. Bode, p. 43.
[3] *Ibid.*
[4] *Ibid.*, p. 44.
[5] *Ibid.*, p. 47; S. Z. Aung, p. 122.
[6] About the literature of Dhammasatthas, see M. Bode, p 85 ff.
[7] M. Bode, PLB, p. 53 f; S. Z Aung, JPTS. 1910-12, p. 122.
[8] M. Bode, P. 54; S. Z Aung, p 122.
[9] S. Z. Aung, p. 122.
[10] *Ibid.*
[11] M. Bode, p. 78 ff.; de Zoysa, Catal., p. 12; Fausböll, JPTS. 1896, p. 28, Nr. 82.

the Saṃgharāja of Burma, author of (*a*) *Peṭakālaṃkāra*, a commentary on the Netti (**19**), (*b*) the *Sādhuvilāsinī* on a part of the D. (**9**.1), and (*c*) of several devotional stories such as *Catusāmaṇeravatthu*, *Rājavādavatthu*. His (*d*) *Rājādhirājavilāsinī* deserves special mention. It is a prose work devoted to the eulogy of the then king Bodōpayā. It is a masterpiece of learned literary work full of references to legends and history and teeming with quotations from various provinces of the literature, particularly from the Jātakas.—Somewhat older is the anonymous Buddha-biography *Mālālaṃkāra*,[1] which has become well known through Bigandet's translation.

44. Last of all I shall mention a number of modern works which cannot be dated accurately, or were composed in the 19th century. Both the time and the author of 1. the *Nalāṭadhātuvaṃsa* are unknown. The work gives the story of the frontal bone relic of the Buddha. It is evidently the Pāli counterpart, or perhaps the original, of the Sinhalese Dhātuvaṃsa, which contains exactly the same number of chapters as this work.[2]—Also 2. the *Chakesadhātuvaṃsa*[3] is devoted to the sacred relics. It is the work of a modern Burmese author and it gives in prose the story of six hairs of Buddha, which the latter had distributed as relics among his disciples, and for which Thūpas have been erected at various places.—Two modern works throw interesting sidelight on the relation between Ceylon and Burma; they are 3. the *Saṃdesakathā*[4] and 4. the *Sīmāvivādavinicchayakathā*.[5] In them are found the dates 2344 and 2345 after Buddha, equal to 1800 and 1801 A.D.

Quite a peculiar importance attaches to 5. the *Gandhavaṃsa*.[6] This work was composed in Burma. It is a sort of library catalogue, a list of authors and works. After the usual introductory votive verses it begins at first with an analysis of the Tipiṭaka. Then it deals with the *porāṇācariyā*, the Theras of the three councils who compiled the words of the Buddha, with the exception of Mahākaccāyana. The same Theras are also the *aṭṭhakathācariyā*. Mahākaccāyana, who is mentioned in the Gandhavaṃsa as the author of the famous grammar,

[1] Bigandet, The life or legend of Gautama the Buddha, Rangoon 1866.

[2] Geiger, Dīpavaṃsa und Mahāvaṃsa, pp. 102-05; de Zoysa, Catal., p. 19.

[3] Edited by Minayeff, JPTS. 1885, p. 5 ff.

[4] Edited by Minayeff, JPTS. 1885, p. 17 ff.

[5] Edited by Minayef, JPTS. 1887, p. 17 ff.

[6] Edited by Minayeff, JPTS. 1886, p. 54 ff. Cf. M. Bode, Index to the Gandhavaṃsa, *ibid*, 1896, p. 53 ff.

Mahā- and Culla-nirutti, and Netti, Peṭakopadesa and the Vaṇṇanīti, is mentioned as the only example of the *tividhanāmakācariyā*. Then follows the long list of *gandhakācariyā*, headed by the authors of the Kurundī and the Mahāpaccarī, who are followed by Buddhaghosa, Buddhadatta, Ānanda, Dhammapāla, etc. Last of all are mentioned Ariyavaṃsa (see 42.1) and Udumbara. Then follows a list of anonymous works. After that the authors are grouped together according as they were active in Laṅkā or Jambudīpa (including Farther India). Last of all is recorded which works were composed at the instance of other persons, and which out of the authors' own initiative (*attano matiyā*).—6. The *Sāsanavaṃsa* of Paññasāmin [1] is dated in the year 1223 of the Burmese era, equal to 1861 A.D. Inspite of the very recent origin of this work it is of great importance in various ways, because it is based on older literature. In ten chapters it gives a complete history of the Buddhist church in India till the third council under Asoka, and then in Ceylon and other countries where Buddhist missions had been sent. The history of Buddhism in Aparantaraṭṭha, *i.e.*, Burma itself, is dealt with very exhaustively in Chap. 6. It has to be mentioned however that in the Burmese tradition, no less than 5 out of the 9 countries, to which missions were sent according to Dpvs. 8.1 ff., Mhvs. 12.1 ff., are assigned to Farther India, namely, Suvaṇṇabhūmi, Vanavāsi, Aparanta, Yonaka and Mahāraṭṭha. The chief sources of the Sāsanvaṃsa are Samantapāsādikā, Dipavaṃsa, Mahāvaṃsa, as well as the Burmese chronicles. The Aṭṭhakathā too is mentioned, but naturally it could have been utilised only indirectly.

45. There was an extraordinary literary activity both in Ceylon and Burma in the field of philology for which I may rely on the description of indigenous Pāli grammar and lexicography given by R. O. Franke.[2] W. Subhúti's Introduction to the Nāmamālā too is very useful.[3]

The grammatical works are divided into three groups: 1. Those which belong to the school of Kaccāyana (*Bālāvatāra*, *Rūpasiddhi*); 2. the grammar of Moggallāna with the ancillary works belonging to it, such as *Payogasiddhi*, *Padasādhana*, etc. ; 3. Saddanīti with the

[1] Sâsanavaṃsa, ed. M. Bode, PTS., London 1897. The Sâsanavaṃsadīpa which appeared in Ceylon is not available to me.

[2] Cf. above, p. 37, f.-n. 2.

[3] Subhúti, Nâmamâlâ or a Work on Pāli Grammar (Ceylonese), Ceylon 1871, with English foreword.

Cullasaddanīti.[1] To each of these three schools belongs a list of roots—the three lists being the *Dhātumañjūsā*, the *Dhātupāṭha* and the *Dhātvatthadīpanī*. For dictionary we have the *Abhidhānappadīpikā*. Finally there are also some works on prosody, etc. The value which these works possess as accessories for the study of Pāli has been rightly judged by Franke.[2] They are not based on the direct knowledge of Pāli as a living and spoken language. The authors have drawn their material from the literature just as we too have to do to-day. Their method also is not based on any homogeneous tradition reaching back to the days when Pāli was actually spoken. Moreover they slavishly imitate the model works of Sanskrit grammar and lexicography and take over their system mechanically into Pāli. Grammatical forms and words of Pāli which are found in the text-books have therefore to be treated with the greatest caution so long as they are not proved actually to occur in literature. In all these cases the possibility is ever there that we have before us merely artificial constructions in imitation of Sanskrit.

46. Of the works belonging to the school of Kaccāyana, the commentary called Nyāsa has been already dealt with in **30**, for it belongs to the preceding age. The next oldest work is 1. the *Suttaniddesa* of Chapada.[3] Subhúti assigns it to the Budda-year 1715 = 1181 A.D. This also is a commentary on Kaccāyana. Approximately to the same age belongs 2. the *Saṃbandhacintā* of Saṃgharakkhita,[4] who has been mentioned in **32**. 1. It deals with Pāli syntax and there is an anonymous Ṭīkā on it.—There is further 3. the *Saddatthabhedacintā* of the Thera Saddhammasiri [5] from Arimaddana in Burma. This work too is furnished with an anonymous Ṭīkā.—4. The *Rūpasiddhi* or *Padarūpasiddhi*[6] is but a reshuffling of Kaccāyana's grammar. In the colophon the author gives his

[1] Subhúti, Preface, p. 10.

[2] PGr., p. 83.

[3] Subhúti Nâm., p. XV; de Zoysa, Catal., p. 29; M. Bode, PLB., p. 17.

[4] Sambandha-Cintâ, the grammar of Śrī Saṅgharakkhita, ed. K. Sarānanda, Colombo 1891 (JPTS. 1912, p. 149). Cf. de Zoysa, Catal., p. 27; Fausböll, JPTS. 1896, p. 47, Nr. 148.11 and p. 48, Nr. 152.2.

[5] Saddatthabbeda-cintâ: Grammar by Saddhamma Siri, ed. Sujâta and Ñānānanda, Colombo 1901 (JPTS. 1912, p. 149). Cf. de Zoysa, p 27; Fausböll, p. 47, Nr. 148.12 and p. 48, Nr. 152.3.

[6] Grünwedel, das sechste Kapitel der Rūpasiddhi, Berlin 1883. Cf. Turnour, Mhvs., p. XXV f.; d'Alwis, Catal., p. 179 ff.; Subhúti, p. XXI; Zoysa, p. 26; Fausböll, p. 49, Nr. 155; Franke, PGr., pp. 25-29.

name as Buddhappiya with the surname Dīpaṃkarā, a pupil of the Thera Ānanda. He is therefore probably the author of the Pajjamadhu (see 37), and the Rūpasiddhi therefore belongs to the second half of the 13th century. The work is divided into seven chapters, and the arrangement of the material is exactly like that of Kaccāyana the only difference being that Kitaka and Uṇādi have been stuffed in one chapter which is the seventh. There is a Ṭīkā[1] on the Rūpasiddhi, as well as a Singhalese adaptation (*sannaya*) of it. The latter is mentioned already in Rāhula's Moggallāyanapañcikāpadīpa, a work of the year 1456 A.D.—5. The *Bālāvatāra*[2] is a handbook very much in use in Burma and Siam. This also is an adaptation of Kaccāyana's grammar, giving the contents of the basic work in a more concise form and a slightly different order. According to tradition its author is Dhammakitti[3] who composed also the Saddhammasaṃgaha (see 39.2). The Bālāvatāra should accordingly have been composed towards the end of the 14th century. In Gnvs, 62[9], 71[26] it is however ascribed to Vācissara, in which case the work would be more than a century older. There is also a Bālāvatāra-Ṭīkā[4] by an anonymous author – 6. The *Saddasāratthajālinī*[5] of the Burmese monk Kaṇṭakakhipanāgita, usually called simply Nāgita, was composed in 1900 after Buddha (=1356 A.D.), *i.e.*, about the same time as the Ṭīkā on Abhidhānappadīpikā. The arrangement of the material is again very much as in Kaccāyana's grammar. The chapters 3-9 of the former correspond to the chapters 1-7 of the latter.

47. To the school of Kaccāyana further belongs—7. the *Kaccāyanabheda*, a commentary by Thera Mahāyasa[6] who is supposed to have

[1] Subhūti, p. XXII; de Zoysa, p. 26

[2] Bālāvatāra : Grammar by Dharmakirti, ed. DAdS. Batuvantudave. Colombo 1869; Bālāvatāra : Pāli Grammar, ed. Sri Dharmārāma. Paliyagoda 1902; Bālāvatāra with Ṭīkā : Pali Grammar, ed. H. Sumaṅgala, Colombo 1893 (JPTS. 1912, p. 139). The Bālāvatāra was edited with English translation by L. Lee in "The Orientalist" II. 1892 Cf. d'Alwis, p. 78 ff. ; Subhūti, p. XXIV; de Zoysa, p. 21 f.; Fausböll, p. 45, Nr. 144.2; Franke, PGr., p. 24. f.

[3] Subhūti, p. XXV; Wickremasinghe, Catal. of Sinh. MSS., p. XIX.

[4] Subhūti, p. XXVI; de Zoysa, p. 22.

[5] Sabdasarartha Jalini, a Pāli work compiled by Nagita, ed. and transl. by Silananda, Colombo 1902. Cf. de Zoysa, p. 27; Fausböll, p. 47, Nr. 148.16 and p. 48, Nr. 152.5.

[6] M. Bode, PLB., p. 36 f.; Subhūti, Nam., p. LXIII f.; de Zoysa, Catal., p. 23; Fausböll, JPTS. 1896, p. 47, Nr. 148.17; p. 48, Nr. 152. 1; Franke, PGr., p. 29. In Gnvs. 74[1] Dhammānanda is mentioned as the author both of Kacc.- bheda and Kacc.-sāra.

lived in the second half of the 14th century. Fausböll however mentions Rassathera as the author of this work. There are two Ṭīkās[1] on this work which consists of 400 strophes and is divided into seven chapters. One of them was composed by the Burmese monk Ariyālaṃkāra about the year 2152 after Buddha (=1608 A.D.), and is titled *Sāratthvikāsinī*. The other is the *Kaccāyanabheda-Mahāṭīkā* of Uttamasikkha. Mahāyasa is also the author of a *Kaccāyanasāra*,[2] on which the author himself is said to have written a Ṭīkā. This is perhaps the *Kaccāyanasāra-Purāṇaṭikā*,[3] of which however Subhúti expressly says that the author and the time of origin are unknown. A *Kaccāyanasāra-Abhinavaṭīkā*, also called *Saṃmohavināsinī*, was composed by the Burmese monk Saddhammavilāsa of Pagan—8. The *Saddabindu*,[4] consisting of 21 strophes, probably belongs to the second half of the 15th century. According to Sāsv. 76[25], King Kyacvā of Arimaddana (Burma) was the author of this work. Subhúti gives for it the year 2025 after Buddha (=1481 A.D.). A Saddabindu-Ṭīkā[5] titled *Linatthasūdanī* was composed by Ñāṇavilāsa toward the end of the 16th century.—9. Neither the author nor the time of origin of the *Bālappabodhanā*[6] is known. The editor Sudhammālaṃkāra gives the approximate date 2100 after Buddha (=1556 A.D.). It is at all events later than Kaccāyanabheda and Saddhattabhedacintā. Also the Ṭīkā on Bālappabodhana is anonymous.—10. I am unable to give any date for the *Abhinavā-Cullanirutti* of Sirisaddhammālaṃkāra.[7] It deals with the exceptions to the rules of Kaccāyana—11. Finally I shall mention the *Kaccāyanavaṇṇanā* of the Burmese Thera Mahāvijitāvin,[8] who lived about 1600 A.D. The work is a commentary on the

[1] Subhúti, pp. XLVI and XLIV; Oldenberg, Catal., p. 90. Nr. 65; de Zoysa, pp. 28, 23.

[2] Subhúti, pp. LXXXIII; Fausböll, p. 47, Nr. 148, 14; M. Bode, de Zoysa, Franke, *Ibid*.

[3] Subhúti, p. LXXXIV, LXXXV; de Zoysa, p. 23.

[4] De Zoysa, p. 27; Subhúti, p. XCI f.

[5] Subhúti, p. XCII f.; de Zoysa, p. 27.

[6] Bálappabódhana, a Pali grammar ed. with a Sinhalese paraphrase by R. Sudhammalankara, Colombo 1913. Subhúti, p. XCI; de Zoysa, p. 21.

[7] Subhúti, p. XXVIII f.; de Zoysa, p. 22. The introductory verses show that the Culanirutti mentioned in Oldenberg, p. 102, Nr. 77 is the same work.

[8] M. Bode, p. 16; Subhúti, p. XVIII ff.; de Zoysa, p. 24; Fausböll, p. 47, Nr. 150 and 151.

saṃdhikappa of Kaccāyana. The authors of the most important earlier works, such as Nyāsa, Rūpasiddhi, saddanīti, etc., are mentioned in the introductory verses. This *Kaccāyanavaṇṇanā* however must not be confused with a much earlier work of the same name, which has been mentioned already in the introductory verses of the Rūpasiddhi.[1] Mahāvijitāvin is also the author of the *Vācakopadesa*,[2] in which—according to Oldenberg—the grammatical categories have been considered from a logical point of view.

48. Besides Kaccāyana, the Thera Moggallāna or Moggallāyana[3] was the founder of a new grammatical school. His works are **1.** the *Moggallāyanavyākaraṇa*, also called *Saddalakkhaṇa*, with the *Vutti* belonging to it, and 2. the *Moggallāyanapañcikā*, which was the author's own commentary on his grammar. This commentary is now lost. For the contents of the grammatical work of Moggallāna I refer to the researches of R. O. Franke. It is doubtless superior to the work of Kaccāyana. Moggallāyana's grammar too is of course not free from the defects of indigenous Pāli grammatical literature, but Moggallāna deals with the linguistic material more exhaustively and with greater understanding of the essence and character of Pāli. There are considerable differences in the arrangement and grouping of the rules, as well as in the terminology. Besides the older Pāli grammars, the Kātantra and the work of Pāṇini, Moggallāna has drawn most upon Candragomin. As for the age of Moggallāna, he himself says in the concluding verses of the Vutti that he composed the work in the reign of Parakkamabhuja. Therewith is surely meant Parakkamabāhu I (1153-1186 A.D.). Moggallāna was an inhabitant of Anurādhapura, where he was a member of the Thūpārāma. According to the Gnvs. 62[9], 71[26] Vācissara is said to have composed a Ṭīkā on his grammar; but it appears that this Vācissara was not the pupil of Sāriputta mentioned in **32**.3. There was evidently a confusion with the Thera Rāhula, the author of the Moggallāyanapañcikāpadīpa, who likewise bore the not unusual surname Vācissara.

49. As in the case of Kaccāyana's grammar, an extensive literature belongs also to the grammar of Moggallāna.

1 See d'Alwis, Catal., p. 179; Subbûti, p. XXIII.

2 Subhûti, p. LXXIII; de Zoysa, p. 20.

3 Moggallāyana-Vyākaraṇa : Grammar, ed. H. Devamitta, Colombo 1890 (JPTS. 1912, p. 147) Cf. d'Alwis. Catal., p. 188 ff.; Subhûti, Nâm., p. XXX; de Zoysa. Catal., p. 24; Oldenberg, Catal., p. 94, Nr. 74; R. O. Franke, PGr., p. 34 ff.

First of all there is to mention 1. Piyadassin's *Padasādhana*.[1] The author was one of the immediate pupils of Moggallāna, and therefore probably belonged to the end of the 12th century. His work is an abridged version of the grammar of his master. De Zoysa says that the relation between Piyadassin and Moggallāna is analogous to that between Bālāvatāra and Kaccāyana. A commentary called *Padasādhana-ṭikā* or *Buddhippasādanī*[2] on the Padasādhana was composed in the year 1472 by the Thera Srī Rāhula of Titthagāma, with the surname Vācissara, who is well known also in the Sinhalese literature.[3]—2. The *Payogasiddhi* of Vanaratana medhaṃkara[4] is considered to be one of the best grammars of Moggallāna's school, and, according to de Zoysa, its position with regard to the Moggallānavyākaraṇa is similar to that of Rūpasiddhi with regard to Kaccāyana's grammar. The author lived in the reign of Bhuvanekabāhu, the son of Parakkamabāhu. Perhaps it is Bhuvanekabāhu III who is meant, in which case Medhaṃkara should have lived about 1300. He is different from the two Medhaṃkaras mentioned in 34.4 and 40.1.—3. The *Moggallāyanapañcikāpadīpa*[5] is a commentary on the lost Pañcikā of Moggallāna. The author is the same Rāhula who composed also the Ṭīkā on Padasādhana. The Pañcikā-commentary is written partly in Pāli and partly in Singhalese. De Zoysa considers it to be one of the most learned works on Pāli grammar that we possess. Very rich material has at all events been collected and discussed in it. Subhúti mentions no less than 50 grammatical works which have been referred to in it, including Candra's Sanskrit grammar. The date of the work is given as the year 1379 of Saka era=1457 A.D.

50. Aggavaṃsa's *Saddanīti*[6] is of peculiar importance for determining the value of indigenous tradition. The author was a native of Arimaddana in Burma, and his work is the fruit of grammatical

[1] Cf. Subhúti, Nâm., p. XXXVIII; de Zoysa, Catal., p. 25 f.; Oldenberg, Catal., p. 99. Nr. 76; R. O. Franke, PGr., p. 44 f. The edition of Padasādhana by Dhammānanda and Ñāṇissara, Colombo 1887, is not known to me.

[2] Buddhippasadani, a commentary on Padasādhana by Sri Rahula ed. Dhirananda and Vachissara, Colombo 1908. Cf. Subhúti, p. XLI; de Zoysa, p. 26.

[3] Geiger, LSprS., p. 10.

[4] Subhúti, p. XLIV; de Zoysa; p 26; Oldenberg, p. 94, Nr. 75; Franke, p. 45.

[5] Moggallāna-Pañcakapradīpa: Grammar, ed. Srī Dharmārāma, Colombo 1896 (JPTS. 1912, p. 147). Cf. Subhúti, p. XXXIV; de Zoysa, p. 24; Franke, p. 44.

[6] Subhúti, Nâm., p. XLVIII ff.; de Zoysa, Catal., p. 27; Fausböll, JPTS. 1896, p. 49, Nr. 159; R. O. Franke, PGr., p. 45 ff.; Saddanīti, la grammaire Pali d' Aggavaṃsa, ed. by Helmer Smith, 3 parts, Lund 1928-30.

studies as carried on in that country independently of Ceylon. The news of the erudition of the Burmese monks in the field of grammar is said to have been brought to Ceylon [1] by the mission of Uttarājīva. In order to test the truth of these rumours Ceylonese monks went themselves to Arimaddana. They were shown the Saddanīti, and they had to admit that in Ceylon there was no grammatical work which was so good as this. The year 1154 A.D. is given as the date of the Saddanīti. Its author Aggavaṃsa was also called Aggapaṇḍita the third and was the nephew of the second Aggapaṇḍita, who himself was a pupil of the first Aggapaṇḍita. Afterwards Aggavaṃsa became the teacher of King Narapatisithu (1167-1202).—On the whole, as R. O. Franke has shown, the Saddanīti is based on Kaccāyana. From the point of view of contents it is hardly justifiable to separate the Saddanīti from the school of Kaccāyana. But Aggavaṃsa utilised for his work also the Sanskrit grammars such as those of Pāṇini, etc. The work of Moggallāna could have been hardly known to him; it was composed probably after the Saddanīti. The Saddanīti consists of 27 chapters; the first eighteen are called Mahāsaddanīti and the remaining nine Cullasaddanīti. It is expressly mentioned in the colophon that this work is based on the writings of the Ācariyā, as well as on the canonical literature, from which therefore it has drawn its material.

51. Of the lexicons only one has been handed down to us from olden times, and that is the *Abhidhānappadīpikā* of Moggallāna.[2] It is generally accepted from the time of d'Alwis that this Moggallāna is not identical with the grammarian of the same name (see **48**). As is mentioned in its concluding verses, he was a member of the Jetavana-monastery in Pulatthipura (Polonnaruwa), whereas, as we have seen, the grammarian Moggallāna lived in the Thūpārāma in Anurādhapura. Also in Gnvs. 62[3] he is called *Nava-Moggallāna* to distinguish him from the grammarian. The difference in age between the two however could not have been very great. From the manner

[1] Sāsvs. 40, 74. Cf. M. Bode, PLB., p. 16 f.

[2] Abhidhānappadīpikā or Dictionary of the Pali Language by Moggallāna Thero...by W. Subhúti, 2nd ed., Colombo 1883. Further: A Complete Index to the Abhidhánappadīpiká by W. Subhúti. Colombo 1893 (Pāli-title: Abhidhānappadīpikāsūci; athavā ... Pāli-Akārādigantho). Cf. d'Alwis, Catal., p. 1 ff.; de Zoysa, Catal. p. 21; Fausböll, JPTS. 1896, p. 46, Nr. 147.2, 148.3; p. 51, Nr. 166 (*ibid.*, Nr. 167, as well as de Zoysa, p. 21 where the Abhp.-Ṭīkā) is mentioned; Oldenberg, Catal., p. 104, Nr. 82, 83 and p. 105. Nr. 85; R. O. Franke, PGr., p. 65 ff.

in which the king Parakkamabhuja (Parakkamabāhu I) has been spoken of in the concluding verses it is clear that the Abhidhānappadīpikā must have been composed shortly after his reign (1153-1186), that is to say, towards the end of the 12th century.—The work is divided into 3 parts: synonyms, homonyms and indeclinables. It consists of 1203 strophes. The model after which this work was composed was the Amarakośa. Large portions, particularly in the part on synonyms, have been taken *in toto* from the Amarakośa, and not infrequently Moggallāna gives as Pāli words straight away those forms which he himself constructed from Sanskrit according to the phonological laws of Pāli. R. O. Franke has shown that beside Amara also another Sanskrit Kośa might have been used. It does not seem to me to be conclusively proved however that another Pāli synonyms-dictionary must have existed before the Abhidhānappadīpikā. A Ṭikā on the Abhidhānappadīpika (see **46.** 6) was composed about the middle of the 14th century.—We have still to mention the *Ekakkharakosa* of the Burmese monk Saddhammakitti,[1] a metrical list of monosyllablic words closely on the model of similar works in Sanskrit. The date of the work is the year 2009 after Buddha = 1465 A.D.

52. So far as the lists of roots are concerned, 1. *Dhātumañjūsā*[2] (cf. **45**) belongs to the school of Kaccāyana. It is therefore also called Kaccāyana-Dhātumañjūsā. According to the colophon, its author was the Thera Sīlavaṃsa of the Yakkhaddilena monastery, now Yakdessāgala near Kurunagala. It is metrical and consists of 150 strophes. According to Subhúti, the work is planned after Vopadeva's Kavikalpadruma. Its relation with the school of Kaccāyana is further proved by the agreement which is found in the arrangement of root-classes. According to Franke, Sīlavaṃsa used both the Pāṇini-Dhātupāṭha and the following work.—2. The *Dhātupāṭha*[3] belonging to Moggallāna's system, as indicated by the order of the root-classes, is shorter and not metrical. The author and the time of origin are unknown. Probably however the Dhātupāṭha is older than the Dhātumañjūsā.—3. The

[1] Edited by Subhúti as appendix to his edition of Abhp. Cf. Nâm, p. LXXX. Here (p. LXXXI) is also mentioned a Ṭīkā on it composed by a Burmese Monk. On the Sanskrit Ekākṣarakośas, see Zachariae, die ind. Wörterbücher, p. 37.

[2] Subhúti, Nâm, XCV (here is also mentioned an edition of the work by Baṭuwantuḍāwē); de Zoysa, Catal., p. 23; Oldenberg, Catal., p. 106, Nr. 87; R. O. Franke, PGr., pp. 57 f., 60 ff.

[3] Probably the Dhātumañjūsā mentioned in de Zoysa, p. 22. Cf. Oldenberg, p. 106, Nr. 86; Franke, pp. 58, 62 f.

Dhātvatthadīpanī,[1] according to Franke, "is a versified form of the roots recounted in a particular chapter of the Saddanīti." The order of the root-classes agrees with that of the Saddanīti. The author of the Dhātvatthadīpanī had made use of the Pāṇini-Dhātupāṭha, like the authors of the works discussed above in 1 and 2.

53. 1. Pāli poetics is dealt with in the *Subodhālaṃkāra* of Saṃgharakkhita[2] who has been mentioned frequently above (**32**.1, **46**.2). There is also a Ṭīkā on it. The same Thera wrote a work on Pāli prosody of the title *Vuttodaya*[3] on which there is likewise a Ṭīkā named *Vacanatthajotikā* —2. Lastly I mention here a number of works of grammatical contents which have been discussed by Subhūti[4] but which I am not in a position to classify accurately: (*a*) *Vaccavācaka* of the Sāmaṇera Dhammadassin[5] of Arimaddana in Burma, consisting of 100 strophes, dating probably from the end of the 14th century. A Ṭīkā on it was composed in the year 2312 after Buddha (=1768 A.D.) by the monk Saddhammanandin of the Khemāvatāra-monastery in Burma.—(*b*) *Gandhaṭṭhi* of Maṅgala,[6] a work on particles, perhaps belonging to the 14th century and probably older than the work mentioned next. *Cf.* **40**.3—(*c*) *Gandhābharaṇa* of Ariyavaṃsa,[7] likewise dealing with particles, composed about the year 1980 after Buddha (=1436 A.D.). A Ṭīkā on it was composed by Suvaṇṇarāsi of Burma (2128 after Buddha =1584 A.D.).—(*d*) *Vibhattyatthappakaraṇa*[8] on the use of cases, in 37 Ślokas, is ascribed to a daughter of the King Kyacvā of Burma. Its date is 2025 after Buddha (=1481 A.D.) according to Subhūti. To it belongs a *Vibhattyattha-Ṭīkā*, which is perhaps identical with the *Vibhattyatthadīpanī* mentioned by de Zoysa and Fausböll. At least in the introductory verse the Ṭīkā ascribes to itself the same title. De Zoysa mentions also a *Vibhattikathāvaṇṇanā*.—(*e*) *Saṃvaṇṇanānayadīpanī*[9] composed

[1] De Zoysa, p. 22; Franke, p 59 f., 63 f. Is the work mentioned in JPTS. 1912, p 142, Nr 82 an adaptation of this list of roots?

[2] Gnvs. 61[15], 70[28]. De Zoysa, Catal. p. 28; Fausböll, JPTS 1896, p. 46, Nr. 148.4, p. 48, Nr. 152.7 and p. 51. Nr. 172.2.

[3] Gnvs. 70[28]. De Zoysa, p. 29; Oldenberg, Catal., p. 106, Nr. 88 and p. 107, Nr. 89; Fausböll, p 46, Nr 148 5, p. 48, Nr. 152.6 and p. 51, Nr. 170-172.

[4] See Nām. p. LXXXVII, LXXXVI, LV etc.

[5] M Bode, PLB. p. 22; de Zoysa, p. 29; Fausböll, p. 50. Nr. 163 and 164.

[6] M. Bode, p. 26; de Zoysa, p. 23.

[7] M. Bode, p. 43; de Zoysa, p. 23; Fausböll, p. 50, Nr. 164.

[8] Edited by Subhūti as Appendix to the Abhp., p. XIII ff. Cf. de Zoysa, p. 29; Fausböll, p. 50, Nr 163

[9] M. Bode, p. 55.

by Jambudhaja in 2195 after Buddha (=1651 A.D.). The same author has written also the *Niruttisaṃgaha* and the *Sarvajñanyāyadipanī*.[1]—(*f*) *Saddavutti* of Saddhammaguru[2] composed before 2200 after Buddha (=1656 A.D.), with a Ṭīkā by the Burmese monk Sāriputta.—(*g*) *Kārakapupphamañjarī*,[3] composed by Attaragama Baṇḍāra Rājaguru of Kandy, dealing with syntax, was written in the reign of Kīrtiśrī Rājasiṃha (1747-1780 A.D.). The same author composed also the work *Sudhīramukhamaṇḍana*[4] dealing with Pāli compounds.—(*h*) The *Nayalakkhaṇavibhāvanī* by the Burmese monk Vicittācāra[5] belongs to the second half of the 18th century.

[1] De Zoysa, pp. 25, 28.

[2] De Zoysa, p. 27; Fausböll, p. 47, Nr. 148.15. According to M. Bode, p. 29, Saddavutti was composed in the 14th century.

[3] De Zoysa, p. 24.

[4] De Zoysa, p. 28.

[5] De Zoysa, p. 25.

PART II

Grammar of Pāli

Literature (general, grammars, dictionaries, chrestomathies).

E. Burnouf et Chr. Lassen, Essai sur le Pāli. Paris 1826.

E. Burnouf, Observations grammaticales sur quelques passages de l'Essai sur le Pâli de Burnouf et Lassen. Paris 1827.

B. Clough, Compendious Pāli Grammar with a copious Vocabulary in the same Language. Colombo 1824.

J. Alwis, Lecture on the Buddhist Scriptures and their Language, the Pāli (1861). Reprinted in JPTS. 1883, p. 39 ff.

J. Minayeff, Grammaire Pâlie, traduite par St. Guyard. Paris 1874—Pāli grammar, a phonetic and morphological Sketch of the Pāli Language, with an introductory Essay on its Form and Character by J. M., 1872; transl. from Russian into French by M. St. Guyard, 1874. Rendered into English by Ch. G. Adams, 1882.

Fr. Müller, Beiträge zur Kenntnis der Pâli-Sprache, I. II. III. Stzber. d. Wiener Ak. d. W., phil.-hist. Cl. Vol. 57, 1867, p. 7 ff.; p. 243 ff.; Vol. 60, 1868, p. 533 ff.

R. C. Childers, A Dictionary of the Pali Language. London 1875 (4. ed. 1909).

E. Kuhn, Beiträge zur Pāli-Grammatik. Berlin 1875.

V. Trenckner Pāli Miscellany, Vol. I. London 1879. Cf. also Trenckner's Notes to the Milinda-pañha, revised and edited by D. Andersen, JPTS. 1908, p. 102 ff.

A. Torp, Die Flexion des Pāli in ihrem Verhältnis zum Sanskrit. Christiania 1881.

O. Frankfurter, Handbook of Pāli, being an elementary Grammar, a Chrestomathy, and a Glossary. London and Edinburgh 1883.

E. Müller, A simplified Grammar of the Pāli Language. London 1884.

Morris, Notes and Queries, JPTS. 1884, p. 69 ff.; 1885, p. 29 ff.; 1886, p. 94 ff.; 1887, p. 99 ff.; 1889, p. 200 ff.; 1891/3, p. 1 ff.

E. Müller, A Glossary of Pāli Proper Names, JPTS. 1888, p. 1 ff.

Morris, Contributions to Pali Lexicography, Academy 1890-91.

V. Henry, Précis de Grammaire Pâlie, accompagné d'un choix de textes gradués. Paris 1894.

Tha Do Oung, Grammar of the Pali Language (after Kaccâyana). Vol. I: Sandhi, Nâma and Kâraka, and Samâsa; Vol. II: Taddhita, Kita, Uṇâdi, Âkhyâta, Upasagga and Nipâta particles; Vol. III: Dictionary of Pali word-roots; Vol. IV: Chandam etc. Akyab 1899-1902.

M. Bode, Index to Pāli Words discussed in translations, JPTS. 1897-1901, p. 1 ff.

H. H. Tilbe, Pāli Grammar. Rangoon 1899 (Student's Pāli Series).

J. Takakusu, A Pāli Chrestomathy, with Notes and Glossary giving Sanskrit and Chinese Equivalents. Tokyo 1900.

D. Andersen, A Pali Reader with Notes and Glossary. Part I: Text and Notes; Part II: a Pāli Glossary including the words of the Pāli Reader and of the Dhammapada. Copenhagen, London and Leipzig 1901, 1907.

R. O. Franke, Pāli and Sanskrit, in ihrem histor. und geogr. Verhältnis auf Grund der Inschriften und Münzen. Strassburg 1902.

H. H. Tibe, Pāli First Lessons. Rangoon 1902 (Student's Pāli Series).

J. Gray, Elementary Pāli Grammar or Second Pāli Course. Calcutta 1905.

J. Gray, First Pāli Delectus or Companion Reader to the Pāli Course. Calcutta 1905.

E. Windisch, Über den sprachlichen Charakter des Pali. Actes du XIVe Congrès Internat. des Orientalistes 1, Sect. I, p. 252 ff. Paris 1906.

Ch. Duroiselle, A Practical Grammar of the Pāli Language. Rangoon 1906.

Ch. Duroiselle, School Pāli Series, I: Reader; II: Vocabulary. Rangoon 1907.

K. P. Johansson, Pāli-Miszellen; Le Monde Oriental 1907-08, p. 85 ff Nyānatiloka, Kleine systematische Pāli Grammatik. Breslau 1911 (Veröffentlichungen d. D. Pāligesellschaft 5).

K. Seidenstücker, Elementargrammatik der Pāli Sprache. Leipzig 1916.

Sri Buddhatta Sthavira, The New Pāli Course, Part 1. Colombo 1937.

Valuable preliminary work for a Pāli dictionary is contained also in: St. Konow, Lexicographical Notes, Words beginning with H, JPTS. 1907, p. 152 ff.; St. Konow and D. Andersen, Lexicography, Words beginning with S, JPTS. 1909, p. 1 ff.; T. W. Davids and W. Stede, The Pali Text Society's Pali-English Dictionary, London, PTS. 1921; Dines Andersen and Helmer Smith, A Critical Pāli Dictionary.

Other monographs on Pāli Grammar and Vocabulary will be mentioned in proper places in the following.

A. PHONOLOGY

1. *Sound-system and Accent*

§ 1. For the writing of Pāli there are used in the Orient various scripts: in Ceylon the Sinhalese, in Burma the Burmese, in Siam the Kamboja script. The Bangkok edition of the Tipiṭaka is printed in Siamese letters.

§ 2. The sound-system of Pāli consists of the following:

1. Vowels: *a*, *ā*, *i*, *ī*, *u*, *ū*, *e*, *o*, as well as the nasal vowels ***aṃ***, ***iṃ***, ***uṃ***.

2. Consonants: Gutturals: *k*, *kh*, *g*, *gh*, *ṅ*.
Palatals: *c*, *ch*, *j*, *jh*, *ñ*.
Cerebrals: *ṭ*, *ṭh*, *ḍ*, *ḍh*, *ṇ*.
Dentals: *t*, *th*, *d*, *dh*, *n*.
Labials: *p*, *ph*, *b*, *bh*, *m*.
Liquids: *r*, *l*, *ḷ*, *ḷh*.[1]
Semi-vowels: *y*, *v*.
Sibilant: *s*.
Aspiration: *h*.

Here should be noticed: 1. The vowels *e*, *o* are of middle length, in closed syllables they are short and in open syllables they are long.—2. The sign of nasalisation (*ṃ*) corresponding to the anusvāra and anunāsika of Sanskrit is called Niggahīta by Pāli grammarians. In Ceylon at present the Niggahīta is pronounced as a guttural nasal.—3. The consonant *ḷ* stands for intervocalic *ḍ*, likewise *ḷh* for *ḍh*. In the MSS. *l* and *ḷ* are always confused. Some spellings seem to be arbitrary. Thus *kāḷa* 'black' is mostly written with *ḷ*, although it is equivalent to Sanskrit *kāla*, probably to distinguish it from *kāla*, 'time.' Surely *ḷ* should be written everywhere where an etymological connection with cerebrals is apparent.—4. The *h* is, where it stands alone, a consonant. In combination with *y*, *r*, *l*, *v*, or with the nasals, it appears to have been pronounced in a particular manner. The grammarians in this case call it *orasa* 'spoken in the breast.'[2]

[1] There is no special sign for this sound. It is usually indicated by the ligature *ḷ+h*.

[2] Minayeff, P Gr. p. 2.

✓ § 3. In its sound-system Pāli stands in Prākritic stage when compared with Old Indian. Also Prākrit has given up the vowels ṝ, ḷ, as well as the diphthongs *ai*, *au*, in all the dialects, and the vowel ṛ in most of the dialects excepting Apabhraṃśa. Moreover Prākrit like Pāli possesses the cerebral consonant ḷ and the middle-length vowels *e*, *o*. Most Prākrit dialects have like Pāli only the dental *s*; the cerebral *ṣ* is found in none of them, and the palatal *ś* is absent in most.[1]

The original diphthongical character of *e*, *o* is brought to light by the circumstance that in Sandhi *a* + *i* becomes *e* and *a* + *u* becomes *o*, Cf. *macchassevodoke gataṃ* = *macchassa iva udake g°* 'like the course of fish in water' Jā. I.295[8]. There was even a tendency to use them (instead of *ai*, *au*) as vṛddhi-vowels. Thus are found forms originated inside Pāli, such as *tepiṭaka*, 'devoted to the *Tipiṭaka*'. DhCo. III. 384[18], Mhvs. 5.84 from *tipiṭaka*, and *opadhika* 'relating to the substratum of existence' Vv. 34.21, 24 = S. I. 233[15,21] from *upadhi*. This strengthening into *e*, *o* may take place even in those cases where originally there was no *i*, *u*. Thus *pothujjanika* 'relating to common people' Vin. I.10[12] from *puthujjana*, where the *u* corresponds to Skr. ṛ (*pṛthagjana*). Cf. *sosānika* 'relating to cemetery' Pu. 69[27], DhCo. I. 69[4] from *susāna* = *śmaśāna*. In *gelañña* 'illness' D.II. 99[16], JāCo. II. 31[20] from *gilāna* = Skr. *glāna*, and in *sovatthika* 'bringing prosperity' Vv. 18.7 from *suvatthi* = Skr. *svasti*, *e* and *o* are the strengthened forms of the svarabhakti-vowels *i*, *u* originated within Pāli. Cf. also *veyyāvacca* 'rendering service' Vin. I.23[10] from **viyāvata* = Skr. *vyāpṛta*; *veyyākarṇa*, 'answering' D. I. 51[5] from *viyākaroti* = Skṛ *vyākaroti*.

In the same way *a* has been strengthened into *ā* within Pāli; *sākhalya*, *lla* 'friendliness' M.I. 446[19], Jā. IV. 57[5] from *sakhila*; *bhākuṭika* 'with frowning eye-brows' Vin. III. 181[6] from *bhakuṭi* = Skr. *bhrakuṭi* (or *bhṛkuṭi*).

§ 4. Nothing has been handed down to us about the nature of Pāli accent. It is, however, improbable that the ancient Indian accent was still in force. Rather, as Jacobi has suggested also for Prākrit,[2] the Sanskritic accent was the rule in Pāli.[3] This is suggested by the

[1] Pischel, PkrGr. § 45.

[2] Different view of Pischel, KZ. 34.568 ff., 35.10 ff.; PkrGr. § 46. Against him Jacobi, ZDMG. 47.574 ff., KZ. 35.578 ff. Cf. Grierson, ZDMG. 49.395 ff.; Michelson, IF. 23.231.

[3] On this cf. Jacobi, ZDMG. 47.574.

changes of vocalism in Pāli, such as the weakening of a vowel after the accented syllable (in the Skr. form) or its strengthening in the main tonic syllable. *Cf.* § 19 ff.

2. *The Law of Mora*

§ 5. In Pāli, as generally in Middle Indian,[1] a syllable can contain only one mora or two moras but never more. The syllable is thus either (1) open with short vowel (one mora) or (2) open with long vowel (2 moras), or (3) closed with short vowel (2 moras). Every syllable with a nasal vowel is considered as closed. Long nasal vowels do not occur. Due to this law, where Skr. has long vowel before double-consonance (*i.e.*, in closed syllable), Pāli has there either (*a*) short vowel before double-consonance[2] or (*b*) long vowel with the following double-consonance simplified.

Examples of (*a*): *jiṇṇa* 'old, exhausted' = *jīrṇa*. Likewise *maṃsa* 'flesh' = *māṃsa*, and the final in *nadiṃ* 'the river' (acc.) = *nadīm*. The vowels *e*, *o* are short in such cases: *sĕmha* 'catarrh' = *śleṣman*; *ŏṭṭha* 'lip' = *oṣṭha*.—Examples of (*b*): *lākhā* 'lac' = *lākṣā*; *dīgha* 'long' = *dīrgha*. In case of the vowels *e*, *o*, the orthography in the mss. varies not infrequently, such as *apĕkkhā* and *apēkhā*, 'expectation' = *apĕkṣā*; *upekkhā* and *upēkhā* 'indifference' = *upekṣā*; *vimŏkkha* and *vimōkha* 'deliverance' D. II.70[28], A. IV. 306[11] = *vimokṣa*.

§ 6. The Law of Mora has led to various changes.[3] Due to it: 1. There can be in Pāli long vowel before single consonant where Skr. has short vowel before double-consonance: *sāsapa* 'mustard seed' (instead of **sass*-) Dh. 401, S. II. 182[17], DhCo. I.107[3] = *sarṣapa*; *vāka* 'bark' (instead of **vakka*) D. I.167[2]. Vin. III. 34[28], JāCo I. 304[2] = *valka*; *nīyāti* 'goes away' = *niryāti*.[4]—2. Pāli shows short vowel before double-consonance where originally there was long vowel before a single consonant: *abbahati* 'draws out' Th. 1. 162, 1007, Sn. 334. Jā. II. 95[5] = *ābṛhati*; *niḍḍa* (sic!) 'nest' Dh. 148 (AMāg. *nĕḍḍa*) = *nīḍa*; *udukkhala* 'mortar and pestle' Vin. III. 6[28], D. II. 341[6], Jā-Co. I. 502[20] (AMāg. *udukkhala* beside *udūhala*) = *udūkhala*; *kubbara*

[1] R. O. Franke, P. und Skr. p. 90 f.

[2] In P. *sutti*, therefore, there have coincided, *e.g.*, Skr. *śukti* 'oyster-shell' (Vin. II. 106[11,12]) and *sūkti* 'good speech' (Saddhammopāyana 340, 617).

[3] For analogous phenomena in Pkr. see Pischel, PkrGr. § 62-65, 90, 74-76.

[4] *Cf.* also *svātanāya* 'for next day' (in Buddhistic Skr. *śvetanāya* etc.) from Skr. *śvastana*. Johansson, Monde Oriental, 1907-08, p. 106 ff.

'pole of a carriage' Vv. 64.2, A. IV. 191[6], VvCo. 269[5]=*kūbara, kūvara*; *pĕttika* 'fatherly' D. II. 232[10], Vin. III. 16[35], JāCo. II. 59[13] for **pētika=paitṛka* (after which has been latterly formed *mettika*). *Cf.* also *mahabbala, mahapphala=mahābala, mahāphala.*—3. As the short nasal vowel has two moras like the long, a nasal not infrequently appears in the place of a pure long vowel [1] and *vice versa*: *maṃkuṇa* 'bug' JāCo. III. 423[13] instead of **māk-, *makk-=matkuṇa*; *saṃvarī* 'night' D.III. 196[22] (verse), Jā. IV. 441[6] instead of **sāv-', *sabb-=śarvarī*; *suṃka* 'toll' (AMāg. *ussuṃka*) instead of **sūka, *sukka*=Skr. *śulka*; *ghaṃsati* 'rubs' instead of **ghās-, *ghass-=gharṣati*; *vidaṃsentī* 'she who shows' Th2. 74 instead of **vidās-, *vidass-=vidarśayantī*. On the other hand: *vīsati vīsaṃ* 'twenty'=*viṃśati*; *sīha* 'lion'=*siṃha*; *sārambha* 'audacity' (beside *saṃrambha* Dāṭhāvs. 4.34)=*saṃrambha*, and other words with *saṃ-*.

§ 7. Sometimes a long vowel is retained before double-consonance. Thus particularly in contractions, as in *sājja=sā ajja* Th2.75, *yathājjhāsayena* 'according to desire' JāCo. IV. 243[8]. Further, in derivatives such as *dussīlya* from *dussīla*. Cf. *bālya* 'stupidity' DhCo. II. 30[3], variant reading of *balya*. These are evidently cases of learned orthography. There are also sporadical cases like *dābbī* (name of a plant) Abhp. 586=*dārvī*; *dātta* 'sickle' Abhp. 448=*dātra* (none of these, forms, however, is quotable from texts).[2] Quite frequent is *svākkhāta* 'well proclaimed' Vin. I. 12[24] etc.=*su-ākhyāta*.

§ 8. It is also due to the action of the Law of Mora that even in the case of the separation a consonant-group by a Svarabhakti vowel (§ 29 ff.) a long vowel preceding the consonant-group is regularly shortened.[3] The two one-mora syllables in these cases represent one two-mora syllable: *suriya* 'sun' (instead of **sūyya*)=*sūrya* but *sūriya* 'heroism' Jā. I.282[17], purposely differentiated from the preceding;

[1] The tendency towards nasalisation is often in evidence in mss.: *naṁgara* instead of *nagara*, *gaṃchi* (*gañchi*) instead of *gacchi* etc. Cf. *uḷumpa* 'raft' D.II. 89[15]=*uḍupa*.

[2] Childers gives also *ājjava* 'straightness' beside *ajjava*. *Sākya* Bodhivs. 22[12], 27[29] instead of *Sakya* (according to the Colombo edition), *Sakka* or *Sakiya* is perhaps a wrong reading. The form *Sākiya* also is not quite correct.

[3] As a rule it is different in Pkr., cf. AMāg. *sūriya vīriya* etc. But still AMāg., JMāh. *veruliya=vaidūrya* (P. *veḷuriya*). In Pāli we have *sīliya*, Jā. III. 7[1] only *metri causa*.

pakiriya gerund of *pakirati* 'loosens (the hair)' = ***prakirya***. In words like *cetiya*= *caitya* and *Moriya*=*Maurya* we have therefore to consider *e* and *o* as short vowels.—The insertion of the svarabhakti-vowel however does not disturb the length of a *following* vowel: thus *gilāna* 'ill'=*glāna*. Only in the case of the originally monosyllabic words *itthĭ* 'woman'=*strī*, *sirĭ* 'fortune' *śri* and *hirĭ* 'modesty' =*hrī* does this law act in some measure.[1] In compounds these words have short vowel[2]: *itthiratana* 'jewel of a woman' D.I. 89[3], *hirimana* 'of modest disposition' D. II. 78[34] etc. Also *sirimant*, *hirimant* and occasionally *sassirika*,[3] *ahirika* etc.

---

3. *The Vowels* ă ĭ ŭ

§ 9. Occasionally *e* appears for *a* before double-consonance: *pheggu* 'empty, worthless' M. I. 194[25], S. IV. 168[2] etc. =*phaigu*; *seyyā* 'bed'=*śayyā*.[4] The word *ettha* 'here' is probably not= *atra*, but=**itra*, Av. *iθra*,[5] and is therefore to be classed with § 10.2. In the same way *heṭṭha* 'below' is derived not from *adhasthāt*, but from an **adheṣṭhāt*[6] as is shown by the cerebrals -*ṭṭh*-.

§ 10. 1. The vowels *i*, *u* are lengthened in the flexional endings -*īhi*, -*ūhi* and -*īsu*, -*ūsu* of *i*- and *u*-declensions (§ 82).—2. Not infrequently *i* and *u* become *ĕ* and *ŏ* before double-consonance[7]: *Veṇhu* (JMāh. *Viṇhu*) D. II. 259[22]=*Viṣṇu*[8]; *nekkha* 'gold ornament' Su. 689, A. I. 181[15] (beside *nikkha* Vin. I. 38[16])=*niṣka*; *koccha* 'bundle, ball, fleshy part' Vin. II. 149[32], 266[23]=*kūrca* (cf. §62.1); *oṭṭha* 'camel' M. I. 80[13], Vin. IV.

[1] On the same words in Pkr. see Pischel, PkrGr. § 98, 147.

[2] Lengthening takes place only *metri causa*, thus *sirīmant* Tbl. 94, *sirīdhara* Mhvs. 5.16.4.

[3] *sassirīka* JāCo., I.504[29]. Smp. 300[23], *nissirīka* JāCo. VI. 456[1].

[4] There might have been intermediate forms like **phiggu*, **siyyā* (Pkr. *sejjā* with the frequent variant reading *sijjā*). Cf. *miṃjā* 'marrow' (§6.3)=*majjā*. For Pischel's explanation see PkrGr. § 101. Jacobi, KZ. 35.573 ascribes the *i* in *sijjā* to the influence of the palatal.

[5] So already Lassen, Instit. Linguae Pracriticae 129. Cf. E. Kuhn, Beitr. p. 21. Pischel, § 107 thinks of connection with Ved *itthā*. I would however like to point out the v. l. *ubhayettha* of *ubhayattha* DhCo. I. 29[13].

[6] Pischel § 107. Not so Johansson, IF. 3.218; Monde or. 1907, 93 and Wackernagel, KZ, 43.293.

[7] Frequently also in Pkr., Pischel, § 119, 122, 125.

[8] Also in S. I. 52[10] should be read *Veṇhu* instead of *Veṇḍu*.

7[16] = *uṣṭra* ; *vokkamati* 'gets deranged' D. I. 230[14], M. III. 117[23], JāCo. I. 23[21] = *vyutkramati* ; *Okkāmukha* (proper name) = *Ulkāmukha*.[1] In words like *rāmaṇeyya* 'charming' = *rāmaṇīya*, *dakkhiṇeyya* 'worthy of veneration' = *dakṣiṇīya*, an intermediate stage with **-iyya* has to be imagined.—The change into *e* takes place even in the case of such *i* as is derived from *ṛ*. Thus in the verb *gheppati* 'grasps,' if it is derived from **ghippati* < **ghṛpyati* like Pkr. *gheppaï* as Pischel (PkrGr. § 107) has suggested.—The double-consonance following after *ĕ*, *ŏ* may be secondarily simplified according to the Law of Mora with concomitant protraction of *e*, *o* : *Uruvelā* (place-name) through **-vĕllā*, **-villā* = *Uruvilvā* ; *ojā* 'strength' D. II. 285[10], M. I. 124[32], DhCo. I. 107[16] through **ŏjjā*, **ujjā* = *ūrjā*. In *vihesati* 'injures, insults' Ud. 44[30], 45[8] (beside *vihiṃsati*) the intermediate steps **vihīsati*, **vihissati*, **vihĕssati* have to be imagined. Out of original *ṛ* this *i*, *e* has been developed in *paligedha* 'desire' A. I. 66[10], *paligedhin* A. III. 265[7] through **-gĕddha*, **-gĕddhin*, **-giddha*, **-giddhin* = *gṛddha*, *gṛddhin*.

§ 11. Intermediate stages with double-consonance have to be imagined where in open syllable *ī*, *ū* have become *e*, *o* : *edi*, *edisa* (*erisa*), *edisaka*, *edikkha* (*erikkha*) 'such a one' Sn. 313, Vin. I. 195[11], Mhvs. 5.56 (beside *idisa* etc. Mhvs. 5.93) through **iddi*, **ĕddi* etc. = *īdṛś*, *īdṛśā*, *idṛkṣā*[2] ; *āveḷā* 'garland' Vv. 36.2, JāCo. I.444[6], 501[29] (Pkr. *āmeḷā*) through **āvēḍā*, **āvĕḍḍā*, **āviḍḍā*, = *āpīḍā*[3] ; *gaḷocī* (a plant ; Pkr. *gaḷoī*) Abph. 581 through **gaḷŏccī*, **gaḷuccī* = *guḍūcī* ; *jambonada* 'gold' Dh. 230, Vv. 84. 17 through **-ŏnnada*, **-unnada* = *jambūnada*. *Mahesī* 'queen' from *mahiṣī*[4] is remarkable.

4. *Representation of the Vowels ṛ, ḷ*

§ 12. The vowel *ṛ* is represented by *a*, *i*, *u* in P.—even in initial position, which is not the case in Pkr.[1] The quality of the vowel is

[1] But always *ukkā* 'flame, meteor' D. I. 49[31], JāCo. IV. 290[23] ; D. I. 10[17] = *ulkā*. The name *Okkāka* = *Ikṣvāku*, which is connected by the Buddhists with *ikṣu* 'sugarcane' is in fact derived from **Ukkhāka* (**ukkhu* side-form of *ucchu*). The analogical influence of *Okkāmukha* was also effective.

[2] Cf. AMāg. *eddaha* beside *erisa* etc Pischel, PkrGr. § 121, 122. Pāli has however only *kīdi*, *kīdisa* etc

[3] Pischel, § 122, 248.

[4] E. Kuhn, Beitr. p. 24 suspects influence of *mahesi* 'wise man.' Cf. here also *gahetvā*, *netvā* which have been wrongly explained by Minayeff, PGr. § 16, p.

largely influenced by the neighbouring sounds (cf. § 16); *u* appears mostly after labials.—1. *a* stands for *ṛ* :*accha* 'bear' Jā. VI. 507^{5}, JāCo. VI. 538^{21} = *ṛkṣa*; *pasada* 'spotted antelope' Jā. VI. 537^{31} = *pṛṣata*; *vaka* 'wolf' Sn. 201, JāCo. I. 336^{17} (verse) = *vṛka*; *hadaya* 'heart' = *hṛdaya*.—2. *i* stands for *ṛ* :*ikka* 'bear' Jā. VI. 538^{1} (Co. = *accha*) = *ṛkṣa* (cf. § 62.2); *iṇa* 'debt' (AMāg. *aṇa*) Sn. 120, D. I. 71^{31}, JāCo. I.321^{20} = *ṛṇa*; *vicchika* 'scorpion' D. I. 9^{8}, Vin. II. 148^{9} = *vṛścika*; *sipāṭikā* 'seed-house' M. I. 306^{2} = *sṛpāṭikā*.—3. *u* stands for *ṛ*: *uju* or *ujju* (Jā. VI. 518^{8}) 'straight' = *ṛju*; *usabha* 'bull' Dh. 422, S. I. 75^{32}, JāCo. I. 336^{20} = *ṛṣabha* (beside *vasabha* = *vṛṣabha*); *pucchati* 'asks' = *pṛcchati*; *muḷāla* JāCo. I. 100^{7} and *muḷāli* Jā. VI. 530^{16} 'lotus-stalk' = *mṛṇāla*; *pāvusa* 'rainy season' Thl. 597 f., Jā. VI. 202^{27} = *prāvṛṣa*.—4. Sometimes representation varies : cf. above, beside *accha* the dialectical form *ikka* 'bear' ; *vṛddhi* has been differentiated into *vaḍḍhi* 'blessing' and *vuddhi* 'growth'; *mṛga* has been differentiated into *maga* 'animal' Sn. 275, Thl. 958, S. I. 199^{21} and *miga* 'gazelle' passim.[2] Beside *iṇa* there is *anaṇa* 'debtless' Th2. 2, M. II. 105^{16} and *sāṇa* (= *sa-aṇa*) 'indebted' M. III. $127^{7, 9}$, S. II. 221^{1}, probably through vowel-assimilation[3] (but *sayiṇa* or *saiṇa* Mhvs. 36.39). Beside *kaṇha* 'black' = *kṛṣṇa* there is found as variant reading *kiṇha* D. I. 90^{15}, S. IV. 117^{6}. Skr. *pṛthivī* appears as *pathavī*, *paṭhavī*, *puthavī*, *puthuvī*, *puṭhuvī*; here the region from where the MSS. are derived is to be taken into consideration: *pathavī*, *e.g.*, is the orthography of the Burmese MSS. Moreover cf. *pitughātaka*, *mātughātaka*, 'parricide, matricide' Vin. I. 88^{20} with *pitipakkhato*, *mātipakkhato* 'from paternal side, from maternal side' etc.

§ 13. In some cases the *ṛ*-vowel becomes consonant: *brahant*, *brahā°* 'big' Thl. 31, Jā. III. 117^{23} = *bṛhant*; *brūheti* 'devotes himself to a cause' Dh. 285, Ud. 72^{17} (verse), JāCo. I. 289^{11} = *bṛṃhayati*, *vṛṃhayati*. *Vṛ* becomes *ru* in *rukkha* 'tree' = *vṛkṣa*[4] and in *pāruta*

[1] In Pkr. initial *ṛ* usually becomes *r*+vowel, Pischel PkrGr. § 56. In P. we have only *iruveda* Dpvs. 5. 62. or *irubbeda* DCo. I. 247^{19} = *ṛgveda*. This word is however an artificial formation.

[2] The form *miga* is found in its general meaning 'animal' in *sākhāmiga* 'monkey' Jā. III. 98^{14}, *migacakka* 'animal magic' D. I. 9^{10}, DCo. I. 94^{6}.

[3] Trenckner, Notes p. 76 (JPTS. 1908, p. 129).

[4] Pischel, PkrGr. § 320 connects *rukkha* with Skr. *rukṣa*. Cf. Wackernagel, Altind. Gr. I, § 184 b. The side-form *rakkha* is found in Jā. III. 144^{15}.

'covered, concealed' Thl. 153, S. I. 167[27], JāCo. I. 347[8]=*prāvṛta* and *apāruta* 'opened up' Vin. I. 7[4] (verse), D. II. 217[15], JāCo. I. 264[4]=*apāvṛta*.

§ 14. The vowel *ḷ* is represented by *u*: *kutta*[1] 'clipped' D. I. 105[9], DCo. I. 274[17]=*kḷpta*.[2] In the same way also *kuttaka* (a kind of woollen cover) D. I. 7[10], Vin. I. 192[8], II. 163[24], perhaps 'shorn cover'.[3] Further *kutta*, *kutti*, 'behaviour, procedure' = *kḷpta*, *kḷpti* in *itthikutta*, *purisakutta* A. IV. 57[6,9], JāCo. I. 296[21] etc., *saṃnatavīrakutti* Jā. V. 215[16] where *kutta*=*kappana*, just as *mata*=*maraṇa*. In DhsCo. 321[11] it is explained by *kiriyā*.

5. *Diphthongs and their Representation*

§ 15. The diphthongs *e*, *o* are as a rule preserved ; *ai* and *au* have become *e* and *o* : *Erāvaṇa* (name of Indra's elephant)=*Airāvaṇa*; *metti* 'friendship'=*maitrī*; *ve* (interj.)=*vai*. *orasa* 'derived from the breast'=*aurasa*; *pora* 'urban'=*paura*; *ratto* 'at night'=*rātrau*.

Not infrequently *e* and *o* are shortened into *i* and *u* before double-consonance[4]; this shortening may take place even where the double-consonance is of secondary origin (according to § 6.2); 1. *i* from *e*= original *e* : *paṭivissaka* 'neighbour' M. I. 126[5], DhCo. III. 155[11] from *-*vĕssaka*=*prativeśya-ka*; *pasibbaka* 'bag' Vin. III. 17[10], JāCo. III. 10[21] etc. through *-*sĕbbaka*=*prasevaka*. The word *ubbilla* 'pleasant surprise' M. III. 159[4] with its numerous derivatives belongs to the root *vell* with *ud*. Also *dvinnaṃ*, *ubhinnaṃ* are traced by E. Kuhn[5] to **dvenaṃ*, **ubhenaṃ* which are directly derived from the Nom. (**ubhe* instead of *ubho* is due to analogy with *dve*[6]).—2. *i* from *e*=original *ai* : *issarıya* 'rulership'=*aiśvarya*; *sindhava* 'horse from Sind'=*saindhava*.—3. *u* from *o*=original *o*: *akuppa*, *asaṃkuppa* 'unshakable' Thl. 182, 649=-*kopya*; *tutta* 'spur' Cp. III. 5.2, D. II. 266[5] (verse)=*tottra*[7]; *sussaṃ* (v.l. *sossaṃ*) 'I shall hear'

[1] E. Leumann, GGA. 1899, Nr. 8, p. 594.

[2] Cf. Rhys Davids, Dial., I. 130, f.-n. 2.

[3] Differently explained by Buddhaghosa as quoted by Rhys Davids and Oldenberg, VT. II. 27, f.-n. 4.

[4] Cf. for Pkr. Pischel, § 84.

[5] Beitr. p. 28.

[6] Cf. S. *duvenaṃ*, *duvehi*, *duvesu*.

[7] E. Müller, PGr. p. 12.

Sn. 694=*śroṣyāmi*; *gunnaṃ* Gen. Pl. of *go* 'cow'=*gonām*.—4. *u* from *o*=original *au*: *ussukka* 'zeal'=*autsukya*; *khudda* 'honey' Jā. VI. 532[30], D. III. 85[16]=*kṣaudra*; *ludda* 'horrible, diabolical' Sn. 247, Vv. 84.5, M. II. 97[26]=*raudra*[1]; *assumha* 'we heard' (§ 159. III)=*aśrauṣma*. In *ussāva* 'dew' JāCo. II. 11[12], DhCo. III. 338[17] (AMāg. *ussā* and *osā*)=*avaśyāya* the *u* is derived from *o*<*ava*.

6. *Influence of Neighbouring Vowels or Consonants on the Vowels*

§ 16. Vowels are not infrequently influenced by neighbouring vowels. Here we have the beginnings of a 'vowel-assimilation' in Pāli.[2] 1. Influence of following vowels: (*a*) *i* becomes *u* before a following *u*: *usu* 'arrow' (also in AMāg.)=*iṣu*; *ucchu* 'sugar-cane' (AMāg. *ucchu* beside *ikkhu*)=*ikṣu*; *kukku* (a measure of length) A. IV. 404[21], Vin. I. 254[38]=*kiṣku*[3]; *susu* 'young'=*śiśu* (nasalised form in *suṃsumāra* 'crocodile'=*śiśumāra*). In *kukkusa* 'powder in rice-ears' Vin. II. 280[20]=*kiknasa*[4] the intermediate steps are **kikkasa*, **kikkusa* (§19.2). Hereto belongs *nuṭṭhubhati*, *-hati* 'spits out' Vin. II. 175[7], JāCo. I. 459[2], II. 105[23] (beside *niṭṭhubhati* Ud. 50[18], *-hati* DhCo. II. 36[7]) from a root **stubh* with *ni*[5].—(*b*) *a* becomes *u* before following *u*: *sumugga* 'basket' JāCo. I. 265[24] (beside *samugga*)=*samudga*; *usūyā*, *usuyyā* 'envy' S. I. 127[8], JāCo. I. 444[8], D. II. 243[2] (§ 6.2)=*asūyā*—(*c*) *a* becomes *i* before following *i*: *siriṃsapa* 'snake'=*sarīsṛpa*; *timissā* 'moonless night' JāCo. III. 433[10]=*tamisrā*.[6]—(*d*) *u* becomes *a* before following *a* in *kappara* (AMāg. *koppara*) 'knuckle' Vin. III. 121[9], JāCo. I. 293[1] =*kūrpara*.

§ 17. There is further 2. the influence of the preceding vowel: (*a*) *a* becomes *u* after preceding *u*: *uḷuṅka* 'ladle' JāCo. I. 235[23], III 71[22]=*udaṅka*; *kuruṅga* (a kind of gazelle) JāCo. I. 173[15]=*kuraṅga*; *pukkusa* (designation of a low caste) Jā. III. 194[30], M. III. 169[28], Pu. 51[23], Milp. 5[12]=*pukkaśa*; *puthujjana* 'ordinary

[1] H. Lüders, GN. 1898, p. 1.

[2] Trenckner, Notes, p. 75 f. For Pkr. see Pischel, § 117. On the vowel-assimilation in modern dialects see Grierson, ZDMG. 49. 400 ff.; Geiger, LSprS. p. 43ff.

[3] E. Müller, PGr. p. 9.

[4] VT. III. 367, f.-n. 4.

[5] Pischel, PkrGr. § 120.

[6] Also *timisā* D. II. 175[17], M. III. 174[26], which presupposes a **tamiṣā*.

(not converted) people' = *pṛthagjana*.—(*b*) *i* becomes *a* after preceding *a*: *arañjara* 'water-pot' Abhp. 456 = *aliñjara*; *kākaṇikā* (small coin) JāCo. I. 120²⁰, DhCo. III. 108¹² = *kākiṇikā*; *pokkharaṇī* 'lotus-tank' = *puṣkariṇī*; *sākhalla*, -*lya* 'friendship' (§ 3) from *sakhila*.¹—(*c*) *u* becomes *a* after preceding *a*: *āyasmant* 'venerable' = *āyuṣmant*; *matthaluṅga* 'brain' Kh. 3 JāCo. I. 493¹⁰ = *mastuluṅga*; *sakkhalī*, -*likā* 'ear-lobe' (JPTS. 1909, p. 17) = *śaṣkulī*.—(*d*) *a* becomes *i* after preceding *i*: *siṅgivera* 'ginger' = *śṛṅgavera*; *nisinna* 'sitting' (but *pasanna*, *saṃsanna*) *niṣaṇṇa*.²

§ 18. The influence of consonants on vowels comes to light in the fact that 1. the vowel *u* appears by preference in the neighbourhood of labials, and that 2. *i* appears by preference in the neighbourhood of palatals. Ad 1 : Of derivatives from the root *majj* with *ni* and *ud* we have *nimujjati* 'drowns', *ummujjati* 'floats,' *nimujjā*, *ummujjā*, *nimugga* etc. Cf. further *saṃmujjani*, -*muñjanī* 'broom' DhCo. III. 168⁶ beside *saṃmajjanī* DhCo. III. 7¹⁹ = *saṃmārjanī*. Also *muta* 'thought' Sn. 714, 793, M.I. 3²² etc., *muti* 'thought' Sn. 846, *mutimā* Sn. 321, Jā. IV. 76¹⁰ = *matimān* should be regarded only as dialectical side-forms of *mata* etc. The existence of a root *mu* however seems to be guaranteed by the Fut. Pass. Part. *motabba* and the verbal noun *motar* A. II. 25¹⁶⁻¹⁸.— Ad. 2: *miṃjā* 'marrow' (see p. 65, f.-n. 4) from *majjā*; *jigucchati* 'conceals' D. I. 213²³, JāCo. I. 422²⁰, *jigucchā* D. I. 174¹⁹ as opposed to *jugupsatc*, *jugupsā*³; *bhiyyo* 'more' from *bhūyas*. On *seyyā* see § 9.

7. Influence of Accent on Vocalism

§ 19. In words of three or four syllables, which on the evidence of Skr. had the accent on the first syllable, the vowel of the second syllable is often reduced. In most cases *i* appears as the reduced vowel; after labials appears frequently, though not always, *u* instead of *i*: 1. After the accent-syllable *a* becomes *i*: *candimā* 'moon' = *candramās*⁴; *carima* 'following, last' Th1. 202 = *carama*; *parima* 'the highest' M. III. 112¹⁵ = *parama*; *puttimā* N. Sg. 'endowed with sons' Sn. 38, 34 = **putramān*; *majjhima* 'middle' =

---

[1] Similarly *kosajja* 'slowness' Dh. 241, A. I. 11²⁹ (from *kusīta*) as opposed to *kauṣīdya*.

[2] Also in *pathavī* (-*ṭh*-) and *puthuvī* (§ 12.4) = *pṛthivī* we have vowel-assimilation; *puthavī* in a cross-form. Not so Pischel, PkrGr § 115.

[3] Forms like *jeguccha* 'contrary' Vin. I. 58²⁸ etc. and *jegucchin* 'disgusting' Vin. III. 3¹, JāCo. I. 390¹⁴ etc. are new formations. *Cf.* § 3.

[4] A different but very 'far-fetched explanation is given by Pischel, PkrGr. § 103

madhyama[1]; *saccika* 'true' Milp. 226[17] = *satyaka*. Cf. the forms *ahiṃkāra*, *mamiṃkāra* 'self-consciousness' M. III. 32[34] beside *ahaṃk-mamaṃk-*. In the same way should be judged the future forms like *dakkhisi* 'you will see', *kāhisi* 'you will do' (beside *dakkhasi*, *kāhasi*), *ehisi* 'you will go', etc. as opposed to Skr. *drakṣyasi*, **karṣyasi*, *aṣyasi*.—2. After the accent-syllable *a* becomes *u*: *navuti* 'ninety' (AMāg. *naüiṃ*) = *navati*; *pāpuraṇa* 'mantle' S. I. 175 f., DhCo. III. 1[9] through *pāvuraṇa* M. I. 359[13] (AMāg. *pāüraṇa*) = *prāvaraṇa*; *saṃmuti* 'consent' (beside *saṃmata*) = *saṃmati* (cf. above §18.1). In the flexional system (§ 92.3) *brahmunā*, *brahmuno*; *kammunā*, *kammuno* (also AMāg. *kammuṇā*, *-ṇo*); *addhunā*, *addhuno*[2] = *brahmaṇā*, *-ṇas*; *karmaṇā*, *-ṇas*; *adhvanā*, *-nas*. After non-labials there is *u* in *ajjuka* (name of a plant) Abhp. 579 = *arjaka*[3]; *kukkusa* (§ 16. 1a) = *kiknasa*; *pekhuṇa* 'wing' Tbl. 211, 1136, JāCo. I. 207[10] = *preṅkhana* 'swing'[4]; *sajjulasa* 'resin' Vin. I. 202[1] = *sarjarasa*.—3. Occasionally after the accent-syllable *i* becomes *u* and *u* becomes *i*: *rājula* (a reptile) Abhp. 651 = *rājila*; *geruka* 'reddish chalk' Vin. I. 48[8] (AMāg. *geruya* beside Māh. *geria*) = *gairika*; *pasuta* 'intent on something' Thl. 28, D. I. 135[25], JāCo. III. 26[4] = *prasita*. Further *muditā* 'softness' M.I. 370,[8] S. V. 118[25] (beside *mudutā* A.I. 9[28]) = *mṛdutā*. On *suṇisā* see § 31.2.

§20. Unstressed short vowels, particularly immediately after the accent, are sometimes syncopated: *jaggati* 'watches' (§142.4) is to be traced from *jāgarati* through **jāgᵃrati*; *oka* 'water' Dh. 34, 91 from *udaka* through **ŏkka*, **ukka*, **utka*, **udᵃka*; *agga* 'house' (in *uposathagga*, *khuragga*, *bhattagga* etc.) from *agāra* through **agᵃra*, **agara*. Syncope is in evidence also in the verbal ending *-mhe* (beside *-mahe*).[5] Finally, there is a number of onomatopoetic words in which syncope may be clearly traced: *cicciṭāyati* 'rustles' Vin. I. 225[25], S.I. 169[6], Sn. S. 14, Pu. 36[32] beside *ciṭiciṭāyati*; *sassara*, *babbhara* M.I. 128[25] (JPTS. 1889, p. 209) for **sarᵃsara*, **bharᵃbhara* beside *sarasara*, *bharabhara*. In enclisis *khalu* has become *kho* through **khᵃlu*, **kkhu*.[6]

[1] This should not be regarded as "Saṃprasāraṇa" as E. Kuhn, Beitr. p. 54, suggests, because the *i* is not derived from *ya*; the *y* is contained in *jjh*. At the most one can say that at an earlier stage of the language the *a* after *y* in *madhyama* had a pronunciation leaning towards *i*.

[2] The same view should be taken as in f.-n. 1.

[3] Subhūti, Abhp.-Sūci under this word gives *ajjaka* beside *ajjuka*.

[4] Pischel, § 89.

[5] E. Kuhn, Beitr., p. 94.

[6] In Pkr. Śaurasenī and Māgadhī we have *kkhu* which causes the shortening of the preceding *e*, *o*. Pischel § 94, 148. Whence the *o* in Pāli *kho*?

§21. Weakening of the syllable preceding the accented one is found in *kăhāpaṇa* (a coin) (Pkr. *kăhāvaṇa*) = *kārṣāpana*; perhaps also in *nigrodha* 'ficus indica' = *nyagrodha* and in *susāna* 'burial ground' from **śvaśāna*, a side-form of *śmaśāna*[1]. Yet however similar instances of saṃprasāraṇa are found also in the syllable with main accent. It is perhaps due to the weakening of the syllable preceding the accented one that *dvi-* appears as *du-* in compounds, e.g., *dujīvha* 'double-tongued' Jā. V. 82^4. Under the accent we have the regular forms *dvi-*, *di-*, e.g., *dipada* 'biped'[2]. The two types having later crossed each other we have on the one hand *duvidha* 'double' = *dvividha*, and on the other *dvibhūmiko* 'consisting of two stories' JāCo. II. 18^8.—In forms like *ṭhăpeti* (*uṭṭhăpeti* etc.) as opposed to *sthāpayati* we have analogical formations after the type *jñăpayati* etc. (§ 180.1); similarly in *kiṇati* 'buys', as opposed to *krīṇāti*, after the types *mināti*, *lunāti*.[3]

§ 22. The effect of accent is perceptible also in the shortening of unstressed final syllables. Thus *o* becomes *u* in *asu* 'that' (§ 109) through **aso* (thus in AMāg.) = *asau*; *udāhu* 'or' = *utāho*; *sajju* 'immediately' Dh. 71 (from which *sajjukaṃ*) through **sajjo* = *sadyas*; *hetu* (in *kissa hetu* 'what for?') through **heto* = *hetos*.[4] With later nasalisation: *-khattuṃ* (adv. numeral suffix) through **-khatto* = *-kṛtvas* and *aduṃ* 'that' through **ado* = *adas*. Cf. § 66.2 *b*. Qualitative change (reduction) is in evidence in *saddhiṃ* 'together with' = *sārdham*,[5] *sakkhi(ṃ)* or *sacchi* 'before one's eyes' (certainly not = *sākṣāt*, but) = **sākṣam* (AMāg. *sakkhaṃ*[6]); *saṇiṃ* 'slowly' Mhvs. 25. 84 (not = *śanais*, but) = **śanam*. Reduction to *u* under the influence of an *u* of the preceding syllable (§ 17. 2 *a*) is found in *puthu* 'separate' Thl. 86, Milp. 4^1 = *pṛthak*. The enclitic *-svid* has become *-su*, *-ssu*: *kiṃ-su*, *kena-ssu* etc. S.I. 36 ff. We have moreover *-si* in *kaṃ-si* DhCo. I. 91^{18}. Cf. § 111. 1.

§ 23. In a series of words even from the beginning the long second syllable was shortened. This is evidently due to the shifting of the accent to the first syllable. Examples: *alika* 'false' Sn. 239,

[1] Pischel, PkrGr. § 104 Johansson (IF. 25. 225 ff.) separates *susāna* from *śmaśāna* and derives the former from *śuvaśayana* 'burial ground'.

[2] Also Pkr. has *du-*, *do-* beside *di-*, *bi-*. Pischel, § 436.

[3] A different explanation is given by Michelson, IF. 23. 127.

[4] Even new nominal stems are formed in this way; Skr. *āgas* 'sin' through **āgo* becomes *āgu*, inflected like *madhu*.

[5] A different explanation in Pischel, PkrGr. § 103

[6] Pischel, § 114.

S. I. 189[2], Rasav. II. 83[14] = *alīka*; *gahita* 'seized' = *gṛhīta*; *paññavant* 'intelligent' Thl. 70, Vin I. 60[1] = *prajñāvant*; *pāniya* 'water' beside *pānīya* (*pāniyāni* D. I. 148[4], *pānīyāni* JāCo. I 450[8]) = *pānīya* (AMāg., JMāh. *pāṇiya*); *vammika* 'ant-hill' JāCo. I. 432[5] beside *vammīka* JāCo. III. 85[8] = *vălmīka*; *sāluka* 'lotus-root' Vin. I. 246[16] = *śālūka*. Similarly *dutiya* 'second', *tatiya* 'third' = *dvitīya*, *tṛtīya*[1].—In other cases, where the vowel of the second syllable was originally short, qualitative change of the vowel took place as a result of this shifting of accent: *Pajjunna* (name of the god of rains) D. II. 260[25], JāCo. I. 331[21] = *Parjanya*; *mutiṅga* 'drum' D. I. 79[13], Vin. I. 15[10] (Pkr. *muiṅga*) = *mṛdaṅga*. Cf. *meraya* 'intoxicating drink' Dh. 247, D. I. 146[20] = *maireya*.

§ 24. The effect of the new expiratory accent is perceptible also in the occasional lengthening of the vowel of the first syllable: *ājira* 'court-yard' Mhvs. 35.3 = *ajira*; *ālinda* 'terrace in front of a house' D.I. 89[30], Vin. I. 248[3], DhCo. I. 26[4] = *alinda*; perhaps we have also to include here *ānubhāva* 'power' JāCo. I. 509[23] = *anubhāva*. This explanation of the lengthening of the vowel of the initial syllable often however remains doubtful, as in *āroga* 'in good health' JāCo. I. 408[1] (reading uncertain) beside *aroga* = *aroga*; *pāṭibhoga* 'surety' Ud. 17[10], Iv, I[6], JāCo. II. 93[14], which in meaning is difficult to connect with *pratibhoga*; *pāṭiyekka* 'individually' JāCo. I. 92[24] beside *pacceka* = *pratyeka*.—Gemination of consonants may take the place of lengthening of vowels: *ummā* 'flax' in *ummāpuppha* (a precious stone) A. V. 61[21] = *umā*; *kummagga* 'evil path' A. III. 420[29]. Pu. 22[7], Milp. 390[8], *kunnadi* 'small (intermittent) river' Thl. 145, S. I. 109[5], JāCo. III. 221[11], *kussubbha* 'small pool' S. V. 63[8] (beside *kusubbha*) = *ku* + *mārga*, *nadī*, *śvabhra*; *mukkhara* 'garrulous' Minayeff, Prātimokṣa 59 (beside *mukhara* S. I. 203[34], JāCo. III. 103[5]) = *mukhara*[2].

8. *Saṃprasāraṇa and the Loss of Syllable through Contraction*

§ 25. Through Saṃprasāraṇa: 1. *yă* becomes *ī* also in stressed syllable: *thīna* 'sloth' = *styāna*; *dvīha*, *tīha* 'period of two (three)

[1] Pischel, KZ. 35. 142, PkrGr. § 82, 91 assumes the basic forms **dvityá*, **tṛtyá*. But see Jacobi, Kalpasūtra (AbhKM. VI. 1), p. 103, f.-n., as well as KZ. 35, 570 f.

[2] The example *suddiṭṭha* quoted in JPTS. 1909, p. 193 is = *su-uddiṭṭha*; *sakkāya* is not = *svakāya*, but = *satkāya* (Franke, D., p. 54, f.-n. 4) and *cikkhalla* 'earthen,' Vin II. 122[31] not = *cikhala* but = **caikhalya* > **cēkhalla* > **cekkhalla* (E. Müller, PGr. p. 19).

days' D. I. 190[15], A. I. 140[15]=*dvyaha*, *tryaha*; *visīveti* 'dries out at fire' JāCo. II. 68[16], DhCo. I. 225[2]=*viśyāpayati*. Of frequent occurrence is *vīti*=*vyati-*, *vi-ati-*, *e.g.*, *vītivatta*=*vyativṛtta* etc. Cf. *niṅka* (a kind of deer) Abhp. 619=*nyaṅku*. Instead of ī there is *e* in (*saṃ*) *pavedhati* 'shakes' Sn. 928. D. II. 22[2] from root *vyath*. Often *yă* is retained: *vyasana* 'misfortune', *vyādha* 'hunter' etc. In *cajati* 'gives up' =*tyajati*, *majjhantika* 'relating to noon-time' from *madhya* etc. we have the assimilation of *y* to the preceding consonant.—2. *vă* becomes *ū* in *sūna* 'dog' Abhp. 519 from the stem *śvān-*.[1] Before double-consonance *ū* becomes *o* through *u* (§ 10): *sotthi* 'welfare' (beside *suvatthi*)=*svasti*; *soppa* 'sleep' (beside *supina*) S. I. 110[32] (verse)=*svapna*; *sobbha* 'tank' (*cf. kussubbha* § 24) =*śvabhra*. The form *ko* 'where ?' S. I. 199[16] (verse), Vin. I. 36[24] (beside *kvaṃ*, *kuvaṃ*, *kva-ci*) is probably a sandhi-form before double-consonance. Before single consonants there is *o* instead of *ū*, *e.g.*, in *sopāka* (AMāg. *sovāga*), 'man of low caste' =*śvapāka* and *soṇa* 'dog'[2]. Moreover *vă* is often retained in the assimilation of *v*, *e.g.*, *assattha* 'ficus religiosa' (AMāg. however has *assottha* etc.)=*aśvattha*. —3. Quite peculiar is *dosa* in which Skr. *doṣa*, 'fault' and *dveṣa* 'hatred' have coincided. *Cf. dosaniya* 'deserving hatred' A. III. 169[28]=*dveṣaṇīya*.

§ 26. Through contraction *aya* can become *e* and *ava* can become *o*[3], clearly through the intermediate stages *ayi*: *aï*, *avu*: *aü* (§ 19). 1. *aya* becomes *e* in *jeti* 'wins' (beside *jayati*) =*jayati*, etc.; *ajjhena* 'study' Sn. 242, M. III. 1[13]=*adhyayana*. Facultatively also in causatives and other verbal stems in *aya*, such as *moceti*. *katheti*.[4] Further *terasa* 'thirteen'=**trayadaśa*, *tevīsa(ti)*=**trayaviṃśati*; *aya* is retained in *nayana* 'eye,' *sayana* 'bed' etc (but *senāsana* 'bedstead and seat' beside *sayanāsana* Sn. 388 f., Dh. 185)—2. *ava* becomes *o* in *odhi* 'limit' D. II. 160[32], JāCo. II. 18[21]=*avadhi*; *oma* 'lowly' Sn. 860, A. III. 359[28] (verse)=*avama*; *poṇa* 'sinking, inclined' Vin.II. 237[19], Ud. 53[9] etc.=*pravaṇa*; *loṇa* 'salt' =*lavaṇa*; *hoti* 'is, becomes'

[1] In *turita* 'hastening' and *kuthita* 'boiled' as opposed to *tvarita* and *kvathita*, we have in fact no Saṃprasāraṇa of the Pāli stage. We are to assume here older basic forms **turita*, **kuthita*.

[2] The intermediate stages seem to have been *iya* and *uva*; thus *dvyaha* : **dviyaha* : *dvīha*, *śvān-* : **suvān-* : *sūna*, *soṇa*. *Cf. soṇṇa*, 'gold' beside *suvaṇṇa*.

[3] Pischel, PkrGr. § 153 f.

[4] In the same way may be explained also *bhāyāmi* 'I fear' and *palāyati* 'flies' beside which are found also *bhemi* and *paleti*. *Cf.* § 138 and 139. 1.

(beside *bhavati*) and many other forms. Also facultatively *o-*=the prefix *ava-*(*orodha* 'harem' =*avarodha*) and *vo*=the prefix *vyava-*, *vi-ava*, (*vosita* 'fulfilled' Dh. 423=*vyavasita*). Cf. *uposatha* (Pkr. *posaha*)=*upavasatha*. *Ava* is retained in *lavana* 'harvest,' *savana* 'hearing' etc. But *loṇa* 'salt'=*lavaṇa*.

§ 27. Further cases of contraction are 1. *aya* becomes *ā*:*patisāllāna* 'meditation' D. II. 9[10], JāCo. II. 77[11] etc.=*pratisaṃlayana*; *sotthāna* 'welfare' Sn. 258, A. IV. 271[20] (verse)=*svastyayana* (§25.2).—2. *āya* becomes *ā*:*vehāsa* 'atmosphere' D. I. 95[10], JāCo. I. 445[20] etc. =*vaihāyasa*; *upaṭṭhāka* 'attendant' Vin. I. 72[17], JāCo. I. 357[4] etc. =*upasthāyaka* (but fem. *upaṭṭhāyikā* Thūpavs. 81[29]); *Kaccāna* (beside *Kaccāyana*), *Moggallāna* n. pr.=*Kātyāyana*, *Maudgalyāyana* etc.[1] Very frequently at the end of a word *-āya* is contracted into *-ā*, such as *sayaṃ abhiññā* 'on the strength of one's own knowledge' instead of *-ññāya*=*abhijñāya* Ger.; *apaṭipucchā* 'without hearing' Vin II. 8[3] instead of *-cchāya* I. Sg. f.; *esanā* '(goes) in search of' JāCo. II. 34[16] instead of *-nāya* D. Sg. m.; *chamā* 'on the earth' instead of *-māya* Loc. Sg. f.[2] Particularly in the first syllables of words *āya* is likely to be retained: *vāyasa*, *jāyati* etc.—3. *āva* becomes *o* in *atidhona* (*cārin*) '(committing) transgressions' Dh. 240=**atidhāvana*.[3] But *āva* is retained in the first syllables: *pāvaka*, *sāvaka*.—4. *avā* becomes *ā* in the *yāgu* 'rice-gruel' A. III. 250[12] etc.=*yavāgū*; *avā* remains uncontracted in *kavāṭa*, *pavāḷa*, as *ayā* in *dayālu* etc.—5. *ayi* and *avi* become *e*: *acchera* 'miraculous' Vv. 84. 12 through **acchayira* (beside *acchariya*)=*āścarya*; similarly *ācera* 'teacher' Jā. IV. 248[9] (beside *ācariya*)=*ācārya*; *macchera* 'envy' Dh. 242, DhCo. III, 2[1] etc.=*mātsarya*[4]; *thera* 'venerable priest'=*sthavira*; *hessati* 'will be' (§ 154.2)=*bhaviṣyati*[5].—6. *āyi* becomes *e* in the technical term *acceka* (*cīvara*) '(garment) given at an unusual hour' Vin. III. 260[33] beside *accāyika* 'pressing' M. II. 112[27], JāCo. I. 338[31]=**atyāyika*. Beside this *e* we have *ī* in *pāṭihīra* 'sign of miracle' D.I. 193[3], Mhvs. 5.188 through **pāṭihāyira* (beside

[1] Also *pācittiya* 'transgression requiring penance' Vin. IV. 1 ff., if it is related to *prāyaścittika* Sylv. Lévi, JAs. Ser. X, t. 20, p. 506 ff. derives it from a * *prāk-citta*.

[2] In analogy with these cases an inorganic *ya* has sometimes been added to a final *ā*: *senāya caturaṅginī* Jā. V. 322[18].

[3] D. Andersen, P. Gl. under the word.

[4] Thus through metathesis in the intermediate step. Cf. E. Kuhn, Bietr. p. 56; E. Müller, PGr. p. 41 f.; V. Henry, Précis de Gramm. Pâlie § 88.4. Pischel, PkrGr. § 176 however suggests epenthesis.

[5] On *hohiti*, *hotabba*. *hotum* see § 151, 206.

pāṭihāriya) = *prātihārya*; similarly (*a*) *saṃhīrā* '(not) to be won' Jā. V. 81[17], A. IV. 141[11] etc. = (*a*) *saṃhārya*.—7. *iya* is changed into *ī* (*i*) in *kittaka* 'how much?' Smp. 304[1] = **kiyattaka*. According to §10. 2 is to be explained *ettaka* 'so much' = **iyattaka*[1].—8. Isolated cases of contraction are found moreover in *koṭṭha* in the names of birds *rukkhakoṭṭhasakuna* JāCo. III. 25[29] if it is = *koyaṣṭi*[2] and *mora* 'peacock' (the same form also in Pkr.; in Pāli also *mayūra* D. III. 201[22]) = *mayūra*[3].

§ 28. As in Pkr.,[4] so also in P. the prepositions *upa-* and *apa-* (through **uva-*, **ava-*) may become *ū-* and *o-*: 1. *upa-* becomes *ū-*, as I think, in *ūhadeti* 'besmears with dung' = *upahadati* and *ūhasana* 'smiling at somebody' Milp. 127[31]. Cf. Pkr. *ūhasia* in Hem. = *upahasita*[5].—2. *apa-* becomes *o-* in *ovaraka* 'inner apartment (of a house)' Vin. I. 217[17], VvCo. 304[14] = *apavaraka*; *ottappati* 'feels shame' A. III. 2[16] (*ottappa* 'shame', *ottappin* or *ottāpin* 'shameful') from the root *trap* with *apa*[6]. Presumably also in (*pacc*)*osakkati* 'falls back' D. I. 230[21], JāCo. I. 383[8], Mhvs. 25.84 (AMāg. *paccosakkai*) from root *ṣvaṣk* with (*prati*)*apa*[7].

9. *Increase of Syllables through Svarabhakti*

§29. Only the consonant-groups containing *r*, *l*, *y*, *v* or a nasal are separated by svarabhakti.[8] An exception is to be found in *kasaṭa* 'bad, false' A. I. 72[8], JāCo. II. 96[22], Milp. 119[13] etc. = *kaṣṭa*. This is perhaps a dialectical expression. In Pkr. we have the Paiśācī form *kasaṭa*.[9] —The added vowel appears mostly in the inside of words. In initial

[1] Not so Pischel, § 153.

[2] Fausböll, Five Jāt., p. 38.

[3] Uncontracted *mayūkha* 'beam of light' as opposed to Pkr. Māh. *moha*.

[4] Hem. I. 173; Pischel, PkrGr. § 155.

[5] It may be thought that also *ūhanti* in the meaning 'defiles' is derived from *han* with *upa*. Yet this is rendered improbable by Vin I. 78[12] where *ummihati* stands parallel to it. It is certain that *ūhanti* = *han* with *ud* and it means 'conquers, annihilates.' Instead of *ūhananti* M. I. 243[23] we have in fact *upahananti* (with v.l. *uh-*) in the parallel passage S. IV. 56[19].

[6] E. Müller, PGr., p. 43.

[7] In Jā. III. 83[6] we have *avasakkati*, but with the variant reading *apa-* in the Burmese MSS. The word *oggata*, Thl. 477 (used about the sun) may be = *apagata* or *a vagata*.

[8] For Pkr. cf. Jacobi, KZ. 23.594; Pischel, PkrGr. § 131.

[9] Vararuci X. 6, Hemacandra IV. 314; Grierson, ZDMG. 66.52[21]; Pischel, § 132; St. Konow, ZDMG. 64. 114[36].

position it is found in *itthī* 'woman' = *strī* and in *umhayati,-te* 'smiles'[1] Jā. II. 131[22], JāCo. III. 44[14] = *smayate*.—Beside forms with the added vowel there are often those showing assimilation of the consonant-groups. The latter are archaic and are found particularly in the gāthās. In the commentary they are explained by the forms with the added vowel, which therefore must have been the current forms. Thus we have in Jā. III. 151[5] *asi tikkho va maṃsamhi*; the Co. replaces *tikkha* 'sharp' = *tīkṣṇa* by *tikhiṇa*. Regarding the action of the law of mora on the quantity of a long vowel preceding a consonant-group separated by svarabhakti, see above § 8. In verse the svarabhakti-vowels are often ignored as also in Pkr.[2] Cf. Dh. 10 *arahati* = *arhati*; Dh. 25 *kayirātha* = *kayrātha*; Th1. 477 *suriyasmiṃ* = *suryasmiṃ*; Th2. 49 *puriso* = *purso* etc. The *i* of *itthī* is always metrically justified; beside it however there is found in verses the form *thī*: Sn. 769, Jā. I. 295[8], Jā. V. 81[16].

§ 30. Of all the added vowels the most frequent is *i* (both prothetic and anaptyctic): 1. In the group *ry*: *iriyati* 'moves' M. I. 74[6], A. III. 451[6] (substantive *iriyā*) = **īryate*, *īryā*; *mariyādā* 'frontier' Mhvs. 34.70 = *maryādā* etc. In the same way are formed the passives like *kariyati* from *karoti* (also *karīyati* D. I. 52[27]), *vāriyati* 'is held back' = *vāryate*.—2. In other combinations with *y*: *kālusiya* 'darkening' DCo. I.95[10] = *kāluṣya*; *jiyā* 'bow-string' D.II. 334[20], Mhvs. 14.4 = *jyā* etc. In the same category are to be included also the passives like *pucchiyati* 'is asked' = *pṛcchyate*. Also in *hiyyo* (AMāg. *hijjo*) 'yesterday' = *hyas* we have svarabhakti with secondary reduplication of *y*.—3. In other combinations with *r*: *vajira* 'thunder, diamond' (AMāg. *vaïra*) Dh. 161, D. I. 95[8], Milp. 118[21] = *vajra*. On *sirī*, *hirī*, see § 8. Svarabhakti by *i* is in evidence also in *purisa* 'man' (cf. § 29). The basic form is **pūrṣa*. In the popular dialects the form with the svarabhakti vowel *i* was preferred to the Skr. form *puruṣa* with *u*[3]. From **pūrṣa* through **pussa*, **possa* is derived also P. *posa* Sn. 110 (and otherwise in verses).—4. In consonant-groups with *l*: *pilakkhu* (name of a tree) Jā. III. 24[26] = *plakṣa*; *hilāda* 'joy' Attanagaluvs. 1. 11. = *hlāda* etc. But we have invariably *sukka* 'white' = *śukla*.—5. In consonant-groups with nasals: *sineha* 'affection' = *sneha*; *tasiṇā* 'thirst' Dh. 342 f. (beside *taṇhā*) = *tṛṣṇā*. On the other hand there occur only *kaṇha* 'black' = *kṛṣṇa* (Pkr. *kaṇha*, *kasiṇa*, *kasaṇa*) and *nagga* 'naked' =

[1] Wenzel, Academy 1890, II, p. 177.

[2] It is however not right to change the orthography for the sake of metre.

[3] Wackernagel, AiGr. I, § 51; Pischel PkrGr. § 124; Michelson, IF, 23.254.

nagna (AMāg. *nagiṇa*, *nigiṇa*). In flexion we have *rājinā*, *rājino* beside *raññā*, *rañño*=*rājñā*, *rājñas*. On *gini* from **agini*, *agni* see § 66.1. On *mihita* see § 50.6.

§ 31. 1. The svarabhakti-vowel *a* is found particularly in those cases where the *a*-vowel is much in evidence before and after: *garahā* 'abuse' JāCo. I. 372[31], 'dishonesty' D. I. 135[14], *garahati* 'abuses' etc. =*garhā*, *garhati*; *palavati* 'swims' Dh. 334, Thl. 399 (beside *pilavati* Thl. 104)=*plavati*; *harāyati* 'is ashamed' (§ 186. 2) beside *hirīyati* from *hrī*. Cf. *nahāyati* in § 50. 5. As link in compound: *antaradhāyati* 'disappears' from root *dhā* with *antar*.—2. The svarabhakti-vowel *u* is found before *m* and *v*: *usumā* 'heat' JāCo. III. 71[18]= *uṣman*; *sukhuma* 'fine'=*sūkṣma*; *duve* 'two' (more frequently *dve*) *metri causa* Sn. 48, 896=*dve*; *maruvā* (v.l. *muruvā* (a kind of hemp) M. I. 429[23]=*mūrvā*. Sometimes *u* is induced by an *u* of the following syllable: *kurūra* 'cruel' A. III. 383[24], Pu. 56[7]=*krūra*. In the same way originated also the form *suṇisā* 'daughter-in-law' through **sunusā* (as in Paiśācī) from *snuṣā*. The *i* in this form[1] is to be explained according to § 19.3. The svarabhakti-vowel *u* is in evidence also in *sakkuṇāti* 'is able' and *pāpuṇāti* 'obtains' from Skr. *śaknoti*, *prāpnoti*. Cf. § 148.

10. *Quantitative Changes in Composition and under Stress of Metre*

§ 32. On account of the metre very often 1. short vowels are lengthened[2]: *satīmati* Th2. 35; *tūriyaṃ* Mhvs. 25. 74; *tatīyaṃ* Dh. 309; *anūdake* Jā. VI. 499[5]. Frequently also in final syllables: *sīho va nadatī vane* Thl. 832. Due to the law of mora, the lengthening of preceding vowel is to be regarded as equivalent to the reduplication of the following consonant: *paribbasāno* for *pariv°* Sn. 796; *sarati bbayo* 'life flies' (cf. § 51. 8) for *saratī vayo* Jā III. 95[18]. The forms *kummiga* Milp. 346[18], *kussobbha* Sn. 720 might be due to metrical exigencies. According to § 24, they may however occur even where there is no pressure of metre.—2. Shortening of long vowels *metri causa*[3] is likewise very frequent: (*bhūtāni*) *bhummāni vā yāni va* (instead of *vā*) *antalikkhe* Kh. 6.1=Sn. 222 (cf. Kh. 9. 6, Dh. 138 f.); *paccanikā*

[1] The *ṇ* in *suṇisā* is perhaps derived from the side-form *suṇhā* (see § 50.8).

[2] Similarly in Pkr., Pischel, § 78.

[3] Pischel, § 99.

instead of *-nikā*. Cp. II. 8. 4 etc. *o* is shortened into *a* in *okamokata* (instead of *-to*) Dh. 34, and *e* is shortened into *i* in *°gimhisu* (instead of *-esu*) Dh. 286. Not infrequently the endings *-inaṃ*, *-unaṃ*, *-ihi*, *-uhi*, *-isu*, *-usu* remain short in verse as opposed to *-īnaṃ* etc. in prose. Thus Th1. 1258, 240, Jā. VI. 579[29], Th1. 1207 etc. Nasal vowels are denasalised: *dīghaṃ addhāna* (instead of *-naṃ*) *socati* Dh. 207. In Th2. 91 should be read *pāpuṇi* instead of *-niṃ*. In sandhi we have further very often cases like *aññā samatimaññi 'haṃ* (instead of *-ññiṃ ahaṃ*) Th2. 72. Also in the inside of words the nasal may be dropped *metri causa*. Thus *jīvato* Jā. III. 539[2] instead of *jīvanto*. Simplification of double-consonance is again equivalent to shortening of vowels. Thus we have, *metri causa*, *dukhaṃ* for *dukkhaṃ* Thl. 734; *dakkhisaṃ* for *-issaṃ*[1] Th2. 84 (*cf. dakkhisāma* Jā. III. 99[7]) and many similar cases.

§ 33. At the end of the first member of a compound 1. the short vowel is often lengthened[2]: *sakhībhāva* JāCo. III. 493[6] (*sakhībh-* JāCo. VI. 424[20]); *abbhāmatta* S. I. 205[4] (in a verse, but not *metri causa*); *rajāpatha* (see Childers, P. D. sub voce), for which there is *rajapatha* in Pu. 57[12]. Equivalent to this lengthening there is also the gemination of the initial consonant of the second member of the compound: *jātassara* 'natural lake' Vin. I. 111[4]; *navakkhattuṃ* 'nine times' DhCo. III. 377[12] and likewise in all compounds with *-khattuṃ* =*-kṛtvas*.—Lengthening of vowels or gemination of consonants is found very frequently in combinations with prepositions: *pāvacana* (AMāg. *pāvayana*) 'word' Th2. 457, D. I. 88[8] etc.=*pravacana*; *pākaṭa* (AMāg. *pāgaḍa*) 'apparent' Th1. 109, VvCo. 267[27]=*prakaṭa*[3]. This may be partially due also to the effect of the stress accent (§ 24). Gemination of the consonant is found also in *abhikkanta* 'glorious' D. I. 85[7] etc.: it belongs rather to the root *kam* (not to *kram*[4]); further in *paṭikkūla* 'contrary' M. III. 301[11], JāCo.

[1] Different explanation by Mrs. Rhy Davids, Psalms of the Sisters, p. 56, f.-n. 2.

[2] Similarly in Pkr.; Pischel, § 70.

[3] In *pāheti* 'sends' (beside *pahiṇati*) the *ā* is perhaps due to forms like *pāhesi* 'he sent'.

[4] The forms *upakkiliṭṭha* 'defiled,' *upakkilesa* 'defilement' are perhaps contaminations of **upakkiṭṭha*, **upakkesa=upakliṣṭa*, *upakleśa* with **upakiliṭṭha* and **upakilesa* (with svarabhakti-vowel according to § 30. 4). Probably a contamination of the root-forms *sraj* and *sarj* is at the root of *ossajjati* 'gives up', *vissajjati* 'gives away' (beside *ossajati*, *vissajati*), *oggata* 'gone down' (see p. 76, f.-n. 7) and *okkasati* 'takes away' D. II. 74[29] from root *karṣ* with *ava* (intermediate steps: **ōgata* **ōkasati*) are cases of § 6,2.

I. 393[24] beside *paṭikūla* Vin. I. 29[28] etc. = *pratikūla*. Perhaps we have to explain in this way also some of the compounds of the type *phalāphala* 'fruits of every sort.'[1] In many cases however, *e.g.*, *maggāmagga* 'paths of every description (good and evil ways),' it is not unnatural to think of the type *subhāsubha* (*subha* + *asubha*).—2. Shortening of the vowel often takes place when stems in *ā*, *ī*, *ū* form the first member of the compound[2]: *upāhanadāna* 'gift of shoes' JāCo. IV. 20[18] from *upāhanā* + *d*-; *dāsigaṇa* 'troop of maid-servants' JāCo. II. 127[28] from *dāsī* + *g*-; *sassudevā* 'worshipping the mother-in-law as god' S.I. 86[14] = Jā. IV. 322[15] (in verse, but without pressure of metre) from *sassū* + *d*-.

11. Irregularities of Vocalism

§ 34. There are now still a number of "sporadical cases" to deal with. Thus from Skr. *punar* the double forms *puna* and *pana* have been developed with different meanings: *puna* means 'again, once more,' *pana* means 'but, on the contrary.'[3]—In many cases the vocalism of Pāli is more archaic than that of Skr. Thus in *garu* 'heavy' as opposed to Skr. *guru*, and also in *agaru*, *agalu* 'aloe' Jā. VI. 510[14], VvCo. 237[1] as opposed to *aguru* (beside *agaru*). Perhaps also in *kilañja* 'mat' M. I. 228[33], Mhvs. 34. 54 as opposed to *kiliñja*; *mucalinda* (name of a tree) Vin. I. 3[12] as opposed to *mucilinda*; *jhallikā* 'beetle' Abhp. 646 as opposed to *jhillikā*.—In other cases the Pāli word is derived from a basic form different from that of the Skr. word: thus *tipu* 'tin' D. II. 351[9], Vin. I. 190[27] is not = *trapu*, but = **tṛpu*; *papphāsa* 'lung' Kh. 3, D. II. 293[15] etc. is not = *pupphusa*; *simbala*, *-li* 'cotton-tree' (AMāg. *simbalī*) is not = *śālmalī* (AMāg. *sāmalī*) but = Ved. *śimbala* 'cotton-flower'[4]; *tekicchā* 'healing,' *atekiccha* 'incurable' (AMāg. *teïcchā*) A. III. 146[32], DhCo. I. 25[21] not = *cikitsā*, but = **cekitsā*.[5] The forms *kissa* G. Sg. and *kismiṃ*, *kimhi* L. Sg. of the Interr. Pron. do not belong to the stem *ka*, but to the stem *ki* which appears in Skr. *kim*.[6]—Not

[1] Fausböll, Dasaratha-Jātaka, p. 26; Trenckner, Notes, p. 74; E. Kuhn, Beitr. p. 31; Andersen, PGl. sub voce *a*-.

[2] *Cf.* Pischel, § 97.

[3] Michelson, IF. 23. 258, f.-n. 1.

[4] Pischel, PkrGr. § 109; Geldner in Pischel and G., Ved. Studien II. 159.

[5] Pischel § 215.

[6] *Cf.* in Pkr. Māg. *kiśa* etc. and Pischel, § 103, 428. Not so R. O. Franke, GN. 1895, p. 529, f.-n. 1.

infrequently, parallels to the Pāli forms are found in Pkr. Thus *pārepata* 'dove' Jā. VI. 539[15] = AMāg. *pārevaya* as opposed to Skr. *pārāpata* = Māh. *pārāvaa*[1]; *milakkha* 'barbarian' S. V. 466[29], *milakkhu* Thl. 965 = AMāg. *milakkhu* as opposed to Skr. *mleccha* = AMāg. *mĕccha*, *miccha*[2]; *timbaru* (name of a tree) Attanagaluvs. 7.15 = Pkr. *ṭimbaru*, *-ruya* as opposed to Skr. *tumburu* = Pkr. *tumburu*[3].—The verb *dhovati* 'washes' as opposed to Skr. *dhāvati* owes its *o* to forms like *dhota* 'washed' = *dhauta*.[4]

12. *Consonants in Free Position*

§ 35. On the whole, the free consonants are well preserved in Pāli. Unlike Pkr.[5], it retains intervocalic mutes. Also *n* and *y* remain as a rule unchanged.[6] The sibilants *ś*, *ṣ*, *s* (see § 3) have coincided in *s*.—It may be said as a general rule (see § 2) that in intervocalic position *ḍ* and *ḍh* change into *ḷ* and *ḷh*[7]: *āveḷā* 'garland' (§ 11) = *āpīḍā*; *peḷā* 'basket' Pv. IV. 1. 42, Mhvs. 36. 20 = *peḍā*; *hīḷeti* 'neglects' (JPTS. 1907, p. 167) from root *hīḍ*; *mīḷha* Vv. 52.11 = *mīḍha* from root *mih*; *vūḷha* 'carried away' Vin. I. 32[13] = *ūḍha*. The *ḍ* is retained in *kuḍumala* 'opening bud' (*kuḍumalakajāta* A. IV. 117[21]). Here the *ḍ* originally stood in a consonant-group (Skr. *kuḍmala*) which was separated by svarabhakti. In Abhp. 482 appears also *kuḍuba* (a certain measure) = *kuḍava*. The form *sahoḍha* 'together with what has been plundered' from *saha* + *ūḍha*[8] is remarkable.

§ 36. The various phenomena of Prākrit are met with sporadically also in Pāli. The words and forms concerned are taken from those dialects which had gone further on the path of Prākritisation than the literary language represented by Pāli. On the corresponding phenomena is sound-groups cf. § 60 ff.

One of these sporadical phenomena is the occasional elision of an intervocalic mute which is replaced by the hiatus-filler *y* or *v*: *suva* 'parrot' (beside *suka*) = *śuka*; *khāyita* 'eaten' Jā. VI. 498[19], M.I.

[1] Pischel, § 112.
[2] Pischel, § 105, 238; E. Kuhn, KZ. 25. 327.
[3] Pischel, § 124.
[4] Jonansson, IF. 3. 223 f. Not so Pischel, § 482.
[5] Pischel, PkrGr. § 186 ff.
[6] In contrast to Pkr.; cf. Pischel, § 224, 252.
[7] The *ḍh* is retained in Pkr.; Pischel, § 240, 242.
[8] JPTS. 1909, p. 137.

83[6], Vin. I. 109[29] = *khādita*[1]; *niya* 'own' Sn. 149 (beside *nija*) = *nija*[2]; *sāyati* 'tastes' D. III. 85[20], A. III. 163[21] (beside *sādiyati*, *sādita*) = *svādate*. Cf. the names *Aparagoyāna* Bodhivs. 74[2] = *Aparagodāna*[3] and *Kusinārā* through **-naara* = *Kuśinagara*. The Pāli forms in these cases very probably reflect the local dialectical pronunciation. Interchange between the endings *-ikă* and *-iyă* is very frequent[4]: *āveṇika* 'particular, separate' S. IV. 239[10] and *āveṇiya* Vin. I. 71[30]; *Kosiya* (name of Indra) Jā. II. 252[8], M. I. 252[32], Milp. 126[7] = *Kauśika*; *posāvanika* 'developed to maturity' JāCo. III. 134[20] and *-niya* DhCo. III. 35[2] from *posati*. But these are not cases of Prākritism; double forms like *lokiko* 'worldly' = *laukika* and *lokiya* = *laukya* have led to the confusion of two suffixes. In this way originated also *sotthika* 'Brahman' Mhvs. 5. 105 as variant reading of *sotthiya* = *śrotriya*. Similarly perhaps also *veyyattikā* 'lucidity' Smp. 323[28] is to be regarded only as a side-form of *veyyattiyă* M. I. 82[35], II. 208[33], which has been derived from *viyatta* (with svarabhakti) = *vyakta* in the same way as *veyyāvacca* from **viyāvata* (§ 3).

§ 37. It is again a phenomenon of Pkr. whan sporadically a sonant aspirate in intervocalic position is represented by *h*[5]; *lahu*, *lahuka* 'light' Dh. 35, Thl. 104, A. I. 10[2] etc. = *laghu*; *ruhira* 'red, blood' Thl. 568, M. III. 122[34] (beside *rudhira* DhCo. I. 140[14]) = *rudhira*; *sāhu* 'good' Thl. 43, VvCo. 284[29] (beside more frequent *sādhu*) = *sādhu*; *āyūhati* 'struggles' Sn. 210, S. I. 48[1] (verse), Jā. VI. 283[2], Milp. 326[8], if, as H. Kern (IF. 25.238) suggests, it is derived from a basic form **āyodhate*; *nuṭṭhuhati* 'spits out' (beside *-bhati* § 16.1*a*) from root *stubh* with *ni*; *pahaṃsati* 'rubs' JāCo. II. 102[6], DhCo. I. 253[5] through **paghaṃsati*[6] = *pragharṣati*; *momŭha* 'mad' S.I. 133[32] (verse), D. I. 27[9] (*momūhatta* A. III. 119[9], Pu. 69[7]) = *momugha*[7]. The ending *-bhis* in Instr. Pl. has become *-hi*; *-bhi* is archaic. The present form *dahati* 'sets, places' is to be derived from **dadhati* as Pischel has

[1] E. Kuhn. Beitr. p. 56.

[2] Minayeff, PGr. § 41.

[3] BR. under the word *aparagaḍāni*.

[4] Sometimes the place of origin of the MSS. is responsible for these discrepancies. The Siamese MSS. have, *e.g.*, *-ika*, where the other MSS. have *-iya*. Mrs. Rhys Davids, Vibhaṅga, preface, p. xiv.

[5] For Pkr. cf. Pischel, § 188. On the *h* instead of an aspirate in sound-groups, see below § 60.

[6] Trenckner, Notes, p. 61. Not so Johansson, Monde Oriental, 1907 8, p. 85 ff.

[7] E. Kuhn, Beitr. p. 42; E. Müller, PGr. p. 37.

suggested[1]. Similarly *dahāsi* Sn. 841 and *dahāti* Sn. 888, Jā. V. 220[8] represent *dadhāsi, dadhāti*. In initial position *h* represents *bh* in *hoti* 'becomes' beside *bhavati* (also Pkr. *hoï*); to the same category belong further *pahoti* 'is able', *pahonaka* 'sufficient' *pahū̆* 'able' Sn. 98, *pahūta* 'much'=*prabhavati* etc. In secondary initial there is *h* for *dh* in *heṭṭhā* 'under'=**adheṣṭhāt* (§ 9). It should be noticed here that in Pāli, as also in Pkr.[2], an old aspirate is sometimes preserved where the Skr. form shows only *h*: *idha* 'here' as opposed to Skr. *iha*=Av. *iδa*; *ghammati* 'goes' as opposed to Skr. *hammati*, Pkr. *hammaï*; *Vebhāra* (name of a hill) (AMāg. *Vebhāra*, *Vĕbbhāra*, *Vibbhāra*) as opposed to *Vaihāra* (but *Vaibhāra* with the Jainas)[3]. Also in *pilandhati* 'decorates', *pilandhana* 'decoration' from the Skr. root *nah*, Pāli has retained the older *dh*.—A surd aspirate has been replaced by *h* in *suhatā* 'happiness' Jā. III. 158[24] from *sukha*[4] and in *samīhati* 'moves away' Vv. 5.1, VvCo. 35[16], which is perhaps connected with Skr. *īkhate* (beside *īṅkh* of the Dhātupāṭha[5]).

§ 38. The softening of surds in intervocalic position is another feature of Pāli which is to be attributed to the influence of dialects.[6] 1. Softening of *k* into *g*: *eḷamūga* 'deaf and dumb' Jā. I. 247[28], M.I. 20[19]=*eḍamūka*; *paṭigacca* 'earlier' D. II. 118[27], DhCo. III. 305[3] etc. (in S. I 57[19] variant reading *paṭikacca*)=*pratikṛtya*.[7] Further, in the proper names *Sāgala* (a city) Milp. 1[3], JāCo IV. 230[21]=*Śākala* and *Māgandiya* (a Brahman; JPTS. 1888, p. 71)= *Mākandika*. *kh* is softened into *gh* in *nighaññasi* 'you will dig' Jā VI. 13[18].—2. Softening of *c* into *j*: *sujā* sacrificial ladle' from Skr. *sruc*[8]—3. Softening of *t* into *d*: *udāhu* 'or'=*utāho*; *niyyādeti* 'hands over' JāCo. I. 507[2] (also *niyyāteti* D. II. 331[2]) and *paṭiyādeti* 'prepares' D. I. 226[7]=*-yātayati*; *pasada* 'spotted antelope' (§ 12.1)=*pṛṣata* *ruda* 'voice' Jā. I. 207[20] (beside *rū̆ta* JāCo. II. 38.[23])=*ruta*; *vidatthi*

[1] Pischel, BB. 15, 121; PkrGr. § 507. [2] Pischel, § 266.

[3] The case of *saṃgharati* (JPTS. 1909, p. 34) beside *saṃharati* is doubtful.

[4] On the other hand *suhita* 'contented' is certainly not=*sukhita* (Minayeff, PGr. § 43), but=*su-hita* (E. Müller. PGr., p. 37).

[5] BR. under the word *īṅkh*.

[6] According to Hem. IV. 396, this is characteristic also of Apabhraṃśa. Pischel, PkrGr. § 192, 202.

[7] Trenckner, Milp., p. 421 (note on p. 48[12]); E. Müller, PGr., p. 37. S. Lévi, JAs. sér. X. t. 20, p. 508 ff. cf. above Introd. IX) connects *jalogi* Vin. II. 301[11] with *jalauka* 'leech.'

[8] Lévi, ibid., p. 505 f. derives *pārājika*, a particular kind of transgression, from **pārācika* (AMāg. *pārañciya*).

'span' DhCo. III. 172[4] = *vitasti*. S. Lévi explains also *saṃghādisesa* (designation of a particular kind of transgression) from *saṃgha* + *atiśeṣa* and *ekodi* 'spiritually united' (°*bhāva*, °*bhūta*) from *eka* + *ūti* 'consisting of a single (woven) chain.' [1]—4. Softening of *th* into *dh*: *pavedhati* 'shivers' (§ 25.1) = *vyathate*; *gadhita* 'greedy' Ud. 75[10], Milp 401[2] beside *gathita* D. I. 245[24], M. I. 162[14] = *grathita*.—5. Softening of *p* into *v*[2] is very frequent: *avaṅga* 'corner of the eye' Vin. II. 267[6] = *apāṅga*[3]; *avāpuraṇa* 'key' JāCo. I. 501[25] (*avāpurati*, *avāpurāpeti* JāCo. I. 263[30], II. 22[9] beside *apāp-* Vv. 64.27, Vin. I. 5[31], V. 80[4]) from root *var* with *apā* (cf. § 39.6); *āveḷā* (§ 11) = *āpiḍā*; *ubbillāvita* 'unduly elated' D. I. 3[24] beside *ubbillāpita* JāCo. II. 10[8]; *kavi* 'monkey' Abhp. 1105 (beside the usual *kapi* Cp. III. 7.1) = *kapi*; *kaviṭṭha* (name of a tree) JāCo. V. 132[4],[7], cf. III. 463[7], V. 115[5] (beside *kapittha* Jā. VI. 529[20], Mhvs. 29.11) = *kapittha*; *theva* 'drop' Vin. I. 50[11] from root *stip*, *step*, of the Dhātupāṭha; *pūva* 'cake' A. III. 76[14] etc. = *pūpa*; *bhindivāḷa* (a kind of weapon) Abhp. 394 = *bhindipāla*; *vyāvaṭa* (Pkr. *vāvaḍa*) 'engaged on something' D. II. 141[20], JāCo. III. 129[15] = *vyāpṛta*[4]; *visīveti* (§ 25.1) = *viśyāpayati*.—In the same way is to be explained also 6. the change of *ṭ* into *ḷ* which presupposes an intermediate *ḍ*: *kakkhaḷa*; 'cruel' = *kakkhaṭa*; *kheḷa* 'village' = *kheṭa* (or from the root *kṣviḍ* of the Dhātupāṭha); *cakkavāḷa* 'horizon JāCo II. 37[19], Mhvs. 31.85 through **cakkavāṭa* from **cakravarta* (Skr. *cakravāḍa*, *-vāla*); *phaḷika* 'crystal' = *sphaṭika*. To this category also belong the proper names: *Āḷavī*, (a city) = *Āṭavī*, *Lāḷa* (a country and a people) Dpvs. 9. 5 (cf. *Lāḷudāyitthera* JāCo. I. 123[12]) = *Lāṭa*.

§ 39. It is again due to dialectical variations that sporadically the sonants are represented by surds.[5] 1. Instead of *g* appears *k* in: *akalu* (a perfume) Milp. 338[13] = *aguru* (§ 34); *chakala* 'goat' Abhp. 1111 =

[1] S. Lévi, ibid. 503, 502. See also R. O. Franke, D. p. 39, f.-n. 6 with p. LVIII. It is quite doubtful whether *dandha* 'slow, dull' is to be classed here. Weber, ZDMG. 14.48 connects it with Skr. *tandra*. He is followed by Childers, Fausböll, E. Kuhn. A different, but wrong, explanation is given by Trenckner, Notes, p. 65 (JPTS 1908. 115, foot-note) and E. Müller. On the other hand Johansson, Monde Oriental, 1907-8, p. 103 connects the word with I.-E. **dhendhro-*.

[2] Similarly also in Pkr.; Pischel. § 192.

[3] VT. III. 342, f.-n. 6.

[4] Trenckner, Notes, p. 63.

[5] See Trenckner, Notes, p. 62 f. For analogous phenomena in Pkr. cf. Pischel, PkrGr. § 191, 27; Grierson, ZDMG. 66.49 f.; St. Konow, ZDMG. 64.108 f.; 114. For similar phenomena in sound-combinations in Pāli see below § 61.2.

=*chagala*; *thaketi* 'closes' Vin. I. 48[35], *thakana* Mhvs. 6.13=*sthagayati*, *sthagana*; *palikuṇṭhita* 'veiled' JāCo. II. 92[24] beside *palig-* DhCo. I. 144[11], verse) from root *guṇṭh* with *pari*; *laketi* 'clings', *lakanaka*, 'anchor' Milp. 377[19], [23] =*lagati*, *lagnaka*; *vākurā* 'snare' Thl 775 (*vākarā* M. II. 65[5]) =*vāgurā*. Hardening of consonant in initial position is found in: *kilāsu* 'indolent' Vin. III. 8[5] (*akilāsu* Vin. III. 9[2] etc.), which is to be connected with *glāsnu* 'loose' (root *glā*) according to Trencker.—2. Instead of *gh* appears *kh* in: *palikha* Jā. VI. 276[3] (beside frequent *paligha*)=*parigha*.—3. Instead of *j* appears *c* in: *pāceti* 'drives' Dh. 135 (*pācanayaṭṭhi* S.I. 115[6]) beside *pājeti* JāCo. II. 122[5] from root *aj* with *pra*.—Instead of *d* appears *t* in: *kusīta* 'slow' Thl. 101, A. III. 3[11] etc.=*kusīda* (but *kosajja* p. 70, f.-n. 1 from **kausadya*); *patara* 'crack' Jā. IV. 32[21]=*pradara*; *mutiṅga* 'drum' (§ 23)=*mṛdaṅga*; *pātu* 'apparent'=*prādur*; *saṃsati* Loc. Sg. 'at the assembly' Jā. III. 493[1]= *saṃsadi*. To this category belong also the names of peoples *Ceti*, *Ceta*, *Cetiya* (metri causa *Cecca*) S.V. 436[19], Cp. I. 9[38], Jā. V. 267[15]=*Cedi*, *Cedika*.—5. Instead of *dh* appears *th* in: *upatheyya* 'pillow' Jā. VI. 490[13] =*upadheya* (cf. *upadhāna*); *pithīyati* 'is covered' Thl. 872, M. III. 184[15] (beside *pidahati*, *pidhāna*)=*pidhīyate*.—6. Instead of *b*, *v* appears *p* in: *avāpuraṇa* etc. (§ 38.5), *apāpurati* 'discloses' Vv. 64.27, Vin. I. 5[31] (verse), II. 148[19] from root. *var* with *apā*; *chāpa(ka)* 'young animal' Vin. I. 193[5] etc.=*śāva*; *pabbaja* (a kind of grass) Thl. 27 (beside *babbaja* Vin. I. 190[3])=*balbaja*; *palāpa* 'chaff' JāCo. I. 467[6]=*pralāva*; *pāpuraṇa* (§ 19.2)=*prāvaraṇa*[1]; *opilāpeti* 'drowns' M. I. 13[6], JāCo. I. 238[12], 330[33]=*-plāvayati*; *lāpa* (a bird) JāCo. II. 59[6]=*lāba*, *lāva*; *lāpu* JāCo. I. 341[2] and *alāpu* Dh. 149 'cucumber' (beside *lābu*, *alābu*)=*lābu*, *alābu*; *hāpeti* 'extinguishes (fire)' Jā. IV. 221[20]=*hāvayati*. Also 3. Sg. Opt. *hupeyya* Vin. I. 8[30] from *bhavati* for *huveyya*.

§ 40. Also the sporadical appearance and disappearance of aspiration have parallels in Prākrit.[2] 1. Unetymological aspiration, (*a*) in initial position: *khīla* (same in AMāg.) 'post' A.I. 141[2], Mhvs. 29.49=*kīla*; *-khattuṃ*=*kṛtvas*; *khujja* 'humped' D. II. 333[21] =*kubja*; *thusa* 'husk' D. I. 9[5]=*tuṣa*; *pharasu* 'axe' A. III. 162[19], JāCo. I. 399[7] (beside *parasu* JāCo. III. 179[1])=*paraśu*; *pharusa* 'harsh, cruel'=*paruṣa phala* (a certain measure) Jā. VI. 510[4] (beside

[1] Not so Johansson, IF. 25. 209 ff.

[2] Pischel, PkrGr. § 206 ff. For similar phenomena in sound-combinations see below § 62.

pala Thl. 97)=*pala*; *phalagaṇḍa* 'carpenter' S. III. 154[29] (beside *pal-* M. I. 119[14])=*phalagaṇḍa*; *phalu* 'knot (of a branch)' D. I. 5[31]= *parus*; *phārusaka* (a flower) DhCo. III. 316[1] =*pāruṣaka*; *phālibhaddaka* (name of a tree) JāCo. II. 163[5]=*pāribhadra*; *phāsukā* 'rib' Dh. 154, JāCo. III. 273[14] etc.=*pārśukā*; *phulaka* (a precious stone) VvCo. 111[25] =*pulaka*; *phusita* (AMāg. *phusiya*) 'drop' M. III. 300[21], DhCo. III. 243[6]=*pṛṣata*; *phussa* (a lunar mansion, name of a month) Vv. 53.4= *puṣya* (*phussaratha* JāCo. III. 238[28]=*puṣyaratha*; *phussarāga* 'topaz' Milp. 118[22]); *bhasta* 'goat' Jā. III. 278[11]=*basta*; *bhisa* 'lotus-sprout' Jā VI. 516[3], JāCo. I. 100[7]=*bisa*; *bhisī* 'mattress' Vin. I. 47[35]=*bṛṣī*; *bhusa* 'chaff' Dh. 252, Ud. 78[10]=*busa*. According to Pischel (PkrGr. §211) this unetymological aspiration of the initial consonant is in evidence also in words like *cha* 'six'[1]=*ṣaṭ*; *chaka*, *chakana* 'dung' Vin. I. 202[25] =*śakṛt*; *chāpa(ka)* (AMāg. *chāva*)=*śāva* (§ 39.6); *cheppā* (AMāg. *chĕppa*, *chippa*) 'tail' Vin. I. 191[2], III. 21[37]=*śepa*; the aspirated *ṣh*, *śh* is said to have developed into *ch* in these cases. Johansson (IF. 3.212f.) assumes Indo-European doublets with *sk̂* and *k̂*; *ch* in his opinion is derived from *sk̂*.—(*b*) Unetymological aspiration in the middle of a word; *sunakha* (Pkr. *suṇaha* 'dog'=*śunaka*; *sukhumāla* 'tender' =*sukumāra*; *kakudha* (Māh. *kaüha*) 'hump' JāCo. 340[3]=*kakuda*. —2 Loss of aspiration is rare: (*a*) initially: '*jalla*' 'dirt' Sn.249, D. I. 167[9], *jallikā* Sn. 198=*jhallikā*.—(*b*) Medially: *kapoṇi* 'elbow' Abph. 265=*kaphoṇi*: *khudā* 'hunger' Sn. 52, Jā.VI. 529[30]=*kṣudhā*; cf. also *katikā* 'agreement' M. I. 171[28], Vin. I. 9[6] etc. beside *kathikā*, a variant reading in JāCo. I. 450[16]=**kathikā*.

§ 41. Dialectical influences are responsible also for sporadical changes of the place of articulation of the consonants.—1. Palatal appears for guttural in: *cunda* 'turner's lathe' *cundakāra* 'turner' JāCo VI. 339[12]=*kunda*; root *iñj* D.I. 56[22] (beside *iṅg* JāCo. II. 408[12])=*ing* —2. Dental appears for palatal[2] in: *dighañña* 'situated behind, to the west' Jā. V. 402[9], 403[30] from *jaghana*); *daddallati* 'glistens' (§ 185)= *jājvalyate*; *tikicchati* 'cures' (§ 184)=*cikitsati* (§ 34); *digucchati* 'feels abhorrence' in Childers (AMāg. *duguccha͏ï*) beside *jigucchati*=*jugupsate*[3]. The last two are probably cases of dissimilation.—3. A dental

[1] Beside it also *sa-*, *saḷ-*, *so-* 'without aspiration.'

[2] Also in Pkr; see Pischel, § 215.

[3] *daddara* 'deep-sounding' A. IV. 171[10]=*jarjara* and *dardara*. In Sinhalese the mutation of *j* into *d* is phonological.

appears for a cerebral in: *deṇḍima* (a drum) D.I. 79[14] (beside *dindima*) = *ḍiṇḍima*, which is clearly derived from popular speech.[1]

§ 42. Quite frequently cerebrals appear in the place of dentals, mostly under the influence of preceding *r*, *ṛ*, even though they may have disappeared in Pāli[2]. Thus there is 1. *ṭ* for *t* in *ambāṭaka* (a tree) Abhp. 554 = *āmrātaka*[3]. Also *vaṭaṃsa(ka)* (§ 66.1) as opposed to *avataṃsa* and *paṭaṃga* 'insect' Jā. VI.506[30], Milp. 272[5] as opposed to *pataṃga*[4]. Moreover sometimes in the participles of *r*-roots we have *ṭ* for *t* : *haṭa* (AMāg. JMāh. *haḍa*) 'taken away' = *hṛta*; *vyāvaṭa* (§ 38.5) = *vyāpṛta*. On the other hand we find only *mata* 'dead', *ābhata* 'brought in,' *saṃvuta* 'restrained'; mostly also *kata* 'done' (*dukkaṭa* term. tech. for a particular kind of transgression). Instead of *prati-*, there appears sometimes *pati-* and sometimes *paṭi-*, the former particularly (but not exclusively) in those cases where other cerebrals occur in the word concerned; thus *patiṭṭhāti* 'stands firm'; but also *patimanteti* 'disputes' D.I. 93[23], Vin. II. 1[12] etc. On the other hand we have *paṭi-* in *paṭimā* 'image' = *pratimā* etc. Michelson[5] would connect *paṭi-* with Skr. *prati-* but *pati-* with Avest. *paiti-*, O. Pers. *patiy-*.—2. *ṭh* appears for *th* in. *paṭhama* 'the first' = *prathama*; *saṭhila* 'uncareful' Dh. 312 f = **śṛthila* (but *sithila* Thl. 277 etc.). Orthography is uncertain in the case of *paṭhavī*, *pathavī* (§ 12.4). Cf. further *kaṭhita* (AMāg. *kaḍhiya*, Māh. *kadhia*) 'made hot', *pakkaṭhita* Thūpavs. 48[33] as against *kvathita*[6].—3. *ḍ* appears for *d* in the two roots *daṃś* 'to bite' and *dah* 'to burn'[7] and their derivatives. Thus *ḍasati*; *saṃḍāsa* 'pincers' Jā. III. 138[12], M. II. 75[12] = *saṃdaṃśa*; *ḍaṃsa* 'gnat' Thl. 31, Vin. I. 3[20] etc. = *daṃśa*. But we have invariably *daṭṭha* 'bitten' = *daṣṭa* and *dāṭhā* (Pkr. *dāḍhā*) 'tooth,' obviously on account of the cerebral inside these words. Further *ḍahati*; *ḍāha* 'glow' M.I. 306[11], JāCo. III. 153[10] = *dāha*. On the other hand we have *daḍḍha*

[1] For changes in the place of articulation of consonants in sound-groups see § 68.

[2] Cerebralisation is much more widespread in Pkr., Pischel, § 218 ff. For cerebralisation in sound-combinations see below § 64.

[3] For *apphoṭā* (a kind of jasmine) Jā. VI. 536[32], the proper reading with cerebral is found also in Skr. *āsphoṭā*.

[4] On the other hand *pataṃga* signifies 'bird' according to Abhp. 624.

[5] IF. 23. 240.

[6] There occurs also *pakkaṭṭhita* (variant reading *pakkuṭṭhita*) DhCo. I. 126[8], III. 310[9] beside *pakkuthita* Th2Co. 292[5]. and *pakkaṭṭhāpeti* 'causes to boil' JāCo, I. 472[7]. How to explain this *ṭṭh* here? On *kuthita* see p. 74, f.-n, 1.

[7] As also in Māh., AMāg., JMāh. ; Pischel, § 222.

'burnt' = *dagdha*. Medially, between vowels, *ḍ* is then further changed into *ḷ*: *āḷāhana* 'pier' D. I. 55²⁶, DhCo. I. 26¹⁸ etc. and *pariḷāha* 'sorrow' Dh. 90 etc. from *dah*. Similarly *uḷāra* 'great' Th1. 65 etc. = *udāra*; *uḷuṅka* (§ 17. 2 *a*) = *udaṅka*; *koviḷāra* (a kind of tree) Jā. VI. 530² = *kovidāra*; *dohaḷa* 'desire during pregnancy' JāCo. III. 28³, DhCo. III. 95⁷, *dohaḷinī* = *dohada*. *dohadinī*[1]; *bubbuḷa(ka)* 'bubble' Dh. 170, Mhvs. 30. 13 = *budbuda*.—4. *ḷh* appears (through *ḍh*) for *dh* in : *dveḷhaka* 'doubt' Smp. 309²¹ from *dvaidha*.—5. *ṇ* appears for *n* in: *sakuṇa* 'bird' = *śakuna*; *saṇa* 'hemp' = *śana*; *saṇiṃ, saṇikaṃ* (§ 22) = **śanam*. A peculiar case is offered by *ñāṇa* 'knowledge' (also *abhiññāṇa* etc.) = *jñāna*. The orthography is sometimes uncertain in Pāli: thus *sanati, saṇati* 'sounds' from root *svan*.

§ 43. Related to the phenomenon of cerebralisation is the sporadical representation of *d* by *r*, of *n* by *l* or *r*, and also of *ṇ* by *ḷ*.—1. For *ḍ* appears (through *d*) an *r²* quite promiscuously in the compound numerals with *dasa* 'ten' such as *ekārasa* (beside *ckādasa*) 'eleven,' etc., as well as in the compounds with *-disa, -dikkha* = *-dr̥kṣa* : *erisa, erikkha* (beside *edisa, edikkha*) = *īdr̥śa, īdr̥kṣa* etc. according to Kacc. IV. 6. 19 (Senart, p. 525). *t* becomes (through *d ḍ*) *r* in *sattari* 'seventy' = *saptati* S. II. 59³⁴, 60¹. Cf. § 112. 3.—2. *l* appears for *n* in : *ela* 'fault' (*anelaka* 'faultless' D. III. 85¹⁷ etc.) = *enas*; *pilandhati, pilandhana* (§ 37) from root *nah*; *Milinda* (proper name) = Menandros (in the last two cases *n* is perhaps due to dissimilation)[3]. For *n* appears *r* in *Nerañjarā* (name of a river) Vin. I. 1⁶ etc. = *Nairañjanā*.— 3. For *ṇ* appear *ḷ*[4] in : *veḷu* (also AMāg. *veḷu* beside *veṇu*) 'bamboo' = *veṇu*; *muḷāla* (§ 12.3) = *mr̥ṇāla*.

§ 44. Representation of *r* by *l* is very common in Pāli, and in Pkr. it is the rule for Māgadhī, although this substitution occurs sporadically also in other dialects[5]. Thus, initially, in *lujjati* 'falls apart', Th1. 929, S. IV. 52⁸ (*palujjati* D. II. 118³¹ etc.) = *rujyate*; *ludda* (§ 15.4) = *raudra*⁶. Sometimes double forms with *l* and *r* occur in Skr. : *lūkha* (AMāg. *lūha* beside *lukkha*) 'gross, bad' Thl. 923, Vin.

---

[1] Lüders, GN. 1908, p. 3.
[2] For Pkr. see Pischel, § 245.
[3] Schulze, KZ. 38 226, f.-n. Cf. Wackernagel, GN. 1906, p. 165, f.-n. 1.
[4] Fausböll, Five Jāt., p. 20.
[5] Pischel, PkrGr. § 256.
[6] In JāCo. IV. 416²⁵ we have *ruddarūpa* with the variant reading *luddarūpa*.

I.55[22] = *lūkṣa*, *rūkṣa*; *lodda* (name of a tree) Jā. VI. 497[25] = *lodhra*, *rodhra*. In Pāli we have *loma*, *roma* (the latter in Abhp. 259, 175) 'hair' and *lohita*, *rohita* (the latter in certain compounds) 'red, blood' as in Skr. Medially *l* stands for *r* in *elaṇḍa* 'Ricinus' M.I. 124[30] = *eraṇḍa*; *taluṇa* 'tender' A. IV. 129[6] (beside *taruṇa* D. I. 114[15]) = *taruṇa*; *tipukkhala* (technical term) Nett. 2[9] etc. = *tripuṣkara*; *daddula* (a kind of rice) D. I. 166[20], A. I. 241[6] = *dardura*; *sajjulasa* (§ 19.2) = *sarjarasa* etc. In the case of *kumbhīla* 'crocodile' we have also in Skr. *kumbhīla* beside *-īra*. Not infrequently there appears *pali-* for *pari-*: *palikhanati* 'exterminates' S.I. 123[6] (verse), II. 88[7] from root *khan* with *pari*; *palissajati* 'embraces' D. II. 266[10] (verse), Jā. V. 204[17] from root *svaj* with *pari*. For other examples see § 39. 1, 2 and Childers. A secondary *r* originating from *d* (§ 43.1) alternates with *l* in *telasa*, *terasa* 'thirteen'.[1]

§ 45. Skr. *l* is more rarely represented by Pāli *r*: *arañjara* (§ 17. 2b) = *aliñjara*; *ārammaṇa* 'basis, object' Sn. 474, M. I. 127[6] etc. = *ālambana*; *kira* (particle) = *kila*; *biḷāla* 'cat' Abhp. 461 (beside the usual *biḷāra* Jā. I. 461[8], *biḷārikā* JāCo. III. 265[10]) = *biḍāra*.—For *l* appears *n* (perhaps through dissimilation) in *naṅgala* (also in AMāg.) 'plough, Thl. 16, D. II. 353[5] etc. = *lāṅgala*; *naṅgula* 'tail' in *goṇaṅgula* (a kind of ape) Thl. 113 = *lāṅgula*[2]; *nalāṭa* 'forehead' D. I. 106[13], JāCo. I. 388[18] = *lalāṭa*. Medially there appears *n* for *l* in *dehanī* 'threshold' Abhp. 219 = *dehalī*[3].

§ 46. Not infrequent is the alternation between *y* and *v*[4]. 1. Pāli *v* appears for Skr. *y*: *āvudha* 'weapon' Dh. 40, A. IV. 107[7], JāCo. 100[1] (*āyudha* Mhvs. 7. 16 etc.) = *āyudha*; *āvuso* Voc. from *āyuṣmant*; *ussāva* (§ 15.4) = *avaśyāya*; *kasāva* 'dirt, sin' Sn. 328, Dh. 9 f. (*kasāyita* Attanagaluvs. 2.2) = *kaṣāya*; *kāsāva* 'yellow robe of monks' = *kāṣāya*; *tāvattiṃsā* (AMāg. *tāvattīsā*) 'the 33 gods' = *trayastriṃśat*; *piṇḍadāvika* 'provision-carrier' D. I. 51[9], D.Co. I. 156[25] for *piṇḍadāyika*; *migavā* 'chase' JāCo. I. 149[28] = *mṛgayā*. The form *kīva(ṃ)* 'how much? how far?' (*kīva-dūraṃ* etc.) is to be compared with Ved. *kīvant* as opposed to Skr. *kiyant*. Beside

[1] For *r* appears *d* in *Puriṃdada* (a name of Indra) D. II. 260[1] (verse) instead of *Puraṃdara*, perhaps through folk-etymology. E. Kuhn. Beitr. p. 43.

[2] Cf. also *naṅguṭṭha* A. II. 245[2], JāCo. I. 370[23] etc., which stands to *naṅgula* as *aṅguṭṭha* 'thumb' to *aṅgula*.

[3] In Abhp. 562 there is also *tintiṇī* 'tamarisk' instead of *tintiḷikā*, *-ḍikā*.

[4] For Pkr. see Pischel, § 254. In the language of Asoka's inscriptions cf *papovā* = *prāpnuyāt*, Michelson, IF. 23.229.

kaṇḍuvati 'scratches' Vin. III. 117[14] = *kaṇḍūyati* there is *kaṇḍūyana* Attanagaluvs. 2. 3. After the svarabhakti-vowel *i* there appears *v* instead of *y* in *paṭiviṃsa*, *-visa* Vin. I. 28[9], DhCo. III. 304[10] = **pratyaṃśa*. Childers cites also *tivaṅgika* out of **tiy-* = **tryaṅgika*, as well as *divaḍḍha* 'one and a half' = **dvyardha* (but in Smp. 285[35], Mhvs. 10.92 there is *diyaḍḍha*). In case of the gemination of *v* there appears (cf. § 51.3) *bb*: *pubba* 'pus' Sn. 671, M. I. 57[19], JāCo. II. 18[16] through **puvva*, **pūva* = *pūya*; *vaṇibbaka* 'begging' D. I. 137[25], DhCo. I. 105[15] = *vaṇīyaka*. Now as in Pāli *b* occasionally appears for Skr. *v*(*kabala* 'morsel' = *kavala*, *kabalikā* 'compress' Vin. I. 205[35] = *kavalikā*, *buḍḍha* 'old' D. II. 162[26] beside *vuḍḍha* = *vṛddha*), so it can naturally appear also for *y* (through the intermediate stage of *v*) *jalābu* 'uterus' M. I. 73[4], S. III. 240[18] (see § 44) = *jarāyu*.—2. Pāli *y* appears for Skr. *v* in: *dāya* 'park' D. II. 4o[19], Vin. I. 8[9] etc. (beside *dāva* JāCo. I. 212[11]) = *dāva*. The Gerund *lāyitvā* Jā. III. 226[24] Vin. III. 64[37], JāCo. I. 215[22], III. 130[5], and the Participle *lāyita* JāCo. III. 130[2] seem to stand for **lāvitvā*, **lāvita* (*lāveti* 'tears out, mows,' root *lū*); E. Kuhn[1] has derived *caccara* 'crossing of roads' Milp. 1[18], JāCo. I. 425[12] through **catyara* from *catvara*. —3. Occasionally *l* appears for *y* as in *laṭṭhi*(*kā*) 'sprout, stick' Jā. III. 161[13], D I. 105[10] beside *yaṭṭhi*(*kā*) JāCo. II. 37[4] = *yaṣṭi*[2]. The mutation of *y* into *r* is however doubtful. The form *antarārati* 'runs risk' cannot be quoted from texts. About the forms *sakhāram*, *sakhāro* instead of *sakhāyam*, *sakhāyas* see below § 84. In *vedhavera* 'son of a widow' Jā. IV. 124[22], VI. 508[13] and *sāmaṇera* 'novice' derived from *vaidhaveya* and *śrāmaṇeya* the suffixes themselves are different. Also *nahāru* 'ligament, string' (§ 50.5) cannot be directly equated with *snāyu*, for it is derived from a side-form with *r* as is shown by Av. *snāvare* and Goth. *snōrjō*[3].—4. *v* and *m* alternate in the people's name Pāli *Damiḷa* = Skr. *Draviḍa*. Cf. also *sāmi* 'porcupine' JāCo. V. 489[32] = *śvāvidh* (Lüders, ZDMG. 61. 643). The forms *vīmaṃsati* 'tests,' *vīmaṃsā*, *-sana*, *-sin* as opposed to Skr. *mīmāṃsate* are to be explained through dissimilation[4].

[1] Beitr. p. 45.

[2] Pischel, § 255.

[3] Johansson, IF. 3.204 f.

[4] Against the derivation given by Fausbõll, Five Jāt. p. 37 (cf. also Andersen, Pāli Glossary, sub voce) from root *mṛś* with *vi* goes the length of *ī* as Senart, Kacc. p. 434 rightly pointed out.

13. Dissimilation and Metathesis

§ 47. Some examples of 1. Dissimilation have been already mentioned in § 41.2, 48.2, 45, 46.4. To them are to be added the following isolated cases: *kipilla, -llikā* 'ant' Sn. 602, Vin. I. 97³, DhCo. III.206¹⁸ = *pipīla, -likā*¹; *takkola* 'bdellium' Abhp. 304 = *kakkola*, but also Skr. *takkola*, Sgh. *takul*. The people's name *Takkola* Milp. 359²⁸ is perhaps = *Karkoṭa*².—2. The liquid *r* is particularly susceptible to metathesis: *ālārika* 'cook' D. I. 51¹⁰ = *ārālika*; *kaṇeru(kā)* 'young elephant' Jā. VI. 497¹, JāCo. VI. 485²² = *kareṇu*; *pārupati* 'covers, dresses' D. I. 246¹⁰, JāCo. II. 24⁴, Mhvs. 22.67, *pārupaṇa*³ 'mantle' JāCo. I. 378⁸, III. 82⁴ beside *pāpuraṇa* (§ 19.2 and 39.6). Metathesis may take place after the insertion of a svarabhakti-vowel: *kayirā* through **kariyā* = **karyāt* from root *kar*⁴; *kayirati* (§ 175) = **karyate*; *payirudāharati* 'utters' D. II. 222¹¹, JāCo. I. 454²⁸ and *payirupāsati* 'sits at the feet (of the teacher)' Thl. 1236 through **pariyud-*, **pariyupa-* = *paryud-*, *paryupa-*; *rahada* 'tank' through **harada* (§ 31.1) = *hrada*. Also *daha* (AMāg. *daha, draha*) Vin. I. 28³, Mhvs. 1.18 is to be explained through **draha* derived from *hrada*. Forms like *acchera* 'wonderful' (§ 27.5) are also cases of metathesis: *āścarya* > **acchariya* > **acchayira* > *acchera*. Finally should be mentioned *makasa* 'mosquito' Sn. 20, A. II. 117³³, JāCo. I. 246²³ through **masaka* = *maśaka*⁵. On *-hīrati, -bhīrati* see § 175.

14. Consonant-groups

Combination of Two Consonants

§ 48. Consonant-groups may be divided by svarabhakti according to § 29. They however remain undivided, 1. if they consist of similar consonants or of a mute with the corresponding aspirate, or 2. if they consist of a nasal with a homorganic mute. In the derivatives

¹ Similarly Sgh. *kubudinu* 'awake' instead of **pubudinu*.

² On these and other doubtful cases see Trenckner, Notes p. 55 f. (JPTS. 1908, p. 109); E. Müller, PGr. p. 39; JPTS. 1888, pp. 18, 37, 50.

³ Johansson (IF. 25. 222 f.) is inclined to derive *pārupati* from an extended root *varp* (I.-E. *verp*).

⁴ On *acchera, ācera, macchera*, where quite the same metathesis is in evidence, see § 27.5.

⁵ Fausböll, Five Jāt., p. 29 derives *makasa* from *makṣa* with svarabhakti; but separation of *kṣ* does not occur anywhere else.

from *pañca* are found however also forms with *nn*, *ṇṇ*, *ññ*: *pannarasa* 'fifteen, fifteenth' (rarely *paṇṇa-*), *paṇṇuvīsa* 'twenty-five' Jā. III. 138[20] beside *pañcadasa* Sn. 402 and *pañcavīsa* Dpvs. 3.29, and only *paṇṇāsa(ṃ)* DhCo. III. 207[12] or *paññāsa(ṃ)* 'fifty' = *pañcāśat*.[1] Assimilation of a mute to a preceding nasal is to be found in *ārammaṇa* (§ 45) = *ālambana*.

§ 49. Consonant-groups containing *h* have to be dealt with separately: 1. Metathesis takes place in the case of groups *h* + nasal, *y* or *v*.[2] Thus *hṇ*, *hn*, *hm*, *hy*, *hv* become respectively *ṇh*, *nh*, *mh*, *yh*, *vh*. Examples: *pubbaṇha* 'forenoon' D. I. 109[29], DhCo. III. 98[20] = *pūrvāhṇa*. Similarly *aparaṇha* 'afternoon' = *aparāhṇa*, and after them also *sāyaṇha* 'evening' = *sāyāhna*; *cinha* 'sign' Abhp. 55 (beside *cihana* with svarabhakti Abhp. 879) = *cihna*; *jimha* 'crooked, false' Jā. III. 111[17], A. V. 289[4] = *jihma*; *vayhā* 'movable chair' Jā. VI. 500[13] from *vāhya*. Similarly in Future Passive Participles: *sayha* 'that which is to be endured' Sn. 253 = *sahya*; in Gerunds: *āruyha* from root *ruh* with *ā* 'to mount' = *āruhya*; in Passives: *duyhati* 'is milked' Milp. 41[1] = *duhyate*.[3] Also *jivhā* 'tongue' D. I. 21[19] etc. = *jihvā*. In compounds we have *bavhābādha* 'ill' M. II. 94[20] = *bahvābādha*; *bavhodaka* 'containing much water' Thl. 390.—2. The combination *hr* undergoes various changes.[4] Initially we find *h* in *hesati* 'neighs' Dāṭhāvs. 44, *hesā*, *hesita* 'neighing' Rasav. II. 98[16], Mhvs. 23.72 = *hreṣate*, *hreṣā*, *hreṣita*; but we have *r* in *rassa* (as opposed to Māg. *hassa*) 'short' Dh. 409, JāCo. I. 356[18] etc. = *hrasva*. Both svarabhakti and metathesis are in evidence in *rahada* = *hrada* (§ 47.2).

§ 50. There should further be mentioned the groups consisting of a sibilant followed by a nasal. As in Pkr.,[5] so in Pāli too, there takes place in these cases, as a rule, metathesis with concomitant mutation of the sibilant into *h*. Frequently there are found parallel forms with svarabhakti which took place in some cases already in the original sound-group and in some cases after metathesis and mutation of *s* into *h*. 1. *śn* becomes *ñh* (Pkr. *ṇh*): *pañha* (AMāg. *paṇha*) 'question,'

[1] Cf. Pkr. AMāg. JMāh. *paṇṇarasa*, *paṇṇāsam* etc. Pischel, § 273. E. Kuhn, KZ. 33.478 tried to explain this phenomenon through dissimilation.

[2] As in Pkr.; Pischel, § 330, 332.

[3] In Pkr. *hy* becomes *jjh*, initially *jh*; Pischel, § 331.

[4] For *hl* may be quoted only *kallahāra* 'white water-lily' Dpvs. 16.19 = *kahlāra*: cf. § 30.4.

[5] Pischel, PkrGr. § 312 ff

=*prañśa*; *pañhipaṇṇī* (sic! not *paṇhi-*) (name of a plant) Abhp. 584=*pṛśniparṇī*.—2. *śm* becomes *mh*: *amhanā* 'with the stone' Sn. 443=*aśmanā*; *amhamaya* 'stony' Dh. 161. Besides also *asmā* Jā. III. 29^{17}. Sometimes *sm*=*śm* is retained in Pāli: *Kasmīra*=*Kāśmīra*; *rasmi* (Pkr. *rassi*) 'ray, rein' Dh. 222, M.I. 124^{21}, JāCo. I. 444^{6} (beside *raṃsi* Sn. 1016, Vv. 52.5)=*raśmi*; *vesma* 'house' Abhp. 206=*veśman*. Initially *ś* is assimilated to *m* (*m*<*mm*) in *massu* (AMāg. *maṃsu*) 'beard' D.I. 60^{17} etc.=*śmaśru*.—3 *ṣṇ* becomes *ṇh*: *uṇha* 'hot, heat' D. Andersen Pāli Gl. sub voce=*uṣṇa*; *uṇhīsa* 'diadem' D. II. 179^{1}, Dpvs. 12.1=*uṣṇīṣa*; *kaṇha* 'black, demoniac' Thl. 140, Vin. III. 20^{30} etc.=*kṛṣṇa*; *taṇhā* 'thirst' (beside rarer *tasiṇā* § 30.5)=*tṛṣṇā*; *tuṇhī* 'silent'=*tūṣṇīm*; *Veṇhu* (§ 10)=*Viṣṇu*; *suṇhā* 'daughter-in-law' through **suṣṇā* from *snuṣā*,[1] beside *suṇisā* (§ 31.2).—4. *ṣm* becomes *mh*: *gimha* 'summer' Dh. 286, Vin. I. 79^{29}, JāCo. I. 390^{26}=*grīṣma*; *semha* (AMāg. *sembha*, *simbha*) 'phlegm'=*śleṣman*; *tumhe*, *tumhākaṃ* etc.=*yuṣme*, *yuṣmākam* etc. (§104). *sm*=*ṣm* is retained in *usmā* 'warmth' D. II. 335^{15} (beside *usumā* §31.2)=*uṣman*; *āyasmant* 'venerable'=*āyuṣmant*; *bhesma* (sic!) 'horrible' Abhp. 167=*bhaiṣma*.—5. *sn* becomes *nh* in: *nhāyati* 'bathes,' *nhāna* 'bath' etc. mostly in verses, beside the forms appearing in prose such as *nahāyati*, *nahāna* (*sunhāta*, *sunahāta* 'well-bathed' D. I. 104^{27}, M. II. 120^{13}, S. I. 71^{11})=*snāyati*, *snāna*; *nhāru* Vin. I. 25^{1} beside the more frequent *nahāru* Sn. 194, M.I. 429^{22} etc. connected with *snāyu* (§ 46.3).—6. *sm* becomes *mh* in: *vimhaya* 'astonishment' Mhvs. 5.92, *vimhita* Mhvs. 6. 19=*vismaya*, *vismita*; *amhe*, *amhākaṃ* etc. (§ 104)=*asmān*, *asmākam* etc. There are moreover the Pāli forms *asme* JāCo. III. 359^{21} (verse), *asmākaṃ* Sn. 102 in which *sm* has been retained. It is retained moreover in *asmi* (beside *amhi*) 'I am', in the endings *-smā* of Abl. Sg. (beside *-mhā*) and *-smiṃ* of Loc. Sg. (beside *-mhi*), in *bhasma* 'ash' Dh. 71, S. I. 169^{25} =*bhasman*. There is svarabhakti in initial *sm* in the case of *sumarati* 'remembers' Dh. 324^{1}=*smarate*; beside it also *sarati* with assimilation. Similarly *sita* 'smile' M. II. 45^{4}, DhCo. III. 479^{7} beside *mihita* JāCo. VI. 504^{30}=*smita*.

§ 51. Moreover, in so far as no svarabhakti intervenes, the assimilation of consonant is characterised by the rule that the consonants of lesser power of resistance are assimilated to those of greater resisting power. The power of resistance diminishes in the order: mutes—

[1] H. Jacobi. Erzählungen in Māhārāshṭrī, p. XXXII. 3 explains Pkr. *suṇhā* through metathesis out of **ṇhusā*. Not so Pischel, § 148.

sibilants—nasals—*l*, *v*, *y*, *r*. Thus an *r* is assimilated to a mute or a sibilant, both when it precedes or follows it. Where a mute is combined with a mute, or a nasal with a nasal, the first consonant is assimilated to the second.

The following details should also be noticed: 1. If the consonant-group contains an aspirate, the aspiration appears at the end of the new group after completed assimilation: *kh* + *y* becomes *kkh*, *k* + *th* becomes *tth*. Aspiration of the resultant group is normally caused also by the presence of a sibilant in the original group: *s* + *t* becomes *tth*.—2. In initial position, there remains only one of the assimilated consonants, which is normally the second one: thus *ṭṭh* becomes *ṭh*. In compounds however the double-consonance normally appears again, and occasionally also in external sandhi. Cf. § 67, 74.1.—3. Wherever according to the laws of assimilation the sound-group *vv* would originate, there appears in P., in contrast to the other Middle Indian dialects, always *bb*[1]; initially however only *v*.—4. Also certain other qualitative changes are concomitant with assimilation: dentals, as well as *n*, are palatalised by a following *y* before the effectuation of assimilation. Sometimes also *k* is palatised in the combination *k* + *ṣ*.—5. Between *m* and a following liquid there is introduced in the first instance the slide-sound *b*[2]. Only after that there takes place assimilation or separation through the svarabhakti-vowel. Examples: *amba* 'mango' Vv 81. 16, JāCo. I. 450[20] etc. through **ambra* = *āmra*; *ambāṭaka* (§ 42. 1) = *ămrātaka*; *tamba* 'red, copper' Vv. 32 3, M. III. 186[15], JāCo. I. 464[7] etc. through **tambra* = *tāmra*; *Tambapaṇṇī* (Ceylon) JāCo. I. 85[11] = *Tāmraparṇī*. Svarabhakti in *ambila* 'sour, acid' JāCo. I. 349[30] etc. through **ambla* = *amla*. In this way is to be explained also *gumba* 'mass, bush' D. I. 84[16], Thl. 23 etc. = *gulma*, with metathesis, from **gumla*, **gumbla*[3].

§ 52. Progressive assimilation takes place 1. in the combination of mute with mute: *chakka* 'collection of six' M. III. 280[33] = *ṣaṭka*; *satthi* 'thigh' Thl. 151, Vv. 81. 17, JāCo. II. 408[5] = *sakthi*; *mugga* 'bean' Jā. III. 55[4], D. II. 293[20], JāCo. I. 274[24] = *mudga*;

[1] Similarly, according to § 6. 2, *yobbana* (Pkr. *jovvaṇa*) 'youth' Dh. 155 f., D. I. 115[16] = *yauvana*.

[2] Also in Pkr.; Pischel. § 295.

[3] No metathesis has taken place in Pkr. *gumma*; here assimilation has been direct.

ugg āta 'blow' Vin. I. 192[2] = *udghāta*.—2. In the combination of sibilant with mute (with aspiration of the resultant group): *acchera* (§ 27.5) = *āścarya*; *nikkha*, *nekkha* (§ 10) = *niṣka*[1]; *apphoṭeti* 'claps the hands' JāCo. VI. 486[17] (*apphoṭana*, *apphoṭita*) = *āsphoṭayati*. Initially: *khalati* 'stumbles' Thl. 45, Milp. 187[12] = *skhalati*; *thaneti* 'thunders' D. II. 260[25] (verse), *thanita* JāCo. I. 470[12] = *stanayati*, *stanita*; *phassa* 'touch' = *sparśa*. There is no assimilation in *bhasta* (§ 40.1 *a*) = *basta* (cf. *bhastā* 'bellows' M. I. 128[21] = *bhastrā*); *vanaspati* 'tree' Jā. I. 329[6], S. IV. 302[23] = *vanaspati*.—3. In the combination of liquid with mute, sibilant or nasal: *kakka* (a precious stone) VvCo. 111[25] = *karka* (*karketana*); *kibbisa* 'sin' Jā. III. 34[13], M. III. 165[5] = *kilbiṣa*; *vāka* (§ 6.1) = *valka*; *kassaka* 'farmer' D. I. 61[16] = *karṣaka*[2]; *ūmi* 'wave' JāCo. I. 498[6], Milp. 3[7] (§ 5 *b*) = *ūrmi*; *kammāsa* 'spotted' D. II. 80[24], A. II. 187[26] = *kalmāṣa*.—4. In the combination of nasal with nasal: *ninna* 'deep, low' Dh. 98, S. IV. 191[1], JāCo. II. 3[6] = *nimna*; *ummūleti* 'uproots' JāCo. I. 328[9] = *unmūlayati*.—5. In the combination of *r* with *l*, *y*, *v*: *dullabha* 'difficult to attain' = *durlabha*; *ayya* 'venerable' Vin. II. 290[28], D. I. 92[13], JāCo. III. 61[13] (beside *ariya* with svarabhakti according to § 30.1) = *ārya*[3]; *udiyyati* 'is heard, resounds' Thl. 1232 = *udīryate*[4]; *niyyāti* 'goes away' D. I. 49[31] (*niyyāna*, *niyyānika*) = *niryāti* etc.; *niyyāma* 'sailor' JāCo. IV. 137[10] = *niryāma*; *niyyāsa* 'resin' Mhvs. 29. 11, Thūpavs. 57[18] = *niryāsa*; *saṃkīyati* 'is mixed up, defiled' S. III. 71[16], A. IV. 246[13] (§ 5*b*) through **-kiyyati* = *saṃkīryate*; *kubbanti* 'they make' Jā III. 118[10] (§ 51.3) = *kurvanti*; *sabba* 'all' = *sarva*; *dubbuṭṭhi(kā)* 'drought' D. I. 11[7], JāCo. VI. 487[6] = *durvṛṣṭi*.[5] In verbs of the type *jīryati*, *pūryate* we have mostly *r* (instead of *yy*, *y*) as the result of the regressive assimilation of *ry*. Thus (*pari*) *pūrati* 'is filled' Dh. 121 f., Jā I. 498[22], JāCo. I. 460[27] = *pūryate*, beside the analogically formed passives *-hīrati*, *-bhīrati* (§ 175). Cf. the doublets *jīyati* 'is digested, becomes old' and *jīrati jīryati*, *-te* (§ 137).

§ 53. Regressive assimilation takes place 1. in the combination of mutes with nasal: *ubbigga* 'anxious' Jā. I. 486[10], JāCo. III. 197[14] =

[1] Similarly *dukkha* 'sorrow' = *duḥkha*.

[2] Cf. *ghaṃsati* 'rubs' (§ 6.3) = *gharṣati*.

[3] In Pkr. *ry* becomes *yy* only in Māg., otherwise *jj*; Pischel, § 287.

[4] The similar form *miyyati* (and *mīyati*) 'dies', which cannot be connected with Skr. *mriyate*, is derived from a **mīryate*.

[5] In analogy with it there appears *bb* also in *subbuṭṭhikā*.

udvigna; *soppa* (§ 25.2) = *svapna*; *abhimatthati* 'rubs, grinds' Dh. 161, S. I. 127[14] = *abhimathnāti*; *chaddan* 'veil, cover' in *vivattacchadda* (of a Buddha) D. I. 89[9], JāCo. I. 56[14] = *chadman*. On the other hand *jñ* becomes *ññ*[1] through progressive assimilation: *paññā*, *paññāṇa* 'knowledge' Sn. 1136, Dh. I. 124[4] = *prajñā*, *prajñāna*; *raññā*, *rañño* Instr. and Gen. Sg. of *rājan* = *rājñā*, *rājñas*. In initial position *jñ* becomes *ñ*: *ñatti* 'request' Vin. I. 56[14] etc. = *jñapti*. For *āṇā* 'order' see § 63.2. The assimilation observed in the form *rumma vati* = *rukmavatī*[2] quoted by E. Kuhn, Beitr. p. 46 from Vuttod. would also be progressive.—2. In the combination of mutes with liquids: *takka* 'whey' JāCo. II. 363[11] = *takra*; *udda* 'otter' Vin. I. 186[21], JāCo. III. 51[26] = *udra*; *sobbha* (§ 25.2) = *śubhra*; *sukka* 'white' = *śukla*. In initial position there appears in these cases only a single mute: *kayavikkaya* 'purchase and sale' D. I. 5[10] = *krayavikraya*; *tāṇa* 'protection' Dh. 288. M. III. 165[5] = *trāṇa*; *bhātar* 'brother' = *bhrātar*. Sometimes the combination mute + *r* remains unchanged: *nigrodha* (§ 21) = *nyagrodha*; *tatra* 'there' Thl. 31, Vin. I. 10[32], D.I. 76[23] (beside *tattha* Thl. 185) = *tatra*; *citra* 'multicoloured' Jā. VI. 497[16], D. I. 7[22] (beside *citta* Dh. 151) = *citra*; *bhadra* 'happy' S. I. 117[24] etc. (beside *bhadda* D. II. 95[17] etc.) = *bhadra*; *udrīyati* 'is split' S. I. 113[15], D. I. 96[17] (*udraya* 'fruit, reward' S. II. 29[12], A. I. 97[31]) from **uddrıyate* for *uddīryate*[3]. The Part. Pres. *atricchaṃ* Jā. I. 414[6], III. 207[15] is explained in the commentary by *atra atra icchanto* 'desiring this and that'; cf. *atriccha* 'desirous' JāCo. III. 206[16], *atricchatā* 'covetousness' JāCo. III. 222[6]. In *atrajā* 'son, daughter' Jā. III. 181[4], Dpvs. 18.29 through **attajā* = *ātmajā* the *tr* originated through folk-etymology.—3. In the combination of mutes with semi-vowels (dental + *y* will be discussed in § 55): *sakka* 'capable' = *śakya*; *vuccati* 'is said' = *ucyate*; *kuḍḍa* 'wall' D. I. 78[3], S. III. 238[25] = *kuḍya*; *pajjalati* 'burns' D. II. 163[20] etc. = *prajvalati*; *labbha* 'attainable' Jā. III. 204[27], M. II. 220[13] = *labhya*; *cattāro* 'four' = *catvāras*; *addhan* 'way' = *adhvan*; *saddala* 'grassy' Thl. 211. Jā. VI. 518[21] = *śādvala*. In initial position there appears only the single mute: *kaṭhita* (§ 42.2) = *kvathita*; *dija* (poetic term) 'bird'

[1] In Pkr. *jñ* mostly becomes *ṇṇ*; Pischel, § 276.

[2] Another *rumma* is to be found in *rummavāsī* 'irregularly dressed' Jā. IV. 380[1], 384[3]; cf. also *rummī* Jā. IV. 322[1] (Com. = *anañjıtāmaṇḍita*).

[3] The verb *udrabhati*, *-bheti* 'tears off' M. I. 306[12],[15] (in 307[2] we have *udraheyyuṃ*) is derived from a root **drabh* or **drah* (Skr *darh*) with *ud*.

D. II. 258[22] (verse), Jā. II. 205[15] = *dvija*; *dhanita* 'resounding' DCo. I. 177[1], Milp. 344[2], JPTS. 1887, p. 26[18] = *dhvanita*[1]. But we find initially *b* for *dv* in *bārasa* 'twelve', *bāvīsati*, *battiṃsa* (§ 116. 2). Sometimes the combination mute + semi-vowel remains unchanged: *vākya* (poetic term) 'word, speech' D. II. 166[5] (verse) etc. = *vākya*[2]; *ārogya* 'good health' Jā. I. 366[24], D. I. 11[9], JāCo. I. 367[3] = *ārogya*; *kvaṃ* 'where, how', *kvaci* 'somewhere' = *kva*, *kvacit*; the gerundial suffixes *-tvā*, *tvāna*; *dve* 'two' (beside *duve*), *dvidhā* D. II. 341[3], *dvedhā* Vin. I. 97[5] etc. = *dve*, *dvidhā*, *dvedhā* etc. In compositional combination *ḍv*, *dv* become *bb*[3] through *vv* due to progressive assimilation (cf. § 55, 57): *ubbiga* (see § 53. 1) = *udvigna*; *ubbilla* (§ 15. 1) from root *vell* with *ud*; *ubbāsīyati* 'becomes depopulated' Mhvs. 6. 22 (Pass. of the Caus. of root *vas* with *ud*); *ubbaṭṭeti* 'anoints' Thūpavs. 39[11] = *udvartayati*; *ubbinaya* 'against the Vinaya' Vin. II. 306[20] = **udvinaya*; *ubbejitar* 'one who causes excitement' Pu. 47[17] from root *vij* with *ud*; *tabbaṃsika* 'descended from this family' Mhvs. 37.89 (= Cūlavs. 37. 39 ed. Colombo) from *tadvaṃś-*. Similarly *chabbaṇṇa* 'six-coloured' Mhvs. 17.48 = *ṣaḍvarṇa*; *chabbīsati* 'twenty-six' = *ṣaḍviṃśati*.

§ 54. **Regressive assimilation** takes place 4. in the combination of sibilant with liquids or semi-vowels: *missa* 'mixed' Thl. 143. JāCo. III. 95[4] = *miśra*; *avassaṃ* 'necessary' DhCo. III. 170[23] = *avaśyam*; *vayassa* 'friend' JāCo. II. 31[9] = *vayasya*; *assa* 'horse' = *aśva*; *palissajati* (§ 44) = *pariṣvajate*[4]. In initial position there is only *s*: *sota* 'stream' = *srotas*; *semha* (§ 5) = *śleṣman*; *sandana* 'chariot' Jā. VI. 511[3] = *syandana*; *seta* 'white' = *śveta*. Initially *sv* is retained in *sve* 'to-morrow' (beside *suve*) = *śvas*, *svātanāya* 'for next day'[5] and in forms like *svākkhāta* 'well-proclaimed' from *su-ākhyāta*, *svāgata* 'welcome' Vv. 63. 4, D. I. 179[16] (variant reading *sāg-*) = *svāgata*.—The combination *ṣy* becomes *h* in future forms like *ehisi* 'you will go,' *ehiti* (beside *essasi*, *essati*) = *eṣyasi*, *eṣyati*. Similarly *kāhāmi* 'I shall do,' *kāhasi*, *kāhati* through **kassāmi*, **kāsāmi* from **karṣyāmi*. See § 153. 1.—5. In the

1 Minayeff, PGr. p. 49, § 3; Morris, Transactions Congr. of Or., London 1892. I. 482 f.

2 For the proper name *Sākya* cf. p 64, f.-n. 2.

3 In Pkr. too *dv* becomes *vv* in combinations with *ud*; Pischel § 298 (towards the end).

4 The verbs *ossakkati*, *paccosakkati* (§ 28.2) are to be explained through **sāsakkati*.

5 Johansson, Monde Oriental 1907/8, p. 106 f.

combination of nasal or liquid *l* with semi-vowels (*n*, *ṇ*+*y* will be discussed in § 55); *saṃmannati* 'agrees' Vin. I. 106[4], II. 295[11] from root *man* (*manve*, not=*manye*)+*sam*; *samannesati* 'seeks' D. I. 105[25], S. I. 194[28] from root *iṣ* with *sam-anu* and similar compounds with *anu*; *kiṇṇa* 'ferment' Abhp. 533=*kiṇva*; *ramma* 'graceful' Thl. 63, Dpvs. 1. 69=*ramya*; *kalla* 'ready, possible' Vin. I. 16[1], D. I. 157[26], S. IV. 25[2]=*kalya*; *billa* (a kind of fruit) A. V. 170[26]=*bilva*; *bella* (the same fruit) Jā. III. 77[24] (besides *beluva* M. II. 6[35])=*bailva*; *khallāṭa* 'bald' (in *Khallāṭanāga* Mhvs. 33. 29)=*khalvāṭa*; *pallaṅka* 'seat with cross-legs'=*paryaṅka* presupposes a **palyaṅka* just as *pallattha*=*paryasta* presupposes a **palyattha*. The combination *nv* is retained in *anvadeva* 'afterwards' D. II. 172[25], M. III. 172[29]; *anveti* follows'=*anveti*; *anvaya* 'progeny' D. II. 261[9] (verse), M. I. 69[5] (besides *durannaya* 'difficult to follow' Dh. 92, Jā. II. 86[2])=*anvaya*, etc. Similarly *my* in °*kamya*, °*kamyatā* 'wishing something, desire for something' Vin. IV. 12[24], Thl. 1241=°*kāmya*, °*kāmyatā*; *ly* in *malya* 'flower' Vv. 1. 1, 2. 1=*mālya*, etc. In flexion we have, *e.g.*, *pipphalyā* (Gāthā-language!) Vv. 43. 6 (I. Sg. of) *pipphalī* 'pepper'.—6. In the combinations *vy*, *vr* which become *bb* (through *vv*): *paribbaya* 'expenditure' JāCo. I. 433[18]=*parivyaya*; *udayabbaya* (in composition) 'origin and decay' Thl. 10, 23=*udaya*+*vyaya*; *tibba* 'sharp' Dh. 349, S. I. 110[15]=*tīvra*; *patibbatā* (in composition) 'devoted to the husband' Jā. VI. 533[7]=*pativratā*. Initially we have *v* in: *vapayanti* 'they go away, disappear' Vin. I. 2[5] from root *i* with *vi-apa*; *vāḷa* 'beast of prey, snake' Jā. VI. 497[13], JāCo. I. 99[14]=*vyāḍa*; *vata* 'religious observance' Vv. 84. 24, S. I. 201[29], JāCo. III. 75[1]=*vrata*[1]; *vo-* (§ 26. 2)=*vyava*. Also in composition as in *udayavaya* A. II. 45[26] besides *udayabbaya* (see above). Frequently however *vy* is retained as in: *vyāseka* 'mixing up' DCo. I. 183[24], *vyāsiñcati* 'is mixed' S. IV. 78[7] from root *sic* with *vi-ā*; *vyeti* 'bifurcates' Thl. 170 (*vyagā*)=*vyeti*; *vyāvaṭa* (§ 38.5)=*vyāpṛta*, etc. In manuscripts from hinter-India *by-* is written for *vy-* in these cases. Medially we have *vy* in *paṭhavyā* Dpvs. 5. 2 (Loc. Sg.) besides *paṭhaviyaṃ*, and in the composition *udayavyaya* D. II. 35[15] (var. reading *-bb-*).

§ 55. Palatalisation takes place in the combination of dentals

[1] The word *sorata* 'kind' and its abstract noun *soracca* should not be derived from *suvrata* which has become *subbata* in Pāli, but from *saurata*, *sauratya*, (the opposite view is expressed in JPTS. 1909, p. 233).

(including *n*) with *y*, as well as in the combination of *ṇ* with *y* (cf. § 51.4): *sacca* 'true' = *satya*; *racchā* 'street' JāCo. I. 425^{12} (besides *rathiyā* D. I. 83^{6}) = *rathyā*; *chijjati* 'is split' = *chidyate*; *dvojjha* 'falsity, uncertainty' A. III. 403^{10} = *dvaidhya*; *añña* 'another' = *anya*[1]. In flexion: *jaccā* Jā. III. 395^{6}, Sn. 136 (besides *jātiyā*) Ins. Sg. from *jāti* 'birth'; *najjā* Vin. I. 1^{6} (besides *nadiyā*) G. Sg. from *nadī*. Initially: *cajati* 'leaves' = *tyajati*; *jotati* 'lightens up' JāCo. I. 53^{4} = *dyotate*; *ñāya* 'method' D. II. 21^{2} etc. = *nyāya*. Examples of *ññ* from *ṇy*: *kammañña* 'ready for use' A. I. 9^{31}, Vin. I. 182^{31} (besides *kammaṇiya* D. I. 76^{14}, Vin. III. 4^{19}) = *karmaṇya*; *piññāka* 'oil-cake' D. I. 166^{22}, Pu. 55^{25} = *piṇyāka*, etc. The rule seems to apply also in the case of the combination cerebral + *y*: *vekurañjā* <**vaikuraṇḍya* from *vikuraṇḍa* 'without testicle' (Skr. *kuraṇḍa*). But *aḍḍha* 'rich' = *āḍhya*. When *ud* precedes a word beginning with *y*, the combination *dy* becomes *yy* through progressive assimilation (cf. § 53.3, 57): *uyyāna* 'garden' = *udyāna*; *uyyutta* 'alert' DhCo. III. 451^{15} = *udyukta*, etc.[2]

§ 56. The Skr. sound-group *kṣ* requires special treatment. 1. Where Skr. *kṣ* = Indo-Iranian *kṣ* or *śṣ*, it is represented as in Prākrit by *kkh* or *cch*. Pischel's hypothesis, according to which Pkr. *kkh* should be derived from Indo-Iranian *kṣ* = Avestan *Xš*, and Pkr. *cch* from Indo-Iranian *śṣ* = Avestan *š*, although both have coincided in *kṣ* in Skr.,[3] can be as little proved from the actual state of things in Pāli as from that in Pkr. Rather it seems that *kkh* and *cch* appear quite promiscuously, sometimes in accordance with, but as often in opposition to, the indication of the Avestan language. Sometimes even Pāli and Pkr. do not agree with each other, and not infrequently both forms are found side by side also in P. as in Pkr. (*a*) We have *kkh* in P. *dakkhiṇa* (similarly Pkr. but Avestan *dašina*) = *dakṣiṇa*; *makkhikā* 'fly' (Av. *maXši*, but Pkr. *macchiā*[4]) = *makṣikā*. Initially: *khudā* (§ 40.2 *b*) = *kṣudhā* (Av. *šuδa*, Pkr. *khuhā* and *chuhā*) etc. (*b*) We find *cch* in *kaccha* (similarly in Māh., *kakkha* in AMāg. JMāh.: Av. *kaša*) 'axis, arm' Sn. 449, Vin. I. 15^{10}, JāCo. II. 88^{18} = *kakṣa*; *tacchati* (Pkr.

[1] In Pkr. *ny* becomes *ṇṇ*, which is also written as *nn* in the Jaina works: Pischel, § 282.

[2] In Pkr. we get *jj*, which however (in analogy with *vv* from *dv*) is not directly derived from *dy*, but from *yy*.

[3] Pischel, GGA. 1881, p. 1322; PkrGr. § 316 ff.

[4] Only Ś. *ṇimmakkhia* = *nirmakṣika*.

takkhaï and *tacchaï*, Av. *tašan*) 'to shape' D. II. 341[1], JāCo. I. 247[14] =*takṣati*, etc. Initially: *chārikā* 'ash' Ud. 93[3], D. II. 164[6]=*kṣārikā*, etc. (c) Sometimes in P. *kkh* and *cch* alternate in one and the same word: *acchi* 'eye' Abhp. 149 besides the usual *akkhi*=*akṣi* (Pkr. *akkhi* and *acchi*, Av. *aši*); *ucchu* (§ 16.1*a*)=*ikṣu* (Pkr. *ucchu*, in AMāg. also *ukkhu*) besides *Okkāka* (p. 66, f.-n. 1) through **Ukk-*, **Ukkh-*= *Ikṣvāku*; *accha* (§ 12.1) besides *ikka* (for **ikkha*, § 12.2 and § 62.2) =*ṛkṣa* (AMāg. *accha* and *riccha*, Av. *arəša*). A differentiation in meaning has come about in *chaṇa* 'festival' JāCo. I. 423[9] and *khaṇa* 'moment' Thl. 231, Vin. I. 12[12]=*kṣaṇa*, as well as in *chamā* 'earth' Sn. 401, M. III. 164[25] and *khamā* 'forgiveness' Abhp. 161 (also *khamā* 'earth' Abhp. 994)=*kṣamā*.[1]—2. Where Skr. *kṣ* corresponds to the Indo-Iranian sonant-group *ẑẓ*=Av. *γž*, there appears in P. *ggh*, *jjh* and in Pkr. *jjh*.[2] Cf. *paggharati* 'drips' Thl. 394 etc. =*prakṣarati*. Similarly *uggharati* Thl. 394, D. II. 347[18]. Initially we have *jh*: *jhāma* (so also in AMāg.) 'burnt' S. IV. 193[17], JāCo. I. 238[14], DhCo. I. 118[24]=*kṣāma*; *jhāyati*(AMāg. *jhiyāï*)'burns (intrans.)' Ud. 93[3], A. I. 137[12], JāCo. I. 485[6]=*kṣāyati*; *jhāpeti* 'burns (transitive)' D. II. 159[26], JāCo. III. 164[6] etc. =*kṣăpayati*.

§ 57. Finally the Skr. sound-groups *ts* and *ps* have to be mentioned. Both become *cch* in P.: *kucchita* 'despicable' VvCo. 215[1]= *kutsita*; *maccharin* 'jealous' Dh. 262, Vv. 52.26, JāCo. I. 345[18]= *matsarin*; *vacchatara* 'ox' D.I. 127[12], A. IV. 41[11] =*vatsatara*; *accharā* 'nymph'=*apsaras*; *jigucchā jigucchati* (§ 18.2)=*jugupsā*, *jugupsate*. Skr. *icchati* and *īpsate* have coincided in *icchati* 'wishes'. Through dialectical influence *ts* appears as *th* initially in *tharu*(also AMāg. *tharu*, besides *charu*) 'handle, sword' A. III. 152[32], JāCo. III. 221[1]=*tsaru*. The representation of *ps* by *ch* in initial position is quite regular: *chāta* 'hungry' Jā. III. 199[2], JāCo. I. 345[29]=*psāta*.—In composition, when *t* (*d*) at the end of a word combines with an initial Skr. *ś* or *s*, the resulting sound-groups **tś* (=Skr. *cch*), *ts* become *ss* through progressive assimilation. In rare cases there appears *cch*[3], mostly in combinations with *ud*. Cf. § 53.3, 55. Examples for *ts*: *ussada* 'friction' DhCo. I. 28[15] (verse), JāCo. IV. 188[13] from Skr. *utsādana*

[1] *khudda* 'small' Thl. 43, Vin. II. 287[31] and *chuddha* 'despised' Dh. 41 are of course not both=*kṣudra* as Childers explains them in his dictionary; the latter rather= *kṣubdha*. We have moreover P. *khubbhati* Jā. VI. 489[13] and *khobheti* JāCo. I. 501[31].

[2] Pischel, § 326.

[3] So also in Pkr.; Pischel, § 327a.

(*ucchādana*); *ussanna* 'increased' Vin. I. 71[34], DhCo. III. 425[10] = *utsanna*; *ussava* 'festival' JāCo. III. 87[3] = *utsava*; *ussahati* 'exerts' D. I. 135[20], JāCo. II. 19[25], *ussāha* Vin. I. 58[19], *ussoḷhi* Dhs. 13, 22, Vbh. 217[7] = *utsahate*, *utsāha*, **utsoḍhi*; *ussiñcati* 'exhausts' JāCo. I. 450[11] = *utsiñcati*; *ussuka* 'eager' Dh. 199, *ussukka* (§ 15.4) = *utsuka*, *autsukya*; *ussūra* 'evening' DhCo. III. 305[12] = *utsūra*. Also *tassāruppa* 'corresponding to that' M. III. 163[19] from *tat* + *sār-*. Examples for **tś* (Skr. *cch*): *ussaṅkin* 'coward' Vin. II. 190[23] from root *śaṅk* with *ud*; *ussīsaka* (JMāh. *ūsīsaa*) 'head-end (of bed)' JāCo. II. 410[20], Mhvs. 30.77 = *ucchīrṣaka* (*ud* + *śīrṣa*); *ussussati* 'dries up' S. I. 126[2] = *ucchuṣyati* (*śuṣ* with *ud*). On the other hand we find in P. *cch* for *ts* in *ucchaṅga* 'lap' Jā. I. 308[5], JāCo. II. 412[8] = *utsaṅga*; *ucchādana* 'annihilation' D.I. 76[18], S. IV. 83[27], 'friction' (besides *ussada*, see above) D. I. 7[19], DCo. I. 88[12] = *utsādana*; *cch* appears also for **tś* in *ucchiṭṭha* 'leaving' Jā. VI. 508[7], DhCo. III. 208[2] = *ucchiṣṭa* (*śiṣ* with *ud*).

Combination of more than two Consonants

§ 58. Under the influence of the general laws of assimilation, groups of more than two consonants are reduced to combinations of two.—1. Where a nasal preceding a mute stands at the beginning of a group, it remains according to § 48, and the following consonants are assimilated and simplified: *ānañca* 'infinity' is derived from *ānantya* through **ānañcca* (§ 55); *randha* 'hole' Jā. III. 192[29], A. IV. 25[15], DhCo. III. 376[10] is derived from *randhra* through **randdha*; *kaṅkhā* 'doubt' from *kāṅkṣā* through **kaṅkkhā*.—2. When a heavy consonant (mute or sibilant) stands between light consonants (nasal, liquid, semi-vowel) at first the first light consonant is assimilated to the heavy one: *macca* 'man' is derived from *martya* through **mattya*, **matya*; *paṇhi(kā)* 'heel' D. II. 17[19], JāCo. I. 491[10] from *pārṣṇi* through **paṣṣni*, **paṣni*; *akamha* 'we did' (§159.III) is likewise derived from *akārṣma*. Svarabhakti is in evidence in *vaṭuma* 'path' D. II. 8[5], S. IV. 52[21] through **vaṭṭma*, **vaṭma* = *vartman*, as well as in *pāṣani*(?) 'heel' Abhp. 277 besides *paṇhi*.—3. In the same manner, assimilation and simplification of the first two consonants take place at first in those cases where a light consonant stands at the end of the group, and two heavy consonants or one light and one heavy consonant stand at the beginning of the group: *oṭṭha* (§ 10) through **uṭṭhra*, **uṭhra* = *uṣṭra*; *tikkha* 'sharp' Jā, III. 151[5], S. I. 191[10], Vin. I. 6[26] through **tikkhṇa*, **tikhṇa* = *tīkṣṇa*; *dāṭhā* 'tooth' besides *daṭṭhā* Milp.

150[8] = *daṃṣṭrā*. Svarabhakti however may take place, though mostly in the last stage: *tikhiṇa* 'sharp' JāCo. II. 18[21] etc. besides *tikkha*; *pakhuma* 'eyelid' D. II. 18[28], Th2Co. 255[14] = *pakṣman*; *sukhuma* 'tender' = *sūkṣma*[1]. Taking into consideration also § 57, we are then in a position to understand also *ussāpeti* 'raises' Vin. III. 203[1] = *ucchrāpayati* (root *śri* with *ud*), (*sam*)*ussita* = (*sam*)*ucchrita*, (*sam*)*ussaya* = (*sam*)*ucchraya*. The *v* is retained in Gerunds like *mutvā* = *muktvā*, *patvā* = *āptvā* with *pra*, *vatvā* = *uktvā*. Similarly *y* is retained in forms like *ratyā* 'at night' = *rātryām*, *ratyo* 'the nights' = *rātryas*,[2] as well as in *agyantarāya* 'hindrance through fire' Vin. I. 112[37], *agyāgāra* D. I. 101[22], Vin. I. 24[21] from *aggi* + *antarāya* (*āgāra*).—4. Groups consisting only of heavy consonants are found in composition in forms like *uggharati* (§ 56.2) from root *kṣar* with *ud* and *nicchubbati* 'thrusts out' Bu. 11.15, Jā. III. 512[11], Milp. 130[19] from root *kṣubh* with *nis*[3]. In these cases *kṣ* at the beginning of the root at first became *gh* and *ch* respectively, to which then the final consonant of the preposition was assimilated.

§ 59. Some details: 1. The sound-groups *kṣṇ*, *kṣm*, *tsn* may be treated as *ṣṇ*, *ṣm*, *sn*,[4] and thus according to § 50.3-5 they may be changed into *ṇh*, *mh*, *nh*: *saṇha* 'tender' = *ślakṣṇa*; *tiṇha* 'sharp' D. I. 56[32], JāCo. III. 89[14] (besides *tikkha*, *tikhiṇa*) = *tīkṣṇa*; *abhiṇhaṃ* 'repeatedly' Jā. I. 190[5], A. V. 87[29], Pu. 48[9], JāCo. II. 39[11] (besides *abhikkhaṇaṃ*) = *abhīkṣṇam*; *abhiṇhaso* 'continuously' Thl. 25 = *abhīkṣṇaśas*; *pamha* 'eyelid' Th2. 383, VvCo. 162[27] (besides *pakhuma*) = *pakṣman*; *juṇhā* (with cerebralisation, for **junhā*, as also Pkr. *joṇhā*) 'moonlight' = *jyotsnā* (cf. § 15.3).—2. *ts* is treated as in composition in *dosina* 'clear' D. I. 47[10], JāCo. I. 509[8] (besides *juṇha*) through **dossna*, **dosna* = *jyautsna* (cf. § 63.3) and in *kasina* 'whole' Abhp. 702 = *kṛtsna*. In the same manner is treated *cch* in *kasira* 'difficult' (besides *kiccha*; cf. *kicchena kasirena* 'with much labour' Vin. I. 195[6], JāCo I. 338[29] etc.) = *kṛcchra*.—3. Besides *uddhaṃ* 'upwards' = *ūrdhvaṃ* there is also *ubbhaṃ*[5] Thl. 163. Here *dhv* is treated like *dv* in composition

[1] In *hammiya* 'but' Vin. I. 58[20], II. 146[29] = *harmya*, as well as in *abhikkhaṇaṃ* 'repeatedly' M.1. 129[25] = *abhīkṣṇam* the Svarabhakti has taken place in the first stage.

[2] The sentences *ratyā ruccati cando*, *ratyo amoghā gacchanti* are quoted by Subhūti, Nām. p. 38.

[3] Wrongly E. Müller, PGr, p. 9.

[4] Also in Pkr.; Pischel, § 312.

[5] Also in Pkr. *ubbha* besides *uddha*; Pischel, § 300.

§53. 3).—4. From Skr. *dṛṣṭvā* Gerund of root *dṛś* 'to see' we get Pāli *disvā*, as also AMāg. *dissā*.[1]

15. *Sporadical Phonological Aberrations in Sound-groups*

§ 60. One of these sporadical phonological phenomena in sound-groups is the representation of a sonant aspirate (cf. § 37) by *h* in the group *bhy*, which became *yh* through metathesis in *tuyhaṃ* = *tubhyam*. But it is perhaps formed in analogy with *mayhaṃ* = *mahyam*. The group *dhv* became *vh* in the ending of the 2. Pl. Pres. Med. *-vhe* = *-dhve*. Moreover, in some words *h* alternates with an aspirated media after a nasal. Thus in *-sumbhati* 'strikes' Jā. VI. 549[6], VvCo. 212[22], Pv. III. 1. 7, 8, Th2. 302 and *-sumhati* Jā. III. 185[9], JāCo. III. 435[9]; *vambheti* 'shames,' *vambhanā* D. I. 90[25], M. I. 523[36], A. V 150[7], Vin. IV. 6[1], DhCo. IV. 38[11] and *vamheti*, *vamhanā* JāCo. I. 454[20], 356[3]. The roots underlying these forms seem to have been *sumbh*, *vambh*.[2] Besides *rundhati* 'encloses' JāCo. I. 409[30], *saṃnirundhati* M. I. 115[32] we have-*rumbhati* JāCo. I. 62[31], II. 341[10] and *-rumhati* JāCo. II. 6[27], VvCo. 217[27] There was thus clearly a root *rubh* (*rumbh*) beside *rudh* (*rundh*)[3]. Similarly, we have further (*sam*)*ūhanti* 'removes' D. II. 254[18], M. II. 193[3], (*sam*)*ūhata* Thl. 223, which stand for *(*sam*)*ūdhanti*, *(*sam*)*uddhanti*, *(*sam*)*uddhata* from root *han* with *sam-ud*.

§ 61. 1. Softening of tenues (cf. § 38) sometimes occurs after a nasal: *nighaṇḍu* 'vocabulary' D. I. 88[5], A. III. 223[19] = *nighaṇṭu*; *gandha* 'book' Mhvs. 34. 66 besides *gantha* DhCo. I. 7[18] = *grantha*; the interjection *handa* = *hanta*; *aḍḍhuḍḍha* 'three and a half' Vin. I. 34[10] instead of *-*uṭṭha*. But *puñjati* 'rubs off' JāCo. I. 318[5] for' *puñchati* JāCo. I. 392[11] etc. = *proñchati* is perhaps merely a graphic error. The group *kkh* was softened in *sagghasi* 'you will be able to ' instead of *sakkhasi* Sn. 834 = *śakṣyasi*. On *leḍḍu* see § 62. 2. —2. Hardening of media (cf. § 39) is found in *bhiṅkāra* ' jug ' (however with the frequent variant reading with *g*) D. II 172[21], Dpvs. 11. 32 = *bhṛṅgāra*; *tippa* ' sharp ' Jā. VI. 507[7], M. I. 10[29], Milp.

[1] Pischel. § 334.

[2] Not so R. O. Franke, WZKM. 8. 331.

[3] Cf. Māh., AMāg. *rumbhai* and *rundhai*; Fausböll, Ten Jātakas, p. 93; E. Kuhn, Beitr. p. 42; Pischel, PkrGr. § 507.

148[16] besides *tibba* Dh. 349, S. I. 110[18]=*tīvra*[1]; *vilāka* 'slim' Jā. IV. 19[29], V. 215[19] through **vilakka *vilagga*=*vilagna*.

§ 62. Unetymological aspiration or de-aspiration of sound-groups (cf. § 40) is not rare.—1. Unetymological aspiration: *siṅghāṭaka* (also AMāg. *siṅghāḍaka*) 'road-crossing'=*śṛṅgāṭaka*; *Khandhapura* (name of a city) Sāsvs. 81[25] from *Skanda* (name of the war-god); *pipphala* 'Ficus Religiosa' Abhp. 909=*pippala*; *pipphalī* 'pepper' Jā. III. 85[24], S. V. 79[22], Vv. 43. 6=*pippalī*. Such aspiration is often caused by *r*: *acchi* 'light' S. IV. 290[27] besides *acci*=*arcis*; *koccha* (§ 10)=*kūrca*.[2] Sometimes the *r* occupies the second position in the original sound-group: *tattha* 'there' (besides *tatra*, § 53.2)=*tatra*; *sotthiya* 'Brahman' (besides *sottiya*)=*śrotriya*; *paripphoseti* 'sprinkles' M. III. 243[17] from root *pruṣ* with *pari* (*paripphosaka* 'besprinkled all around' D. I. 74[3], M II. 15[13] etc.). Initial aspiration: *khiḍḍā* 'play' (beside *kīḷā*) through **khīḍā*=*krīḍā*; *phāsu(ka)* 'comfortable,' if it is connected with Vedic *prāśu*.[3]—2. De-aspiration: *lodda* (§ 44)=*lodhra*, *rodhra*; *babbu(ka)* 'cat' Jā. I. 480[1]=*babhru*; *bunda* 'root' Abhp. 549 (with concomitant metathesis)=*budhna* (cf. *bondi* 'body' Pv. IV. 3. 32); *muccati* 'coagulates' Dh. 71, DhCo. II. 67[22]=*mūrchati*.[4] The form *milāca* 'forest-dweller' Jā. IV. 291[3] is perhaps a variant of *milakkha* (§ 4, and derived from **milacca*, **milaccha*. The form *ludda(ka)* 'hunter' DhCo. III. 31[7], Mhvs. 28. 41=*lubdha(ka)* is perhaps due to contamination with *ludda* 'cruel' (§15.4, 44). On *aṭṭa* =*artha* see §64.1. Not infrequently the expected aspiration (according to § 51.1) does not take place in groups containing a sibilant. Thus, when the sibilant is first in the group: *saccessati* 'will interrupt(?)' A. IV. 343[25] from root *saśc*; *kukku* (§ 16.1 *a*)=*kiṣku*; *catukka* 'a collection of four, crossing of roads' Dāṭhāvs. 1. 58, JāCo. III. 44[6], Milp. 1[18]=*catuṣka*; *nippesika* 'cheat' (?) D. I. 8[30]=*naiṣpeṣika*; *bappa* 'tear' Abhp. 260=*bāṣpa*[5]; *maṭṭa* 'polished' D. II. 133[6] (besides *maṭṭha* Vv. 84. 17, DhCo. I. 25[9])=*mṛṣṭa*; *(abhi)vaṭṭa* 'he who has

1 On account of its meaning the form cannot be derived from *tṛpra*.

2 Similarly to be considered perhaps also *dubbhati* 'injures' Thl. 1129, S.I. 225[10] etc. (*dūbhin* 'malignant' Jā. III. 73[28], *mittadubbhika* 'treacherous' Mhvs. 4. 1.), which I am inclined to connect not with *druh*—from it is derived *mittaddu* S. I. 222[31] (verse), Mhvs. 4. 3—but with *durv dūrvati* (*dhurv*).

3 Not so Pischel, PkrGr. § 208.

4 Besides it *muccheti* 'sounds, plays (on the lyre)' JāCo. III 188[23]=*mūrchayati*.

5 According to Mārkaṇḍeya in Pischel § 305 the form *bappa* in the sense of 'tears is said to have been current also in Śaurasenī.

showered rain ' JāCo. I. 487[28]; Milp. 176[1] (besides *vaṭṭha*, *vuṭṭha*) = *vṛṣṭa*; (*pacc*)*osakkati* (p. 97, f.-n. 4) from root *ṣvaṣk*; *takkara* 'thief' Abhp. 522 = *taskara*; *saṃtatta* 'horrified' = *saṃtrasta*; as well as *Indapatta* (name of city) (beside *-pattha*) = *Indraprastha*.[1] In *leḍḍu* 'clod of earth' M.I. 123[32], JāCo. III. 16[18] through **leṭṭhu*, **leṭṭu* = *leṣṭu*[2] there is concomitant softening of the group (§ 61.1). In composition, the expected aspiration is missed in: *niccala* 'immovable' = *niścala*; *duccarita* 'bad deed' = *duścarita*; *duttara* 'difficult to cross' = *dustara*; *namakkāra* 'obeisance' JāCo. II. 35[1] = *namaskāra*; also *majjhatta* 'impartial' JāCo. I. 300[18], Mhvs. 21.14 = *madhyastha*. Missing aspiration in sound-groups with the sibilant in second position: *dhaṅka* 'crane' ThI. 151, Jā. II. 208[19], 'crow' S. I. 207[29] (verse), VvCo. 334[30] through **dhaṅkha* = *dhvāṅkṣa*; *ikka* (§ 12.2) = *ṛkṣa*; *Okkāka* (p. 66, f.-n. 1) from *Ikṣvāku*; *Takkasilā* (name of a city) = *Takṣaśilā*. Expected aspiration missing in initial position: *kuḍḍa*[3] 'small' D. II. 146[12], 169[9], Jā. V. 102[24] (cf. § 64.1) besides *khudda* = *kṣudra*; *culla*, *cūla* (also AMāg., JMāh. *culla*) 'small' (for *chulla*) = *kṣulla*, which in itself is very probably a popular form of the word *kṣudra*.

§ 63. Change of consonant-classes in sound-groups (cf. § 41): 1. Guttural appears for palatal perhaps in *bhiṣakka* 'physician' M.I. 429[4], A. III. 238[6], Milp. 247[11] as against *bhesajja* 'medicine'.—2. Cerebral appears for palatal in *āṇā* 'order' JāCo. I. 369[23] etc. (*āṇāpeti*, *āṇatta*, *āṇatti*) = *ājñā* (*ājñāpayati*[4]). But we have also *aññā* 'highest knowledge', *aññātar* 'one who knows well', *aññāya* Gerund from root *jñā* with *ā*. Similarly to be explained also *paṇṇarasa*, *paṇṇuvīsa*, *paṇṇāsa* (§ 48.2).—3. Dental appears for palatal in *uttiṭṭha* (Skr. *ucchiṣṭa*) 'rest of a mental' Milp. 213 f. (*uttiṭṭhapatta* 'alms-bowl with grains of food attaching to it'[5]), a dialectical side-form of *ucchiṭṭha* § 57). For initial *jy* there is *d* instead of *j* in *dosina* (§ 59.2) = *jyautsna*.

§ 64. Cerebralisation of dental-groups is the most frequent case of the change of place of articulation (cf. § 42). 1. Under the influence of *r*: thus *rt*, *rd*, *rdh* become *ṭṭ*, *ḍḍ*, *ḍḍh*: *aṭṭa* 'pained' ThI. 1106,

[1] E. Müller, JPTS. 1888, p. 12.
[2] Also in Pkr. *leḍu* etc. beside *leṭṭhu*: Pischel, § 304.
[3] The reading of the MSS. is however uncertain.
[4] Similarly Pkr. *āṇā āṇavei*.
[5] VT. I. (= SBE. XIII), p. 152, f.-n. 1. Wrong interpretation in SBE. XXXV, p. 4.

Vin. I. 121[3], JāCo. I. 265[7] = *ārta*; *kevaṭṭa* 'fisherman' D.I. 45[29], JāCo. III. 171[12] = *kaivarta*; *chaḍḍeti* 'throws away' = *chardayati*; *vaḍḍhati* 'increases' with numerous derivatives) = *vardhate*. Besides *vuddha*, *vaddha* 'grown up, old' Jā. I. 177[1], D. I. 90[4] there is *buḍḍha*, *vuḍḍha* (§ 46.1); beside *vuddhi* (§ 12.4) there is also *vaḍḍhi*. In *aṭṭa* 'law-suit' (de-aspiration according to § 62.2) as opposed to *attha* 'property etc.'[1] = *artha* the change in sound has been accompanied by a change in meaning Forms both with *tt* and *ṭṭ* are to be found side by side among the derivatives of the root *vart*: always *vaṭṭati* when it signifies 'it is proper', but *vattati* signifies 'becomes, originates etc.'; similarly *vaṭṭa* 'round, circle', but *vatta* 'duty, responsibility', both = *vṛtta*. The spelling with *ṭṭ* is preferred also in *vaṭṭati* in composition, when the sense of rolling is emphasised: *āvaṭṭati pavaṭṭati* 'rolls hither and thither' D. II. 140[1], JāCo. VI. 504[15] etc. Hence also *āvaṭṭa* 'turn, whirl', *saṃvaṭṭa* 'overturning, annihilation', *vivaṭṭa* 'renewal (of an aeon)' D.I. 14[26], Vin. III. 4[25]. The group *nt* became *ṇṭ* under the influence of an original *ṛ* in *vaṇṭa* 'stalk' Jā VI. 537[22], D. I. 46[13], *tālavaṇṭa* 'fan' Vin. II. 137[7], JāCo. I. 165[29] = *vṛnta*, *tālavṛnta*. Cf. also *alla* 'dapm' D. II. 332[26], Vin. I. 109[3] etc. through **aḍḍra*, **aḍḍa* = *ārdra*.—2. Under the influence of a sibilant: *ṭhāti*, *ṭhahati* 'stands', *ṭhāna* 'place', *saṃṭhāna* 'figure', *paṭṭhāya* 'beginning from', *kūṭaṭṭha* 'standing firm as a rock' etc. from root *sthā*, *sthāna*, *saṃsthāna*, *prasthāya*, *kūṭastha* etc.—3. Irregular cerebralisation is found in *jaṇṇuka* 'knee' (perhaps this form should be corrected) JāCo. VI. 332[16] besides *jannu(ka)* = *jānu*, as well as *kaviṭṭha* (§ 38.5) besides *kapittha*. Cf. also the cerebrals in *daḍḍha* (§ 42 3) = *dagdha*.

16. *Metathesis in Sound-groups and Loss of Syllable through Haplology.*

§ 65.1. Metathesis in sound-groups takes place in combinations of *h* with nasal or semi-vowel (§ 49, 60), and further in combinations of sibilant with nasal, which become nasal + *h* (§ 50). The sibilant is retained, inspite of the metathesis, in *raṃsi* 'ray' = *raśmi*. On the metathesis of *ry* into *yr* with concomitant insertion of svarabhakti see § 47.2; for *gumba* = *gulma* see § 51.5; for *bunda* = *budhna* see § 62.2. Unique is the case of *gadrabha* 'ass' D. II. 343[14], JāCo. II. 96[24] as opposed to *gardabha*.

2. Haplology and the loss of syllable caused by it is in evidence in *aḍḍhatiya* (for **aḍḍhatatiya*) 'three and a half' JāCo. II. 93[4] (also

[1] On the other hand the usual spelling is *aṭṭhakathā* 'commentary'.

aḍḍhateyya Vin. I. 39[24], DhCo. I. 95[6]) ; *viññāṇañcāyatana* (for *viññāṇānañcāy-*) 'sphere of infinite knowledge' M. III. 106[13] etc. As sporadical cases may be mentioned : *pavissāmi* (for *pavisissāmi*) 'I shall enter' Cp. I. 9.56, JāCo. II. 68[20], *sossi* (for *sossasi*) 'you will hear' Jā. VI. 423[8], *vipassi* (for *vipassasi*) 'you apprehend' Th2. 271, *gacchisi* (for *gacchissasi*) ' you will go ' Th1. 356. Cf. also *sakkhī* Jā. V. 116[5] for **sakkhisi* (Co: *sakkhissasi*), *āsāduṃ* Jā. V. 154[19] (Co: *āsādituṃ*). It is however impossible to decide whether the optatives of ī-roots such as *jeyyam* from *ji*, *neyyaṃ* from *nī* should be regarded as "haplologies" for **jayeyyaṃ*, **nayeyyaṃ*.

17. Sandhi

§ 66. Initial and Final. 1. In Pāli the initial may be only one vowel or (as a rule) only one consonant (§51.2). In a number of cases in Pāli the initial sound shows peculiar variations which should be regarded as due to petrified sandhi-forms. Thus an initial vowel has been lost in *va*=*iva* and *eva*, in *pi*=*api*, *ti*=*iti* (beside *iva*, *eva*, *api*, *iti*), *dāni* ' now ' (beside *idāni*)=*idānīm*[1], *heṭṭhā* (§9)=**adheṣṭhāt*, and in the Pronominal stem *na*=*ena*[2]. The following too are sandhi-forms originated in position after a vocalic final: *posatha* ' holiday ' (beside *uposatha*)=*upavasatha*, *gini* ' fire ' from **agini*=*agni*; *vaṭaṃsa(ka)* ' ear-ornament ' Vv. 38.5, JāCo VI. 488[25] etc.=*avataṃsa*; *valañja* ' use ', *valañjeti* ' he uses ' from root *lañj* with *ava*. The doublets *daka*, *udaka* ' water ' occur also in Skr. Similarly we have in Skr. *ratni* and *aratni* ' one cubit '=Pāli *ratana*[3]. Also of Skr. *yūka* and Pāli *ūkā* ' louse ' JāCo. I. 453[29], Dhco. III. 342[15], one or the other is probably a sandhi-form. Similarly, words containing a prothetic *y* before *i*(*e*) and *v* before *u* (*o*) should be regarded as frozen sandhi-forms : *yiṭṭha* 'sacrificed'=*iṣṭa*; *vutta* ' spoken '=*ukta*; *vutta* ' sown '=*upta*; *vutta* ' shorn '=*upta*; *vusita* ' inhabited,=*uṣita*; *vūḷha* ' carried '=*ūḍha* (cf. *saṃyūḷha* D. II. 267[19], M.I.386[33]besides *saṃvūḷha* DCo.I.38[8]=*samūḍha*); also *ubbūḷha-(vant)* ' firm ' M. I. 414[30]=*udūḍha*. In some cases the form varies. Thus we have both *vuṭṭhahitvā* D. II. 156[5] and *uṭṭhahitvā* M. III, 183[30] after vowel. There is *vuṭṭhiṭa* beside *uṭṭhita*, *vuṭṭhānas* besides

1 D. Andersen, PGl- under the word.

2 Johansson, Le Monde Oriental 1907-08, p. 89 ff.

3 Johansson, ibid., p. 98. ff.

uṭṭhāna, vonata 'bent down' Thl. 562 beside *onata* Vin. I. 29[1] = *avanata*. In a number of cases it is doutful whether *vo-* is derived from *ava-* through *o-*, or is derived from *vyava-*. There are moreover the frozen sandhi-forms *yeva* = *eva* and *viya* = *iva*, the latter of which I consider to be derived from **yiva* through metathesis[1]. To the same category belong also the short forms *va*, *pi*, *ti* mentioned above. All of them have become independent side-forms. In the cas of *pi*, *ti* this is proved by their occurrence after the anusvāra, which becomes *m* and *n* respectively before them: *yam-pi...tam-pi* M. I. 48[33,34]; *ālapitun-ti* JāCo. III. 453[11]. As regards the use of *eva*, *yeva*, *va*[2], the state of things according to my collections seems to be as follows: 1. *eva* occurs most frequently after a vowel which is itself elided (*tass' eva*), then after *-aṃ*, *-iṃ*, which become *-am*, *-im*, and after *-i* which is itself elided. It is ten to twelve times as frequent as 2. *yeva*, which occurs after *-a*, *-i*, *-u*, *-e* as well as after nasal vowel. 3. *va* occurs about half as often as *yeva* and that after *-ā*, *-e*, *-o*. After nasal vowel we find not infrequently orthographic forms such as *tvaṃ ñeva* or *tvañ ñeva* JāCo. IV. 155[17], which indicate a particularly close combination. Of the three forms corresponding to Skr. *iva*, we find (*a*) *iva*, particularly in verses, after *-a*, with which it coalesces into *-eva*; (*b*) *viya* occurs, mostly in prose, after *-a*, *-ā*, *-o* and nasal vowel; (*c*) the short form *va* occurs, mostly in verses, after long or nasal vowel.—2. In final position there can be only a vowel (also nasal vowel). The consonants which originally occurred in final are dropped; *n* and *m* become anusvāra. Final *m* is dropped in *tuṇhī* 'silent' = *tūṣṇīm*. The following details should be noted:—(*a*) Final *-as* and *-ar* became *-o*: *tato* 'therefrom' = *tatas*, *pāto* 'early in the morning' = *prātar*. Both the forms *puno* and *puna* 'again' = *punar* are found to occur. In verbal flexion there often appears *-ă* for Skr. *-as* (§ 157, 159. II). Sporadically there appears *-e* instrad of *-o* (Māgadbism)—in *pure* 'former' (compar. *puretaraṃ*) = *puras*; cf. also *sve*, *suve* (§ 54.4) = *śvas*. Similarly also in flexion, see § 80, 82.5, 98 3.—(*b*) The vowel which becomes final after a consonant is dropped, can remain unchanged. But it may also be lengthened; *dhī* 'fie!' Dh.389 = *dhik*; *papatā* 'hurled down' Vin.III. 17[26] = *prāpatat*; *madhuvā* 'honey-like' Dh.69 (according to Fausböll) = *madhuvat*; in this way a new stem *parisā* originated out

[1] Not so Pischel, Pkr. Gr. § 336.

[2] Cf. also Windisch, Ber. d. K. Sächs. Gesellsach. d. W. 1893, pp. 230 f.

of *pariṣat* 'retinue'. Or it may be shortened: *abravi* 'he spoke' = Skr. *abravīt*. Or it may be nasalised: *manaṃ* 'a little' Jā. I 405[16], Vin. I. 109[3], 'in short' DhCo. III. 147[22] = *manāk*; *tiriyaṃ* 'obliquely' = *tiryak*; *sakiṃ* (beside *saki*) 'once' = *sakṛt*; °*khattuṃ* (§22.1)°*kṛtvas*; *aduṃ* 'that' (§ 109) = *adas*. In verbal flexion there are endings in-*uṃ* which are derived from -*us* (§ 127, 159. I, III, IV).

§ 67. COMPOSITIONAL SANDHI on the whole follows the rules of Skr., particularly in the case of compounds derived from an older period. Consonant-groups undergo assimilation according to § 49 ff. For vowel-sandhi I mention here *mahodadhi* 'ocean' (as in Skr.); *kākolūkā* 'crows and owls' DhCo. I. 50[13] (from *kāka* + *ul*-); *mahesakkha* 'powerful' from *mahā* + *īs*-; *accuggamma* Vin. I. 6[35] Ger. from root *gam* with *ati-ud* (Skr. *atyud*). More like Skr. forms are *agyantarāya* (§ 58.3), *anveti* (§ 54.5), etc. Examples of consonant-sandhi are: ***tammaya*** (§52.4) 'consisting of that' = ***tanmaya*** (from ***tad*** + ***maya***); ***tannissita*** 'issued out of that' M. III. 243[28] = *tad-ni*; *jaraggava* 'old bull' Thl. 1154, Jā. III. 156[11] (§ 52.1) = ***jaradgava***; ***tabbiparīta*** 'opposite of that' JāCo. I. 337[29], DhCo. III. 275[10] (§ 53.3) from ***tadviparīta***, etc. Original final consonant of the first component often reappears in composition: ***punabbhava*** 'rebirth' = ***punarbhava***; ***chappañcavācāhi*** 'with five or six words' Vin. IV. 21[25] from ***cha*** = *ṣaṭ* + ***pañca*** + *v.*; ***sakadāgāmin*** 'one destined to be born once more only, = ***sakṛd*** (Pāli *sakiṃ*) + *āgāmin*. Also the original double-consonance at the beginning of the second component reappears in composition: ***subbata*** 'virtuous' from ***su*** + ***vata*** = ***vrata***.—But Pāli is not always consistent. Quite often in vowel-sandhi one of the vowels is simply elided: ***satipaṭṭhāna*** 'earnest meditation' from ***sati*** + ***upaṭṭhāna*** = ***smṛtyupasthāna***. Hiatus too is allowed in composition: ***patto saüdako*** 'vessel with water' Vin. I. 46[15]; ***atiagginā odanaṃ uttarati*** 'cooking food on blazing fire' Milp. 277[29]. Sometimes however one of the two confronting vowels is extended: ***hitūpacāra*** 'beneficial help' JāCo. I. 172[6] = ***hita*** + ***upacāra***. Sometimes inorganic consonants are introduced to avoid hiatus: ***nisīda puppha-m-āsane*** 'sit on the seat decorated with flowers' DhCo. I. 108[20] (verse); ***su-h-uju*** 'quite straight' Kh. 15. In mixed sandhi the re-introduction of the initial double-consonance of the second component is often omitted: ***supaṭipanna*** 'keeping on the righteous path' M. II. 120[10] beside *suppaṭipanna* Pu. 48[33] = ***supratipanna***. In consonant-sandhi the first component often appears in its peculiar Pāli form: ***pātubhāva*** 'appearance' (without assimilation into ***bbh***) = ***prādurbhāva***; ***antovana*** 'interior part of the jungle' M. I. 124[33] = ***antarvana***.

§ 68. External Sandhi of Pāli is fundamentally different from that of Skr[1]. It is always arbitrary. Neither does it apply equally to all the words of a sentence but only to those which are syntactically closely connected. Windisch rightly said that such a sandhi, as opposed to that of Sanskrit, certainly appears to be older and more natural. The cases in which sandhi can take place are the following combinations: 1. subject and the verb of the predicate, 2. verb and the object, 3. substantive and attribute, 4. attribute and attribute, 5. adverb and verb, 6. noun of the predicate and copula, 7. adverb and object, 8. vocative and the word preceding it; 9. particles and pronouns may join in sandhi with preceding or following words. In general, sandhi in Pāli is much more frequent in verses under the stress of metre than in prose.

§ 69. When two similar vowels meet: 1. ā̆ + ā̆ become *ā* by contraction when the second word begins with an open syllable: ***duggatāhaṃ*** Th2. 122 = ***duggatā ahaṃ***. If the second word begins with a closed syllable, one *a* is simply elided[2]: ***piyo c' assaṃ*** M. I. 33[9]; ***chāt' amha*** = ***chātā amha*** JāCo. III. 416[4]. Frequently however also in this case contraction takes place, the length of the resulting vowel being retained against the general rule § 5. (cf. § 7): ***gavāssā ca*** = ***gavā assā ca*** Jā. III. 408[21]; ***nācceti*** = ***na acceti*** Jā. IV. 165[22]; ***tassākkhibhedaṃ*** = ***tassa akkhi-*** JāCo. III. 431 [8].—2. The result is similar in the case of ī̆ + ī̆, ū̆ + ū̆; yet here elision can take place also when the initial syllable is an open one, and that not only—as demanded by Jacobi's law[3]—when the prefinal syllable of the preceding word is long. We have thus contraction in numerous cases such as ***gacchatīti*** = ***gacchati iti***, at the side of elision as in ***yaṃ p'icchaṃ na labhati*** 'what he longs to get, but cannot' M.I. 48[33]; but elision may take place also when the initial syllable is open, *e.g.*, ***cattār' imāni*** M. I. 66[1] and even ***pañcas, upādānakkhandhesu*** M.I, 61 [1].

[1] F. Kuhn, Beitr. p. 59 ff.; E. Müller, PGr. p. 59 ff.; Windisch, Über die Sandhikonsonanten des Pāli, Ber. d. K. Sächs. Gesellsch. d. W. 1893, p. 228 ff.

[2] In the case of the most frequent sandhi combinations handed down from the older period of the language (*e.g.*, *n'atthi* = *nāsti*, it is possible that the contraction was followed by the shortening of the vowel according to the Law of Mora. But those cases of sandhi which took place only in the Pāli period, as well as the undoubted cases of elision such as *pañcas' upādānakkhandhesu*, and finally the analogy of the treatment of confronting dissimilar vowels (§ 70 f.), speak rather for elision.

[3] Jacobi. Über eine neue Sandhiregel in Pāli und in Prākrit der Jainas, IF. 31 211 ff.

§ 70. Confrontation of dissimilar vowels: 1. When *a* is followed by *i* or *u*: (*a*) there is contraction of *a*+*i* into *e* and *a*+*u* into *o*. This form of sandhi applies mainly to the language of the Gāthās. Example: *macchassevodake* (§ 3). From later poetic literature: *ceme*=*ca ime* Mhvs. 1. 10.; *maṃ nopeti*=*na up-* Mhvs. 32. 13. We have even *mamedaṃ*=*mama idaṃ* JāCo. III. 446[12].—(*b*) The *ă* is elided: *satt' imāni ca suttāni* Iv. 22[12] (verse); *Bodhisattass' upaṭṭhāko* JāCo. III. 463[20]; *manas' icchasi*=*manasā icchasi* Jā. III. 493[4]. Elision may take place also when the penultimate syllable of the preceding word is short: *iminā pan' upāyena* JāCo. III. 420[1]. This form of sandhi (:elision) is met with in all periods of the language. The elision may take place also before *e*, *o*: *dhuttā mūlen' ekaṃ bhattapātiṃ āharāpesuṃ* JāCo. III. 287[22].—(*c*) Finally, after the elision of *a*, the remaining vowel may be lengthened: *idh' ūpapanno* Iv. 99[11]. Frequently however, when *iti* follows a word ending with *a*, the initial *i* is elided with concomitant lengthening of the preceding *a*: *bhavissāmā 'ti*[1] M.I. 42[4].—2. Confrontation of *i*, *u* with dissimilar vowels: (*a*) *i* and *u* become *y*, *v*, particularly in the Gāthā language, but occasionally also in the later period of the language: *manussesvetam na vijjati* Sn. 611; *na te dukkhā pamuty-atthi* (from *pamutti atthi*) Th2. 248. In *icc-eva* (*iti eva*) Jā. III. 481[22] the sandhi is accompanied by consonantal assimilation. In canonical and post-canonical prose: *app-ekacce* (<*api ek-*) Vin. I. 6[27] etc.; *Brahmāyvāham* (from *Brahmāyu ahaṃ* with lengthening of the initial vowel) M. II. 144[26]; *pātv-ăkāsi* JāCo. III. 405[25], DhCo. III. 411[8].—(*b*) Any one of the two vowels may be elided (in every period of the language): *karom' ahaṃ* Th2. 114; *karissas' eko* Th2. 231; *paṇḍiteh' atthadassibhi* Th1. 4; *gacchant' eva* JāCo. IV. 149[23]; *yaṃ hi 'ssa* M. I. 9[26]; *saddahissat' eva* JāCo. III. 499[3]; *anabhijjhālu 'ham- asmi* M.I. 17[37]. The remaining vowel may be lengthened: *labhiṃsū 'ti*[1] JāCo. III. 403[22]; *ās' ūpasampadā* (*āsi upasampadā*) Th2. 109; *idān āhaṃ* M.I. 13[5].

§ 71. Confrontation of *e*, *o* and nasal vowels with vowels. 1. *e*, *o* before vowel. (*a*) The initial vowel is elided: *sutto 'smi* Jā. III. 404[18]; *tato 'gacchi* (from *āgacchi*) Th2. 129; *cattāro 'me puggalā* M. I. 24[17].—(*b*) Sometimes *e*, *o* is elided with

[1] It is to be transliterated like this. Where on the other hand the long vowel is original, I would prefer to omit the elision-sign ' in view of the independent existence of *ti*, *pi*.

concomitant protraction of a following short in open syllable: *y' āham* (from *yo ahaṃ*) JāCo. III. 364[24]; *y' āhu* (from *yo ahu*) Thl. 632; *y' assa* (from *ye assa*) M. I. 7[26]; *sac' āhaṃ* (from *sace ahaṃ*) JāCo. III. 475[21].—(*c*) In monosyllabic words such as *te*, *me*, *so*. *yo*, *kho* the vowels *e*, *o* are changed into the sami-vowels *y*, *v*, in which case a following short vowel is always protracted in an open syllable, but is optionally so in closed one [1]: *namo ty·atthu* Th2. 157; *ty-āhaṃ* (from *te ahaṃ*) M. I. 13 [1]; *ty-āssa* (from *te assa*) DhCo. I. 116[20]; *sv-āyaṃ* (from *so ayaṃ*) Vin. I. 29[26]; *yv-āssa* (from *yo assa*) M. I. 137[17]; *khv-āssa* (from *kho assa*) M. I. 68[12]. Like these monosyllabic words is treated *ito* in *itv-eva* Thl. 869. —2. Nasal vowel before vowel. In such cases (*a*) all the phenomena of vowel-sandhi may appear. Thus contraction: *nandeyyāhaṃ* (from *nandeyyaṃ ahaṃ*) Jā. III. 495[20]; *yesāhaṃ* (from *yesaṃ ahaṃ*) M. I. 33[17]. Elision: *paripucch' ahaṃ* (from *-cchiṃ ahaṃ*) Th2. 170; *catunn' etam* (from *-nnam etam*) S. IV. 174[23]. Elision with compensatory lengthening: *tes' ūpasammati* (from *tesaṃ up-*) Jā. III. 488[8]. Transformation into semi-vowel after denasalisation is in evidence in *ky-āhaṃ* (from *kiṃ ahaṃ*) Jā. III. 206[21].—(*b*) The retrograde mutation of Anusvāra into *m* is very frequent: *bandhitum-icchati* Th2. 299; *atītam-addhānaṃ* M. I. 8[4]; *saddam-akāsi* JāCo. III. 287[25]; also *antalikkhasmim-eḷiki* Jā. III. 481[16]. An original long vowel shortened before Anusvāra gets back its original quantity in this process: *āloko passatām-iva* (from *-taṃ+iva*) Sn. 763; *pappoti mām iva* (from *mam+iva*) Jā. III. 468 [4]. It should be noted that in *n' etaṃ ajjatanām-iva* Dh. 227 the lengthening is due merely to metrical exigencies.

§ 72. The hiatus due to confrontation of vowels in a sentence is often filled, 1. by restoring at the end of the first word a consonant which originally formed part of it. Thus, *e.g.*, by restoring *r*: *punar -ehisi* Th2. 166; *pātur · ahosi* Vin. I. 5 [21] etc. (as opposed to *pātu bhavati*). This restitution is in evidence also in flexional forms [2]: *raṃsir-iva* Vv. 52. 5; *pathavīdhātur-ev' esā* M. III. 240 [29] (analogically also *vijjur-iva* Vv. I. 1); *bhattur-atthe* (Skr. *bhartur-arthe*) Jā. II. 398[15]; *sabbhir-eva* (Skr. *sadbhir-eva*) Thl. 4. Restitution of *d* to avoid hiatus: *etad-avoca* (passim), *yad-idaṃ* (passim), *yad-icchiaṃ* Th2. 46; *ahud-eva bhayaṃ* D.I. 49[35]; *sakid-eva* 'once only' Pu. 16[17].

[1] Cf. on it Michelson, IF. 23. 269.

[2] Cf. AMāg. *sihir-iva*, *vāyur-iva* etc ; Pischel, Pkr. Gr. § 353.

Restitution of *g*: *pag-eva* (Skr. *prāg-eva*) JāCo. I. 354[20]; *puthag-eva* (Skr. *pṛthag-eva*) from *puthu* Kacc. I. 5. 1 (Senart, p. 221). Restitution of *m*: *tuṇhīm-āsīne* D. II. 212[21] (verse) from *tuṇhī*=Skr. *tūṣṇīm*. Finally, *ḷ* is restituted at the end of the numeral *cha* 'six': *chaḷ-ete* (Skr. *ṣaḍ-ete*) Jā. I. 366[27]. After the analogy of *punar-ahosi* etc. also *haṃsar-iva* Jā. I. 403[21]; *bahud-eva* S. IV. 183[27] after *aññad-eva* M. I. 372[18].—2. By prothesis of *y* before *i* (*e*) and of *v* before *u* (*o*). For frozen sandhi-forms of this type see § 66. 1. In numerous cases a prothetic *y* precedes the pronominal stem *ima*: *na-y-idaṃ* Th2. 166, DhCo. I. 201[3]; *cha-y-ime* M. I. 51[16]; also *na-y-ito* Jā. III. 466[28] etc. Further *ādicco-v-udayaṃ* 'the rising sun' Iv. 85[4] (verse); *ubhaya-v-okiṇṇo* 'scattered in both directions'[1] D. III. 88[6–7] beside *okirati* JāCo. I. 88[20]; *kati-v-uttari*, *pañca-v-uttari* S. I. 8[15–17] (in Windisch).

§ 73. The phenomena described above have led—particularly in the Gāthā language—to the introduction of inorganic sandhi-consonants for the purpose of avoiding hiatus. Thus there is 1. *y* occasionally also before *a*: *khaṇi-y-asmani* Jā. III. 433[11]; *yā-y-aññaṃ* Jā. I. 429[27]. —2. Frequently *m* serves as a sandhi-consonant: *Sattukā-m-iva* Jā. III. 438[16], *isi-m-avoca* Sn. 692, *saki-m-eva* Milp. 10[12]. According to § 72.1 one would rather expect instead: *Sattukād-iva*, *isir-avoca*, *sakideva* (so A. IV. 380[20]). Other examples are: *nīcakulā-m-iva* Sn. 411; *puno-m-ahaṃ* Th2. 292; *ekañ-ca-jeyya-m-attānaṃ* 'one should conquer one's own self' Dh. 103 etc. With characteristic shortening: *hitva-m aññaṃ* (from *hitvā aññaṃ*) Sn. 1071.—3. Further we find *r* as sandhi-consonant: *dhi-r-atthu* Th1. 1134, Jā. III. 29[18], as against *dhig-atthu* (Skr. *dhig-astu*) according to § 72.1; *jalanta-r-iva* (from *jalantaṃ iva*) Jā. VI. 181[6]; *jīva-r-eva* (from *jivaṃ eva*; Comm. *jīvanto yeva*) Jā. III. 464[17]. According to § 71. 2 *b* these two forms should rather have been *jalantam-iva*, *jīvam-eva*. Very frequently there is *r* before *iva*, particularly after *ā*, *e*, *o*: *turiyā-r-iva* Th2. 381; *jana-majjhe-r-iva* Th2. 394; *thambo-r-iva* Sn. 214; *so-r-iva suṃsumāro* Jā. II. 228[21]. Shortening is in evidence in *haṃsa-r-iva* Sn. 1134(there is however the variant reading *haṃso-r-iva*); *suriyan-tapantaṃ sarada-r-iva* from *sarado* (Gen. Sg.) *iva* Sn. 687 etc.—4. Sometimes we find *d* as sandhi-consonant: *puna-d-eva* Vv. 53.22, JāCo. I. 96[8]; *samma-d-eva* D. II. 126[11] (against Skr. *samyag-eva*); *bahu-d-eva rattiṃ* Th1. 366.—

[1] R. O. Franke, D. 275.

5. Occasionally *t* serves as sandhi-consonant: *ajja-t-agge* 'from to-day' M. I. 24[9], D. I. 85[14] etc. But it is uncertain whether *yasmātiha* (*tasmātiha*) is to be explained as *yasmā-t-iha*. I would rather divide it into *yasmā ti ha* like Windisch (p. 244)[1].—6. For the sandhi-consonant *n* Kacc. 1.4.6 (Senart, p. 218) gives the examples *ciran-n-āyati* 'since long' and *ito-n-āyati* 'from now on.'—7. It is uncertain whether *h* too should be regarded as a sandhi-consonant[2] in cases like *mā-h-evaṃ avaca* S. I. 150[7] or *na-h-eva* M. II. 223[8] etc.; *Kokanadāhasmiṃ* S. I. 30[1] may be explained as *Kokanadā ahaṃ asmiṃ*.

§ 74. Confrontation of vowels and consonants (mixed sandhi): 1. Frequently an original initial consonant-group at the beginning of the second word reappears in sandhi. Often this is due to exigencies of metre, as in *sarati-bbayo* (from *vayo* = Skr. *vyaya*) Jā. III. 95[18]; but sometimes also without the stress of metre and in prose: *muni-ppakāsayi* Sn. 251; *tatra-ssu* (from *su* = Skr. *svid*) M. I. 77[28]; *na-ppajahanti* M. I. 14[15]; *na-ppamajjasi* JāCo. III. 424[4] etc.—2. The ending *o* is sometimes retained in its original form *as* before *s*: *tayas-su dhammā* Sn. 231; *lūkhas-sudaṃ homi* M. I. 77[25]. In the same way we find *-us* in *Soṇena Suhanus-sahā* Jā. II. 31[24], *pitus-sutaṃ* Jā. III. 484[24], in which case however a different explanation is possible.—3. When a nasal vowel is confronted with a consonant, the Anusvāra before mutes and nasals is very frequently changed into the corresponding nasal: *karissañ-ca* Jā. III. 437[25]; *bheriñ carāpetvā* JāCo. III.410[11]; *āsabhaṇ-ṭhānam* M.I.69[32]; *man-tāta* Th2. 274; *kahan no mātā* JāCo. III. 427[20]; *cittuppādam-pi* M. I. 43[26]; *diṭṭham-me* JāCo. III. 449[26]. The Anusvāra may be changed into *ñ* before *h*: *cittañ-hi 'ssa padūsitam* Iv. 13[9].

[1] Not so E. Kuhn, Beitr. p. 62.
[2] As in composition; cf. *su-h-uju* § 67.

B. WORD-FORMATION

Note : The flexion of Pāli is throughout determined by the laws of analogy. The old historical forms have been more and more replaced by new formations in course of the development of the language. The relation between archaic and later forms in particular periods of the language has been discussed already in Introduction II.

I. Noun (Substantive and Adjective)

1. Generalities

§ 75. In Pāli the nominal stems have undergone multifarious changes. Due to the phonetic law entailing the elision of final consonants, the consonant stems become vowel ones and are inflected like the latter. Thus we get *sumedha* 'wise' Dh. 208, Vin. I. 5^{35} (verse) from *sumedhas*; *āpā* 'misfortune' (Loc. Pl. *āpāsu* Jā. II. 317^{13}) from *āpad*. In this way originated *sappi* 'butter' (Abl. Sg. *sappimhā* D. I. 201^{26}) from *sarpis*; *acci* or *accī* (the latter form in M. III. 273^{17}) 'brightness' from *arcis*; *tādi* 'like this' from *tādṛś*, etc.; similarly *vijju* 'lightning' (N. Pl. *vijjū* Mhvs. 12.13) from *vidyut*; *maru* 'god' from *marut*, etc.—Very often the transfer to vowel-flexion is effected by adding *ă* to the consonantal stem. The *a*-flexion has supplied most of the types of new formations.[1] Besides *sumedha* we have *sumedhasa* (N. Sg. *sumedhaso* Dh. 29; Fem. *sumedhasā* Mhvs. 22. 36). Similarly *āpadā* Thl, 371, JāCo. III. 12^{13} beside *āpā* (in JāCo. II. 317^{21} *āpāsu* is explained by *āpadāsu*); *vijjutā* Loc. Pl. *vijjutāsu* D. II. 131^{10}) besides *vijju*. Analogous stems are *sarada* 'autumn' =*śarad*; *barihisa* 'sacrificial grass' D. I. 141^{29}=*barhis*; *sarita* 'flowing stream' D. III. 196^{26}=*sarit*, etc. In this way the consonantal flexion is reduced more and more, and at the side of older consonantal forms new forms according to the vowel flexion appear in the language and gradually come to be regarded as the only possible correct forms.

§ 76. Gender is distinguished on the whole according to the rules of Sanskrit. Syntactical irregularities however often show

[1] R. O. Franke, Die Sucht nach *a*-Stämmen im Pali, BB. 22. 202 ff.

that the sense for grammatical Gender had already become hazy. Thus the L. Sg. Masc. Neut. *asati* Ud. 81 [7-8] is connected both with the Feminine forms *passaddhiyā*, *ratiyā*, *āgatigatiyā* as well as with *calite*, *cutūpapāte*. In Dh. 104 there is *attā jitaṃ* instead of *jito*[1]; Th2. 518: *sakhiyo tīṇi janiyo* 'we three women friends' instead of *tisso*; in Ud. 79[21] the Subject *upāsikāyo* is connected with the Predicate *anipphalāni kalaṃkatāni* etc. Particularly the Neuters in *-as* are occasionally treated as Masculine[2]: *yattha me nirato mano* (instead of *niratam*) Jā. III. 91[15]; *tapo sukho* (instead of *sukhaṃ*) Dh. 194; *sukhumo rajo paṭivātaṃ va khitto* (instead of *sukhumaṃ*, *khittaṃ*) Sn. 662; *mahāvegena āgato nadīsoto* 'the current of the stream coming with great force' DhCo. IV. 45[17] etc. Also Neuters in *-a* are not seldom treated as Masculine and *vice versa*. We have, *e.g.*, *je keci rūpā. . . . sabbe vat' ete* S.I. 67[8]; *sabbe te rūpā* M. III. 217[31]; *ime diṭṭhiṭṭhānā* D.I. 16[34] (cf. A. II. 42 [2,4]). In Jā. I. 289[29] there is *sabbe kaṭṭhamayā vanā*, although *vana* is Neuter, and in M.I. 67[15] *cattāro upādānā* besides the regular *cattāri upādānāni*. Cf. below § 80. 4. On the other hand, Masculines too show flexional forms of the Neuter. Thus we have *dhammāni* from Masc. *dhamma* Jā. V. 221[27]; *vandati pādāni* Vv. 51. 1 has been explained in the commentary 218[14] by *pāde*; *petāni puttāni* (Acc.) Th2. 312 stands for *pete putte* according to the commentary: "*liṅgavipallāsena*". Cf. also Ud. 17[33]. There is *bhujāni poṭhenti* Bu. 1. 36 beside *poṭhayaṃ bhuje* Rasav. II. 92[4], and the Acc. *tālataruṇe* immediately before the Nom. Pl. *tālataruṇāni* Vin. I. 189[10],[11]. Accusatives like *puttāni* should be regarded as cases of Ardha-Māgadhism, Pischel § 358. There are also cases of confusion between Feminines in *ā* and Neuters in *-a*: Thus Pl. *sabhāni* Jā. IV. 223[7] from Fem. *sabhā*, which has been explained by *sabhāyo* in the commentary. The stem *kucchi* 'womb' =*kukṣi* which was originally Masc., has besides the forms *kucchismā*, *kucchimhā*, *kucchismiṃ*, *kucchimhi* also *kucchiyā*, *kucchiyaṃ* JāCo. I.52[8], 293[18], like the Feminine stems of § 86. From *sāli* 'rice'=*śāli* Masc. we have the Acc. Pl. *sāliyo*. Also *dhātu* 'element', although originally Masc., knows forms like Nom. Acc. Pl. *dhātuyo* Dhs. 67, Th2. 14, Inst. Sg. *dhātuyā* D.II. 109[1], A. I. 28[2], IV. 313[21], but Gen. Sg. *dhātussa* Mhvs. 20. 19. The usually Neuter stem *massu* 'beard' has in Gen. Sg. *massuyā* Jā. III. 315[22] etc. Examples of

[1] *Cf.* SBE. XI. 1, p. 31.

[2] Similarly in Pkr., Pischel § 356.

confusion in Gender have been discussed in connection with the changes of word-stems in § 75.

§ 77. 1. Of the Numbers Pāli has given up the Dual [1]. Its place has been taken by the Plural. Of Dual there have been preserved only *dve*, *duve* 'two' = *dve*, and *ubho* 'both' = *ubhau*. It is therefore usual to say *dve cakkhūni* 'the two eyes' JāCo. IV. 137[16], *dve antā* Nom. Pl. and *ubho ante* Acc. Pl. 'the two extremes' Vin. I. 10[10,11,15]. The same use of Plural also in Dvandva-compounds: Acc. Pl. *ime candimasuriye* M.I. 69[16], Gen. Pl. *candimasuriyānaṃ* D.I. 10[14].—2. As for the Cases (cf. R. O. Franke, BB. 16.64 ff.), Pāli replaces the Dative in both Numbers by the Genitive [2]. Only the *a*-stems have retained in Singular a Dative in *-āya* [3]. It serves to express direction and purpose. Thus, *e.g.*, *saggāya gacchati* Dh. 174; *jahassu rūpaṃ apunabbhavāya* 'give up the body in order not to be born again' Sn. 1121. It is also used quite frequently as Infinitive, as in *na ca mayaṃ labhāma bhagavantaṃ dassanāya* 'we do not get permission to see the Blessed One' Vin. I. 253[11]. This Dative is used particularly to express longing after something (cf. *icchā lābhāya*, A. IV. 293 [20]) and exertion for something (*ghaṭati vāyamati lābhāya*, ibid.). It is further used in the sense of 'it suffices to, it servs to' (*sallekhāya subharatāya viriyārambhāya saṃvattissati* M.I. 13 [30]), in connection with *hetu*, *paccaya* 'reason for' (*ko paccayo mahato bhūmicālassa pātubhāvāya* D. II. 107 [11]), and in connection with *alaṃ* 'enough' (*alaṃ vacanāya* A. III. 5 [27]) etc.—Frequently the Abl. Sg. is formed with the suffix *-to* = Skr. *-tas*. It can be also included in the paradigm as has been actually done by V. Henry. As examples let us mention: *gharato* 'from the house' JāCo. I. 290 [26], *mukhato* Ud. 78 [10], *dūrato* 'from afar', *cāpāta* (with lengthening, from *cāpa* 'bow') Dh. 320 (see § 78-80); *Nālāto* Th2. 294, *cūḷāto* JāCo. II. 410[19], *nāvāto* DhCo. III. 39 [14], *jivhāto* S. IV. 178 [15] besides *jivato* S. IV. 175 [1] with shortening as also in *sīmato* JāCo. II. 3[1] (see §81); *aggito* D. II. 88 [2], *aṭṭhito* Jā. II. 409 [3], *dadhito* Milp. 41 [1], *bhikkhuto* Thl. 1024, *kāmaṇḍaluto* DhCo.

[1] The two examples given by E. Müller, PGr. p. 65 f., as instances of retained Dual are unconvincing. One of them (*paṭhamaṃ*) *to idhāgato* Dpvs. 9. 32, even if the reading is not corrupt, goes back only to the author of this work whose knowledge of Pāli was very imperfect. The second form *mātāpitu* (*ca vanditvā*) Cp. II. 9. 7 is certainly no Dual at all.

[2] As in Pkr., Pischel § 361.

[3] Cf. R. O. Franke, BB. 16. 82.

III. 448[3], *cakkhuto* S. IV. 174[33] (see § 82, 85); *kucchito* JāCo I. 52[31], *aṅgulito* DhCo. I. 164[7], *Bārāṇasīto* Th2. 335 besides *-sito* (with shortening) JāCo. II. 47[18], *pokkharaṇīto* JāCo. II. 38[4] besides *-ṇito* VvCo. 217[21], *dhātuto* JāCo. I. 253[29], *jambuto* Bu. 17. 9 (see § 86); *abhibhūto* D. I. 18[7], M. I. 2[27] (see § 87. 2); *pitito* 'from father', *mātito* 'from mother' D. I. 113[25], A. III. 151[16] etc. = *pitṛtas*, *mātṛtas*; *rājato* Dh. 139; *attato* S. III. 46[16]; *hatthito* (from *hatthin* 'elephant') JāCo. IV. 257[20]., *Himavantato* JāCo. I. 140[24] (see § 96); *manato* S. IV. 175[2] (see § 99).—In Plural the suffix *-bhyas* of Dat.-Abl. has been lost. The Abl. formally coincides with Instr. as Dat. with Gen. Also in Singular the form of Instr. is often used as Abl. (§ 82. 2, 90. 1, 91, 92, 95, 96).

2. *a*-declension

§ 78. A. Masculine stems in *-a*; stem: *dhamma* 'law'.

	Singular	Plural
N.	*dhammo*	*dhammā*
Acc.	*dhammaṃ*	*dhamme*
I.	*dhammena*, *dhammā*	*dhammehi*
G. D.	*dhammassa*	*dhammānaṃ*
Abl.	*dhammā*, *dhammasmā*,*-amhā*	*dhammehi*
L.	*dhamme*, *dhammasmiṃ*,*-amhi*	*dhammesu*
V.	*dhamma*	*dhammā*

B. Neuter stems in *-a*; stem: *rūpa* 'figure'.

	Singular	Plural
N.	*rūpaṃ*	*rūpāni*, *rūpā*
Acc.	*rūpaṃ*	*rūpāni*, *rūpe*
V.	*rūpa*	*rūpāni*, *rūpā*

In other cases as in Masculine. On the Dative of *a*-stems in *āya* cf. § 77 (with § 27. 2).

On flexion: 1. The Instrumental Sg. in *-ā* corresponds to the same form of the Vedic language[1]. It is found not infrequently in the Gāthā-language and in canonical prose; but only occasionally in post-canonical prose. A form to the point is the frequent

[1] R. O. Franke, ZDMG. 46. 316ff.

sahatthā [1] 'with one's own hand' JāCo I. 286 [5], D. I. 109 [33], Vin. I. 18[30], JāCo. I. 7[3], Mhvs. 5. 72 besides *sahatthena* JāCo. VI. 305[3]. Also *yogā* DhCo. III. 233[21] (verse), explained by *yogena* in the word-analysis; *pādā* 'with the foot' Jā. III. 269 [16], DhCo. I. 202[6] (verse); *saha vacanā* 'along with the word, in the moment he spoke the word' Ud. 16 [3]; *mā sokā* (=*sokena*) *pahato bhava* Thl. 82; *bhikkhusaṃghā* (parallel to the Instr. *bhagavatā*) Vin. II 198 [23] etc. That these forms were later felt to be archaisms is clear from the fact that as *yogā* is explained by *yogena*, so also is *pādā* explained by *pādena* in the commentary (JāCo. III. 269 [28])—2. The suffixes *-asmā*, *-amhā* of Ablative Sg. and *-asmiṃ*, *-amhi* of Locative Sg. are taken from the pronominal declension.—3. The suffix *-e* of Accusative Pl. is taken f om the pronominal declension [2]. Here the forms *te*, *ime*, *sabbe* are used both in N. and Acc. From *te* **dhammān* gradually originated *te dhamme*.—4. The Instr. Pl. in *-ehi* is either derived from the Vedic forms in *-ebhis*, or is taken over from pronominal declension.—5. As for the Vocative Sg. of neutral declension, cf. *citta* 'O soul' Thl. 1108 f.—6. The Nominative Plural in *-ā* [3] of Neuter stems is not rare in the first two periods of the language: *rūpā* Thl. 455, Vin. I. 21 [19], D. I. 245[17] etc; *sotā* 'ears' Sn. 345; *nettā* 'eyes' Th2. 257; *phalā* 'fruits' Jā. IV. 203 [22], Vv. 84. 4. These forms were still felt to be Neuter. Cf., *e.g.*, *tīṇ' assa lakkhaṇā gatte* Sn. 1019; *moghā* (Com. *moghāni*) *te assū pariphanditāni* Jā. III. 24 [25]. They correspond to the Vedic Plurals in *-ā* like *yugā* 'yokes.'—7. As these forms however formally coincided with Masc. Plurals, they gave rise also to Accusative Plurals in *-e* as in Masc.: *rūpe* M. III. 281[8], S. IV. 8[10] (in Thl. 1099 it occurs at the side of Masc. Accusatives); *sarīre* DhCo. III. 208[9]; *pupphe* VvCo. 174[14]; *te chidde* S. I. 43[20] (verse), where *chiddāni* as Nom. occurs immediately before. Confusion of Gender is thus in evidence.

§ 79. Individual forms. 1. Not at all rare are Sg. Instrumentals in *-asā*[4], formed on the analogy of *as*-stems on the basis of the proportion *mano* : *manasā*=*dhammo* : X. Examples are found specially in the first two periods of the language, and again in the artificial poetry;

[1] Sten Konow and D. Andersen however consider it to be Abl.; JPTS. 1909, p. 131.

[2] E. Kuhn, Beitr p. 72. Cf. Pischel, ZDMG. 35.715 f. Scepticism about this interpretation has been expressed by V. Henry, Préc. de Gramm. Pâlie § 153, note 3.

[3] Frequently also in Pkr.; see Pischel, § 367.

[4] Such forms occur also in Pkr. "through the influence of preceding Instrumentals of *s*-stems," Pischel § 364.

they are rare in post-canonical prose. Cf. *balasā* 'with force' (instead of *balena*) Thl. 1141; Cp. II. 4. 7; *damasā* Sn. 463 beside *damena* Sn. 655; *vāhasā* (instead of *vāhena*) Thl. 218, Vin. IV. 158[20], D. II. 245[9]; *padasā* 'on foot' (instead of *padena*) JāCo. III. 300[29], Mhvs. 14.2. Moreover *mukhasā* 'with the mouth' Pv. I.2.3 is explained by *mukhena* in the Pv.Co. and *vegasā* 'with speed' Jā. III. 185[2] is explained by *vegena* in the Co.[1]—2. According to Moggallāna II. 108 ff., Singular Locatives in *-asi* are formed analogically on the basis of Instrumentals in *-asā*[2].—3. In Vocative Sg. the final is sometimes extended[3]. The Voc. *ayyo* is used in respectful address for both Numbers and Genders (beside *ayya*, *ayyā*; *ayye*, *ayyā*), as for instance in Vin I. 75[8] in Voc. Pl. Masc.—4. In Nom. Pl. the forms in *-āse* are quite common in the Gāthā-language. They correspond to the Vedic forms in *-āsas*, and the ending *-e* instead of *-o* suggests the influence of Māgadhi[4]: *upāsakāse* Sn. 376; *paṇḍitāse* Sn. 875; *dhammāse* Sn. 1038; *brāhmaṇāse* Sn. 1079ff.; *vañcitāse* Thl. 102; *gadhitāse* Thl. 1216; *ussitāse* Vv. 84. 15; *rukkhāse* Jā. III. 399[2]; *ariyāse* Jā. IV. 222[21]; *duṭṭhāse* (and a number of other forms) Iv. 1[10]ff.; *Gotamasāvakāse* D. II. 272[26] (verse), *gatāse* D. II. 255[3] (verse), S.I. 27[8] (verse), Jā. I. 97[1]; *upapannāse* S. I. 60[4] (verse); *niviṭṭhāse* S. I. 67[4] (verse) etc.—[5].An Acc. Pl. Masc. in *-ān* as in Skr. has perhaps been preserved in *vehāsān-upasaṃkamiṃ* Thl. 564 through the influence of Sandhi. But it should rather be construed as *vehāsāni up°* according to §70.2*b*.—6. Besides the ending *-ehi* in Instr. Pl. there is also the archaic form *-ebhi*: *ariyebhi* Ud. 61[2]. To the Skr. ending *-ais* corresponds *-e*[6] in *guṇe dasah' upāgataṃ* Bu. 2.32. Or is it merely a shortened form of *guṇehi dasahi*?[7].

§ 80. Māgadhisms. Forms of the Māgadhi-language are used in isolated passages of the canon. Such forms are: the Singular Nominatives in *-e*—in Masc. instead of *-o*. and in Neuter instead of *-am*; (*a*) Masculine[8], *attakāre*, *parakāre*, *purisakāre* (instead of *-kāro*)

1 The same form is used also by secondarily originated *s*-stems. Cf. § 94

2 Cf R. O. Franke, PGr. p. 35.

3 Also in Pkr.; Pischel, § 71, 366 b.

4 Oldenberg, KZ. 25, 315.

5 Cf. in Pkr. forms in *ā* like Mah. *guṇān* = Skr. *guṇā*, AMāg. *rukkhā*, *purisā* etc. Pischel, § 367.

6 E. Müller, PGr. p.69. I consider the other forms quoted here to be Locative Sg.

7 Cf. similar phenomena in Skr.; R. Roth, Über gewisse Kürzungen des Wortendes im Veda, Vhdl. des Wiener Or. Kongr., Ar. Sect, p. 1 ff. (Vienna 1888),

8 R. O. Franke, D. übersetzung, p. 56, note 5,

D. I. 53^{29}; *bāle ca paṇḍite ca* ' the fool and the wise ' D. I. $55^{29,30}$; *ke chave sigāle ke sīhanāde* (instead of *ko* etc.) D. III. 24^{19}; *bahuke jane pāsapāṇike* (comm. *bahuko jono-ṇiko*) Jā. III. 288^{15}. (*b*) Neuter: *sukhe dukkhe jīvasattame* D. I. 56^{26} instead of *sukhaṃ* etc. Further *ye avitakke avicāre se paṇītatare* D. II. $278^{16,30}$, 279^{12} instead of *yaṃ avitakkaṃ avicāraṃ taṃ paṇītataraṃ*. The passage *ye lokāmisasaṃ. yojane se vante* M. II. 254^{25} instead of *yaṃ -janaṃ taṃ vantaṃ* has been already discussed by Trenckner[1]. Cf. also *navachandake dāni* (var. lec. *dāne*) *diyyati* Jā. III. 288^{13}, which has been replaced in the comm. by *-kaṃ dānaṃ diyyati*.—2. I consider as " Māgadhism " the voc. sg. in *-e* of *a*-stems: *Bhesike* D. I. 225^{7}, 226^{9} from the proper name *Bhesika*; *Takkāriye* Jā. IV. 247^{24} from *Takkāriya*. Cf. Māg. *puttake, ceḍe, bhaṭṭake* etc. These are nominatives used as vocatives[2]. In a Māgadhesque passage in D. I. 54^{12}, M. I. 518^{5} there occur gen. pl. in *-uno*: *cullāsīti mahākappuno satasapassāni* (DCo. I. 164= *mahākappānaṃ*). Also *pañcakammuno satani* (=*kammānaṃ*) D. I. 54^{2}.

§ 81. Feminines in *-ā*. Stem *kaññā* ' girl '.

	Sg.	Pl.
N.	*kaññā*	*kaññā, kaññāyo*
Acc.	*kaññaṃ*	*kaññā, kaññāyo*
Instr.	*kaññāya*	*kaññāhi*
Abl.	*kaññāya*	*kaññāhi*
G.D.	*kaññāya*	*kaññānaṃ*
L.	*kaññāya, -āyaṃ*	*kaññāsu*
V.	*kaññe*	*kaññā, -āyo*

On flexion: 1. The forms of Instr. sg. (as well as of Abl., Gen., Dat.) in *-āya*, like the Prākrit endings in *-āa*[3], are derived from the old ending *-āyās* in Abl.- Gen.; the old Instr. in *-ayā* has disappeared. Beside *-āya* there is also *-ā*. But I do not believe that they are to be connected with the Vedic Instrumentals like *doṣā, barhaṇā*. The forms are rather the result of a phonetical process (§ 27.2). The ending *-ā* appears, for instance, also in loc., e.g. *rathiyā* 'on the street' Dpvs. 6.34.—2. For voc. sg. cf. the frequent *bhadde* JāCo. II. 29^{4} etc. and *ayye* JāCo. I. 405^{5} etc.; further *therike* Th2. 1 (the *i* is extended *metri causa*); *devate* Vv. 29. 2; *lohitape* (scil. *biḷārike*) Jā. III.

[1] Trenckner, Notes, p. 75.

[2] Cf. Pischel, PkrGr. § 366 b.

[3] Pischel, PkrGr. § 375.

266[17] etc. According to Kacc. II. 1.64 (Senart, p. 256), an exception is to be made of *ammā*, *annā*, *ambā*, *tātā*—all used in addressing the mother. The form *ammā* is well attested: Thl. 44, D. I. 93[6] etc.—3. The nom., acc. and voc. pl. *kaññāyo* is analogically formed after the corresponding forms *rattiyo*, *kumāriyo* etc. of the ī-declension[1]. The form is written with ī, for instance, in *pokkharaṇīyo* A. I. 145[10].

3. *i*- and *u*-declension.

§ 82. Masculine stems in *i* and *u*: Stems: *aggi* 'fire', *bhikkhu* 'monk'.

	Sg.	Sg.	Pl.	Pl.
Nom.	*aggi*	*bhikkhu*	*aggayo*, *aggī*	*bhikkhavo*, *bhikkhū*
Acc.	*aggiṃ*	*bhikkhuṃ*		
Instr.	*agginā*	*bhikkhunā*	*aggīhi*	*bhiikkhūhi*
Abl.	*aggismā*, *aggimhā*, *agginā*	*bhikkhusmā*, *bhikkhumhā*, *bhikkhunā*		
Gen.-Dat.	*aggissa*, *aggino*	*bhikkhussa*, *bhikkhuno*	*aggīnaṃ*	*bhikkhūnaṃ*
Loc.	*aggismiṃ*, *aggimhi*	*bhikkhusmiṃ*, *bhikkhumhi*	*aggīsu*	*bhikkhūsu*
Voc.	*aggi*	*bhikkhu*	*aggayo*, *aggī*	*bhikkhavo*, *bhikkhave*, *bhikkhū*

On flexion: 1. The forms in *-ismā*, *-imhā*, *-usmā*, *-umhā* in Abl. Sg. are analogy-formations after the *a*-declension, as also those in *-ismiṃ*, *-imhi*, *-usmiṃ*, *-umhi* in Loc. Sg., those in *-issa*, *-ussa* in Gen. Sg., and those in *-ī*, *-ū* in Nom. and Voc. Pl.[2]—2. The forms in *-ino*, *-uno* of Gen.-Dat. Sg. are either modelled on the neuter *n*-declension of Skr., or they are derived from the declension of *in*-stems[3].—3. The forms of Abl. Sg. in *-inā*, *-unā* are transfers from the Instr.[4] The forms of Acc. Pl. in *-ayo*, *-avo*, like those in *-ī*, *-ū*, are transfers from the Nom.; cf. Acc. Pl. *isayo* S. I. 226[13], *sattavo* Jā. V. 95[26], *aggī* Vin.I. 31[6]. *bhikkhū* M. I. 84[9].—4. The protraction of the stem-vowel in

1 Oldenberg, KZ. 25. 317.

2 The same forms also in Pkr.; Pischel, § 377 ff.

3 Similarly Pkr. *aggiṇo*, *vāuṇo* beside *aggissa vāussa*.

4 The grammarians (E. Kuhn, Beitr, p. 82) give also *kasmā hetunā* in Abl.

-īhi, *-ūhi* of Instr.-Abl. Pl. and in *-īsu*, *-ūsu*, of Loc. Pl. is probably due to analogy with the form in Gen. Pl.—5. The form *bhikkhave* in Voc. Pl. is a "Māgadhism" which has penetrated into the literary language from the popular speech in this word of address so often used by Buddha towards his followers. In Sg. the Nominative form is used as Vocative.

§ 83. Isolated forms: 1. In Acc. Sg. there are sometimes found the forms *bhikkhunaṃ* Sn. 513, *ādiccabandhunaṃ* D. II. 287[21] (verse)—after the analogy of *in*-stems. An *agginaṃ* too would be expected accordingly.—2. The form corresponding to the old Gen.-Abl. in *-os* is to be found in the postposition *hetu* 'on account of, for the sake of' (§ 22).—3. To the Skr. ending *-au* in Loc. Sg. corresponds *-o* in *ādo*, instead of which however occurs *-ādu* in Th1. 1274 (§22). Cf. § 86. 5.—4. The old ending of Voc. Sg. is to be found in *ise* 'O wise one!' Sn. 1052. E. Müller (PGr. p. 73) cites an analogous Voc. Sg. *Sutano* Jā. III. 329[8] (treated as Nom. in JāCo. III. 325[2], 329[28]).—5. The mixing up of *in*- and *i*-flexions (§ 95) has led also in the case of original *i*-stems to the construction of forms according to the *in*-decl.[1] Thus *aggino* Saddhammopāyana 584; *dummatino* Mhvs. 4. 3 (where also the analogous form *mittadduno*); *sāramatino* Dh. 11; *vajjamatino* Dh. 318; also Instr. Sg. *nivātavuttinā* Th1. 71, 210 (in Skr. too occasionally °*vṛttin* for °*vṛtti*).—6. An isolated Acc. Pl. with transfer to the *a*-decl. is to be found in *ise* Jā. V. 92[24]. It is preceded by *samaṇe. brāhmaṇe.*—7. Archaic forms in *-bhi* instead of *-hi* in Instr. Pl. are *isibhi* Th1. 1065, Jā. III. 29[10] (with protraction in *isībhi* Th2. 206); *ñātibhi* Cp. I. 9. 56, Jā. III. 329[19], 495[23]. 8. Forms with shortened stem-vowel in Instr. (Dat. Abl.), Loc. and Gen. Pl. are not at all rare. The shortening takes place mostly *metri causa*. Cf. *pāṇihi* Jā. VI. 579[29]; *kimihi* Th1. 315; *akkhihi* (n.) Sn. 608; *sādhuhi* Dpvs. 4. 6; *ādisu* JāCo. I. 61[15]; *asisu* M. I. 86[31]; *bhikkhusu* Th1. 241, 1207; *usūsu* M. I. 86[30]; *appabuddhinaṃ* Th1. 667; *ñātinaṃ* Th1. 240; *sādhunaṃ* Mhvs. 37. 232 (=Cūlavaṃsa, Colombo ed., 37. 182); *bhikkhunaṃ* Th1. 1231, S. I. 190[15], *bandhunaṃ* Th1. 240.

§ 84. The stem *sakhi* 'friend'[2], which belongs to the poetic language and is represented by *sahāyaka* in prose, has the two

[1] E. Kuhn. Beitr. p. 80; E. Müller, PGr. p. 41.

[2] Cf. JPTS. 1909, p. 18 f. All the forms quoted here from "J. A." i.e., Jātakaṭṭhakathā, are taken from verses ("J").

supplementary stems *sakha* and *sakhāra*. The latter originated from Acc. Sg. *sakhāraṃ*, which is itself an analogy-formation after the flexion of agent nouns (*satthā*: *satthāraṃ* = *sakhā*: x). The flexion is as follows: Sg. Nom. *sakhā* (as in Skr.) Sn. 253, Jā. II. 29[16], III. 50[21], 296[3], V. 509[20], S. I. 36[2] (verse), Dpvs. 11. 26, Mhvs. 19. 13 and (*sabba*)*sakho* Th¹. 648.—Acc. *sakhāraṃ*[1] Jā. II. 348[20], III. 296[3], V. 509[20].—Instr. *sakhinā* (on the analogy of *agginā*) Jā. IV. 41[29].—Abl. *sakhārasmā* Jā. III. 534[2].—Gen. *sakhino* Jā. IV. 426[23], VI. 478[1] (and *sakhissa* according to Kacc. II. 3. 34, in Senart, p. 288). —Loc. (*sakhe* Kacc. II. 3. 32, in senart, p. 283).—Voc. *sakhā* (= Nom.) Jā. III. 295[29].—Pl. Nom. *sakhā* Jā. III. 323[10], Dpvs. 11. 24 and *sakhāro* Jā. III. 492[14], IV. 292[27] (cf. what has been said above about *sakhāraṃ*), (moreover according to Kacc. II. 3. 30: *sakhāno* after the *n*-flexion, as well as 31: *sakhāyo* and *sakhino*). —Instr. (*sakhehi* and *sakhārehi* according to Kacc. II. 3. 34.)— Gen.-Dat. *sakhīnaṃ* Jā. III. 492[14], IV. 42[8] and *sakhānaṃ* Sn. 123, Jā. II. 228[20] (and *sakhārānaṃ* Kacc. II. 3. 36).—Loc. (*sakhesu* and *sakhāresu* Kacc. II. 3. 36).

§ 85. Neuters in *i*, *u*. Stems: *akkhi* ' eye ', *assu* ' tear '.

	Sg.		Pl.	
Nom. Acc. Voc.	*akkhi*	*assu*	*akkhīni*	*assūni*
	akkhiṃ	*assuṃ*	*akkhī*	*assū*

For the rest as in Masc. (§82). There occurs however a Sg. Loc. *ambuni* ' in the water ' Jā. V. 6[5] like Skr. *madhuni*.

On flexion: 1. Analogical formations after the *a*-decl. are the forms in *-iṃ*, *-uṃ* of the Sg. (after *rūpaṃ*), as well as those in *-ī*, *-ū* of the Plural (after *rūpā*).—2. As forms in Nom. Sg. are used, *e.g.*, *dadhiṃ* JāCo. IV. 140[6]; *suciṃ* (*sugandhaṃ salilaṃ*) Jā. VI. 534[11]; *assuṃ* JāCo. III. 163[25]; *vatthuṃ* (= *vastu*) JāCo. III. 39[8]; *kusalaṃ bahuṃ* Vv. 18. 15. On the other hand, *dadhi* Milp. 48[17], *assu* Th2. 220.—3. For the forms in *-ī*, *-ū* cf. Nom. *akkhī bhinnā* Jā. I. 483[29], *madhū* Jā. VI. 537[20]; Acc. *akkhī* DhCo. I. 9[20].

§ 86. Feminines in *i* (*ī*) and *u* (*ū*). Stems: *jāti* ' birth, existence ' (*nadī* ' river ') *dhenu* ' cow ' (*sassū* ' mother-in-law ').

[1] Instead of *sakhaṃ* (as Acc. Sg. of *sakhi*) Jā. II. 299[13] we should perhaps read *sakaṃ* as in the Burmese mss.

	Sg.		Pl.	
Nom.	*jāti (nadī)*	*dhenu (sassū)*	*jātiyo*	*dhenuyo*
Acc.	*jātiṃ*	*dhenuṃ*	*jātī*	*dhenū*
Instr.-Abl.	*jātiyā*	*dhenuyā*	*jātīhi*	*dhenūhi*
Dat.-Gen.	*jātiyā*	*dhenuyā*	*jātīnaṃ*	*dhenūnaṃ*
Loc.	*jātiyā,-yaṃ*	*dhenuyā,-yaṃ*	*jātīsu*	*dhenūsu*
Voc.	*jāti (nadi)*	*dhenu (sassu)*	*jātiyo,-tī*	*dhenuyo, -nū*

On flexion: 1. The flexions of short-vowel stems and long-vowel stems coincide with each other in Pāli excepting in Nom. Sg. Here the latter mostly retain their length. But shortening too is found in this position, as, *e.g.*, in *sassu* Vv. 29. 7, 8.—2. As a rule ī at the end of the stem is changed into *iy* before vowel-endings. The flexion is thus like that of monosyllabic ī-stems in Sanskrit. In analogy with it ū too is then changed into *uy*. Yet, however, there are numerous forms of the ī-stems in which ī is changed into *y*,—particularly, *metri causa*, in the Gāthā-dialect; but analogous forms occur also in canonical prose. Cf. *ratyā* Thl. 517, 628, Jā. VI. 491[21] (instead of *rattiyā*) 'of the night'=*rātryās*; Nom. Pl. *ratyā* Jā. VI. 26[16] (com. *rattio*) and Loc. Sg. *rattimhi* Jā. V. 102[23]; Instr. Sg. *nikatyā* Jā. III. 88[14] (com. *nikatiyā*) 'through treachery' =*nikṛtyā*; Gen. Sg. *pathavyā* Dh. 178 (instead of *-viyā*) 'of the earth'=*pṛthivyās*; Nom. Pl. *nābhyo* (com. *nābhio*) Vv. 64. 4. The laws of assimilation act in most of these cases when the consonant is immediately followed by *y*: Instr. Sg. *jaccā* (§ 55) Dh. 393, Sn. 136, Jā. III. 395[6] (com. *jātiyā*); *sammuccā* (for *-tiyā*) Sn. 648; *uppaccā* (for *-ttiyā*) S. I. 209[6] (verse); Loc. Sg. *Naliññaṃ* (for *-niyaṃ*) Jā. VI. 313[9]; Nom. Pl. *pokkharañño* (for *-ṇiyo*) Vv. 44. 11, S. I. 233[1] (verse); *dasso* (com. *dāsiyo*) Jā. IV. 53[29]; *najjo* (for *nadio*) Vv. 6. 7. In prose: Gen. Sg. *najjā* Vin. I. 1[6], D. II. 112[22]; Nom. Pl. *najjo* S. III. 202[6], 221[11] etc. A remarkable form in Nom. Pl. is *najjāyo* 'rivers' Jā. VI. 278[1], which presupposes a stem **najjā*, abstracted out of an Acc. Sg. **najjaṃ*=Ved. *nadyam*[1]. —3. The forms in Pl. with extended stem-vowel may again undergo shortening: *naranāriṇaṃ* 'of men and women' Cp. I. 6. 2; *nārisu* Dh. 284; *jātisu* Thl. 346 etc.—4. For the double-forms in Nom. Acc. Pl. let us mention, for Nom. Pl., *kumāriyo* JāCo. I. 337[8], *pokkharaṇī* Vv. 81. 5, *jambuyo* Thl. 309, (*accharā*) *puthū* Thl. 1190;

[1] Franke, PGr., p. 35, note 4. According to E. Kuhn, Beitr. p. 82 the forms of Gen. Pl. in *-iyānaṃ* collected by Storck are to be explained in the same way.

Acc. Pl. *pokkharaṇiyo* D. II. 178^{23}, *ramsī* Vv. 53. 5, *dhenuyo* Vv. 80. 6.—5. A form corresponding to Skr. Loc. Sg. in *-au* of *i*-stems has been retained in *ratto*: *divā ca ratto ca* ' day and night ' Sn. 223, Dh. 296, Th2. 312, Ud. 15^{3} (verse), Vv. 84. 32, S. I. 33^{16}, Sdhs. 51^{16} (prose). A Loc. Sg. *bhuvi*[1] is formed from *bhū* ' earth ' according to Kacc. A case of transfer from the *ī*-flexion to *ā*-flexion is presented by *aḍḍharattāyaṃ* ' in the middle of night ' (com. *-ttiyaṃ*) Vv. 81. 16.

§ 87. 1. Flexion of the stems *sirī* ' prosperity, fortune ' (*Sirī* goddess of prosperity) = *śrī*; *hirī* 'modesty ' = *hrī*; *itthī* ' woman ' = *strī*. (*a*) *sirī*: Sg. Nom. *Sirī* Jā. V. 112^{30} and *sirĭ* S. I. 44^{12} (verse);—Acc. *siriṃ* JāCo. II. 410^{9};—Instr. *siriyā* Sn. 686, VvCo. 328^{16};—Voc. *Siri* DCo. 97^{18}.—(*b*) *hirī*: Sg. Nom. *hirī* S. I. 33^{11} (verse), A 1. 95^{25} and *hirĭ* Iv. 36^{6}, A. I. 51^{17}, IV. 11^{22}, Nett. 82^{27}, JāCo. I. 207^{17};—Acc. *hiriṃ* Sn. 719 etc.; Instr. *hiriyā* Jā. II. 65^{4}, A. III. 6^{16}, Nett. 50^{26}, JāCo. I. 129^{23}.—(*c*) *itthī* (*thī*, § 29): *itthī* Jā. I. 307^{14}, A. I. 28^{9}, Mhvs. 9. 24 and *itthĭ* Th1. 151, D. II. 273^{18} (verse), A. III. 68^{23}, JāCo. I. 437^{11};—Acc. *itthiṃ* Th1. 315, Vin. I. 23^{14}, JāCo. I. 307^{23};—Instr. *itthiyā* Vin. I. 23^{15}, JāCo. I. 290^{21};—Dat.-Gen. *itthiyā* S. I. 33^{13} (verse), JāCo. I. 307^{10} (*thiyā* Jā. V. 81^{16}).—Pl. Nom. *itthiyo* S. I. 185^{26} (verse), Vin. I. 36^{18}, JāCo. III. 392^{17};—Acc. *itthiyo* JāCo. I. 289^{10} (*thiyo* Sn. 769, Jā. III. 459^{13});—Instr. *itthīhi*;—Gen.-Dat. *itthīnaṃ* JāCo. III. 392^{18} (*thīnaṃ* Jā. I. 295^{8});—Loc. *itthīsu* Th1. 137, S. IV. 346^{21}.—2. Flexion of masculines in *ŭ̄*[2]: Sg. Nom. *abhibhū* S. I. 121^{16} (verse), D. I. 18^{7} etc. *sayaṃbhū* Bu. 14. 1, *pāragū* D. I. 88^{5}, JāCo. II. 99^{20}, *viññū* Iv. 98^{13} etc., and *pāragŭ* Th1. 66, *mataññŭ* S. IV. 175^{29};—Acc. *abhibhuṃ* Dh. 418, Sn. 534, M. I. 2^{27}, *sabbaññuṃ* JāCo. I. 335^{31};—Instr. *sabbaññunā*, *sayaṃbhunā* Milp. 214^{29};—Dat.-Gen. *amattaññūno* S. IV. 103^{27} and *viññussa* A. I. 138^{30}, M. III. 179^{25}, *abhibhussa* S. I. 157^{10};—Loc. *abhibhusmiṃ* M. I. 2^{28}.—Pl. Nom.-Acc. *mattaññūno* S. IV. 105^{8}, *gotrabhŭno* M. III. 256^{7}, *sahabhŭno* Dhs. 1197 f., *vedagŭno* Ud. 14^{17} (verse), and *sahabhŭ* D. II. 260^{6} (verse), *vadaññū* S. I. 34^{21} (verse), *addhagū* Th2. 55 (neut. *sahabhūni* Nett. 16^{28});—Instr. *viññūhi* D.II. 93^{33}, S. I.9^{14}, *lokavidūhi*

[1] E. Kuhn, Beitr. p. 83; E. Müller, PGr. p. 74.

[2] On the analogy of compounds formed with *bhū* also words compounded with *ā*-roots are transferred to the *ŭ̄*-flexion: *viññŭ̄* ' wise ' = *vijña*, *sabbajñū* ' omniscient ' = *sarvajña*; *pāragŭ̄* ' reaching the other side ' (beside *pāraga*) = *pāraga* etc,

Vv.44.25.—Dat. -Gen. *viññūnaṃ* Thl. 667, S. IV. 93[22], *rattaññūnaṃ* A. I. 25[18]—Loc. *viññūsu* A. III. 153[24], V. 15[16].

4. Diphthong-stems.

§ 88. 1. The Skr. stem *rai* ' wealth ' is unknown in Pāli.—2. From *nau* a new stem *nāvā* ' ship ' has been formed[1], which is inflected according to § 81 (cf. *nāvāyo* DhCo. III. 184[19], *nāvāsu* ib. 185[1]).—3. Of *go* ' cattle ' the following old forms have been preserved: Sg. Nom. *go* S. I. 221[34] (verse), *go-r-iva* Jā. V. 15[27].—Pl. Nom. *gāvo* Sn. 20, A. II. 43[18]; Acc. (transferred from Nom.) *gāvo* Jā. VI. 549[6], S. IV. 181[12], DhCo. III. 43[2];—Instr. *gohi* S.I. 6[9] (verse), Sn. 33.—Dat.-Gen. *gavaṃ* Jā. III. 111[17], *gonaṃ* (=Ved. *gonām*) Dpvs. I. 76 and its phonetic variant (according to § 15. 3) *gunnaṃ* S. II. 188[9], A. I. 229[13], DhCo. III. 243[15]. *Gava* [2] is a new stem which is the basis of Sg. Abl. *gavā* D. I. 201[25], Dat.-Gen. *gavassa* M. I. 429[32], Loc. *gave* Sn. 310. From a third stem *gāva* is derived *gāvī* ' cow ' which is quite common. Finally we have also a stem *goṇa*[3]: Sg. Nom. *goṇo* Vin. IV. 7[16], S. IV. 195[32], DhCo. III. 262[6]; Acc. *goṇaṃ* M. I. 10[36], JāCo. I. 494[11]. Pl. Acc. *goṇe* DhCo. III. 302[18]; Gen. *goṇānaṃ* DhCo. III. 239[22].—4. Of the Skr. stem *div*, *dyu* ' day, sky ' only the adverbially used form *divā* ' by day ' has been preserved in Pāli.

5. Radical Stems.

§ 89. Only meagre rests have been preserved of the flexion of radical stems. Thus, *e.g.*, Sg. Instr. *vācā* ' with the word ' Sn. 232 from Skr. *vāc* which otherwise appears as *vācā* in P. (§ 81); Sg. Instr. *padā* ' with the foot ' Thl. 457, Sn. 768 from Skr. *păd* (cf. pl. Gen *khattiyo dvipadaṃ seṭṭho* S. I. 6[22] (verse) =Skr. *dvipadām*); Pl. Acc. *sarado sataṃ* 'hundred autumns' Jā II. 16[15] from Skr. *śarad*; Pl. Gen. *sāgaraṃ saritaṃ patiṃ* 'the ocean, the lord (husband) of the rivers ' Jā. II. 442[8] from Skr. *sarit*. All the quotable examples belong to the Gāthā-language[4]. In Mhvs. 36. 93 there is the Sg. Loc. *pathi*

[1] Similarly also in Pkr. *ṇāvā*; Pischel, § 394.

[2] Cf. AMāg. Sg. Nom. *gave*, Pl. Nom. *gavā* in Pischel, § 393.

[3] AMāg *goṇa*; beside it fem. *gāvī*.

[4] It seems unlikely to me that in *āpo ca pathavī ca* ' water and earth ' Sn. 307 *āpo* is the Nom. Pl. = Skr. *āpas*. Beside the Acc. Sg. *āpaṃ* Sn 391 we have also the Loc. Sg. *āpe* Sn. 392. A stem *āpa* has therefore to be accepted. In the first member of a compound is found *āpo°*, *e.g.*, in D. II. 108[5].

'on the road' as var. lec. in the Ceylonese mss. for *pathaṃ* (Acc. Sg.) of the Burmese mss. (§ 93. 4).

6. *r*-declension

§ 90. Nomina agentis. Stem: *satthar* 'teacher'.

	Sg.	Pl.
Nom.	*satthā*	*satthāro*
Acc.	*satthāraṃ*[1]	
Instr.	*sattharā, satthārā, satthunā*	*satthūhi, satthārehi*
Abl.	*sattharā, satthārā*	
Dat.-Gen.	*satthu, satthuno, satthussa*	*satthūnaṃ, satthārānaṃ*
Loc.	*satthari*	*satthūsu, satthāresu*
Voc.	*satthā, sattha, satthe*	*satthāro*

On flexion: 1. The following are historical forms used in every period of the language: Sg. Nom. *satthā* (JāCo. III. 20[19]), Acc. *satthāraṃ* (JāCo. III. 21[1]), as well as Pl. Nom. Voc. *satthāro*. The last form was then used also as Acc. Also the following forms are historical: Sg. Gen. *satthu* (Iv. 79[8], JāCo. III. 20[29], *bhattu* Vv. 15[5]) = Skr. *śāstur*; Sg. Loc. *satthari* (Dhs. 1004, DhCo. II. 38[11]) = *śāstari*; also Sg. Instr. *sattharā* = *śāstrā* with Svarabhakti. The Instr. is then used also as Abl.—2. In compounds the *ṛ* of the stem appears in Pāli as *u*. Thus *satthukappa* 'like the master' Mhvs. 14. 65, *bhattuvasānuvattinī* 'obedient to the will of the husband' Jā. II. 348[16]. A stem *satthu* was abstracted out of these *u*-forms, from which: Sg. Instr. *satthunā* (Mhvs. 17. 12), Dat.-Gen. *satthuno* (Sn. 547, 573, Thl. 131, *bhattuno* VvCo. 110[11]), *satthussa* (Mhvs. 4. 32); Pl. Instr. Abl. *satthūhi*, Gen. *satthūnaṃ* (DCo. I. 20[28]: *sotūnaṃ*), Loc. *satthūsu*.—3. A stem *satthāra* was abstracted analogically out of the proportion *kammāraṃ* : *kammāra* = *satthāraṃ* : x. From it are derived the forms Pl. Instr. *satthārehi*, Gen. *satthārānaṃ* (JāCo. I. 509[3]), Loc. *satthāresu*; perhaps also Sg. Instr. *satthārā* (D. I. 163[8], JāCo. II.24[16], DhCo. II. 45[1], Mhvs. 5. 77) and the form in Sg. Abl. which is identical with it[2].—4. Transfer to the *a*-declension through the elision of *r* should also be noticed. Thus

[1] Shortened *metri causa*: *sattharaṃ* Bu. 23. 14.

[2] Also in Pkr. the stems *bhattu* and *bhattāra* cross the historical forms; Pischel, § 389.

nahāpita 'barber' (Sg. Nom. *-to* D. I. 225[16], Acc.*-taṃ* D. I. 225[6], Pl. Acc. *-te* Mhvs. 29. 20) presupposes a stem **snāpitar* (cf. Skr. *nāpitá*); *sallakatta* 'physician' (Sg. Nom. *-tto* Sn. 560, Acc. *-ttaṃ* M. I. 429[4], Milp. 247[12] is = *śalyakartar*[1]. From the stem *khattar* 'door-keeper' = *kṣattar* we have beside the Sg. Nom. *khattā* D. I. 112[29], M. II. 164[31] the Acc. *khattaṃ* D. I. 112[8], M. II. 164[19].—5. The form *satthā* of Voc. Sg. is taken from the Nom. The form *sattha* is shortening of the same on the analogy of *nadi* from *nadī*, *vadhu* Vin. III. 16[25] from *vadhū*. As for the form *satthe*, cf. *khatte* from *khattar* D. I. 112[10], M. II. 164[26]; *katte* from *kattar* Jā. V. 220[24], VI. 492[3]. They are based on the analogy of the Voc. *kaññe* of the Nom. *kaññā* (§ 81).

§ 91. Words signifying personal relation. Stems: *pitar* 'father' m., *mātar* 'mother' f.

	Sg.		Pl.	
Nom.	*pitā*	*mātā*	*pitaro*	*mātaro*
Acc.	*pitaraṃ*	*mātaraṃ*	*pitaro, -tare*	*mātaro*
Instr.	*pitarā*	*mātarā*	*pitūhi,*	*mātūhi*
Abl.	*pitarā*	*mātarā, mātuyā*	*pitarehi*	
Dat.-Gen.	*pitu, pituno, pitussa*	*mātu mātuyā.*	*pitūnaṃ, pitunnaṃ, pitarānaṃ*	*mātūnaṃ*
Loc.	*pitari*	*mātari, mātuyā, -yaṃ*	*pitūsu, pitaresu*	*mātūsu*

On flexion. The stems *pitar* (with short stem-vowel in the strong cases) and *pitu*, which are in use in all the periods of the language, are distributed as in the case of *satthar*. I can find no form to justify the assumption of a stem *pitara*[2]. The stem-vowel is long in *nattar* 'grandson' as in Skr. *naptar*. Cf. Pl. Acc. *nattāro* Ud. 91[23] = Skr. Nom. *naptāras*, also Pl. Instr. *nattārehi* Ud. 92[3].—2. Attestation of the most important forms: Sg. Instr. *pitarā* JāCo. III. 37[15], *bhātarā* JāCo. I. 308[2]. *mātarā* Th2. 212; Sg. Abl. *pitarā*, *mātarā* JāCo. V. 214[22], *dhītuyā* Mhvs. 8. 7; Sg. Dat.-Gen. *pitu* Th2. 419, JāCo. IV. 137[13], *mātu* Th1. 473, Vin. I. 17[13], JāCo. I. 52[29], *duhitu* Th2Co. 269[5], *pituno* Vin. I. 17[1], VvCo. 170[4], *bhātussa* Mhvs. 8. 9; *mātuyā* JāCo. I. 53[5], Mhvs.

1 Cf. E. Müller, PGr. p. 82.

2 In Pkr. there are the stems *pitu*, *piti* (cf. Pāli *pitito*, *mātito* § 77) and *pitara* beside *pitar*. Pischel, § 391.

10. 80; Sg. Loc. *bhātari* JāCo. III. 56[23]; Pl. Instr. *mātāpitūhi* Th2. 516, JāCo. II. 103[3]; Pl. Gen. *pitūnaṃ* Iv. 110[6], *pitunnaṃ* DhCo. I. 161[12]; Pl. Loc. *mātāpitūsu* Th2. 499, JāCo. I. 152[7].—3. Isolated forms: Sg. Acc. *pituṃ* Cp. 2. 9. 3; Pl. Nom. *bhātuno* Th2. 408; Acc. *-pitū* (in *mātāpitū*) Th2. 433; further Sg. Nom. *jāmāto* 'son-in-law' JāCo. IV. 219[25]; Pl. Acc. *bhāte* Dpvs. 6. 21, 22 with transfer to the *a*-flexion (§ 90. 4). Transfer of feminine stems to *ā*-decl. is also found to occur. Cf. Sg. Gen. *mātāya* JāCo. I. 62[13]. Such transfer is very frequent in the case of *dhītar* 'daughter': Sg. Nom. *dhītā* Th2. 46, Acc. *dhītaraṃ* Th2. 98, JāCo. III. 19[16] etc., but also Dat.-Gen. *dhītāya* VvCo. 270[28], Mhvs. 5. 169 (beside *dhītu* JāCO. VI. 366[10]), Voc. *dhīte* JāCo.III. 21[28], DhCo. III. 8[12]; Pl. Nom. *dhītā* Mhvs. 2. 18 (beside *dhītaro* JāCo. III. 3[8]), Instr. *dhītāhi* VvCo. 161[17], Mhvs. 7. 68, Gen. *dhītānaṃ* JāCo. III. 4[7], Loc. *dhītāsu* JāCo. I. 152[8].

7. *n*-declension.

§ 92. Masculines in *-an*. Stems *rājan* 'king' and *attan* 'self, soul'.

<table>
<tr><th></th><th colspan="2">Sg.</th><th colspan="2">Pl.</th></tr>
<tr><td>Nom.</td><td>rājā</td><td>attā</td><td rowspan="2">rājāno</td><td rowspan="2">attāno</td></tr>
<tr><td>Acc.</td><td>rājānaṃ</td><td>attānaṃ[1]</td></tr>
<tr><td>Instr.</td><td>raññā, rājinā</td><td>attanā</td><td rowspan="2">rājūhi</td><td rowspan="2">(attanehi) (attehi)</td></tr>
<tr><td>Abl.</td><td>raññā</td><td>attanā</td></tr>
<tr><td>Dat.-Gen.</td><td>rañño, rājino</td><td>attano</td><td>raññaṃ, rājūnaṃ</td><td>(attānaṃ)</td></tr>
<tr><td>Loc.</td><td>rājini</td><td>attani</td><td>rājūsu</td><td>(attanesu)</td></tr>
<tr><td>Voc.</td><td>rajă</td><td>attă</td><td>rājāno</td><td>attāno</td></tr>
</table>

On flexion. 1. The forms of the Singular (with the exception of Abl., which is = Instr.) are historical and used in all the periods of the language. The forms Instr. *rāññā* (DhCo. I. 164[6]) and Dat.-Gen. *rañño* (Vv. 74. 4, DhCo. I. 164[5], JāCo. III. 5[19]) are = *rājñā*, *rājñas* according to § 53. 1; *rājinā* (Mhvs. 6. 2) and *rājino* (Th2. 463, Sn. 299, 415, Mhvs. 2. 14) are affected by Svarabhakti, as also *rājini* = *rājñi*. The long-vowel forms in the Voc. Sg. are transferred

[1] With Svarabhakti *ātumānaṃ* Sn. 782.

from the Nom. The stems, which like *attan* 'soul, self' end in Skr. with *-man -van* following after a consonant, retain the *a* in the weak cases. Cf. Instr. *amhanā* (§ 50. 2) = *aśmanā*; *attani* JāCo. III. 25[2]. Also *muddhanā* 'with the head' Mhvs. 19. 30 = *mūrdhnā*; Loc. *muddhani* Sn. 689, M. I. 168[29] (verse), JāCo. IV. 265[17], Mhvs. 36. 66 = *mūrdhni*, *-dhani*. In Plural the forms in Nom. Voc. are historical (used also as Acc., *e.g.*, DhCo. II. 15[6]), as well as the Gen. *raññaṃ* (D. II. 87[3], Mhvs. 18. 32) = *rājñām*. Moreover, a new stem *rāju* appears in Plural (*rājūhi* Ud. 41[7], M. II. 120[22], JāCo. III. 45[4], Mhvs. 5. 80, 8. 21, archaic *rājubhi* D. II. 258[14]; *rājūnaṃ* Ud. 11[3], JāCo. II. 104[29], III. 487[21]), probably in analogy with the *r*-stems (§ 90) according to the proportion *satthā* : *satthūhi* = *rājā* : x. I cannot find attestation for the forms *attanehi* etc.—2. Transfer to the *a*-decl. takes place often as a consequence of the dropping of the final nasal; cf. forms of the stem *rāja*[1] such as Sg. Gen. *rājassa* Dpvs. 17. 41, Pl. Nom. *rājā* Mhvs. 37. 89 (= Colombo ed. II. 37. 39); Sg. Acc. *brahmaṃ* (instead of *brahmānaṃ*) Vv. 17. 4, Sn. 151, 285, M. I. 2[11], 328[18] like Pkr. Māg. *bamhaṃ*; *muddhaṃ* (from *muddhan*) Dh. 72, Sn. 987, D. I. 95[13]; *attaṃ* Dh. 379; also Pl. Instr. *attehi*, Gen. *attānaṃ*. A stem *rañña* was developed out of the weak-grade form *rājñ-*: Sg. Nom. *rañño* A. II. 113[21], 116[24], 117[3]; Gen. *raññassa* Jā. III. 70[7]; Loc. *raññe* D. II. 145[16], III. 83[27]; Pl. Instr. *raññehi*[2] A. I. 279[14]. The weak stem extended by *a* gave rise to the forms *attanehi*, *attanesu*. In the same way a stem *addhāna*[3] was abstracted out of the strong-grade form of *addhan* 'way, time' (Sg. Acc. *addhānaṃ*): *atīta-m-addhāne* 'in past time' JāCo. III. 43[1] (verse), *addhānamagga-paṭipanno* D. I. 1[5].—3. Under the influence of the preceding labial (§ 19. 2), in the weak cases of the stem *brahman* 'the god Brahman, Brahmin' the *a* is changed into *u*. Thus Sg. Acc. *brahmānaṃ*, but Instr. *brahmunā* Thl. 1168, Ud. 77[10], D. II. 237[4] etc., Dat.-Gen. *brahmuno* Thl. 182, D. I. 220[33], 222[2], S. I. 141[2]. The Loc. Sg. is *brahmani* M. I. 2[12], the Voc. *brahme* (cf § 90. 5) Jā. VI. 525[15], M. I. 328[20], Vin. I. 6[8]. Similarly also *addhunā* S. I. 78[26], II. 179[27], *addhuno* D. I. 17[19], M. III. 184[9].

[1] At the end of a compound there is used in Pāli sometimes °*rāja*, sometimes °*rājan*. Cf. *supaṇṇarājassa* JāCo. III. 188[28] and *supaṇṇarañño* JāCo. III. 189[7]. Also °*rāju* : *nāgarājūnaṃ* Mhvs. 1. 68.

[2] This is probably the proper reading for *raññāhi*. Pkr. knows neither the *u*-stem nor any stem corresponding to Pāli *rañña*.

[3] Also in Pkr. there are forms such as Sg. Nom. *addhāṇo*, *muddhāṇo*.

§ 93. 1. Of the stem *san* 'dog' = *śvan* the Sg. Nom. *sā* is quite common: S. I. 176^{13} (verse), D. I. 166^{8}, M. I. 77^{35}, II. 232^{25}, Pu. 55^{13}. In JPTS. 1909, p. 61 also the Pl. Nom. *sāno* is cited, but no reference is given[1]. From the Skr. weak stem *śun-* a new stem *suṇa* (sic! with *ṇ*) has been derived: Sg. Instr. *suṇena* Jā. VI. 353^{20,29}, 354^{6,12}; Voc. *suṇa* JāCo. VI. 357^{1}. The frequent form *sunakha* is another derivative. From the strong Skr. stem *śvān-* is further derived *suvāna*, *-ṇa*: Pl. Nom. *suvānā* Jā. VI. 247^{16}, Instr. *suvāṇehi* M. III. 91^{25}.—2. Of *yuvan* 'youth' the Sg. Nom. *yuvā* Dh. 280, Sn. 420, D. I. 80^{16} is quotable. The reading of the Sg. Gen. *yuvino* Jā. IV. 222^{23} is uncertain. The stem *yuva* is to be found in *yuvassa* Mhvs. 18. 28. *Yūna* and *yuvāna*[2] are new formations from the weak and the strong stem respectively.—3. Of *maghavan*, name of Indra, we have the Sg. Nom. *maghavā* Dh. 30, Voc. *maghavā* S. I. 221^{24} (verse) as should be read instead of *mathavā*.—4. Corresponding to the Skr. stems *path* and *panthan* 'path' there are in Pāli the thematised stems *patha* (Sg. Nom. *patho* D. I. 63^{3}, Acc. *pathaṃ* JāCo. II. 39^{13}, Abl. *pathā* Jā. VI. 525^{31}, Gen. *pathassa* Thl. 69, Loc. *pathe* Sn. 176 f., Mhvs. 21. 24) and *pantha* (*panthasakuna* Jā. VI. 527^{22}, *panthadevatā* JāCo. VI. 527^{30}, Sg. Acc. *panthaṃ* Milp. 157^{23}, Loc. *panthasmiṃ* Sn. 121).—5. From *puman* 'man' we have the Sg. Nom. *pumā* Rasav. II. 83^{6}. In Kacc. II. 2. 33 ff. (Senart, p. 271ff.) are given also Voc. *pumaṃ* and Pl. Nom. Voc. *pumāno*, besides Sg. Instr. *pumunā* like *brahmunā*. There is moreover a stem *puma* (Sg. Nom. *pumo* D. II. 273^{18} (verse) and Pl. Nom. *pumā* Jā. III. 459^{13}), as well as *pumāna* (according to Kacc.). There is no trace of the weak stem *puṃs* in Pāli.

§ 94. Neuters in *-an*. Stem: *kamman* 'work, deed' = *karman*. In Sg. the forms are historical in Nom.-Acc.-Voc.—*kamma* Dh. 96, 217; Instr. *kammanā* Sn. 136 etc. and *kammunā*[3] Thl. 143, 786, Vv. 32. 7, Mhvs. 5. 189; Gen. *kammuno*[1] Jā. III. 6?^{17}; Loc. *kammani*. The old forms are however more and more ousted by those of the *a*-flexion on the basis of the agreement in Pl. Nom.-Acc.-Voc. *kammāni* Sn. 263, Dh. 136. Thus Sg. Nom.-Acc. *kammaṃ*, Instr. *kammena* etc. Cf. even in the oldest literature *nāmaṃ* (Sg. Nom.) Sn. 808; *kammehi* Sn. 215, *kammesu* Sn. 140 etc. In the same way

[1] The paradigm given by Minayeff, PGr. p. 28 is artificially constructed: Sg. Nom.-Voc. *sa*, Acc. *saṃ* (etc. like an *a*-stem; but Pl. Instr.-Abl. *sāhi*, *sābhi*, Loc. *sāsu*). Pl. Nom. *sā* 'dogs' S. I. 176^{13}.

[2] Cf. Childers, Pāli Dictionary, under the words.

[3] Cf. § 92. 8, 19. 2.

Sg. Loc. *pabbe* JāCo. I. 245[12], Pl. Loc. *pabbesu* S. IV. 171[20] from *pabba* (*n*) 'knot in a reed, section' = *parvan*; *thāmena* 'forcibly' JāCo. I. 443[7], Milp. 4[3] (beside which, according to § 79. 1. with footnote 1, p. 120, *thāmasā* D. II. 282[27], Mhvs. 23. 83) from *thāma*(*n*) = *sthāman*. New neuter stems are formed also by adding an *a*. Thus Sg. Acc. *jammanaṃ* Sn. 1018 from *jamman* 'birth' = *janman*; Sg. Nom. *yakanaṃ* Kh. 3, M. I. 57[17], D. II. 293[14] from *yakan* 'liver' = *yakan*. —Masculine compounds with neuter second components in *-an* are inflected mostly according to the *a*-decl. after dropping the final nasal. Thus Pl. Nom. *puññakammā* S. I. 97[30]; Sg. Gen. *puthulomassa* Attanagaluvihāravs. 2. 2 from *loman* 'hair'; stem *Vissakamma* (name of a god) = *Viśvakarman* (*e.g.*, Sg. Nom. °*kammo* JāCo. IV. 325[13], Acc. °*kammaṃ* JāCo. V. 132[5], Instr. °*kammena* JāCo. I. 315[11]); but we have also °*kamman* in Acc. °*kammānaṃ* Mhvs. 28. 6 and Instr. °*kammunā* Mhvs. 31. 76.

§ 95. Substantives and adjectives in *-in*. Stem: *hatthin* 'elephant'.

	Sg.	Pl.
Nom.	*hatthī—hatthi*	*hatthino—hatthī*
Acc.	*hatthinaṃ—hatthīṃ*	*hatthino—hatthī*
Instr.	*hatthinā*	*hatthīhi*
Abl.	*hatthinā—hatthismā,-imhā*	*hatthīhi*
Dat.-Gen.	*hatthino—hatthissa*	*hatthinaṃ*
Loc.	*hatthini—hatthismiṃ, -imhi*	*hatthīsu*
Voc.	*hatthi*	*hatthino—hatthī*

On flexion: 1. Two distinct types are in evidence[1]: the old one in *-in* and the new one in *-i* (flexion according to § 82), which is derived either from the stem-form in which the *in*-stems appear in compounds, or from the case-form in Instr. Sg. where both declensions show the same form. Both the types were living in all the periods of the language. Cf., *e.g.*, Sg. Gen. *jhāyino* (from *jhāyin* 'thoughtful') Dh. 110, *seṭṭhino* JāCo. I. 122[17] (from *seṭṭhin* 'merchant'), *hatthino* DhCo. I. 168[12] and °*anupassissa* (from *-ssin* 'observing') Dh. 253, *seṭṭhissa* S. I. 90[1], Vin. I. 218[38], JāCo. IV. 229[10], *hatthissa* Vin. II. 195[26], JāCo. I. 187[26]. Pl. Nom. *jhāyino* Dh. 23, *sāmino* 'the masters' JāCo. II. 3[20], *gāmavāsino* 'the villagers' JāCo. III. 9[27], *pāṇino* 'living beings' Mhvs. 12. 22 and *hatthī* S. I. 211[14] (verse), Vin. I.

[1] As in Pkr. Cf. Pischel, §405.

218[38], JāCo. II. 102[22], *dhaṃsī* 'the brave ones' M. I. 236[1]; Pl. Acc. *hatthi* DhCo. II. 45[25]. Cf. also Sg. Acc. *hatthinaṃ* Thl. 355 and *sāmiṃ* Sn. 83, *gāmavāsiṃ* JāCo. III. 10[11], Sg. Loc *seṭṭhimhi* Vin. I. 17[33]. Long-vowel forms, *i.e.* forms of the *i*-type, are the rule in Pl. Instr.-Abl., Dat.-Gen. and Loc.; metrical shortening is not rare: *pāṇīhi* Vv. 4. 6; *pāṇīnaṃ* Dh. 135, Jā. VI. 594[19].—2. Occasionally *in*-stems too are thematised by adding an *a*[1], thus giving rise to new stems. Cf. Sg. Acc. neut. *ohāriṇaṃ* Dh. 346 from *ohārin* 'dragging down'; Sg. Loc. *ariyavuttine* JāCo. III. 12[24] (verse); Pl. Nom. *verinā* DhCo. II. 37[1] from *verin* 'inimical' = *vairin*; Pl. Acc. *palokine* Th2. 101 from *palokin* 'doomed to destruction', *pāṇine* Sn. 220; pl. Loc. *verinesu* Dh. 197. We have even Sg. Voc. fem. *āveḷine uppalamāladhārine* Vv. 48. 2 from *āveḷin* 'decorated', °*dhārin* 'carrying lotus-wreaths' beside Vocatives like *alaṃkate*. Otherwise the *in*-stems form their feminines as in Skr.: *sāminī* 'mistress', *gabbhinī* 'pregnant' etc.—3. There are some isolated unusual forms, *e.g.*, Pl. Nom. *pāṇayo* Sn. 201, *hatthiyo* Jā. VI. 537[30] and the archaic Instrumentals in *-bhi*: *atthadassībhi* Thl. 4, *nettiṃsavaradhārībhi* Jā. II. 77[23], *jhāyībhi*, *jhānasīlībhi* M. III. 13[25] etc.—4. The stem *tādi* = *tādṛś* (cf. §75) is treated as an *in*-stem; cf. Sg. Gen. *tādino* Vv. 82.7, Pl. Gen. *-naṃ* Vv. 81. 26; also Sg. Loc. *tādine* (cf. 2) Thl. 1173.

8. *nt*-declension

§ 96. Adjectives in *-ant*. Stem: *sīlavant* 'virtuous'.

	Sg.	Pl.
Nom.	*sīlavā— -vanto*	*sīlavanto— -vantā*
Acc.	*sīlavantaṃ*	*sīlavanto— -vante*
Instr.-Abl.	*sīlavatā— -vantena*	*sīlavantehi*
Dat.-Gen.	*sīlavato— -vantassa*	*sīlavantaṃ— -vantānaṃ*
Loc.	*sīlavati— -vante, -vantamhi, -vantasmiṃ*	*sīlavantesu*
Voc.	*sīlavă— -vanta*	*sīlavanto— -vantā*

On flexion. 1. Out of the older historical type the later one has been developed through transfer to the *a*-flexion. The Sg. Acc. in *-antaṃ* was the connecting link. Both types persist side by side through all the stages of the language. The younger type completely

[1] Similarly in Pkr. stems like *sakkhiṇa* = *sākṣin*, *barahina* = *barhin*. Pischel, § 406.

monopolised the Instr., Abl. and Loc. Pl. even from the beginning. Examples of forms of the later type out of the Gāthā-language: Sg. Gen. *sīlavantassa* Dh. 110; Loc. *sīlavante* JāCo. III. 12[22] (verse); Voc. *yasavanta* Vv. 63. 30; Sg. Nom. neut. *vaṇṇavantaṃ* (*pupphaṃ*) Thl. 323. 324; Pl. Acc. *mahante* Jā. IV. 222[28]. From canonical prose. Sg. Nom. *mahanto* 'great' M. III. 185[1]; Pl. Acc. *mahante* Vin. I. 85[31]; Gen. *sīlavantānaṃ* M. I. 334[4], *satimantānaṃ* A. I. 24[33], *dhitimantānaṃ* A. I. 25[2], *bhagavantānaṃ* S. V. 164[6] etc. Also Pl. Instr. *sīlavantehi* D. II. 80[21] etc. Yet the regular flexion is still the older one. From the stem *cakkhumant* 'endowed with eyes, seeing' we have in Sn. the forms Sg. Nom *cakkhumā*, Voc. *-ma*, Instr. *-matā*; Pl. Nom. *-manto*. From *satimat* 'of retentive memory' we have in Dh. Sg. Nom. *satimā*; Gen. *-mato*; Pl. Nom. *-manto*; Gen. *-mataṃ* etc.[1] In canonical prose the forms of the older type are: Sg. Nom. *satimā* D. I. 37[25], *vusitavā* Perf. Part. Act. 'he who has dwelt' M. I. 5[10], *sutavā* 'he who has heard, learnt' M. I. 8[32]; Instr. *mahatā* S. V. 163[26], *sīlavatā* S. III. 167[23]; Gen. *sīlavato* S. IV. 303[20], *sabbāvato* (from *sabbāvant* 'full, complete') M. II. 15[10]; Pl. Gen. *sabbāvataṃ* M. II. 16[18] etc. Also *bhagavā*, *-vatā*, *-vato*, *-vati*; *āyasmā*, *-matā* etc. passim. Forms of the older type in post-canonical prose: Sg. Nom. *sīlavā* Milp. 224[3], JāCo. I. 187[1]; Instr. (*Mārena*) *pāpimatā* Milp. 155[11]; Gen. *mahato* Milp. 224[16], JāCo. III. 23[18], (*Mārassa*) *pāpimato* Milp. 155[8]; *balavato yasavato* Milp. 234[16]; quite commonly *bhagavā*, *-vatā*, *-vato*, *-vati*: *āyasmā*, *-matā*. Beside them however the forms of the *a*-flexion go on increasing: Sg. Nom. *sumahanto* Milp. 155[2]; Instr. *mahantena* JāCo. III. 24[20], 40[3]; Pl. Acc. *sīlavante* JāCo. I. 187[28]; Gen. *bhagavantānaṃ* Milp 226[13]; Sg. Nom. neut. *mahantaṃ* (*pāṭihāriyaṃ*) JāCo. IV. 229[15], *ojavantaṃ* (*raṭṭhaṃ*) JāCo. III. 111[6]; Pl. Nom. neut. *ojavantāni* JāCo. III. 110[20] etc. Of the stem *Himavant*[2], for instance, there occur in JāCo. only the following forms: Sg. Nom. *Himavā* JāCo. VI. 580[8], Gen. *Himavato* JāCo. V. 392[19], 419[18], Loc. *Himavati* seven times (of which five times with the variant reading *-vante*). Otherwise the stem *Himavanta* is used throughout. Cf. also the abstracts like *sīlavantatā* JāCo. I. 320[4] etc., derived from a stem extended by *-a*.—2. Transfer to the *a*-flexion follows also from the dropping of *nt*[3]. Forms of this

[1] Cf. Fausböll, Sn. II. Glossary, under the word *cakkhumat* (p. 118), D. Andersen, PGL. under the word *sīlavat*.

[2] D. Andersen, Index to Fausböll, JāCo. VII, under the word.

[3] Similarly in Pkr.; Pischel, § 398.

type are found in the Gāthā-language: Sg. Acc. *satīmaṃ* Sn. 212, *bhānumaṃ* Sn. 1016, *Himavaṃ* Jā. VI. 272[4]; Pl. Nom. *mutīmā* Sn. 881. Also Sg. Nom. fem. *kittimā* Jā III. 70[6], VI. 508[21]. The fem. name *Sirimā* occurs in all the stages of the language[1]. The neutral form *ojavaṃ* Th2. 55 may be derived from a stem *ojava*, or it may be directly derived from Skr. *ojavat*. These forms perhaps facilitated the shortening of *ant*-stems into *a*-stems.—3. The Nominative-form of the Pl. in *-anto* is used also in Acc., just as that of the Sg. in *-ā* is used in Voc.

§ 97. Present Participles in *-nt*. 1. Their flexion is distinguished from that of the adjectives in *-nt* firstly by the fact that the Sg. Nom. has retained the ending *-aṃ* = Skr. *-an* in the Gāthā-language and in the canonical prose. Thus *jīvaṃ* 'living' Sn. 427, 432, Th1. 44 = *jīvan*; *kubbaṃ* 'making' Jā. III. 278[12] = *kurvan*; *viharaṃ* 'sojourning' Th1. 435 = *viharan*; *bhaṇaṃ* 'speaking' Sn. 429 = *bhaṇan* etc. Similarly *jānaṃ* 'knowing' M. II. 9[23] = *jānan*; *passaṃ* 'seeing' M. II, 9[24] = *paśyan*. But beside it the ending *-nto* occurs already in the oldest period of the language: *kandanto* 'weeping, Th1. 406; *patthento* 'desiring' Th1. 264; *gavesanto* 'seeking' Th1. 183; *apaṭikujjhanto* 'not getting angry with it' S. I. 162[30] (verse) etc., and frequently in the canonical prose: *kandanto* M. II. 3[20], *appajānanto* 'not comprehending, M. I. 7[22]. In post-canonical prose the form in *-nto* becomes predominant, and that in *-aṃ* is considered to be archaic. Hence *nihanaṃ* 'killing' Jā. II. 407[1] is explained by *nihananto* in the Co., as also in similar other instances. In the first two periods of the language the flexion retained the archaic forms: Sg. Instr. *icchatā* (from *icchati* 'wishes') Th1. 167 = *icchatā*; Gen. *vasato* (from *vasati* 'dwells') Jā. III. 17[9] = *vasatas*; Pl. Gen. *vijānataṃ* (from *vijānāti* 'comprehends') Th1. 14; *vadataṃ* (from *vadati* 'speaks') Vv. 53. 1 (Comm. = *vadantānaṃ*); Sg. Gen. *passato* = *paśyatas* M. I. 7[4], *viharato* M. I. 9[27] etc. Along with them should be counted also the forms Sg. Gen. *karoto* Dh. 116, Th1. 98, 99 and Pl, Gen. *karotaṃ* Vv. 34. 21 (but *kurutaṃ* M. I. 516[23]). They belong to the stem *karont-* abstracted out of the Acc. of the new form *karonta-*, and their relation to the Acc. *karontaṃ* is as that of *vasato*, *vasataṃ* to *vasantaṃ*[2]. We should also note the Pl. Nom. *icchato* Th1. 320 for *icchanto* = *icchantas*. At the side of the older forms there are found, already from the Gāthā-language onwards, forms of the *a*-flexion: Sg. Gen.

[1] JPTS. 1909, p. 166.

[2] Cf. E. Kuhn, Beitr. p. 77.

namantassa (from *namati* 'bows') Jā. II. 205[9], *passantassa* Thl. 716; Loc. *kandante* Thl. 774; Pl. Nom. *vicarantā* (from *vicarati* 'wanders about') Thl. 37, *a-vijānantā* Thl. 276; Pl. Gen. *nadantānaṃ* (from *nadati* 'roars') Thl. Introd. verse 1; cf. also Pl. Loc. *uppatantesu nipatantesu* (root *pat*) Thl. 76. These forms become more frequent in the canonical prose (cf. Pl. Nom. *jānantā*, *passantā* M. II. 10[8'9]; Acc. *pavisante*, *nikkhamante* 'the incoming, the outgoing' M. II. 21[26]), and in the post-canonical prose they are the only current ones.—2. More rarely, in the Gāthā-language, the participles in *-ant* go over to the *a*-flexion also by dropping the final *nt*. Cf. *jāno* 'knowing' Jā. III. 24[2] for *jānaṃ*, *jānanto*; *passo* 'seeing' Thl. 61 for *passaṃ*, *passanto*. In this way is to be explained the form *anu-kubbassa* Jā. II. 205[10] instead of *-kubbato*=*kurvatas* (Comm. *anukubbantassa*). The Sg. Nom. neut. *asaṃ* 'worthless' Jā. II. 22[2] would be thus directly =Skr. *asat*.

§ 98. 1. The stem *arahant* 'the perfect one'[1], originally a Part. Pres., has in Sg. Nom. both *arahaṃ* S. I. 169[24] (verse), Sn. p. 100, 103, A. II. 234[36], Iv. 78[22] etc. as well as *arahā* Sn. 1003. The reading of the mss. is ofren uncertain, as in A. III. 436[21], 437[2], IV. 364[22], Iv. 95[12]. Moreover the stems *arahant* and *arahanta* are in evidence side by side. The Sg. Loc. *arahantamhi* occurs already in Thl. 1173; the Pl. Gen. is *arahataṃ* in Dh. 164, D. I. 88[2], S. I. 161[27] and *arahantānaṃ* in A. IV. 394[23], Milp. 208[21] etc.—2. Of the stem *sant* 'existing, good' the old Pl. Inst. *sabbhi*= *sadbhis* has been retainad in verses: Dh. 151, Thl. 1096, D. II. 246[7] (verse), *sabbhir-eva* Thl. 4, S. I. 17[3] (verse), *asabbhi* Sn. 245. The other forms are derived from the stems *sant* or *santa*; *e.g.* Sg. Dat.-Gen. *sato* Thl. 180, D. I. 34[11], Milp. 235[25]; Loc. *sati* Sn. 81, D. II. 31[13], Vin. I. 112[35], Milp. 231[13] (in connection with a fem. substantive JāCo. I. 328[2], 348[8] etc.) and *sante* Sn. 94, M. II. 24[22], DhCo. II. 134[4]; Pl. Nom. *santo* Dh. 83, 151 and *santā* Vin. I. 103[1]; Pl. Loc. *santesu* Milp. 28[8] (verse) etc. The Sg. Nom. masc. is always *santo* Sn. 98, 124, Thl. 198, Milp. 32[6]. On the neut. *asaṃ* see § 97. 2; beside it we have *santaṃ*, *asantaṃ* Vin. I. 94[32'33]. But I consider *asataṃ* Sn. 131 to be Pl. Gen.=*asajjanānaṃ* as in the Comm.; var. lec. of the Comm. is *asantaṃ*=*abhūtaṃ*.—3. The form of address *bhavant* 'venerable', used for the Pron. of the second person, has the following forms: Sg. Nom. *bhavaṃ* Sn. 486, D. I. 249[19], M. I. 484[6], neut.

[1] Cf. R. O. Franke, D. übers., p. 297 foot-note 1.

bhavaṃ M. III. 172[26]; Acc. *bhavantaṃ* Sn. 597, D. II. 231[28]; Instr. *bhotā* D. I. 93[23], S. IV. 120[14], Sn. p. 15; Gen. *bhoto* Sn. 565, M. I. 486[10]; Voc. *bhavaṃ* D. I. 93[18] and *bho* D. I. 93[19], M. I. 484[5], JāCo. II. 26[19]. Pl. Nom. *bhavanto* Sn. p. 103 and *bhonto* Sn. p. 101, 103, M. II. 2[4], Milp. 25[14]; Acc. *bhavante* M. II. 3[22]; Instr. *bhavantehi* M. III. 13[24]; Gen. *bhavataṃ* M. II. 3[19]; Voc. *bhonto* Thl. 832, M. II. 2[5]. The form *bhante*, a 'Māgadhism'[1], is used absolutively in address: Vin. I. 76[32], D. II. 154[14], 283[21], JāCo. II. 111[13], III. 46[4], or in connection with a Voc.: Milp. 25[18], or attributively in any case: it is in Nom. in D. I. 179[16], DhCo. I. 62[21], in Gen.-Dat. in D. I. 179[16] etc. The fem. of the stem *bhavant* is *bhotī*. Cf. Sg. Nom. *bhotī* Sn. 988, Jā. III. 95[13], Acc. *bhotiṃ* Jā. VI. 523[19], Loc. *bhotiyā* Jā. VI. 523[18], Voc. *bhoti* Jā. VI. 523[7], D. II. 249[8] etc.[2]

9. *s*-Declension

§ 99. Neuters in *-as*. Stem *sotas* 'stream'.

Of the historical forms there are preserved only Sg. Nom.-Acc.-Voc. *soto*[3]—Instr. *sotasā*—Dat.-Gen. *sotaso*—Loc. *sotasi*. Transfer to the neutral *a*-declension is also achieved by dropping the final *s* (§ 78 B). The new stem serves as the basis of all the cases in Plural, and, apparently, also of Abl. Sg. Sometimes also the other cases of Sg. are formed from it.

On flexion. 1. The historical forms are found mostly in the Gāthā-language and in the canonical prose: Sg. Nom. (*paramaṃ*) *tapo* 'the (highest) penance' Dh. 184; Acc. *siro* 'the head' Sn. 768, *yaso* 'reputation' Jā. III. 87[25]; Instr. *urasā* 'with the breast' Thl. 27, 233, *sirasā* 'with the head' Vin. I. 4[23], M. II. 120[1], *cetasā* 'with the heart' Vin. I. 4[17], *jarasā* 'through age' DhCo. III. 320[7] (verse); Dat.-Gen. *cetaso* Vin. I. 4[33], M. III. 196[27]; *manaso* 'of the mind' Dh. 390; Loc. *urasi* Jā. III. 148[13], *aghasi-gama* 'moving through the

[1] Cf. AMāg. *bhante*; Pischel. § 366 b.

[2] The feminines of participles are usually derived from the strong stem. Cf. *gacchantī* JāCo. I. 291[3], *labhantī* JāCo. II. 128[15], *passantī* Vin. I. 16[10], JāCo. I. 61[2], *ārocentī* JāCo. VI. 522[34], *khajjantī* (from *khajjati* 'is devoured' = *khādyate*) Thl. 315 etc. The feminines of adjectives are however derived from the weak stem. Cf. *sīlavatī* D. II. 12[27]. *mahatī* DhCo. II. 41[12], and the proper names like *Bandhumatī* (a city) D. II. 12[2], *Ketumatī* (a river) Jā. VI. 518[12], *Yasavatī* (a woman) JāCo. IV. 237[7] etc. Flexion according to § 86.

[3] The coincidence of this form with the Sg. Nom. *dhammo* of masc. *a*-stems has led to a confusion in gender as pointed out in § 76.

atmosphere' Vv. 16. 1. But beside them, already in the oldest period, forms of the *a*-type are frequently used: Sg. Nom. *siraṃ* Th2. 255, *manaṃ* Dh. 96; Acc. *siraṃ* A. I. 141[13]; Instr. *tapena* Sn. 655; Gen. *manassa* S. IV. 4[17]; Loc. *ure* D. I. 135[27], *urasmiṃ* A. I. 141[5], *nabhamhi* 'in the atmosphere' Jā. V. 14[20], *aghe* Jā. IV. 322[1] and *aghasmi* Jā. IV. 484[12]. This becomes the normal flexion in the post-canonical prose[1]. The archaic forms are confined to a limited number of words and expressions: Sg. Nom. *mano* JāCo. IV. 217[25,26]; Acc. *vaco* JāCo. IV. 234[17]; Instr. *manasā* JāCo. IV. 218[4], 227[15], as well as, for instance, Milp. 227[10], in the old phrase *kāyena vācāya manasā*; Loc. *manasi* in *manasi-karoti* 'pays attention to, ponders in mind over' JāCo. I. 393[29], 500[15] etc. On the other hand *mane* DhCo. I. 23[3].— 2. For the Plural it is sufficient to point out from the oldest literature the forms *sotāni* Sn. 433 and *sotā* Sn. 1034; Acc. *sote*[2] Thl. 761; Instr. *sotehi* Sn. 197, *sirehi* Jā. IV. 250[15]; Gen. *sotānaṃ* Sn. 1034.—3. The transfer to the *a*-decl. may take place also through the addition of *a* to the *s*-stem: Sg. Acc. *sirasaṃ* JāCo. V. 434[8].

§ 100. Masculines and feminines in *-as*. 1. The masc. stem *candimas* 'moon' has in Sg. Nom. *candimā* Dh. 172 f., 382= *candramās*. For the rest the flexion is just like that of *a*-stems. The same applies as a rule to compounds with *as*-stems. Cf. Sg. Nom. *attamano* 'joyous' Dh. 328, D. II. 352[11], M. I. 432[3]; *dummano* 'sad' Vin. I. 21[22], JāCo. II. 160[18]; fem. *attamanā* JāCo. I. 52[30]; Pl. Nom. *attamanā* D. I. 46[27]; *sumanā* Sn. 222; Acc. *muditamane* Sn. 680. Forms of the *as*-type are however found in the Gāthā-language: Sg. Gen. *ananvāhatacetaso* Dh. 39; perhaps Sg. Acc. *vyāsattamanasaṃ* Dh. 47. Transfer to the *a*-flexion may take place also through extension of the stem by *a*: Sg. Nom. *avyāpannacetaso*[3] S. V. 74[19,20]; Pl. Nom. *adhimanasā* Sn. 692.—2. The Participles Perf. Act. in *-vas* assume various forms. Historical are the forms *avidvā* 'unknowing' Sn. 535 etc., M. I. 311[7] = *avidvān*, as well as °*dassivā* in *bhaya-dassivā* Dh. 31 f. = °*darśivān* 'seeing'. The form which is most in use is *vidū*, derived from the weak stem *viduṣ* and inflected according to § 87. 2. Moreover we have also a stem *viddasu*: Sg. Nom. *aviddasu* Dh. 268, Gen. *viddasuno*, *av*- M. I. 65[5,6,8]; Pl. Nom. *aviddasū* Sn.

[1] As also in Pkr. (see Pischel, § 408 f.), which has however also retained the old forms, particularly in AMāg. and JMāh.

[2] On *sotā* and *sote* cf. § 78. 6, 7.

[3] Also in Skr. the form *cetasa* is allowed at the end of a compound according to Vopadeva, BR. *sub voce*.

762, *-suno* M. I. 65^{26}.—3. The comparatives in *-yas* drop the final *s* and are transferred to the *a*-flexion. Cf. Sg. Nom. *seyyo* Dh. 308, Sn. 918, S. IV. 88^{3}; Acc. *seyyaṃ* Dh. 61, Thl. 208; Pl. Nom. *seyyā* Dpvs. 4. 51 and *seyyāse* (§ 79. 4) Vv. 18. 12; from this stem also fem. *seyyā*, neut. *seyyaṃ* JāCo. III. 237^{13}, Pl. *seyyāni* Jā. III. 196^{12}. The old Sanskritic form is retained in the neut. *seyyo* 'superior' Dh. 76, Thl. 194, Jā II. 44^{24}, VI. 498^{10}, Vin. III. 73^{14} etc. = *śreyas*. The opposite of it is *pāpiyo* 'inferior' Jā. II. 44^{8} etc. (beside *pāpiyaṃ* Milp. 155^{16}) = *pāpīyas*. The indeclinable *seyyaso* Dh. 42 f., Jā. IV. $241^{4,13}$ is identical in meaning with *seyyo*. *Seyyatara* may be regarded as the usual form for *seyya* in the post-canonical prose, and in VvCo. 96^{22-23}, for instance, *seyya* is explained by *seyyatara*. Also from the old stem the fem. *seyyasi* (shortened from *seyyasī* metri causa) Jā. V. 393^{21}.—4. Pāli *accharā*[1] corresponding to Skr. fem. *apsaras* 'nymph' is a case of transfer to the *ā*-decl., § 81. The stem *jarā* beside *jaras* is known also in Skr.

§ 101. The neuter stems in *-is*, *-us* are treated almost exclusively as *i*-, *u*-neuters (§ 85). Historical forms are found only occasionally, as Sg. Instr. *āyusā*[2] from Skr. *āyus* 'age' Sn. 149. Usually however the stem is as in Pāli *sappi* from Skr. *sarpis* 'butter', Pāli *cakkhu* from Skr. *cakṣus* 'eye'. Thus Sg. Nom *sappi* D. I. 201^{26}, A. I. 278^{31} and *sappiṃ* JāCo. I. 457^{22}, *āyu* 'age' Thl. 145, Dh. 109 and *āyuṃ* JāCo. I. 138^{5}, *cakkhuṃ* Vin. II. 157^{3}; Acc. *sappiṃ* Mhvs. 5. 217, *cakkhuṃ* JāCo. III. 18^{7}; Instr. *sappinā* Ud. 38^{33}, *cakkhunā* JāCo. III. 18^{9}; Abl. *sappimhā* D. I. 201^{26}; Dat.-Gen. *sappissa* Ud. 93^{4}, *āyussa* Mhvs. 35. 78, *cakkhuno* JāCo. IV. 206^{19}; Loc. *cakkhusmiṃ* Vin. I. 34^{32}, *cakkhumhi* Dpvs. 4. 4. Pl. Nom. *cakkhūni* JāCo. IV. 137^{16}; Instr. *cakkhūhi* Dpvs. 17. 26 etc.—The neuter Sanskrit stem *arcis* 'flame' was changed into *acci* and then inflected as a fem. stem: Sg. Instr. *acciyā* M. II. 130^{6}, Pl. Nom. *acciyo* Vin. I. 25^{30} (*acci vātena khittā* A. IV. 103^{5}, S. IV. $399^{23,26}$).—Masculine compounds like *dīghāya* 'long-lived' = *dīrghāyus* are inflected according to § 82.

10. Adverbs and Comparison.

§ 102. The accusative of the neuter adjective serves as the adverb in Pāli: *jaha sīghaṃ samussayaṃ* 'give up quickly the totality (of all that lead to rebirth)' Thl. 83; *sādhu kho mayaṃ palāyimha* 'we have

[1] So also in Pkr.; Pischel, § 410.

[2] As also Pkr. AMāg. *cakkhusā*; Pischel, § 411.

fied just in the right manner' Vin. I. 88[34]; *tumhe sanikaṃ āgaccheyyātha* 'come hither slowly!' JāCo. III. 37[13]; *palāyatha lahuṃ* 'fly quickly!' Mhvs. 7. 66. But other case-forms too are used as adverbs; thus Instrumentals: *kicchena katā paṇṇasālā* 'the hut made with great labour' JāCo.II.44[6]; *api ca me āvuso satthā pariciṇṇo dīgharattaṃ manāpena na amanāpena* 'moreover the master has been served by me for a long time in a fitting manner, and not in an unfitting manner' S. IV. 57[25]. The Abl. is used, for instance, in *kicchā laddho ayaṃ putto* 'this son has been acquired with great difficulty' Thl. 475 (cf. VvCo. 229[18]). Or should *kicchā* here be regarded as Instr.?

§ 103. Comparison. 1. Several of the old comparatives and superlatives in *-īyas* and *-iṣṭha* have been preserved. Thus *seyya(s)* = *śreyas*, *pāpiya(s)* = *pāpīyas* (§ 100. 3); *bhiyyo*, *bhīyo* 'more' (adv.) Dh. 17 f., Thl. 110, 173, S. I. 108[17] etc. = *bhūyas*. The comp. *nīceyya(s)* Sn. 855, 918 has been formed clearly on the analogy of *seyya(s)*. Moreover we have the superlatives *seṭṭha* 'the best' = *śreṣṭha*; *pāpiṭṭha* 'the worst' = *pāpiṣṭha*; *kaniṭṭha* 'the youngest' = *kaniṣṭha*; *jeṭṭha* 'the eldest' = *jyeṣṭha*. *Seṭṭho* in Vv. 64. 33 is used in the sense of a comparative. As in Skr., so also in Pāli, these comparatives and superlatives may undergo further gradation[1]: *seyyatara* (§ 100. 3); *seṭṭhatara* Jā. V. 148[7]; *pāpiṭṭhatara* Vin. II. 5[11]. The compound *pāpissika* is difficult to explain. According to Childers *sub voce* it is = *pāpīyas* + *ika*. A less contracted from is perhaps to be found in *pāpiyyasika* of the technical term *tassapāpiyyasikā*.—2. The comparative suffix-*tara* is very productive in Pāli. It seems to have almost completely ousted the superlative suffix-*tama*. An example of the superlative is *uḷāratama* 'the highest' VvCo. 320[14]; *sattama* 'the best' Sn. 356 is another. Regular examples of the comparative are *piyatara* 'dearer' JāCo. III. 279[24], *sādutara* 'sweeter' Sn. 181 (used in the superlative sense in S. I. 214[19]), *bahutara* 'more' Vin. I. 129[4] etc. There are also new formations such as *mahantatara* 'greater' M. III. 170[13], JāCo. II. 417[16], *sīlavantatara* 'more virtuous' JāCo. II. 3[21], *vaṇṇavantatara* 'more beautiful' D. I. 18[21], in which the suffix has been added to the stem extended by *a*. In *balavatara* 'stronger' Milp. 234[21] it has been added to the shortened stem. Cf. the comparatives *purimatara* 'the earlier' S. IV. 398[8], *paramatara* 'the higher' Thl. 518, *varatara* 'the more excellent' DhCo. I. 332[8] and the Adv. *paṭhamataraṃ* 'earlier' Vin. I. 30[4], DhCo. I. 138[7],

[1] Cf. also in Pkr. AMāg. *jeṭṭhayara* etc.; Pischel, § 414.

JāCo. VI. 510[25]. In *sappurisatara* 'the more efficient man' S. V. 20[7] the suffix *-tara* has been added to the substantive *sappurisa*= *satpuruṣa*; in *puretaraṃ* 'earlier' it has been added to the adv. *pure*. Even the adverb *pageva* 'much more still' has been intensified to *pagevataraṃ* M. III. 145[5]. The comparative has been extended by the suffix *-ika* in *lahukatarika* M. II. 70[13]. The intensity of meaning —'much', 'exceedingly' etc.—may be expressed also by the reduplication of the adj.: *mahantamahanto* JāCo. I. 347[29]. Cf. D. II. 78[6].—3. The simple positive is not infrequently used in the comparative sense.[1] Cf. *etesu kataraṃ nu kho mahantaṃ* 'which is the greater of the two?' JāCo. III. 194[3]; *santi te ñātito bahū* 'they are more numerous than the relatives' Mhvs. 14. 20. Cf. DhCo. I. 94[15].

II. Pronoun

§ 104. A. Personal pronoun of the first person (stem-form in Sg. *maṃ-*, cf. S. IV. 315[23]):

	Sg.	Pl.
Nom.	*ahaṃ* 'I'	*mayaṃ* (*amhe*) 'we'
Acc.	*maṃ*(*mamaṃ*)	*amhe* (*asme*, *amhākaṃ*, *asmākaṃ*)
Instr.-Abl.	*mayā*	*amhehi*
Dat.-Gen.	*mama*, *mayhaṃ* (*mamaṃ*, *amhaṃ*)	*amhākaṃ* (*asmākaṃ*, *amhaṃ*)
Loc.	*mayi*	*amhesu*

Enclitic: Sg. Instr.-Dat.-Gen. *me* Pl. Acc.-Instr.-Dat.-Gen. *no*

B. Personal pronoun of the second person:

	Sg.	Pl.
Nom.	*tvaṃ* (*tuvaṃ*) 'thou'	*tumhe* 'you'
Acc.	*taṃ* (*tvaṃ*, *tuvaṃ*)	*tumhe* (*tumhākaṃ*)
Instr.-Abl.	*tayā* (*tvayā*)	*tumhehi*
Dat.-Gen.	*tava*, *tuyhaṃ* (*tavaṃ*, *tumhaṃ*)	*tumhākaṃ* (*tumhaṃ*)
Loc.	*tayi* (*tvayi*)	*tumhesu*

Enclitic: Sg. Instr.-Dat.-Gen *te* Pl. Acc.-Instr.-Dat.-Gen. *vo*.

[1] Cf. Geiger, Mhvs. ed. p. LIV. The same usage also in Pkr.; Pischel, § 414 (towards the end of the paragraph)

Notes: 1. The unbracketed forms are the regular ones in the post-canonical prose, in which, for instance, clear distinction is made between *tvaṃ* 'thou' and *taṃ* 'thee'. All these forms are used also already in the oldest periods of the language. The bracketed forms are archaic or rarer. Attestation of the Pronoun of the first person: Sg. Acc. *mamaṃ* Jā. III. 55[5], S. I. 88[21], 219[34]; Gen. *mamaṃ* Sn. 694, D. II. 90[11], A. II. 1[11], *amhaṃ*[1] Thl. 1045 (or Pl. Dat.-Gen.?); Pl. Nom. *amhe* S. I. 118[12], DhCo. III. 56[17]; Acc. *asme* Jā. III. 359[21] (Comm. = *amhe*), *amhākaṃ* JāCo. I. 221[29]; Dat.-Gen. *asmākaṃ* Sn. p. 102, *amhaṃ* Th2. 287, Jā. III. 300[16], VI. 509[30], Mhvs. 5. 200. Pronoun of the second person: Sg. Nom. *tuvaṃ* Sn. 377 a, Vv. 64. 23 c, Pv. II. 3. 2; Acc. *tvaṃ* Mhvs. 10. 50 c, *tuvaṃ* Sn. 377 d, Vv. 84. 10; Pl. Acc. *tumhākaṃ* JāCo. I. 221[29]; Dat.-Gen. *tumhaṃ* D. I. 3[5], JāCo. III. 19[15].—2. The *m* of *mayaṃ* = Skr. *vayam* is taken over from the forms of the Sg. such as *maṃ*, *mayā* etc., just as the *t* of *tumhe*, *tumhākaṃ* etc. (as opposed to Skr. *yuṣmākam* etc.) has been taken over from the forms *taṃ*, *tayā* etc.—3. The Nom.-Acc. Pl. *amhe* (*asme*) and *tumhe* correspond to the Vedic forms *asme*, *yuṣme*, which according to Pāṇini VII. 1. 39 may be used for various plural cases[2].—4. The *e* of *amhehi*, *amhesu*, *tumhehi*, *tumhesu* as opposed to *asmābhis*, *asmāsu*, *yuṣmābhis*, *yuṣmāsu* are to be explained by the analogy of the forms *tehi*, *tesu* etc. (§ 105).

§ 105. Pronoun of the third person. (Stem-form *taṃ*- Vv. 84. 44, *tad*- in *tadahe* Mhvs. 5. 43, *tappaccayā* Thl. 719 etc.)

	Sg.		Pl.	
	Masc.	Fem.	Masc.	Fem.
Nom.	*so* (*sa*)	*sā*	*te*	*tā* (*tāyo*)
Acc.	*taṃ*	*taṃ*	*te*	*tā* (*tāyo*)
Instr.	*tena*	*tāya*	*tehi*	*tāhi*
Abl.	*tamhā*, *tasmā*	*tāya*	*tehi*	*tāhi*
Dat.-Gen.	*tassa*	*tassā* / *tissā* (*tissāya*, / *tāya*	*tesaṃ* (*tesānaṃ*)	*tāsaṃ* (*tāsānaṃ*)
Loc.	*tamhi*, *tasmiṃ*	*tassaṃ* (*tāsaṃ*) / *tissaṃ* (*tāyaṃ*)	*tesu*	*tāsu*

[1] Also in Prākrit the grammarians give the forms *amhaṃ*, *tumhaṃ* for Gen. Sg. Pischel, § 415, 420.

[2] Cf. E. Kuhn, Beitr. p. 72, 86; Pischel, ZDMG. 35. 715 f.; PkrGr. § 419, 422

The Neuter has Sg. Nom.-Acc. *taṃ* (in vowel-sandhi *tad-* § 72. 1). Pl. Nom.-Acc. *tāni*. Elsewhere as in Masc.

Notes: 1. The more isolated or archaic forms are again given in brackets. The remaining forms are found in all the periods of the language and become the regular ones in the post-canonical prose. Attestation of the former: For Sg. Gen. fem. *tissāya* cf. *etissāya* (§ 107. 1) VvCo. 106^{14}; Sg. Loc. fem. *tāsaṃ*[1] Milp. 136^{11}, (*tissaṃ* M. II. 55^{25}), *tāyaṃ* (*velāyaṃ*) Vin. I. 2^{2}, Ud. 1^{18}, S. I. 5^{24}. As for the forms of Pl. Gen. *tesānaṃ*, *tāsānaṃ* (double ending!), cf. *esānaṃ* (§ 108) M. II. 154^{2}, *sabbesānaṃ* (§ 113. 1) M. III. 60^{24}, *katamesānaṃ* (§ 111. 2) Vin. III. 7^{22}. Sg. Nom. masc. *sa* is from the first rarer than *so*. In Sn. *sa* occurs 40 times but *so* 124 times; in the first 500 Theragāthās *sa* occurs 4 times (of which twice in the favourite construction *sa ve*) and *so* 37 times. At the end *sa* becomes quite rare. —2. Instead of the Sg. Nom.-Acc. neut. *taṃ* we have sometimes also the Māgadhesque form *se*[2]: D. II. $278^{16, 30}$, 379^{12}, M. II. 254^{25}, 255^{6}. Cf. § 80*b*. I think the same form is contained in *seyyathā* 'just as', *seyyathīdaṃ* 'as follows, namely'[3]. Instead of the former we find *taṃyathā* in Milp. 1^{11}. The *sa-* in *sayathā* 'as' Thl. 412, *sace* 'if' is analogous to Skr. *sa* in *sa-yadi*, *sa-yathā* etc.[4]—3. There is an isolated form with double-ending: Sg. Nom. neut. *tadaṃ* Sn. p. 148, in apposition with the Rel. Pron. *yaṃ*[5].—4. The Pl. Nom. *te* appears also in Acc. Similarly in the flexion of other pronominal stems as well.

§ 106. 1. It is worthy of note that (mostly in the two oldest periods of the language) the Pron. *so*, *sā*, *taṃ* is used to strengthen other pronouns. It is used (*a*) before the personal Pron. of the first and the second persons: *so ahaṃ* Sn. 190; *svāhaṃ* (§ 71. 1c) JāCo. I. 298^{3}; *taṃ taṃ* (=*taṃ tvaṃ*) Jā. VI. 516^{19}; *tesaṃ vo* A. V. 86^{8}. We have even *tesaṃ vo, bhikkhave, tumhākaṃ*......Iv. 32^{1}; *tesaṃ no amhākaṃ* M. III. 194^{19}. The Pron. *so* may refer also to the person contained in a verbal form: *so karohi* '(you) do' Dh. 236; *so tato*

[1] Unnecessarily changed by Trenckner into *tāyam*.

[2] As Pkr. Māg *śe* (*śe muṇḍe*=*tan muṇḍam*), AMāg. *se* (*se diṭṭhaṃ*=*tad dṛṣṭam*). Pischel, § 423.

[3] Not so Pischel, § 423, in whose opinion *se*=Ved. *sed* (*sa-id*). Yet his arguments do not seem to be convincing.

[4] Pischel, *Ibid.*; BR. under the word *sa*, col. 452.

[5] The form *tasmassa* given by E. Müller, PGr. p. 88 from Spiegel's Anecdota p. 15 is of course nothing but *tasmā assa*. The Colombo ed. of the Rasav. (2^{3}) rightly reads *tasmā 'ssa*.

cuto amutra udapādiṃ 'departed from there I was born again at that place' D. I. 13[23]. (*b*) It is used also after the Rel. Pron., which thereby gets the general meaning 'whoever': *yā sā sīmā . . . taṃ sīmaṃ* Vin. I. 109[6]; *ye te dhammā...tathārūpā 'ssa dhammā* M. III. 11[20]; *yo so ... mama sahāyako* DhCo. IV. 128[3]. (*c*) It is used before or after the Dem. Pron. *ayaṃ*: *ta-y-idaṃ* (= *taṃ idaṃ*) D.I. 91[4], M. II. 230[3]; *svāyaṃ* (= *so ayaṃ*) Vin. I. 29[26]; *ayaṃ so* JāCo. II. 16[12].—2. When repeated, the Pron. *so* signifies 'this and that, any, various': *tāsu tāsu disāsu, tesu tesu janapadesu* Vin. I. 21[34]. Or it may refer to the indefinite Rel. Pron. *yo yo*, as for instance in Thl. 144, JāCo. I. 417[6] etc.

§ 107. 1. The Dem. Pron. *eso* (*esa*), *esā*, *etaṃ* 'this' is inflected like *so*. In Sg. Nom. masc. both the forms *eso* and *esa* are equally in use, and that not only as substantive (*esa* JāCo. II. 6[24], *eso* JāCo. II. 7[18]) but also as adjective (*esa* JāCo II. 10[5], *eso* Sn. p. 102). The stem-form is *etaṃ-* which appears, for instance, in *etaṃkāraṇā* 'for this reason' Vin. I. 57[35]. *Eso* too like *so*, is used in connection with other pronouns. Thus *esāhaṃ* (= *eso ahaṃ*) D. I. 110[23], or *ayaṃ eso* Mhvs. 1. 42; or *yāni etāni* (*yānāni*) DhCo. IV. 6[7].—2. The Pron. *ena* (= Skr. *enad*) is found to occur only in the forms *enaṃ* and *enena*[1]. *Enaṃ* occurs as Acc. masc. in Sn. 981, 1114, M. III. 5[7] etc., and as Acc. fem. in Jā. III. 395[5] (changed into *ena* for sake of metre), as Acc. neut. in Sn. 583, Dh. 118, 313. The combination *tam-enaṃ* occurs in M. II. 248[11], III. 5[7], JāCo. I. 350[6] etc., and as fem. in Vv. 21 4. The Sandhi-form of *ena* is *na* which is very common (cf. § 66 1, p. 107, with f.-n. 2). The form *naṃ* in Sg. Acc. masc.-fem.-neut. is very well attested, as well as Dat.-Gen. *nassa* Jā. V. 203[21]; Pl. Acc. *ne* Vin. I. 42[35], S. I. 224[22], JāCo. I. 99[28], 201[17]; Pl. Dat.-Gen. *nesaṃ* Sn. 293, Thl. 130, Th2. 277, JāCo. I. 153[10] etc. —3. Quite an isolated form is *tyamhi* Jā. VI. 292[21], which might belong to the pronominal stem *tya* = Ved. *tya*, mentioned by Moggallāna[2]. The Comm. explains *tyamhi* by *tamhi*. The reading however is not quite certain.—4. Finally we have to mention the pronominal stem *tuma* of the third person which belongs to the two oldest periods of the language and which may be connected with the Ved. *tman*[3].

[1] On Pkr. *eṇa* see Pischel, § 431.

[2] R. O. Franke, PGr. p. 35f.

[3] This according to Oldenberg, KZ. 25. 319, while Johansson Monde Oriental 1907-8, p. 99f. refuses to recognise any connection between the two words.

The following forms of it are found to occur: Sg. Nom. *tumo* Sn. 890, Vin. II. 186[31], A. III. 124[10], 125[6] and the Sg. Gen. *tumassa* Sn. 908.

§ 108. The Demonstrative Pronoun *ayaṃ* 'this' (stem-form *idaṃ*, cf. *idappaccaya* D. I. 185[27]).

	Sg. masc.	Sg. fem.	Pl. masc.	Pl. fem.
Nom.	*ayaṃ*	*ayaṃ*	*ime*	*imā*, (*imāyo*)
Acc.	*imaṃ*	*imaṃ*	*ime*	*imā*, (*imāyo*)
Instr.	*iminā*, (*anena*)	*imayā*	*imehi* (*ehi*)	*imāhi*
Abl.	*imasmā*, *imamhā*, (*asmā*)	*imāya*		
Dat.-Gen.	*imassa*, *assa*	*imissā* (-*ssāya*), (*imāya*), *assā*, (*assāya*)	*imesaṃ*, (*imesānaṃ*), (*esaṃ*, *esānaṃ*)	*imāsaṃ*, (*sānaṃ*) (*āsaṃ*)
Loc.	*imasmiṃ*, *imamhi*, (*asmiṃ*)	*imissaṃ*, -*ssā*, (*imāyaṃ* (*assaṃ*)	*imesu*, (*esu*)	*imāsu*

The neuter has in Sg. Nom.-Acc. *idaṃ*, *imaṃ*; Pl. Nom.-Acc. *imāni*. Otherwise as in masc.

Notes: 1. The pronominal stem *a*-, *ana*- is gradually supplanted by the stem *ima*- in course of the development of the language. It made its way also into Nom.-Acc. Sg. neut.[1] Thus we have *imaṃ* as Nom. neut. in Milp. 46[7] and as Acc. neut. in S. IV. 125[19], JāCo. I. 307[8], DhCo. II. 29[4], 31[12], Mhvs. 5. 157. Examples of forms of the *a*-, *ana*-stem: Sg. Instr. *anena* Mhvs. 5. 55; Abl. *asmā* Dh. 220, Thl. 237; Loc. *asmiṃ*[2] Dh. 168 f., 242, Sn. 634, 990; Pl. Gen. Masc. *esaṃ* M. II. 86[2] and *esānaṃ* M. II. 154[2], III. 259[4], fem. *āsaṃ* Jā. I. 302[4] (Comm. = *etāsaṃ*). The two forms *assa* and *assā* of Sg. Dat.-Gen. masc. and fem. have been retained and are frequently used enclitically also in the post-canonical literature. Of the rarer forms of the stem *ima*-I should mention here *imāyo* Pl. Nom. fem. Sn. 1122 and Acc. Mhvs. 15. 20. Instead of the Sg. Gen. masc. *imassa* there also occurs, *imissa* JāCo. I. 333[2] in analogy with the fem. form *imissā*, and instead of *iminā* there is *aminā* in the compound *tad-aminā* 'thereby, therefore' S. I. 88[18], M. II. 939[9'15], D. III. 83[21] (beside *tad-iminā* M. II. 239[23],

[1] In Pkr. the process has gone further still. Here we find also Sg. Nom. masc. *imo*, fem. *imā*; Pischel, § 430.

[2] The reading *ath' asmiṃ rukkhe* JāCo. III. 208[17] is probably wrong. Cf. the var. lec.

240[8] with var. lec.).—2. The pron. *ayaṃ* appears again in combination with other pronouns. Thus with the relative: *yāyaṃ* (=*yā ayaṃ*) Thl. 124; (=*yo ayaṃ*) Dh. 56; *yam-idaṃ kammaṃ ... taṃ* M. II. 220[11]; *yān' imāni alāpūni* Dh. 149. With the interrogative pron.: *ko nu kho ayaṃ bhāsati* 'who is speaking there?' A. IV. 307[25]. On the connection with *so* see § 106. 1 *c*.—3. When repeated, *ayañ-ca ayañ-ca* signifies 'this and that' and stands for an indefinite person or thing: *ayañ-ca ayañ ca amhākaṃ rañño s'lācāro* 'such and such are the virtues of our king' JāCo. II. 3[23]; *idañ-c' idañ-ca kātuṃ vaṭṭati* 'it is proper to do this and that' JāCo. II. 4[28].

§ 109. The Demonstrative Pronoun *asu*, *amu* 'that'.

	Sg. masc.	fem.	Pl. masc.	fem.
Nom.	*asu, amu*	*asu.*	*amū*	*amū, (amuyo)*
Acc.	*amuṃ*	*amuṃ*	*amū*	*amū, (amuyo)*
Instr.	*amunā*	*amuyā*	*amūhi*	
Abl.	*amusmā, amumhā*	*amuyā*	*amūhi*	
Dat.-Gen.	*amussa*	*amussā, (amuyā)*	*amūsaṃ, (-sānaṃ)*	
Loc.	*amusmiṃ, amumhi*	*amussaṃ, (amuyaṃ)*	*amūsu*	

The Neuter has Sg. Nom.-Acc. *aduṃ*, Pl. *amū*, *amūni*. Otherwise as in Masc.

Notes: 1. The stem *amu* has made its way also into Sg. Nom. masc.[1] (We have, e.g., *amu* M. II. 206[29], 223[30], Mhvs. Ṭī. 118[3] and *asu* M. III. 275[7], S. IV. 315[6], 398[14]). It is found also in Pl. Nom. Instr. Abl. Dat.-Gen. Loc. masc. neut. (as against Skr. *amī*, *amībhis* etc.), so that in Pāli masc. and neut. have coincided with fem. The neut. *aduṃ* occurs in S. IV. 315[8], Jā. I. 500[18], JāCo. I. 500[23].—2. When repeated twice, this Pron. signifies 'the one. . . the other'. Cf. D. II. 200[7]. It is in apposition with the Rel. Pron., e.g., in *yaṃ vā aduṃ khettaṃ aggaṃ* 'that field which is valuable' S. IV. 315[8].—3. The pronouns *amuka* and *asuka* are derived from the stems *amu* and *asu*, and like Lat. *quidam* they are used for indefinite person or thing: *amukasmiṃ gāme* 'in the village so and so' D.I. 193[12] (cf. S. IV. 46[7]);

1 As also Pkr. *amū*; beside it AMāg. *aso*=*asau*. Pāli *asu*. Pischel, § 432. In Pkr. also Nom. Acc. neut. *amuṃ*.

asukasmiṃ kāle JāCo. II. 29[4] (cf. JāCo. I. 122[3]). *Amuka* can be used in this sense also when it is repeated: see A. IV. 302[26]. *Amuka* in M. III. 169[15] has been used in the sense of *amu*.

§ 110. Relative Pronoun *yo* 'which' (stem-form *yaṃ-*, *yad-*; e.g., *yaṃvipāko* D. II. 209[26], *yadattho* Thl. 60):

	Sg. masc.	fem.	Pl. masc.	fem.
Nom.	*yo*	*yā*	*ye*	*yā*, (*yāyo*)
Acc.	*yaṃ*	*yaṃ*	*ye*	*yā*, (*yāyo*)
Instr.	*yena*	*yāya*	*yehi*	*yāhi*
Abl.	*yasmā*, *yamhā*	*yāya*	*yehi*	*yāhi*
Dat.-Gen.	*yassa*	*yassā*, (*yāya*)	*yesaṃ*, (*-sānaṃ*)	*yāsaṃ* (*-sānaṃ*)
Loc.	*yasmiṃ*, *yamhi*	*yassaṃ*, (*yāyaṃ*)	*yesu*	*yāsu*

The Neut. has Sg. Nom.-Acc. *yaṃ*, Pl. *yāni*. Otherwise as in Masc.

Notes: 1. On the sandhi-forms *yv-*(=*yo*), *yad-*see § 71.1c, 72.1—2. The Māgadhesque form *ye* (in apposition with *se*=*taṃ*) occurs in D. II. 278[16] etc. Cf. § 105.2.—3. On the connection of the Rel. with other pronominal stems see § 106. 1*b*, 107.1, 108.2, 109.2. —4. When repeated, the Rel. Pron. has the indefinite meaning 'whoever': *yassaṃ yassaṃ disāyaṃ viharati, sakasmiṃ yeva vijite viharati* 'in whichever region he may be sojourning, he lives in his own kingdom' A. III. 151[13]. The same meaning attaches to *yo koci*, *yā kāci*, *yaṃ kiñci*=*yaḥ kaścit* etc.

§ III. 1. The Interrogative Pronoun *ko* 'who?' has in Sg. Nom. Acc. neut. *kiṃ*. It serves also as stem-form; cf *kiṃnāmo* Vin. I. 93[31] (immediately after it *konāmo*!), *kiṃkāraṇā* 'what for?' JāCo. I. 439[11]. For the rest the flexion is the same as that of the Rel. Pron. Yet in Sg. Abl. Dat.-Gen. and Loc. there are also found derivatives from the stem *ki*-which is in evidence in *kiṃ*: *kismā* S. I. 37[22] beside the usual *kasmā*; *kissa* Ud. 79[6] (verse), Vv. 22. 3, Pv. II, 1.3, D. II. 185[29] beside *kassa* Sn. 1040, Milp. 27[17], Mhvs. 5.191; *kimhi* Vin.

I. 28[31], D. II. 57[21] or *kismiṃ* D. II. 277[4,5], S. IV. 85[20] beside *kamhi, kasmiṃ*. Cf. the frequent construction *kissa hetu* 'on what ground? why?' D.I. 14[4], 15[9], M.I. 1[18] etc.; *kissa* alone in Vin. I. 73[3], JāCo. I. 477[25]. In Jā. V. 141[11,12] we find *kissa* as neut. and *kassa* as masc. A Māgadhesque Sg. Nom. masc. *ke* for *ko* occurs in D. III. 24[19]. The Interrogative Pron. is strengthened by an appended *-su, -ssu, -si*= *-svid* (cf. § 22): *kaṃ-su* S. I. 45[2], *kena-ssu* S. I. 39[8], *kissa-ssu* S. I. 39[4], 161[4] (this is the proper reading, not *kissassa*!), *kaṃ-si* DhCo. I. 91[18]. The Indefinite Pron. *koci, kāci, kiñci* 'any one' is formed by appending *ci*=*cid*[1] to the forms of *ka-*: *kocid-eva puriso* Milp. 40[20]. In construction with the negation *na* it signifies 'none': *n'atthi koci bhavo nicco* 'there is no permanent existence' Thl. 121. The form *na. . . kañcinaṃ* 'none' Thl. 879 is worthy of note, for *kañci* is here further inflected like an *in*-stem.—2. Also *katama* 'who? which one?' (as also in Skr.) is inflected like the Rel. Pron.: Sg. Nom. masc. *katamo* Milp. 26[5]; Sg. Nom. neut. *katamaṃ* D. I. 99[17]; Sg. Instr. masc. *katamena* Vin. I. 30[7], Sg. Loc. fem. *katamassaṃ* M. II. 160[26]; Pl. Nom. masc. *katame* Vin. I. 3[2], Pl. Gen. masc. *katamesā-naṃ* Vin. III. 7[22].—3. *Katara* (as also in Skr.) signifies 'which of the two?' (also 'who,' 'which' in a general sense): Sg. Nom. masc. *kataro* JāCo. I. 352[29]; Sg. Gen. fem. *katarissā* DhCo. I. 215[14].—4. *kati* 'how many' (as also in Skr.): Nom. masc. *kati (samaṇā)* Sn. 83, *kati (uposathā)* Vin. I. 111[23], neut. *kati (kammāni)* M. I. 372[8]; Instr. *katīhi* S. IV. 240[20], D. I. 119[31], DhCo. I. 9[1]. Derivatives from it are: *katipayā* 'some, a few'; *katici* 'some, a few' (*katīhici* JāCo. I. 464[13]); *katipāhaṃ* (from *-payāhaṃ*) 'a few days' JāCo. II. 38[11], *-pāhena* 'in a few days' Mhvs. 17. 41; *katikkhattuṃ* 'how often?' M. III. 125[7].—5. *kīva, kīvaṃ* Adv. 'how? how much?'=Ved. *kīvat* (§ 46. 1) in *kīva-dūra* 'how far distant' M. II. 119[3]; *kīva-ciraṃ* 'how long?' Vv. 24. 14; *kīva-bahukā* 'how many?' Ud. 91[25]; *yāva-kīvaṃ* 'so long' Vin. I. 11[19], S. IV. 8[21], A. IV. 304[22]. From it is also derived *kīvatikā* 'how many?' Vin. I. 117[16].—6. Cf. finally *kittaka* (§ 27. 7) 'how much? how big': *kittakaṃ addhānaṃ* 'how long a time?' VvCo. 117[8] (in explanation of *kīva-ciraṃ*). To it correspond *ettaka*

[1] The noun *kiñcanaṃ* is a compound of *kiṃ* with the particle *cana*. Cf. *yassa natthi kiñcanaṃ* Dh. 421. Whence *akiñcano* 'he who does not call anything his own' Thl. 36, Dh. 88, etc. Its opposite is *sakiñcano*. The word *kiñcāpi* is a conjunction 'although, in spite of the fact that' Sn. 230, D I. 237[9].

'this much' Milp. 316^{25}, DhCo II. 15^{6} etc. and *tattaka* DhCo. II. 16^{11} etc. From the same stem is derived the Adv. *kittāvatā* 'how far ?' Vin. I. 3^{1}, M. I. 14^{2}, S. IV. 38^{32} etc.

§ 112.1. The Possessive Pronoun for all three persons is *sa*= *sva* (*saṃ* 'property'; Instr. *sena* Jā II. 22^{23}, Pl. *sāni* M. I. 366^{5}) and *saka*=*svaka* (Sg. Instr. *sakena dārena* Vv. 83. 20, Abl. *sakamhā gāmā* D. I. 81^{23}, cf. *samhā raṭṭhā* Jā. VI. 502^{34}, Loc. *samhi āsane* D. II. 225^{17}. Pl. Acc. *sake* 'one's own people' Jā. VI. 505^{16} etc.). The Poss. Pron. of the first person *madīya* (in Childers, PD.)=Skr. *madīya* seems to be unattested. The Adj. *māmaka*, fem. *-ikā*=Skr. *māmaka* signifies 'lovable, valuable' Iv. 112^{15}; at the end of a compound it signifies 'loving, worshipping' JāCo. III. 182^{10}, 183^{12}. —2. The oblique cases of *attan* 'soul, self' (§92) are used as reflexive pronoun: *attānaṃ damayanti subbatā* Thl. 19; *attānaṃ nāsesi* JāCo. I. 510^{11}; *attana kataṃ pāpaṃ* Dh. 161. Cf. *attadutiya* 'with one companion' D. II. 147^{21}; *attasattama* 'in group of seven' Smp. 320^{5}, *attaṭṭama* 'in group of eight' VvCo. 149^{17} etc.—3. From pronominal stems are derived: *yāvant* 'how big, how much' (Pl. Nom. *yāvant' ettha samāgatā* Dh. 337; retained also in the conjunctions *yāva* or *yāvaṃ*, *yāvatā*, correlative *tāva*, *tāvatā*) and *yāvataka* 'how big, how much' (Sg. Nom. neut. *-kaṃ* S.IV. 320^{23}, 321^{7}; Pl. Acc. masc. *-ke* Vin. I. 83^{27}), *tāvataka* 'so big, so much' (Sg. Nom. neut. *-kaṃ* S. IV. 320^{23}, 321^{7}, Instr. *-kena* DhCo. III. 61^{14}, Milp. 312^{9}; Pl. Acc. masc. *-ke* Vin. I. 83^{28}), as well as the frequent formations with *-di*, *-di a*,*-risa*,*-dikkha*,*-rikkha*=Skr.*-dṛś*, *-dṛśa*,*-dṛkṣa* (cf. § 43. 1): *mādisa*, *mārisa* 'such as I' (cf. Pl. Nom. fem. *mādisiyo* DhCo. II. 17^{12}) *amhādisa* 'such as we' (Pl. Acc. masc. *-se* Mhvs.5. 128); *tādisa* 'such as you' JāCo. I. 445^{23}; *tumhādisa* 'such as you (pl.)' (DhCo. II. 39^{19}, III. 235^{6}); *yādisa*(*ka*) 'of what sort' and *tādi*, *tādisa*(*ka*), *etādisa*(*ka*) 'of that sort' (Sn. 522, S. I. 227^{27} (verse), D. II. 109^{13}, DhCo. II. 16^{9}, PvCo. 10^{25} (verse); Thl. 201, Vv. 84. 54, D. II. 157^{4} (verse), S.I. 202^{6}(verse)); *īdi*, *īdisa*(*ka*), *īdikkha*, *īrisa* 'of this sort' (Mhvs. 10. 54, 14, 13, JāCo. I. 60^{33} (verse); *edisa*(*ka*), *erisa* 'of this sort' (Sn. 313, Vin. I. 195^{11}); *kīdi*, *kīdisa*, *kīrisa* 'of what sort?' (Sn. 836, 1088, JāCo. I. 496^{21}, II. 3^{23}; *kiṃdisa* S. I. 34^{10} (verse)); *yādisakīdisa* 'of whatever sort' (Jā. I. 420^{7}),

§ 113. The following are pronominal adjectives: 1. *sabba* 'all, whole, every'=*sarva*. It is inflected like the Rel. Pron. Cf. Pl. Nom. masc. *sabbe* Sn. 179, M. III. 61^{12}, JāCo. I. 280^{1}, Gen. masc. *sabbesaṃ* Sn. 1030, M. II. 201^{7}, JāCo. II. 352^{17} and *sabbesānaṃ* M. III.

60[24]; Gen. fem. *sabbāsaṃ* S. I. 17[27]; Sg. Loc. fem. *sabbāya* Vin. I. 165[27].—2. *vissa* 'all' = *viśva* is archaic and quite rare. We have the Sg. Acc. masc. *vissaṃ* (*dhammaṃ*) Dh. 266. The Comm. however explains the word by *visamaṃ*.—3. *añña* 'another' = *anya* is inflected like *sabba*. Cf. Pl. Nom. masc. *aññe* Sn. 201 etc. Gen. *aññesaṃ* Sn. 213, JāCo. I. 254[21] etc. But an *i*-vowel appears in the stem in Sg. Dat.-Gen. and Loc. fem.: Dat.-Gen. *aññissā* Vin. I. 15[10], Loc. *aññissā* (*guhāya*) JāCo. II. 27[16]. When repeated, *añño*... *añño* signifies 'the one...the other' JāCo. I. 456[6]. In *aññamañña* 'one another' only the last component is inflected: *aññamaññassa* D. I. 56[29], *aññamaññamhi* D. I. 20[17], *aññamaññehi* Sn. 936, Thl. 933.—4. *aññatara* 'one of two' D. I. 228[2], M. I. 62[35] or 'any one' Vin. I. 23[4], D. I. 62[34]. The Sg. Gen. fem. is *aññatarissā* S. I. 140[20].—5. *aññatama* 'any one' Mhvs. 38. 14.—6. *itara* 'another' too is inflected like *sabba*: Pl. Nom. masc. *itare* DhCo. IV. 40[13], Dat.-Gen. fem.-*rāsaṃ* JāCo. II. 27[19]. 'The one...the other' is expressed by *eko*... *itaro* VvCo. 149[7], or *itaro*...*itaro* Mhvs. 25. 62; *itarītara* signifies 'the one and the other, everyone, any one' Thl. 230, Jā. I. 467[28] (Comm. = *yassa kassaci*), M. II. 6[1], A. V. 91[6] (*itarītarena* 'reciprocally' Vv. 84[1], likewise *itaretarehi* Attanāgaluvs. 10.5).—7. Also *para* and *apara* 'a different one' are inflected like *sabba*: Pl. Nom. masc. *pare* Sn. 762, Vin. I. 5[4], D. I. 2[33], *apare* JāCo. III. 51[25]; Dat.-Gen. *paresaṃ* Thl. 743, 942, Vv. 80. 6, D. I. 3[9]; *paro*...*paro* 'the one...the other' D. I. 224[13]. As for *paraṃ* Adv. 'beyond, later' and Prep. 'after', as well as for *aparāparaṃ* Adv. 'from one side to the other, up and down,' see Childers, PD. and D. Andersen, PGl. under the words.—8. *pubba* 'the fore part, eastern', *uttara* 'the upper part, northern', *adhara* 'the lower part' are said to be inflected like *sabba*. Of *pubba*, however, only the Sg. Loc. *pubbe* 'earlier, formerly' is attested, the other forms occurring only at the end of compounds. Of *uttara* we have the Loc. Sg. fem. *uttarāya* (*disāya*) D. I. 74[23] beside *uttarassaṃ. di āyaṃ* S. I. 148[4] (verse), Adv. *uttarena* 'to the north' and *uttarato* 'from the north'.—9. Of *ekacca* 'one, any one' (Adj. Vin. I. 183[29], Subst. S. III. 243[14]) the Pl. Nom. is *ekacce* 'some' S. IV. 102[1], Sn. p. 101, JāCo. III. 126[17], Dat.-Gen. *ekaccānaṃ* Vin. I. 45[18], III. 20[12]; *ekacco*...*ekacco* signifies 'the one ...the other' S. IV. 305[10,11], Vin. I. 88[30,31], DhCo. II. 12[8,9]; *ekaccaṃ*... *ekaccaṃ* 'partly...partly' D.I. 17[12]. Its derivative is *ekacciya* 'individually': Sg. Nom. masc. *ekacciyo* Jā. I. 326[8], Vin. I. 290[1], Acc. -*yaṃ* Vin. I. 289[2], Nom. fem. *ekacciyā* (*itthī*) S. I. 86[13] (verse); Pl.

Nom. masc. *ekacciyā* Jā. I. 326[7] (Comm. = *ekacce*), S. I. 199[20] (verse).

III. Numerals

1. Cardinal Numbers.

§ 114. The numbers one and two. 1. *eka* 'one' is inflected like *añña* (§ 113. 3). Thus Sg. Dat.-Gen. masc. *ekassa* Sn. 397, DhCo. II. 23[15], but fem. *ekissā* Vin. II. 38[26], JāCo. I. 151[3]; Loc. masc. *ekasmiṃ*, but fem. *ekissā* M. III. 65[15], JāCo. VI. 32[20] or *ekissaṃ* DhCo. III. 346[6]. The Pl. *eke* signifies 'some' D. I. 12[29]; when repeated, *eko...eko* signifies 'the one...the other' D. I. 181[1], Mhvs. 5. 103; *ekameko* is 'everyone separately, individually' D. II. 171[1], Mhvs. 4. 52. On *ekacca*, *ekacciya* see § 113. 9.—2. *dvi* 'two' (in compound also *dī-*, cf. *diguṇa* 'double') has the following forms for all three genders: Nom. *dve* (masc. DhCo. II. 9[14], JāCo. I. 151[5], fem. Sn. p. 102, neut. JāCo. IV. 137[16]) and *duve* (masc. Th1. 245, fem. Sn. 1001); Acc. *dve* (masc. JāCo. II. 27[20], DhCo. II. 4[14], fem. DhCo. II. 42[4]) and *duve* (masc. Mhvs. 5. 213, neut. Mhvs. 10. 47); Instr. *dvīhi* (masc. JāCo. I. 338[6], II. 153[14], fem. M. I. 78[2], II. 162[6]); Dat.-Gen. *dvinnaṃ* (masc. Mhvs. 24. 19, JāCo. II. 154[22], DhCo. II. 12[8], fem. M. I. 65[23], JāCo. II. 27[19]) and *duvinnaṃ*; Loc. *dvīsu* (masc. Mhvs. 6. 25, neut. JāCo. I. 338[6], DhCo. II. 8[8]). Similar is the flection of *ubho* 'both': Nom.-Acc. *ubho* Dh. 74, Sn. 582, JāCo. I. 510[26], Vin. I. 10[15] etc. (and *ubhe*); Instr.-Abl. *ubhohi* D. II. 176[22], JāCo. IV. 142[10] (and *ubhehi*); Dat.-Gen. *ubhinnaṃ* Jā. I. 353[14], JāCo. I. 338[10], Mhvs. 2. 25; Loc. *ubhosu* Sn. 778, JāCo. I. 264[13] VvCo. 275[17] (and *ubhesu*). The Sandhi-form *vubho* occurs in Jā. VI. 509[24]. The word *ubhaya* 'both' is used both in Sg. and Pl.: thus *puññe ca pāpe ca ubhaye* 'both in virtue and sin' Sn. 547; *ubhayena saṃyamena* 'through both (kinds of) self-control' PvCo. 11[2]; *gihihi ca anāgārehi ca ubhayehi* 'with both the laity and the priests' DhCo. IV. 174[1]; *candimasuriyā ubhay' ettha* (= *yā ettha*) *dissare* 'both sun and moon are visible here' Vv. 83. 4. Cf. DhCo. I. 29[13] (verse). In Voc. we have *ubhayo nisāmetha* 'listen to me, you two!' Th2. 449 (cf. 457); *ubhayaṃ* 'both' Dh. 404. In the same way *dubhaya* is used in the Gāthā-language, of which the initial *d* might be derived from *dvi*: *dubhayaṃ cutūpapātaṃ* 'both degeneration and regeneration' Sn. 51;

dubhayāni paṇḍarāni 'both kinds of intelligence' Sn. 526; *Todeyya-Kappā dubhayo* 'the two (the pair)' T. and K.' Sn. 1007, 1125; Acc. *dubhayaṃ lokaṃ* 'both worlds' Jā. III. 442⁴. Cf. *dubhato* Jā. VI. 497⁴, which is explained in the Comm. by *ubhato*.

§ 115. The numbers three to ten[1]: 3. *ti* 'three' (in compound *ti-*, cf. *tiguṇa* 'three times','*tipiṭaka* 'collection of three baskets'): Masc. Nom.-Acc. *tayo* Sn. 311, JāCo. III. 51²⁵, DhCo. II. 4¹¹ etc. (*tayas-su* Sn. 231); Instr.-Abl. *tīhi* Dh. 391, S. IV. 175²⁶; Dat.-Gen. *tiṇṇaṃ* Th1. 127, S. IV. 86¹⁹, DhCo. II. 46²⁰ and (the later form) *tiṇṇannaṃ*[2] Milp. 309⁸, Mhvs. 15. 34; Loc. *tīsu* DhCo. II. 27⁴. Fem. Nom.-Acc. *tisso* Th1. 24. JāCo. II. 33¹⁶; Instr.-Abl. *tīhi* Th2. 11, S.I. 166³⁰ (verse), Sn. 656; Dat.-Gen. *tissannaṃ* D. II. 66¹⁷, S IV. 234²⁸; *tīsu* Sn. 842, DhCo. II. 25⁹. Neut. Nom.-Acc. *tīṇi* Th2. 134, Mhvs. 6. 25; for the rest as in masc.—4. *Catu* ' four ' (in compound *catu-*, *catur-*, cf. *catukaṇṇa* ' quadrangular ' A. I. 141³⁰ (verse), *caturassa* ' quadrilateral ' Jā. VI. 518²⁹, *catugguṇa* 'four times' JāCo. I. 422²⁷): Masc Nom.-Acc. *cattāro* D. I. 91²⁹, DhCo. II. 9¹⁶, JāCo. IV. 139³ and *caturo* (Nom. Sn. 84, Acc. Sn. 969); Instr.-Abl. *catūhi* Sn. 231, DhCo. II. 8⁶, *catuhi* JāCo. I. 279³¹ and (only archaically) *catubbhi* Sn. 229, Jā. III. 207¹⁴ (*catubbhi ṭhānesu* Vv. 32. 7); Dat.-Gen. *catunnaṃ* D. I. 91³⁰, DhCo. II. 15¹⁴; Loc. *catūsu* DhCo. II. 42¹⁰, IV. 56¹² and *catusu* JāCo. I. 262⁹. Fem. Nom.-Acc. *catasso* Vv. 78. 6, S. III. 240¹⁷, JāCo. I. 262¹⁰ (Acc. *caturo disā* Vv. 6. 10); Instr.-Abl. *catūhi* JāCo. I. 339⁴ and *catuhi* D. I. 102²; Dat.-Gen. *catunnaṃ* D. I. 116¹¹ and *catassannaṃ*; Loc. *catūsu* and *catusu* JāCo. III. 46²⁰. Neut. Nom.-Acc. *cattāri* Sn. 227, Th2. 171, DhCo. II. 24¹⁵; for the rest as in masc.—5. *Pañca* ' five ', *cha* ' six ', *satta* ' seven ', *aṭṭha* 'eight', *nava* 'nine', and *dasa* 'ten' are inflected in all three genders in the following manner: Nom.-Acc. *pañca*, *cha* etc.; Instr.-Abl. *pañcahi*, *chahi* DhCo. II. 28⁵ etc. [with protraction *aṭṭhāhi* Jā. III, 207¹⁴, archaic: *dasabhi* Vin. I. 38²² (verse)]; Dat.-Gen. *pañcannaṃ* S. IV. 173¹⁵, *channaṃ* Sn. 169, A. I. 22³¹ etc.; *sattānaṃ* beside °*annaṃ* M. III. 81²³; Loc. *pañcasu*, *chasu* and *chassu* Sn. 169, *sattasu* Ud. 65¹⁷ etc. In compound these numerals appear in the form *pañca-* etc. given above. On *cha-* *chaḷ-* cf. § 67, 72. 1.

[1] For parallels in Pkr. cf. Pischel, § 438 f.
[2] On this double-formation cf. R. O. Franke, PGr. p. 13.

§ 116. The tens, hundreds etc. 1. The numbers from 20 to 100 are: 20: *vīsa, vīsaṃ, vīsā, vīsati = viṃśati*.—30: *tiṃsa, tiṃsaṃ, tiṃsā, tiṃsati = triṃśat*.—40: *cattārīsa, -rīsaṃ, -rīsā; cattālīsa, -līsaṃ, -līsā; tālīsa, -līsaṃ, -līsā = catvāriṃśat*.—50: *paññāsa, saṃ, -sā; paṇṇāsa = pañcāśat*.—60: *saṭṭhi = ṣaṣṭi*.—70: *sattati, sattari = saptati*.—80: *asīti = aśīti*.—90: *navuti = navati*.—100: *sata = śata*.—200: *dve satāni* or *dvisata*.—300: *tīṇi satāni* or *tisata* etc.—1000: *sahassa = sahasra*.—2000: *dve sahassāni* etc.—100 000: *lakkha*.—10 millions: *koṭi*[1].—2. Intermediate numbers: 11: *ekādasa, ekārasa = ekādaśa*.—12: *dvādasa, bārasa = dvādaśa*.—13: *terasa, telasa = trayodaśa*.—14: *catuddasa, cuddasa = caturdaśa*.—15: *pañcadasa, pannarasa, paṇṇarasa = pañcadaśa*.—16: *soḷasa, sorasa = ṣoḍaśa*.—17: *sattadasa, sattarasa = saptadaśa*.—18: *aṭṭhādasa, aṭṭhārasa = aṣṭādaśa*.—19: *ekūnavīsa, ekūnavīsati = ekonaviṃśati, ūnaviṃśati*—22: *dvāvīsa, sati, bāvīsa, -sati*; 23: *tevīsa*; 24: *catuvīsa*; 25: *pañcavīsa, paṇṇavīsatī, paṇṇuvīsa* etc.—32: *dvattiṃsa, battiṃsa*; 36: *chattiṃsa*; 49: *ekūnapaññāsa*; 55: *pañcapaññāsa*; 56: *chappaññāsa* etc.[2]

§ 117. The mode of using the numerals is unusually varied in character. 1. The numbers 1 to 18 are adjectives. Cf. *dve vā tīṇi vā rattindivāni* 'two or three days and nights' D. II. 327[19]; *catunnaṃ māsānaṃ accayena* 'after the expiry of four months' Sn. p. 99; *soḷasannaṃ puggalānaṃ* 'of 16 individuals' Milp. 310[18]. On the analogy of the tens, however, also the numeral compounds of *dasa* may take a final *ṃ* and thus become substantives: *nava satta dvādasañ-ca...pañcavīsaṃ dvādasañ-ca, dvādasañ-ca navāpi ca* '9 and 7 and 12..., 25 and 12 and (again) 12 and 9 (kings)' Mhvs. 2. 9.—2. Of the decades those in *-ā* are feminine substantives, of which the form in *-āya* (Instr. Dat.-Gen) actually occurs: *ekassa pi dadāmi dvinnam-pi dadāmi ... dasannam-pi dadāmi vīsāya pi dadāmi tiṃsāya pi dadāmi cattārīsāya pi dadāmi paññāsāya pi dadāmi satassa pi dadāmi* 'I give (alms) to one, to 2,...to 10, to 20, to 30, to 40, to 50, to 100' Sn. p. 86. The decades in *-a* may be declined, but are mostly left uninflected; those in *-aṃ* are used as nominatives and accusatives; those in *-ti* are fem. substantives and are inflected according to § 86 or remain undeclined. The numerals *sata* and *sahassa* are neuter.—3. When connected with substantives, the numerals from 20 upwards may be used appositionally in the same case

[1] The designations for higher numbers, such as *abbuda* etc. (see Abhp. 475, Dpvs. 3. 11 f.) are confined to lexicons.

[2] On the numerals in Pkr. cf. Pischel, § 445 f., 443 f.

as the substantive: Loc. *vīsatiyā yojanesu tiṃsāya yojanesu* 'at (the distance of) 20 (30) miles' M. II. 162[30]; Instr. *dvattiṃsāya mahāpurisalakkhaṇehi asītiyā anuvyañjanehi* 'with the 32 major and 80 minor insignia of a Buddha' VvCo. 323[14]; *ekūnapaññāsāya kaṇḍehi* 'with 49 arrows' JāCo. III. 220[21]; *chattiṃsatiyā sotehi* 'with 36 streams' DhCo. IV. 48[16]; Acc. *vīsatim-pi bhikkhū tiṃsam-pi bhikkhū cattārīsam-pi bhikkhū* '20 or 30 or 40 monks' M. III. 79[6]; *vīsam-pi jātiyo tiṃsam-pi jātiyo cattālīsam-pi jātiyo paññāsam-pi jātiyo* '20 and 30 and 40 and 50 existences' Iv. 99[3]; *aṭṭhacattārīsaṃ vassāni* '48 years' Sn. 289; Gen. *imesam tevīsatiyā buddhānaṃ santike* 'before these 23 Buddhas' DhCo. I. 84[3]. In the following examples the decades remain uninflected: Nom. *paṇṇāsa yojanā saṭṭhi yojanā* '50, 60 miles' DhCo. III. 217[8]; *tiṃsa rattiyo* D. II. 327[10]; *pañcapaññāsa vassāni...pañcavīsati vassāni* Thl. 904; *dvattiṃsa mahāpurisalakkhaṇāni* Sn. p. 102 (but *dvattiṃsā mah-* Sn. 1000); Acc. *ekūnapaññāsa jane* '49 people' JāCo. III. 220[20]; *sattasattari ñāṇavatthūni* 'the 77 items of knowledge' S. II. 59[34]; Instr. *dvattiṃsa mahāpurisalakkhaṇehi* M. II. 135[21].—3. Also *sata* and *sahassa*, as well as numerals with them as components, may be used in apposition with a substantive: Nom. *gandhabbā cha sahassāni* '6000 G.'s' Thl. 164; *bhikkhuniyo sahassaṃ* '1000 nuns' Mhvs. 5. 187; Acc. *pañcasatāni Caṇḍālapurise* '500 Caṇḍālas' Mhvs. 10. 91; *gāthā sataṃ* '100 verses' Dh. 102; Instr. *pañcasatehi therehi* 'with 500 Theras' Dpvs. 4. 6. The substantive in such constructions appears sometimes in the Sg., as in Acc. *aṭṭhasataṃ bhattaṃ* (instead of *bhattāni*) '800 meals' Milp. 88[4]. The numeral is treated as an Adj. in Nom. *pañcasatā vāṇijā*, fem. *pañcasatā yakkhiniyo*, Acc. *pañcasate vāṇije* JāCo. II. 128[17,22].—4. The numerals may further be used in Sg. as abstracta and substantives may be connected with them as genitive attributes: *paro-sahassaṃ bhikkhūnaṃ* 'over 1000 monks' Thl. 1238 (but appositionally *paro-sahassaṃ puttā* 'over 1000 sons' D. I. 89[4]); *sahassam-pi aṭṭhānaṃ* '1000 things' S. I. 229[13]; *vihārānaṃ pañcasataṃ* '500 monasteries' Mhvs. 12. 33; *saṭṭhiṃ arahataṃ akā* 'he made 60 Arhats' Mhvs. 1. 14.—5. Finally, a numeral and a substantive may unite into a compound. Cf. *aṭṭhavassaṃ sattamāsaṃ rājā rajjaṃ akārayi* 'the king reigned for 8 years and 7 months' Mhvs. 35. 46. The compound *vassasataṃ* of this type, signifying 'hundred years', is very frequently used. Compounds like the following are also very much in evidence: *satta manussasatāni* '700 people' JāCo. IV. 142[3]; *dvīsu vassasatesu (atikkantesu)* '(after the expiry of) 200 years' Mhvs. 33. 80; *pañca-itthi-satehi* 'with 500 women' Mhvs. 14. 57, etc.

2: Ordinals, Distributives, Fractional Numbers, Numeral Adverbs, Numeral Adjectives and Numeral Substantives.

§ 118. 1. The ordinals from 1 to 10 correspond to those of Skr.: 1. *paṭhama* = Skr. *prathama*.—2. *dutiya* (§ 23) = *dvitīya*.—3. *tatiya* (§ 23) = *tṛtīya*.—4. *catuttha* = *caturtha*.—5. *pañcama* = *pañcama*.—6. *chaṭṭha* (*chaṭṭhama* Sn. 101), *saṭṭha* = *ṣaṣṭha*.—7. *sattama*, fem. *-mī* Th2. 41 = *saptama*.—8. *aṭṭhama* (fem. *aṭṭhamī* 'the 8th day' Th2. 31) = *aṣṭama*.—9. *navama* = *navama*.—10. *dasama* (fem. *dasamī* 'the 10. day' Mhvs. 19. 33) = *daśama*.—2. The same is the case with the decades, the only difference being that in the longer forms (excepting 60 and 80) it is not *-tama*, but only *-ma* that is attached to the basic form in *-ti*: 20. *vīsatima* or *vīsa* = *viṃśatitama* or *viṃśa*.—30. *tiṃsatīma* or *tiṃsa* = *triṃśattama* or *triṃśa*.—40. *cattārīsatima*, *-līsatima* or *cattārīsa*, *līsa* = *catvāriṃśattama* or *catvāriṃśa*.—50. *paññāsatima* = *pañcāśattama*.—60. *saṭṭhitama* = *ṣaṣṭitama*.—70. *sattatima* = *saptatitama*.—80. *asītitama* = *aśītitama*.—90. *navutima* = *navatitama*.—100. *satama* = *śatatama*.—3. The intermediate numbers from 11 to 19 agree on the one hand with Skr., and on the other with Pkr.[1]: 11. *ekādasama* fem. *-mī* M. III. 255[9] = AMāg. *ekkārasama*; or *ekādasa*. fem. *ekādasī* 'the 11. day' = Skr. *ekādaśa*.—12. *dvādasama*, fem. *-mī* M. III. 255[10] = AMāg. *duvālasama*; or *dvādasa*, in fem. *dvādasī* 'the 12. day' = Skr. *dvādāśa*.—13. *terasama*, fem. *-mī* M. III. 255[11] = AMāg. *terasama*; or *terasa* Mhvs. 16. 2. = Skr. *trayodaśa* —14. *cuddasama*, fem. *-mī* M. III. 255[13] = Pkr. *coddasama*; or *cuddasa*, fem. *cuddasī* 'the 14. day' Mhvs. 19. 39; also *cātuddasa* Vin. I. 87[30], 132[18], or *-sī* Th2. 31 = Skr. *caturdaśa*.—15. *pañcadasama* DhCo. III. 27[11]; *paṇṇarasama* = AMāg. *pannarasama*; or *paṇṇarasa* D. II. 207[17], more frequently *pannarasa* Th1. 1234, D. I. 47[6], Vin. I. 87[30] (*pañcaddasī* 'the 15. day' Th2. 31) = Skr. *pañcadaśa*.—16. *soḷasama* = AMāg. *soḷasama*; and *soḷasa*, fem. *-sī* Dh. 70, Vv. 43. 8, A. IV. 252[9] = Skr. *ṣoḍaśa*.—17. *sattarasama*.—18. *aṭṭharasama* = AMāg. *aṭṭhārasama*.—19. *ekūnavīsatima* = AMāg. *egūṇavīsaīma*.—Cf. further

[1] Pischel, PkrGr. § 449

21. *ekavīsatima*; 22. *bāvīsatima*; 23. *tevīsatima*; 24. *catuvīsatima*; 25. *pañcavīsatima*; 26. *chabbīsatima*, etc.—33. *tettiṃsatima*; 36 *chattiṃsatima*, etc.—4. On the use of the ordinals: In some isolated cases the ordinal number stands for the cardinal: *pañcamehi bandhanehi* 'with 5 bonds' S. IV. 201[22], 202[9]. Worthy of notice are the compounds with *attan*, such as *attadutiya* 'with one companion' D. II. 147[21] etc. Cf. § 112. 2.

§ 119. 1. The distributive numbers are expressed by repeating the cardinals or the ordinals as the case may be: *aṭṭhaṭṭha there 'macce ca pesayi* 'to each he sent 8 theras and court-officials' Mhvs. 5. 249. Cf. DhCo. I. 89[6-7].—*Addha*, *aḍḍha* 'half' is the fractional number. Like Skr. *ardha*, Pkr. *addha*, *aḍḍha*[1], it is compounded with the next higher ordinal number, as in German 'dritthalb, vierthalb': *aḍḍhatiya*, *aḍḍhateyya* JāCo. I. 450[21], II. 93[4] (cf. § 65. 2) is 2½; *aḍḍhuḍḍha* Vin. I. 34[10], DhCo. I. 87[21] (=Pkr. *addhuṭṭha* out of *addha*+**turtha*, Skr. *ardhacaturtha*) is 3½. Cf. *saddhiṃ addhatelasehi bhikkhusatehi* 'with 12½ hundred monks' Sn. p. 100, D. I. 47[4]; *aḍḍhanavamasahassāni* '8500 (persons)' Mhvs. 15. 201. If on the other hand *addha*, *aḍḍha* stands *after a cardinal number*, it signifies half thereof: *dasaddha* is thus=5, Thl. 1244. Thus *purisānaṃ dasaḍḍhehi satehi parivārito* 'surrounded by 500 men' Mhvs. 5. 122.—3. Numeral adverbs: 'once' is expressed by *sakiṃ*, *saki* (*sakid-* or *sakad-* in sandhi before a vowel, § 67, 72. 1)=*sakṛt*, or *ekadā* (*appekadā* 'sometimes' M. II. 7[1], A. V. 83[18]). These adverbs are formed moreover by affixing the formans °*khattuṃ* (§ 22)= °*kṛtvas*[2]: *tikkhattuṃ* '3 times' Vin.I. 104[28]; *catukkhattuṃ* '4 times' Th2. 37, 169; *chakkhaṭṭuṃ* '6 times' D. II. 198[24], DhCo. III. 196[20]; *satakkhattuṃ* '100 times' Th2. 519 etc. Also *katikkhattuṃ* 'how many times?' M. III. 125[7]. Moreover the Sg. or the Pl. Acc. *vāraṃ* and *vāre* is used to express 'time': *eka-vāraṃ* 'once' JāCo. III. 150[21]; *dve vāre* 'twice' DhCo. I. 47[11]; *tayo vāre* '3 times' DhCo. I. 48[8]; *nava vāre* '9 times' Mhvs. 30. 52; *bahu-vāre* 'many times' JāCo. II. 88[8]. Cf. also *dvīsu vāresu* 'twice' Mhvs. 6. 25; *tatiye vāre* 'the third time, on the third chance' Mhvs. 6. 26. Otherwise 'the first time', 'the second time' are simply *paṭhamaṃ*, *dutiyaṃ* etc. *Ekaso* =*ekaśas* means 'individually'.—4. Numeral adverbs in 'times' are constructed with °*dhā*= Skr. °*dhā*, Pkr. °*hā*: *sattadhā* 'seven times, in seven parts or pieces' D. I. 94[24], II. 234[23]. Similarly *satadhā*,

[1] BR. *sub voce*; Pischel, PkrGr. § 450.

[2] Pkr. AMāg °*khutto*. Māh. °*huttaṃ*; Pischel, § 451.

sahassadhā—5. Numeral adjectives in 'kinds, fold' are constructed with °*vidha* = Skr. °*vidha*, Pkr. °*viha*, or with °*guṇa* = Skr., Pkr. °*guṇa*: *anekavidha* 'of many kinds' Dpvs. 6. 70; *sattavidha* 'of seven kinds, seven-fold' JāCo. I. 91[33], Milp. 102[13]; *aṭṭhaguṇa* 'eight-fold' Th2. 153. —6. As for numeral substantives, we have *duka* neut. 'aggregate of two', *tika* 'aggregate of three' DCo. I. 24[27] = Skr. *dvika*, *trika*, Pkr. *duka* or *duya*, *tiya*; *catukka* 'aggregate of four' (§ 62.2) = Skr. *catuṣka*; *sataka* 'aggregate of hundred' JāCo. I. 74[22] = *śataka*.

IV. Verbal System

1. Generalities

§ 120. In verbal forms Pāli is still farther removed from the basic Sanskrit than in nominal flexion. The historical forms are on the whole well preserved, particularly in the older periods of the language. But the actual life of the language lies in the new formations, which were created in such numbers, either on the basis of analogy, or after existing types, that it is scarcely possible to lay down rules covering all the individual cases.—It is a prominent feature of Pāli distinguishing it off from Skr., that it has lost the dual.—The medium is also disappearing. Passive forms too have active endings already in the oldest period of the language. The Gāthā-language still shows, it is true, a considerable number of medial forms. But they are in part due to the exigencies of metre, and everywhere bear the stamp of archaism. They become rare already in the canonical prose, and rarer still in the non-canonical, in which they are confined only to a few fixed forms (*e. g.* Imp. 2. Sg. in *-ssu*, Pret. 3. Sg. in *-ittha*). The medial forms appear again in the later artificial poetry. The Part. Pres. Med. in *-māna* was productive in every period of the language. —As for the temporal, the perfect has almost completely disappeared, leaving but slight traces behind. Unlike Prākrit, Pāli has retained the conditional. Imperfect and aorist are no longer sharply distinguished between in Pāli. Both of them have coincided in the preterite which is mostly called "aorist". The various periphrastic formations are of great importance: they are originated by the combination of participles, gerunds or verbal substantives with the verbs "to be" or "to become", or with other verbs of an indefinite meaning. They represent quite a characteristic feature of the language.—The modes are the same as in Sanskrit. The Gāthā-language has apparently still retained isolated forms of the Vedic subjunctive.—Another important feature is the predominance of *a*-stems in the present system. Their analogy has decided the character of many verbs which are athematic in Skr. It is no longer possible to set up a complete system of paradigms for the different 'conjugation-classes' as they are distinguished in Sanskrit. The present-stems of these classes will be discussed, as is proper, in connection with one chief paradigm, as supplement to it. Besides the expansion of the sphere of the *a*-flexion we have also to notice that of *e*-stems.—The preponderance of the present-stem is of particular importance. Tenses, as well as verbal nouns etc., which in Skr. are based directly on the root, may be derived in Pāli from the present-stem. This applies to preterite (aorist), future, past part. in *-ta*, future pass. part. in *-tabba*, infinitive in (*-tuye* and) *-tuṃ*, and gerund in *-tvā*, *-tvāna* and *-ya*. Moreover new passive and causative stems may be derived from present-stems. The innovated forms in all these cases appear side by side with the historical ones—sometimes rare in comparison with the latter, but occasionally even surpassing them in the frequency of use. In particular cases the process goes even further, when, for instance, an historically attested future or passive-stem is made the basis of further new formations.[1]

2. Present-system

with Indicative, Subjunctive, Imperative and Optative.

A. Present Indicative

§ 121. The flexion may be shown by a verb of the I. Class, *labhati* 'gains, receives'.

		Sg.	Pl.
Act.	1.	*labhāmi*	*labhāma*
	2.	*labhasi*	*labhatha*
	3.	*labhati*	*labhanti*
Med.	1.	*labhe*	(*labhamhe*)
	2.	*labhase*	(*labhavhe*)
	3.	*labhate*	*labhante*, *labhare*.

[1] I am thinking here, for instance, of the stem *dakkh-* = Skr. *drakṣ-* (cf. § 152, 204. 1c, 213), or of the stem *chijj-* = *chidy-* (§ 196), etc.

§ 122. 1. Act. Sg. 1. Instead of *-āmi* there is also found in the Gāthā-language the shorter ending *-aṃ*: *tassāhaṃ santike gacchaṃ* 'I am going to him' Th2. 306. For the rest the endings correspond to those of Sanskrit; *-ma* is the secondary ending.—2. Med (the examples are mostly from the Gāthā-language or the artificial poetry) Sg. 1: *rame* 'I enjoy myself' S. I. 180^{8} (verse), *kuppe* 'I am angry' Jā III. 120^{15}. In the post-canonical prose we find, for instance, *maññe* 'I think' JāCo. II. 249^{7} etc. Sg. 2: *anupucchase* 'you ask' Vv. 17. 5; *labhase* Jā. II. 220^{12} (Comm. *labhasi*). Sg. 3: *labhate* Th1. 35; *sobhate* 'is beautiful' Th2. 255 ff.; *rocate* 'suits (one's) taste' Th2. 415; *bhāsate* 'speaks' Sn. 452. Pl. 3: *lambante* 'they hang' Th2. 265; *haññante* 'they are beaten' Th2. 451. The ending *-are* in 3. Pl. is quite frequent: *labhare* S. I. 110^{32} (verse); *khādare* 'they consume' Jā. II. 223^{14} (Comm. *khādanti*); *jāyare* 'they are born' S. I. 34^{16}; *socare* 'they suffer pain' Sn. 445 (against *socanti* Sn. 333); *obhāsare* 'they light up' Vv. 9. 3 (v. l. *obhāsate*); *jīyare* 'they vanish away' Jā. VI. 528^{5} (Skr. *jīryante*); *miyyare* 'they die' Sn. 575 (Skr. *mriyante*); *haññare* 'they are killed' S. I. 76^{22} etc. These forms are connected with the Vedic presents like *śere*, *iśire*, and they correspond to the forms in *-ire* in Pkr.[1]—The 1. Pl. Med. deserves special consideration. Kacc. 3. 1. 2 and 18 (Senart, pp. 423, 429) gives as ending *-mhe*, which is probably derived from *-mahe* through syncope. The fuller form occurs in *bhavāmahe*[2] Mhvs. 1. 60. Also the ending *-mase* (and *-mhase*) seems to have been in existence at its side. All the forms with this ending have not a subjunctive meaning (cf. below § 126), as for instance (*na*) *tappāmase* (*dassanena taṃ*) 'we are (not) tired of (looking at you)' Vv. 17. 4. which is indicative in meaning (cf. Skr. *tṛpyate*). Same perhaps also with *abhinandāmase* 'we are glad' Vv. 17. 7; *saremhase* (according to *e*-flexion) 'we remember' Th2. 383. The ending *-mase* is evidently the medial counterpart of the Act. Vedic *-masi*, and *-mhase* looks like a cross of *-mhe* and *-mase*.

B. Subjunctive

§ 123. It is not possible to set forth a paradigm, because we have to do here only with isolated forms preserved in the Gāthā-language. The Subjunctive is distinguished from the Indicative by

[1] Whitney, Sanskrit Gramm. § 550; Pischel, PkrGr. § 458; Windisch, Abhdl. Sächs. Ges. d. W., Nr. VI, 1887, p. 478 f.; E. Kuhn, Beitr. p. 94; E. Müller, PGr. p. 97.

[2] E. Kuhn, loc. cit.

the extended stem-vowel. Yet only those forms may be relied upon as Subjunctive without any hesitation in which the Subjunctive (Imperative) meaning is quite clear and the possibility of a mere metrical protraction is out of the question. This appears to be the case with one of the two passages pointed out by Pischel[1]: *no vitarāsi bhottuṃ* 'do not go on eating!' Jā. II. 14[17] (Fausböll. Ten Jāt. 19[4]). The Comm. gives the explanation: *mā nāgamamṃsakhādako ahosi*. I add to it: *attānaṃ yeva garahāsi ettha* 'scold yourself for this affair!' Jā. IV. 248[8], which is explained in the Comm. by *attānam-eva garaheyyāsi*. True Subjunctives are to be found perhaps also in the forms *kāmayāsi* and *cajāsi* Jā. V. 220[20,24], which are dependent on *sace* and *ce* respectively. Pischel's second example is, however, doubtful: *ātāpino saṃvegino bhavātha* 'be zealous and enthusiastic' Dh. 144[b]. The form in question here may be simply that of Imp. 2. Pl. protracted *metri causa*. Similar cases are: *adhimanasā bhavātha* Sn 692; *taṃ ca* (i.e. *dhammaṃ*) *dharātha*[2] *sabbe* 'all should hold fast to it (the truth)!' Sn. 385; *pāpāni kammāni vivajjayātha, dhammānuyogañ-ca adhiṭṭhahātha* 'give up sinful practices and hold fast to zeal for the truth!' Vv. 84. 38; *abhinibbajjiyātha naṃ* 'avoid that!' Sn. 281 (from root *varj, varjayati*). Of the three examples given by E. Müller[3], *dahāsi* and *dahāti* Sn. 841, 888 are certainly no Subjunctives: they are simply the representatives of Skr. *dadhāsi, dadhāti* (§ 37) Also *saddahāsi* Jā. I. 426[8] is reproduced in the Comm. simply as *saddahasi*. But even the third *ko taṃ paṭibhaṇāti me* 'who can give me answer to that?' Jā III. 404[4] is very doubtful on account of the *paṭibhaṇāmi* and *-bhaṇāsi* in the parallel verses 404[10,20] and 404[13], 405[8], where the latter certainly has no Subjunctive meaning. It is wanting also in *āvahāti* Thl. 303 (cf. Sn. 181, 182, S. I. 42[5,9], 214[18,22]) for which there occurs *rakkhati* in the parallel passages, and it cannot be traced either in *hanāsi* Jā.III. 199[2] (Comm.=*paharasi*), V. 460[19] and *hanāti* Jā. V. 461[28].

C. Imperative

§ 124. The paradigm is:

Sg. Act.	1.	*labhāmi*	Pl.	*labhāma*
	2.	*labha, labhāhi*		*labhatha*
	3.	*labhatu*		*labhantu*

1 Pischel, KZ. 23, p. 424.

2 It should be noticed that in this passage the Imp. *suṇātha* 'hear!' occurs immediately before.

3 E. Müller, PGr p. 180. Also the 1. Pl. Med of the Imperative is of Subjunctive origin. See § 125. 2.

Med.	1.	*labhe*	*labhāmase*
	2.	*labhassu*	*labhavho*
	3.	*labhataṃ*	*labhantaṃ*

§ 125. Active. The 1. Sg. and Pl. are simply transfers from the Indicative: *vandāma* 'let us praise!' D. III. 197[24] (verse); *dhunāma* 'let us destroy!' Thl. 1147. Hence it is also said *kassa naṃ dema* 'to whom should we give it?' JāCo. II. 196[24], *handa karomi* M. III. 179[27], *handa karoma* Vin. II. 295[5]. Similarly we have in Thl. 1146 *dālemu* 'let us smash!' (with the ending *-mu*, cf. § 128) = Skr. *dālayāma* parallel to *dhunāma*.— In the 2. Sg. the type *labha* corresponds to the Skr.-form of the thematic conjugation. Thus *piva* 'drink!' JāCo. III. 110[22] = *piba*; *siñca* 'pour out!' Dh. 369 = *siñca*; *nipajja* 'seat yourself!' JāCo. II. 223[2] from *nipadyate*. Also *kara* 'do!' JāCo. IV. 1[14] may be regarded as an historical form = Ved. *kára* Verbs which were not originally thematic gradually began to form their Imperatives after the type *labha*. Thus *gaṇha* 'seize!' JāCo. II. 159[5] from *gaṇhāti* = *gṛhṇāti*,—even *paṭiggaha* 'accept!' Jā. I. 233[10]; *saddaha* 'believe!' JāCo. IV. 52[18] from *saddahati* = *śraddadhāti* etc. The second form *labhāhi* has derived its *-hi* from the forms of the athematic conjugation. Historical are the forms like *akkhāhi* 'describe!' Jā. III. 279[7] = *ākhyāhi*; *brūhi* 'speak!' Sn. 76 = *brūhi*; *dehi* 'give!' JāCo. I. 223[19] = *dehi*. On the analogy of these types were further formed *uggaṇhāhi* 'learn!' M. III. 192[22] from *uggaṇhāti* = *udgṛhṇāti*; *sāvehi* 'proclaim!' JāCo. I. 344[14]; *ānehi* 'bring here!' JāCo. II. 254[19]; *vissajjehi* 'give up!' JāCo. I. 228[20]; *karohi* 'do!' JāCo. III. 188[18] etc. from long-vowel stems. Similarly, also from *a*-stems: *jīvāhi* Sn. 1029; *sarāhi* 'remember!' Milp. 79[25] (beside *sara* Thl. 445); *pakkosāhi* 'call here!' DhCo. IV. 28[4]; *tussāhi* 'be content!' JāCo. I. 494[26] etc.[1]—The 3. Sg. and Pl. in *-tu* and *-ntu* are frequent: *passatu* 'he should see' Sn. 909; *etu* 'he should go' D. I. 179[16]; *ijjhatu* 'should succeed' Th2. 329 (from Skr. *ṛdhyate*); *hanantu* 'they should kill' Jā. IV. 42[26]; *vinassantu* 'they should die' JāCo. IV. 2[24], The 2. Pl. in *-tha*, as also in Pkr.[2], is a transfer from the Indicative, and is thus different from the Skr. suffix *-ta*: *āharatha* 'bring here!' JāCo. I. 266[9]; *anurakkhatha* 'protect!' Dh. 327; *vijānātha* 'learn to distinguish!' Sn. 720; *gaṇhatha* 'take!' JāCo. III. 126[25];

[1] Similarly in Pkr. Māg. *bhaṇāhi*, AMāg. *harāhi*, *vandāhi*, JMāh. *kadhehi*. etc; Pischel, § 468.

[2] The suffix in Pkr. is *-ha*. Cf. Māh. *ṇamaha*, AMāg. *haṇaha*, *ḍahaha* etc. Pischel. § 471.

karotha 'do!' Th2. 13, JāCo. II. 196[20]; *voropetha* 'rob!' D. II. 336[4] etc.

§ 126. Medium. The 1. Sg. is a transfer from the Indicative. The 2. Sg. in *-ssu*[1] = Skr. *-sva* is very common. Thus in the Gāthā-language: *labhassu* Th2. 432 = *labhasva*; *pucchassu*[2] 'ask!' Sn. 189; *jahassu* 'give up!' (from *jahāti*) Sn. 1121 and frequently elsewhere. In *bhikkhasu* 'go to beg!' Thl. 1118 the *ss* has been simplified *metri causa*. Further in the canonical prose: *bhāsassu* 'speak!' M. II. 199[8] = *vhāṣasva*; *sikkhassu* 'learn!' A.V. 79[20]; *payirupāsassu* 'worship!' M.II. 196[25]; *nivattassu* 'return!' Vin. II. 182[33]; *pātu-bhavassu* 'appear' Vin. II. 185[12] etc. Also in the post-canonical prose: *bhāsassu* Milp. 27[25]; *tikicchassu* 'cure!' JāCo II. 213[23]; *naccassu* 'dance!' JāCo. I. 292[23]. The medial meaning of the suffix does not seem to have been felt any more, for it is taken also by those roots which were never medial, as, for instance, by *nart*.—In the 3. Sg., suffix *-taṃ* = Skr. *-tām*; cf. *acchataṃ* 'she should remain' Jā. VI. 506[8] (Comm. *acchatu*); *labhataṃ* D. II. 150[13]. In Sandhi: *vaḍḍhatām-eva* 'he should indeed grow' Jā. III. 209[9].—A true Subjunctive form is to be found in the 1. Pl. in *-mase*, *-mhase*. The suffix is probably derived from *-masai*, which is related to the suffix *-mase* discussed in §122 (at the end) as Skr. *-mahai* to *-mahe*. The two suffix-forms necessarily coincided with each other in Pāli. Forms with Subjunctive (Imperativistic or Futural) meaning are not rare in the Gāthā-language: *labhāmase* 'we should attain' Jā. III. 26[19]; *ramāmase* 'we would enjoy' Th2. 370 f.; *bhaṇāmase* 'we wish to speak' S. I. 209[28] (verse) (parallel to it are to be found there the optatives *sikkhema*, *muccema*); *carāmase* 'we wish to do (carry out)' and *bhavāmase* 'we wish to be' Sn. 32 etc. Similarly *karomase* D. II. 288[1] (verse). On *vademase*, *mahemase* etc. see § 129. The suffix-form *-mhase* occurs in *labhamhase* Pv. 3. 2. 24, 29 (governed by *yathā*, explained as *labheyyāma* in the Comm. 185[1]); *mā pamadamhase* 'we do not wish to neglect' Jā. III. 131[16] etc.—Examples for the 2. Pl., of which the suffix *-vho* in contrast to Skr. *-dhvam* is difficult to explain, are the following: *passavho* 'look up!' Sn. 998; *bhajavho* 'seek out!' Jā I. 472[16] (Comm, *bhajatha, gacchatha*); *pucchavho* 'ask!' Sn. 1030; *kappayavho* 'carry out' Sn. 283. Also in the canonical prose: *mantavho* 'take counsel!' D. I. 122[14], instead of *mantayavho* (as in Jā. II. 107[18] beside *mantavho* 107[19]). If the reading is correct,

[1] In Pkr. the corresponding suffix is *-su*, which Pischel § 467 however would separate from Skr. *-sva* and connect with *-si*.

[2] In the parallel passage S. I. 215[6] there is *pucchassa* in the text.

a remarkable double-ending is to be found in *pamodathavho*[1] 'rejoice!' Jā. IV. $162^{22,26}$ in which both the active and the medial endings have been combined.—An interesting form of the 3. Pl. is presented by *visīyaruṃ* 'they should dissolve' Thī. 312, from Skr. *śyā, śīyate*. The Comm. says: *visīyantu ito c' ito viddhaṃsantu*. The suffix *-ruṃ* is pretty certainly the descendant of Ved. *-rām*[2].

D. Optative (Potential)

§ 127. **Paradigm:**

		Sg.	Pl.
Act.	1.	*labheyyaṃ, labhe* / *labheyyāmi*	*labhema, labhemu* / *labheyyāma*
	2.	*labhe* / *labheyya, labheyyāsi*	*labhetha* / *labheyyātha*
	3.	*labhe* / *labheyya, labheyyāti*	*labheyyuṃ, -yyu*
Med.	1.	(*labheyyaṃ*)	(*labheyyamhe*) *labhemase*
	2.	*labhetho*	(*labheyyavho*)
	3.	*labhetha*	(*labheraṃ*)

§ 128. Active. Two types of forms are in vogue side by side. The forms given first: *labheyyaṃ, labhe, labhe*; *labhema, labhetha, labheyyuṃ* are direct continuations of the Skr. -flexion. Only in the 2. Pl. the ending *-tha* (against Skr. *ta*) is taken from the Indicative. On the analogy of the Imperfect a 1. Sg.* *labhem* (=Pāli *labhe*) was formed to match *labhes, labhet*.—The forms given second: Sg. 2. *labheyya* etc., have been formed, by similar analogy, on Sg. 1. *labheyyaṃ*, Pl. 3. *labheyyuṃ*[3]. Then, further, on the analogy of the relation between *labhāmi* and *labhāma* of the Indicative, primary endings were introduced into the Sg. of the Opt., at first into the 1. Person *labheyyāmi*, and then also into the 2. and 3. Sg.,—the

[1] R. O. Franke, BB. 22. 215.

[2] Macdonell, Vedic Grammar § 412 a, with foot-note 16.

[3] The corresponding forms in Pkr. are evidently those of Opt. in *-ejjā̆ -ejjāmi* (Paiś. *-eyya*) etc. Differing from Jacobi, KZ. 36. 577, Pischel § 459 is inclined to derive them from the Optatives of the athematic conjugation (Skr. *duhyām*), on which hypothesis, indeed, the *ā* of the Pkr.-forms, as well as of Pāli *-eyyāsi*, would be at once explained.

long *ā* of the 1. Sg. being extended also to the latter[1].—Considered historically, the forms should be grouped according to types in the following way: The older type is predominant in the Gāthā-language: Sg. 1. *nisumbheyyaṃ* 'I would strike down' Th2. 302; *kareyyāmi* 'I would do' Jā. V. 308[18]. Also the new formations in *e* are found in the Gāthā-language: *passe* 'I would see,' *suṇe* 'I would hear' (Comm. *suṇeyyaṃ*), *saṃvase* 'I would live together (with)' Jā. IV. 240[29] (cf. 240[30], 241[8,9]); *ānaye* 'I could have brought' (Comm. *āneyyaṃ*) Jā. I. 308[6]; *jīve* '(if) I live' Sn. 440.—Sg 2. *yājeyya* '(if) you offer sacrifice' Jā. III. 515[24].—Sg. 3. *icche* 'he should wish for' Th1. 228, *hane* 'he should kill' Sn. 394, *vaje* 'he should go' and *pamuñceyya* 'he should free himself' Jā. II. 247[10]; *iccheyya* Sn. 148, *rakkheyya* 'he should protect' Sn. 702.—Pl. 1. *sikkhema* 'we would learn' Sn. 898, and with the ending *-mu*: *vasemu* 'we would stay' (Comm. *vaseyyāma*), *jānemu* 'we would know' Jā. III. 259[13,14], *viharemu* 'we would stay' Jā. II. 33[25].—Pl. 2. *bhuñjetha* 'you should enjoy' Mhvs. 25. 113.—Pl. 3. *saheyyuṃ* 'they should withstand' Sn. 20; *pajaheyyu* 'they should give up' Sn. 1058.—In the canonical and non-canonical prose on the other hand the older type of flexion (*labhe* etc.) has been given up. Apart from isolated forms of the athematic flexion which have been retained in the language (see below), the regular endings now are: Sg. 1. *-eyyaṃ* and *-eyyāmi*. 2. *-eyyāsi*, 3. *-eyya* and *-eyyāti*; Pl. 1. *-eyyāma*, 2. *-eyyātha*, 3. *-eyyuṃ*. This is apparent also from the fact that in the word-explanations these forms are substituted for the older ones. Thus in JāCo. II. 205[18] *bhajeyya* is given as explanation of *bhaje* and in 223[19] *udabbaheyya* is given as explanation of *udabbahe*. Cf. also above. Examples are: Sg. 1. *pabbajeyyaṃ* Vin. II. 180[15], *puccheyyāmi* D. I. 51[3]; Sg. 2. *kareyyāsi* Vin. II. 190[19], *āgaccheyyāsi* JāCo. II. 212[26]; Sg. 3. *bhāseyya* Vin. II. 189[19], *dadeyya* JāCo. II. 241[25], *jāneyyāti* Vin. II. 190[22]; Pl. 1. *āroceyyāma* Vin. II. 186[28], *vādeyyāma* JāCo. II. 254[25]; Pl. 2. *āneyyātha* 'may you bring' S. I. 221[7], *gaccheyyātha* JāCo. II. 249[20]; Pl. 3. *khādeyyuṃ* Vin. II. 197[11], *vissajjeyyuṃ* JāCo. II. 241[24].

§ 129. Medium. A form of the 2. Sg. is to be found in *labhetho* Sn. 833. The suffix corresponds to Skr. *-thās*. Not infrequently the suffix is *-etha* in 3. Sg., taken also by those verbs which are otherwise inflected in the Active. Examples of this *-etha* are: *rakkhetha* Dh. 36; *labhetha* Sn. 45; *sevetha* Sn. 72, Vin. II. 203[18] (verse); *jāyetha* Dh.

[1] The length of the vowel *ā* was then transferred also to the 2. Pl.

58; *nametha* Sn. 806; *saṅketha* Jā. II. 53[22]; *atmaññetha* Sn. 148; *saddahetha* Jā. III. 192[26]; *jhāyetha* Sn. 709; *kubbetha*[1] Sn. 702. 719, 917 etc.; *āsetha* in *sukhaṃ manussā āsetha* 'men should live happily' Jā. V. 222[16] (Comm.=*āseyyuṃ*) has been used in the plural sense. Also in the post-canonical prose: *jahetha* 'he should forsake' JāCo. II. 206[30]. The aspirate in the ending as against Skr. *-ta* is remarkable. It is found also in the 3. Sg. Cond. and Aor.; cf. § 157, 159. II.—A form of the 1. Pl. is to be found in *sādhayemase* 'we would accomplish' Jā. II. 236[19], which is explained in the Comm. by *sādheyyāma*. There are also other forms in *-emase*: *vademase* 'we would speak' D.III. 197[22]; *mahemase* 'we would worship' (Comm. *mahāmase*) Vv. 47. 11; *samācaremase* 'we would wander' (Comm. *paṭipajjāmase*) Vv. 63. 7; also *viharemasi* '(if) we stay' (Comm. *vasāma*) Th2. 375. It is however not always possible to decide whether the forms in question are those of the 1. Pl. Imp. (§ 126) of the *e*- flexion or simple Optatives. Cf. also *saremhase* in § 122.

E. The Verbal Classes of Sanskrit in Pāli

1. Thematic Conjugation

§ 130. Examples of present-stems of Cl. I are: 1. from roots with a medial *a*: *patati* 'falls, flies', *pacati* 'cooks', *vasati* 'stays', *vadati* 'speaks' (all as in Skr.), *vajati* 'goes'=*vrajati*, *kamati* 'strides'=*kramate*, but *krāmati*[2], *bhamati* 'roams about'=*bhramati*; *khamati* 'forgives'=*kṣamate* etc.—2. From long-vowel roots: *khādati* 'eats', *jīvati* 'lives', *nindati* 'slanders' (all as in Skr.), *vandati* 'worships' =*vandate*, *sandati* 'flows'=*syandate*; *dhovati* 'washes' (cf. § 34) Vin. I. 28[27], Sn. p. 101=AMāg. *dhovatī*, as against Skr. *dhāvati* etc.—3. From roots with a final *u* (on roots in *ī* cf. § 131): *savati* 'flows' =*sravati* etc.—4. From roots with a final *r*: *sarati* 'goes', *carati* 'goes, does, etc.' (both as in Skr.), *sarati* 'remembers' (*sumarati* Dh. 324, comp. *anussarati* D. I. 13[15])=*smarati* etc.—5. From roots with medial *i*, *u*, *ṛ*: *lehati* 'licks' JāCo. II. 44[21] as against Skr. *leḍhi* (Cl. II), *jotati* 'lightens' JāCo. I. 53[4]=*dyotate*, *vassati* 'rains'=*varṣati*;

[1] Also in S. I. 17[3] (verse)=Jā. II. 112[21] we have to take *kubbetha* (against Andersen, PGl, under the word *karoti*, who considers it to be a 2. Pl) as 3. Sg. Med. in the sense 'one should do', as also *samāsetha* 'one should be with' in the same verse.

[2] Also in Pkr. (Pischel, § 481) there is no protraction of the radical vowel.

vattati 'becomes, originates' =*vartate*; *ghaṃsati* 'rubs' (cf. § 6. 3) =*gharṣati*; *haṃsati* 'stands on end (as hair of the body)' Vin. III. 8[33] = *harṣati*; *kaḍḍhati* 'draws' = **kardhati*, side-form of *karṣati*, etc.—6. The secondary verval stems too take after the paradigm *labhati* in the present-flexion. On Passives, Causatives and Denominatives in *ya*, *aya* see particularly § 136. 4, 138, 139. For Desideratives (§ 184), Intensives (§ 185) and Denominatives in *a* (§ 188. 1.) cf. Pres. Sg. 1. *jigucchāmi* Vin. III. 8[4], 3. *dandhati* Jā. III. 141[2]; Pl. 3. *sussūsanti* A. IV. 393[13], Med. *dicchare* S. I. 18[27], *siṃsare* Vv. 64. 7. Imp Sg. 2. *tikiccha* S. I. 238[34] and *tikicchāhi* Vin. I. 71[36], Med. *sikkhassu* Th2. 4; Pl. 2. *vīmaṃsatha* JāCo. VI 367[20]. Opt. Sg. 1. *vīmaṃseyyaṃ* M. I. 125[16], 3. *jigucckeyya* Th2. 471 etc.

§ 131. The following details should be noted regarding Class I: 1. The roots in *i*, *ī* show contracted forms[1] besides those corresponding to Skr. forms. Such contracted forms are: *jemi* 'I conquer', *nemi* 'I lead', *jesi*, *nesi* etc. In the oldest period of the language both types are found side by side. Cf. *ānenti* Jā. VI. 507[4], *vinayanti* Thl. 3. The contracted forms get the upper hand later: *ānemi* JāCo. VI. 334[10], *ānema* JāCo. VI. 334[12]. The Imp. Sg. 2. is *nehi* JāCo. II. 160[2], beside *vinaya* Sn. 1025, *vinayassu* Sn. 559; Pl. 2. *ānetha* Mhvs. 5. 253. In Opt. we have *jeyyaṃ* and *neyyaṃ* (instead of *jayeyyaṃ*, *nayeyyaṃ*) etc. Cf. Sg. 1. *apaneyyaṃ* JāCo. III. 26[6]; Sg. 3. *vijeyya* Sn. 1002, *vineyya* M. I. 56[5], beside the older form *naye* Dh. 256 = *nayet* and *nissayeyya* Sn. 798 from root *śri* with *ni*. Like *jeti* also *ḍeti* 'flies' = *ḍayati* D. I. 71[7], M. I. 268[34], III. 34[26]. The root *ci* 'to collect' too may take this contracted form although it otherwise belongs to Cl. IX: Opt. Sg. 1. *abhisaṃceyyaṃ* 'I would heap up' (Comm. *-cineyyaṃ*) Vv. 47.6; Sg. 3. *niccheyya* (*ci* with *nis*) Sn. 785, 801. Also in DhCo. III. 381[14] we should probably read *viniccheyya*. From the root *hi* 'to send' we have the pres. *pāheti* (p. 79, foot-note 3) beside *pāhiṇati* (§ 147. 2). On the other hand the root *ji* (corresponding to Ved. *jināti*) may form the pres.-stem also according to Cl. IX[2]: Ind. Sg. 2. *jināsi* D. II. 348[23], Sg. 3. *jināti* Sn. 439; Imp. Sg. 2. *jināhi* Thl. 415, *abhivijina* M. II. 71[32]; Opt. Sg. 3. *jine* Dh. 103; Pl. 3. *jineyyuṃ* S. I. 221[5].—2. Similarly there is found an uncontracted and another contracted form of the root *bhū* 'to be'

[1] In Pkr. the form *jedu* = Pāli *jetu* as against *jaadu* = Pāli *jayatu* is not well attested; Pischel, § 473. With roots in *i* on the other hand, contraction is the usual rule (Māh. *ṇei* = Pāli *neti*); Pischel, § 474.

[2] Similarly AMāg. *jiṇāmi* etc. Pischel, § 473.

in the Indic. Pres. and in Imp.[1] The contracted forms are (cf. § 37):

	Sg.	Pl.
Ind.	1. *homi*	*homa*
	2. *hosi* Vv. 84 20, M. III. 140[2]	*hotha* JāCo. I. 307[2]
	3. *hoti* pass.	*honti* pass.
Imp.	2. *hohi* Sn. 31, M. III. 134[14], JāCo.I.32[30]; *hehi* Bu.2.10.	*hotha* Dh. 243, D. II. 141[20], JāCo. II. 302[6]
	3. *hotu* Sn. 224, JāCo. III. 150[25]	*hontu* Sn. 145, JāCo. II. 4[13]

Beside these there are the archaic forms *bhavāmi* etc., Imp. Sg. 2. *bhava* Th2 8, Sn. 701 and *bhavāhi* Sn. 510; Pl. 1. Med. *bhavāmase* Th1. 1128, Sn. 32; 2. *bhavatha* JāCo. II. 218[6] and *bhavātha* Sn. 692, Dh. 144[b] (cf. § 123); 3. *bhavantu* Sn. 145. Moreover Opt. Sg. 1. *bhaveyyaṃ* JāCo. VI. 364[16]; 2. *bhaveyyāsi* Ud. 91[33], PvCo. 11[23]; 3. *bhave* Sn. 716 and *bhaveyya* JāCo. II. 159[22]; Pl. 2. *bhavetha* Sn. 1073; 3. *bhaveyyuṃ* Sn. 906. A dialectical side-form is to be found in Sg. 3. *hupeyya* (§ 39. 6) which is clearly = Paiś. *huveyya*[2]. As for compounds, we have Ind. Sg. 1. *anubhomi* Vv. 15. 10; 2. *anubhosi* Vv. 40. 3; 3. *vibhoti* Sn. 873, *sambhoti* Sn. 743 (cf. D. II. 232[19-21]), *anubhoti* JāCo. II. 202[11], 252[1] and *sambhavati* Milp. 210[4], *anubhavati* JāCo. II. 202[14]; Pl. 1. *abhisambhoma* 'we attain' Jā III. 140[24]; 3. *anubhonti* Th2. 217. Sometimes certain compounds of *bhū* form the present-stem after Cl. IX[3]: *sambhuṇāti* 'attains' Vin. I. 256[8], *abhisambhuṇāti* VinCo. Rangoon ed. I. 2[2] etc. Cf. also § 190, 191.

§ 132. Of reduplicating roots of Cl. I., *pivati* 'drinks' (cf. *pivāmi* M. I. 77[37], *pivasi* JāCo. II. 417[7]; *piva* JāCo. III. 110[22], *pivatha* JāCo. II. 128; *piveyya* D. I. 123[23]) and *pipati* (in Gen.-Dat. Pl. Part. Pres. *pipataṃ* Sn. 398) correspond to Skr. *pibati* (root *pā*); *sīdati* (cf. *nisīda* 'sit down!' Th1. 411, *nisīdatha* Th2. 13) is = *sīdati* (root *sad*). The root *ghrā* 'to smell' assumes in Pāli the form *ghāyati* D. II. 338[20] as against Skr. *jighrati*.—The present-stems of *sthā* 'to stand' are multifarious. We have 1. the stem *tiṭṭha-*[4] = Skr. *tiṣṭha-*. Thus

[1] For Pkr. cf. Pischel, § 475.

[2] The form *huveyya* presupposes a pres. *huvai* (Māh. *huvanti*). For Pāli *heyya* (Minayeff, PGr. p. 77) I cannot find attestation. The corresponding form in Pkr. would be *hojjā*.

[3] Kern, Revue Celtique 22. 337 ff. and Festschrift Thomsen 70 ff.

[4] In Pkr. the corresponding stem is *ciṭṭha-* in Māh., AMāg., JMāh. There are besides the stems *ṭhā-*, *ṭhāya-* and *ṭhe-*; see Pischel, § 483.

Ind. Sg. 1. *tiṭṭhāmi*, 2. *tiṭṭhasi*, 3. *tiṭṭhati*; Pl. 1. *tiṭṭhāma*, 2. *tiṭṭhatha*, 3. *tiṭṭhanti*. Imp. Sg. 2. *tiṭṭha* Mhvs. 7. 13. and *tiṭṭhāhi* Thl. 461, DhCo. III. 194[17], 3. *tiṭṭhatu* D. I. 94[4]. Opt. Sg. 2. *tiṭṭheyyāsi* M. III. 129[7], 3. *tiṭṭhe* Sn. 918 and *tiṭṭheyya* Sn. 929, Milp. 28[10] etc. Also in compounds, as Ind. Sg. 1. *saṃtiṭṭhāmi* A. IV. 302[17], Opt. Sg. 3. *uttiṭṭhe* Dh. 168 etc.—2. Stem *ṭhā*- (according to Cl. II) formed on analogy of roots like *yā* (Pāli *yāti*): Ind. Sg. 3. *uṭṭhāti* Dpvs. 1. 53, *saṃṭhāti* Pu. 31[21], A. I. 197[34], *adhiṭṭhāti* A. II. 45[10]; Imp. Sg. 2. *uṭṭhāhi* Thl. 411, S. I. 233[32], 3. *uṭṭhātu* Jā. III. 297[15].—3. Stem *ṭhāya*- (Cl. IV.) formed after roots like *dhyā* (Pāli *jhāyati*): Ind. Sg. 1. *ṭhāyāmi* Thl. 888.—4. Stem *ṭhaha*-, formed after the stem *daha* of root *dhā*: Ind. Pl. 1. *upaṭṭhahāma* Jā. III. 120[26], 3. *vuṭṭhahanti* Mhvs. 5. 124; Imp. Sg. 2. *adhiṭṭhaha* Vin. I. 183[2], *vuṭṭhaha* Vin. I. 128[21] and *upaṭṭhahassu* S. I. 167[12] (verse); Pl. 2. *uṭṭhahatha* Sn. 331; Opt. Sg. 3. *samuṭṭhahe* Jā III. 156[12] and *saṃṭhaheyya* S. V. 329[9], *adhiṭṭhaheyya* Vin. I. 125[21]; Pl. 2. *uṭṭhaheyyātha* S. I. 217[18].—5. Stem *ṭhe*- in Ind. (and Imp.) Pl. 1. *adhiṭṭhema* Vin. IV. 23[24]; Imp. Sg. 2. *uṭṭhehi*, (on analogy of *dehi* from *dā*) S. I. 198[7] (verse), Ud. 52[19], Vin. I. 6[3], JāCo. I. 151[23]; Pl. 2. *uṭṭhetha* Jā VI. 444[1].

§ 133. 1. The form corresponding to Skr. Pres. *gacchati* from root *gam* is *gacchati* also in Pāli. Cf. Ind. Sg. 1. *gacchāmi* Milp. 26[32], 2. *gacchasi* etc.; Imp. Sg. 2. *gaccha* Jā. II. 160[12], *gacchāhi* S. I. 217[4] (verse) and *gacchassu* Thl. 82, Pl. 2. *gacchatha* Vin. II. 191[35], JāCo. I. 222[19]; Opt. Sg. 1. -*gaccheyyaṃ* D. II. 340[3]; 3. -*gacche* Thl. 11 and *gaccheyya* Sn. p. 14, Pl. 3. *gaccheyyuṃ* Milp. 47[24] etc. On the other hand the present-stem of *yam* 'to restrain' is however *yama*- (Ind. Pl. 1. Med *saṃyamāmase* S. I. 209[27]), not *yaccha*- as in Skr.—2. To Skr. *daśati* (from root *daṃś*-) corresponds *ḍasati* (§ 42. 3) in Pāli.—3. Of the roots with a medial *u*, *ruh* 'to mount' in compounds may both retain it unchanged[1] or lengthen it. Thus *ārūhati* 'climbs up' besides *ārohati*, *virūhati* 'sprouts, grows' JāCo. III. 12[21]; *orūhati* 'climbs down' besides *orohati*. It thus takes after Cl. VI, or is treated like the root *guh*, *gūhati* 'to conceal': *nigūhati* JāCo. I. 286[25], III. 392[14]; Imp. Sg. 2. Med. *upagūhassu* JāCo. III. 437[28].

§ 134. Present-stems after Cl. VI are: *kasati* 'ploughs' = *kṛṣati* (besides *kassati* after Cl. I = *karṣati*: cf. Imp. Pl. 2 *apakassatha* Sn. 281); *khipati* 'hurls' = *kṣipati*; *tudati* 'goads' Jā. I. 500[18] = *tudati*; *disati* 'directs' = *diśati*; *nudati* 'presses' Sn. 480, 928, Dh. 383 = *nudati*;

[1] Similarly in Pkr.; Pischel, § 482.

pucchati 'asks' = *pṛcchati*; *phusati* 'touches' = *spṛśati* (Ind. Sg. 1. *phusāmi* Dh. 272, Imp. Sg. 2. *phusāhi* Thl. 212, Opt. Pl. 3. *phuseyyu* Dh. 133; on the other hand Opt. Sg. 3. *phasse*[1] Sn. 967 after Cl. I, and Imp. Sg. 2. *phusehi* Th2. 6 according to *e*-flexion); *rudati* 'laments' = Ved. *rudati*; *vidati* 'knows' = *vidati*; *-visati* 'goes' = *viśati* etc. Also the verbs *kirati* 'scatters' (Ind. Sg. 3. Med. *ākirate* Dh. 313, Sg. 2. *ākirasi* Sn. 665; Opt. Pl. 3. *parikireyyuṃ* Thl. 1210) = Skr. *kirati* (root *kṝ* according to Indian grammarians) and *girati* (JāCo. I. 150[10]), *gilati* 'devours' (Imp. Sg. 2. *gila* Jā. I. 380[10] and *gilāhi* JāCo. I. 380[14], Opt. Sg. 3. *gileyya* JāCo. I. 508[17]) = *girati* (root *gṝ* according to Indian grammarians).—Also from the root *svap* 'to sleep' (Skr. *svapiti*) the pres.-stem *supati*[2] is formed similarly after Cl. VI: Ind. Sg. 3. *supati* Sn. 110, JāCo. III. 101[15]; Imp. Sg. 2. *supa* Vin. III. 110[15] and *supāhi* Th2. 1 etc. Cf. below § 136. 2.

§ 135. 1. Corresponding to Skr. *icchati* from root *iṣ* 'to wish', we have *icchati* also in Pāli: Ind. Sg. 1. *icchāmi* Thl. 186, D. I. 193[5], JāCo. I. 292[22], Med. *icche* Th2. 332, DhCo. III. 199[4] (verse); Opt. Sg. 1. *iccheyyāmi* Ud. 17[33], 2. *iccheyyāsi* Ud. 17[32], Pl. 2. *iccheyyātha* M. II. 79[8] etc.—2. Here I include also Pāli *acchati* 'sits, remains', which I consider to be an old inchoative formation related to root *ās* in the same way as *icchati* to *iṣ*[3]. Forms: Ind. Sg. 2. *acchasi* Vv. 11. 2, 12. 1, 3. *acchati* D. I. 101[23], Pl. 3. *acchanti* Vin. III. 195[9], Th2Co. 60[30] and Med. *acchare* Th2. 54, *samacchare* Jā. II. 67[19]; Imp. Sg. 2. *acchassu* Jā. VI. 516[16], 3. *acchatu* Jā. VI. 506[13] and Med. *acchataṃ* Jā. VI. 506[8].—3. Roots which show nasal stems in present in Skr.[4] do the same also in Pāli. Thus *muñcati* 'liberates', *limpati* 'besmears', *lumpati* 'robs', *vindati* 'finds' (*nibbindati* 'feels disgust'), *siñcati* 'pours out' (the same forms also in Skr.), *kantati* 'cuts' = *kṛntati*. Cf. *sumbhati*, *sumhati* 'strikes' (§ 60); Opt. Sg. 1. *nisumbheyyaṃ* Th2. 302.

§ 136. Present-stems after Cl. IV. 1. Example of root ending in vowel: *allīyati* 'attaches' JāCo. I. 433[4], 502[8], III. 65[22] (*o-līyati* Iv.

1 Like Pkr. *saṃphāsai* in Hem. 4. 182. Cf. Pischel, PkrGr. § 486.

2 In agreement with Pkr.; Pischel, § 497.

3 Pischel, PkrGr. § 480 derives the verb and the forms corresponding to it in Pkr. from *ṛcchati*. This is, however, impossible on account of the meaning. See *ibid*, the various attempts to explain the forms by Ascoli, Childers, E. Müller, Trenckner, Torp, E. Kuhn, Johansson. Cf. also Johansson, IF. 3. 205-212.

4 Unnasalised forms, which are normal in Pkr. Māh., JMāh., AMāg. (Pischel, § 485), are unknown in Pāli.

43[14], *nilīyati* JāCo. I. 292[18]) = *ā-līyate*, root *lī*. In the case of roots ending in consonant the *y* is assimilated to the preceding consonant. Thus *ijjhati* 'flourishes' = *ṛdhyati*; *kujjhati* 'is angry' = *krudhyati*; *kuppati*; 'is angry' = *kupyati*; *gijjhati* 'is eager' = *gṛdhyati*; *naccati* 'dances' = *nṛtyati*; *nassati* 'is destroyed' = *naśyati*; *saṃnayhati* 'guards up, prepares' = *saṃnahyati*; *āpajjati* 'gets involved in something' and many other compounds of the root *pad* = *āpadyate*; *bujjhati* 'wakes up, perceives' = *budhyate*; *maññati* 'thinks' = *manyate*; *yujjhati* fights' = *yudhyate*; *sussati* 'dries up' = *śuṣyati* etc. Also *siniyhati* (§ 49. 1) DhsCo. 192[31] = *snihyati*. There are found moreover, in agreement with Skr.: *majjati* 'rejoices' Jā. II. 97[15], A. IV. 294[6] (Opt. Sg. 3. *majjeyya* Jā. III. 87[25]) = *mādyati* (root *mad*); *sammati* 'rests' = *śāmyati* (root *śam*). Also *bhassati* 'falls down' Jā. VI. 530[11] = *bhraśyati* (root *bhraṃś*); *rajjati* 'takes delight in somthing' S. IV. 74[21] (verse), DhCo. III. 233[3, 4] = *rajyati* (root *rañj*); *vijjhati* 'bores through' = *vidhyati* (root *vyadh*). To the Skr. pres.-stem *krāmya-* from root *kram* (not attested) corresponds *kamma-* in Imp. Sg. 2. *paṭikamma* 'go back!' S. I. 226[28] (verse), and to Skr. *medya-* from root *mid* 'to feel oneself drawn towards something' corresponds the stem *mejja-* DhsCo. 192[31] (var. lec. *mijja-*).—2. Though not in Skr.[1], a pres.-stem *lagga-* after Cl. IV is derived in Pāli from the root *lag* 'to hang' (Imp. Sg. 3. *laggatu* DhCo. I. 131[12]). Similarly from root *ruc* 'to be liked' *ruccati* ' Vv. 63. 8, DhCo. I. 13[23] against *rocate*. In the same way Pāli has besides *supati* (§ 134) from root *svap* 'to sleep' also *suppati*, *soppati* (§ 10) S. I. 107[19] (verse).—3. To the Skr. Pres. *paśyati* from root *darś* corresponds Pāli *passati*. Cf. Ind. Sg. 1. *passāmi* Sn. 776, Vin. I. 126[3], 2. *passasi* etc. Imp. Sg. 2. *passa* Sn. 435, JāCo. II. 159[25], 3. *passatu* Sn. 909, Pl. 2. *passatha* Sn. 176, JāCo. III. 126[20], Med. *passavho* Sn. 998; Opt. Sg. 1. *passe* Jā. IV. 240[29] and *passeyyaṃ* JāCo. I. 356[29], 2. *passeyyāsi* M. III. 131[1], JāCo. I. 137[29]. 3. *passe* Dh. 76 and *passeyya* JāCo. III. 55[22] etc. Beside it a new pres.-stem *dakkha-* has arisen in the language. It is abstracted out of the future-stem (*drakṣyati*, § 152). Cf. Opt. Pl. 1. *dakkhema* or *-mu* DhCo. III. 217[19], 218[7] (verse).—4. The Passives (§ 175 f.) and the *ya*-Denominatives (§ 188. 2, 3) have formally coincided with the presents of Cl. IV. Cf. Ind. Sg. 1. *ñāyāmi* 'I am mentioned' Milp. 25[8], *vediyāmi* 'I feel' Vin. III. 37[35], *namassāmi* 'I worship' Sn. 1058, *aṭṭiyāmi* 'I suffer' D. I. 213[22]; 2. *vediyasi* M. II. 70[14], 3. *sūyati suyyati*

[1] As also in Pkr.; Pischel, § 463.

'is heard' Jā. IV. 141[20], JāCo. I. 72[1], *khīyati* 'weakens' Thl. 145; Pl. 1. *jiyyāma* 'we lose' Jā. II. 75[22], *posiyāmase* 'we are nourished' Jā. III. 289[7]; 3. *sūyanti* M. I. 30[19], *sūyare* Jā. VI. 528[30], *vuccanti* 'are mentioned' D. I. 245[16]. Imp. Sg. 2. *samādiya* 'take up!' Bu. II. 118, *samādiyāhi* Th2. 249; Med. *samādiyassu* Vv. 83. 16, *muccassu* 'be free!' Th2. 2; 3. *bhijjatu* 'should be destroyed' Thl. 312; Pl. 2. *namassatha* Mhvs. 1. 69. Opt. Sg. 1. *vediyeyyaṃ* M. II. 70[13]; 3. *upādiye* 'he should cling' Sn. 400, *mucceyya* D. I. 72[8], *namasseyya* Dh. 392, *hāyetha* 'may decrease!' D. I. 118[3], *nīyetha*, *niyyetha* 'may be guided!' Sn. 327, 931; Pl. 3. *palujjeyyuṃ* 'may they be destroyed' M. I. 488[29], *hāyeyyuṃ* D. I. 118[3].

§ 137. The root *jar* (*jṝ*) 'to grow old', Skr. *jīryati*, gives in Pāli (besides *jīriyati* M. I. 188[7] with Svarabhakti) the forms *jīrati* Jā. III. 38[8] (Ind. Pl. 3. *jīranti* Dh. 151, Imp. Sg. 3. *jīratu* Mhvs. 22, 76) and *jīyati* (Ind. Pl. 3. *jīyanti* M. III. 168[9], Med. *jīyare* Jā. VI. 528[5], Opt. Sg. 3. Med. *jīyetha* D. II. 63[27]) and *jīyyati* M. III. 246[20] (*parijīyyati* Thl. 1215). Cf. § 52. 5. From the root *śar* (*śṝ*) 'to wither', Skr. *śīryati*, *-te*, we have Ind. Sg. 2. *seyyasi* (instead of **siyyasi*, § 10) Jā. I. 174[9], in Comm. = *visiṇṇaphalo hoti*. Similarly from root *mar* 'to die', Skr. *mriyate*, we have in Pāli *mīyati* (Ind. Pl. 3. *mīyanti* Dh. 21, M. III. 168[9], Opt. Sg. 3. Med. *mīyetha* D. II. 63[27]) and *miyyati*[1] Sn. 804 (Ind. Pl. 3. Med. *miyyare* Sn. 575, Opt. Sg. 1. *miyye* in *miyyāhaṃ* Jā. VI. 498[20]). Moreover *marati* (as in vedic) in Ind. Pl. 3. *maranti* Mhvs. spurious verse after 5. 27, Opt. Sg. 1. *mareyyaṃ* JāCo. VI. 498[30], 2. *mareyyāsi* JāCo. III. 276[22].

§ 138. To Skr. *jāyate* from root *jan* 'to be born' there corresponds in Pāli *jāyati*; to Skr. *ā-hvayati* from root *hvā* 'to call' the Pāli forms *avhayati* and *avheti* (§ 49. 1.): Ind. Pl. 1. *avhayāma* D. I. 244[25], 3. *avhayanti* Jā. VI. 529[1]; Opt. Sg. 3. *avheyya* D. I. 244[16]. Various roots in *ā* form their present-stems in the same way as *jāyati*, partly in agreement with Skr. (the roots in *ai* of the Indian grammarians), and partly deviating from it[2]. Thus *vāyati* 'blows' besides *vāti*, Skr. *vāti* (Ind. Pl. 3. *vāyanti* Jā. VI. 530[12], Vin. I. 48[35], D. II. 107[25]; also *nibbāyati* 'is extinguished' JāCo. I. 61[3], Opt. Sg. 3. *nibbāyeyya* M. I. 487[23] besides *parinibbanti* Dh. 126, *parinibbātu* D. II. 105[5]). Similarly

[1] AMāg. *Mijjai*, *mijjanti*, might be the corresponding forms in Pkr.; Pischel, § 477.

[2] On *ghāyati* and *ṭhāyati* see § 132. The deviating forms get the upper hand in Pkr. according to Pischel, § 487.

yāyati 'goes' besides *yāti*, Skr. *yāti* (Ind. Pl. 3. *yāyanti* Vin. I. 191[18], Opt. Sg. 3. *yāyeyya* Vin. 191[22]); *gāyati* 'sings' = *gāyati*; *milāyati* 'withers' S. I. 126[2,3] = *mlāyati*; *jhāyati* 'meditates' = *dhyāyati*; *jhāyati* 'burns' (§56.2.) = *kṣāyati* (*vijjhāyati* 'is extinguished' Vin. I. 31[29]); *nahāyati* 'bathes' = *snāyati* besides *snāti*; *khāyati* 'becomes clear' (Ind. Pl. 3. *pakkhāyanti* D. II. 99[23] besides *pakkhanti* Th1. 1034) = *khyāyate*; *tāyati* 'protects' DCo. 18[1] (Imp. Sg. 2. Med. *tāyassu* DhCo. 1. 218[4] (verse)) = *trāyate* besides *trāti*; *antaradhāyati* 'disappears' D. II. 109[19] A. IV. 30.[27] = *antardhāyate*. In the same way is formed also *bhāyati* 'fears'[1]; Ind. Sg. 1. *bhāyāmi* Th1. 21, Sn. p. 47, 2. *bhāyasi* Th2. 248, Sn. p. 47; Pl. 1. *bhāyāma* JāCo. II. 21[22], 3. *bhāyanti* Dh. 129; Imp. Pl. 2. *bhāyatha* Ud. 51[9], JāCo. III. 4[4]; Opt. Sg. 3. *bhāye* Sn. 964 and *bhāyeyya* Milp. 208[26], Pl. 3. *bhāyeyyuṃ* Milp. 208[20]. *Palāyati* 'flees' = *palāyate* is inflected in the same way: Imp. Sg. 2. *palāyassu* DhCo. III. 334[9], Pl. 2. *palāyatha* Mhvs. 7. 66, 3. *palāyantu* JāCo. II. 90[17]. Denominatives of the type *cirāyati*, *dhūpāyati* (also *sajjhāyati*) along with forms like *gahāyati*, *phusāyati*, *saṃkasāyati* are to be grouped herewith so far as the form is concerned. Cf. § 186.

§ 139. The formans *aya* is contracted into *e* also in the present-stems of Cl. X.—1. To this group belong verbs like *cinteti* 'thinks' Sn. 717, JāCo. I. 221[30] = *cintayati*, *pūjeti* 'worships' = *pūjayati*, particularly however denominatives like *katheti* 'relates' = *kathayati*, *gaṇeti* 'counts' = *gaṇayati*, *pattheti* 'begs' = *prārthayati* and the whole category of causatives. Similarly also *bhemi* 'I fear' S. I. 111[2] (verse) besides *bhāyāmi* and *paleti* 'flees' Dh. 49, Sn. 1074 besides *palāyati* (see p. 74, f.-n. 4 and § 138). In the Gāthā-language both uncontracted and contracted forms are found side by side. In Sn., for instance, they almost hold the balance if the prose portions are left out of consideration. But already in the canonical prose contraction is the rule. But occasionally even later there are found forms like *tappayati* Milp. 227[9,12], *pihayāmi*, *patthayāmi* Th2Co. 239[30], *mantayatha* JāCo. II. 107[22]. The flexion will be clear from the following examples:

Older type:

Ind. Sg. 1. *sāvayāmi* Sn. 385; *āmantayāmi* D. II. 156[1]; Med. *patthaye* Th2. 341 (*patthe* Th2. 32).
2. *patthayasi* Sn. 18; *maggayasi* Th2. 384.
3. *patthayati* Sn. 114; Med. *kārayate* Jā. VI. 360[10].
Pl. 1. *ṭhapayāma* D. I. 120[33], Med. *ujjhāpayāmase* S. I. 209[14] (verse).

[1] Cf. in Pkr. Māg., S. *bhāāmi* etc., in Pischel, § 501.

2. *bhamayatha* Sn. 680.
3. *dassayanti* Dh. 83; *vādayanti* Sn. 682; *ramayanti* Thl. 13.

Imp. Sg. 2. *sāvaya* Jā. III. 437[13]; *nīyādayāhi* Th2. 323; Med. *parivajjayassu* Vv. 53. 15.
Pl. 2. Med. *kappayavho* Sn. 283. Pl. 3. *pālayantu* Jā. II. 34[13].

Opt. Sg. 1. *papothayeyyaṃ* Jā. III. 175[22].
3. *pūjaye* Dh. 106 f.; *kāraye* Milp. 211[9] (verse); *phassaye* Sn. 54; *kathayeyya* Sn. 930.
Pl. 1. Med. *sādhayemase* Jā. II. 236[19].

Later Type:

Ind. Sg. 1. *kathemi* PvCo. 11[12], *vattemi* Sn. 554.
2. *kathesi* JāCo. I. 291[29].
3. *katheti* JāCo. I. 292[12]; *dasseti* JāCo. III. 82[7] *vaḍḍheti* Sn. 275.
Pl. 1. *pavedema* M. II. 200[9]; *nisāmema* Vin. I. 103[22].
2. *sobhetha* DhCo. I. 56[11].
3. *gamenti* Sn. 390; *paññāpenti* D. I. 13[7]; *pūjenti* D. I. 91[4]; *kathenti* JāCo. II. 133[26].

Imp. Sg. 2. *kārehi* Jā. III. 394[7], *kathehi* JāCo. III. 279[22], *palehi* Sn. 831.
3. *desetu* M. II. 207[9]; *dhāretu* Sn. p. 25.
Pl. 2. *bhāvetha* Thl. 980, *paletha* Vv. 84. 36.
3. *āgamentu* Sn. p. 103; *pālentu* JāCo. II. 34[25].

Opt. Sg. 1. *manteyyaṃ* Sn. p. 103.
2. *āroceyyāsi* M. II. 210[17]; *dhāreyyāsi* Milp. 47[25].
3. *jāleyya* M. II. 203[20]; *dasseyya* Milp. 47[4].
Pl. 1. *saṃvejeyyāma* S. I. 146[35]; *sādheyyāma* JāCo. II. 236[25].
2. *katheyyātha* Ud. 11[18]; *pāteyyātha* DhCo. III. 201[8].
3. *vāceyyuṃ* D. I. 97[14]; *tāseyyuṃ* Milp. 209[6].

2. The *e*-flexion has however extended its sphere on all sides, and verbs which originally did not belong to Cl. X were transferred to it. Thus from root *vad* 'to speak' we have not only *vadati* but also *vadeti* (the causative is *vādeti*) Sn. 825, D. I. 36[30], Vin. II. 1[11], JāCo. I. 294[21]; *bhajehi* 'worship!' occurs in Jā. III. 148[11, 13] for the usual *bhaja*, *bhajāhi* (Comm. *bhajeyyāsi*); to Skr. *upahadati* corresponds Pāli *ūhadeti* 'defiles with dung'; *maññesi* Pret. Sg. 2. 'you thought' pre-

supposes *maññeti* besides *maññati*; *gaheti*, without any Causative sense (the Causative is *gāheti*), is the oft-used side-form of *gaṇhāti* 'seizes'. Instead of the usual *akkhāhi* (§ 140.2) there also occurs *akkhehi* in Jā. VI. 318[20] etc.

2. Athematic Conjugation.

§ 140. 1. An isolated form of athem. flexion after Cl. II. is to be found in *hanti*[1] 'strikes' Sn. 118, 125, Dh. 72, 355, S. I. 154[3] (verse); also Milp. 214[7], besides thematic *hanati* Jā. I. 432[13], Milp. 220[4], 2. Pl. *hanatha* JāCo. I. 263[3], Opt. Sg. 3. *haneyya* Sn. 705 etc. Similarly *veti* 'knows' Thl. 497=*vetti*. In other cases however the thematic flexion has taken the place of athematic in Pāli: *āsati* 'sits' (Dh. 61; Opt. Pl. 1 -*āseyyāma* JāCo. I. 509[1]) as against Skr. *āste* (Ved. also *āsate*), *ghasati* 'eats', *lehati* 'licks', *rodati* 'cries', *ravati* 'roars', *abhi-tthavati* 'praises' S. I. 190[6] against *stauti* (but Ved. also *stávate*) etc.—2. More numerous are the athematic forms of roots in *ā*, which are otherwise transferred to the flexion of Cl. IV. Individual examples have been given in § 138. Cf. Ind. Sg. 2. *yāsi* 'you go' JāCo. I. 291[15]. 3. *yāti* Sn. 720, Dh. 29, Pl. 1. *āyāma* D. II. 81[14], 3. *āyanti* Th2. 337; Imp. Sg. 2. *yāhi* Mhvs. 13. 15, Pl. 2. *yātha* Mhvs. 14. 29 from root *yā*. Similarly Ind. Sg. 2. *vāsi* Jā. II. 11[21], Pl. 3. *pavanti* Th2. 371 from root *vā* 'to blow' Ind. Sg. 1. *akkhāmi* Sn. 172, Imp. Sg. 2. *akkhāhi* Thl. 168 from root *khyā* with prefix *ā*- 'to proclaim'; Imp. Sg. 2. *sināhi* 'bathe!' M. I. 39[21] (verse), or *nahāhi* JāCo. VI. 32[10] (besides *nhāya* Vin. III. 110[15]); Ind. Pl. 3. *ābhanti* 'they light up' Vv. 6. 10, *paṭibhanti* 'they become clear' JāCo. II. 100[19] from root *bhā* etc.—3. The root *i* 'to go', after generalising the strong stem, has given rise to the forms *emi*, *esi*, *eti*; *ema*, *etha*, *enti*[2], both as simplex and also in numerous compounds. On the basis of such historical forms as *eti* (*sameti* etc.) the pres.-flexion has been completely adapted to that of verbs like *nī*, *ji* (§ 131), or to that of *e*-stems (according to § 139) as the case may be. Examples are numerous: Ind. Sg. 1. *paccemi* D. I. 186[1], 2. *paccesi* D. I. 185[33], 3. *pacceti* Dh. 125, Pl. 1. *paccema* Milp. 313[6], 3. *accenti* Thl. 231; Imp. Sg. 2. *ehi* Thl. 175, JāCo. II. 159[15], 3. *etu* D. I. 179[16], Pl. 2. *etha* D. II. 98[26], *apetha* DhCo. III. 201[13]; Opt.

[1] The form Imp. Sg. 3. *samūhantu* D. II. 154[17] is not quite certain. Buddhaghosa (DCo. ed. Rangoon, II. 165[30]) reads -*hanatu*. So also in the quotation in Milp. 142[18].

[2] The Pl. 3. is *enti* also in Pkr. Māh., AMāg.; Pischel, § 493. It is doubtful if *inti* Jinālaṃkāra is right.

Sg. 2. *upeyyāsi* Jā. IV. 241[24], 3. *pacceyya*[1] Nett. 93[14], *upeyya* M. III. 178[33]. The analogy of *e*-stems then also gave rise to forms like Ind. Pl. 3. *accayanti* Thl. 145, S. I. 109[1] (verse), Opt. Sg. 3. *accayeyya* Sn. 781.—4. The flexion of the root *śī* should be judged precisely in this light. Forms such as Ind. Sg. 2. *sesi* Jā. III. 34[12], S. I. 110[23] (verse) and Sg. 3. *seti* Dh. 79, Jā. I. 141[25] may be direct continuations of Skr. *śeṣe*, *śete*. After them was formed (as *nenti* to *neti*) the 3. Pl. *senti* Sn. 668 (against Skr. *śerate*). And just as there are forms like *nayāmi* etc. besides *nemi*, *kathayāmi* etc. besides *kathemi*, so we have also forms like *sayāmi* Thl. 888, S. I. 110[26] (verse), *sayati* Vin. I. 57[30], Jā. II. 53[16] (cf. Ved. *śayate*); Imp. Sg. 2. *saya* JāCo. III. 23[21]; Opt. Sg. 3. *saye* Iv. 120[10] (verse), Med. *sayetha* Thl. 501.

§ 141. 1. The present-flexion of *as* 'to be' is as follows:—

		Sg.	Pl.
Ind.	1.	*asmi* / *amhi*	*asmă* (*asmase* Sn. 595), / *amhă* [*amhăse* Jā. III. 309[27], D. II. 275[11] (verse)]
	2.	*asi*	*attha*
	3.	*atthi*	*santi* (*sante* Sn. 868)
Imp.	3.	*atthu*	
Opt.	1.	*siyaṃ*, *assaṃ*	*assāma* M. III. 250[15]
	2.	*assa*	*assatha* D I. 3[5]
	3.	*siyā*, *assa*	*siyuṃ*, *assu*.

The Medial forms in Ind., occurring only in the Gāthā-language, are innovations on the analogy of *labhāma* : *labhāmase*, *labhanti* : *labhante*. In Opt. the forms *siyaṃ*, *siyā*, *siyuṃ* correspond to Skr. *syām*, *syāt*, *syus*; the form *siyaṃsu* M. II. 239[1] in Pl. 3. is remarkable. It is a new formation in the place of *siyuṃ*, just as in Aor. there is *addasaṃsu* besides *addasuṃ*. The forms *assaṃ* etc. are derived from the strong stem like Greek *eiēn*. They occur already in the Gāthā-language. In the post-canonical prose the forms of *atthi* are used mostly in periphrastic perfect. But they were more and more replaced by forms of *bhavati-hoti*. Quite frequently *atthi* is used, also with a plural subject, as a petrified form in the indefinite sense of 'there is'. Cf., e.g., DhCo. I. 41[25], JāCo. III. 126[19] etc.—2.

[1] Also of the simplex the Opt. Sg. 3. is *eyya*. Cf. M. III. 159[26], where the proper division of words would be *matam-eyya* 'he goes unto death, dies'.

In the pres.-forms of the root *brū* the stem of the 1. Pl. Skr. *brūmas* was generalised[1]. We have Sg. 1. *brūmi* Sn. 458, Dh. 385, Th1. 214, *pabrūmi* Sn. 870, 2. *brūsi* Sn. 457, Jā. II 48[23], Th2. 53, S. I. 8[10,11], 3. *brūti* Sn. 122, *pabrūti* Sn. 131, Pl. 3. *pabrūnti* Sn. 649; Imp. Sg. 2. *brūhi* Sn. 76, *pabrūhi* Sn. 599. Quite remarkable is the Imp. Sg. 3. *brūmetu* D. I. 95[19]; but the form is not above all doubts. This verb may be regarded as an archaism when it occurs still in the post-canonical prose (e.g., Milp. 327[3]). That is why *brūmi* is explained as *kathemi* in PvCo. 11[12].

§ 142. Present-stems after Cl. III. 1. A stem *jaha-* (besides *jahā-*) has been abstracted out of *jahāmi* from root *hā-* 'to leave', and it is the basis of the forms of the present: Ind. Pl. 3. *jahanti* Dh. 91; Imp. Sg. 2. *jaha* Th1. 83 (also *jahi* Th2. 508) and Med. *jahassu* Sn. 1121, Th1. 1219, Pl. 2. *pajahatha* S. IV. 81[10]; Opt. Sg. 1. *jaheyyaṃ* JāCo. I. 153[1], 2. *pajaheyyāsi* S. IV. 350[23]; 3. Med. *jahetha* (§ 129) etc. The stem *jahā-* in Sg. 3. *jahāti* Sn. 1. ff., 506, 589, *pajahāti* Sn. 789.—2. The stem *daha-* stands in the same relation to the root *dhā* 'to set' (cf. particularly also *saddahati* 'believes'= *śraddadhāti*). The forms *dahāsi*, *dahāti* (§ 123) are older. From the stem *daha-* we have Ind. Sg. 1. *samādahāmi* M. I. 116[15], 2. *saddahasi* S. IV. 298[12], JāCo. I. 426[10], 3. *saṃdahati* Milp. 40[29], Pl. 1. *saddahāma* D. II. 328[1], 2. *saddahatha* JāCo. I. 222[6], 3. *dahanti* Sn. 882, D.I. 92[15]; Imp. Sg.2. *saddaha* JāCo. IV. 52[18], Med. *odahassu* Sn. 461, Pl. 2. *pidahatha* Thūpavs. 76[33]; Opt. Sg. 2. *nidaheyyāsi* Jā. VI. 494[17], 3. *vidahe* Sn. 927 and *padaheyya* M. II. 174[11], Med. *saddahetha* Jā. III. 192[26], Pl. 1. *saddaheyyāma* Milp. 330[4], 3. *saddaheyyuṃ* S. II. 255[26] etc. The root *dhā*, however, also takes the *e*-flexion, particularly in the Gāthā-language[2]: Ind. Sg. 1. *samādhemi* Th2. 50, 114, Pl. 3. *odhenti* Th1. 1233=S. I. 190[30]; Imp. Sg. 2. *paṇidhehi* Th2. 197, S. IV. 302[25]; Opt. Sg. 3. *saddheyya* Jā. II. 446[14] (Comm.=*saddaheyya*) etc.—3. From root *hu* (*juhoti*) 'to pour into the fire' we have the stem *juha-*[3]: Ind. Sg. 1. *juhāmi* Th1. 343, 3. *juhati* S. I. 167[21], Sn. p. 79.—4. The pres.-stem of root *gar* (*jāgarti*, *jāgarati*) 'to wake up' is *jāgara-* or (with the elision of *a* according to

[1] The form *brūmi* may be found occasionally also in Skr. In Pkr, we have AMāg. Ind. Pl. 1. *būma*, Imp. Sg. 2. *būhi*. In AMāg. the Ind. Sg. 1. is *bemi*, Pl. 3. *benti*, Pischel, § 494.

[2] On the basis of the 2. Sg Imp. *dhehi*. Similarly in Pkr. Cf. Pischel, § 500.

[3] As var lec. we have *jūhati* Sn. p. 79, and its Part. Pres. Sg. Gen. *jūhato* Sn. 428. *Jūh-* may be derived also from *juvh-*=*juhv-* (Skr. *juhvati* 3. Pl).

§ 20 and the assimilation of *gr) jagga-*. From the first we have, e.g., Imp. Sg. 2. Med. *jāgarassu* Th1. 411, as well as the Participles *jāgarant* Dh. 39, Vin. III. 31[35] and *jāgaramāna* Dh. 226. From the second the Ind. Sg. 1. *paṭijaggāmi* JāCo. I. 438[30], 3. *jaggati* A. III. 156[9], Pl. 3. *jagganti* A. III. 156[7]; Opt. Sg. 3. *paṭijaggeyya* Dh. 157.

§ 143. The present forms of the root *dā* 'to give' have had a multifarious development. There are found (*a*) the stems *dadā-* and *dada-*: Ind. Sg. 1. *dadāmi* Sn. 421, Th2. 245, 2. *dadāsi* Mhvs. 10. 50, 3. *dadāti* D.I. 103[33], Sn. p. 86, Pl. 1. *dadāma* Th1. 475, JāCo. III. 47[19], Med. *dadamhase* Jā. III. 47[8], 3. *dadanti* Vv, 44. 25; Imp. Sg. 2. *dada* Jā. III. 412[6] and *dadāhi* Jā. III. 109[14], JāCo. III. 109[17], Pl. 1. Med. *dadāmase* Jā. III. 131[15], 2. *dadātha* Vv. 44. 19. Moreover Opt. Sg. 1. *dadeyyaṃ* Vin. I. 39[14], S. I. 97[7], JāCo. I. 254[18], 2. *dadeyyāsi* JāCo. III. 276[21], 3. *dade* Vv. 62. 5 and *dadeyya* Vin. I. 49[21], Milp. 28[11], Med. *dadetha* S. I. 32[4] (verse), Pl. 1. *dademu* Jā. VI. 317[16] and *dadeyyāma* M. II. 116[23], S. I. 58[13], 2. *dadeyyātha* JāCo. III. 171[16], IV. 230[18], 3. *dadeyyuṃ*.—(*b*) The stem *de-* abstracted out of 2. Sg. Imp. *dehi*: Ind. Sg 1. *demi* JāCo. I. 307[17], DhCo. I. 42[13], 2. *desi* D.I. 50[5], JāCo. I. 279[15], 3. *deti* Sn. 130, S. III. 245[9], JāCo. II. 154[5], Pl. 1. *dema* JāCo. III. 127[1], 2. *detha* JāCo. III 126[25], 3. *denti* Sn. 244, JāCo. II. 104[26]; Imp. Sg. 2. *dehi* Th2. 49, JāCo. I. 254[17], DhCo. I. 33[2], 3.*detu* JāCo. II. 104[8], Pl. 2. *detha* JāCo. II. 103[22], 3. *dentu* Mhvs. 5. 179. Also Opt. Sg. 1. *deyyaṃ* Mhvs. 7. 31. Already the Gāthā-language knows the flexion *demi* etc. in Ind. and Imp. Along with the Opt. *dadeyyaṃ* etc. this can be regarded as the regular flexion in the canonical and the post-canonical prose—(*c*) An old form which is met with in all the periods of the language is to be found in the Ind. Sg. 1. *dammi* Sn. p. 14, Vin. I. 39[17], JāCo. I. 127[26], II. 231[21], DhCo. I. 100[9]. It is derived from *dadmi* which is current in epic Sanskrit. Also Pl. 1. *damma* in Kacc. 3. 4. 1 (Senart, p. 452).—(*d*) The following Optative forms are also old: Sg. 1. *dajjaṃ* Vin. I. 148[25], 2. *dajjāsi* Jā. VI. 251[26], 3. *dajjā* Dh. 224, Th1. 468, D. II. 267[10] (verse), S. I. 57[32] (verse). They are derived from Skr. *dadyām* etc. and are a special feature of the Gāthā-language. The JāCo. I. 322[15] explains *dajjā* by *dadeyya*. A present-stem *dajja-* or *dajje-*[1] was abstracted out of these forms. Hence, e.g., Imp. Sg. 2. *dajjehi* Vin. III. 217[4] and the double-forms-*dajjeyya*, -*dajjeyyāma* Vin. III. 259[35,36], *dajjeyyātha* Vin.

[1] Cf. Childers, PD. under the word *dajjati*; E. Kuhn, Beitr. p. 105. The form *dajjāmi* Jā. VI. 437[18] is Sg. 1. Opt.

I. 232[7]. On the analogy of *dadāmi*: *dajjaṃ* there was formed also from the root *vad* 'to speak' a similar Opt.: Sg. 1. *vajjaṃ* Th2. 308, 2. *vajjāsi* Th2. 307, and *vajja*(?) Th2. 323, 3. *vajjā* Sn. 971, Jā. VI. 526[35], Pl. 3. *vajju*(*ṃ*) Sn. 859, Jā. V. 221[31]. These forms too are a peculiar feature of the Gāthā-language; in JāCo. VI. 527[4] *vajjā* is explained by *vadeyya*, as *vajjāsi* by *vadeyyāsi* in Th2Co. 228[6].

§ 144. The present-stems of Cl. VII have generalised the weak form, and their flexion is thematic (*a*-flexion) throughout[1]. These presents, therefore, have coincided with *muñcati* etc. discussed in § 135.3. Cf. *kantati* 'spins' (root *kart*, *kṛṇatti*); *chindati* 'cuts off' (root *chid*, *chinatti*); *bhañjati* 'breaks' (root *bhaj*, *bhanakti*); *bhindati* 'splits' (root *bhid*, *bhinatti*); *bhuñjati* 'enjoys' (root *bhuj*, *bhunakti*); *yuñjati* 'joins' (root *yuj*, *yunakti*); *riñcati* 'leaves' (root *ric*, *riṇakti*); *rundhati* (cf. § 60) 'surrounds' (root *rudh*, *ruṇaddhi*); *hiṃsati* 'injures' (root *hiṃs*, *hinasti*). I give here a combined paradigm: Ind. Sg. 1. *bhuñjāmi* Sn. p. 12; 2. *niyuñjasi* Th1. 1114, *hiṃsasi* M. I. 39[23] (verse); 3. *yuñjati* JāCo. I. 149[26], Med. *yuñjate* Dh. 382; Pl. 2. *yuñjatha* Th2. 346; 3. *anuyuñjati* Dh. 26, JāCo. II. 96[7], *riñcanti* Vin. I. 190[5].—Imp. Sg. 2. *chinda* JāCo II. 153[18], *chindāhi* JāCo. III. 184[17], Med. *yuñjassu* Th2. 5; 3. *bhunjatu* Sn. 479, S. I. 141[28] (verse), Pl. 2. *anuyuñjatha* D. II. 141[22].—Opt. Sg. 1. *paribhuñjeyyaṃ* Sn. p. 91; 3. *chinde* Dh. 370, *hiṃseyya* Sn. 368, *chindeyya* JāCo. III. 65[1]; Med. *bhuñjetha*, Dh. 70; Pl. 3. *sambhañjeyyuṃ* S. I. 123[26], *chindeyyuṃ* D. II. 322[2].

§ 145. In the present-stems of Cl. IX, the form with the suffix *nā* has been generalised. The analogy of *labhāmi*; *labhati* has then led to frequent transfers to the *a*-flexion. The forms with the suffix *nī* have disappeared. Examples: 1. Root *jñā* (*jānāti*) 'to know'. It derives (*a*) from the stem *jānā*-(here I give also those forms in which the stems *jānă*-would coincide): Ind. Sg. 1. *jānāmi* Sn. 908, JāCo. I. 266[29], Med. *jāne* Mhvs. 37. 220 (ed. Colombo 170), 2. *jānāsi* Sn. 504, JāCo. I. 223[15], 3. *jānāti* Sn. 276, S. I. 103[23], JāCo. III. 26[9], Pl. 1. *jānāma* JāCo, VI. 337[9], Med. *jānāmase* Vv. 84, 47, 2. *jānātha* Th2. 346, JāCo. VI. 337[9], 3. *jānanti* Sn. 441 etc.; Imp. Sg. 2. *jānāhi* Th2. 59, D.I.88[22], JāCo. III. 392[16], Med. *pajānassu* D.II. 243[20] (verse), 3. *jānātu* Iv. 28[9], 29[10], Mhvs. 13. 13, Pl. 2. *jānātha* JāCo. II. 250[24], 3. *jānantu*.

[1] As also in Pkr.; Pischel, § 506 f. The nasal has been dropped *metri causa* in the form Opt. Sg. 3. *paṭisaṃyuje* S. S. I. 221[27] (verse).

—(*b*) From the stem *jāna-*[1] we have Ind. Sg. 3. *avajānati* Sn. 132, 438 (? *metri causa*), Pl. 3. Med. *-jānare* Sn, 601; Imp. Sg, 2. *jāna* S. IV. 374[13], *vijāna* Sn. 1091 (*vijānahi* under stress of metre Jā. III. 32[7]) Pl. 2. *jānatha* DhCo. III. 438[14]. I mention in this connection also *vikkiṇatha* 'sell!' JāCo. I. 121[20] (as for the *i* as against Skr. *krīṇāti* see § 21). On *jināti* cf. § 131.—(*c*) The Opt. is regularly formed: Sg. 1. *jāneyya(ṃ)* M. I. 487[13], Sn. P. 21, 2. *jāneyyāsi* M. I. 487[12], DhCo. I. 125[7], 3. *jāneyya* Mhvs. 23. 31. Pl, 1. *jāneyyāma* Milp. 330[4] and *jānemu* S. I. 34[11] (verse), Sn. 76, Vv. 62. 2, 2. *jāneyyātha* M. II. 215[22], JāCo. II. 133[5], 3. *jāneyyuṃ* Jā. I. 168[6]. Another type is found besides in the oldest period of the language: Sg. 1. *vijaññaṃ* Sn. 482, 3. *jaññā* Dh. 157, Thl. 10, Sn. 116. In the Comm. on Jā. II. 42[12] *jaññā* is explained by *jāneyya*. This type is analogical, formed after the Opt. *dajjaṃ* from *dadāmi*. The form *jāniyāma* Sn. 873 is very probably historical and the same as Skr. *jānīyāma*.

§ 146. Similarly in the case of 2. root *grah* (*gṛhṇāti*) 'to seize' there are side by side the stems *gaṇhā-* and *gaṇha-*: (*a*) From *gaṇhā-* we have for instance Ind. Sg. 2. *gaṇhāsi* DhCo. III. 57[4], 3. *gaṇhāti* JāCo. III. 28[9]; Imp. Sg. 3. *gaṇhātu* DhCo. III. 200[9], *paṭigaṇhātu* Sn. 479, Vin. II. 192[15] (for metrical reasons *paṭiggahātu* Jā. I. 495[2]). (*b*) From *gaṇha-*: Ind. Sg. 3. *gaṇhati* JāCo. I. 303[23]; Imp. Sg. 2. *gaṇha* JāCo. II. 159[5] and beside it *gaṇhāhi* D. II. 102[6], JāCo. I. 279[24] and Med. *gaṇhassu* DhCo, III. 302[19], 3. *gaṇhatu* JāCo. I. 207[8], Pl. 2. *gaṇhatha* JāCo. I. 111[17], III. 126[25] or *gaṇhātha* M. I. 459[6]. The Opt. is *gaṇheyyaṃ* JāCo. I. 255[9] etc. On *gahāyati* see § 186. 5. Futures, Preterites, Infinitives and Gerunds are derived from the secondarily formed stem *gahe-* of the *e*-flexion (§ 139. 2). —3. Of the root *mā* (*māti, mimīte*) the present-stem is *minā-*. Cf. Opt. Pl. 1. *abhinimmineyyāma* S. I. 124[32].—4. The root *bandh* (*badhnāti*) 'to bind' has, as in Pkr. (Pischel, § 513) the present-stem *bandha-*, and is inflected, therefore, according to § 144. Cf. Imp. Sg. 2. *bandha* D. II. 350[4], Pl. 3. *bandhantu* JāCo. I. 153[7]; Opt. Pl. 3. *bandheyyuṃ* Vin. III. 45[17] etc.

§ 147. The present-stems of Cl. V are often transferred to Cl. IX The formation of fhe present-stem with the suffix *no* has in most

[1] Similarly there are found in Pkr. JMāh., AMāg. *jāṇasi, jāṇai, jāṇa* beside *jāṇāsi* etc.; Pischel, § 510. Also Māh. *vikkiṇai*, AMāg. *kiṇai*, Ś. Imp *kiṇadha*, Pischel § 511. In some Pkr. dialects also the root *bhaṇ* follows the analogy of stems of Cl. IX, e.g., Ś. *bhaṇāsi* (Pischel, § 514); this does not seem to have been the case in Pāli.

cases gone out of use altogether[1]. Thus we have 1. from root *ci* 'to collect', against Skr. *cinoti*, the present-stem *cinā̆-* in compound. Cf. Ind. Sg. 2. *pacināsi* Jā. III. 22[2], 3. *vicināti* Sn. 658, S. I. 149[21] (verse), Pl. 3. *vicinanti* Vin. I. 133[12]; Imp. Sg. 2. *vicina* JāCo. I. 453[29] and *vicināhi* JāCo. III. 91[6]; Pl. 2. *vicinātha* Smp. 328[19]. On the analogy of roots like *ji jeti* the root *ci* too easily went over to the *e* flexion. Cf. § 131.—2. Also the root *hi* 'to send' gets in compound the present-stem *hiṇā̆* as against Skr. *hinoti*. Thus Ind. Pl. 3. *pahiṇanti* D. II. 321[1], 323[27]; Imp. Sg. 3. *pahiṇatu* DhCo. III. 34[24]; Opt. Pl. 2. *pahiṇeyyātha* DhCo. III. 318[8].—3. From the root *dhū* 'to shake' we find, as against Skr. *dhū̆noti* (in Dhātup. also *dhunāti*), the stems *dhūnā-* or *dhunā̆*. Cf. Ind. Pl. 3. *dhunanti* Th2. 276, *o- saṃ-nid-dhunanti* D. II. 336[19,20]; Imp. Sg. 2. *niddhunāhi* Th1. 416, Pl. 1. *dhunāma* Th1. 1147, 2. *dhunātha* Sn. 682, Th1. 256, *o- saṃ- nid-dhunātha* D. II. 336[17,18]. Also Ind. Sg. 3. *vidhūnati* JāCo. II. 90[1]; Imp. Pl. 2. *vidhūnatha* JāCo. I. 335[9].—4. The two stems *suṇo-* and *suṇā̆-* are derived from the root *śru* (*śṛṇoti*) 'to hear'. Both are found side by side already in the Gāthā-language, and isolated forms of *suṇo-* occur also later. But the stem *suṇā̆-* is by far the more predominant one. In Opt. it is naturally the only stem in use: (*a*) Stem *suṇo-* in Ind. Sg. 1. *suṇomi* Jā. IV. 443[22], Pl. 1. *suṇoma* Sn. 350, 1110, Vv. 84. 12; Imp. Sg. 2. *suṇohi* Sn. 273, D. I. 62[20], Milp. 315[1], Pl. 2. *suṇotha* Sn. 997, Vv. 84. 1, Milp. 1[12] (verse). (*b*) Stem *suṇā̆-*: Ind. Sg. 1. *suṇāmi* DhCo. III. 172[7], 2. *suṇāsi* Sn. 696, 3. *suṇāti* D. I. 62[33], A. III. 162[2], Milp. 5[34], Pl. 3. *suṇanti* S. I. 114[31], JāCo. II. 24[12]; Imp. Sg. 2. *suṇa* Th2. 404, S. III. 121[34], JāCo. III. 231[4] and *suṇāhi* Sn. p. 21, JāCo. IV. 1[14], 3. *suṇātu* Vin. I. 56[16], Pl. 1. *suṇāma* Sn. 354, 2. *suṇātha* Iv. 41[15] (verse), Vv. 84.1, D II. 2[11], 3. *suṇantu* Sn. 222, D.II. 166[5] (verse), Milp. 25[14]; Opt. Sg. 1. *suṇeyyaṃ* Ud. 48[32], 3. *suṇe* Jā IV. 240[29] and *suṇeyya* Sn. 325, Vin. I. 7[22], Pl. 1. *suṇemu* Vv. 53. 23 (according to VvCo. 242[16]), and *suṇeyyāma* M. II. 90[18].

§ 148. Roots of Cl. V. with consonantal final are: *śak* (*śaknoti*) 'to be able to' and *āp* 'to get' mostly with *pra* (*prāpnoti*). 1. From the root *śak* we have (*a*) the present-stem *sakko-* = *śakno-* preserved in the Ind. which completely ousted the weak stem *śaknu-* and is met with in every period of the language: Sg. 1. *sakkomi* Mhvs. 32. 17, 2. *sakkosi* JāCo. I. 433[28], II. 214[5], 3. *sakkoti*, Pl. 1. *sakkoma* Sn. 597, Vin. I. 31[9], JāCo. I. 437[17], DhCo. I. 90[20], 2. *sakkotha* JāCo.

[1] The same phenomenon in Pkr. Cf. Pischel, § 502 f. The root *star* (*sṛṇoti* and *stṛṇāti*) 'to stretch out' is inflected according to Cl. I. Cf. also Skr. *starati*, *-te*.

II. 405^{25}, 3. *sakkonti* Vin. I. 31^{16}, DhCo. I. 23^{3}. Beside it there is the stem (*b*) *sakkuṇā-*[1] after Cl. IX (with Svarabhakti) whence Opt. Sg. 2. *sakkuṇeyyāsi* JāCo. III. 301^{22}, Mhvs. 12. 18, 3. *sakkuṇeyya* JāCo. I. 361^{6}; Pl. 1. *sakkunemu* Jā. V. 24^{26} or *sakkuneyyāma* M. I. 457^{22}. (*c*) Ind. Sg. 1. and 2. *sakkāmi sakkasi* JāCo. I. 290^{33}, 3. *sakkati* Thl. 533 is =*śakyati*; Passive *sakkate* 'it is possible' Nett. 23^{3}=*śakyate*.—2. From the root *āp+pra* we have (*a*) the present-stem *pappo.*=*prāpno-* : Ind. Sg. 3. *pappoti* Dh. 27, Sn. 584, Thl. 35, 292, D.II. 231^{11,16} (verse), Pl. 1. *pappoma* Jā. V. 57^{19}; 3. *papponti* Jā. III. 256^{18}; Imp. Pl. 3. *pappontu* Thl. 603. All the examples belong to the Gāthā-language. The stem *prāpnu-* is to be found in the Opt. Sg. 3. *pappuyya* Thl. 364 etc.=*prāpnuyāt*. Beside it there is found from the earliest times (*b*) the stem *pāpuṇā-*[2] formed according to Cl. IX. with Svarabhakti-vowel. This is the only form used in the later period. Cf. Ind. Sg. 3. *pāpuṇāti* Milp. 337^{8}, Pl. 3. *pāpuṇanti* Milp. 314^{18}, JāCo. I. 150^{21}; Imp. Sg. 2. *pāpuṇa* Th2. 432, Sg. 3. *pāpuṇātu* JāCo. I. 150^{25}; Opt. Sg. 3. *pāpuṇe* Sn. 324, Dh. 138 and *pāpuṇeyya* S. I. 126^{1}, Milp. 307^{30}; Pl. 2. *pāpuṇetha* Jā. V. 208^{2}. From *āp+pari*: Imp. Pl. 2. *pariyāpuṇātha* 'learn!' S. I. 50^{13}.

§ 149. A probable example of a present-stem of Cl. VIII is to be found in *munāti* 'comprehends, understands' Dh. 269. But itself it seems to stand for **munoti*=Skr. *manoti* (Act. to *manute*, root *man*), with transfer to Cl. IX. I would explain in the same way also *thunāti* 'roars' from root *stan*[3]. We have to do here with a formation according to Cl. VIII. (and Cl. IX). There is besides an *abhi-tthanati* and *-tthanayati* 'thunders' (§ 52.2) Jā. I. 332^{1}, JāCo. I. 330^{18}=*stanati stanayati* after Cl. X, just as beside *munāti* there is *maññati* after Cl. IV. The forms are: Ind. Sg. 3. *anutthunāti* Sn. 827, Pl. 3 *thunanti* Sn. 884, Vv. 52. 3, *anutthunanti* Sn. 901, *nitthunanti* VvCo. 224^{1}. Cf. also the Part. Pres. Sg. Nom. *anutthunaṃ* Jā. III. 114^{6}, explained in the Comm. as *nitthunanto*.—Present-formations of the root *kar* 'to do' are multifarious. We have (*a*) in Ind. and Imp. the stem *karo-* abstracted

[1] The form expected is *sakuṇa-*; the *kk* is probably taken from the form *sakko-*, which was in living use. Also in Pkr. are found *sakkaṇomi* and *sakkuṇomi*; Pischel, § 505.

[2] In Pkr. we have AMāg. *pāuṇai* beside *pappoi*; Pischel, § 504.

[3] Pāli *thunāti* cannot be connected with root *stu* (cf. Pischel, § 494) on account of its meaning, even though it remains difficult to explain (as in *munāti*) the *u* in the first syllable (? weakening before the stressed syllable).

out of *karoti*. Its forms are met with in every period of the language, and are to be regarded as the regular forms in canonical and post-canonical prose. Ind. Sg. 1. *karomi* Sn. 78, *karosi* M. III. 140[3] (*vyāk-*), DhCo. I. 45[13], 3. *karotī* Sn. 216, M. III. 247[9], JāCo. I. 278[26], Pl. 1. *karoma* JāCo. I. 221[33], DhCo. I. 53[2], 2. *karotha* Ud. 51[16] (verse), DhCo. III. 201[5], 3. *karonti* Sn. 246, DhCo. I. 52[12]; Imp. Sg. 2. *karohi* Sn. 1062, Milp. 330[17], JāCo. II. 223[4], DhCo. I. 52[17], 3. *karotu* Mhvs. 5. 273, Pl. 2. *karotha* Th2. 13, JāCo. I. 253[23], Mhvs. 4. 44; 3. *karontu* JāCo. I. 155[7].—(*b*) Stem *kubba*[1], abstracted out of *kubbanti* Sn. 794, Jā. III. 118[10] = *kurvanti*: Ind. Sg. 2. *kubbasi* S. I. 181[10] (verse), 3. *kubbati* Sn. 168, Jā. III. 118[10]; Opt. Sg. 3. *vikubbeyya* Dpvs. 1. 40 and Med. *kubbetha* (cf. p. 166, foot-note 1) Sn. 702, 719 (also, after Cl. X, *kubbaye* Sn. 943). Forms derived from this stem belong to the Gāthā-language and the artificial poetry).—(*c*) Stem *kara-*[2] corresponds to Ved. *kárati*. It is in use in all periods of the language; in the second and the third periods the Opt. is formed regularly from this stem. Ind. Sg. 1. Med. *kare* Jā. II. 138[13]; Imp. Sg. 2. *kara* JāCo. IV. 1[14], Dpvs. 1. 56 and Med. *karassu* Thl. 46, S. I. 120[15] (verse), Jā. III. 74[1]; Opt. Sg. 1. *kareyyaṃ* M. I. 487[19] (*vyāk-*), 2. *kareyyāsi* M. I. 487[10] (*vyāk-*), JāCo. II. 102[7], 3. *kare* Dh. 42 f. and *kareyya* Sn. 920, 923, Vv. 84. 40, DhCo. I. 38[11], Pl. 1. *kareyyāma* S. I. 58[14], 2. *kareyyātha* Sn. p. 101, 3. *kareyyuṃ* JāCo. I. 168[4], III. 300[9].—(*d*) Stem *kar-* of athematic conjugation (cf. Ved. *kárṣi*) is found only in the archaic forms of the Opt. occurring in the Gāthā-language: Sg. 3. *kayirā* (from **karyā*, § 47. 2) Dh. 42 f., Sn. 728, Thl. 152 (for metrical reasons *kayirā* Jā. IV. 127[8]); Pl.2. *kayirātha* Dh.25, Ud.92[22](verse), S.I. 2[25](verse).—(*e*) Stem *kuru-*, abstracted out of Ind. Sg. 3. Med. *kurute* Dh. 48 = *kurute* or Imp. Sg. 2. *kuru* Mhvs. 4. 40 = *kuru*, also in Imp. Sg. 3. *kurutu* Jā. IV. 396[8].—(*f*) There is moreover the isolated form Ind. Sg. 1. *kummi* Jā. II. 435[19], VI. 499[16] (Comm. = *karomi*), formed after **kumma* = *kurmas*.

3. Future
with Conditional

§ 150. In Pāli there are two types of future, derived from *-sya*-future and *-iṣya*-future of Skr. The flexion corresponds to that of

[1] Cf. Pkr. AMāg. *kuvvai*, Opt. *kuvvejja*; Pischel, § 508. Forms like Māh. *kuṇai*, *kuṇa* etc. are however wanting in Pāli.

[2] Pkr. *karai* etc. in Pischel, § 509. But again in Pāli there is no trace of forms like Pkr. *karei*.

Skr.; in 1. Sg. there is, besides *-āmi*, also *-aṃ*[1]; in 1. Pl. there is *-ma* instead of *-mas*. For Type I the paradigm may be shown by *dassāmi* (vowel root)=*dāsyāmi* and *lacchāmi*=*lapsyāmi* (consonant root), for Type II by *karissāmi*=*kariṣyāmi*.

		Ia	Ib	II
Sg.	1.	*dassāmi, dassaṃ*	*lacchāmi, lacchaṃ*	*karissāmi, karissaṃ*
	2.	*dassasi*	*lacchasi*	*karissasi*
	3.	*dassati*	*lacchati*	*karissati*
Pl.	1.	*dassāma*	*lacchāma*	*karissāma*
	2.	*dassatha*	*lacchatha*	*karissatha*
	3.	*dassanti*	*lacchanti*	*karissanti*

Examples of medial forms are: Sg. 2. *gamissase* 'you will go' Th1. 359; Sg. 3. *hessate* 'will be' Mhvs. 25. 97; Pl. 1. *sikkhissāmase* 'we shall learn' Sn. 814, *lacchāmase* Vv. 32. 9; Pl. 3. *karissare* Mhvs. 30. 55, *vasissare* Th1. 962, *bhavissare* Jā. III. 207[9].

In the Gāthā-language (particularly in the 2. 3. Sg. and the 3. Pl.) *ss* may be replaced by *h*[2]. Thus *padāhisi* Th2. 303 for *-dassasi*; *parinibbāhisi* 'you will attain extinction' Th1. 415; *hāhasi* 'you will forsake' Jā. III. 172[26] and *vihāhisi* Jā. I. 298[26] from root *hā*; *palehiti* 'he will fly' Th1. 307 from *palāy-*; *ehisi* 'you will go' Dh. 236; *ehiti* 'he will come' Jā. II. 153[18]; *karihiti* 'he will do' Th2. 424 etc. Other examples in § 151 (at the end) and § 153. 1. On the *i* after *h* cf. § 19.1.

§ 151. The future is formed after Type Ia by 1. roots in *ā*: *dassāmi* 'I shall give' JāCo. III. 53[14], DhCo. III. 190[1] (Sg. 2. *dassasi* JāCo. II. 160[1], Pl. 1. *dassāma* DhCo. III. 194[9], 2. *dassatha* D. II. 96[20] etc.); *ṭhassati* 'he will stand' D. I. 46[10]=*sthāsyati* (Pl. 3. *ṭhassanti* D. II. 75[28] etc.); *hassāmi* 'I shall forsake' Jā. IV. 420[20] (*pahāssaṃ* M. II. 100[3] (verse)=*hāsyati* (Pl. 2. *pahassatha* Dh. 144), *pāssati* 'he will drink' Jā. VI. 527[20]=*pāsyati*. In the oldest period of the language *ā* is not unfrequently transmuted into *i*[3]: *pissāmi* 'I shall drink' Jā. III. 432[12]; *paccupadissāmi* from root *dā* Jā. V. 221[7]; *upaññissaṃ* from root *ñā* Sn. 701, 716 (Pl. 3. *viññissanti* Th1.

[1] As also in Pkr.; Pischel, § 520.

[2] The substitution of *h* is much wider in Pkr.; Pischel, *loc. cit.*

[3] Analogous forms in Pkr. are Futures like AMāg. *saṃ-dhissāmi*, *pari-hissāmi* Pischel, § 530.

703); *parinibbissaṃ* 'I shall attain Nirvāṇa' from root *vā* Th1. 658; *akkhissaṃ* 'I shall proclaim' from root *khyā* with *ā* Jā. VI. 523[21]; *vyakkhissaṃ* Sn. 600; *upaṭṭhissaṃ* 'I shall serve' Jā. VI. 523[19]. Mutation into *e* is rarer: *hessāmi*, *-ma* from root *hā* Jā. IV. 415[19], VI. 441[16].—2. Roots in *u*: *sossāmi* 'I shall hear' S. I. 210[9] (verse) =*śroṣyāmi* (Sg. 2. *sossi* for *sossasi* § 65. 2, 3. *sossati* D. II. 131[2]). Also *sussaṃ* Sn. 694 according to § 15.—3. Roots in *ī* and *e*-stems: *jessasi* 'you will conquer' Jā. II. 252[15]=*jeṣyasi*; *nessāmi* 'I shall lead' JāCo. I. 222[23], II. 159[14]=*neṣyāmi* (Pl. 2. *nessatha* Dh. 179 f.); *pacessati* 'he will collect' Dh. 44 f.=*ceṣyati* (besides *pacissati* Jā. III. 22[4] according to § 15); *essāmi* 'I shall go' JāCo. VI. 365[5], *essasi* JāCo. VI. 365[6], *essati* Dh. 369, JāCo. VI. 365[4], *essanti* Dh. 86=*eṣyāmi*, etc. Similarly of compounds: *paccessaṃ* Vin. I. 255[24], *samessati* S. IV. 379[19], *samessanti* Iv. 70[12]. Also verbs which have an *e*-stem in present take after this type. Thus *nidhessāmi* 'I shall lay down' from stem *dhe-* (§ 142. 2); *gahessāmi* 'I shall take' JāCo. I. 268[12] from the stem *gahe-* of root *grah*; *sessaṃ* 'I shall lie' Sn. 970, *sessati* S. I. 83[30], DhCo. I. 320[14] from stem *se-* (§ 140. 4) of the root *śī* as against Skr. *śayiṣyate*. (On *hessati* 'will be' cf. § 154. 2). The forms derived from the contracted stems of verbs of Cl. X and of Denominatives and Causatives are very numerous: Sg. 1. *kathessāmi* JāCo. IV. 139[20], *saṃgāmessāmi* JāCo. II. 11[4], 2. *kappessasi* A. IV. 301[20], 3. *pūjessati* Vin. I. 105[29], *damessati* JāCo. I. 506[30], Pl. 1. *dassessāma* JāCo. I. 59[4], 2. *vassāpessatha* JāCo. I.253[26], 3. *ropessanti* Vin. II. 12[16] etc. In the same way there came to be formed from *anubhoti* 'enjoys' (§ 131. 2) an *anubhossati* Jā. I. 500[19], and with *h* instead of *ss*: *anubhohisi* Th2. 510 (*anubhossasi* Vv. 52. 18); from *saṃbhoti* a *saṃbhossāma* Mhvs. 5. 100, from *pahoti* 'suffices' a *pahossati*[1] DhCo. III. 254[12]. Similarly from *hoti* (§ 131. 2): *hohisi* Th1. 382 and *hohiti*[2] Th1. 1137, Th2. 465.

§ 152. The type I b includes a number of historical forms, belonging particularly to the older literature. But quite a number of examples are found also in the post-canonical prose[3]. From root *śak* 'to be able to' we have Sg. 3. *sakkhati* Sn. 319=*sakṣyati*, Pl. 3. *sakkhinti* Sn.28, Fut. Sg. 2. *sakkhasi* A. I. 111[6] or *sakkhī* (for **sakkhisi*) Jā. V. 116[5]; also *sagghasi* with softening of medial consonants

[1] In Pkr. cf. Māh- *hossaṃ*.

[2] Cf. Pkr. *hohimi*, *hohisi*, *hohii*; Pischel, § 521.

[3] Analogous futures in Pkr. are *dacchaṃ*, *mocchaṃ*, *vocchaṃ*, *checchaṃ*, *bhocchaṃ*, etc.; Pischel, § 525, 526, 529, 532.

(§ 61. 1). From root *vac* 'to speak': Sg. 1. *vakkhāmi* JāCo. I 346[2] =*vakṣyāmi*, 3. *vakkhati* S. I. 142[32], JāCo. II. 40[10], Pl. 1. *vakkhāma* S. IV. 72[9], M. III. 207[23], 3. *vakkhanti* Vin. II. 1[21]. From root *bhuj* 'to enjoy': *bhokkhaṃ* Jā. IV. 127[20]=*bhokṣyāmi*. From root *chid* 'to cut off': Sg. 1. *checchaṃ* Jā. III. 500[23]=*chetsyāmi*, 3. *checchati* Dh. 350, Th1. 761. From root *bhid* 'to split': Sg. 3. *bhecchati* A. I. 8[4]=*bhetsyati*. From root *labh* 'to attain': Sg. 1. *lacchāmi* M. II. 71[6], JāCo. I. 395[15]=*lapsyāmi*, 2. *lacchasi* Vv. 83. 5, M. II. 71[1], JāCo. I. 279[3], 3. *lacchati* S. I. 114[19], Pl. 1. *lacchāma* Jā. IV. 292[21]. From root *viś* 'to enter': Sg. 1. *pavekkhāmi* Jā. III. 86[5], Mhvs. 25. 42. From root *vas* 'to live': Sg. 1. *vacchāmi* Jā. VI. 523[11] and *vacchaṃ* Th2. 414, 425=*vatsyāmi*, 3. *vacchati* Th2. 294. From root *darś* 'to see': Sg. 1. *dakkhaṃ* Th1. 1099=*drakṣyāmi*, 2. *dakkhasi* S. I. 116[11] (verse) and *dakkhisi* Th2. 232, Jā. VI. 497[15], 3. *dakkhati* S. II. 255[23] and *dakkhiti* Sn. 909, D. I. 165[19], M. II. 202[6], Pl. 3. *dakkhinti* Vin. I. 16[34]. The forms *mokkhasi* Vin. I. 21[18] (verse) =S. I. 111[29] (verse) and *mokkhanti* Dh. 37 from root *muc*=*mokṣyasi*, *mokṣyanti* have a passive meaning. These futures were apparently still felt to be such. Thus in M. III. 130[1] *dakkhati* stands beside *ñassati* and *sacchi-karissati*. But that the futural sense was already getting blurred is proved (already in the oldest period of the language) by doublets[1] such as *dakkhisaṃ* (instead of *-issaṃ* for metrical reasons) Th2. 84 (Comm. 89[19]: *passissaṃ*); 2. *dakkhissasi* M. III. 5[10]; Pl. 1. *dakkhisāma* Jā. III. 99[7] (Comm *dakkhissāma*), 2. *dakkhissatha* M. II. 60[5]. Similarly Sg. 1. *sakkhissāmi* 'I shall be able to' JāCo. I. 290[7], 2. *sakkhissasi* Vin. III. 19[33], JāCo. I. 222[11], 3. *sakkhissati* DhCo. III. 176[4], Pl.1. *sakkhissāma* JāCo. II. 129[5], 2. *sakkhissatha* DhCo. III. 80[7], 3. *sakkhissanti* JāCo. I. 255[25],—in all of which the future-suffix has been added to *sakkh-* which itself is the future-stem of root *śak*[2].

§ 153. The Type I b includes 1. a number of futures of roots in *r*. A form **karṣyāmi* is evidently presupposed by *kassaṃ* Th1. 381, *kassāmi* Th1. 1138 (in the same verse *karissāmi*!) from root *kar* 'to do'. Instead of *kassaṃ* there is also *kāsaṃ* Jā. IV. 287[13], and this leads easily over to the forms Sg. 1. *kāhāmi* Th1. 103, Jā. II. 257[1], III. 47[15], Vv. 52. 17, 2. *kāhasi* Dh. 154, Th1. 1134, II. 57; 3. *kāhati* Jā. II. 443[14] and *kāhiti* Jā. VI. 497[2], Pl. 1. *kāhāma* Vv. 84. 37, 3.

[1] Cf. Māh *dacchihisi* in Pischel, § 525.

[2] Does the verb-form *pavecchati* 'throws, gives, bestows' Sn. 463 ff., 490 ff., Th2. 272, S. I. 18[26 27] (verse), Jā. III. 12[1-3], 172[7], VI. 502[12] contain a future-stem like this?

kāhanti Jā. VI. 510[3] and *kāhinti*[1] Th2. 509. From root *har* with *vi* 'to sojourn, live' we have *vihassaṃ* Th1. 1091 ff. = **viharṣyāmi*, 3. *vihassati* S. I. 157[1] (verse). Then with *h* Sg. 2. *vihāhisi* Dh. 379, and also the simplex Sg. 3. *hāhiti* Jā. VI. 500[6]. Instead of *a* we have *i* in the root-syllable in Sg. 1. *vihissāmi* Th2. 181, 360, Pl. 1. *vihissāma* Th2. 121; also Sg. 1. *āhissaṃ* 'I shall bring in' Jā. VI. 523[7] (Comm. *āharissāmi*); and further *e* in *vihessati*[2] Th1. 257. All these forms belong exclusively to the Gāthā-language.—2. Finally there are still to mention some difficult futural forms of the root *han* 'to strike, kill', occurring in the Gāthā-language and the canonical prose: Sg. 1. *patihaṅkhāmi* S. IV. 104[26] (= **haṅkṣyāmi?*); *hañchati* Jā. IV. 102[9] (Comm. *hanissati*); the Opt. *hañchema* Jā. II. 418[11] (Comm. *hanissāma*) proves that the futural meaning of the stem *hañch-* had become blurred. Finally I have to mention the Sg. 1. *āhañhi* 'I shall strike' Vin. 1. 8[26] (verse). D. II. 72[6, 19], which however may have to be emended into *āhañhaṃ*[3].

§ 154. Futures of Type II likewise contain many historical forms. 1. Examples: Sg. 1. *pakkamissaṃ* Th2. 294 = *prakramiṣyāmi*, *asissāmi* Sn. 970 = *aśiṣyāmi*, *khādissāmi* JāCo. III. 52[19] = *khādiṣyāmi*; 2. *karissasi* JāCo. III. 54[25] = *kariṣyasi*, *harissasi* JāCo. VI. 364[26] = *hariṣyasi*; 3. *jayissati* (besides *jessati*) Jā. II. 252[15] = *jayiṣyati* (besides *jeṣyati*); *nayissati* Vin. I. 43[17] (verse) = *nayiṣyati* (besides *neṣyati*), *hanissati* JāCo. IV. 102[25] = *haniṣyati*; Pl. 1. *yācissāma* Vin. II. 196[35] = *yāciṣyāmas*, *vasissāma* Mhvs. 14. 26 = *vasiṣyāmas* (besides *vatsyāmas*); 2. *labhissatha* JāCo. III. 126[24] = *labhiṣyatha* (besides *lapsyatha*), *pabbajissatha* Mhvs. 5. 199. = *pravrajiṣyatha*; 3. *gamissanti* Sn. 445 = *gamiṣyanti*, *samanumodissanti* M. I. 398[9] = *modiṣyante*, etc.—2. The forms *bhavissāmi*, etc. = *bhaviṣyāmi*, etc. are historical, and they are the usual forms in the canonical and post-canonical prose. But beside them there are in the Gāthā-language (and artificial poetry), and archaistically also in the canonical prose, the contracted forms (§ 27. 5) such as Sg. 1. *hessaṃ* Th1. 1100, Jā. III. 224[3] and *hessāmi* Th2. 460, 3. *hessati* Jā. III. 279[16], Med. *hessate* Mhvs. 25. 97, Pl. 2.

[1] The corresponding forms in Pkr. are *kāhaṃ*, *kāhisi*, *kāhii*, etc.; Pischel, § 533.

[2] The forms of the root *har* have thus coincided with those of the root *hā*. Cf § 150, 151.

[3] Franke, D. 180, foot-note 7, adopts for the passage D. II. 72[6, 19] the very plausible reading *āhañh' ime Vajjī* (= *āhañhaṃ ime*) instead of *āhañhi' me* as in the text-edition; but the form *āhañhi* occurs also in Vin. I. 8[26]: *āhañhi amatadudrabhiṃ*. The text here should then have to be emended into *āhañh' amata-*.

hessatha S. IV. 179[24]. Formally these forms have coincided with those of the *e*-stems of Type I.—3. According to Type II are derived future forms also from the uncontracted stems of Cl. X and Causatives and Denominatives discussed in § 187, and they correspond to the analogous forms in Skr. Thus *bandhayissāmi* 'I shall have bound' Mhvs. 24. 6 = *bandhayiṣyāmi*; *pālayīssāmi* 'I shall protect' JāCo. IV. 129[15] = *pālayiṣyāmi*.—4. Also Desideratives (§ 184) and Intensives (§ 185) form their future after Type II: Sg. 1. *titikkhissaṃ* Dh. 320, *vīmaṃsissāmi* JāCo. I. 390[17], *caṅkamissāmi* Thl. 540; Pl. 1. *sussūsissāma* S. II. 267[21], 3. *sussūsissanti* S. II. 267[8].

§ 155. The Type II has extended its sphere to an unusual extent within Pāli[1]. Practically from every pres.-stem a future of this Type may be derived. Examples from thematic conjugation: 1. Cl. I. With reference to § 132: Sg. 1. *pivissāmi* Thl. 313, JāCo. IV. 2[9], *tiṭṭhissāmi* M. III. 129[13], *vuṭṭhahissāmi* Mhvs. 36. 76; 2. *pivissasi* JāCo. VI. 365[8], *nisīdissasi* A. IV. 301[19]; 3. *nisīdissati* Vin. I. 9[4], *patiṭṭhahissati* DhCo. III. 171[21]; Pl. 1. *upaṭṭhahissāma* DhCo. IV. 7[15]; *pivissāma* JāCo. I. 99[8]; 2. *pivissatha* Vin. I. 78[7]; 3. *vuṭṭhahissanti* D. II. 74[6]. With reference to § 133: Sg. 1. *gacchissāmi* JāCo. III. 10[3], *gacchissaṃ* Thl. 95, Vv. 63. 21; 2. *gacchisi* (§ 65. 2); 3. *āgacchissati* JāCo. III. 53[7]; Pl. 2. *gacchissatha* JāCo. II. 128[7], etc.—2. Cl. VI. With reference to § 134: Sg. 1. *pavissāmi* (§ 65. 2) and *pavisissāmi* JāCo. III. 86[7], *ādisissāmi* Th2. 308, *pucchissāmi* Sn. p. 32, Jā. VI. 364[18], *phusissaṃ* Thl. 386; Pl. 1. *pucchissāma* Sn. p. 112, etc. The form *panudahissāmi* Thl. 27, 233 is remarkable. With reference to § 135: Pl. 3. *acchissanti* Vin. II. 76[3]. Sg. 1. *muñcissāmi*[2] JāCo. I. 434[1, 19]; Pl. 3. *siñcissanti* Vin. II. 12[17] etc.—3. Cl. IV. With reference to § 136. 1: Sg. 1. *naccissāmi* JāCo. I. 292[21]; 2. *maññissasi* Vin. I. 59[27]; 3. *ijjhissati* JāCo. I. 15[14], *vinassissati* JāCo. I. 256[15], *pabujjhissati* JāCo. I. 62[19]; Pl. 1. *naccissāma* DhCo. III. 102[2]; 2. *āpajjissatha* M. I. 124[28]; 3. *kujjhissanti* DhCo. III. 101[6], *naccissanti* Vin. II. 12[22]. With reference to § 136. 3: Sg. 1. *passissāmi* Vin. I. 97[25], JāCo. I. 62[12]; 2. *passissasi* Vin. I. 97[24]; 3. *passissati* Ud. 40[28]; Pl. 1. *passissāma* JāCo. II. 213[8] etc. With reference to § 136. 4: Sg. 1. *vihaññissaṃ*

[1] It is significant that in the commentaries future forms of Type I are frequently explained by those of Type II. Thus, of the example given in § 150, 151, 152, *hāhisi* is explained by *jahissasi*, *jessasi* by *jinissasi*, *bhokkhaṃ* by *bhuñjissāmi*, *vacchati* by *vasissati*. For all the new formations of Type II there are parallels in Pkr.; Pischel, § 520 ff.

[2] In both cases in passive sense; it therefore should perhaps be read *muccissāmi*. In that case also *pamuñce* 'may he be released' Jā. III. 236[19], 237[2] should be emended to *pamucce*.

Thl. 386; 3. *paññāyissati* JāCo I. 484[23], *niyyissati* A. V. 195[10]; *sūyissati* S. IV. 344[22], *khīyissati* JāCo. I. 290[4]; Pl. 1. *muccissāma* JāCo. I. 434[20]; 2. *muccissatha* DhCo. III. 242[14]. With reference to § 137: Sg. 3. *jiyyissati* and *miyyissati* M. III. 246[22]. With reference to § 138: Sg. 1. *nahāyissāmi* JāCo. I. 265[25], *nibbāyissaṃ* Thl. 162, 919, *parinibbāyissāmi* D. II. 104[19], *tāyissāmi* JāCo. II. 252[17]; Sg. 3. *antara-dhāyissati* Vin. I. 43[21]; Pl. 3. *gāyissanti* Vin. II. 12[22] etc. Sg. 1. *palāyissāmi* JāCo. II. 247[23] (also *sajjhāyissāmi* JāCo. II. 243[12] with reference to § 138. 1).

§ 156. Athematic Conjugation. 1. Cl. III. With reference to § 142: Sg. 1. *jahissāmi* Jā. IV. 415[19], JāCo. IV. 420[26], *saddahissāmi* Milp. 148[31], *paṭijaggissāmi* JāCo. II. 200[2]; 2. *jahissasi* JāCo. III. 173[4]; 3. *jahissati* Jā. III. 279[16]; Pl. 2. *saddahissatha* DhCo. I. 117[23], *paṭijaggissatha* DhCo. IV. 10[15] etc.—2. Cl. VIII. With reference to § 144: Sg. 1. *bhañjissaṃ* Thl. 1095, (*pari*) *bhuñjissāmi* Vin. I. 185[21], II. 300[29], JāCo. IV. 129[14]; 3. *chindissati* JāCo. II. 252[21], *bhindissati* Vin. II. 198[33]; Pl. 3. *samucchindissanti* D. II. 74[15], *bhuñjissanti* Vin. II. 196[13], *riñcissanti* Vin. I. 190[19].—2. Cl. IX. With reference to § 145: Sg. 1. *jānissāmi* JāCo. III. 53[22], *vikkiṇissāmi* DhCo. III. 430[1], *jinissāmi* JāCo. III. 5[3]; 2. *jinissasi* JāCo. II. 252[18]; 3. *janissati* JāCo. VI. 364[19], *jinissati* JāCo. III. 5[2]; Pl. 1. *anujānissāma* M. II. 57[5]; 3. *samanujānissanti* M. I. 398[8]. With reference to § 146: Sg. 1. *gaṇhissāmi* JāCo. I. 222[24], 2. *gaṇhissasi* JāCo. I. 222[24], 3. *gaṇhissati* JāCo. III. 280[22], Pl. 1. *gaṇhissāma* JāCo. II. 104[9], 2. *gaṇhissatha* JāCo. II. 197[17] etc.—3. Cl. V and IX. With reference to § 147: Sg. 1. *suṇissāmi* DhCo. III. 195[10], 2. *suṇissasi* DhCo. III. 195[9]; Pl. 1. *sakkuṇissāma* JāCo. II. 415[22], 2. *suṇissatha* DhCo. I. 97[11], *pāpuṇissatha* JāCo. I. 253[26], 3. *pāpuṇissanti* JāCo. I. 256[4] etc.

Conditional.

§ 157. As in Skr., the Conditional is formally a Preterite to the Future. It is used as Irrealis of the present and the past. Excepting in compounds, the augment seems to be obligatory. The flexion is as in Skr., only the 3. Pl. derives its ending *-aṃsu* from the Aorist (§159. III). Examples are: Sg. 1. *abhavissaṃ* JāCo. I. 470[15] = *abhaviṣyam*; *adassaṃ* JāCo. III. 30[6] = *adāsyam*; *apāpessaṃ* (from Causative of *āp* + *pra*[1]) JāCo. II. 11[18]; *olokessaṃ* 'I would watch' or 'I would have watched' JāCo. I. 470[15].—Sg. 2. *abhavissa* JāCo. II. 11[18], III. 30[6]

[1] *Pāp-* was no longer felt to be a compound, hence the augment.

=*abhaviṣyas*; *āpajjissa* DhCo. III.137[17].—Sg.3. *abhavissa* 'would be' or 'would have been' Vin. I. 13[38], D.II.57[6]. M.III. 163[11], Ud.80[24], JāCo. II. 112[16](should it be read *nābhavissa*?), V.264[1]=*abhaviṣyat*; *anassissa*[1] 'he would have died' JāCo. II. 112[17]; *adassa* JāCo. V. 264[1]; *uppajjissa* DhCo. III. 137[19], *payojayissa*, *pabbajissa*, *pāpuṇissa*, *patiṭṭhahissa* DhCo. III. 131[16], *akarissa* DhCo. I. 147[19], *asakkhissa* DhCo. I. 147[20] (should it be read *nāsakkhissa*?), III. 8[23], *alabhissa* DhCo. III. 4[1].—Pl. 1. *alabhissāma* and *āgamissāma* JāCo. III. 35[10,11].—Pl. 3. *abhavissaṃsu* Vin.I.13[31].—Here should be mentioned a series of medial forms of the Conditional in the Sg. 3. occurring in D. II. 63[3] ff.: *okkamissatha* 'would have climbed down', *samucchissatha*[2] 'would have originated', *nibbattissatha* (root *vart*) 'would have come about', have originated', *nibbattissatha* (root *vart*) 'would have come about', *āpajjissatha* 'would have been attained', *alabhissatha* 'would have attained.' The suffix is -*tha* as against Skr. -*ta* as in Pres. Opt. (§ 129) and Aor. (§ 159. II).

4. Aorist.

§ 158. The Aorist of Pāli is derived from old Imperfects and Aorists. Apart from the endings, it is characterised by the augment, which is however frequently left out. Wackernagel[3] has succeeded in formulating definite rules according to which the augment is retained or dropped: 1. The augment is retained by monosyllabic verbal forms: *adaṃ* 'I gave', *agā* 'he went'. Also *acc-agā*, *samajjh-agaṃ* (besides *adhi-gaṃ* Th2. 122).—2. The augment is always retained, also in the later language, by dissyllabic forms derived from the Imperfect, the simple Aorist or the *s*-Aorist: *agamā* 'he went', *adāsi* 'he gave', *akāsi* 'he did', *avocuṃ* 'they spoke'. Also *ajjh-agamā*, *pacc-assosi*, *pāyāsi*.—3. In the two oldest periods of the language the use of the augment is arbitrary in the dissyllabic forms derived from the -*iṣ*-Aor.: *alabhiṃ* 'I received' beside *labhi* 'he received.' Omission of the augment is the rule in the post-canonical prose: *khādi* 'he ate,' *bhindi* 'he broke'.—4. The augment is always retained by the trisyllabic forms (*a*) of the extended type (§ 165)

[1] It should be read as does Speyer, Ved. u. Skr. Syntax, p. 60, foot-note 2: *nassissā 'ti* (more properly: *yev' anassissā 'ti*). Cf also D. Andersen, PR. p. 119.

[2] E. Windisch, Buddha's Geburt, p 39, foot-note, hesitatingly derives the form from Skr. *sam-mūrch*. In that case we would have to read *saṃmucchissatha* Not so R. O Franke, WZKM.8. 327.

[3] Wortumfang und Wortform, GN. 1906, p. 154 ff. It was held hitherto that the use of the augment was quite arbitrary as laid down by Kacc. Cf. eg. V. Henry, Prècis de Gramm. Pâlie, p. 88, § 220.

such as *agamāsi* 'he went,' *addasāsiṃ* 'I saw' or (*b*) derived from thematic Imperfects and Aorists, such as *abhāsatha* 'he spoke'.—5. For the rest, forms of three or more syllables began early to drop the augment, at first quite at random, but regularly later in the post-canonical prose. Thus in the Gāthā-language we have still *apucchiṃsu* 'they asked' beside *pucchiṃsu*; but the forms which later predominate and finally usurp the field are *desesiṃ* 'I taught,' *khādimha* 'we ate', *kathayiṃsu* 'they related.'

§ 159. The different types of Aorist[1] may be classified according to origin.

1. Type. Example: root *dā* 'to give.'

	Sg.	Pl.
1.	*adaṃ* Jā. III. 41[10]	(*adamha*) Jā. II. 71[4], Vv. 68. 4, 5
2.	*ado* (*adā*) Jā. IV. 240[14], V. 161[12]	(*adattha*) JāCo. II. 106[21]
3.	*adā* Sn. 303, Mhvs. 7. 70.	*adū*, *aduṃ*.

This Type is derived from the root-aorist, Skr. *adām*, *adās*, *adāt* ...*adus*. The forms of the Pl. 1. and 2 are however taken from Type III (as against Skr. *adāma*, *adāta*).

II. Type. Example: root *gam* 'to go.'

	Sg.	Pl.
1.	*agamaṃ* Th1. 258	*agamāma* (*agamamha* Sn. 349)
2.	*agamā* Sn. 834	*agamatha* (*agamattha*)
3.	*agamā* Sn. 408, Mhvs. 5. 42	*agamuṃ* Sn. 290, Mhvs. 4.36.

This Type is based on the *a*-Aor. (Skr. *asicam*, *asicas*, *asicat*... *asican*) or the thematic Imperfect (*asiñcam* etc.). The endings *-amha* *-attha* are taken from Type III. But there occur also the endings *-āma*, *-atha*: *akarāma* 'we did', *addasāma* 'we saw', *addasatha* 'you saw.' Cf. § 162. 1, 3—There are also medial forms of this Type: Sg. 3. *-tha*: *abhāsatha* 'he spoke' Sn. 30, *vindatha* 'he found' Th2. 420; Pl. 1. *-mhase*: *akaramhase* Jā. III. 26[18]; Pl 3. *-re*, *-ruṃ*: *abajjhare* 'they were bound' Jā. I. 428[1], *amaññaruṃ* 'they thought' Jā. III. 488[2]. The suffix *-tha* again shows (cf. § 129, 157) the aspirate instead of the tenuis. For *-amhase* (Type III) cf. § 126; *-re* and *-ruṃ* correspond to the Ved. endings *-re* and *-ran* or *-ram*[2].

[1] In Pkr. only the AMāg. has retained Aorist-forms; Pischel, § 516 f.

[2] Macdonell, Vedic Grammar, § 412 a.

III. Type. Example: root *śru* 'to hear,' *kar* 'to do.'

	Sg.	Pl.
1.	*assosiṃ* Th1. 131	*assumha* S. I. 157[12], JāCo. III. 278[4]
2.	*assosi*	*assuttha* D. II. 272[2] (sic!), S.I. 157[9]
3.	*assosi* D I. 87[11], Sn. p. 99	*assosuṃ* D. I. 111[10], Vin. I. 18[35]
1.	*akāsiṃ* Th2. 74, Vv. 1. 5	*akamha* Jā. III. 47[4]
2.	*akāsi* Vv. 1. 3, Th1. 1207	*akattha* Vv. 84. 38, Mhvs. 12. 22
3.	*akāsi* JāCo. III. 188[24], DhCo. I. 39[6]	*akāsuṃ* Mhvs. 31. 99 var. lec., *akaṃsu* Sn. 882, JāCo. I. 262[6].

This Type is derived from Skr. *s*-Aor.: *aśrauṣam*, *akārṣam*; *aśrauṣīs*, *akārṣīs*; *aśrauṣīt*, *akārṣīt*; *aśrauṣma*, *akārṣma*; *aśrauṣṭa*, *akārṣṭa*; *aśrauṣus*, *akārṣus*. The *u* in *assumha*, *assuttha* is to be explained according to § 15; the suffix *-mha* according to § 50. 4 or 58. 2. The ending *-ttha* = *ṣṭa*, instead of the expected *-ṭṭha*, is remarkable.—The medial forms are: Sg. 3. *-tha*: *udapattha* 'flew up' (root *pat*) Jā. V. 255[14] (conjecture by Fausböll), *pāpattha* 'he fell' Jā. V. 255[20]; a new formation based on this *pāpattha* is to be found in the Sg. 1. *pāpatthaṃ* 'I fell' Jā. VI. 16[29]; *mā laddhā* 'she should not receive' Jā. III. 138[21] = Skr. *alabdha*, but also *alattha*[1] 'he received' Jā. IV. 310[3], M. II. 49[3], S. IV. 302[9], Sn. p. 107. The *s* has been dropped in all these forms as in Skr.

IV. Type. Example: root *gam* 'to go.'

	Sg.	Pl.
1.	*agamisaṃ*, *agamiṃ* Th1. 9	*agamimha* S. I. 202[33] (verse)
2.	*agami* Sn. 339, JāCo. IV. 2[17]	*agamittha* JāCo. I. 263[4], DhCo. III. 22[7]
3.	*agami* D. II. 264[9], JāCo. VI. 366[24]	*agamisuṃ*, *agamiṃsu* JāCo. II. 416[23]

This Type is derived from Skr. *iṣ*-Aorist *abodhiṣam*, *abodhīs*, *abodhīt*, *abodhiṣma*, *abodhiṣṭa*, *abodhiṣus*. The form *agamiṃ* is derived from the Vedic 'contracted' forms such as *akramīm*, *avadhīm*[2]. Instead of *-isaṃ* we find also *-issaṃ* in Sg. 1. exactly as also in Pkr. (Pischel, § 516), e.g. *adhigacchissaṃ* Sn. 446; *nandissaṃ* S. I. 176[12] (verse). Besides *-isuṃ*, *-iṃsu* there is also *-uṃ* in Pl. 3., taken from Type II. Also Imperfects

[1] The hardening of the sonant group into a surd one is explained by the influence of forms like *apattha* in conjunction with those like *abhāsatha*.

[2] Whitney, Sanskrit Gramm. § 904 a, Macdonell, Ved. Gr. § 529 a, 3.

with *i* in Sg. 2. and 3. have contributed to the building up of this type. Thus *abravī* Sn. 355, Thl. 430 and *abruvī* Jā. III. 62[20] 'he spoke' = *abravīt* (its Sg. 1. is then *abraviṃ* Cp. 2. 6. 8; Pl. 3. *abravuṃ* Jā. V. 112[30]). Also *āsi* 'he was' Sn. 286, Mhvs. 2. 1 = *āsīt* (its Sg. 1. *āsiṃ*, *āsi* Th1. 157, Pv. 1. 2. 2, Cp. 3. 7. 1, but Pl. 1. *āsuṃ* Th2. 224; Pl. 3. *āsuṃ* Sn. 284, Mhvs. 1. 32).—Medial forms: Sg. 2. *-ittho* = *-iṣṭhās*: *mā paṭisevittho* 'do not expose yourself (to poison)!' Jā. IV. 222[9], *pucchittho* 'you asked' D. II. 284[3], *amaññittho* Thl. 280, M. III. 247[6] (cf. Jā. II. 29[17]), *vihaññittho* Thl. 385; Sg. 3. *-ittha* = *-iṣṭa*: *pucchittha* Mhvs. 17. 33; *mā jīyittha* 'may it not disappear' Jā. I. 468[2]; *sandittha* 'flowed' (root *syand*) D. II. 129[33]; *mā vo āvuso evaṃ ruccittha* 'may it not please you to do so!' DhCo. I. 13[23]. From Passive stems: *sūyittha* 'was heard' DhCo. I. 16[3]; *adissittha* 'showed himself' Thl 170; *dīyittha* 'was given' S. I. 58[9]. Here again we find dentals in the place of expected cerebrals[1].

Type I.

§ 160. The forms of Type I belong for by far the most part to the Gāthā-language, individual forms occurring also in the canonical and post-canonical prose. Mostly roots in vowels take these for us. Thus 1. root *gā* 'to go': Sg. 1. *ajjhagaṃ* Thl. 405, Th2. 67, *adhigaṃ* Th2. 122, *samajjhagaṃ* S. I. 103[10]; 2. *ajjhagā* Vv. 34. 7; 3. *agā* Sn. 538, *ajjhagā* D. I. 223[3]; Pl. 3. *ajjhagū* Jā. I. 256[7], Sn. 330, *upaccaguṃ* A. I. 142[21] (verse). To these belongs also the Pl. 1. *āgamhā* Sn. 597, though formally of Type III.—2. Root *sthā* 'to stand': Sg. 3. *aṭṭhā* Sn. 429 = *asthāt*.—3. Root *bhū* 'to be': Sg. 1. *ahuṃ* Jā. III. 411[5], Thl. 316 as against Skr. *abhūvam* on the analogy of *adaṃ*; 2. *ahū* Th2. 57, 190, PvCo. 11[10] (verse) = *abhūs*; 3. *ahū* Dh. 228, Sn. 139, M. I. 487[3], *ahud-eva* S. IV. 350[12] = *abhūt*; Pl. 3. *ahū*, *ahuṃ* D. II. 256[8] (verse), Mhvs. 2. 25 as against Skr. *abhūvan* on the analogy of *aduṃ*. As for Pl. 1. there is *ahuṃ* Th2. 225. The form *ahumha* belongs to § 163. 3.—4. The form *akā* 'did' Jā. V. 29[2] (Comm. *akāsi*) = Ved. *ákar* is also historical. On the analogy of *adā*: *adaṃ* there was formed a Sg 1. *akaṃ* Jā. V. 160[1] (Comm. *akariṃ*) to *akā*. Similarly *assuṃ* 'I heard' Jā. III. 542[1], *assu* 'you heard' Jā. III. 541[10] (Comm. *assosiṃ*, *assosi*) presuppose a Sg. 3. **assu* = Ved. *áśrot*. Historical are moreover Sg. 3. *addā* 'he saw' Thl. 1244 = Ved, *adrāk* and Pl. 3. *āgu*

[1] Such forms with *tth* instead of *ṭṭh* are found also in Pkr. Cf. AMāg. *sevitthā bhuñjitthā*. Pischel (§ 517) doubts whether these forms belonged to the Aorist from the beginning. Cf. also Johansson, KZ. 32. 450 ff.

(root *gā* + *ā*) D. II. 258[8] = *āguḥ* (new formation Sg. 3. *āga* D. II. 258[20] on the analogy of *āha* : *āhu*), and perhaps *pāvā* Sn. 782, 888 from root *vac* + *pra*.

Type II.

§ 161. What has been said at the beginning of the preceding paragraph applies also to the use of Type II in the different periods of the language. Examples: (*a*) Forms of Imperfect origin are Sg. 1. *kasaṃ* 'I ploughed', *pavapaṃ* 'I sowed' Th2. 112, *pāpataṃ* 'I fell' Jā. V. 70[12]; *amaññaṃ* 'I thought' Jā. V. 215[6], *adadaṃ* 'I gave' Vv. 34. 8; Sg. 2. with primary ending *apucchasi* 'you asked' Sn. 1050; Sg. 3. *papatā* Vin. III. 17[26], *asarā* 'went' Jā. VI. 199[7], *amarā* 'died' (Ved. *marati*, cf. § 137) Jā III. 389[18]; Pl. 2. *amaññatha* 'you meant' Th2. 143. Moreover Sg. 3. Med. *ajāyatha* 'originated' Dpvs. 5. 40, *samapajjatha* 'became' Jā. V. 71[30], *upapajjatha* 'originated' Thl. 30, *abhassatha* 'fell down' Sn. 449, *samakampatha* 'shook' Jā. VI. 570[12] etc. (*b*) The forms in Sg. 2. with the ending -o are Aorist-forms: *mā pamādo* 'do not tire!' Dh. 371, Thl. 119, S. IV. 263[20], 264[13]; *āsado* 'you came in, reached' Jā. I. 414[6], Vin II. 195[28] (verse); Sg. 3. *abhida* 'broke to pieces' Jā. III. 29[17], D. II. 107[3] (verse) or *abbhidā* Jā I. 247[29] = *abhidat*, *acchida* 'tore asunder' Sn. 357, *āsadā* Thl. 774; Pl. 3. *acchiduṃ* S. I. 35[14].—2. A remarkable innovation[1] has taken its origin from the medial forms *alattha*, *pāpattha* of Type III (§ 159. III). As these forms came to be regarded as analogous to *abhida* there were formed after them also the Sg. 1. *alatthaṃ* Vv. 81. 22. Thl. 747, D. II. 268[6], JāCo. I. 141[21], DhCo. I. 51[24], 2. *alattha* S. 1. 114[14]; Pl. 1. *alatthamha* M. II. 63[1], 3. *alatthuṃ* D. II. 274[22]. (verse). Beside them there is also *alatthaṃsu* S. I. 48[34] after Type III. Precisely in the same way, from *asayittha* of Type IV (§ 169. 1). there has been evolved a Sg. 1. *asayitthaṃ* A I, 136[29], and *alabhitthaṃ* Thl. 217 from an **alabhittha*.

§ 162. 1. The Aorist of Type II of the root *kar* 'to do' is derived from the Ved. Impf. *ákaram* etc.: Sg. 1. *akaraṃ* Jā. III. 206[21], V. 70[12], 2. *akarā* Jā. III. 135[17], V. 69[13], 3. *akarā* Jā. II. 230[15]; Pl. 1. *akarāma* M. II. 214[27] and *akaramha* M. II. 214[28], 3. *akaruṃ* D. II. 256[4] (verse), Mhvs. 3. 33.—2. The following forms of the root *bhū* 'to become' are derived from an Impf. of Cl. VI (**bhuvati*, cf. § 131. 2 with f.-n. 2, p. 168): Sg. 1, *ahuvā* S. I. 36[2] (verse). 2. *ahuvā* S. I. 36[9] (verse), 3. *ahuvā* Jā. II. 106[1], III. 131[11], Vv. 81. 24; Pl. 1.

[1] See E. Kuhn, Beitr. p. 111; R. O Franke, BB. 22 216.

ahuvāma M. I. 93[13], II. 214[24] and *ahuvamha* M. I. 93[14], II. 214[25], 2. *ahuvattha* S. IV. 112[6], M. I. 445[26], DhCo. I. 57[10].—3. The root *darś* 'to see' forms an Aorist from the base *draś*: Sg. 1. *addasaṃ* Sn. 837, Th2. 48, Jā. III. 380[8], M. I. 79[6], JāCo. III. 380[25] and, with primary ending, *addasāmi*[1] Th1. 1253, Th2. 135, S. I. 168[18], Vv. 50. 12, 2 *addasă* S. I. 115[10], 3. *addasă* Vin. II. 192[7], JāCo. I. 222[20]; Pl. 1. *addasāma* Sn. 31, Jā. II. 355[17] S. I. 196[13] (verse) JāCo. III. 304[2], 2. *addasatha* M. II. 108[32], JāCo. III. 304[3] and (for metrical reasons) *addasātha* Jā. V. 55[23], 3. *addasuṃ* D. II. 256[7] (verse).—4. The Aor. of the root *vac* shows two series of forms. One series is derived from a thematic Impf. **avacam*, the other form the Aor. *avocam*: Sg. 1. *avacaṃ* JāCo. III. 280[19], DhCo. III. 194[17] and *avocaṃ* Th2. 124, Vv. 79. 7, S. I. 10[23], DhCo. III. 285[21], 2. *avaca* Th2. 415 and *(a)voca* Dh. 133; 3. *avaca* JāCo. I. 294[21] and *avoca* Th2. 494, S. I. 150[4], JāCo. II. 160[8]; Pl. 1. *avacumha* and *avocumhă* M. II. 91[28], III. 15[5], 2. *avacuttha* Vin. II. 297[10], DhCo. I. 73[24] and *avocuttha*, 3. *avacuṃ* Jā. V. 260[4,10] and *avocuṃ* M. II. 147[29].

Type III.

§ 163. A considerable number of historical forms of this Type were retained in all the periods of the language. 1. Aorists of roots in *ā*. Thus from *jñā* 'to know' (*ajñāsīt*) Sg. 1. *abbhaññāsiṃ* Vin. III. 5[23], 3. *aññāsi* Sn. 540, Vin. I. 18[13], JāCo. VI. 366[10]; Pl. 3. *abbhaññāsuṃ* Sn. IV. 11[30] or *abbhaññaṃsu* D. II. 150[31] or (under the influence of Type IV) *aññiṃsu* JāCo. III. 303[17]. Also Sg. 3. *pāyāsi* D. II. 73[8], JāCo. I. 223[6], Pl. 3. *abhiyaṃsu* S. I. 216[10] and *pāyiṃsu* D. II. 96[24], DhCo. III. 257[19], JāCo. I. 254[11] from root *yā* 'to go' (*ayāsīt*); Sg. 3. *pahāsi* Sn. 1057 from root *hā* 'to leave' (*ahāsīt*). Similarly from the root *dā* 'to give': Sg. 1. *adāsiṃ* JāCo. I. 167[9], DhCo. I. 19[10], 2. *adāsi*, 3. *adāsi* JāCo. I. 279[17]; Pl. 1. *adamha* Vv. 65. 4, Jā. II. 71[4] and (with tranfer to Type IV) *adāsimha* Th2. 518, Jā. III. 120[11], 2. *adattha* JāCo. II. 166[21], 3. *adaṃsu* JāCo. I. 222[9]. From root *sthā* 'to stand': Sg. 1. *aṭṭhāsiṃ* Th2. 73, 3. *aṭṭhāsi*[2] Vin. II. 195[25], JāCo. II. 19[22]; Pl. 3. *aṭṭhaṃsu* D. II. 84[28], JāCo. II. 96[21] etc. From root *pā* 'to drink': Pl. 3. *apaṃsu* (sic!) Ud. 78[11]. From root *mā* 'to measure': Pl. 3. *pāmiṃsu* Th1. 469.—2. Aorists of roots in *ī*. From root *nī* 'to lead' (*anaiṣīt*): Sg. 3. *nesi* JāCo. V. 281[23]. Pl. 3. *ānesuṃ* JāCo. IV. 137[22], Mhvs. 5. 24 etc. From root *ji* 'to conquer'

[1] Cf. R. O. Franke, ZDMG. 63. 6.

[2] Cf. Pkr. AMāg. *ṭhāsi*; Pischel, § 516.

(*ajaiṣīt*): Sg. 3. *ajesi* Vin. II. 1^{12}. From root *hi* 'to send' (*ahaiṣīt*): Sg. 3. *pāhesi* Th1. 564, Vin. I. 92^{35}, JāCo. II. 90^{12}, Pl. 3. *pāhesuṃ* Mhvs. 25. 104. Forms of 1. and 2. Pl. are not attested. On Aor. IV. of uncontracted stem, see § 167. 1.—3. Aorists of roots in *ū*. Cf. *śru* § 159. III. From root *dhū* 'to shake' (*adhauṣīt*): Sg. 3. *adhosi* Sn. 787. After this form was constructed also that Aor. of root *bhū* 'to be, to become' which became the predominant one in course of the development of the language: Sg. 1. *ahosiṃ* Th1. 620, JāCo. I. 106^{10}, 2. *ahosi* JāCo. I. 107^{9}; 3. *ahosi* Sn. 835 Vin. I. 23^{7}, JāCo. I. 279^{8}, *anubhosi* JāCo. III. 112^{24}, *adhibhosi* S. IV, 185^{32}; Pl. 1. *ahumha* Jā. I. 362^{19}, DhCo. I. 57^{9}, 3. *ahesuṃ*[1] Vv. 74. 4, D. II. 6^{7}, JāCo. I. 149^{19}. The form Pl. 3. *adhibhaṃsu* S. IV. 185^{31} as compared with the Sg. *adhibhosi* is to be explained by the analogy of *adaṃsu*.—4. Aorists of roots in *r*. Cf. *kar* § 159. III^{2}. From root *har* 'to take away' (*ahārṣīt*): Sg. 1. *pahāsiṃ* Th2. 99, *vihāsiṃ* Th1. 513, Ud. 42^{8}, Vin. III. 4^{8}, 3. *ahāsi* Dh. 3, *pahāsi* Jā. III. 85^{12}, Vv. 29^{8}, Pl. 3. *ahaṃsu* Jā. V. 200^{6}, also *vihiṃsu* Th1. 925.

§ 164. Historical forms are preserved also by roots in mutes and sibilants. Thus Sg. 3. *acchecchi*[3] 'cut off' Sn. 355, Th1. 1275, M. I. 12^{4}, A. I. 134^{6}=*acchaitsīt* from root *chid*. In the same way, (*a*)*sakkhi* 'was able to' D. I. 96^{10}, Vin. I. 10^{6}, Milp. 5^{2} may be derived from an **aśākṣīt* from root *śak* (whence Sg. 1. (*a*)*sakkhiṃ* Th1. 88, Mhvs. 32. 43, Sg. 2. *asakkhi* DhCo. I. 16^{15}); *akkocchi* 'howled' Dh. 3, Jā. III. 212^{6} from an **akraukṣīt* from root *kruś*; *pāvekkhi* 'entered' Jā. III. 460^{2} from a **pra-avaikṣīt* from root *viś*. Old Aorist forms of the root *darś* 'to see' (*adrākṣam*, *-kṣīs*, *-kṣīt*, *-kṣus*) are quite numerous: Sg. 1. (*ad*)*dakkhiṃ* Sn. 939, Th1. 510, Th2. 147, Vv. 83. 14; 2. *addakkhi* Jā. III. 189^{23}, 3. *addakkhi* Sn. 208, Th1. 916, S. I. 117^{3} (verse), Vin. II. 195^{35}; Pl. 3. *addakkhuṃ*[4] D. II. 256^{6} (verse). The form *addā* 'saw' Th1. 986, 1244 is also very old. It is the Ved. *adrāk*. On the analogy of *adā*: *adaṃ* there was formed also here a Sg. 1. *addaṃ* Jā. III. 380^{6} (Comm. *addasaṃ*).

§ 165. 1. Double-forms such as *akā*: *akāsi*, *adā*: *adāsi* have given rise to remarkable new formations which are based on Type II, but are brought about by the transfer of forms of this type to the

[1] AMāg Sg. 3. *ahesi*.

[2] AMāg Sg. 2. *akāsi*.

[3] Also in S. IV. 205^{17}, 207^{13}, Iv. 47^{10} we have to read *acchecchi taṇhaṃ*.

[4] Cf. Pkr. AMāg. *addakkhu*; Pischel, § 516.

[5] Johansson, Monde Oriental 1907/3, p. 95 f. Aorists of the same construction occur also in AMāg.; Pischel, § 516.

mode of flexion characteristic of Type III[5]. Thus from *addasā* 'he saw' (§ 162. 3) there was formed an *addasāsi* Th2. 309, Jā. V. 158[16] (Comm. *addasa*), and also Sg. 1. *addasāsiṃ* Thl. 287, Jā. II. 256[23], Pl. 3. *addasāsuṃ* M. II. 98[7], Vin. II. 190[24] and *addasaṃsu* M. I. 79[5], Vin. I. 8[11]. Similarly *agamāsi* 'went' Thl. 490, JāCo. I. 113[12], II. 160[3], Mhvs. 4. 41 besides *agamā*; Pl. 3. *agamaṃsu* Vv. 80. 6, JāCo. I. 143[1], IV. 3[5], DhCo. I. 64[2]. In the same way Sg. 1. *ahuvāsi(ṃ)* Vv. 82. 6 beside *ahuvā* (§ 162. 2); Sg. 2. *avacāsi* 'you spoke' Vv. 35. 7, 53. 9 and Sg. 3. *avacāsi* Jā. VI. 525[14] beside *avacā*; Sg. 1. *pivāsiṃ* 'I drank' Ud. 42[14]; Sg. 3. *viramāsi* 'ceased' Th2. 397 etc.—2. The Type III has been greatly extended due to the fact that *e*-stems of various origins form their Aorists on the analogy of *ajesi*, *anesi* (§ 163 2) just as the *ā*-and *o*stems form their Aorists after *akāsi*, *assosi*. A few examples will suffice: Sg. 1. *sesiṃ* 'I lay' Jā. V. 70[14] (from *set*: § 140. 4), *vadesiṃ* 'I spoke' DhCo. III. 174[16] (§ 139. 2), *kathesiṃ* 'I related' JāCo. III. 369[17] (§ 139. 1), *cintesi (ṃ)* 'I thought' Jā. VI. 570[19], Cp. 1.8.1, *kāresiṃ* 'I had...made' JāCo. III. 11[21]; Sg. 2. *vadesi* DhCo. III. 173[21], *paccesi* M. I. 445[29] (from *eti* § 140. 3); Sg. 3. *pūjesi* 'he worshipped' JāCo. I. 422[31], *kathesi* Vin. I. 15[36], JāCo. II. 154[7], *pidhesi* 'covered' Mhvs. 24. 52 (stem *dhe*, § 142. 2, from root *dhā* with *pi*). *aggahesi* 'seized' JāCo. I. 52[25], *kāresi*, *kārāpesi* JāCo. I. 63[4], 143[11] etc., *saṃyāmesi* (§ 187. 1) JāCo. V. 417[17]; Pl. 3. *samesuṃ* 'they assembled' JāCo. II. 30[16], *pūjesuṃ* Dpvs. 16. 31, *kathesuṃ* JāCo. II. 250[16], *aggahesuṃ* Sn. 847, *kāresuṃ* JāCo. III. 1[10] etc. Forms of 1. and 2. Pl. are not attested. On Aor. IV. of uncontracted stems see § 168. 4.

Type IV.

§ 166. The Aorists of Type IV occur most frequently in canonical and non-canonical prose. Quite a number of forms may be regarded as historical. Thus from root *khād* 'to eat': Sg. 3. *khādi* Mhvs. 6. 21 = *akhādit*; from *grah* 'to seize': Sg. 1. *aggahiṃ* Thl. 97 = Ved. *agrabhīm*, 3. *aggahī* Jā. V. 91[4] = *ágrabhīt*.—Similarly from root *kram* 'to stride' (*ákramiṣam*, *ákramīt*), with facultative lengthening of the radical vowel as is found also in Skr. in the case of various roots with a medial *a*: Sg. 1. *pakkāmiṃ* Thl. 34, 3. *pakkāmi* Vin. I. 8[10], JāCo. II. 110[25] and *pakkami* Mhvs. 19. 56; Pl. 1. *upasaṃkamimha* S. IV. 97[8], 3. *pakkāmuṃ* Sn. 1010 and *pakkamiṃsu* JāCo. I. 150[15].—From root *tras* 'to fear': Sg. 2. *mā vitthāsi* Vin. I. 94[34]. Various compounds of the root *pad*: Sg. 1. *udapādiṃ* 'I was born' D. I. 13[23], 3. *udapādi* Jā. III. 29[5], D. I. 235[16]; Pl. 3. *āpādu* 'fell into...'

D. II. 273[20] (verse).—Of the roots in *ar* the forms in *ā* may be regarded as historical. Thus from root *car* 'to live, do, carry on' (Skr. *acāriṣam*): Sg. 1. *(a) cāri (ṃ)* Th1. 423, Th2. 79, 3. *acāri* Dh. 326, Sn. 354; Pl. 3. *acārisuṃ* Sn. 284. From root *tar* 'to cross': Sg. 3. *atāri* Sn. 355 (= Ved. *atārīt*); Pl 3. *atāru(ṃ)* Sn 1045. There are besides forms with *ă*, which probably have to be judged according to § 167: Sg. 1. *(a)cariṃ* Th2. 107, Jā. V. 10[16], 3. *acari* Sn. 344 and *atarī* Jā. III. 453[16], *otari* JāCo. II. 154[21]; Pl. 1. *vicarimha* Th2. 305, 3. *acariṃsu* Sn 809, *vicariṃsu* JāCo II. 96[27] and *atariṃsu*[1] Sn. 1046. Similarly from root *kar*: Sg. 1. *kariṃ* JāCo. III. 393[29] 2. *kari* Th2. 432, JāCo. II. 22[15], III. 276[13], 3. *akarī* D.II. 157[13] (verse); Pl. 2 *karittha* JāCo. I. 263[5], 492[23], DhCo. I. 64[21], 3. *kariṃsu* JāCo. II. 352[8].—I give here further a number of forms a part of which are historical: Sg. 1. *(a)labhiṃ* 'I attained' Th1. 218, Th2. 78, *udikkhisaṃ* 'I noticed' Th1. 268, *paccavekkhiṃ* 'I observed' Th1. 395 (cf. Skr. *aikṣiṣṭa*) *nandissaṃ* 'I was pleased' S. I. 176[12] (Skr. *anandīt*); *adassiṃ* 'I was' Cp. 1.2.2, *saṃdhāvissaṃ* 'I ran through' Th1. 78, *asevissaṃ* 'I visited' Jā. IV. 178[4] (Skr. *aseviṣṭa*); Sg. 2. *mā vadi* 'do not say!' JāCo. II. 133[11]; Sg. 3. *vedi* 'he knew' Dh. 419, 423 (=*avedit*), *vandi* 'he praised' Sn. 252, *vasī* 'he lived' Sn. 977, JāCo. II. 158[27], *pabbaji* 'he left the life of the laity' D. II. 29[30] (but Skr. *avrājīt*), *pāvassi* 'poured rain' Sn. 30 (Skr. *avarṣīt*); Pl. 1. *paṭikkosimha* 'we disputed' M. I. 85[8], *labhimhā* D. II. 147[18], *āvasimhā* Vv. 65. 4; Pl. 3. *khādiṃsu* 'they ate' JāCo. II. 129[25], *avattiṃsu* 'they existed' Sn. 298, *vaḍḍhiṃsu* 'they grew' (Skr. *avardhiṣṭa*) JāCo. II. 105[17], *paṭikkosiṃsu* M. I. 84[19] etc.—With the exception of Passives, Causatives and Denominatives (§ 168. 3, 4), the secondary stem—the Desideratives (§ 184) and the Intensives (§ 185)—form their Aorist after Type IV: Sg. 1. *abhisiṃsiṃ* Vv. 81. 18, *caṅkamiṃ* Th1. 272; Pl. 3. *sussūsiṃsu* Vin. I. 10[8].

§ 167. The type IV became very productive, and that due to the fact that Aorists of this Type could be derived from all present-stems with the exception of those in long vowels (§ 163, 165. 2) in every period of the language[2]. Examples: Thematic Conjugation: (1) Cl. 1. With reference to § 130. 4: *parilehisaṃ* 'I licked' Vv.

[1] It is quite clear that the variation between *acāriṃsu* and *acariṃsu* was partly determined by the word-rhythm.

[2] Aorists of other Types are often replaced by those of Type IV in the Commentaries: thus *akkocchi* DhCo. I 43[20] by *akkosi ahaṃsu* in Jā V 200[6] by *āhariṃsu akaṃha* in Jā. III. 47[4] by *karimha* etc.

81. 21, VvCo. 316[20]. With reference to § 131: The roots in *ī* form Aor. IV from the uncontracted stem (Aor. III from the contracted stem, § 165. 2): Sg. 3. *ānayi* Mhvs. 1. 30 (beside *ānesi*); Pl. 1. *ānayimha* JāCo. III. 127[15], 3. *ānayiṃsu* JāCo. IV. 138[3] (beside *ānesuṃ*). Also from root *bhū*: Pl. 3. *bhaviṃsu* DhCo. IV. 15[5] (Skr. *abhāviṣus*) beside the (possibly contracted) form *ahesuṃ*. With reference to § 132: Sg. 1. *nisīdiṃ* Th2. 44, *patiṭṭhahiṃ* Cp. 3. 7. 3; 3. *apivi* Mhvs. 6. 21. *nisīdi* Vin. I. 1[8], *uṭṭhahi* JāCo. III. 104[23], *adhiṭṭhahi* Th1. 1131; Pl. 3. *nisīdisuṃ* Mhvs. 7. 40 and *nisīdiṃsu* D. I. 118[28], *uṭṭhahiṃsu* JāCo. I. 202[21], DhCo. I. 20[1]. With reference to § 133 1: Sg. 1. *agacchisaṃ* Th1. 258, *adhigacchissaṃ* Sn. 446, *upāgacchiṃ* Th2. 69; 3. *āgacchi* Sn. 379, *samāgacchi* Vin. I. 96[15]; Pl. 2. *upagacchittha* Mhvs. 5. 101; 3. *upagacchiṃsu* Vin. I. 92[10]. There are besides, particularly in Ceylonese manuscripts, forms with *ñch* instead of *cch*[1]: Sg. 3. *āgañchi* Sn. 979, JāCo. III. 190[19], *upagañchi* Cp. 2. 6. 9, D. I. 1[19], II. 99[2]; Pl. 3. *upagañchuṃ* D. II. 99[1]. With reference to § 133. 3: Sg. 3. *āruhi* Mhvs. 35. 26; Pl. 3. *āruhuṃ* Mhvs. 11. 8.—(2) Cl. VI. With reference to § 134: Sg. 1. *pāvisiṃ* Th1. 60, *apucchiṃ* Cp. 2. 6. 5 and *apucchissaṃ* Sn. 1116; 2. *mā gilī* 'do not devour!' Dh. 371; 3. *phusi* S. I. 120[24], *(a)pucchi* Sn. 698, JāCo. II. 133[9], III. 401[7], *ākiri* Mhvs. 15. 25, *supi* Milp. 89[4]; Pl. 1. *apucchimhă* Sn. 875, M. II. 132[21]; 176[25]; 3. *pavisiṃsu* Mhvs. 18. 56, *pucchiṃsu* JāCo. I. 221[29] and *pucchisuṃ* Mhvs. 10. 2, *supiṃsu* Vin. II. 78[2]. Also Sg. 2. *abbuhi* 'you drew out' Th2. 52 (var. lec. DhCo. I. 30[17]: *abbahi*) from root *barh* (*bṛhati*) with *ā*. With reference to § 135. 1: Sg. 1. *icchiṃ* Jā. I. 267[20] and *icchisaṃ* S. I. 176[12] (verse), 3. *icchi* JāCo. I. 492[27], VI. 367[22]. With reference to § 135. 2: Sg. 1. *acchisaṃ* Th1. 487. With reference to § 135. 3: Sg. 1. *nibbind' ahaṃ* 'I felt aversion' Th2. 26 (from *vindati*); 3. *osiñci* Vv. 83. 8; Pl. 3. *muñciṃsu* JāCo. IV. 142[5], *abhisiñciṃsu* Mhvs. 11. 41.

§ 168. Thematic conjugation. (3) Cl. IV. With reference to § 136.1: Sg. 3. *nilīyi* 'sat down' JāCo. II. 208[8]; Pl. 3. *nilīyiṃsu* JāCo. II. 200[26], *allīyiṃsu* JāCo. I. 347[32]. Also Sg. 1. *amaññissaṃ* D. II. 352[13] M. III. 247[2]; 2. *āpajji* Jā. III. 83[4], *pamajji* Mhvs. 17. 15; 3. *kuppi* JāCo. I. 437[15], *nipajji* JāCo. I. 279[4], *vijjhi* JāCo. II. 18[16], *rucci* Vin. II. 188[32]; Pl. 1. *upapajjimha* Th2. 519; 3. *nacciṃsu* JāCo. I. 362[6] or *anaccuṃ* Th1. 164, *nipajjisuṃ* Mhvs. 7. 29 or *nipajjiṃsu* JāCo.

[1] Cf. Trenckner, Notes, p. 71 (JPTS. 1908. 123).

I. 61[20], *amaññisuṃ* Sn. 286. With reference to § 136. 3: Sg. 1. *apassi* Th2Co. 52[26]; 3. *passi* JāCo. II. 66[18]; Pl. 1. *passimha* JāCo. III. 278[7]; 3. *passiṃsu* JāCo. IV. 141[14]. With reference to § 136. 4 (Passives and Denominatives): Sg. 3. *chijji* 'ceased' JāCo. I. 329[27], with medial ending *bhijjittha* JāCo. I. 468[10], *ḍayhittha* JāCo. I. 215[18], *khīyi* JāCo. I. 489[18] and *khīyittha* Vin. I. 57[33], *sampūri* 'was filled' JāCo. IV. 458[20]; Pl. 3. *mucciṃsu* JāCo. II. 66[16], *haññiṃsu* D. I. 142[23] etc. Also Sg. 1. *namassi* Th2. 87; Pl. 3. *namassiṃsu* Sn. 287, Thl. 628. With reference to § 137: Sg. 3. *jīyittha* Jā. I. 468[2]. With reference to § 138: Sg. 1. *bhāyiṃ* DhCo. III. 187[3]; 2. *bhāyi* Thl. 764, JāCo. I. 222[26], DhCo. III. 187[2]; 3. *jāyi* JāCo. III. 391[20] and Med. *ajāyittha* Dpvs. 5. 16, *anupariyāyi* 'transformed' DhCo. III. 202[17], *vāyi* S. IV. 290[1], *parinibbāyi* D. II. 156[34], JāCo. II. 113[5], *samādiyi* JāCo. I. 219[14]; Pl. 2. *bhāyittha* Vin. II. 1[14], JāCo. I. 253[23]; 3. *jāyiṃsu* Mhvs. 28. 40 and *ajāyisuṃ* Mhvs. 4. 45; *gāyiṃsu* JāCo. I. 362[6]. In the same way: Sg. 2. *palāyi* JāCo. II. 26[19], 3. *palāyi* JāCo. III. 72[21], Med. *palāyittha* Vin. I 23[9], JāCo. III. 76[26]; Pl. 3. *palāyiṃsu* Mhvs. 24. 20 (cf. Skr. *apalāyiṣṭa*); Sg. 3. *dhūpāyi* (§ 136. 2.) JāCo. I. 347[20] etc.—(4) Cl. X. With reference to § 139: The verbs of Cl. X, the causatives and the *aya*-Denominatives form Aor. IV. from the uncontracted stem: Sg. 1. *kampayiṃ* 'I shook' Thl. 1164; *paññāpayiṃ* 'I set aright' Th2. 428; 2. *mā cintayi* 'do not think!' DhCo. I. 16[19]; 3. *pakāsayi* 'proclaimed' Sn. 251, *adesayi* 'taught 'Sn. 233; *pūjayi* 'worshipped' Milp. 222[14]; Med. *amohayittha* 'was befooled' Sn. 332. *arocayittha* 'was p'easing' Sn. 252; Pl. 1. *pāpayimha* 'we had ... attained' DhCo. III. 39[22]; 2. *mā vaḍḍhayittha* 'do not increase!' DhCo. I. 93[4], *mā dassayittha* 'do not show!' DhCo. III. 201[7]; 3. *pātayiṃsu* 'they felled' Thl. 252, *akappayiṃsu* 'they performed' Sn. 458 and *akappayuṃ* Sn. 295, *parivārayiṃsu* 'they surrounded' JāCo. II. 253[13], *kathayiṃsu* 'they related' JāCo. II. 216[26] etc. On Aor. III. from the contracted stem, see § 165. 2. In verses the choice between forms after one type or the other is often determined by the metre.

§ 169. Athematic Conjugation. (1) Cl. II. With reference to § 140. 1: Sg.3. *hani* Mhvs. 25. 42, *ravi* JāCo. II. 110[9], III. 102[23], *aravi* Mhvs. 32. 79 and the historical form *arāvi* Mhvs. 10. 69; Pl. 3. *haniṃsu* Sn. 295, Vin. I. 88[30], *raviṃsu* JāCo. I. 202[28]; from root *i* + *sam* (*sameti*) Pl. 3. *samiṃsu* S. II. 154[25–27]. With reference to § 140. 4: Sg. 3. *asayittha* A. I. 136[28] from *sayati* (besides *settha* Sn. 970 from *seti*).—2. Cl. III. With reference to § 142: Sg. 1. *pajahiṃ* M. III. 160[30], *juhiṃ* Thl 341; 3. *vijahi* JāCo. I. 489[29], *saddahi* JāCo. II. 38[6], Med. *saddahittha* DhCo. I. 117[24]; Pl. 3. *jahiṃsu* JāCo. III. 19[23] and *jahuṃ*[1] Jā. III. 19[23], *pidahiṃsu* Mhvs. 31. 119, *paṭijaggiṃsu* JāCo. III. 127[5]. With reference to § 143: Pl. 2. *dadittha* JāCo. III. 171[3].—3. Cl. VII. With reference to § 144: Sg. 1. *bhuñjiṃ* Milp. 47[23], *anuyuñjisaṃ* Thl. 157; 3. *acchindi* Mhvs. 5. 240, (*a*)*bhindi* A.IV. 312[3] (verse). JāCo. I. 467[15], *rundhi* JāCo.I. 409[20]; Pl. 1. *pajahimhā* M. I. 448[15]; 2. *anuyuñjittha* Thl. 414; 3. *acchindiṃsu* Vin. I. 88[29], *bhindiṃsu* Dpvs. 7. 54, *abhuñjiṃsu* Thl. 922 and *abhuñjisuṃ* Mhvs. 7. 25.—4. Cl. IX and V. With reference to § 145: Sg. 1. *paṭijāniṃ* DhCo. I. 21[2], *abhijānissaṃ* Thl. 915; 3. *ajāni* Sn. 536, *saṃjāni* DCo. I. 261[29] (cf. *ajini* 'conquered' Jā. III. 212[8]); Pl. 3. *jāniṃsu* JāCo. II. 105[4] (cf. *kiṇiṃsu* Sn. 290). With reference to § 146: Sg. 2. *gaṇhi* JāCo. VI. 337[12]; 3 *gaṇhi* JāCo. VI. 337[10]; Pl. 2. *gaṇhittha* JāCo. I. 254[4]. III. 127[14]; 3. *gaṇhiṃsu* JāCo. III. 127[13]. From *bandhati*: Sg. 1. *anubandhiṃ* Sn. 446 and *anubandhissaṃ* Jā. VI. 508[30]. With reference to § 147. 1, 2: Sg.3. *pahiṇi* JāCo. I. 290[25]; Pl. 3. *pahiṇiṃsu* JāCo. II. 21[11], *vinicchiniṃsu* JāCo. II. 2[9]. With reference to § 148: Sg. 1. *pāpuṇiṃ* Thl. 865, JāCo. I. 167[11]; 3. *sakkuṇi* Mhvs. 7. 14, *pāpuṇi* JāCo. I. 151[3]; Pl. 3. *pāpuṇiṃsu* JāCo. II. 111[23]. With reference to § 149: Pl. 3. *anutthuniṃsu* D. III. 86[22], 88[6].

§ 170. It remains still to discuss a few isolated forms which may be interpreted in different ways. Thus we have in Th2Co. 85[26] (verse from Apadāna) the form *dakkhisaṃ* 'I saw'. As *dakkh-* =*drākṣ-* is already itself a stem of Type III (cf. § 164), the transfer to the flexional mode of Type IV is effected by means of the ending *-isaṃ*. Probably the parallel forms in *-isaṃ* and *-iṃ* of Type IV have led to the new formation' out of *adakkhiṃ*. Similarly (*a*)*sakkhissaṃ* 'I was able to' M. III. 179[28], A. I. 139[10,28], Pl. 1. *sakkhimha* D. II. 155[2], 3. *sakkhiṃsu* Mhvs. 8. 23 and *sakkhisuṃ* Mhvs. 23. 11. Of course it may also be assumed that the future-stem of the roots *darś* and *śak* provided the basis to these new formations. *Dakkhati* and *sakkhati* were no longer felt to futures, but as presents (cf. § 136. 3), which now formed their Aorist after Type IV. An Aorist stem of Type III is however doubtless the basis of the form

[1] Wackernagel, GN. 1906. 157 considers it to be a Pl. 3. Prf.=Skr. *jahus*, which is, of course, formally possible.

adāsimhā 'we gave' Th2. 518 (Comm. 295[17]=*adamhā*), as well as of the form *ahesumha* 'we existed' M.I. 265[1-4]. I am therefore inclined to consider all the forms referred to as 'double constructions' in which both the Types III and IV have crossed each other. This hypothesis seems to be more probable to me than the assumption that these are forms of the *iṣ*-Aorist of Skr. Also *pamādassaṃ* 'I was unexerting' M. III. 179[29], A. I. 139[1'28] is probably nothing but an elaboration of **pamādaṃ* (Type II, § 161) after Type IV, which might have been facilitated by the form *sakkhissaṃ* which immediately precedes it.

5. Perfect

§ 171. With the exception of a few petrified forms, the Perfect has been almost completely eliminated from the Pāli language. Forms like *bubodha susoca*[1] (but cf. also *jagāma* Jā. 203[2]) as they are found, for instance, in the artificial poetry, are merely learned reminiscences. To set forth a paradigm for the Perfect, as is done by the Grammarians, is therefore unnecessary. The last vestiges of the perfect are: *āha* 'he has said' (=*āha*) Sn. 790, Vin. I. 40[28] (verse). M. I. 14[15], JāCo. I. 121[3] and its Plural *āhu* (=*āhus*) Th1. 188. Dh. 345. JāCo. I. 59[31], Mhvs. 1. 27, to which was added the new formation *āhaṃsu* (after *adaṃsu*) JāCo. I. 121[12], 222[14] etc. Finally, we have also *vidū* or *viduṃ* 'they know' (=*vidus*) Sn. 758, Th1. 497, Mhvs. 23. 78. The Sg. corresponding to it is the form *vedi* (§ 166), which is very probably=Skr. *avedit*.

6. Periphrastic Constructions

172. Traces of the use of the periphrastic future, as in Skr., are present in Pāli. Thus *āyantāro punabbhavaṃ* (the copula has to be supplied) Sn. 754. Cf. M. II. 130[16]. A periphrastic Optative is to be found in... *iti ce, bhikkhave, pucchitāro assu* 'if, you monks, would ask this' Sn. p. 135; cf. also *bhavanti vattāro* 'it will be said' M. I. 469[14] and *bhavanti upasaṃkamitāro* 'they will come along' M. III. 111[9]. I mention here further *tassa kumbhe patitāmi* 'I will throw myself on his head' JāCo. III. 113[24], where we

[1] Cf. Childers, PD. under the word *bujjhati*; E. Müller, PGr. p 117, On the paradigm cf. Minayeff, PGr. § 182, p. 65; E. Kuhn, Beitr. p. 114. On *jahuṃ* cf. § 169. 2 with foot note.

have either to read *patitā 'mhi* or to accept analogical contamination by the flexion of the simple future (*patissāmi*).[1]

§ 173. A periphrastic Perfect arose out of the combination of the Preterital Participle with the copula[2]. In the third Person the copula *atthi* is always omitted, and *hoti* is often so. Examples are numerous in every period of the language.—1. For Intransitive verbs we have thus: Sg. 1. *pabbajito 'mhi* 'I have retired from worldly life' Thl. 72; *otiṇṇo 'mhi* 'I have dismounted' M. I. 192[6]; *sītibhūto 'smi* 'I have been forsaken' Thl. 79, fem. *sītibhūt' amhi* (=-*tā 'mhi*) Th2. 15; *āgato 'mhi* 'I have come' JāCo. II. 20[13]; Sg. 2. *ṭhito 'si* 'you are standing' JāCo. III. 53[12], fem. *sītibhūtāsi* Th2. 16, *gatāsi* 'you are gone' JāCo. II. 416[8]; Sg. 3. *uppannaṃ* (*hoti*) 'is originated' M. I. 130[5'10]; *nahāto* 'has bathed' JāCo. I. 184[29]. Pl. 1. *vutth' amha* (=*vutthā amha*) 'we have lived' JāCo. IV. 243[11], *sītibhūta' amha* (fem.) Th2. 66, *āgat' amhāse* D. II. 275[11] (verse); Pl. 2. *āgat' attha* JāCo. I. 20[11], *jāt' attha* 'you have become' DhCo. III. 59[4]; Pl. 3. *āgatā* Mhvs. 14. 12.—2. In the case of transitive verbs the Periphrastic Perfect has naturally a passive meaning: Sg. 1. fem. *mutt' amhi* (=*muttā amhi*) 'I am released' Th2. 11; *vañcit' ammi* (sic ! =*vañcitā amhi* fem.) 'I am betrayed' JāCo. I. 287[26]; *nimantit' amha, nimantit' attha* 'we, you, have been invited' Vin. III. 10[37], 11[3]. The agent is in Instr. or also in Gen.-Dat.[3], as, for instance, in *Mahākaccāno Satthu c' eva saṃvaṇṇito sambhāvito* 'M. has been praised and honoured by the Master himself' M. III. 194[2], S. IV. 93[21], or *patto me āsavakkhayo* 'I have achieved the conquest of carnal weaknesses'[4] Thl. 116. In the case of certain transitive verbs the Periphrastic Perfect however sometimes assumes an active meaning: *patto 'si nibbāṇaṃ* 'you have attained Nirvāṇa' Dh. 134. Cf. Vv. 53. 20, Mhvs. 4. 65 etc.—3. Also other tenses and moods may be expressed by the combination of the Past Participle with the auxiliary verb. Thus we have a Pluperfect Potential in *patto abhavissaṃ* 'I would have attained' JāCo. I. 470[15], or an Exact Future in *gato bhavissati* 'he will be gone' JāCo. II. 214[4] etc.

§ 174. Periphrastic constructions are further resorted to when continuous action, whether of the past or the present, has to be

[1] Cf. also the form *vañcitammi* in § 173 2.

[2] Exclusively these forms are used in Pkr. to express past tense, excepting in AMāg.; Pischel, § 519.

[3] Cf. R. O. Franke, BB. 16. 111.

[4] According to R. O. Franke, D., p. 83. note 1.

expressed. Formally they are combinations of Participle Present or Gerund with the Copula or Verbs with an indefinite meaning[1]. We have thus 1. Part. Pres. with Copula; e.g. *sayāno 'mhi* 'I am lying' M. I. 57[1] (as also immediately preceding *ṭhito 'mhi, nisinno 'mhi*). —2. Part. Pres. with *tiṭṭhati*. Thus *te aññam-aññaṃ patvā sarīrāni lehentā aṭṭhaṃsu* 'they were licking each others' body' JāCo. II. 31[18], in which however the original meaning 'they stood there licking......' can still be distinctly felt. Likewise in DhCo. III. 93[2].—3. Gerund with *tiṭṭhati*. Thus *mūlam-pi tesaṃ palikhañña tiṭṭhe* 'attempt should be made to pull out even their roots' Sn. 968; *mahantaṃ phaṇaṃ karitvā aṭṭhāsi* 'he formed an enormous hood' Vin. I. 3[18-19]; *hatthilaṇḍaṃ..... ekasmiṃ gumbe laggitvā aṭṭhāsi* 'remained hanging from a bush'. Cf. S. IV. 60[15], Th1 98, M. I. 247[21] etc.—4. Part. Pres. with *carati* or *vicarati*. Thus *nāññesaṃ pihayaṃ care* 'one should not be jealous of others' Dh. 365; *Bodhisatto ekaṃ upamaṃ upadhārento vicarati* 'B. was busy thinking out a simile' JāCo. III. 102[16]. Cf. D. I. 26[24], JāCo. III. 16[9]; D. II. 287[7] (verse), JāCo. I. 503[5] etc.—5. Gerund with *viharati*. Thus *paṭhamajjhānaṃ upsampajja viharati* 'he has attained the first stage of the trance (and is continuing to be in that stage)' D.I. 37[3]. Cf. M. I. 33[26], Sn. p. 15 etc.—6. Gerund with *vattati*. Thus *Gotamo ime dhamme anavasesaṃ samādāya vattati* 'G. is observing these rules to the letter' D.I. 164[5]. Cf. D.I. 230[14] etc.—7. Gerund with *voharati*. Thus *so tad-eva abhinivissa voharati* 'he is holding on to it firmly' M. III. 210[28-29]. Cf. M. I. 410[18].

7. Passive

§ 175. The Passive may be formed in two ways: by means of *ya*, or by means of *īya*[2]. The Passive formed with *ya* formally coincides with the Present-class IV (§ 136. 4). The *ya* is retained unchanged after vowels; it is assimilated to the final consonant of a root according to the respective phonetic laws. 1. Roots in vowels: Roots in *ā*: *ñāyati* 'becomes known' Milp. 25[8]; *paññāyati* D. I. 93[3], JāCo. I. 435[5] = *prajñāyate*; the roots *dā* and *dhā* have *dīyati* (*diyyati*) Th2. 467, D. I. 144[25] and *dhīyati* (*dhiyyati*) D. I. 73[23], M. I. 37[33],

[1] Many of these constructions are reminiscent of the similar usage in Singhalese. Cf. Geiger, LSprS. § 67. Thus, for instance, *kiṃ pana te imaṃ dhanaṃ gahetvā va na gamiṃsu* 'why have they not taken their money with them (in death)?' DhCo. III. 87[15]. Sgh. *gen-enu, gena-yanu*.

[2] Both the constructions are known also in Pkr. Pischel, § 535.

Milp. 289[7] = *dīyate*, *dhīyate*. In *ādiyati* (*samād-*, *upād-*) 'takes unto himself' (§ 136. 4) the passive has a medial meaning. Cf. Skr. *ādatte*, as well as § 176. 1. The root *hā* has besides *hīyati* (*hiyyati*) 'decreases' Th1. 114 (*nihīyati* Th1. 555, *pahiyyati* S. IV. 31[3]) = *hīyate* also *hāyati* Jā. I. 181[20], DhCo. I. 11[10] (verse), D. II. 208[10], JāCo. I. 279[9]. From the root *śyā* 'to congeal' we have *sīyati* Th1. 312, Vv. 335[21] = *śīyate*. Roots in *ī*. *ū*: *jīyati* (*jiyyati*) 'is defeated' Dh. 179, Jā. II. 75[22], M. III. 170[8] = *jīyate*; *parājīyati* 'goes under' JāCo. I. 290[20]; *nīyati* (*niyyati*) 'is led' Sn. 580, M.I. 371[7] = *nīyate*; *parikkhīyanti* 'they are being annihilated' Th2. 347 = *kṣīyate*. Root *bhū*: *anubhuyyati* 'is enjoyed' VvCo. 181[20]; root *śru* 'to hear': *sūyati* (*suyyati*) Jā. IV. 141[20], VI. 528[30], M. I. 30[19], JāCo. I. 72[1], Milp. 152[12].—2. Roots in *r*: root *kar* 'to do': *kayirati* (§ 47. 2) Dh. 292, S. I. 180[3] (verse), Vin. II. 289[17] = **karyate*; root *par* 'to fill': *pūrati*[1] Dh. 121 f., Jā. I. 498[22], JāCo.I. 460[27] = *pūryate*; cf. moreover forms of root *har*: *parihīrati* 'is avoided' Th1. 453, Sn. 205, *saṃhīrati* 'is fettered' M. III. 188[28], 189[7], and also of root *bhar*: *anubhīrati*[2] 'is carried to' M. III. 123[20].—3. Roots in consonants: *vuccati* 'is spoken' Dh. 63, D. I. 168[2] = *ucyate*; *paccati* 'is cooked' = *pacyate*; *lujjati* 'falls to pieces' (§ 44) = *rujyate*; *kacchati* 'is related' M. II. 253[21] = *kathyate*; *vijjati* 'exists' Th1. 132, Sn. 21, D. I. 18[24] = *vidyate*; *bajjhati* 'is bound' Th1. 137, JāCo. I. 428[17] = *badhyate*; *bhaññati* 'is spoken' Vin. I. 11[33], JāCo. I. 444[13] = *bhaṇyate*; *haññati* 'is killed' = *hanyate*; *patāyanti* (root *tan*) 'they arise out of......' D. III. 201[17] (verse), Jā. III. 283[16] = *pratāyante*[3]; *vuppati* 'is sown' Th1. 530 = *upyate*; *dissati* 'is seen' Th1. 44, Vin. I. 16[12] = *dṛśyate*; *kassate* 'is ploughed' Th1. 530 = *kṛṣyate*; *gayhati* 'is seized' (§ 49) Vin. I. 88[35] = *gṛhyate*; *ḍayhati* 'is burnt' Sn. 63, Vin. I. 109[24], M. III. 184[11] (*viḷayhase* Jā. II. 220[12]) = *dahyate*; *vuyhati* 'is carried away' Th1. 88, Vin. I. 106[31] (*nibbuyhati* 'saves himself' Th2. 468) = *uhyate*.

§ 176. The construction with *īya* is found very frequently 1. in Causative (and analogous) stems[4]. Thus *bhājiyati* 'is divided' Ud.

[1] Cf. § 52. 5. Also Pkr. Māh. *pūrai*.

[2] I believe that *hriyate*, *bhriyate* at first became **hiryate*, **bhiryate* through metathesis, and then *hīrati*, *bhīrati* like *pūrati*. In the same way is formed also *kīrati* 'is treated' Th1. 143 from root *kar*.

[3] E. Müller, PGr. p. 121. Not so O. Franke. WZKM. 8. 323.

[4] The corresponding forms in Pkr. are Māh. *kārijjai*, *cheijjanti* etc. Pischel, § 543.

48[24] from *bhājeti* (root *bhaj*)=*bhājyate*; *paricāriyati* 'is served' Vin. I. 15[4], D. II. 325[9] from *paricāreti*; *dassiyati* 'is shown' D. II. 124[10] from *dasseti*=*darśyate*; *addiyati* 'is pained' Th2. 140=*ardyate*; *paññāpiyati* 'is elucidated' DhsCo. 113[14] from *paññāpeti* (root *jñā*); *vesiyati* 'is introduced' M. I. 88[25] from *veseti*; *sodhīyati* 'is purified' Bu. 2. 40 from *sodheti*=*śodhyate*; *posiyati* 'is nourished' Jā. III. 289[7], JāCo. I. 492[12] from *poseti*. Similarly *sāriyati* 'is reminded', *māriyati* 'is killed', *codiyati* 'is impelled' etc. Also *pūjiyati* 'is worshipped' Mhvs. 17. 17 from *pūjeti* of Cl. X. Sometimes the causative meaning cannot be traced in such Passives. Thus *vediyati* 'is made to experience, feels' M. I. 59[12], A. I. 141[6] from *vedeti* (root *vid*); *vādiyati* 'is made to speak, speaks' Sn. 824, 832. The Passive has medial meaning in *sādiyati* 'enjoys for himself, takes pleasure in' Vin. II. 294[20], III. 29[18], D. I. 166[4] from **sādeti* (=Skr. *svādayati*) from root *svad*[1].—2. Passives may be constructed with *īya* also from various Present-stems[2]. Firstly, in the case of a number of verbs of which the Present-stem is the same as the root. Thus *yācīyati* 'is asked for' MLvs. 7. 14 from root *yāc*; *pucchīyati* 'is asked' DhCo. I. 10[10] from the weak-grade root *pṛch*; *samanugāhiyamāna* 'interrogated regarding motives' A. V. 156[5] from root *gāh* etc. In the words quoted above the Pāli form is distinguished from the Skr.-form only by the Svarabhakti; cf. Skr. *yācyate*, *pṛcchyate*, *gāhyate*. But we have also *harīyati* 'is carried away' M. III. 148[14] from *harati*, as against Skr. *hriyate*=*hīrati*; *yuñjiyati* in *samanuyuñjiyamāna* 'exorted, interrogated' A. V. 156[5] from *yuñjati* (§ 144)—3. We have a "double-construction" in which a new Pass. in *iya* is derived from a Passive-st. formed according to § 175. 3 in *parichijjiyamāna* 'clearly marked off' DhCo. I. 22[1], 35[15] from *chijjati*=*chidyate*. Similar double-construction also in *an-upalabbhiyamāna* from *upa-labhati* =*upa-labhyate* S. III. 112[6], A. I. 174[11].

§ 177. The flexion of the Passive is like that of a verb of Cl. IV. For the Present-system cf. § 136. 4, for the Future § 155. 3, for the Aorist[3] § 168. 3. The Sg. 3. Aor. Pass. in *i* derived from the strong-grade form of the root has been retained in a few isolated forms:

[1] In Sn. 281 I am inclined to read *abhinibbajjiyātha* 'avoid!' from root *varj*, *varjayati* and explain the Passive form in the same way. If we read *abhinibbijjiyātha* (root *vid*) then it would be a case of "double-construction."

[2] These forms are more frequent in Pkr. than in Pāli. Cf. Pischel, § 536 ff.

[3] An Aor. from the Passive-stem is found only in AMāg. in Pkr. a Future however almost in all the dialects. Pischel, § 549.

abhedi 'was destroyed' and *nirodhi* Ud. 93[12] (verse) = *abhedi, arodhi*; *samatāni* 'stretched itself out' D. III. 85[11] = *atāni*.

8. Causative

§ 178. Many Causatives in Pāli are historical continuations of corresponding constructions in Skr. The formans *aya* may be contracted to *e*[1]. 1. Unmodified roots: *pāpeti* 'makes attain' JāCo. I. 223[14], II. 11[8] (root *āp* with *pra*) = *prāpayati*; *saṃsandeti* 'joins together' JāCo. I. 403[19] = *syandayati*. Similarly with roots with medial *r* and *l*: *dasseti* 'shows' Thl. 86, Dh. 83, JāCo. III. 276[4] = *darśayati*; *kappeti* 'performs' Sn. 295, JāCo. I. 140[26] = *kalpayati*. Cf. *chaḍḍeti* = *chardayati*; *vatteti* = *vartayati*; *vaḍḍheti* = *vardhayati*; *vissajjeti* = *visarjayati*; *haṃseti* = *harṣayati*.—2. Roots with medial *a* before a single consonant: (*a*) the *a* is lengthened as in Skr. Thus *vādeti* 'makes speak, plays (musical instrument)' Sn. 1010, Jā. I. 293[23], JāCo. II. 110[7] = *vādayati*; *ubbāheti* 'heaves up' D. II. 347[17] = *udvāhayati*; *hāseti* 'makes laugh' Vin. III. 84[21] = *hāsayati*. Similarly *gāheti* = *grāhayati*; *tāpeti* = *tāpayati*; *pāteti* = *pātayati* -*pādeti* = -*pādayati*; -*yādeti* (§ 38.3) = -*yātayati*; *vāseti* = *vāsayati*; *sādeti* = *sādayati*; *sāmeti* = *śāmayati*. For **lābheti* as against *lambhayati* we have *labbheti* 'lets attain' Vin. IV. 5[38] (verse) = JāCo. I. 193[10], DhCo. III. 213[10]. From roots with final *r*: *kāreti* 'causes to do' Jā. III. 394[7], JāCo. I. 107[21] etc. = *kārayati*; *pūreti* 'fills' Sn. 30, 305, JāCo. II. 1[19] etc. = *pūrayati*. Similarly *tāreti* = *tārayati*; -*thāreti* = -*stārayati*; *dhāreti* = *dhārayati*; *māreti* = *mārayati*; *vāreti* 'holds back' and 'chooses' = *vārayati*; *sāreti* = *sārayati*; *sāreti* = *smārayati*.—(b) The *a* remains short as also in Skr. in *gameti* 'makes go' M. III. 166[21], A. I. 141[3] (*āgameti* 'waits' Vin. I. 78[6], JāCo. II. 21[14]) = *gamayati*. Similarly *janeti* = *janayati*, *dameti* = *damayati*; *yameti* Dh. 37, 380 = *yamayati*; *bhameti* Mhvs. 23. 80 = *bhrămayati*.—(c) The quantity varies: *jăleti* 'kindles' (*ă* Milp. 47[2], *ā* JāCo. II. 44[1], 104[27]) = *jvălayati*; *namayanti* 'they bend' Dh. 80, Thl. 19, but *panāmeti* 'sends away, stretches out' Jā. II. 28[12], Vin. I. 5[23], II. 303[13] etc., (in Skr. only *namayati*); *nikkhămeti* 'lets go out' (*ă* JāCo. II. 112[12], *ā* Vin. I. 187[35], 188[1'5], JāCo. III. 99[10]) = *kramayati*, *niṣkrāmayati*.

§ 179. Causative stems 3. of roots with non-final *i, u*: *chedeti* 'causes to be cut off' Jā. III. 179[17], Mhvs. 21.18 = *chedayati* (root *chid*); *deseti* 'shows, teaches' Sn. 722, Vin. I. 5[4], D. I. 195[31], JāCo. II. 12[24] =

[1] For the sake of brevity I give in the following always the form in *e*.

deśayati (root *diś*); *paveseti* 'lets enter, introduces' Vin. III, 29[2], M. III. 169[16], JāCo. I. 419[23] = *praveśayati*; *codeti* 'pushes forward' Dh. 879, Vin. I. 114[16], A. V. 79[9] = *codayati* (root *cud*); *sodheti* 'purifies' Dh. 141, M. I. 39[18] (verse), Vin. I. 47[32], JāCo. I. 291[1] = *śodhayati*. Similarly *peseti* = *preṣayati* (root *iṣ* with *pra*); *ceteti* Vv. 84. 40, D.I. 184[15], Vin. III. 19[38] = *cetayati* (root *cit*); *vedeti* = *vedayati*; *sineheti* 'makes tender' Milp. 172[6] = *snehayati*; *poseti* = *poṣayati*; *āroceti* = *ārocayati*; *bhojeti* = *bhojayati*; *yojeti* = *yojayati*; *palobheti* = *pralobhayati*; *soceti* = *śocayati*.—4. From roots with final ī, ū: *bhāyayate* 'frightens' Jā. III. 99[14] = *bhāyayati* (root *bhī*); *cāveti* 'drives forth' Sn. 442, Vin. I. 120[32] = *cyāvayati* (root *cyu*); *bhāveti* 'brings about' Thl. 83, 166, Jā. II. 22[25], D. II. 79[14], JāCo. I. 415[5] = *bhāvayati*; *sāveti* 'lets hear, proclaims' Jā. III. 437[13], Vin. I. 36[6], JāCo. I. 344[14], Mhvs. 5. 238 = *śrāvayati*. Also *nāyeti* = *nāyayati* from root *nī*[1], as well as *opilāpeti* (§ 39.6) = *plāvayati* and *hāpeti* (ibid.) = *hāvayati* from roots *plu*. *hu*.—5. Miscellaneous: In agreement with Skr. the root *duṣ* (*dussati* 'is defiled' Vin. I. 188[17]) forms the Causative *dūseti* 'defiles, insults' Jā. I. 454[16], Vin. I. 85[17], JāCo. I. 358[28] = *dūṣayati*; *padoseti* Sn. 659, S. IV. 70[32] (verse), M. I. 186[13] (in the parallel passage M. I. 129[16] *-dūs-*); from *han* we have *ghāteti* 'causes to be killed' Sn. 629, Dh. 129, S. I. 116[19], JāCo. I. 255[5], Mhvs. 6. 41 = *ghātayati*; from root *prī*: *pīṇeti* 'pleases' D. I. 51[15], Mhvs. 36. 77, Rasav. II. 96[20] = *prīṇayati*. The Causative is based on the Pres.-stem in *nacceti* 'causes to dance' D. I. 135[27], DhCo. III. 231[14] from *naccati* (§ 136); *laggeti* 'hangs up' JāCo. III. 107[14], DhCo. I. 138[2] from *laggati* (ibid.).

§ 180. As in Skr., the roots in *ā* take the formantic element *paya*, *pe*. And as in Skr. some roots may shorten the *ā*, the vowel in some cases is of variable quantity—even in those roots which are never shortened in Skr.[2] 1. Examples: *dāpeti* 'causes to give' Vin. I. 55[37], JāCo. IV. 138[1] = *dāpayati*, but *samādăpeti* 'causes to take, exhorts'; *nidhāpeti* 'causes to lay down' Mhvs. 20. 12, *niddhāpeti* 'turns out' Jā. IV. 41[26] = *-dhāpayati*; *vijjhāpeti* 'extinguishes' Vin. I. 31[26] (root *kṣā* § 56. 2); *ñāpeti* 'causes to know, informs' Vin. I. 56[10], JāCo. II. 133[26], *paññăpeti* 'explains, designates', *āṇāpeti* 'orders' (§ 63. 2) etc. = *jñăpayati*; *māpeti* 'causes to measure', *nimmāpeti* 'causes to build' = *māpayati*; *yāpeti* 'passes (time), lives on......' Jā. VI. 532[15], D. I. 166[12], JāCo. III, 67[21] = *yāpayati*; *nibbāpeti* 'extinguishes' D. II.

[1] In Minayeff, PGr. § 208.

[2] Also in Pkr., *e.g.*, *ṭhăvei*; Pischel, § 551.

164[17], JāCo. I. 472[10]=*nirvāpayati*; *ṭhăpeti* 'establishes' (*ā*) Dh. 40, Thl. 38, D. I. 120[33], JāCo. I. 223[21], (*ā*) Sn. 112, A. II. 46[13] (verse) with numerous compounds=*sthāpayati*; *nahāpeti* 'bathes (trans.)' D. I. 93[6], II. 19[35], JāCo. I. 166[20]=*snăpayati*; *hāpeti* 'causes to leave, releases' (JPTS. 1906-7, p. 163)=*hāpayati*[1].—2. The course of this type was taken also by some other roots, as also in Skr. Thus *ropeti* 'plants' Sn. 208, Vin. II. 2[22], JāCo. II. 87[5], *āropeti* 'causes to climb up', (*v*) *oropeti* 'robs'=*ropayati* (besides *rohayati*) from root *ruh*; *ussāpeti* 'raises up' (§ 58. 3)=*ucchrāpayati* from root *śri* with *ud*; *jāpeti* 'causes to conquer' S. I. 116[19], M. I. 231[2'3]=*jāpayati* from root *ji*. Peculiar to Pāli is the form *ānāpeti*[2] 'causes to be brought' Vin. I. 116[37], JāCo. III. 391[24], Mhvs. 9. 25 from root *nī* with *ā*.—3. From root *pā* we have *pāyeti* 'gives to drink' Vin. II. 289[30], D. II. 19[24], JāCo. III. 98[1], VI. 336[35] (Skr. *pāyayati*).

§ 181. Numerous new forms were constructed after the Causatives of roots in *ā*. The formantic elements *āpaya*, *āpe* serve 1. to form causatives out of all Present-stems, and 2. to form new double-causatives out of older causatives. These new formations are not yet current in the Gāthā-language, but are met with already in the canonical prose and are unusually numerous later. 1. Causatives from Present-stems[3]. With reference to § 130: *vasāpeti* JāCo. I. 290[12], II. 27[16]; *paccāpeti* JāCo. II. 15[24]; *khamāpeti* 'excuses' Vin. I. 54[13], JāCo. II. 29[23], Mhvs. 4. 40; *sandāpeti* Milp. 122[2]; *harāpeti* JāCo. II. 38[6], 106[14]; *uddharāpeti* 'causes to bring out' Vin. IV. 39[17]; *sarāpeti* 'causes to remember' Vin. III. 44[6]. With reference to §132: *nisīdāpeti* JāCo. III. 392[7], VI. 367[17]. With reference to § 133: *ḍasāpeti* JāCo. II. 31[1]. With reference to § 134: *khipāpeti* JāCo. II. 36[21], Mhvs. 20. 35; *pucchāpeti* Mhvs. 10. 75; *okirāpeti* Smp. 339[3], Mhvs. 34. 44. With reference to § 135: *icchāpeti* (Childers, PD. sub voce); *muñcāpeti* D. I. 148[3]; *vilimpāpeti* JāCo. I. 254[7]; *siñcāpeti* JāCo. II. 20[3], 104[24]. With reference to § 136: *nipajjāpeti* JāCo. I. 492[30], II. 21[26], Mhvs. 9. 25; *bujjhāpeti* 'leads to true knowledge' JāCo. I. 407[13]; *vijjhāpeti* 'causes to be bored through' Mhvs. 25. 70. The form *chejjapessāmi* Milp. 90[11], which is however doubtful, would seem to

[1] On *hāpeti*=*hāvayati* see § 179. 4.

[2] Often wrongly written with *ṇ* through the attraction of *āṇāpeti* 'orders'.

[3] See Pischel, § 552, for the corresponding forms in Pkr.

be derived from a Passive-stem. The form expected is *chijjāpessāmi*[1]. With reference to § 187: *jīrāpeti* 'digests' JāCo. I. 419^{29}. With reference to § 138: *gāyāpeti* DhCo. III. 231^{14}, *dāyāpeti* 'causes (crops) to be mowed' DhCo. III. 285^{1} from root *dā* (*dyati*); *palāpeti* 'chases away' JāCo. II. 69^{22}, DhCo. III. 97^{1}.—With reference to § 140: *hanāpeti* JāCo. I. 262^{28}; *sayāpeti* 'lays down' JāCo. I. 245^{13}, V. 461^{11}, Mhvs. 31. 55. With reference to § 142. 2: *nidahāpeti* 'causes to lay down' JāCo. II. 38^{3}, *saddahāpeti* JāCo. I. 294^{16}, VI. 575^{5}. With reference to § 144: *chindāpeti* JāCo. I. 438^{16}, II. 104^{3}, III. 179^{14}; *bhindāpeti* JāCo. I. 290^{22}; *hiṃsāpeti* PvCo. 123^{16}. With reference to § 145: *jānāpeti* JāCo. I. 452^{20}, II. 21^{7}. With reference to § 146: *gaṇhāpeti* JāCo. I. 264^{6}, II. 105^{13}. With reference to § 147: *suṇāpeti* DhCo. I. 206^{13}. From the Desid. *tikicchati* (§ 183) is derived *tikicchāpehi* 'cause to be cured!' DhCo. I. 25^{13}.

§ 182. The number of 2. Double-causatives too is very large. With reference to § 178. 1, 2: *kappāpeti* D. I. 49^{22}, II. 189^{27}, JāCo. II. 96^{17}, *chaḍḍāpeti* JāCo. I. 357^{15}; *vaḍḍhāpeti* JāCo. I. 455^{28}; *vissajjāpeti* JāCo. I. 294^{28}, II. 31^{6}, Mhvs. 6. 43; *gāhāpeti* JāCo. I. 166^{19}, II. 37^{12}; *paṭiyādāpeti* D. II. 88^{14}, 127^{5}, JāCo. I. 453^{9}; *adhivāsāpeti* JāCo. I. 254^{22}; *kārāpeti* Vin. I. 89^{15}; *ohārāpeti* 'causes to decrease' Vin. I. 22^{12}; *mārāpeti* JāCo. II. 417^{9,12}, Mhvs. 22. 19; *pūrāpeti* Mhvs. 35. 7. With reference to § 179: *chedāpeti* D. I. 52^{22}, Mhvs. 35. 42; *sodhāpeti* JāCo. I. 305^{3}, II. 19^{27}, Mhvs. 25. 5; *yojāpeti* D. II. 95^{18}, 96^{3}; *posāpeti* JāCo. I. 290^{14}; *ārocāpeti* D. II. 127^{6}, JāCo. I. 153^{5}; *ghātāpeti* Vin. I. 277^{7}; *laggāpeti* Mhvs. 33. 11. With reference to § 180: *ṭhapāpeti* JāCo. II. 20^{17}, Mhvs. 36. 104; *ropāpeti* D. II. 179^{15}, Smp. 341^{10}, Mhvs. 34. 40. The form *cetāpeti* 'causes to collect' Vin. IV. 250^{13} ff. is remarkable. Formally it is a double-causative from *ceteti*, but, as the meaning shows, it belongs to the root *ci* 'to collect'. The double-causative meaning has often become obscure in the forms reviewed above, but in some cases it is still quite clear. Thus, e.g., when in Vin. I. 49^{15} *vinodāpeti* occurs in the immediate vicinity of *vinodeti*, or when the simple Causative is derived from a basic transitive verb and through further suffixation becomes a double transitive, as in the case of *ṭhapeti* and *ṭhapāpeti* 'erects' and 'causes to erect'.

[1] R. O. Franke, BB. 22. 220. But *nibbijjāpema* Sn. 448 = S I. 124^{8} and *nibbijjāpetha* S. I. 127^{17} (verse) are to be divided *nibbijja-apema* (*apetha*), as Fausböll (Sn. Wtb. p. 335) has already done following the Comm.

§ 183. Flexion of the Causative: for the Present-system cf. § 139; for the Future § 151 and 155; for the Aorist § 165. 2 and 168. 4. Passive of Causative § 176. 1.

9. Desiderative.

§ 184. The Desideratives of Pāli are stems derived from an older stage of the language[1]. The construction of Desideratives is no longer a living motif in Pāli. Examples: *jigucchati* 'dislikes, loathes' Sn. 215, 958, Th2. 469, 471, D. I. 213[27], Vin. I. 87[1], 88[6], JāCo. I. 422[26,32] = *jugupsate* from root *gup*; *jighacchati* 'wishes to eat' D. II. 266[1] (verse) = *jighatsati* from root *ghas* (*jighacchā* 'hunger' Dh. 203); *vicikicchati* 'hesitates' D. I. 106[17], S. II. 17[19] = *vicikitsati* from root *cit*, but *tikicchati* 'treats (medically)' Vin. I. 71[36], JāCo. I. 485[11] and *tikicchā* 'medical treatment', *tekiccha* 'curable' (§ 41.2); *jigiṃsati*, *jigīsati* 'wishes to attain, conquer' Sn. 700, Th1. 743, 1110 = *jigīṣati* from root *ji*[2]; *titikkhati* 'tolerates' Dh. 321, 399, Jā. III. 38[5], S. I. 221[24] (verse) = *titikṣati* from root *tyaj*; *pivāsati* 'wishes to drink' (Kacc. III. 2. 3, Senart, p. 434) = *pipāsati* from root *pā*; *bubhukkhati* 'wishes to eat' (Kacc. III. 2. 3) = *bubhukṣate* from root *bhuj*; *vīmaṃsati* 'puts to test' M. I. 125[16], JāCo. I. 279[11], Mhvs. 5. 258, 14. 16 = *mīmāṃsati* (§ 46. 4) from root *man*; *vavakkhati* 'wishes to speak' D. II. 256[9] (verse) = *vivakṣati* from root *vac*; *sussūsati*[3] 'wishes to hear' D. I. 230[13], M. III. 133[2], A. IV. 393[3] = *śuśrūṣate* from root *śru*. Weakened and shortened stems too are met with as in Skr.: *dicchati* 'wishes to give' S. I. 18[27] (verse) = *ditsati*, Pl. 3. *dicchare* S. I. 18[27], from root *dā*; *sikkhati* 'wishes to succeed, learns (JPTS. 1909, p. 157) = *śikṣate* from root *śak*; perhaps also *siṃsati* 'wishes to go' Vv. 64. 7 f., 81. 18 = (*si*) *sīrṣati* from root *sar*[4]. Skr. *icchati* and *īpsati* have coincided in Pāli *icchati*.—On the flexion cf. § 130. 6, 154. 4, 166 (end), 181. 1 (end).

10. Intensive.

§ 185. Also the Intensives of Pāli are derived from Skr. stems[5]. Of very frequent occurrence is *caṅkamati* 'walks up and down' Vin.

[1] Similarly in Pkr.; Pischel, § 555.
[2] According to Kacc. III. 2. 3 (Senart, p. 434) from root *har* (Skr. *jihīrṣati*).
[3] The spelling *sussūyati* M. III. 221[8] etc. is very probably wrong.
[4] But (*pacc*) *āsiṃsati* is derived from Skr. *śaṃs*.
[5] For Prākrit see Pischel, § 556.

I. 15[25], 87[13], D. I. 89[19], Sn. p. 101, 11 =*caṅkramate* from root *kram*. Cf. further *daddallati* 'ligh(s up, sparkles' S. I. 127[18] (verse), D. II. 258[7] (verse)=*jājvalyate* (§ 41. 2) from root *jval*; *lālappati*[1] 'chatters' Sn. 580, Jā. III. 217[10], Mhvs. 32. 6∂ (*lālappita* 'conversation' Jā. VI. 498[17])=*lālapyate* from root *lap*. The substantive *loluppa* 'desire' Jā. I. 429[27], JāCo. I. 340[25] (cf. Skr. *lolupa* 'desirous') is derived from a root *lup*. Cf. also *kākacchati* JāCo. I. 61[24], 160[28], 318[2], Milp. 85[22], probably meaning 'talks (in sleep)' from the verb *kathayati*. Sometimes the stem in Pāli ends in *a* as against *ya* in Skr.: *jaṅgamati* against *jaṅgamyate* from root *gam* 'to go', *cañcalati* against *cañcalyate* from root *cal* 'to move'[2], *momuhati* Sn. 841 (besides the Adj. *momuha* § 37) as against *momuhyate* from root *muh* 'to lose control over one's own mind'. On *jāgarati*, *jaggati*=*jāgarti* see § 142. 4.—For the flexion of Intensives cf. § 130. 6, 154. 4, 166 (end).

11. Denominative.

§ 186. The number of Denominatives with the formantic element *āya* is very large: 1. From Adjectives in *a*: *cirāyati* 'hesitates' JāCo. I. 426[30], III. 498[4], VI. 521[11]=*cirāyati, -te*; *dandhāyati* 'is slow' JāCo. III. 141[10] from *dandha* (p. 84, foot-note 1); *piyāyati* 'loves' Th2. 285, JāCo. II. 27[23], 133[14] from Skr. *priya*; *maccharāyati* 'is jealous' JāCo. III. 158[2], VI. 334[13] from Skr. *matsara*; *sukhāyati* 'is happy' JāCo. II. 31[4]=*sukhāyate*.—2. From Substantives in *a*: *kukkuccāyati* 'feels remorse' Vin. I. 191[32], JāCo. II. 15[12] from *kukkucca*; *dhūpāyati* 'spits forth smoke' Vin. I. 180[27], S. I. 169[7], DhCo. III. 244[4]=*dhūpāyati*; *dhūmāyati* 'smokes' M. III. 184[13], Dpvs. 15. 67=*dhūmāyati, -te*; *mahāyati* 'honours by a festival' Jā. IV. 236[2] from *maha*; *rahāyati* 'wishes to be alone' M. II. 119[29] from *raha(s)*; *verāyati* 'rages' Dpvs. 15. 67; *saddāyati* 'makes noise' Ud. 61[6-7], Milp. 258[29], 259[1], JāCo. III. 288[2]=*śabdāyate*; *sārajjāyati* 'is embarrassed' S. III. 92[31] from *sārajja*. In Kacc. III. 2. 4 (Senart, p. 434), *pabbatāyati* 'he is like a mountain' from *pabbata* and III. 2. 24 (Senart, p. 442) *samuddāyati* 'resembles the ocean' from *samuddo*. Anomalous is the case of *harāyati* 'feels shame' Vin. I. 87[1], 88[5], D. I. 213[22] from *hirī*=*hrī*.—3. From a pronominal form: *mamāyati* 'loves, worships' Th1. 1150, DhCo. I. 11[10] (verse), Mhvs. 20. 4=*mamāyate*.—4. Onomatopoetic expressions[3]

[1] *Cf. the var. lec. of the text: lālapataṃ.*

[2] *E. Kuhn, Beitr. p. 118; E. Müller, PGr. p. 122.*

[3] Morris, JPTS. 1884, p. 106 f. These constructions are found in large numbers alsↄ in Pkr.; Pischel, § 558.

are quite numerous: *kiṇakiṇāyati* 'rings' Jā. III. 315[9] (Comm. *kiṇi-kiṇāyati*); *gaggarāyati* 'gurgles' Milp. 3[7] from Skr. *gargara*; *gaḷa-gaḷāyati* 'trickles' Thl. 189, D. II. 131[9], S. I. 106[21]; *ghurughurāyati* 'snores' JāCo. III. 538[21] = *ghuraghurāyate*; *ciccitāyati* or *citicitāyati* (§ 20) 'rustles'; *taṭataṭāyati* '(voice) shakes (with anger)' JāCo. I. 347[12], VvCo. 121[10]; *tintiṇāyati* 'sighs, groans' JāCo. I. 244[3], III. 223[6]; *daddabhāyati* 'crackles' Jā. III. 77[10]; *dhamadhamāyati* 'hums, roars' Milp. 117[21];—5. Here are to be included also forms like *uggahāyanti* 'they learn' Sn. 791, which is connected with Ved. *gṛbhāyati*[1]; *phu-sāyati* 'touches' (besides *phusati*) S. I. 104[3,21], 106[14]; *pacalāyati* 'shakes the head (in sleep)' Thl. 200, JāCo. I. 384[2]; *ocināyati* 'turns back' Jā. VI. 4[19]; *patāyanti* 'go out of' Jā. III. 283[16] (Comm. *nikkhamanti*); perhaps also *saṃkasāyati* 'accommodates oneself to, S. I. 202[23], A. I. 69[10] (S. II. 277[12] *saṃkāsāyati*).

§ 187. Denominatives with the formantic element *aya* (contracted to *e*) or *āpaya* (contracted to *āpe*), after the manner of the causatives: 1. With *aya* (*e*): *gopayati*, *-eti* 'protects' Dh. 315, DhCo. III. 488[9,10] = *gopayati*, *-te*; *vijaṭeti* 'unravels' Milp. 3[17] from *jaṭā*; *tīreti* 'leads to the goal' Ud. 13[5], Vin. III. 12[32], D. II. 341[9], JāCo. III. 292[20] = *tīrayati*; *theneti* 'steals' JāCo. II. 410[10], III. 18[27] = *stenayati*; *thometi* 'praises' VvCo. 102[21] = *stomayati*; *dhūmayati* 'smokes' Smp. 315[15] besides *dhūmāyati*; *patthayati*, *-eti* 'prays for' Thl. 51, Th2Co. 38[28] = *prārthayate*; (*saṃ*) *piṇḍeti* 'heaps up, collects' JāCo. I. 230[25], DhCo. 171[19], Mhvs. 36. 108 = *piṇḍayati*; *pihayati*, *-eti* 'desires' Dh. 94; Thl. 62 etc. = *spṛhayati*; *baleti* 'strengthens' Jā. III. 225[14] = *balayati*; *bhuseti* 'increases' Jā. V. 218[28] (Comm. *bhusaṃ karoti*, *vaḍḍheti*), Skr. *bhṛśāyate*; *maggayati* 'pursues' Th2. 384 from *magga*; *mantayati*, *-eti* 'takes counsel' A. I. 199[15] (verse), Vin. II. 299[11], Mhvs. 4. 20 and *āmanteti* 'invites, demands' Thl. 34, D.I. 88[12], II. 209[15], Vin. I. 55[31] = *āmantrayati*; *yanteti* 'hurls' JāCo. I. 418[14] = *yantrayati*; *saṃgāmeti* 'fights' Iv. 75[16], S. I. 83[2], JāCo. II. 11[4], V. 417[17]; *samodhāneti* 'connects' JāCo. I. 9[36], 106[7] from *samo-dhāna*; *sākaccheti* 'talks with somebody' (JPTS. 1909, p. 137) from *sākacchā*; *sukheti* 'makes happy' D. I. 51[15] = *sukhayati*[2].—2. With *āpaya* (*āpe*): *ussukkāpeti* 'exerts himself' Th2Co. 5[30], VvCo. 95[12]

[1] Whitney, Ind. Gr. § 1066 b.

[2] Further examples in Kacc. III. 2. 8 (Senart, p. 437): *atihatthayati* 'covers the distance on the back of an elephant', *upavīṇayati* 'accompanies with the lute', *daḷhayati* 'makes firm', *visuddhayati* 'becomes purified.'

besides *ussukkati* from *ussukka* *muramurāpeti* (onomatopoetic) 'crackles' JāCo. III. 134[24]; *opuñjāpeti* 'heaps up with something' Vin. III. 16[19] from *puñja*, Skr. *puñjayati*. Causative meaning is quite clear in *āmantāpeti* 'causes to call' D. I. 134[30] and in *sukhāpeti* 'makes happy', *dukkhāpeti* 'makes unhappy' D. II. 202[12], Milp. 79[7,10].

§ 188. Denominatives 1. with the stem-vowel *a*: *atricchati* 'desires this and that' Jā. I. 414[6], III. 207[15] from *atricchā*; *usūyati*, *usuyyati* 'is jealous' from *usūyā* (§ 16. 1 *b*)=*asūyati*; *ussukkati* 'takes interest in' D. I. 230[21] from *ussukka*; *paripañhati* 'questions' M. I. 223[33], A. V. 16[2] from *pañha*; *vijjotalati* 'sparkles' M. I. 8![31], 87[1]; *sajjhāyati*, 'recites' Milp. 10[10], JāCo. I. 435[23] from *sajjhāya*=*svādhyāya* (whence the Causative *sajjhāpayati*, *-peti* Jā III. 28[21], JāCo. III. 29[6] and *sajjhāyāpeti* Milp. 10[8]). Further *tintiṇati* JāCo. I. 243[6] besides *tintiṇāyati* (§ 186. 4), *dandhati* Jā. III. 141[2] besides *dandhāyati* (§186. 1), *dhūpati* Mbvs. 12. 14 besides *dhūpāyati* (§ 186. 2), *sārajjati* A. IV. 359[8] besides *sārajjāyati* (§ 186. 2).—2. With the stem in *ya*: from substantives in *ā*: *karuṇāyati* 'takes pity' VvCo. 100[6] from *karuṇa* (or according to § 186. 1 from *karuṇa*)=*karuṇāyate*; *mettāyati* 'acts like a friend' JāCo. I. 365[17] from *mettā* (or directly from the adj. *metta*). From a substantive in *i*: *vyādhīyati* 'becomes ill' A. II. 172[7]. Y becomes *v* after *u* in *kaṇḍuvati* (§ 46. 1)=*kaṇḍūyati*; it is assimilated to the preceding consonant in *tapassati* 'practises austerities' DhCo. I. 53[3]=*tapasyati*; *namassati* 'makes obeisance'=*namasyati*.—3. With stems in *īya*: *aṭṭīyati* 'suffers' S. I. 131[12] (verse), Vin. I. 86[36] from *aṭṭa*=*ārta*; *paṭiseniyati* 'behaves like an enemy' Sn. 390 from *paṭisenā*=*pratisenā* 'enemy army' (SBE. X. 2, p. 64). Also in Kacc. III. 2. 5 and 6 (Senart, p. 435): *puttiyati* 'treats like a son', *pattīyati* 'desires an alms-bowl for himself', *dhanīyati* 'desires money' etc.

§ 189. For the flexion of Denominatives see 1. Present-system: § 136. 4, 138 (at the end), 139; 2. Future: § 151. 3, 154. 3, 155 (at the end); 3. Aorist: § 165. 2, 168. 3 and 4.

12. Verbal Nouns.

1. Participles of the Present and the Future—Active.

§ 190. The Present Participles in *-nt(a)*—flexion § 97—are derived from multifarious Present-stems[1]. Examples: With

[1] I give the stem-forms *-nt* and *-nta* respectively according to the passages quoted. On the feminine in *-ntī* cf. p. 188, foot-note 2.

reference to § 130: *vasant(a)* Sn. 43, Jā. III. 396[5], JāCo. III. 190[17]; *jīvant* Sn. 427, Thl. 44; *khādanta* JāCo. III. 276[25]; *carant(a)* Dh. 61, Sn. 89, 1079, JāCo. I. 152[9]; II. 15[24]. From Desiderative stem *jigucchanta* JāCo. I. 422[32]; *vicikicchanta* Nett. 11[27]; *tikicchanta* S. I. 162[33] (verse). From Intensive stem: *caṅkamanta* Vin. I. 133[32].—With reference to § 131: *jinant* S. I. 116[19]; *bhavant* (§ 98. 3); *pahonta* 'sufficing' DhCo. III. 137[11]; *abhisambhonta* Thl. 351; *a-sambhuṇanta* Sn. 396.—With reference to § 132: *pivant(a)* Dh. 205, DhCo. III. 269[5], JāCo. I. 460[12]; *tiṭṭhant* Sn. 151, 1092 and *ṭhahanta* Vin. I. 9[6].—With reference to § 133: *gacchant(a)* Sn. 579, 960, JāCo. II. 39[28] etc.—With reference to § 134: *phusant* Iv. 68[1] (verse); *supanta* Vin. I. 15[10].—With reference to § 135: *icchant* Thl. 167; *muñcant* Sn. 791; *vilimpanta* JāCo. III. 277[7].—With reference to § 136 and 137: *naccant(a)* Jā. VI. 497[7,15]; *sussanta* JāCo. I. 503[3], II. 424[15]; *passant(a)* Sn. 837, M. I. 64[9], JāCo. I. 168[2]. From Passive stems with passive meaning: *muccanta* JāCo. I. 118[8] (read *nalāṭato sede muccante*); *khajjant* 'one who is being devoured' Thl. 315; *yāciyanta* 'he who is being implored' Mhvs. 7. 14; *vāriyanta* 'he who is being dissuaded' Mhvs. 34. 86. From Denominative stem (§ 188. 2): *namassanta* D. II. 208[16] (verse), —With reference to § 138. *jhāyant(a)* 'meditating' Thl. 85, Dh. 395, Vin. I. 2[3] (verse), M. II. 105[20] (verse); *upavāyanta* Thl. 544. From Denominative stem (§ 186. 1): *cirāyanta* JāCo. VI. 521[11], *dhūmāyanta* Mhvs. 25. 31.—With reference to § 139: *nandayanta* 'gladdening', *socayanta* 'depressing' Milp. 226[24]; *bhāvayant* Thl. 166; *nivārayant* Thl. 730 f.; *viheṭhayanta* 'injuring' Dh. 184; *pācenta* D. I. 52[31]; *kārenta* JāCo. I. 107[21]; *dāpenta* D. I. 52[33]; *ghātenta* D. I. 52[30].—With reference to § 140: *hanant(a)* Jā. II. 407[1], D. I. 52[20], JāCo. II. 407[8]; *paccakkhant* (Nom. Sg. *-akkhaṃ*) Thl. 407 (root *khyā*); *enta* (root *i*) JāCo. VI. 365[6]; *sayant(a)* Sn. 193, Jā. VI. 510[11].—With reference to § 141: *sant(a)* see § 98.2.—With reference to § 142 and 143: *samādahant* S. V. 312[11]; *saddahanta* JāCo. I. 222[5]; *jāgarant* Dh. 39 and *jaggant* S. I. 111[2] (verse); *dadant* Sn. 187, Vv. 67. 5, D. II. 136[22] (verse), *dadanta* Vv. 83. 13, D. I. 52[33], VvCo. 294[18] and *denta* PvCo. 11[8], JāCo. I. 265[2].—With reference to § 144-148: *bhuñjanta* JāCo. III. 277[11]; *bhindanta* Mhvs. 5. 185; *jānant* Sn. 320, 508, Dh. 384, M. I. 64[9], Milp. 48[21] and *jānanta* JāCo. I. 223[3], II. 128[5]; *gaṇhanta* JāCo. III. 52[15], 275[13]; *vicinanta* JāCo. III. 188[12]; *suṇanta* Sn. 1023 and (according to Cl. I) *savant* Jā. III. 244[22]; *sakkonta* Milp. 27[25], JāCo. II. 26[16]; *kubbant* Thl. 323 f., Dh. 51,

Jā. III. 26[24] (=*kurvant*), *karont* (Sg. Gen. *karoto*, Pl. Gen. *karotaṃ*, § 97. 1), *karonta* JāCo. I. 98[11], II. 109[24], III. 188[21], DhCo. III. 123[11] (the usual form in post-canonical prose) and *karant* Thl. 146.

§ 191. In every period of the language the Present Participles in *-māna*, even from non-medial verbs, are found in very large numbers, often along with the Participle in *-nt*. With reference to § 130: *vasamāna* JāCo. I. 291[13]; *labhamāna* Sn. 924, Jā. II. 106[2]; *jīvamāna* JāCo. I. 307[18]; *caramāna* Sn. 413, D. I. 87[3]. From Desiderative-stem: *sussūsamāna* Sn. 383. From Intensive-stem: *jāgaramāna* Dh. 226; *daddallamāna* S. I. 127[18] (verse). From Denominative-stem (§ 188. 1): *sārajjamāna* A. IV. 359[9].—With reference to § 131-135: *an-abhisaṃbhuṇamāna* D. I. 101[3, 11]; *tiṭṭhamāna* JāCo. I. 52[27]; *gacchamāna* JāCo. IV. 3[3]; *saṃphusamāna* Sn. 671.—With reference to § 136: frequently from Passives (cf. § 175 ff.): *diyyamāna* DhCo. III. 191[12] (=*dīyamāna*); *hiyyamāna* (root *hā*) Thl. 114; *nīyamāna* S. I. 127[8] (verse); *kayiramāna* Vin. II. 289[17], D. II. 103[10]; *anubhīramāna* M. III. 123[20]; *vuccamāna* Vin. I. 60[2], III. 221[2]; *vijjamāna* JāCo. I. 214[4], III. 127[6]; *bhaññamāna* Vin. I. 11[33], 70[21], D.I. 46[29]; *tappamāna* Thl. 32; *gayhamāna* DhsCo. 18[15] (=*gṛhyamāṇa*); *vuyhamāna* Thl. 88, Vin. I. 33[15], S. IV. 179[9]; *ḍayhamāna* Thl. 39, Dh. 371; *desiyamāna* Vin. I. 17[2]; *posiyamāna* JāCo. I. 492[12]; *sāriyamāna* Vin. III. 221[34]; *vāriyamāna* JāCo. IV. 2[22]; *dassiyamāna* D. II. 124[10]; *pūjiyamāna* Bodh. 141[10]; *vuṭṭhāpiyamāna* A. I. 139[21]; *pucchiyamāna* DhCo. I. 10[10]; *yāciyamāna* JāCo. IV. 138[27]; even from a double Passive: *-chijjiyamāna* (§ 176. 2 at the end). From Denominative-stem (§ 188. 2, 3): *aṭṭiyamāna* Vin. II. 292[17], JāCo. I. 292[12]; *namassamāna* Vin. I. 3[25].—With reference to § 137-138: *jīramāna* Thl. 32 or *jiyyamāna* M. III. 246[22]; (=*jīryamāṇa*); *miyyamāna* M. III. 246[22]; *jhāyamāna* 'burning' Ud. 93[3]. From Denominative-stem (§ 186. 1): *sukhāyamāna* JāCo. II. 31[4].—With reference to § 139: Only from uncontracted stems: *sārayamāna* JāCo. I. 50[1], *kārayamāna* JāCo. I. 149[16] etc. From Denominative-stem (§ 187. 1.): *patthayamāna* JāCo. I. 279[20].—With reference to § 140 and 142 f.: *sayamāna* Thl. 95 and *semāna* Jā. I. 180[1], D. II. 24[8], A. I. 139[21]; *saṃdahamāna* DhsCo. 113[2]; *dadamāna* S. I. 19[3] (verse), JāCo. II. 154[22] (Vedic *dádamāna*).—With reference to § 144-148: *bhuñjamāna* Thl. 12, Sn. 240; *jānamāna* Sn. 1064, JāCo. I. 168[3]; *pariganhamāna* JāCo. II. 2[28]; *aṇhamāna* 'eating' Sn. 239 f. (from **aṇhāna*=*aśnāna*); *suṇamāna* JāCo. III, 215[17], DhCo. III. 156[3]; *kubbamāna* Sn. 897

and *kurumāna* JāCo. I. 291[15], Dpvs. 9. 17.—The suffix *-māna* has been pleonastically added to Past Participles in *paduṭṭhamāna* DhCo. I. 179[9] = *paduṭṭha*; *vibhātamāna* DhCo. I. 165[11] = *vibhāta*, *aladdhamāna* Rasav. I. 35[10] = *aladdha*. These are constructions of later age.

§ 192. Present Participles in *-āna*[1] are rarer. They belong to the Gāthā-language; occasionally some forms may be found also in the canonical prose. Examples are: *esāna* 'seeking, desiring' Dh. 131 (Skr. *eṣamāṇa*); *abhisaṃbudhāna* 'attaining the highest knowledge' Dh. 46; *an-uṭṭhahāna* 'not getting up' Dh. 280; *a-heṭhayāna* 'not injuring' S. IV. 179[3] (verse); *patthayāna* 'begging for' Sn. 976, Vv. 84. 7; *sayāna* 'lying' Jā. III. 95[17], D. I. 90[13] (= *śayāna*); *saddahāna* 'faithful' S. I. 20[25] (verse) and *samādahāna* S. I. 169[16] (verse) (= *-dadhāna*); *kubbāna* 'making' Dh. 217 (= *kurvāṇa*) and *a-saṃkharāna* S. I. 126[26] (verse), *purekkharāna* Sn. 910. From a Passive-stem: *paripucchiyāna* 'interrogated' Sn. 696. The root *ās* 'to sit' has *āsīna* Dh. 227, 386, Jā. I. 363[12], 390[32], III. 95[17], D. II. 212[21] (verse) as in Skr. The form is however archaic.

§ 193. Very rare is the construction of Future Participle in *-nt* from the futural stem. Thus Sg. Acc. *marissaṃ*[2] (cf. § 97. 2) Jā. III. 214[11] for *marissantaṃ* = *mariṣyantam* (Comm. *yo idāni marissati taṃ*); *paccessaṃ* 'one who will return' Vin. I. 255[24] (root *i* + *prati*).

2. Participles of the Preterite.

§ 194. The Past Participle in *-ta* has mostly a passive meaning in the case of transitive verbs, and an active meaning in the case of intransitive verbs. There are numerous forms of historical origin. Thus from roots in *ī*, *ū*: *ita* 'gone' (*samita*, *atīta*, *peta* etc.), *jita*, *nita* as in Skr.; *suta* = *śruta*; *bhūta* = *bhūta*. As there is *suta* from *suṇāti*, so there is *pariyāputa* D. III. 203[6] from *pariyāpuṇāti* 'learns'. From roots in *ā*: *ñāta* = *jñāta*, *sināta* Jā. V. 330[3], M. I. 39[1] = *snāta*; *gīta* 'sung' D. I. 99[11], JāCo. III. 61[25] = *gīta*; *ṭhita* = *sthita*; *hita* (*ohita*, *pihita*, *vihita* etc.) = *hita*; *atta* 'seized' in *attadaṇḍa* Dh. 406 = *ātta* (root *dā* with *ā*).—Roots in *ṛ*: *kata* = *kṛta*, *mata* = *mṛta*; *saṃsita* 'one who has wandered about (in the existences)' Sn. 730, D. II. 91[2] (verse) = *saṃsṛta*; *saṃvuta* 'restricted' = *saṃvṛta*; *nibbuta* 'released'

[1] In Pkr. these Participles are quite rare; Pischel, § 562 (at the end).

[2] E. Müller, PGr. p 123 quotes from Dāṭhāvs. 3. 80 the form *karissaṃ*. It is, however, clearly the 1. Sg. = *kariṣyāmi*. The Sgh. paraphrase has *keremi*. On the Part. Future Active in Pkr. see Pischel, § 560.

Dh. 406, 414, Th1. 79, 96, Vin. I. 8[21] (verse)=*nirvṛta*[1]; *haṭa*=*hṛta*; *aṭṭa* (§ 64)=*ārta* (root *ar* with *ā*). Also from root *star* 'to stretch out' we have *atthata, saṃthata, vitthata* as against Skr. *stīrṇa*.—Roots in nasal: *hata, mata, tata; nata, gata; nikhāta* Sn. 28, Jā. III. 24[28], D. II. 171[1] as also in Skr. Similarly *santa* 'quieted'=*śānta* (root *śam*); *santa* 'tired'=*śrānta*; *kanta* 'dear, charming'=*kānta*; *nikkhanta* 'gone out', *pakkanta* etc.=*-krānta*; *jāta* 'born, originated' from *jan*.—Roots in surds and sonants: *sitta* Th1. 110, JāCo. III. 144[1]=*sikta*; *vutta*=*ukta*, *durutta*=*durukta*; *bhutta*=*bhukta*; *yutta*=*yukta*; *puṭṭha* 'interrogated'=*pṛṣṭa*; *yiṭṭha* 'sacrificed' Jā. VI. 522[6], M. I. 82[15], A. II. 44[6] (verse)=*iṣṭa* (root *yaj*); *saṃsaṭṭha*=*-sṛṣṭa* (root *sarj*), *suddha* 'purified'=*śuddha*; *khitta* 'hurled'=*kṣipta*; *vutta* 'sown' JāCo. I. 340[19], III. 12[20]=*upta*; *sutta* 'one who has slept' Dh. 29, Th1. 22 etc.=*supta*. On *vatta*, *vaṭṭa*=*vṛtta*[2] see § 64. 1.—Roots in aspirates: *duddha* 'milked' Sn. 18=*dugdha*; *siniddha* 'oily, smooth' Th2Co. 139[18], JāCo. I. 89[23] (verse), 481[1]=*snigdha*; *daḍḍha* (§ 42. 3)=*dagdha*; *vuḍḍha*, *vuddha* etc. (§ 64)=*vṛddha*; *laddha* 'attained'=*labdha*; *luddha* 'eager' Iv. 1[10] (verse)=*lubdha*.—Roots in sibilants: *diṭṭha*=*dṛṣṭa*; *phuṭṭha* 'touched'=*spṛṣṭa*; *naṭṭha* 'destroyed'=*naṣṭa*; *kaṭṭha* 'ploughed' S. I. 173[3] (verse)=*kṛṣṭa*; *sattha* 'taught' commanded' Jā. II. 298[23], III. 3[24]=*śāsta*; *saṃtatta* 'frightened' Jā. III. 77[25]=*-trasta*.—Roots in *h*=Indo-Iranian *źh*: *vūḷha* (§ 35)=*ūḍha*; *mūḷha* 'foolish' Iv. 2[16] (verse)=*mūḍha*; *saṃyūḷha* (*saññūḷha*) 'spoken, composed' D. II. 267[19], M. I. 386[33] (*saṃvuḷha* DCo. I. 38[8])=*sam-ūḍha* (root *ūh*); *abbūḷha* 'torn out' Sn. 593, 779, D. II. 283[27], M. I. 139[17] from *abbahati*=*ā-bṛhati*.

§ 195. Past Participles in *-ita* too have been handed down in large numbers in historical forms. Examples: *patita, carita*; *khādita, saṃdhāvita* D. II. 90[14] etc., as in Skr.; *sayita* 'laid down to rest' D. II. 353[8], JāCo. I. 338[24], III. 33[18]=*śayita*; *paritasita* 'thirsty' Milp. 253[26]=*-tṛṣita* (root *tarṣ*); *vusita* Th1. 258, D. II. 206[10] (verse) (besides *vuttha* Jā. I. 183[22] etc.)=*uṣita* from root *vas* 'to dwell'; *gahīta*=*gṛhīta*. Often from Causatives: *dassita*=*darśita*; *pesita*=*preṣita*; *kārita, codita, dāpita* as in Skr.; *addita* 'pained' Th2. 77, 328=*ardita*[3].

[1] But the users of the language felt that *(pari)nibbuta* was the Past Participle of *(pari)nibbāyati*.

[2] Instead of *kanta* 'spun' M. III. 253[9] I should like to read *katta*=*kṛtta*.

[3] From the Causative of root *jñā* we have *ñatta* Dh. 72 (cf. SBE X 1, p. 22, note); *āṇatta* 'ordered' Dpvs. 6. 75, Mhvs. 5. 183, 10. 1; *paññatta* 'declared, fixed legally' Vin. I. 83[23], D. II. 74[3] etc.=*jñāpta, ājñapta, prajñapta*.

Similarly from Desideratives: *jighacchita* 'hungry' M. III. 186[2], DhCo. III. 263[13] = *jighatsita*; *jigucchita* 'scared' Mhvs 6. 3 = *jugupsita*. From Intensives: *caṅkamita* Mhvs. 15. 208 = *caṅkramita*. From Denominatives, § 186: *cirāyita* DhCo. III. 305[1], *dhūpāyita* Thl. 448, *mamāyita* DhCo. I. 11[10] (verse) as in Skr. With reference to § 187: *patthita* JāCo. I. 408[26], II. 36[16], DhCo. I. 112[26] = *prārthita*; *mantita* Thl. 9, M. II. 105[21] (verse) = *mantrita*; *dukkhita* Th2. 29 = *duḥkhita*.

§ 196. The type of Past Participle in *-ita* has moreover been very productive for the reason that new forms were evolved after it from every kind of Present stem[1]. They are met with in every period of the language. With reference to § 130-133: *kilamita* 'tired' JāCo. III. 36[26] (besides *kilanta* = *klānta*); *saṃtasita* (root *tras*) Milp. 92[2] (besides *-tatta*); *vasita* 'inhabited' Mhvs. 20. 14, 16 (besides *vusita* and *vuttha* § 195); *āharita* S. IV. 59[25], 60[5] (besides *āhaṭa* § 194); *saṃsarita* Th2. 496, D. II. 90[14] (besides *saṃsita* § 194); *jinita* JāCo. II. 251[20] (besides *jita*); *gacchita* Th2Co. 126[11] (as explanation of *gata*).—With reference to § 134-135: *phusita* Th2. 158 (besides *phuṭṭha*); *pucchita* JāCo. II. 9[18], Mhvs. 20. 8 (besides *puṭṭha*); *supita*, Sn. 331, S. I. 198[7] (verse) (besides *sutta*); *icchita* Th2. 46, D. I. 120[1], DhCo. IV.5[9], Mhvs. 7.22 (besides *iṭṭha*); *sampaṭicchita* DhCo.III.439[3]; *pamuñcita* Vv. 53. 8 (or *pamuccita* VvCo. 237[11]?).—With reference to § 136 138: *gijjhita* 'desired' Th2. 152; *samāpajjita* D. II. 109[27] (besides *samāpanna*), *maññita* M. III. 246[12], S. IV. 21[32], 22[3]. Even *chijjita* Jā. III. 389[17] from the Passive-stem *chijja-* (Comm. *chinna*); *vāyita* 'woven' M. III. 253[9] (besides *vāta*); *gāyita* 'sung' DhCo. III. 233[17] (besides *gīta*).—With reference to § 142-145: *jahita* JāCo. III. 32[3'4]; *saddahita* M. II. 170[30]; *paṭijaggita* DhCo. III. 138[19]; *saṃjānita* in the abstract noun *saṃjānitatta* Dhs. 4 (in elucidation of *saññā*).—Also *khādayita* 'fed' Vin. I. 278[12] (Caus. of *khād*), *patthayita* 'implored' Jā. III. 218[25] (Comm. *patthita*).

§ 197. Many Past Participles are formed also with the suffix *-na* as in Skr. Thus from roots in *d*: *chinna*, *bhinna*, *-panna*, *-sanna* (but *nisinna* = *niṣaṇṇa*); *pakkhanna* 'fallen into something' Thl. 95, 253, 342 = *praskanna*; *tunna* 'goaded' Th2. 162 and *nunna* 'pushed, propelled' A. II. 41[13], JāCo. VI. 527[20], Mhvs. 34. 60, as in Skr. Also *ruṇṇa* 'bewailing' Jā. VI. 525[4], 'wail, lamentation' Thl. 554, A. I. 261[2] (besides *roṇṇa* Thl. 555) as against Skr. *rudita* (root *rud*).[2]—

[1] Analogous constructions from the Present-stem also in Pkr., Pischel, § 565.

[2] Also Pkr. Māh. *ruṇṇa*; Pischel, PkrGr. § 566.

Further from certain roots in *ā*, *ī*, *ū*: *hīna* (JPTS. 1907. 163) from root *hā*, *sīna* 'frozen' M. I. 79[29] (verse), Milp. 117[18] = *śīna* (root *śyā*); *līna* (*a-līna* 'unattached, passionless' Dh. 245, Sn. 68, 717, *nilīna* 'concealed' Vin. III. 35[4], JāCo. III. 26[4], *patisallīna* 'withdrawn' Vin. I. 4[33] etc.) = *līna* (root *lī*); *vikkhiṇa* 'destroyed' Th2. 22 = *vikṣīṇa*; *lūna* 'cut off' Th2. 107 = *lūna*.—From certain roots in *ṛ*: *jiṇṇa*, *tiṇṇa*, *puṇṇa* = *jīrṇa*, *tīrṇa*, *pūrṇa*. Also *patthiṇṇa* 'spread out' Vin. I. 286[34] = *prastīrṇa* (besides *patthata* § 194), as well as *ciṇṇa* 'done, performed' Sn. 181 f., Vin. II. 39[15], JāCo. I. 300[6] (*āciṇṇa* 'done, customary' M. I. 372[10] etc., *pariciṇṇa* Th1. 178, M. III. 264[23]) besides *carita* as Skr. *cīrṇa* and *carita*.—From some roots in *j* and *g*: (*saṃ*)*bhagga* 'broken' Dh. 154, Th1. 184, S. I. 123[28] = *bhagna*; *nimugga* 'drowned' (§ 18) Vin. I. 6[31], D. I. 75[17], II. 324[5], JāCo. III. 47[1] = *nimagna* (root *majj*); *saṃvigga* 'disturbed, anxious' D. I. 50[1], S. IV. 290[30], JāCo. I. 59[10], *ubbigga* Jā. I. 486[10], JāCo. I. 503[13] = *vigna* (root *vij*); *olagga* 'bound fast' Th1. 356 = *avalagna*.—The root *dā* 'to give' has *dinna* = Pkr. *diṇṇa*, *dinna*[1] against Skr. *datta* (this, e.g., in *dattūpajīvin* 'one who lives on what he receives as charity' DhCo. IV. 99[18] as well as in proper names like *Brahmadatta*, as also in *atta* § 194).—Finally, there is the dialectal form *paṭimukka* 'bound down' Th2. 500, S. IV. 91[23], 92[1] (opposite of *ummukka* S. IV. 92[7]) as against Skr. *pratimukta*[2].

§ 193. Past Participle Active. 1. The meagre traces of the Participle in *-vas* have been discussed in § 100.—2. We do not find any large number of Participles formed by affixing *-vant* to Participles in *-ta*. Thus *vusitavant* 'he who has lived' in the transferred sense 'perfect, complete', Sg. Nom. *-vā* Sn. 514, Iv. 96[14], M. I. 4[23], D. I. 90[20], Pl. Gen. *-vataṃ* D. II. 223[19], 229[13]; *bhuttavant* 'he who has enjoyed' Sg. Gen. *-vato* VvCo. 244[6]. In Kacc. IV. 2. 6 (Senart, p. 483) we have moreover *hutavā*. Of analogous construction is the Sg. Nom. *ādinnavā* 'he who has seized, utilised'[3] Mhvs. 7. 42.—3. The Participles in *-tāvin* (flexion according to § 95) are an innovation of Pāli: *bhuttāvin* 'he who has eaten', Sg. Acc. *-viṃ* D. I. 109[35], 227[4], Gen. *-vissa* D. II. 195[32]; *vijitāvin* 'he who has been victorious', Sg. Nom. *-vī* Th1. 5 ff., S. I. 110[8] (verse), D. I. 88[34],

[1] Kieckers. IF. 32. 88 ff.

[2] As var. lec. to *mutta* we have *mukka* in M. III. 61[15]. The corresponding form in Pkr. is *mukka*; Pischel, § 566.

[3] D. Andersen, PR. 112[31] (PGl. *sub voce*) reads *ādiṇṇavā* 'he who has torn asunder', Skr. *dīrṇa* from root *dar*.

Acc. *-vinaṃ* Dh. 422, Pl. Gen. *vinaṃ* A. III. 151[26]; *katāvin* 'expert', Sg. Nom. *-vī* M. II. 69[7]; *kīḷitāvin* 'he who has played', Sg. Nom. *a-nikīḷitāvī* S. I. 9[6], Pl. Nom. *-vino* S. IV. 110[27]; *samitāvin* 'he who has come to rest', Sg. Nom. *-vī* S. I. 188[4] (verse); *sutāvin* 'he who has heard and learnt, learned', Pl. Nom. *a-ssutāvino* Th1. 955.

3. Participles of Future—Passive.

§ 199. Of Future Passive Participles those in *-tabba*[1] = *-tavya* are the most numerous. 1. The following are some of the historical forms: *dātabba* 'that which has to be given' Vin. I. 46[6], JāCo. III. 52[2] = *dātavya*, *pahātabba* Sn. 558, M. I. 7[11] (root *hā* 'to forsake') = *-hātavya*; *saddhātabba* JāCo. II. 37[25] = *śraddhātavya*; *paccuṭṭhātabba* 'he who is to be greeted by standing up' M. III. 205[17] = *-sthātavya*; *netabba* = *netavya*; *sotabba* = *śrotavya*; *gantabba* Vin. I. 46[19] = *gantavya*; *vatthabba* Mhvs. 3. 12 (root *vas* 'to live') = *vastavya*; *daṭṭhabba* PvCo. 10[18] (root *darś* 'to see') = *draṣṭavya*; *kattabba* Dh. 53, JāCo. I. 453[22] and (§ 6. 1) *kātabba* Vin. I. 47[20], JāCo. II. 112[15] = *kartavya*; *vihātabba* (from *viharati*) M. III. 294[27] = *-hartavya*. Similarly also forms with *i*: *bhavitabba* JāCo. I. 440[4] = *bhavitavya*; *tikicchitabba* DhCo. III. 264[1] = *cikitsitavya*; *rakkhitabba* JāCo. III. 52[2] = *rakṣitavya* etc.—2. After this latter type are moreover constructed numerous new forms from Present-stems[2]. With reference to § 130-132: *vasitabba* Sn. 678 from *vasati*; *pacitabba* Vin. I. 50[5] from *pacati* as against *paktavya*; *-kamitabba* Vin. I. 59[11], D. I. 179[10] from *-kamati*; *uddharitabba* Vin. I. 47[6] from *uddharati*, *saṃharitabba* Vin. I. 46[29] (from root *har*); *jinitabba* DhCo. III. 313[9] (from root *ji*); *nisīditabba* Vin. I. 47[19] (from root *sad*). With reference to § 134-138: *-khipitabba* Vin. I. 46[35], 47[1] as against *kṣeptavya*; *pucchitabba* Vin. I. 46[33] from *pucchati* as against *praṣṭavya*; *-visitabba* Vin. I. 47[16] as against *veṣṭavya*; *ālimpitabba* Vin. II. 267[1] (from root *lip*); *āsiñcitabba* Vin. I. 49[11] (from root *sic*); *-pajjitabba* Vin. I. 164[10], D. II. 141[11] from *-pajjati* (root *pad*); *paṭivijjhitabba* 'that which is to be comprehended' DCo. I. 20[25] from *-vijjhati* (root *vyadh*). From Passive *-bhijjati*: *bhijjitabba* JāCo. III. 56[23] as against *bhettavya*; from *jāyati* 'is born, originated': *jāyitabba* Th2. 455. With reference to § 142, 144: *vijahitabba* Vin. III. 200[17] (from root *hā*); *nidahitabba* Vin. I. 46[28], *saddahitabba* Milp. 310[2]

[1] The suffix may occasionally be extended by *ka*. Cf. *khāditabbaka* DhCo. III. 137[9].

[2] As in Pkr.; Pischel, § 570.

from *dahati* (root *dhā*); *bhañjitabba* Vin. I. 74[10] (from root *bhaj*, *bhañj*), *bhuñjitabba* Mhvs. 5. 127 (from root *bhuj*).

§ 200. The Future Passive Participle of root *bhū* too may be constructed on the Present-stem[1]: *hotabba* Vin. I. 46[19], *paribhotabba* that which should be deprecated' S. I. 69[7], Sn. p. 91 from *hoti*, *-bhoti* (§ 131. 2). The *aya*-stems (Cl. X., Causatives, Denominatives) too derive it in the same way directly from the contracted *e* stem[2]. Examples are numerous: *codetabba* Vin. II. 2[21] as against *coditavya*; *sāretabba* Vin. II. 2[22] from *sāreti* (root *smar*); *pūjetabba* M. III. 205[20] (stem *pūjay-*); *lañchetabba* Vin. II. 267[3] from *lañcheti* 'seals'; *ñāpetabba* Vin. II. 2[23] from *ñāpeti* (*jñā*); *ghaṃsāpetabba* Vin. II. 266[28] from *ghaṃsāpeti* 'causes to rub' (root *ghars*); *koṭṭāpetabba* Vin. II. 266[29] from *koṭṭāpeti* 'causes to hit'; *paṭiggahetabba* 'that which should be accepted' Vin. I. 46[13] from *gaheti* (§ 139. 2) etc. A whole list of such froms is to be found in Vin. I. 46-50. I cite from there *otāpetabba* 'that which is to be heated', *paṭiyādetabba* 'that which is to be constructed' (root *yat*), *ṭhapetabba* 'that which is to be erected' (root *sthā*), *thaketabba* 'that which is to be closed' (root *sthag*, § 39. 1) etc. We have a curious form in *chedātabba* 'that which is to be cut off' Vin. I. 50[15], the form expected being *chedetabba*. Besides it there is *chedāpetabba*[3].

§ 201. Moreover there is in Pāli the Future Passive Participles in *-anīya* or *-aneyya*[4] = Skr. *-anīya*. Thus *labhanīya* Th2. 513 (*alabbhaneyya* 'unattainable' Jā. III. 205[9] is due to contamination of *labbha* § 202 with *labhanīya*); *pūjanīya* Sn. 259 or *-neyya* Th1. 186 = *pūjanīya*; *anatthaneyya* 'what should not be striven after, useless' Th1. 1073 from *arthay-*; *dassanīya* 'that which is worth seeing, charming' Vin. I. 38[25], D. I. 47[11], JāCo. I. 509[8] and *dassaneyya* Dpvs. 15. 39 = *darśanīya*. These forms have very often a substantive meaning. Thus *karaṇīya* 'task, duty'; *mohaneyya* 'enchantment' Jā. III. 499[10]; *yāpanīya* 'sustenance' Jā. VI. 224[13], Vin. I. 59[10]; *bhojanīya* 'liquid food' and *khādanīya* 'solid food' Vin. I. 18[29], D. I. 108[7] etc., Skr. *karaṇīya*,

[1] As in Pkr AMāg., JMāh *hoyavva*, Ś. Māg. *hodavva* besides Ś. *bhavidavva*; Pischel, § 570.

[2] Cf. Pkr. AMāg. *paritāveyavva*, *dameyavva*.

[3] Instead of *tuvaṭṭitabba* Vin. II. 121[11] from *tuvaṭṭeti* 'lies down' one would expect *tuvaṭṭetabba*.

[4] In Pkr. *-aṇijja* and *-aṇia*. Cf. AMāg. *pūyaṇijja*, *daṃsaṇijja* etc.; Pischel, § 571.

mohanīya etc.; *khamanīya* 'toleration' Vin. I. 59[10], D. II. 99[22], JāCo. I. 408[11] = *kṣamaṇīya*.

§ 202. The Future Passive Participles in *-ya* mostly belong to the two oldest periods of the language.[1] Hence, for instance, even *haññа* 'he who should be killed' Jā. IV. 273[27] is explained in the Comm. by *hanitabba*, *saddheyya* 'worthy of credence' Jā. III. 62[18] by *saddhātabba*. Examples from roots in vowel: *neyya* 'that which should be led' Sn. 803 = *neya* (root *nī*); *bhabba* 'capable of' Vin. I. 17[18], A. III. 8[30] = *bhavya* (root *bhū*); *pameyya* 'that which is to be measured' A. I. 266[18], Pu. 35[3] = *prameya* (root *mā*); similarly *viññeyya* 'that which can be perceived' Vin. I. 184[20], D. I. 245[17] etc, *deyya* Sn. 982, Vin. III. 11[3], D. I. 87[10], *peyya* 'drinkable' D. I. 244[14], II. 89[14], Milp. 2[14] = *vijñeya*, *deya*, *peya*. Also *suppahāya* 'that which should be easily forsaken' Sn. 772 (root *hā*) as Rv. 10. 103.5 *vijñāya*. From roots in *r*: *a-kāriya* 'unfeasible' Dh. 176 = *kārya* (besides *kicca* 'that which should be done, task, duty' Dh. 276, Thl. 167 etc. = *kṛtya*), *a-saṃhāriya* 'indestructible' S. V. 219[2] = *-hārya*, both with Svarabhakti. From other consonant roots: *khajja* 'masticable' and *bhojja* 'edible' Milp. 2[14] = *khādya*, *bhojya*; *vajja* 'that which should be avoided, sin' Dh. 252, D. I. 63[15] etc. = *varjya*; *vajjha* 'he who must be killed' Jā. VI. 528[2], JāCo. I. 439[4] = *vadhya*; *a-bhejja* 'inseparable' JāCo. III. 51[4] = *bhedya*; *labbha* 'attainable, possible' D. II. 118[29], M. II. 220[13] = *labhya*; *sayha* 'that which is to be borne' Sn. 253 = *sahya*. Form root *lih* 'to lick' we have in Milp. 2[14] *leyya* instead of **leyha* = *lehya*, due to attraction of *peyya* occurring at its side. Svarabhakti is in evidence in *a-sādhiya* 'incurable' Mhvs. 5. 218 = *sādhya*. We have a new construction in *a-sakkuṇeyya* 'impossible' JāCo. I. 55[3] from the Present *sakkuṇāti*, after the pattern of *deyya* from *dadāti*.

§ 203. The Future Passive Participles in *-tāya*, *-tayya* or *-teyya* are a peculiarity of Pāli.[2] Examples out of the two oldest periods of the language: *ñātayya*, *daṭṭhayya*, *pattayya* 'that which is to be known, seen, attained' S. IV. 93[6-7], *ñāteyya*, *daṭṭheyya*, *patteyya* S. I. 61[26-27] (root *jñā*, *darś*, *āp* with *pra*); *a-tasitāya* 'where one need not

[1] The corresponding Prākrit forms (cf. AMāg. *bhavva*, *pejja*, JMāh. *neya* = *jñeya*) in Pischel, § 572.

[2] R. O. Franke, PGr. p. 35, N. 4. II; Trenckner, Notes 66, foot-note 27 (JPTS, 1908, p. 117).

fear' S. III. 57[27]. From Causatives: *ghātetāya* 'to be killed', *jāpetāya* 'to be conquered', *pabbājetāya* 'to be banished' (root *vraj*) M. I. 231[2-3], II. 122[1-2]. Also *lajjitāya*[1] 'that of which one has to be ashamed' Dh. 316.

4. Infinitives.

§ 204. 1. The Infinitives in *-tave* = Ved. *-tave* or *-tavai*, as well as some forms in *-tāye*, *-tuye*[2] are confined to the Gāthā-language (and the artificial poetry). (*a*) Infinitives in *-tave*. From roots in vowel: *netave* Dh. 180, S. I. 107[24] (verse); *sotave* Kacc. IV. 2. 12 (Senart, p. 485); *dātave* Sn. 286, Jā. I. 190[3], *yātave* Sn. 834, *hātave* Dh. 34, Sn. 817. Also *nidhetave* Jā. III. 17[6] (Comm. *nidhānatthāya*) from the *e*-stem of root *dhā*. From other e-stems: *rajetave* Thl. 1155 from *rajeti* 'colours, paints', *lapetave* Ud. 21[11] (verse) from *lapeti* 'speaks, addresses'. From roots ending in consonant: *gantave* 'to go' Th2. 332, Jā. IV. 221[26] (Comm. *gantuṃ*), *vattave* 'to say' S. I. 205[2] (verse) = *gántave*, *váktave*. (*b*) Infinitives in *-tuye*: *kātuye* Th2. 418 (root *kar*, Comm. *kātuṃ*); *marituye* Th2. 426; *gaṇetuye* Bu. 4. 28 from *gaṇeti* 'counts'; *hetuye* Bu. 2. 10 from *hoti*. (*c*) Infinitives in *-tāye*: *dakkhitāye* D. II. 254[7] (verse) = S. I. 26[25] from the new Present-stem *dakkha-* derived from the Future of *darś*; *jagghitāye* 'to laugh' Jā. III. 226[10] (Comm. *hasitvā*, or *hositena*), *pucchitāye* 'in order to ask' Jā. V. 137[6] (Comm. *pucchituṃ*); *khāditāye* 'to eat' Jā. V. 33[7] governed by *arahati*.—2. A rare and archaic Infinitive form is to be found in *etase* Th2. 291 'to go' (Comm. *etuṃ*, *gantuṃ*), governed by *nāsakkhiṃ*.—3. Finally, the Datives of Verbal Nouns are not seldom used as Infinitives: thus *savanāya* (governed by *labhati*) '(is fortunate enough) to hear' D. III. 80[16]; *dassanāya* (governed by *pahoti*) '(is in a position) to see' M. II. 131[24]; *karaṇāya* (governed by *arahati*) '(can) do' Jā. III. 172[23-24]; *idhāgamanāya* (governed by *pariyāyamakāsi*) '(has made it possible) to come here' D. I. 179[18] etc.; *vicakkhukammāya* 'in order to dazzle' S. I. 112[13]; *adubbhāya* (governed by *sapassu*) '(swear) not to injure' S. I. 225[19] etc.

[1] Norman in his edition of DhCo. III. 490 wrongly divides the words into *alajjitā ye* and *lajjitā ye*. Cf. the Commentary.

[2] In Pkr. there are corresponding Infinitives in *-ttae*, *-ittae*, such as AMāg. *ittae*, *hottae*, *pucchitae*; E. Müller, Beitr. z. Pkr. Gr., p. 61; Pischel, PkrGr. § 578.

§ 205. The Infinitive which is most current in every period of the language is however that in *-tuṃ*. The number of historical forms is very large. Thus from roots ending in vowels: *dātuṃ*, *saddhātuṃ*, *ñātuṃ* from roots *dā*, *dhā*, *jñā*; *nibbātuṃ* 'to die' Mhvs. 5. 219 (root *vā*); *vinetuṃ* JāCo. I. 501[15], III. 103[4] (root *nī*); *etuṃ* Th2Co. 224[29] (root *i*); *ketuṃ* 'to buy' Jā. III. 282[14]; *vikketuṃ* 'to sell' JāCo. III. 283[12]=(*vi*)*kretum*; *ocetuṃ* 'to collect' Th1. 199=*avacetum*; *sotuṃ* Sn. 384, D. II. 2[7]=*śrotum*. From roots in *r*: *kātuṃ*=*kartum*; *uddhātuṃ* 'to draw out' Th1. 83, *āhattuṃ* M. I. 395[5]=*āhartum* from root *har*=*-hartum*. From roots in nasal: *gantuṃ*; in mute: *vattuṃ* Sn. 431, S. I. 129[27] (verse)=*vaktum*; *puṭṭhuṃ* Sn. 91, S. I. 15[7] (verse)=*praṣṭuṃ*; *avabhottuṃ* 'to enjoy' Jā. III. 272[23]=*-bhoktum* (root *bhuj*); *yaṭṭhuṃ* 'to sacrifice' Sn. 461=*yaṣṭum* (root *yaj*); *chettuṃ* Th1. 188=*chettum*; *pattuṃ* 'to attain' DhCo. III. 399[4]=*prāptum*; *sottuṃ* S. I. 111[2] (verse), apparently derived directly from *svaptum* 'to sleep'; *laddhuṃ* 'to attain' JāCo. II. 352[14], DhCo. III. 117[14]=*labdhum*. From roots in sibilant: *daṭṭhuṃ*=*draṣṭum*.—Also constructions with *i* are quite numerous: *jīvituṃ* JāCo. I. 263[3]=*jīvitum*; *kīḷituṃ* JāCo. III. 188[28]=*krīḍitum*; *bhavituṃ* JāCo. IV. 137[25]=*bhavitum*; *uddharituṃ* (besides *uddhātuṃ*) JāCo. I. 313[6] from root *har* (Skr. *haritum* besides *hartum*). From Desideratives: *tikicchituṃ* JāCo. I. 485[11]=*cikitsitum*; *vīmaṃsituṃ* Mhvs. 37. 234 (Colombo ed. 184)=*mīmāṃsitum*. From a Causative: *dhārayituṃ* Anāgatavs., JPTS. 1886. 35[23]=*dhārayitum*. From a Denominative: *gopayituṃ* DhCo. III. 488[10].

§ 206. The Infinitive is very often derived directly from the Present-stem[1]. Thus *pappotuṃ* 'to attain' Th2. 60=S. I. 129[16] from *pappoti*; *hotuṃ* from *hoti*. Also in the case of *e*-stems (Causative etc.) the Infinitive may be directly derived from the Present-stem: *sodhetuṃ* Vin. II. 34[5], JāCo. I. 292[14]; *bhāvetuṃ* DhCo. III. 171[10]; *vāretuṃ* JāCo. IV. 2[18]; *gahetuṃ* Vin. I. 92[37], JāCo. I. 222[31], Mhvs. 8. 23 (cf. § 139. 2), *gāhetuṃ* Mhvs. 33. 48 and *gāhāpetuṃ* JāCo. I. 506[28]; *ṭhapetuṃ* Vin. II. 194[33], D. II. 177[7]; *kārāpetuṃ* Mhvs. 5. 80. The form *tārayetuṃ* Sn. 319 is a double-construction,—a contamination of *tārayituṃ* and *tāretuṃ*.—The type in *-ituṃ* has been very productive. In later literature it has in many cases supplanted the historical forms in *-tuṃ*. The form *bhottuṃ*, for instance (see § 205), has been explained in the Comm. by *bhuñjituṃ*. Examples of new construc-

1. Corresponding innovations also in Pkr. Cf. AMāg. *vārcuṃ*, Māh. JMāh. *mariuṃ*, Māh. *pucchiuṃ*, Ś *bhuñjiduṃ*, *suṇiduṃ* etc.; Pischel, § 573 ff.

tions: With reference to § 130-132: *cajituṃ* JāCo. III. 69[4] as against *tyaktum* (root *tyaj* 'to forsake'); *marituṃ* D. II. 330[8] as against *martum*; *abhivijinituṃ* M. II. 71[32] (root *ji*); *nisīdituṃ* Dpvs. I. 55; *uṭṭhahituṃ* JāCo. II. 22[17], *upaṭṭhahituṃ* DhCo. III. 269[20] from *ṭhahati*. With reference to § 134-135: *pucchituṃ* Sn. 510, Vin. I. 93[27]; *ukkhipituṃ* JāCo. I. 264[9] as against *kṣeptum*; *phusituṃ* Thl. 945, DhCo. III. 199[4] (verse) as against *spraṣṭum*; *pavisituṃ* JāCo. III. 26[6] as against *veṣṭum*; *supituṃ* Thl. 193; *paṭicchituṃ* JāCo. IV. 137[28]; *muñcituṃ* D. I. 96[10]; *siñcituṃ* JāCo. VI. 583[27]; *nibbindituṃ* 'to feel disgust' D. II. 198[22] from root *vid, vindati*. With reference to § 136-138: *naccituṃ* DhCo. III. 102[7]; *-pajjituṃ* Thl. 1140, A. III. 8[18]; *pamajjituṃ* Thl. 452; *virajjituṃ* 'to be free' D. II. 198[22]; *vijjhituṃ* Mhvs. 6. 28; *passituṃ* JāCo. I. 222[7], Mhvs. 4. 21. Also from a Passive stem: *pamuccituṃ* 'to free oneself' Thl. 253; *vimuccituṃ* D. II. 198[22]. Further: *sināyituṃ* M. I. 39[6]; *jhāyituṃ* 'to meditate' Vin II. 147[34] (verse); *palāyituṃ* JāCo. II. 19[26]; *sajjhāyituṃ* (§ 188. 1) DhCo. III. 445[21]. With reference to § 142: *jahituṃ* JāCo. I. 138[9], III. 94[17]; *saṃvidahituṃ* Vin. I. 287[13] from root *dhā*; *paṭijaggituṃ* Thl. 193. With reference to § 144-148: *bhañjituṃ* Thl. 488; *bhuñjituṃ* (see above); *chinditum* V.vCo. 119[7]; *kiṇituṃ* JāCo. III. 282[10] and *vikkiṇituṃ* JāCo. III. 283[23] (in explanation of *vikketuṃ*); *bandhituṃ* Th2. 299; *gaṇhituṃ* JāCo. II. 159[4], III. 26[2]; *suṇituṃ* Milp. 91[16]; *pāpuṇituṃ* A. II. 49[16], M. III. 197[20], JāCo. IV. 267[6].

§ 207. As in Skr., in compounds with *-kāma* the Infinitive has the ending *-tu*[1]: *jīvitukāma* 'he who desires to live' Dh. 123, D. II. 330[8]; *pabbajitukāma* 'he who desires to forsake the world' DhCo. III. 273[8]; *gantukāma* 'he who wishes to go' JāCo. I. 222[13]; *daṭṭhukāma* 'he who wishes to see' Sn. 685; *amaritukāma* 'he who does not wish to die' D. II. 330[8] etc.

5. Gerunds.

§ 208. The Gerunds are formed with the suffixes *-tvā* and *-ya*, for the first of which there often appears, particularly in the Gāthā-language, also the suffix *-tvāna*. The suffix *-ya* appears particularly after compounds, but this rule is not so strictly followed in Pāli as in Skr. The suffix *-tvā*, *-tvāna* is clearly widening its sphere progress-

[1] Similarly also in Pkr.; Pischel, § 577.

ively, and is by no means confined only to the simplex. According to statistics prepared by me on the basis of a large section of the Jātaka-Commentary, the Gerunds in *-tvā* occur 8 to 9 times more frequently than those in *-ya*. In the canonical prose the difference is not so great. In the Commentaries too the forms in *-ya* are readily replaced by those in *-tvā*, as *saddhāya* Jā. V. 176^{8} by *saddahitvā*, *aññāya* Jā. I. 308^{21} by *ajānitvā*. The few forms in *-tūna*[1] are confined to the Gāthā-language, as also those in *-yāna*, which is evidently a new construction on the analogy of *-tvā* : *-tvāna*.

§ 209. There are many historical forms among the Gerunds in *-tvā*, *-tvāna*. From roots in vowel: *ñatvā*, *ñatvāna* = *jñātvā*, *nhatvā* = *snātvā*, *datvā* = *dattvā* (in analogy with these forms also *pidhatvā* Th2. 480 from root *dhā* as against *(d)hitvā*, and *ṭhatvā* from root *sthā* as against *sthitvā*); *pītvā(na)* Dh. 205, Th1. 103, 710, Jā. II. 71^{6} = *pītvā* (root *pa*); *hitvā(na)* Sn. 60, 284 etc. = *hitvā* (root *hā*). Also *jitvā* Th1. 336 fr m root *ji*; *sutvā* = *śrutvā*, *hutvā* = *bhūtvā*. From roots in *r*: *katvā(na)* = *kṛtvā* (*purakkhatvā* D. II. 207^{23}, Jā. VI. 516^{19} or *purakkhitvā* Vv. 84. 49). From roots in mutes: *mutvā* (§ 58. 3) Jā. I. 375^{5} = *muktvā* (root *muc*); *vatvā* = **vaktvā*; *bhutvā(na)* Th1. 23, S. I. 8^{25} (verse), Jā. III. 53^{17} = *bhuktvā* (the *o* of *bhotvā* S. IV. 74^{7} (verse) is to be explained according to § 10. 2); *chetvā(na)* Dh. 283, 346, Vin. I. 83^{1}, JāCo. III. 396^{75} = *chittvā* (*e* according to § 10. 2, or due to analogy of *jetvā*, *netvā*, § 210); *bhetvā(na)* Th1. 753 = *bhittvā*[2]; *patvā* from root *āp* (Skr. *āptvā*) with *pra*; *laddhā(na)* Sn. 67, 228 etc., *paṭiladdhā* Vv. 80.7 = *labdhvā*. From root *darś* the Gerund is *disvā(na)* = *dṛṣṭvā*.[3] The roots in *n*, *m* retain the nasal through the influence of forms like Skr. *śāntvā*. Thus we have also *hantvā* as against *hatvā*; *mantvā* Mhvs. 12. 50 (besides *mantā*[4] Vv. 63. 6), as against *matvā*; *gantvā(na)* (*āgantvā* Sn. 415, JāCo. I. 151^{1} etc.) as against *gantvā*.—Historical forms in *-itvā*: *patitvā*, *pacitvā*, *vanditvā*, *khāditvā* as in Skr.; *nikkhamitvā* JāCo. III. 26^{14}, *akkamitvā* Vin. I. 188^{29} etc. = *kramitvā* (besides *krāntvā*); *sayitvā* JāCo. II. 77^{14} = *śayitvā*

[1] The same suffix occurs also in Pkr. in the form *-tūṇa*, *-ūṇa*; Pischel, § 584, 586. The distinction made in Skr. between the use of *-tvā* and *-ya* is unknown also in Pkr.; ibid., § 581.

[2] Also in Pkr. AMāg *chettā*, *bhettā*; Pischel, § 582.

[3] As AMāg. *dissā*; Ibid. § 334. According to H. Kern (Toevoegselen op 't Woordenboek van Childers I. 63) the form *dṛṣṭvā* is retained in *a diṭṭhā* (*var lec.* of *adaṭṭhā*) Jā. IV. 192^{6}.

[4] As AMāg. *hantā*, *mantā*.

(root *śi*). Similarly from Causative[1]: *bhojayitvāna* Jā. VI. 577[29] = *bhojayitvā*; *gāhayitvā* Mhvs. 10. 31 = *grāhayitvā*, *ghātayitvā* Milp. 219[16] from *ghāteti* (root *han*), *janayitvā* Milp. 218[21] as in Skr.; *ṭhapayitvāna* Mhvs. 19. 31 = *sthāpayitvā*, and in the same way from double-causatives: *gāhāpayitvā* Mhvs. 7. 49 etc. From Desideratives. Intensives and Denominatives: *a-jigucchitvā* JāCo. I. 422[20] = *jugupsitvā*; *vīmaṃsitvā* JāCo. VI. 368[2] = *mīmāṃsitvā*; *vavakkhitvāna* D.II. 256[9] (verse) = *vivakṣitvā*; *cirāyitvā* Mhvs. Ṭī. 124[22] etc.

§ 210. New constructions out of Present-stems are again quite frequent. Thus we have forms from Causatives, Denominatives etc. with the contracted *e*-stem, and in fact these forms are more frequent than those in *-ayitvā*. Examples: *dosetvā* JāCo. I. 152[10]; *codetvā* Vin. II. 2[22]; *sāretvā* (root *smar*) Ibid.; *bhāvetvā* A. V. 105[15]; *ghātetvā* Mhvs. 25.7; *ṭhapetvā* Dh. 40, D. I. 105[27] etc.; *gahetvā* (§ 139.2); *vandāpetvā* Vin. I. 82[23], *kārāpetvā* Ibid.; *āmantetvā* (§ 187. 1) Th1. 34, JāCo. II. 133[2]; *a-gaṇetvā* JāCo. II. 229[11] etc. occurring very frequently. The roots in *ī* too take after them: *jetvā* Sn. 439, Th2. 7 from *jeti* (root *ji*) as against Skr. *jitvā*; *netvā(na)* Sn. 295, Vin. II. 11[11] as against *nītvā*. Also *abhibhotvāna* Th1. 429, from an *abhibhoti* 'overcomes'.—The number of new constructions in *-itvā*[2] derived from Present-stems is extraordinarily large. With reference to § 130: *labhitvā* JāCo. I. 150[20] as against Skr. *labdhvā*; *vasitvā* JāCo. I. 78[26] as against *uṣitvā*; *uddharitvā* D. I. 234[6], JāCo. III. 52[14], *saṃharitvā* JāCo. I. 265[27] from *harati* as against *hṛtvā*; *otaritvā* JāCo. I. 223[19], II. 19[5] as against *tīrtvā*; *sarivā* Th2. 40 as against *sṛtvā*; *ghaṃsitvā* JāCo. III. 226[1] as against *ghṛṣṭvā*. With reference to § 131: *vinayitvāna* Sn. 485 besides *netvāna*; *a-jinitvā* Mhvs. 32. 18 besides *jetvā*; *-bhavitvā* Sn. 52 as against *bhūtvā*. With reference to § 132: *pivitvā* JāCo. I. 419[29] besides *pītvā*; *nisīditvā* passim; (*v*)*uṭṭhahitvā* Vin. I. 2[29], JāCo. I. 208[1] etc. Also *ghāyitvā* DhCo. III. 270[3] as against Skr. *jighṛtvā*. With reference to § 133: *ārohitvā* Vin. I. 15[16], *orohitvā* Vin. I. 15[33] as against *rūḍhvā*. With reference to § 134: *pakkhipitvā* JāCo. I. 265[3] etc. as against *kṣiptvā*; *ādisitvāna* Th2. 311 from root *diś*; *pavisitvā* D. II. 331[19] etc. from root *viś*; *gilitvā* Mhvs. 31. 52; *okiritvā* JāCo. III. 59[14]; *supitvāna* Th1. 84 as against *suptvā*. With reference to § 135: *icchitvā* JāCo. I. 256[17] from root *iṣ*; *muñcitvā* JāCo. I. 375[11], in explanation of *mutvā*; *siñcitvā* Sn. 771; *vilimpitvā* JāCo. I.

[1] As AMāg. *uttāsaittā*, *vigovaittā*.

[2] Corresponding Pkr. forms, particularly in AMāg., in Pischel, § 582 Cf. *vasittā*, *jiṇittā*, *bhavittā*, *jāṇittā*, *kiṇittā*, *giṇhittā*, *karittā* etc.

265[29] as against *liptvā*. With reference to § 136: *niliyitvā* JāCo. I. 500[13], III. 26[16]; *kujjhitvā* Mhvs. 5. 141; *saṃnayhitvā* D. II. 175[15], M. II. 99[6], JāCo. I. 129[7]; *-pajjitvā* Thl. 158, JaCo. I. 138[8], II. 70[18]; *sussitvā* JāCo. II. 5[28], 339[10]; *pamajjitvā(na)* Dh. 172, Thl. 871; *vijjhitvā* JāCo. I. 150[18]; *laggitvā* JāCo. II. 19[22]; *passitvā* Thl. 510, JāCo. II. 155[4]; *chijjitvā(na)* JāCo. I. 167[27], Mhvs. 17. 47; *namassitvā* S. I. 234[33](verse); *ādiyitvā* JāCo. I. 430[26]. With reference to § 138: *yāyitvā* Sn. 418; *nhāyitvā* Vin. III. 110[16]; *nahāyitvā* JāCo. II. 27[6]; *gāyitvā* DhCo. I. 15[14]; *sajjhāyitvā* (§ 188. 1) DhCo. III. 447[19]. With reference to § 140 and 142 f.: *hanitvāna* Jā. III. 185[20]; *a-vijahitvā* Thūpavs. 8[17]; *-dahitvā* Vin. I. 287[16], III. 53[4], JāCo. V. 176[13] from *dahati* (root *dhā*); *paṭijaggitvā* DhCo. III. 30[10]; *daditvā* Thl. 532. S. I. 174[9] (verse). With reference to § 144: *chinditvā* D. I. 224[14], JāCo. I. 222[29], II. 90[15], and *bhinditvā* JāCo. I. 425[4]. 490[29] besides *chetvā*, *bhetvā*; *bhuñjitvā* JāCo. III. 53[20] in explanation of *bhutvā*; *riñcitvā* Th2. 93 as against *riktvā*. With reference to § 145 f.: *jānitvā* Jā. I. 293[14], JāCo. II. 246[18] besides *ñatvā*; *kiṇitvā* Milp. 48[16]; *gaṇhitvā* passim, as against *gṛhitvā*; *nimminitvāna* Thl. 563; *bandhitvā* Vin. I. 46[17], JāCo. I. 428[26] as against *baddhvā*. With reference to § 147-149: *vicinitvā* Vin. I. 133[14] as against *citvā*; *suṇitvā(na)* Th2. 44, Jā. V. 96[9]; *a-pāpuṇitvāna* Th2. 494; *karitvā* Sn. 444, Jā. VI. 577[30], JāCo. I. 267[31] besides *katvā*.

§ 211. Of examples of Gerunds in *-tūna* there occur in Kacc. IV. 3. 15, 4. 6 and 7 (Senart, p. 497, 503): *janitūna*, *kātūna* (*kattūna*), *gantūna*, *khantūna*, *hantūna*, *mantūna*. I quote here from literature: *hātūna* Jā. IV. 280[17] from root *har* (Comm *haritvā*), *apakiritūna* Th2. 447 (Comm. *chaḍḍetvā*), *nikkhamitūna* Thl. 73; *āpucchitūna* Th2. 426. Also *chaḍḍūna* Th2. 469 from **chardtūna*. Comm. *chaḍḍetvā* 'after throwing away.'

§ 212. Gerunds in *-ya*[1]. From roots ending in vowel: *abhiññāya*[2], *aññāya* = *abhi-*, *ā jñāya*; *ādāya* (and other compounds of *dā*) = *ādāya*; *nidhāya* Dh 142, 405 and other compounds of *dhā* = *nidhāya* *uṭṭhāya* (*paṭṭhāya* as postposition 'starting from.........') = *utthāya*. From root *i* (Skr. *-itya*) we have *pecca* 'after dying' Dh. 15 ff., JāCo. II. 417[1] (verse) = *pretya*, *paricca* Th2. 71 = *parītya*, *samecca* D. II. 273[20] (verse) = *sametya*, *paṭicca* 'in consequence of' = *pratītya*. From root *bhū*: *abhibhuyya* Dh. 328, Sn. 45, Thl. 1242, D. II. 110[8]. In

[1] Corresponding Pkr. forms in Pischel, § 589 ff.

On the contraction of *-āya* into *-ā* see above § 27. 2.

analogy of *abhibhoti* : *abhibhuyya* there has been formed from *pappoti* a Gerund *pappuyya* Sn. 593, 829, Th1. 364, 876, S. I. 7[25] (verse), 212[18] (verse). In Vin. II. 156[28] (verse) there is *appuyya* from the simplex **appoti* = *āpnoti*. From root *kar*: *nikacca* Vin. III. 90[24] (verse) = *nikṛtya*, *sakkacca* Vv. 11.6 (mostly *sakkaccaṃ*) = *satkṛtya*, *paṭigacca* (§ 38. 1). From roots in nasal : *āhacca*, *ūhacca* Jā. II. 71[16], III. 206[22], *nihacca* Th2. 109 = -*hatya* (root *han*) ; *palikhañña* Sn. 968 or *palikhāya* S. I. 123[6] (verse) from root *khan* with *pari* 'to dig out, exterminate' = Skr. -*khanya* and -*khāya* ; *āgamma*, *saṃgamma* etc. = -*gamya* ; *nikkhamma* Mhvs. 5. 221 = *niṣkramya* ; also simplex *gamya* Jā. V. 31[3] (Comm. *gantvā*). From roots in mute : *āpuccha* Th2. 416 (Comm. *āpucchitvā*), *sampuccha* S. I. 176[13] (verse), DhCo. IV. 9[2] = -*pṛcchya* ; *pariccajja* 'after forsaking' Jā. III. 194[29] = *parityajya* ; *pavibhajja* 'after separating' Th1. 1242 = -*bhajya* ; *saṃcicca* 'after deliberation' Vin. I. 97[2] = *saṃcitya* ; *pabhijja* Th1. 1242 = *prabhidya* ; -*pajja* = -*padya*; -*sajja* = -*sadya*; *panujja* 'after frightening away' Sn. 359, 1055 = *pranudya* ; *atívijjha* 'after piercing through' M. II. 112[1] = -*vidhya* (root *vyadh*) ; *ārabbha* 'beginning with ......' = *ārabhya* ; *olubbha* 'hankering after......' Th2. 17, S. I. 118[3], JāCo. I. 265[14] = -*lubhya*. From a root in sibilant : *okkassa* 'by dragging after' (p. 79, foot-note 4) D. II. 74[29, 31] = *avakṛṣya*. From roots in *h* : *ā*-, *abhi*-, *o-ruyha* Th1. 147, JāCo. I. 438[24], II. 27[5] = -*ruhya* ; *abbuyha* 'after tearing out' Th1. 298, Th2. 15 = *ābṛhya* ; -*gayha* = -*gṛhya* ; *pasayha* 'forcibly' D. II. 74[29] = *prasahya*. Besides -*gayha* there is also *gahāya* 'after seizing' Sn. 791, *samuggahāya* Sn. 797, clearly from *gahāyati* (§ 186. 5). The proportion *gaheti* : *gahāya* has also led to the formation of *anvāya* (post-position) 'on account of, by means of' D. I. 13[12], JāCo. II. 39[16] from *anveti*[1] (root *i* with *anu*) and *uñchāya* 'having searched' Jā. V. 90[10] (Comm. *uñchitvā*).

§ 213. The Svarabhakti-vowel *i* appears not seldom before the suffix -*ya*. Thus in *pakiriya* 'letting (the hair) loose' D. II. 139[30] = *prakīrya* ; *liṅgiya* Th2. 398 = -*liṅgya* (Comm. *āliṅgetvā*) ; *abhirūhiya* Th2. 27 (besides -*ruyha*) ; (*saṃ*)*avekkhiya* Sn. 115, Mhvs. 5. 195 ; *pekkhiya* Mhvs. 5. 194 = -*īkṣya* ; *nikujjiya* Th2. 28, 30 from *nikujjati* (Skr. *kubj*) 'turns round, upsets' ; *vivajjiya* Th2. 167 from *vivajjeti* ; *virājiya* Th2. 18 from *virājeti* 'sends away from oneself, is displeased

[1] A double-construction with the suffixes -*ya* and -*tvā* is to be found in *abhiruyhitvā* quoted in Kacc. II. 6. 5 (Senart, p. 321), as against the usual *abhirūhitvā* and *abhiruyha*. Similarly *ogayhitvā* from *ogāhati* 'dips in' Mhvs. 38 102 (ed. Colombo).

with'; *cintiya* Mhvs. 7. 17 = -*cintya*; *kāriya* Mhvs. 3. 5 = -*kārya*. On the analogy of *kāretuṃ*, *kāreti*: *kāriya* there has been formed a *nicchiya* 'after deciding' Mhvs. 37. 233 (Colombo ed. 183) to *niccheti* (= *nicchinati* § 131), *nicchetuṃ* (§ 205).—A new type of Gerunds in -*iya* was originated in this way, and the new formations derived from the Present-stem took after this type. Thus with reference to § 130: *sumariya* Mhvs. 4. 66, as against -*smṛtya*; *atitariya* Sn. 219 as against -*tīrya*. With reference to § 135: *nisiñciya* Mhvs. 7. 8 as against -*sicya*. With reference to § 136: *passiya* Th2. 399. With reference to § 144: *chindiya* Th2. 480 as against -*chidya*. With reference to § 145 f.: *avajāniya* Sn. 713 as against -*jñāya*; *bandhiya* Th2. 81 as against -*badhya*. With reference to § 147ff.: *suṇiya* Mhvs. 23. 102 as against -*śrutya*; *kariya* Th2. 402 as against -*kṛtya*. Also the new Present-stem *dakkha*- (§ 136. 3) has given rise to *dakkhiya* Th2. 381 f.

§ 214. Examples of Gerunds in -*yāna* are: *uttariyāna* Jā. V. 204^9 (Comm. *uttaritvā*, *avattharitvā*); *ovariyāna* Th2. 367, 369 (instead of it *ovadiyāna* Th2Co. 250^{26} explained as *ovaditvā*); *pakkhandiyāna* Vv. 84. 11 (in VvCo. 338^{13} explained as *pakkhanditvā*) from root *skand*.—Nasal ending is to be found in *khādiyānaṃ* 'having eaten' Jā. V. 24^4, *anumodiyanaṃ* 'having been pleased' Jā. V. 143^9, etc.

INDEX TO PART I, PĀLI LITERATURE

Figures refer to *paragraphs* in Part I, pp. 9-58 excepting where page is specifically mentioned.

A. NAMES OF AUTHORS

Aggavaṃsa 50
Attaragama Baṇḍāra Rājaguru 53.2
Anuruddha 26.7, 32.4
Ariyavaṃsa 42.1, 44.5, 53.2
Ariyālaṃkāra 47.7
Ānanda 25.2, 26.1, 44.5
Uttamasikkha 47.7
Udumbara 44.5
Upatissa 29.2
Upasena 26.2
Kaccāyana 19.1 & 2, 30, 45, 46, 47, 52.1
Kassapa 26.4 29.1
Kyacvā 47.8
Khema 26.6
Culla Dhammapāla 26.1 & 6
Chapada 30, 33, 46.1
Jambudhaja 53.2
Ñāṇavilāsa 47.8
Ñāṇābhivaṃsa 43.5
Tipiṭakālaṃkāra 43.1
Tilokaguru 43.2
Dāṭhānāga p. 38 f.-n. 3
Dhammakitti 34 1—36—39.2, 46.5
Dhammadassin 53.2
Dhammapāla 25.3, 30, 44.5
Dhammavilāsa 33
Dhammasiri 27
Dhammasenāpati p, 33 f.-n. 2
Nāgita 46.6
Paññasāmin 44.6
Piyadassin 49 1
Buddhaghosa 21, 22, 23, 24, 25, 30, 31, 44.5—42.6
Buddhadatta 26.1 & 3, 32.3, 34 3, 44.5
Buddhanāga 32.2
Buddhappiya 37, 39.1, 46.4
Buddharakkhita 34.3
Maṅgala 53.2
Mahākaccāyana 44.5
Mahākassapa 43.4
Mahānāma 26.3—28—42.6
Mahāmaṅgala (cf. Maṅgala) 40.3
Mahāyasa 32.1—47.7
Mahāvijitāvin 47.11
Mahāsāmin 27
Medhaṃkara 34.4—40.1—49.2
Moggallāna (Moggallāyana) 45, 48, 49, 51—52.2
Yamaka p. 38 f. n. 1
Raṭṭhasāra 42 4
Rassathera 47.7
Rāhula 46.4, 48, 49.1 & 3
Vajirabuddhi 26.5
Vanaratana Medhaṃkara=the third Medhaṃkara
Vācissara 32.3, 34.2 & 4, 46.5, 48
Vicittācāra 53.2
Vimalabuddhi 30
Vimalasāra 32.3
Vedehathera 36, 37
Saṃgharakkhita 32.1, 46.2, 53.1
Saddhammakitti 51
Saddhammaguru 53.2
Saddhammajotipāla *see* Chapada
Saddhammanandin 53.2
Saddhammapālasiri 42.2
Saddhammavilāsa 47.7
Saddhammasiri 46.3
Saddhammālaṃkāra 42.5
Sāradassin 43.3
Sāriputta 31—34, 43.1—*see* Dhammavilāsa
Siddhattha 39.1
Sirisaddhammālaṃkāra 47.10
Sīlavaṃsa 42.3—52.1
Sumaṅgala 32.4, 42.1
Suvaṇṇarāsi 53.2

B. TITLES OF WORKS

Aṅguttara-Nikāya 8, 10.4, 22
Aṭṭhakathā 2 (end), 18, 21, p. 31 f.-n. 3, 35, 44.6
Attanagaluvihāravaṃsa 37
Atthasālinī 22, 31, 42.1, 43.1
Anāgatavaṃsa 29.1
Andhaṭṭhakathā 18
Apadāna 14.13, 22
Abhidhammatthagaṇṭhipada 43.4
Abhidhammatthavikāsanī 32.4
Abhidhammatthavibhāvanī 32.4, 42.1
Abhidhammatthasaṃgaha 26.7, 32.4

Abhidhammatthasaṃgahasaṃkhepaṭīkā 33
Abhidhamma-Piṭaka 1, 15-16, 22
Abhidhammamūlaṭīkā *see* Mūlaṭīkā
Abhidhammāvatāra 25 1; Ṭīkā thereon, 32.3 & 4
Abhidhānappadīpikā 45, 46.6, 51; Ṭīkā thereon, 46.6, 51
Abhinava-Cullanirutti 47.10
Itivuttaka 11.4, 25 3
Uttaravinicchaya 25.1; Ṭīkā thereon, 32.3
Udāna 11.3 25 3
Ekakkharakosa 51 (end)
Kaṅkhāvitaraṇī 22, 32.2
Kaccāyanagandha *see* Kaccāyana vyākaraṇa
Kaccāyanabheda (with Ṭīkās) 47.7 & 9
Kaccāyanavaṇṇanā 47.11
Kaccāyanavyākaraṇa 30, 44.5, 49.2
Kaccāyanasāra (with Ṭīkās) 47.7
Kathāvatthuppakaraṇa 1, 16.3
Kammavācā 7.2
Kāyaviratigāthā 42.4
Kārakapupphamañjarī 53.2
Kārikā p. 38 f.-n. 2
Kurundī 18, 44.5
Khandhaka *see* Vinaya-Piṭaka
Khuddaka-Nikāya 11-14, 19, 22, 25.3
Khuddakapāṭha 11.1
Khuddasikkhā 27: Ṭīkā thereon 32.1 & 3
Khemappakaraṇa 26 6; Ṭīkā thereon 32.3
Gandhaṭṭhi 53 2
Gandhavaṃsa 44.5
Gandhasāra 33
Gandhābharaṇa 53.2
Catusāmaṇeravatthu 43 5
Cariyāpiṭaka 14, 15, 25.3
Culaniruttigandha 30, 44 5
Cullapaccarī 18
Cullavagga *see* Vinaya-Piṭaka
Cullasaddanīti 45
Cūlavaṃsa 38
Chakesadhātuvaṃsa 44.2
Jātaka 13.10
Jātakatthavaṇṇanā 23, 25.3, 42.3 & 4
Jātakavisodhana 42.1
Jinacarita 34.4
Jinālaṃkāra 25.1, 34.3
Ñāṇodaya 22
Tipiṭaka 1 ff
Telakaṭāhagāthā 41 2
Thūpavaṃsa 34.2, 35
Theragāthā, Therīgāthā 13.8 & 9, 25.3
Dāṭhāvaṃsa 34 1
Dīgha-Nikāya 8, 9 1, 22
Dīpavaṃsa 18, 21, 28, 44.6
Dhammapada 11.2
Dhammapadaṭṭhakathā 24
Dhammavilāsa-Dhammasattha 33, 42
Dhammasaṅgani 16.1, 22
Dhātukathā 16.5 -Ṭīkāvaṇṇanā, -Anuṭīkāvaṇṇanā 43 2; -yojanā, 43.3
Dhātupāṭha 45, 52.2
Dhātumañjūsā 45, 52.1
Dhātvatthadīpanī 45, 52.3
Nayalakkhaṇavibhāvanī 53.2
Nalāṭadhātuvaṃsa 44.1
Nāmacāradīpa 33
Nāmarūpaparicchcda 26.7; Ṭīkā thereon 32.3
Nidānakathā 23, 29.2, 42.3
Niddesa 14. 11, 26.2
Niruttisaṃgaha 53.2 *e.*
Niruttisāramañjūsā p. 38 f.-n. 3
Nettippakaraṇa 19.1, 30 42 2, 43 5, 44.5
Nettippakaraṇassa Atthasaṃvaṇṇanā 25.3
Nettibhāvanī 42 2
Nyāsa 30, 46, 47.11
Nyāsapradīpa 30
Paccayasaṃgaha 32.3
Pajjamadhu 37, 39.1, 46.4
Pañcagatidīpana 40 2
Pañcappakaraṇ aṭṭhakathā 22, 31
Pañcikā *see* Moggallāyanapañcikā
Paṭisaṃbhidāmagga 14.12, 26.3
Paṭṭhānagaṇanānaya 33
Paṭṭhānadīpanī 42 5
Paṭṭhānappakaraṇa 16.7, 42 5, 43.2
Paṭṭhānavaṇṇanā 43.2
Paṇṇavāra 18
Padarūpasiddhi *see* Rūpasiddhi
Padasādhana 45, 49.1
Papañcasūdanī 22, 31
Payogasiddhi 45, 49.2
Paramatthakathā 22
Paramatthajotikā 22
Paramatthadīpanī 25.3
Paramatthappakāsinī 31
Paramatthamañjusā 25.3
Paramatthavinicchaya 26.7
Paritta 17
Parivāra *see* Vinaya-Piṭaka
Pātimokkha 7.1, 22
Pātimokkhavisodhanī 33
Puggalapaññatti 16.4
Peṭakālaṃkāra 43.5
Peṭakopadesa 19.2, 30, 44.5
Petavatthu 12.7, 25 3
Bālappabodhana (with Ṭīkā), 47.9
Bālāvatāra 45, 46. 5, 49.1; Ṭīkā thereon, 46.5
Buddhaghosuppatti 40.3
Buddhavaṃsa 14.14, 25.1
Buddhālaṃkāra 42.3
Buddhippasādanī = Padasādhana-Ṭīkā 49 1
Bodhivaṃsa 29.2, 35
Majjhima-Nikāya 8, 9.2, 22
Maṇidīpa 42.1
Maṇisāramañjūsā 42 1
Madhuratthavilāsinī 25.1 & 3
Madhusāratthadīpanī 42.6
Manuvaṇṇanā 42.7
Manusāra 42.7
Manorathapūraṇī 22, 31
Mahāaṭṭhakathā *see* Aṭṭhakathā
Mahāṭīkā *see* Paramatthamañjūsā
Mahāniruttigandha 30, 44.5
Mahāpaccarī 18, 44.5
Mahāpaṭṭhāna *see* Paṭṭhānappakaraṇa
Mahāparitta *see* Paritta
Mahābodhivaṃsa *see* Bodhivaṃsa
Mahāvaṃsa 28, 29.2, 34, 35, 36, 38, 41.2, 44.6; Ṭīkā thereon, 35

Mahāvagga *see* Vinaya-Piṭaka
Mātikatthadīpanī 33
Mālālaṃkāra 43 5
Milindapañhā 20
Mukhamattadīpanī *see* Nyāsa
Mūlaṭīkā 25.2, 42.6
Mūlasikkhā 27; Ṭīkās thereon 32 3
Moggallāyanapañcikā 48.2
Moggallāyanapañcikāpadīpa 39.1, 46.4, 48.2, 49.3
Moggallāyanavyākaraṇa 48.1
Mohavicchedanī 26.4 – 42.6
Yamaka 16 6, 43 2
Yamakavaṇṇanā 43.2
Yasavaḍḍhanavatthu 43.1
Yogavinicchaya 32 3
Rasavāhinī 36
Rājādhirājavilāsinī 43.5
Rājovādavatthu 43.5
Rūpasiddhi 45, 46.4, 47 11, 49.2
Rūpārūpavibhāga 32.3
Līnatthapakāsanā 31
Līnatthapakāsanī 25.3
Līnatthavaṇṇanā 25 3
Līnatthasūdanī 47.8
Lokappadīpasāra 40.1
Vaṃsatthappakāsinī *see* Mahāvaṃsa-Ṭīkā
Vacanatthajotikā 53.1
Vaccavācaka 53.2
Vajirabuddhi 18, 26.5
Vaṇṇanīti 44.5
Vācakopadesa 47.11
Vinayagaṇḍhi 26 5
Vinayagūḷhatthadīpanī 33
Vinayatthamañjūsā 32.2
Vinaya-Piṭaka 1, 7, 22, 24
Vinayavinicchaya 25 1; Ṭīkā thereon 32.3
Vinayasaṃgaha 31, 43.1
Vinayasamuṭṭhānadīpanī 33
Vinayālaṃkāra 43.1
Vibhaṅga 16.2, 22
Vibhattikathāvaṇṇanā 53.2
Vibhattyattha-Ṭīkā or -dīpanī 53.2
Vibhattyatthappakaraṇa 53.2
Vimaticchedanī 26.4
Vimativinodanī p. 35 f.-n. 3
Vimānavatthu 12.6, 24, 25.3
Visuddhimagga 22, 25 3
Vīsativaṇṇanā 43.1
Vuttodaya 53 1
Saṃyutta-Nikāya 8, 10.3, 22
Saṃvaṇṇanānayadīpanī 53.2
Saṃkhepaṭṭhakathā 18
Saccasaṃkhepa 26.1; Ṭīkās thereon 32.3 & 4
Saddatthabhedacintā 46 3, 47.9
Saddanīti 45, 47.11, 50, 52 3
Saddabindu 47.8
Saddalakkhaṇa *see* Moggallāyana-vyākaraṇa
Saddavutti 53.2
Saddasāratthajālinī 46.6
Saddhammaṭṭhitikā *see* °ppajotikā
Saddhammappakāsinī 26.3
Saddhammappajotikā 26.2
Saddhammasaṃgaha 39.2
Saddhammopāyana 41 1
Saṃdesakathā 44.3
Samantakūṭavaṇṇanā 36
Samantapāsādikā 18, 22, 26.5, 31, 44 6
Saṃbandhacintā 46.2
Saṃmohavināsinī 47 7
Saṃmohavinodanī 22, 31
Sarvajñanyāyadīpanī 53.2
Sahassavatthaṭṭhakathā p. 43 f.-n. 4
Sahassavatthuppakaraṇa 36
Sādhuvilāsinī 43 5
Sāratthadīpanī 18, 31
Sāratthappakāsinī 22, 31
Sāratthamañjūsā 31
Sāratthavikāsinī 47.7
Sārasaṃgaha 39 1
Sāsanavaṃsa 44.6
Sīmālaṃkārasaṃgaha 32.3; Ṭīkā thereon 33
Sīmāvivādavinicchayakathā 44.4
Suttaniddesa 46 1
Suttanipāta 12 5, 24
Sutta-Piṭaka 1, 8—14
Suttavibhaṅga *see* Vinaya-Piṭaka
Suttasaṃgaha 19.8
Sudhīramukhamaṇḍana 53.2
Subodhālaṃkāra 53 1
Sumaṅgalappasādanī 32.3
Sumaṅgalavilāsinī 22, 31

INDEX TO PART II, GRAMMAR OF PĀLI

Figures refer to *paragraphs* in Part II, pp. 61-231 excepting where page is specifically mentioned.

A. INDEX OF CONTENTS

Ablative, in *-to* 77.2, of *a*-st. in *-asmā*, *-amhā* 78.2. Abl.=Instr. 77.2, 82.3, 90.1,3, 91, 92, 95, 96

Accent 4. Influence on vocalism 19 ff.

Accusative,=Nom. 82.3, 88 3, 90.1, 92 1, 96.3, 105. Acc. Pl. of *a*-st. in *-e* 78.3, 7 and *-ān* 79.5

Adverbs 102

Aorist 158 ff. ; of Pass. 168.3, 177

Aspirates, represented by *h* 37 ; in cons.-groups 60. Retention of original Asp. 37. Aspiration of sound-groups, 51.1, Appearance and disappearance of Aspiration, 40, 62

Aspiration *h* in consonant-groups 49 ; from sibilants 50, 54 4, 59.1, 2 ; in place of Aspirate 37, 60

Assimilation 51 ; progressive 52, 53.1, 3, 55 ; regressive 53 ff.

Augment in Conditional 157 (with fn. on p 189), in Aorist 158

Case, look under Nom , Acc. etc.

Causative, stems 178 ff. ; Present 139 ; Fut. 151, 154.3 ; Aor. 165.2, 168.4 ; Passive 176.1. Part., Inf., Ger. look under these.

Cerebrals 35, 38.6, 42, 43 3, 63.2, 64

Comparison 103 ; comparatives in *-yas* 100.3

Compositional Sandhi 33, 51 2, 53.3, 54.6, 55 57, 58.4, 67

Conditional 157

Consonants, in free position 35ff. ; Gemination 5, 6, 32, 33 ; Influence of double-consonance on vowels 9, 10, 15. Cf. Cerebrals, Dentals, Gutturals, Labials etc.

Consonant-groups look under Assimilation ; retained 48 ; with *h* 49 ; with sibilant 50, 56, 57

Contraction 26, 27, 28, 139

Dative,=Gen. 77.2 ; Dat. of *a*-st. in *-āya* loc. cit.

Declension, *a*-st. 78 ff. ; *ā*-st. 81, *ĭ*-, *ŭ*-st. 82 ff. ; diphth.-decl. 88 ; decl. of radical st. 89 ; *r*-st. 90 f. ; *n*-st. 92 ff., *nt*-st. 96 ff. ; *s*-st, 99. Transfer to other decl. 83.5, 6, 86 5, 88.2, 90.4, 92.2, 93, 94, 95, 96, 99, 100

Denominatives, stems 186 ff ; Pres 130.6, 136 4, 138, 139 ; Fut. 151, 154.3 ; Aor. 165 2, 168 3,4 ; Part, Inf., Ger. look under these.

Dentals 41.2, 3, 63.3

Desideratives, stems 184 ; Pres 130.6, 136.4, 138, 139 ; Fut. 151, 154.3 ; Aor. 165 2, 168.3,4 ; Part., Inf., Ger. look under these.

Diphthongs 15 ; Diphth. *e* 3, 9, 10 25 1, 26.1, 27 5,6 ; Diphth. *o* 3, 10, 25.2, 26.2, 27.3, 28.2

Dissimilation 43.2, 45, 46.4, 47.1, 63.3

Double-constructions 105 1,3, 115.3, 126, 143, 152, 165.1, 170, 176 3 (with f.n. 1 on p 206), 182, 201, 206

Dual, wanting in Pāli 77.1, 120

Elision, of initial vowels 66.1 ; of final consonants 66 2

Enclisis 20

Feminine formations 95.2, 98, fn. 2 p. 138

Final sound 66.2

Future 150 ff. ; Periphr. Fut. 172 ; Fut. Exact, 173.3

Gender of Subst 76 ; confusion in 76, 78.7

Genitive used as Dat. 77.2

Gerund, in *-tvā* 208-210 ; in *-tūna* 211 ; in *-ya* 212 f. ; in *-yāna* 214. Ger. in periphr constructions 174.3,5,6

Glide-sound *b* 51.5

Gutturals 63.1

Haplology 65.2

Imperative, of Present, look under this.

Imperfect preserved in Aorists 159.II, IV

Indicative, of Present, look under this.

Infinitives in *-tave*, *-tuye*, *-tāye* 204.1-2 ; in *-tum* 205 f. ; Dat. of verbal nouns as Inf. 204.3

Initial sound 66.1

Instrumental Pl. in *-bhi* 79.6, 83.7, 92.1, 95.3, 115.5 ; Sg. of *a*-stems in *-ā* 78.1, in *-asā* 79.1, Pl in *-ehi* 78.4, in *-e*=Skr. *-ais* 79 6. Instr. used as Abl. 77 2, 82.3, 90.1,3, 91, 92, 95, 96

Intensive, stems 185; Pres. 130.6; Fut. 151.4; Aor. 166 (end); for Part., Inf., Ger. look under these.
Labials 46.1, 51.4
Law of mora 5 ff.
Liquids 43.1,2, 44, 45; in sound-groups 52.3,5, 53.2, 54
Locative, of *a*-st. in *-asi* 79.3; of *ĭ* st. in *-o* 83.3, 86.5
Māgadhism 66, 2*a*, 80, 82.5, 98.3, 105.2, 110.2
Medium 120, 122.2, 126, 129, 131.2, 133.1,3. 135.2, 137, 138, 139, 140.4, 145, 146, 149; Fut. 150, 154.2. Cond. 157; Aor. 159 II.III,IV.
Metathesis 47.2, 65.1
Metre, influence on vocalism 32
Modes 120; *see* Ind., Imp., Opt., Subj.
Mutes 35, 36, 38; in consonant-groups 52.3,4, 53.1, 55, Nasalisation 6.3 (with fn. 1 on p. 61). Nasal presents 135.3
Nominal stems 75
Nominative, Sg. of *a*-st. in *-e* 80.1; Pl. of *a*-stems in *-āse* 79.4, Neut. in *ā* 78.6, Nom. used as Acc. 82.3, 88,3, 90.1, 92.1, 96.3, 105.4; as Voc. 80.2, 82.5, 84, 96.3
Numerals, Card. 114 ff., 117; Ord. 118; Distrib. 119.1; Fractional 119.2; Num.- Adv., -Subst., -Adj. 119.3-6
Onomatopoetic verbs 186
Optative of Present, look under this.
Palatals 40.1 *a*, 41.1; Palatalisation of sound-groups 55, 57
Participles of Pres. Act. 97, 190; Med. in *-māna* 191, in *-āna* 192; of Fut. Act. 193; of Perf. Act. 100.2, 198; of Perf. Pass. in *-ta* 194-196, in *-na* 197; of Fut. Pass, in *-tabba* 199, 200, in *-anīya* 201, in *-ya* 202, in *-tāya*, *-tayga*, *-teyya* 203. Part. in periphr. formations 173, 174
Passive, stems 175 ff., Pres. 136.4, Fut. 155.3, Aor. 168.3, 177, Part. look under this.
Perfect, vestiges of in Pāli 171; Periphr. Perf. 173
Periphrastic formations 120, 172, 173, 174
Pluperfect 173.3
Present, stems 130 ff., Indic. 121 f., Imp. 124-126, Opt. 127-129, Subj. 120, 123. Expansion of *a*-flexion 120, 140, 142.3; of *e*-flexion 120, 139.2, 142.2, 147.1, Expansion of Pres.-stem 120. 155, 165.2, 167 f., 176.2, 179.5, 181.1, 196, 199 f., 202 (end), 206, 210
Pretonic syllable weakened 21
Primary endings in Aor. 161, 162.3
Pronoun, Personal 104 f.; *sa*, *esa* 106, 107.1; *ena* 107.2; *tya* 107.3; *tuma* 107.4; *ayaṃ* 108; *amu(ka)* 109; Rel. 110; Interrog. 111; Indef. 111.1; Poss. 112.1; Refl. 112.2 Derived stems 112.3; Pron. Adj. 113
Pronominal declension penetrating into Nom.-flexion 78.2,3
Reduction of Vowels 19, 23
Relationship, terms of 91
Saṃprasāraṇa 25
Sandhi 66 ff; frozen forms 66; Compositional S 67; External S. 68 ff.; Vowel S. 69, 70, 71; Organic Sandhi-consonants 72; Inorganic Sandhi-consonants 73
Sibilant 3, 35; in consonant-groups 50, 52.2,3; 54, 56, 57, 59.1,2. *s* from *ch* 59.2
Sonants, represented by surds 39; in place of surds 38. Old son. asp. preserved 37
Stem, expansion of *a*-st. among Subst. 75, among Verbs 120 140, 142.3; of *e*-st. among Verbs 120, 139.2, 142.2, 147.1
Subjunctive of Pres., look under this.
Suffix *-are* 122.2; *-ittha* 159.IV; *-emase*, *-emasi* 129; *-ttha* 159-III; *-tha* (= *-ta*) 125; 129, 157, 159.II,III; *-mase* 122.2, 126, 129; *-mu* 125, 128; *-mha* 159.III; *-mhase* 122.2; *-ruṃ* 126 159.II; *-re* 122.2, 159.II; *-vhe* 60; *-vho* 126; *-ssu* 126
Svarabhakti 29-31; in Law of Mora 8; strengthened 3
Surds *see* Sonants
Syncope 20
Vedic forms in P. 78.1,4, 159.II, IV, 160.4, 204
Vocative, of *a*-st. in *-e* 80.2 of *i*-st. in *-e* 83.4, Cf. Nom.
Vowels, *a* into *e* 9; *a* from *ṛ* 12; *a* as Svarabhakti 31.1; *ā* from *aya*, *āya* 27.1,2, from *avā* 27.4.—*ĭ* into *e* 10.2, 11; from *ṛ* 12, from *e* 15.1,2; from *u* 19.3; *ī* from *yă* 25.1; from *āyi* 27.6 from *-iya* 27.7; *i* as Svarabhakti 30.—*ŭ* into *o* 10.2, 11; *u* from *ṛ ḷ* 12, 14; from *o* 15.3,4; from *a* 19.2; from *i* 19.3; *ū* from *vă* 25.2; from *upa* 28.1; *u* as Svarabhakti 31.2—Vowel-assimilation 16, 17; Vowel influenced by Consonant 18; Reduction of 19, 23; Syncope 20; Shortening and Lengthening 8, 21, 22, 32 33, 82.4, 83.8, 86.3.—Nasal vowels 6.3, 32.3,—*ṛ*, *ḷ* in P. 12, 13, 14.—Vowel-strengthening 3

B. INDEX OF WORDS

akaṃ, akamha, akaraṃ. akā etc. see *kar*
akalu 39 1
akilāsu 39.1
akuppa 15.3
akkocchi 164
akkhāti, akkhissaṃ see *khyā*
akkhi, acchi 56.1, 85
agamaṃ etc. see *gam*
agaru, agalu 34
agga 20
aggahiṃ etc. see *grah*
aggi 82
agyantarāya, agyāgāra 58.3, 67
acāriṃ etc. see *car*
accayanti etc. see *i*
acci 101
acceka 27.6
accha 12 1, 56 1
acchati, acchataṃ 126, 135.2
accharā 57, 100.4
acchi, akkhi 56.1, 85
acchi=*acci* 62.1
acchidā, acchindi, acchecchi see *chid*
acchera, acchariya 27.5, 47.2, p. 91 f.-n. 4
ajini, ajesi see *ji*
ajjuka 19.2
ajjhena 26.1
añña, -tara, -tama 113, 3—5
aññāsiṃ etc. see *jñā*
aṭṭa (1) 64. 1; (2) 64.1, 194
aṭṭiyati 136.4, 188.3, 191
aṭṭhā, -āsi etc. see *sthā*
aḍḍha, addha 55, 119.2
aḍḍhatiya 65.2, 119 2
aḍḍhuḍḍha 61 1, 119.2
atāri etc. 166
atāni 177
atidhona 27.3
atta 194
attan 92, 112.2, 118.4
atrajā 53.2
atriccha, -atā, ati 53.2
adaṃ, adāsiṃ etc. see *dā*
aduṃ Pron., 22, 66.2*b*, 109
addakkhiṃ, addā, addasaṃ, addasāsiṃ see *darś*
addiyati, addita 176 1, 195
addha, aḍḍha 119.2
addhan, -unā etc 19.2, 92.3
addhāna 92.2
adhosi 163.3
anaṇa 12 4
anubhomi etc, 131; see *bhū*
anumodiyanaṃ 214
anelaka 43.2
antaradhāyati 31.1, 138
antarārati 46.3
antovana 67
anvadeva 54.5
anvaya, anveti 54.5, 67; see *i*
anvāya 212 (end)
apaṃsu see *pā*
apaṭipucchā 27.2
apattha, -aṃ 159.III, 161.2
apara 113.7
aparagoyāna 36
aparaṇha 49.1
apāpessaṃ 157
apāruta 13
apucchasi 161
appuyya 212
apphoṭā 42, p. 87 f.-n. 3
apphoṭeti 52.2
abbahati, abbuhi etc see *barh*
abbuyha 212; see *barh*
abhikkanta 33.1
abhikkhaṇaṃ p. 102 f.-n 1.
abhiññā 27.2
abhiṇhaṃ, -haso 59.1
abhitthavati see *stu*
abhinibbajjiyātha 123
abhimatthati 53.1
abhiruyhitvā p. 230 f -n. 1
abhivaṭṭa 62 2
abhedi 177; see *bhid*
amaññaṃ etc. see *man*
amu(ka) 109
amba 51.5
ambāṭaka 42.1, 51.5
ambila 51.5
ambuni Loc. Sg. 85
amma 81.2
amhanā 50.2, 92.1
amhi 50.6; see *as*
amhe, -hehi etc. 50.6, 104.1-4
ayaṃ Pron 108
ayya, ayyo 52.5, 79.3
arañjara 17 2*b*, 45
arahant 98.1
ardh root, Pres. 125, 136; Fut. 155
arodhi 177
alattha, aṃ 159.III, 161.2
alabbhaneyya 201
alāpu 39.6
alika 23
alla 64 1
allīyati see *lī*
avaṅga 38.5
avacaṃ, -cāsi etc. see *vac*
avassaṃ 54 4
avāpurati, -puraṇa 38.5, 39.6
avidrā 100 2
avekkhi see *īkṣ*
avocaṃ etc. see *vac*
avhayati, -eti 138
as root 50.6; Pres. 141.1; Aor. 159. IV
asaṃ Sg. Nom. neut. 97.2, 98.3
asakkhiṃ see *śak*
asayittha, -aṃ see *śī*
asu(ka) see *aduṃ*
asmā 50.2
asmi see *amhi, asme* see *amhe*
assu 85
assu(ṃ), assosi etc. see *śru*

ahāsi (1) 163.1; see *hā*; (2) 163.4; see *har*
ahiṃkāra 19.1
ahuṃ, ahuvā, -vāsi, ahosi, ahesuṃ etc. see *bhū*

āgu p. 72 f.-n. 4, 160.4
ācera 27.5, p. 91 f.-n. 4
ājira 24
āṇā, āṇatti, āṇāpeti etc. 63 2; see *ñā*
āṇumānaṃ p. 130 f.-n. 1
ādinnavā 198
ādiyati 136.4, 175.1; see *dā*
ādu, ādo 83.3
ānañca 58.1
ānāpeti 180.2; see *ni*
ānubhāva 24
āp root with *pra* (*pāpuṇāti*) 31; Pres. 148.2; Fut. 156.3, Aor. 169.4; Caus. 157, 168.4, 178.1; Part. 204; Inf. 205, 206; Ger. 210, 212
āpā 75
āpo, āpe, āpaṃ p. 127 f.-n. 4
ābhanti see *bhā*
āyūhati 37
ārammaṇa 45, 48
āroga, -gya 24, 53.3
Āḷavī 38.6
ālārika 47.2
āḷāhana 42.3
ālinda 24
āvaṭṭa 64.1
āvudha 46.1
āvuso 46.1
āveṇiya, -ka 36
āveḷā 11, 35, 38.5
āveḷine 95.2
ās root, Pres. 126, 129, 140.1; Part. 192
āsado, -dā 161; see *sad*
āsāduṃ for *āsādituṃ* 65.2
āsi etc. see *as*
āha, āhu, āhaṃsu 171
āhañhi 153.2

i root, Pres. 125, 140.3; Fut. 19.1, 54.4, 150, 151.3; Inf. 204, 205; Part. 190, 194; Ger. 212
ikka 12.2, 56.1, 62.2
-ikkhisaṃ, -ikkhiya see *ikṣ*
iñj=iṅg 41.1
icchati etc. see *iṣ*; =*īpsate* 57.1, 184
iṇa 12.2
itara, itarītara 113.6
itthī 8, 29, 87.1
idāni 66.1
idha 37
Indapatta 62.2
ima Pron. st. 108
iriyā, -yati 30.1
irubbeda, iruveda p. 67 f.-n. 1
iṣ root (1) 57.1, 97.1; Pres. 128, 135.1; Aor. 167.2; Caus. 181.1; Part. 190, 196; Inf. 206; Ger. 210.—(2) 179.3
ise Sg. Voc. 83.4; Pl. Acc. 83.6
issariya 15.2

īkṣ root, Aor. 166; Ger. 13

uggharati 56.2, 58.4
ugghāta 52.1
ucchaṅga 57
ucchādana 57
ucchiṭṭha 57
ucchu 16.1 *a*, 56.1
uju, ujju 12.3
uṇha, uṇhīsa 50.3
uttara 113.8
uttiṭṭha 63 3
udayabbaya 54.6
udāhu 22, 38.3
udiyyati 52.5
udukkhala 6.2
udūḍha 66.1
udda 53 2
udrabhati, -hati p. 96 f.-n. 3
udraya, udrīyati 53.2
upakkiliṭṭha, -kkilesa p. 79 f.-n. 4
upaṭṭhāka 27.2
upaṭṭhissaṃ 151; see *sthā*
upatheyya 39.5
uposatha 26.2
ubbaṭṭeti, ubbāsīyati 53.3
ubbigga 53.1.3
ubbinaya 53 3
ubbilla 15.1, 53.3
ubbillāvita 38.5
ubbūḷha(vant)=udūḍha 66.1
ubbejitar 53.3
ubbhaṃ 59.3
ubhaya, ubho 114.2
ubhinnaṃ 15.1
ummā 24
ummujjā etc. 18.1
ummūleti 52.4
umhayati 29
uyyāna, uyyutta 55
Uruvelā 10
uḷāra 42.3
uḷuṅka 17.2*a*, 42.3
uḷumpa p. 64 f.-n. 1
usabha 12.3
usu 16.1*a*
usumā, usmā 31.2, 50.4
usūya, usuyyā 16.1*b*
usūyati 188.1
ussaṅkin 57
ussada, ussanna, ussava 57
ussaya 58 3
ussahati 57
ussāpeti 58.3, 180.2
ussāva 15.4, 46.1
ussāha, ussīsaka 57
ussita 58.3
ussukka, -kkati 15.4, 57, 188.1
ussussati 57; see *śuṣ*
ussūra 57

ū=upa 28.1
ūkā 66.1
ūmi 52.3
ūhadeti 28.1, 139.2

ūhanti p. 76 f.-n. 5
ūhasana 28.1

eka 114.1
ekacca, -cciya 113.9
ekārasa 43.1
ekodi 38.3
eta Pron. st. 107.1
etase Inf. 204
eti see *i*
ettaka 27.7, 111.6
ettha 9
edi, edisa etc. 11, 43 1
ena, na Pron. st. 66.1, 107.2
eyya 140.3; see *i*
erisa, erikkha etc. 43.1
eba 43.2
elaṇḍa 44
elamūga 38.1
esa 107.1
esanā 27.2
esāna 192
essāmi, ehisi etc. see *i*

o=ava 26.2; *=apa* 28.2
oka 20
okkasati, okkassa see *karṣ*
Okkāka p. 66 f.-n. 1, 56 1, 62.2
Okkāmukha 10
ogayhitvā p. 230 f.-n. 1
oggata p. 76 f.-n. 7, p. 79 f.-n. 4
ojavaṃ 96.2
ojā 10
oṭṭha (1) 5; (2) 10, 58.3
ottappa etc. 28.2
odhi 26.2
opadhika 3
oma 26.2
orodha 26.2
ovaraka 28.2
ovariyāna 214
osakkati 28.2 p. 97 f.-n, 4, 62.2
osajjati p. 79 f.-n. 4

ka Pron. st. 111.1
kakudha 40.1*b*
kakka 52 3
kakkhaḷa 38.6
kaṅkhā 58.1
kaccha 56.1
kañcinaṃ 111.1
kaññā 81
kaṭhita 42.2, 53 3
kaḍḍhati 130
kaṇeru 47.2
kaṇḍuvati 46.1, 188.2
kaṇha 12.4, 30.5. 50.3
katama, katara 111.2, 3
katāvin 198.3
kati 111.4
katte Sg. Voc. 90.5
kanta p. 218. f.-n. 2
kapoṇi 40.2*b*
kappara 16.1*d*
kabala, -likā 46.1
kammaṇiya, -ñña 55
kamman 19.2, 94
kammāsa 52.3
kayirā, -rati 47.2, 149, 175.1; see 1. *kar*
(1) *kar* root 'to do', Pres. 125, 126, 128, 129, 149; Fut. 19.1, 54.4, 150, 153.1; Cond. 157; Aor. 58, 159. III, 162.1, 166; Pass. 175.1; Caus. 178.2 182.2; Part. 97.1, 2, 190, 191, 192, 194, 195, 198, 199.1, 201, 202; Inf. 204, 205, 206; Ger. 38.1, 209, 210, 211, 212, 213
(2) *kar* root 'to strew' Pres. 134; Aor. 167.2; Caus. 181.1; Ger. 8, 210, 213
kart root 114
karṣ root p. 79 f.-n. 4, 134, 161, 212
kalp root 14, 126, 182
kalla 54.5
kallahāra p. 92 f.-n. 4
kavi=kapi 38.5
kaviṭṭha 38.5, 64.3
kasaṭa 29
kasati see *karṣ*
kasāyati 186.5
kasāva 46.1
kasina, kasira 59.2
Kasmīra 50.2
kassa 111.1
kassaṃ 153.1; see (1) *kar*
kassaka 52.3
kahāpaṇa 21
kākacchati 185
kākaṇikā 17.2*b*
kālusiya 30.2
kāsaṃ 153.1; see (1) *kar*
kāsāva 46.1
kāhasi, kāhisi etc. 19.1, 54.4, 153.1; see (1) *kar*
kiṃ 111.1
kiñcana p. 149 f.-n. 1
kiṇāti etc. see *krī*
kiṇṇa 54.5
kiṇha 12.4
kittaka, kittāvatā 27.7, 111.6
kipilla, -llikā 47.1
kibbisa 52.3
kira 45
kirati etc. see (2) *kar*
kilañja 34
kilāsu 39.1
kissā, kismiṃ, kimhi 34, 111.1
kīḷituṃ 205
kīva. -vatikā 46.1, 111.5
kukku 16.1*a*, 62 2
kukkusa 16.1*a*, 19.2
kucchita 57
-kujjiya 213
kuḍuba, kuḍumala 35
kuḍḍa (1) 53.3; (2) 62.2
-kuṇṭhita 39.1
kutta, kuttaka, kutti 14
kuthita p. 74 f.-n. 1
kunnadī 24
kup root 122.1
kubbati etc. see (1) *kar*
kubbara 6.2
kummagga 24

kummi, kuru, kurute see (1) *kar*
kuruṅga 17.2a
kurūra 31.2
Kusināra 36
kusīta 39 4
kusubbha, kuss- 24
kūṭaṭṭha 64.2
ke=ko 111.1
kevaṭṭa 64.1
ko=kva 25.2
koccha 10, 62.1
koṭṭha 27.8
kosajja p. 70 f.-n. 1, 39.4
Kosiya 36
kram root, Pres. 130.1; Fut. 154; Cond. 157.1; Aor. 166; Caus. 178.2 *c*; Int. 185; Ger. 209, 211, 212
krī root, Pres. 21, 145; Fut. 156; Aor. 196.4; Inf. 205, 206; Ger. 210
krīḍ root, Inf. 205
kvaṃ, kvaci 53.8
kṣar root 56.2
kṣā root 56.2, 191
kṣi root 186.4, 197
kṣip root, Pres. 134; Inf. 206; Ger. 210

khajja 202
khaṇa, chaṇa 56.1c
khattar 90.4, 5
-khattuṃ 22.1, 33.1, 40.1*a*, 66.2*b*, 119.8
khan root, Part 191; Ger. 212
-khanna, -khandiyāna see *skand*
Khandhapura 62.1
khamaniya 201
khamā, chamā 56.1c
khalati 52.2
khallāṭa 54.5
khād root, Pres. 122, 128, 130; Fut. 154; Aor. 166; Part. 36, 190, 195, 201, 202; Ger. 209, 214
khāyita 36
khiḍḍā 62.1
khīyati 136.4; see *kṣi*
khila 40.1*a*
khujja 40.1*a*
khudā 40.2*b*, 56.1*a*
khudda (1) 15.4; (2) p. 100 f.-n. 1
kheḷa 38.6
kho 20
khyā root, Pres. 125, 140; Fut. 151.1; Part. 190

gacch- see *gam*
gaṇh- see *grah*
gadrabha 65.1
gandha 61.1
gam root, Pres. 122.1, 128, 133.1; Fut. 65.2, 150, 155; Aor. 159 II, IV, 165. 1, 167; Caus. 178.2 *b*; Int. 185; Part. 190, 191, 196, 199.1; Inf. 204.1*a*, 205; Ger. 209, 211, 212
(1) *gar* root 'to devour', Pres. 134; Aor. 167; Ger. 210
(2) *gar* root 'to wake up', Pres. 20, 142.4; Fut. 156; Aor. 169.2; Part. 190, 191, 196. Ger. 206, 210
garaha, -hati 31.1
garu 34
gardh root, Pres. 136; Part. 196
galocī 11
gava 88.3
gahāya 212; see *grah*
gahāyati 146, 186 5: see *grah*
gahita, gaheti etc. see *grah*
(1) *gā* root 'to go', Aor. 160.1
(2) *gā* root 'to sing', Pres. 138; Aor. 168.3; Caus. 181.1; Part. 194, 196; Ger 210
gijjh- see *gardh*
gini 30 5, 66.1
gimha 50.4
gir-, gil- see (1) *gar*
guṇe=guṇehi 79.7
gunnaṃ 15.3, 88.3
gumba 51.5, 65.1
guh root 133 3
geruka 19 3
gelañña 3
go, goṇa 88.3
grah root, Pres. 125, 139.2, 146.2; Fut. 151.3, 156; Aor. 165.2, 166, 169.4; Pass. 175.3; Caus. 178.2*a*, 181 1; Den. 186 5; Part. 190, 191, 195, 200; Inf. 206; Ger. 209, 210, 212

ghaṃs see *gharṣ*
ghammati 37
gharṣ root, Pres. p. 95 f.-n. 2, 130.5; Part. 200; Ger. 210
ghāteti see *han*
ghāyati see *ghrā*
gheppati 10
ghrā root. Pres. 132; Ger. 210

cakkavāḷa 38.6
cakkhu 101
cakkhumant 96
caṅkamati 185, 195
caccara 46.2
cañcalati 185
catu 115.4
catukka 62.2, 119 6
candimas 19.1, 100.1
car root, Pres. 129, 130; Aor. 166; Part. 195, 197
carima 19.1
-calāyati 186.5
cāpāto 77
ci root, Pres. 131, 147.1; Fut. 151.3; Aor. 169.1; Part. 190; Inf. 205; Ger. 210, 213
-cikicchati 184, 190; see *cit*
cikkhalla p. 73 f.-n. 2
-cicca 212; see *cit*
ciccitāyati, ciṭiciṭ- 20, 186.4
ciṇṇa 197; see *car*
cit root, Des. 41.2, 181.1, 184; Part. 190; Ger. 212
citra, citta 53.2

cin- see *ci*
cint root, Pres. 139.1; Aor. 165.2; Ger 213
cinha, cihana 49.1
cirāyati 138, 186.1, 190, 195, 209
cunda(kāra) 41.1
cūla, culla 62.2
ce- see *ci*
Ceta, Ceti, Cetiya, Cecca 39.4

cha 40.1*a*, 67, 72.1, 115.5
chaka(na) 40.1*a*
chakala 39.1
chakka 52.1
chaḍḍūna 211
chaḍḍeti, -ḍḍāpeti 64.1, 178.1, 182.2
chaṇa, khaṇa 56.1c
chaddan 53.1
chabbaṇṇa, chabbīsati 53.3
chamā 56.1c
chāta 57
chāpa(ka) 39.6, 40.1*a*
chārikā 56.1*b*
chijj- see *chid*
chid root, Pres. 144; Fut. 152, 156; Aor. 161, 164, 168.3, 169.3; Pass. 55, 176.3; Caus. 179.3, 181.1, 182.2; Part. 191, 196, 197, 200; Inf. 205, 206; Ger. 209, 210, 213
chuddha p. 100 f.-n. 1
checchaṃ, -ati 152; see *chid*
chejjapessāmi 181.1
chedātabba 200
cheppā 40.1*a*

jagg- see 2. *gar*
jagghitāye 204c
jaṅgamati 185; see *gam*
jaccā=jātiyā 55, 86.2
jaññaṃ, -ā 145; see *jñā*
jaṇṇuka 64.3
jan root, Pres. 122.2, 129, 138; Aor. 168.4; Caus. 178.2*b*; Part. 194, 199.2; Ger. 209
jambonada 11
jammanaṃ 94
jay- see *ji*
jar root, 52.5; Pres. 122.2, 137; Fut. 155; Aor. 159 IV, 168.3; Caus. 181.1; Part. 191, 197
jalābu 46.1
jalogi p. 83 f.-n. 7
jalla, -kā 40.2*a*
jah- see *hā*
jāgarati see 2. *gar*
jāti 86
jān- see *jñā*
jāno=jānaṃ 97.2
jāpeti 180.2; see *ji*
jāy- see *jan*
ji root, Pres. 26.1, 131, 136.4; Fut. 151.3, 154, 156; Aor. 163.2, 169.4; Pass. 175.1; Caus. 180.2; Des. 184; Part. 194, 196, 198, 199.2, 203; Inf. 206; Ger. 209, 210
jigucchā, -ati 18.2, 57, 184, 190, 195, 209
jigīsati, -iṃsati 184; see *ji*

jighacchati 184, 195
jin- see *ji*
jimha 49.1
jiyā 30.2
jiyy- see *jar*
jivhā 49.1
jīy-, jīr-, jīrāp- see *jar*
jīv root, Pres. 125, 127, 128, 130.1; Part. 190, 191; Inf. 205
juhati, juhāmi 142.3
jūhati, -to p. 177 f.-n. 3
je- see *ji*
jotati 130
jñā root, 63.2; Pres. 128, 145; Fut. 151.1, 156; Aor. 163.1, 169.4; Pass. 136.4, 175.1, 176.1; Caus. 180.1, 181.1; Part. 97.2, 190, 191, 194, p. 218 f.-n. 3, 200, 202, 203; Inf. 205; Ger. 209, 210, 212, 213
jval root, 41.2; Caus. 178.2 *c*; Int. 185, 191.

jhallikā 34
jhāyati, jhāpeti, jhāma 56.2, 191; see *kṣā*
jhāyati see *dhyā*

ñatti 53.1
ñāṇa 42.5
ñāya 55
ñāyati, ñissaṃ see *jñā*

ṭhap-, ṭhass-, ṭhah-, thāy- see *sthā*
ṭhāti, ṭhāna etc. 64.2

ḍaṃsa 42.3
ḍas, ḍaṃs see *daś*
ḍah see *dah*
ḍāha 42.3
ḍeti 131.1

ta Pron. st. 105
taṃ=tvām 104
taṃyathā 105.2
takka 53.2
takkara 62.2
Takkasilā 62.2
Takkāriye Sg. Voc. 80.2
takkola, Takkola 47.1
tacchati 56.1*b*
taṇhā 30.5, 50.3
tatiya 23, 118
-tatta see *tras*
tattaka 111.6
tattha, tatra 53.2, 62.1
tadaṃ 105.3
tadaminā 108.1
tan root, Pass. 175.3, 177
tabbaṃsika 53.3
tabbiparīta 67
tamba, Tambapaṇṇi 51.5
tar root, Pres. 130.4; Aor. 166; Part. 197; Inf. Caus. 206; Ger. 210, 213, 214
taruṇa, taluṇa 44
tasiṇā 30.5, 50.3
-tasita, tasitāya see *tras*
tasmātiha 73.5

tāy- see *tan* and *trā*
tārayetuṃ 206; see *tar*
tāvattiṃsā 46.1
tālavaṇṭa 64.1
ti = *iti* 66.1
ti Numeral 115.3
tikicchati 41.2, 126, 181.1, 184. 190, 205; -see *cit*
tikkha, tikhiṇa 58.3
tiṭṭh- see *sthā*
tiṇṇannaṃ 115.3
tiṇha 59.1
titikkhati 184
tintiṇī p. 89 f.-n. 3
tipu 34
tipukkhala 44
tippa 61.2
tibba 61.2
timissā 16.1 *c* with f.-n. 6, p. 69
timbaru 34
tiriyaṃ 66.2 *b*
tivaṅgika 46.1
tīha 25.1
tuṇhī 66.2
tutta 15.3
tud root, Pres. 134; Part. 197
tuma Pron. st. 107.4
tumhe, -hehi etc. 50.4, 104
tuyhaṃ 60
turita p. 74 f.-n. 1
tuṣ root 125
tekicchā 34
tepiṭaka 3
terasa, telasa 26.1, 44, 116.2
tevīsa 26.1, 116.2
tyamhi 107.3
tras root, Part. 62.2, 194, 196, 203
trā root, Pres. 138
tvaṃ 104

thaketi, thakana 39.1
thaneti, -ita 52.2
tharu 57
-thavati 140; see *stu*
thāmasā, -mena 94
thī = *itthī* 29, 87.1 *c*
thīna 25.1
thunāti, -niṃsu 149, 169.4
thusa 40.1 *a*
thera 27.5
theva 38.5

dakkh- see *darś*
dakkhiṇa 56.1 *a*
dakkhiṇeyya 10
dajj- see *dā*
daṭṭha 42.3; see *daś*
daṭṭhā, dāṭhā 58.3
daḍḍha 42.3, 64.3; see *dah*
dattūpajīvin 197
dad- see *dā*
daddara p. 86 f.-n. 3
daddallati 41.2, 185, 191
daddula 44
dandha p. 84 f.-n. 1
Damiḷa 46.4
dammi see *dā*
darś root, Pres. (*passati*) 125, 128, 136.2; Fut. 19.1, 32.2, 152, 155; Aor. 161.3, 162.3, 164, 165.1, 166, 168.3, 170; Pass. 175; Caus. 6.3, 176.1; Part. 97.2, 100, 190, 191, 194, 199.1, 201, 203; Inf. 204, 205; Ger. 59.4, 209, 210, 213
daś (*ḍas*) root 42.3; Pres. 153.2; Caus. 181.1
-dassivā 100
dasso = *dāsiyo* 86.2
dah (*ḍah*) root 42.3, 64.3; Pass. 175.2; Part. 191, 194
dah-, see *dhā*
daha = *hrada* 47.2
dā root, Pres. 125, 143; Fut. 150, 151.1; Cond. 157; Aor. 159.1, 163, 169.2, 170; Pass. 136.4, 175.1; Caus. 180.1; Des. 130.6, 184; Part. 190, 191, 194, 197, 199.1, 202; Inf. 204, 205; Ger. 209, 210, 212
dāṭhā 42.3, 58.3
dātta 7
dāni 66.1
dābbī 7
dāya, dāva 46.1
dāḷemu 125
dāhisi 150; see *dā*
di-, dvi, 21
digucchati 41.2
dighañña 41.2
dicchati, -re 130.6, 184; see *dā*
dindima, deṇḍima 41.3
dinna 197; see *dā*
divaḍḍha, diy- 46.1
divā 88.4
diś root, Pres. 134; Caus. 179.3; Ger. 210
disvā 59.4; see *darś*
dīghāyu 101
du- 21
duka 119.6
dukkha p. 95 f.-n. 1
duccarita 62.2
dujivha 21
dutiya 23
duttara 62.2
dubbuṭṭhi(kā) 52.5
dubbhati, -dubbhika p. 104 f.-n. 2
dubhaya 114.2
duyhati 49.1
dullabha 52.5
durannaya 54.5
duvidha 21
dūseti 179.5
deṇḍima, dindima 41.3
demi etc. 143; see *dā*
dehanī 45
dosa, dosanīya 25.3
dosina 59.2, 63.3
dohaḷa, -ḷinī 42.3
dvi-, di- 21
dvi Numeral 114.2
dvidhā 53.4
dvinnaṃ 15.1
dvipadaṃ Pl. Gen. 89

dvīha 25.1
dvejjha 55
dvedhā 53.4
dveḷhaka 42.4

dhaṅka 62.2
dhanita 53.3
dhamma 78
dhā root, Pres. 37, 123, 125, 142.2; Fut. 151.3, 156; Aor. 165, 169.2; Pass. 39.5, 175.1; Caus. 180.1, 181.1; Part. 190, 191, 192, 194, 196, 199.1, 2, 202; Inf. 204, 205, 206; Ger. 210, 212
dhītar 91.3
dhū root 125, 147.3
dhe- see *dhā*
dhenu 86
dhovati 34, 130
dhyā root, Pres. 138; Part. 190; Inf. 203

na Pron. st. 66.1, 107.2
nagga 30.5
naṅgala 45
naṅguṭṭha p. 89 f.-n. 2
naṅgula 45
nacc- see *nart*
namakkāra 62.2
najjā, *-jjo*, *-jjāyo* 55, 86.2
nattar 91.1
nadi 86
namassati 188.2; Pres. 136.4; Part. 190, 191
nāmeti 178.2c
nay- see *nī*
nart root, Pres. 126, 136.1; Aor. 168.3; Part. 190
nalāṭa 45
navuti 19.2
naś root Pres. 125, 136.1; Cond. 157
nahā-, *nahāy-* see *snā*
nahāna 50.5
nahāpita 90.4
nahāru, *nhāru* 46.3, 50.5
nāvā 88.2
nikkha, *nekkha* 10, 52.2
nigrodha 21, 53.2
nighaññasi 38.1
nighaṇḍu 61.1
niṅka 25.1
niccala 62 2
nicchiya 213; see *ci*
nicchubhati 53.4
niḍḍa 6.2
ninna 52.4
nippesika 62.2
nibbāy- see *vā*
nibbijj-, *nibbind-* see 2. *vid*
nimujjā etc. 18.1
niya 36
niyy- see *nī*
niyyāti etc., *niyyāsa* 52.5
nisinna 17.2*d*, 197; see *sad*
nī root, Pres. 128, 131.1, 136.4; Fut. 151.3, 155; Aor. 163.2, 167.1; Pass. 175.1; Caus. 180.2; Part. 191, 194, 199.1, 202; Inf. 204, 205; Ger. 210

nuṭṭhubhati, *-hati* 16.1*a*, 37
nud root, Pres. 134; Part. 197; Ger. 212
ne- see *nī*
nekkha, *nikkha* 10, 52 2
Nerañjarā 43.2
nh- see *nah-*

pakiriya 8; see 2. *kar*
pakkaṭhita, *-ṭṭhita* 42.2 with f.-n. 6 on p. 87
pakkuṭṭhita, *-thita* p. 87 f.-n. 6
pakhuma 58.3
pagevataraṃ 103.2
paggharati 56.2; see *kṣar*
pac root. 130.1, 175.3, 181.1, 199 3
paccosakkati 28.2, p. 97 f.-n. 4, 62.2
-pajj- see *pad*
Pajjunna 23
paññatta p. 218 f.-n. 3
paññavant 23
paññā, *paññāṇa* 53.1
paññāsa 48
pañha, *pañhipaṇṇī* 50.1
paṭaṃga 42.1
paṭi, *pati* 42.1
paṭikkamma 136.1
paṭikkūla 33.1
paṭigacca 38.1, 212
paṭiviṃsa 46.1
paṭivissaka 15.1
paṭiseniyati 188.3
paṭṭhāya 64.2
paṭhama 42 2
paṭhamataraṃ 103.2
paṭhavī, *pathavī* etc. 12.4, p. 70 f.-n. 2, 42 2
paṇṇararsa *paṇṇāsa* 48, 63.2, 116.2
paṇhi(ka), *pāsaṇi* 58.2
pataṃga p. 87 f.-n. 4
patara 39.4
pati see *paṭi*
patitāmi 172
patibbatā 54.6
patisallāna 27.1
patthay- 187.1, 191, 192, 195
patha 93.4
pathi Sg. Loc. 89
pad root, Pres. 125, 136.1; Fut. 155; Cond. 157; Aor. 161, 166, 168.3; Caus. 178.2*a*, 181.1; Part. 197, 199.2; Ger. 210, 212
padā Sg. Instr. 89
pana 34
pantha 93.4
pannarasa, *paṇṇ-* 48
pappuyya, *pappoti* etc. see *āp*
papphāsa 34
pabbaja, *babbaja* 39 6
pabbe, *pabbesu* 94
pamādassaṃ 170; see *mad*
pamādo 161*b*; see *mad*
paṃha 59.1
payirud- 47.2
par root, Pass. 52.2, 168.3, 175.2; Caus. 178.2*a*, 182.2; Part. 197
para 113.7

parinibbāyi, *-bbāhisi* see *vā*
parip̣phoseti, *-saka* 62.1
paribbaya 54.6
parima 19.1
pariḷāha 42.3
parisā 66.2
palavati, *pil-* 31.1 ; see *plu*
palāpa 39.6
palāy-, *pale-* p. 74 f.-n. 4, 139.1, 150, 206
palikuṇṭhita, *palig-* 89 1
palikha, *-gha* 39.2
palikhanati 44
paligedha, *-dhin* 10
palissajati 44, 54.4
palujjati 44
pale- see *palāy*
palokine 95.2
pallaṅka 54.5
pallattha 54.5
pavissāmi, *-sissāmi* 65.2, 155
pavecchati p. 186 f.-n. 2
pasada 12.1. 38.3
pasibbaka 15.1
pasuta 19 3
pass- see *darś*
passo=passaṃ 97,2
pahaṃsati 37
pā root, Pres. 125, 132; Fut. 151.1, 155; Aor. 163.1, 165.1, 167,1; Caus. 180.3; Des. 184; Part. 190, 202; Ger. 209, 210
pākaṭa 33,1
pācittiya p 75 f,-n. 1
pāceti 39.3
pāṭibhoga 24
pāṭiyekka 24
pāṭihīra 27.6
pāṇine 95.2
pātu 39.4
pātubhāva 67
pāto 66 2*a*
pāniya 23
pāpattha see *apattha*
pāpay- see *āp*
pāpiṭṭhatara 103.1
pāpiyas 100.3, 103.1
pāpissika 103.1
pāpuṇ- see *āp*
pāpuraṇa 19.2
pāmiṃsu 163.1 ; see *mā*
pāyāsi, *-yiṃsu* 163.1 ; see *yā*
pārājika p. 83 f -n. 8
pāruta 13
pārupati, *-pana* 47.2
pārepata 34
pāvā 160.4
pāvacana 33.1
pāvusa 12.3
pāvekkhi 164 ; see *viś*
pāsaṇi 58.2
pāssati 151.1 ; see *pā*
pāheti, *-si* see *hi*
pi 66.1
piññāka 55
piṇḍadāvika 46.1
pilar 91
pitito 77 2, p. 120 f.-n. 2
pithīyati 39.5 ; see *dhā*
pipataṃ 132 ; see *pā*
pippḥala -*lī* 62.1
pilakkhu 30.4
pilandhana, *-ti* 37, 43.2
pilav-, *pilāp-* see *plu*
piv- see *pā*
pukkusa 17.2*a*
pucch- see *prach*
puñjati 61.1
puṭṭha 194 ; see *prach*
puttāni 76
puttimā 19.1
puthu 22
puthujjana 17 2*a*
puna, *puno* 34, 66.2
pubba (1) 46.1 ; (2) 113 8
pubbaṇha 49.1
puman 93.5
Puriṃdada p. 89 f.-n. 1
purisa 29, 30.3
pure 66.2
pūjay- Pres. 139 ; Fut. 151.3 ; Aor. 168.4 ; Pass 176.1 ; Part. 200, 201
pūr- see *par*
pūva 38.5
pekhuṇa 19 2
pettika 6.2
peḷā 35
poṇa 26.2
pothujjanika 3
posa 30.3
posatha 66.1
posāvanika *-ya* 36
prach root, *Pres.* 122.2, 126 128, 134 ; Fut. 155 ; Aor. 167 ; Pass. 176.2 ; Caus. 181.1 ; Part. 191 192, 194, 196, 199.2 ; Inf. 205,206 ; Ger. 211, 212
plu root 31.1, 179.4

pharasu 40.1 *a*
pharusa 40.1 *a*
phala (*gaṇḍa*) 40.1 *a*
phalāpeala 33.1
phalika 38.6
phalu 40.1 *a*
*phass-*see *sparś*
phassa 52.2
phārusaka 40.1 *a*
phālibhaddaka 40.1 *a*
phāsu(*ka*) 62.1
phāsukā 40. 1 *a*
phuṭṭha 194 see *sparś*
phulaka 40.1 *a*
*phus-*see *sparś*
peusita 40.1 *a*
phussa 40 1 *a*
pheggu 9

battiṃsa 53 3, 116.2
bandh root, Pres. 146.4 ; Fut. 154 3 ; Aor. 169.4 ; Pass. 175.3 ; Caus. 154 3 ; Inf. 206 ; Ger. 210, 213
bappa 62.2
babbu(*ka*) 62.2

babbhara 20
barh root 6. 2, 128. 167, 194, 212
bavhābādha, *bavhodoka* 49. 1
bārasa, *bāvisati* f3. 3, 116.2
bilāra. -*rikā*, -*la* 45
billa, *bella* 54.5
bujjh-see *budh*
buḍḍha, *vuḍḍha* 46. 1, 64. 1
budh root 136. 1, 181. 1, 192
bunda 62.2
bubhukkhati 184 see *bhuj*
bella, *billa* 54. 5
brahant, *brahā* 13
brahman 19. 2. 92. 2, 3
brū root 125, 141. 2, 159. IV
brūheti 13

bhaj- *bhañj* root Pres. 144; Fut. 156. 2; Part. 197, 199.2; Inf. 206
bhajeti 139.2
bhaṇ root 126, p. 180 f.-n. 1
bhadda. *bhadra* 53.2
bhante 98. 3
bhar root, Pass. 52. 5, p. 205 f. -n 2, 191
bhavant 98. 3
bhasta 40. 1 *a*, 52. 2
bhastā 52. 2
bhasma 50. 6
bhassati 136. 1
bhā root 140. 2
bhākuṭika 3
bhātar 91. 2, 3.
bhāy-see *bhī*
bhāṣ root 'to speak' 122. 2, 126, 128
-*bhāsare* 122. 2
bhikkhu 82, -*ave* 82. 5
bhiṅkhu, *gāra* 61. 2
bhijj. see *bhid*
bhid root. Pres. 144; Fut. 152, 156 9; Aor 161. 1 *b*, 168. 3, 169. 3; Pass. 136. 4. 177; Caus. 181. 1; Part. 190, 197, 199. 2; Ger. 209, 210, 212
bhindivāḷa 38. 5
bhiyyo 18. 2, 103. 1
bhisa 40. 1 *a*
bhisakka 63. 1
bhisī 40. 1 *a*
bhī root 138, 168 3, 179. 4
bhīrati Pass. from *bhar*
bhuj root, Pres. 128, 144; Fut. 152, 156; Aor. 169. 3; Caus. 179. 1; Des. 184; Part. 190, 191. 198, 199. 2, 201, 202; Inf. 205, 206; Ger. 209, 210
-*bhuṇāti* 131. 2; see *bhū*
bhuvi Sg. Loc. 86.5
bhusa 40. 1 *a*
bhū root, Pres, 26. 2. 37, 39. 6, 122. 2, 126, 131. 2; Fut. 27. 5, 151. 3, 154. 2; Cond. 157; Aor. 162. 2, 163. 3, 165. 1, 167, 170; Pass. 175. 1; Caus. 179. 4; Part. 190, 191, 199. 1, 240. 202; Inf. 204. 1 *b*, 206; Ger. 209, 210, 212
bhecchati 152; see *bhid*
bhokkhaṃ 152; see *bhuj*
bhetā etc. 98. 3
-*bhoti*. *bhossaṃ* etc. see *bhū*

makasa 47. 2
makkhikā 56. 1 *a*
maga 12. 4
maghavan 93. 3
maṃkuna 6. 3
macca 58. 2
maccharin 57
macchariya, -*era* 27. 5, p. 91 f. -n. 4
majj-see *mad*
majjhatta 62. 2
majjhima 19. 1
maññ see *man*
maṭṭa *maṭṭha* 62. 2
mata 42. 1
matameyya p. 176 f. -n. 1
-*matthati* 53. 1
matthaluṅgā 17. 2 *c*
mad root Pres. 126, 136. 1; Aor. 161. 1 *b*, 169. 3, 170; Inf. 206; Ger. 210
madhuvā 66 2 *b*
man root, Pres. 129, 136. 1, 139. 2. 149; Fut. 155; Aor. 159. II, 161, 168 3; Des 46. 4, 184; Inf. 205; Ger. 209
manaṃ 66. 2 *b*
mantavho 126
mamāy 186. 3, 195
mamiṃkāra 19 1
mayaṃ 104. 2
mayūkha *mayūra* 27. 9 (with f.-n. 3 on p. 76)
mar root, Pres. p. 95 f.-n. 4, 122. 2. 137; Fut. 155. 3; Caus. 176 1. 178. 2 *a*, 182. 2 *a*; Part. 191, 193; Inf. 204. 1 *b*, 206. 207
mariyādā 30. 1
maruvā 31. 2
malya 54. 5
massu 50. 2
mahemase 129
mā root, Pres. 146. 3; Aor. 163. 1; Part. 202; Ger. 210
Māgandiya 38. 1
mātar 91
mātito 77. p. 129 f.-n. 2
māmaka 112. 1
miga 12 4
migavā 46. 1
miṃjā p.-65 f.-n. 4. 18. 2
mināti etc. see *mā*
miyy-, *mīy*-see *mar*
milakkha, -*kkhu* 34
milāca 62 2
Milinda 43. 2
missa 54. 4
mihita *sita* 50. 6
mu root 18
-*mukka* 197; see *muc*
mukkhara 24
mugga 52. 1
-*mugga* 197
muc, *muñc* root Pres. 128, 135. 3, 136. 4; Fut. 152, 155; Aor. 167. 2, 168. 3;

Pass. 175. 3; Caus. 181. 1; Part, 109, 196, 197; Inf. 206; Ger 209, 210
mucalinda 34
muccati, muccheti 62. 2 with f.-n. 4 on p. 104
muta muti 18 1
mutiṅga 28. 39, 4
muditā 19. 3
muddhan 92. 1 2
muḷāla, -li 12.3 43.3
much root 194, 201
mejjati 136. 1
mettika 6. 2
meraya 23
mokkh-see *muc*
motabba, motar see *mu*
-*modathavho* 126
momuha. -*hati* 87, 185
mora 27. 8

ya Pron. *st*. 110
yakanaṃ 94
yaj root 66 1, 12[8], 194, 205
yaṭṭhuṃ 205 see *yaj*
yam root 133
yasmātiha 73. 5
yā root, Pres. 138, 140. 2; Aor. 163. 1, 168. 3; Caus. 180. 1; Inf. 204. 1 *a*; Ger. 210
yāgū 27. 4
-*yādeti*, -*yādāpeti* 88. 3, 178. 2, 182. 2, 200
yāpeti, yāpanīya 180. 1, 201
yiṭṭha 66. 1, 194; see *yaj*
yuj root, Pres. 144; Aor. 169. 3; Pass. 176.2; Caus. 179. 3, 182.2; Part. 194
yuvan 93. 2
ye=yaṃ 110. 2
yeva 66. 1

raṃsi, rasmi 50. 3, 65. 1
racchā, rathiyā 55
rajetave 204 1 *a*
rajjati 136. 1, 206
ratto 86 5
ratana 66. 1
-*rattāyaṃ* 86. 5
ratyā -*o* 58. 3 86. 2
randha 58. 1
ram root 126, 165. 1
-*rasa=dasa* 43. 1
rasmi see *raṃsi*
rassa 49. 2
rahada 47. 2, 49, 2
rājan 92
rājula 19. 3
rāmaṇeyya 10
ric root 144, 156. 210
-*risa*. *rikkha* 43. 1, 112. 3
ru root 140. 1, 169. 1
rukkha 13
ruc root 122. 2, 128, 136. 2, 179. 3, 181. 2
ruṇṇa, roṇṇa 197
ruda, ruta 38. 3
rudda p. 88 f -n. 6
-*rumbhati*, -*rumhati*, -*rundhati* 60, 144
rummavatī 53. 1
rummavāsi, rammī p. 96 f.-n. 2
ruh root, Pres. 133. 3; Aor. 167; Caus. 180. 2, 182. 2; Ger. 210, 212 with f.-n 1 on p. 230
ruhira 37
rūpa 78
roṇṇa see *ruṇṇa*

lakunka, laketi 39. 1
lag root, Pres. 136. 2; Caus. 179. 5, 182. 2; Part. 197; Ger. 210
lacch- 150, 152; see *labh*
lajjitāya 203
laddhā Aor. 159. III see *labh*
laṭṭhi(kā) 46 3
lapetave 204 1 *a*
labh root, Pres. 121, 122 2, 124, 126-129; Fut. 150, 152; Cond. 157; Aor. 159 III 161. 2, 166; Caus. 178[5] 2 *a*; Part. 194, 201; Inf. 205; Ger. 209, 210
lahu ka) 37
lākhā 5
lāpa, lāpu 39. 6
lālappati 185
lāyita -*tvā* 46. 2
Lāḷa 38. 6
lip. limp root, Pres. 135. 3; Caus 181 1; Part. 190, 199. 2; Ger. 210
lih root 130. 5, 167
lī root 136. 1, 168 3, 197, 210
lujjati 44. 136. 4. 175. 3
ludda 15. 4, 44
ludda(ka) 62. 2
-*lubbha* 212
lūkha 44
lūna 197
leḍḍu 62. 2
loṇa 26. 2
lodda 44, 62. 2
loma, roma 44, 94
loluppa 185
lohita, rohita 44

va=iva, eva 66. 1
vaka 12, 1
vakkh- see *vac*
vac root, Pres. 136. 4; Fut. 152; Aor. 162. 4, 165. 1; Pass. 175. 3: Des, 184; Part 66. 1, 191, 194; Inf. 204. 1 *a*, 205; Ger. 209
vacch-see *vas*
vajira 30. 8
vajjaṃ 143 *e*
vañcit' ammi p. 203 f.-n. 1. 173.2
vaṭaṃsa(ka) 42. 1, 66. 1
vaṭuma 58. 2
-*vaṭṭa* 62. 2
-*vaṭṭa*. *vaṭṭati* 64. 1; see *vart*
vaḍḍh, see *vardh*
vaḍḍhi, vuddhi 12. 4, 64. 1
vaṇibbaka 46. 1
vaṇṭa 64. 1
vata 54. 6
vatt- see *vart*

vad root, Pres. 128, 129, 139, 2, 143 *e*; Aor. 165. 2; Pass. 176. 1; Caus 178. 2*a*
vanaspati 52. 2
vap root, Pass. 175. 3; Part. 66. 1, 194
vapayanti 54. 6
vambheti, *vamheti* 60
vammīka 23
vayassa 54. 4
vayhā 49. 1
var root, Caus. 178. 2 *a*; Part. 190. 191; Inf. 206; Ger. 214
vart root 53. 3, 64. 1, 130. 5, 178. 1
vardh root 64. 1. 178. 1, 182 1
valñja, *-jeti* 66 1
vavakkhati 184 209 see *vac*
vas root. Pres 128. 130. 1; Fut. 150, 152. 154; Caus. 178. 2 *a*. 53. 3, 181. 1. 182. 2; Part. 66. 1, 191, 195, 196, 198, 199. 1, 2; Ger. 210
vah root, Pass. 175 3; Caus. 178. 2 *a*; Part. 35, 66. 1, 191, 194
(1) *vā* root 'to weave' 196
(2) *vā* root 'to blow', Pres. 138, 140. 2; Fut. 150, 151. 1; Aor. 168. 3; Caus. 180. 1; Part. 190; Inf. 205
vāka 6. 1
vākarā, *-urā* 39. 1
vākya 53. 3
vācā Sg. Instr. 89
-vigga 197
-vāraṃ, *vāre* 119. 3
vāḷa 54. 6
vikkhīṇa 197 see *kṣi*
vicchika 12 2
vijitāvin 1́8 3
vijjh- see *vyadh*
viññāṇañcāyatana 65. 2
(1) *vid* root 'to know' Pres. 140. 1; Aor. 166; Pf. 171; Caus. 136. 4, 176. 1, 179. 3; Part. 100. 2
(2) *vid*. *vind* root 'to find'. Pres. 135 3; Aor. 167. 2; Pres. 175. 3; Caus. f.-n. 1 on p. 210; Part. 191; Inf. 206
vidaṃsentī 6. 3; see *darś*
vidathi 38. 3
viddasu 100. 2
vipassi 65. 2
vimhaya. *-hita* 50. 6
viya 66 1
vilāka 61. 2
viś root, Pres, 134; Fut 65 2, 152, 155. 2; Aor. 164; Pass. 176. 1; Caus. 179. 3; Ger. 210
visīyaruṃ 126; see *śyā*
vissa 113. 2
vissakamma 94
vissajj -see *sarj*
vihesati 10
vīta- 25. 1
vīmaṃsati. *-sā* 46. 4, 184, 205, 209
vīsaṃ, *vīsati* 6.3., 116. 1
vuḍḍha, *vuddha* see *vardh*
vutta see *vac*, *vap*
vuddhi, *vuḍḍhi* 12. 4, 64. 1
vuppati see *vap*
vuyhati, *vūḷha* see *vah*
vasita(*vā*) see *vas*
vekurañja 55
vekkh-, *vecch-* 152 (with f.-n 2 on p. 186)
Veṇhu 10, 50. 3
veti, *vedi* etc. see 1. *vid*
-vedhati see *vyath*
vedhavera 46. 3
Vebhāra 37
veyyattikā, *-ya* 36
veyyāvacca 3
verinesu 95. 2
veḷu 43. 3
veḷuriya p. 64 f.-n. 3
vesma 50. 2
vehāsān Pl. Acc. 79. 5
vo- 26. 2, 54. 6
vokkamati 10
vonata. *onata* 66 1
vosita 26. 2
vyath root 25. 1, 38. 4
vyadh root 136. 1. 199. 2. 210. 212
vyāvaṭa 38. 5 42. 1, 54. 6
vyāsiñcati, *vyāseka*. *vyeti* 54. 6

śak root. Pres. 148. 1; Fut. 61. 1, 152, 156; Cond. 157; Aor. 164. 170; Des. 126, 128, 150, 184; Part. 190
śam root 136, 1
śar root 137
śī root Pres. 140. 4; Fut. 151. 3; Aor. 161. 2, 165. 2 169. 1; Caus. 181. 1; Part. 190, 191, 192. 195; Ger. 209
śudh root 176. 1, 179. 3, 194
śuṣ root 57, 136, 1, 210
śyā root 25. 1, 38. 5, 126 175. 1
śru root, Pres. 128, 147 4; Fut. 15. 3, 4, 65 2, 151. 2, 156. 3; Aor. 159. III, 160. 4, 169 4; Pass. 136. 4. 175.1; Caus. 179. 4, 181. 1; Des. 184; Part. 190, 191, 194. 198. 4, 199. 1; Inf. 204. 1 *a*. 205, 206; Ger, 209, 210, 213
sa Pron. 105
saṃyūḷha 194
saṃvarī 6. 3
saṃsati Sg. Loc. 39. 4
saṃsarita, *-sita* see *sar*
saṃhīra 27. 6
sakiṃ 66. 2 *b*, 67, 72. 1, 119. 3
sakuṇa 42 5
sakk., *sakkuṇ-*, *sakkh-* see *śak*
sakka 53 3
Sakka, *Sakya*, *Sākiya* p. 64. f.-n. 2, p. 97 f.-n. 2
sakkāyā p 73 f.-n. 2
sakkhalī, *-likā* 17, 2 *c*
sakkhi(*ṃ*), *sacchi* 23
sakkhī for *sakkhisi* 65. 2
sakhi. *sakhāraṃ*. etc. 46. 3. 84
saggasi 61. 1, see *śak*
saṃkīyati 52. 5
saṃghaṭati p. 83 f.-n. 3
saṃghādisesa 38. 3
sace 105. 2
saccika 19. 1
saccessati 62. 2
sacchi see *sakkhi*(*ṃ*)

sajju 22
sajjulasa 19. 2, 44
sajjhāyati 188. 1, 206, 210
saṭhila 42. 2
saṇa 42. 5
saṇati, *sanati* 42, 5
saṇiṃ 22, 42. 5
saṃḍāsa 42. 3
saṇha 59. 1
satimat 96
sattama 103. 2
sattari 43
satthar 90
satthi 52. 1
sad root, Pres. 132, Fut. 155; Aor. 161.1*b*, 167. 1; Caus. 178. 2 *a*, 181. 1; Part. 17. 2 *d*, 197, 199. 2; Ger. 210
saddala 53. 3
saddhiṃ 22
san 93. 1
sant(a) 98. 2
saṃtatta 62. 2; see *tras*
sappi 101
sabba 113 1
sabbhi 98. 2
sabbāya Loc. Sg. fem. 113. 1
samannesati 54. 5
samīhati 37
samucchissatha 157
samussaya, *-ssita* 58. 3
samūhati *-hata* 60
saṃbhuṇāti 131. 2, see *bhū*
sammati 136 1, see *śam*
sammannati 54. 5
saṃmujjanī 18. 1
saṃmuti 19. 2
say- see *śī*
sayathā 105. 2
sar- see *sar*, *smar*
sar root 'to go', Pres. 130. 4; Caus. 178. 2 *a*; Des. 130. 6, 166, 184; Part 194, 196; Ger. 210
sarado Pl. Acc. 89
sarj root p. 79 f.-n 4, 128, 178. 1, 182. 2, 194
sallakatta 90. 4
sassara 20
sassū 86
sahatthā 78. 1
sahoḍha 35
sā 'dogs' p. 132 f.-n. 1
Sākiya (*Sākya*) see *Sakka*
Sākhalya 3 17. 2 *b*
Sāgala 38. 1
sāṇa 12. 4
sādiyati 176. 1
sādhayemase 129
sāmaṇera 46. 3
sāmi 46. 4
sāyati 36
sāyaṇha 49. 1
sārambha 6. 3
sāluka 23
sāsapa 6. 1
sāhu 37
-si=*svid* 22, 111. 1
siṃs- Des. from *sar*
sikkh- Des. from *śak*
siṅgivera 17. 2 *d*
siṅghāṭaka 62. 1
sic, *siñc* root, Pres. 125, 135. 3; Fut. 155; Aor. 167; Caus. 181. 1; Part. 194, 199. 2; Ger. 210, 213
sita, *mihita* 50. 6
sithila 42. 2
siniyh-, *sinih-* see *nih*
sineha 30. 5
sindhava 15. 2
sipāṭikā 12. 2
simba'i *-la* 34
siyaṃ etc. 141. 1; see *as*
sirī 8, 30. 3, 87 1
Sirimā 96
siriṃtapa 16. 1 *c*
sīd see *sad*
sīna 197
sīlavant(a) 96
-sīvcti see *śyā*
-su, *-ssu*, *-si*=*-svid* 22, 111. 1
sukka 30. 4
-sukhuma 31. 2, 58. 3
sukkumāla 40 1 *b*
suṃka 6. 3
sujā 38. 2
suṇ- see *śru*
suṇa 93 1
suṇisā *suṇhā* 31. 2, 50. 3
suddiṭṭha p. 73 f.-n. 2
sunakha 40. 1 *b*
sunahāta, *sunh-* 50. 5
sup-, *supp-* see *svap*
subbata 67
subbuṭṭhikā p. 95 f.-n. 5
sumar- see *sar*
sumugga 16. 1 *b*
sumedha (*sa*) 75
-sumbhati, *-hati* 60, 128, 135. 3
sūriya 8
suva 36
suvāna, *-ṇa* 93. 1
suve *sve* 54. 4, 66. 2
susāna 21
sussaṃ, *sussūs-* see *śru*
suhatā 37
suhita p. 83 f.-n 4
su-h-uju 67
sūna 25. 2
se=*taṃ* 105 2
seṭṭhatara 10? 1
seti, *senti*, *settha* see *śī*
senāsana 26. 1
semha 5. 50. 4, 54, 4
seyyasi 137; see *śar*
seyya(s), *seyyatara* 100, 103. 1
seyyathā 105. 2
sesiṃ, *sessaṃ* see *śī*
soṇa 25. 2
soṇṇa p. 74 f.-n. 2
sotas 99
sottuṃ see *svap*
sotthāna 27. 1
sotthi 25. 2

sodh- see *śudh*
sopāka 25. 2
sopp- see *svap*
soppa 25. 2, 53 1
sobbha 25. 2. 53. 2
sorata p. 98 f.-n. 1
sovatthika, sosānika 3
sossati, sossaṃ, sossi see *śru*
skand root 197, 214
stan root 149, 169. 4
star root p. 181 f.-n. 1, 194, 197
stu root 140
sthā root, Pres. 64. 2, 132; Fut. 151. 1, 155; Cond 157; Aor. 160. 2, 163. 1, 167. 1; Caus. 21, 180. 1, 182. 2; Part. 190, 191, 192, 194, 199. 1, 200; Inf. 206; Ger. 209, 210. 212
snā root 50. 5, 138, 140. 2, 180. 1, 206, 209
snih root 136. 1. 179. 3
sparś root, Pres. 134; Fut. 155; Aor. 167. 2; Den. 186. 5; Part. 194, 196; Ger. 206
smar root, Pres. (*sumarati, sarati* 50. 6, 122 2, 125, 129; Caus. 178. 2 *a*; Part. 191, 200; Ger. 210, 213
smi root 29, 50. 6
svap root, Pres. 134, 136. 2; Aor. 167. 2; Part. 190, 194; Inf. 205, 206: Ger. 210
svākkhāta 7, 51. 4
svāgata 54. 4
svātanāya p. 63 f.-n. 4, 54. 4
sve see *suve*
-ssu=svid 22, 111. 1

haṃsati, -eti 130. 5, 173 1
haṅkh-, hañch, hañña- see *han*
haṭa 42. 1, see *har*
hadaya 12 1
han root, Pres. p. 76 f.-n. 5, 60, 140. 1; Fut. 153. 2; Aor. 169. 1; Pass. 122. 2, 168. 3, 175. 3; Caus. 179. 5, 181. 1, 183. 2; Part. 190, 202, 203; Ger. 209, 210, 211, 212
hammiya p. 102, f.-n. 1
har root, Pres. 125. 128, 129; Fut. 153. 1. 151. 1; Aor. 163. 4; Pass. 53. 5, 175. 2, 176. 2; Caus. 183. 2; Part. 42. 1, 194, 196, 199. 1, 2; Inf. 205; Ger. 210, 211
harāyati 81. 1, 186. 2
hassaṃ etc. 153. 1 from root *har*
hassāmi etc. 151 from root *hā*
hā root, Pres. (*jahāti*) 126. 128, 129. 136. 4, 142. 1; Fut. 150. 151, 1, 156. 1; Aor. 163 1, 169. 2; Pass. 175 1; Caus. 180. 1; Part. 196. 197, 199. 1, 2, 203; Inf. 204, 206; Ger. 209, 210
hāpeti 39. 6. 179. 4
hāhisi 153. 1 from root *har*; 150 from root *hā*
hi root, Pres. p. 79 f.-n. 3. 131 1 147. 2; Aor. p. 79 f.-n 3, 163. 2, 169. 4
hiṃsati, sāpeti 144, 181. 1
-hiṇāti etc. see *hi*
Himavant (*a*) 96
hiyyo 30.2
hirī 8 30 3, 87. 1
hilāda 30. 4
-hissāmi 153. 1 from root *har*
-hīrati Pass. from root *har*. Look under *har*
hīḷeti 35
hu root 142 3
hupeyya 39. 6, see *bhū*
heṭṭhā 9, 37, 66. 1
hetu 22 p. 122 f.-n. 4
hetuye 201. 1 *b*
heyya p. 168 f.-n. 2
hesati, hesā, hesita 49. 2
hessati 27. 5 from root *bhū*
-hessati 153. 1 from root *har*
hessāmi 151. 1 from root *hā*
hotabba hoti, hotuṃ, hohisi, hohiti from root *bhū*